Second Edition

Recr and Selection

in Canada

Second Edition

Recruitment and Selection in Canada

Victor M. Catano
Saint Mary's University

Steven F. Cronshaw
University of Guelph

Willi H. Wiesner
McMaster University

Rick D. Hackett
McMaster University

Laura L. Methot
Methot Associates
Applied Performance Solutions

Series Editor: Monica Belcourt

NELSON

™

THOMSON LEARNING

Australia • Canada • Mexico • Singapore • Spain • United Kingdom • United States

NELSON
THOMSON LEARNING

Recruitment and Selection in Canada

by Victor M. Catano, Steven F. Cronshaw,
Willi H. Wiesner, Rick D. Hackett, and
Laura L. Methot

Editorial Director and Publisher:
Evelyn Veitch

Acquisitions Editor:
Edward Ikeda

Marketing Manager:
Anthony Rezek

Developmental Editor:
Karina TenVeldhuis

Production Editor:
Natalia Denesiuk

Production Coordinator:
Hedy Sellers

Art Director:
Angela Cluer

Cover Design:
Anne Bradley

Interior Design:
Julie Greener

Copy Editor:
Jim Leahy

Proofreader:
Dawn Hunter

Compositor:
Carol Magee

Printer:
Webcom

Canadian Cataloguing in Publication Data

Main entry under title:
Recruitment and selection in Canada

(Nelson series in human resources management)
2nd ed.
Includes bibliographical references and index.
ISBN 0-17-616843-5

1. Employees – Recruiting – Canada.
2. Employee selection – Canada.
I. Catano, Victor M. (Victor Michael), 1944– II. Series.

HF5549.5.R44R417 2000
658.3'11'0971
C00-932853-X

BRIEF CONTENTS

TABLE OF CONTENTS

CHAPTER 3   SCIENTIFIC METHODS   71

CHAPTER 6   PERFORMANCE MEASUREMENT: THE ROLE OF CRITERIA IN SELECTING EMPLOYEES   193

CHAPTER 7   RECRUITMENT: IDENTIFYING, CONTACTING, AND ATTRACTING THE TALENT POOL   229

CHAPTER 8   SELECTION I: APPLICANT SCREENING AND SELECTION   285

CHAPTER 9   SELECTION II: TESTING   343

CHAPTER 10   SELECTION III: INTERVIEWING   401

CHAPTER 11   DECISION MAKING   435

PREFACE TO THE SERIES

The importance of the profession of human resources management (HRM) is growing, as reflected in the number of students choosing HRM as their field of study, by the dramatic increases in memberships in professional HR associations, and by the titles and compensation packages being given to HR executives. Human resource professionals do make a difference to employers and employees. Knowledgeable HR professionals can have a significant impact on their organization's ability to attract, motivate, and retain productive employees.

The Nelson Series in Human Resources Management is dedicated to ensuring that HR professionals are knowledgeable and well-grounded in their disciplines. In addition to this book, texts in the series include

- *Occupational Health and Safety*
- *Managing Performance through Training and Development*
- *Strategic Human Resources Planning*
- *Compensation in Canada: Strategy, Practice and Issues*
- *Research, Measurement, and Evaluation of Human Resources*
- *An Introduction to the Canadian Labour Market*

The Nelson Series in Human Resources Management is important for many reasons. Each book in the series (except for *Compensation*) is the first Canadian text in the area. Human resource practitioners must work with Canadian laws, Canadian facts, Canadian policies, and Canadian values. This series serves these needs.

These texts, for the first time, also provide a standardized guide to the management of various HR functional areas. The standardization enables readers to locate material quickly, and to link and cross-reference information, thus providing an encyclopedia of knowledge about HRM. This one-stop resource will prove useful to anyone involved in the management of people.

Most importantly, the publication of these texts signals that the HR field has advanced to the stage where theory and applied research guide practice. Additionally, because HRM is an applied discipline, examples of best practices used by organizations that are leaders in HR are woven into the texts, thus allowing students to learn about emerging tools and methods.

Observers agree that this is the decade of human resources management. It is an incredibly exciting time to be learning about HRM, and to be embarking on a career in this profession. I know that this text, and others in the series, will provide you with the very best preparation to practice.

Monica Belcourt, Ph.D., CHRP
Series Editor
September 2000

ABOUT THE AUTHORS

VICTOR M. CATANO

Dr. Victor M. Catano is Professor and Chairperson of Psychology at Saint Mary's University in Halifax, Nova Scotia. He obtained a B.Sc. in electrical engineering from Drexel University in Philadelphia and went on to complete both a master's and a Ph.D. in psychology at Lehigh University in Bethlehem, Pennsylvania. He is a registered psychologist in Nova Scotia. Dr. Catano joined the Saint Mary's faculty following completion of his doctoral degree and was instrumental in establishing the university's master's program in industrial/organizational psychology. He has also served as a Special Lecturer at the Technical University of Nova Scotia and as a Visiting Research Fellow at the Canadian Forces Personnel Applied Research Unit in Toronto; he is currently an Honorary Adjunct Professor in the graduate faculty at Dalhousie University. Dr. Catano has served as President of the Association of Psychologists of Nova Scotia, a member of the Nova Scotia Board of Examiners in Psychology (the body responsible for regulating the profession within Nova Scotia), and President of the Canadian Society of Industrial/Organizational Psychology. He is currently the editor of *Canadian Psychology*, the flagship journal of the Canadian Psychological Association, and a member of the editorial board for *Advances in Organizational Behavior* and has acted as a reviewer for numerous scholarly journals and granting agencies.

Dr. Catano has extensive consulting experience in personnel selection and assessment, job analysis, utility analysis, occupational families, attitude surveys, leadership, productivity issues, statistical analyses and research methodology, and industrial relations. His clients have included the Department of National Defence, Royal Canadian Mounted Police, Asea Brown Bovari, Nova Scotia Government Employees Union, and Manufacturing Research Corporation of Ontario, among others. He has published over 150 scholarly articles, conference papers, and technical reports. His current research interests include personnel psychology, the psychology of labour relations, organizational and environmental constraints on productivity, and the impact of psychological environments on the health, safety, and productivity of workers. In recognition of his contributions to the science and practice of psychology in Canada, Dr. Catano was elected a Fellow by the Canadian Psychological Association, and an Honorary Member by the Canadian Forces Personnel Selection Officers Association.

STEVEN F. CRONSHAW

Dr. Cronshaw is Associate Professor of Psychology at the University of Guelph, Ontario. He earned his B.A. and B.Comm. degrees at the University of

Saskatchewan in Saskatoon and his M.A. and Ph.D. degrees in industrial/organizational psychology at that university, with much of his teaching activity centred on graduate courses and supervision of graduate students. Dr. Cronshaw also founded and was the first Executive Director of the Guelph Centre for Occupational Research Inc. (GCORI), which is a research consulting company devoted to transferring human resources management concepts and practical solutions between university environments and external organizations. Largely under the aegis of GCORI, he has consulted widely to Canadian organizations on human rights, selection systems, job analysis, attitude surveying, leadership programs, and other issues related to human resources management. His research activities, spanning numerous journal articles, book chapters, and conference papers, cover a range of topics, including leadership, personnel selection, human rights, utility analysis, and job analysis. He is the author of *Industrial Psychology in Canada*, published in 1991. A biographical entry containing Dr. Cronshaw's personal and work history is published in Marquis' *Who's Who in the World*, 14th edition (1997).

WILLI H. WIESNER

Dr. Wiesner received his Ph.D. in industrial/organizational psychology from the University of Waterloo, where he specialized in personnel psychology. He has taught in the Faculty of Commerce at Concordia University in Montreal and is currently Associate Professor of Human Resource Management and Chair of the Human Resources and Management Area of the Michael G. DeGroote School of Business at McMaster University. Dr. Wiesner is a member of the Canadian Psychological Association, the American Psychological Association, the Canadian Society for Industrial and Organizational Psychology, the Society for Industrial and Organizational Psychology (U.S.), the Administrative Sciences Association of Canada, and the Academy of Management. He has served as Institute Coordinator and President of the Canadian Society of Industrial and Organizational Psychology.

Dr. Wiesner has extensive consulting experience in the areas of employee selection, performance appraisal, and other personnel issues. His recent clients include the RCMP, Drake Personnel, the Bartlett Group, the McQuaig Institute, St. Peter's Hospital, Grand River Hospital Corporation, Halton Regional Police Services, Tires Only, AFG Glass, and Canada Post (as an associate of Hackett & Associates in Dundas), the Department of National Defence, and the Public Service Commission of Canada (as an associate of EER Technologies in Ottawa). Dr. Wiesner has also presented workshops on employee selection, performance appraisal, training and development, and team building through the Executive Development Office in the School of Business at McMaster University. His recent research and publication activities have focused on employment interviewing and selection, group decision-making, and team effectiveness.

Rick D. Hackett

Dr. Hackett received his Ph.D. in industrial/organizational psychology in 1985 from Bowling Green State University in Ohio. He is Professor of Human Resource Management at McMaster University's Michael G. DeGroote School of Business and served as Associate Dean from July 1, 1997, to December 31, 2000. He is President of Hackett & Associates Human Resources Consultants Inc., as well as Past President of the Canadian Society for Industrial and Organizational Psychology (CSIOP) of the Canadian Psychological Association, a professional association of approximately 170 Canadian industrial/organizational psychologists. In June 1997 he was elected a Fellow of the Canadian Psychological Association. Additionally, Dr. Hackett is an ad hoc reviewer for several scholarly journals in management and has been appointed editor of the *Canadian Journal of Administrative Sciences* (Human Resources Division) for two three-year terms spanning January 1, 1997, to December 31, 2002. Dr. Hackett was guest editor of a special issue of *Canadian Psychology* published in 1998 and was elected a member of the *International Who's Who of Professionals* in October 1997.

Dr. Hackett's primary research and consulting interests lie in the areas of recruitment, personnel assessment, selection, work attitudes, employee commitment, absenteeism, performance appraisal, and team development.

Laura L. Methot

Dr. Laura L. Methot is a senior consultant with the Continuous Learning Group (CLG). She specializes in designing and implementing performance and process management systems that assist client organizations in meeting their strategic needs. She has extensive international experience working as a consultant and performance coach to health care organizations, government agencies, and private-sector businesses. Dr. Methot's projects have included designing and implementing large-scale leadership and organizational development systems, leading executive coaching and training, and facilitating cross-functional teams in re-designing process and implementing change in global organizations.

Dr. Methot holds a B.A. in psychology from Saint Mary's University in Halifax, Nova Scotia. She also holds an M.A. in industrial/organizational psychology and a Ph.D. in applied behaviour analysis from Western Michigan University. Prior to joining CLG, Dr. Methot was Assistant Professor of Industrial/Organizational Psychology at Saint Mary's University, where she designed and taught graduate courses in behavioural systems analysis, organizational change, and training and development. She has co-authored *Fundamentals of Behavior Analytic Research* with Alan Poling and Mark LeSage and has presented her research at conferences of the Association for Behavior Analysis, the Atlantic Conference on Ergonomics, the Canadian Psychological Association, and the Canadian Society for Industrial and Organizational

Psychology. She is a past member of the executive council of the Association for Behavior Analysis and the Canadian Society for Industrial and Organizational Psychology. She has also served as a reviewer for academic journals and has been invited to speak at various academic and professional meetings.

PREFACE

Recruitment and Selection in Canada, Second Edition, is designed to meet the needs of both students and practitioners working in human resources or personnel psychology. It provides an up-to-date review of the current issues and methodologies that are used in recruiting and selecting employees for Canadian organizations. Over the years the field of personnel selection has become more quantitative and subject to both federal and provincial human rights legislation. This book provides an introduction to these more technical areas through an easy-to-read style. Each chapter includes examples and cases that illustrate how the practices discussed in the text are carried out in both private- and public-sector organizations. Many of these illustrations are drawn from current events reported in the media.

The text provides an introduction to sound procedures in recruitment and selection that meet scientific, professional, and Canadian legal standards. It presents recruitment and selection as essential components of strategic human resource planning and emphasizes their role in enhancing productivity. Starting with a solid scientific and legal foundation, the text introduces organizational and job analyses as the key to developing a recruitment and selection system and to understanding the relationship between improved selection systems and increased organizational productivity. The book includes contemporary developments related to competencies, interviewing, cognitive ability testing, personality testing, and drug and honesty testing. Recognizing the constraints under which organizations operate, the text presents recruitment and selection within the context of a global market and competition. One of the most remarkable developments since publication of the first edition of this book has been the rise of the Internet as a resource tool. We have included references to relevant Web sites and interactive material throughout the text and as part of the end-of-chapter exercises and cases.

This new edition of *Recruitment and Selection in Canada* offers several advantages to both students and practitioners. First it provides an up-to-date introduction to the current developments in recruiting and selecting employees within a Canadian context. The approach taken with this text has been to incorporate the Canadian material organically into the development of the text rather than "Canadianizing" a popular American text. This approach has allowed us to focus in greater detail on issues of concern to Canadian organizations and to Canadian human resource practitioners. We feature, wherever possible, Canadian examples and Web sites.

We have attempted to provide as complete coverage as possible on current issues in recruitment and selection. We do this by integrating the role of recruitment and selection in a context of strategic human resource planning. At all stages of the recruitment and selection process, the text emphasizes the necessity of satisfying both professional and legal requirements and offers guidelines on how this can be accomplished. Increasingly, both students and practitioners must understand the scientific, technical, and legal aspects that form the basis of current recruitment and selection practices. Often, texts on recruitment and selection make little attempt to explain the statistical and technical underpinnings of these topics, or do so in a way that those new to the material cannot comprehend. Unlike these other texts, we have provided a complete and thorough introduction to this essential material in a readable, non-technical style that minimizes scientific jargon and emphasizes understanding of the basic concepts in a context of application. To assist understanding, we have also included learning points at the start of each chapter, definitions of important concepts throughout each chapter, and both exercises and case material at the end of each chapter to illustrate important principles and concepts.

This text is designed for one-semester courses in Human Resource Management, Personnel Psychology, and Personnel Selection. It is also an ideal text for short courses that form part of diploma or professional upgrading programs. The first edition of *Recruitment and Selection in Canada* was adopted for courses taught as part of degree programs in colleges and universities; as well, it is used as a standard reference for graduate courses. One of the strengths of the text is the systematic integration of the different aspects of recruitment and selection with current legal and technical practices. However, the needs of students and instructors may differ across the settings in which this text may be used. Some students may already have had a substantial introduction to the scientific method and measurement issues in other courses that form part of their program. In those cases, Chapter 3, or parts of it, can be omitted. Later chapters in the text, however, do refer to material contained in Chapter 3 or to concepts introduced in it. If these have been omitted, the student can easily read the relevant sections of Chapter 3 in conjunction with the later reference. We have not placed Chapter 3 in an appendix because it is our firm believe that any human resource practitioner must be familiar with the content of Chapter 3 in order to practice recruitment and selection in a professionally acceptable manner.

Similarly, Chapter 6 includes a discussion of issues related to the measurement of performance. It is our firm belief that students must be conversant with all aspects of the recruitment and selection system. Measurement of performance is essential to evaluating the effectiveness of any selection system. Often the problem with poor selection systems is not the selection instruments used, but how performance is measured. Performance is the bottom line and we have integrated that into the text. Again, if performance measurement and evaluation have been covered elsewhere in a student's program, Chapter 6 can serve as a brief, useful review.

In developing both Chapters 3 and 6, we have tried to strike a balance by presenting only the information that any human resource practitioner is likely to need to know. A guiding rule has been, "Is this information essential for a human resource practitioner to meet both legal and professional standards in the conduct of their practice?" We feel we have met this standard.

What's changed in this new edition? The most notable changes involve the addition of a separate chapter on competencies and the deletion of the chapter on "future trends." Competency assessment has played a more prominent role in recruitment and selection over the past few years. In Chapter 5, we review developments in this area from a legal and scientific perspective. We have also included conceptual information on job performance in this chapter, as the two issues are related. We have placed material on performance measurement in Chapter 6. Since the "future" has become the "now," we have integrated the material from Chapter 11 of the first edition into the appropriate chapters of the current edition.

There are significant changes in the other chapters as well. Chapter 1 has been revised to emphasize the importance of recruitment and selection to the economic well-being of organizations competing in a global marketplace. Chapter 2 incorporates the most recent human rights cases that have changed the legal foundation for human resources, particularly the new, more stringent tests needed to establish bona fide occupational requirements. We have moved the discussion of utility analysis from Chapter 3 to Chapter 11's discussion on decision making. We have also updated our presentation on validity in Chapter 3 to reflect the most recent changes in professional standards; as well, we have expanded our presentation on the topics of bias and fairness. Chapter 4 now includes more detailed information on how knowledge, skills, abilities, and other requirements are derived from different job analyses. We have also included new job analysis procedures. Chapter 7, on recruitment, has expanded to include the phenomenal growth of the Internet as a recruitment tool. Chapter 8 updates research on the use of application blanks, résumés, and screening interviews and contains a new section on work experience as a screening tool. Chapter 9 presents an expanded section on the role of personality in selection and the use of honesty and drug/alcohol tests, and also contains a new section on "emotional intelligence." Chapter 10 presents the most recent information on the interview as a selection device and provides more information on developing situational or behavioural interviews. The book now concludes with our discussion on decision making; Chapter 11 reviews recent developments, including legal precedents, on the use of procedures designed to enhance employment equity. As noted previously, we have included many new features throughout the text to enhance learning opportunities and to make the text more "interactive," including the use of Web sites, expanded exercises, and case material. We believe we have succeeded in this endeavour.

ACKNOWLEDGMENTS

The production of any book is a collaborative effort. Many people, other than the authors whose names appear on the cover, play an important role. We would like to acknowledge their assistance and to thank them for their valuable contributions to this process. We have tried to present in this book the latest scientific foundation for human resources management. We could not have done that without the research compiled by our academic colleagues throughout North America and the experience of human resources practitioners in adapting that research to the workplace. This book would not exist if it were not for their work.

We are also indebted to our past and present students who have challenged our ideas and made us be clear in the exposition of our arguments. In particular, we owe a debt to the students in Psychology 428 and Psychology 605 at Saint Mary's University; their feedback on early drafts of this text was invaluable. Likewise, the book benefited immensely from the feedback of reviewers at various colleges and universities across Canada. For taking the time to read the early drafts and share with us their extensive and detailed comments, we thank Eli Levanoni, Brock University; Herman Schwind, Saint Mary's University; Diane White, Seneca College; Robert McManus, Algonquin College; Rick Goffin, University of Western Ontario; Bob Russell, Assiniboine Community College; Dan Scarlicki, University of Calgary; Alan Saks, York University; Edward Rowney, University of Calgary; Barbara Marshall, Sheridan College; and Anne Harper, Humber College.

Monica Belcourt, the editor for the series, deserves special praise. She was the glue that held everything together and kept the project on track. It is truly the case that without her efforts, this book would not have materialized. We must also acknowledge the patience and professionalism of the team at Nelson; first, John Horne and Edward Ikeda, who handled the early development of the book, and then Jenny Anttila, Anita Miecznikowski, Jackie Wood, Lynda Chiotti, Karina TenVeldhuis, and Natalia Denesiuk, who shepherded this project to completion.

Finally, we are most grateful to our families and friends who provided us with support and understanding throughout the long nights. They inspired us to think and write clearly.

Victor M. Catano
SAINT MARY'S UNIVERSITY

Steven F. Cronshaw
UNIVERSITY OF GUELPH

Willi H. Wiesner
MCMASTER UNIVERSITY

Rick D. Hackett
MCMASTER UNIVERSITY

Laura L. Methot
METHOT ASSOCIATES
APPLIED PERFORMANCE SOLUTIONS

1

INTRODUCTION

CHAPTER GOALS

This chapter introduces the topics of recruitment and selection in Canadian organizations.

After reading this chapter you should

- appreciate the importance and relevance of recruitment and selection to Canadian organizations;
- understand the terms recruitment and selection;
- understand the impact that the global economy, technology, and a changing workforce have on recruitment and selection;
- understand the economic context in which recruitment and selection take place;
- know where recruitment and selection fit into the organization as a whole and the human resources management system in particular;
- know which professional associations and groups in Canada have a stake in recruitment and selection;
- become familiar with basic ethical issues in recruitment and selection; and
- understand how the rest of the chapters in this book work together to present a detailed picture of both the practice and theory of recruitment and selection in Canada.

"Hi, my name is Joe, and until recently I worked for the Beaver Beer Company. I was Beaver's director in charge of human resources. You may have heard a lot about Beaver Beer; it's been in the news lately. This is my story.

"I graduated from college with a diploma in human resources and worked my way up from an entry-level position. I kept up with all the developments in HR. Over the years I insisted that Beaver Beer do things the right way in recruiting and selecting. I applied all the best HR principles and practices that I learned over the years. We had some of the best people working for us. They were committed, knew what to do, and worked hard to get their jobs done. Sometimes it took a while to demonstrate that these best practices, which cost a fair bit of money to implement, would pay off in the long run for Beaver Beer. Hiring the best people would lead to more productivity and to higher profits for Beaver Beer; those new profits would more than cover the recruiting and selection costs.

"The beer industry is pretty competitive, and when the recession hit, the human resources department was the first to be downsized. This was bad enough, but my new boss did not think human resources was contributing to the company's profits. He thought we were too 'scientific' in our approach. He couldn't understand why we had to spend so much time and money showing our selection procedures were 'valid.' He felt that the beer industry had to 'catch the next wave' before it happened and this meant hiring people in the 19–34 age group, the same demographic as most of our customers. He wanted us to hire people 'who knew beer.' He kept showing me all these articles he read on the airplane; you know the ones, where the newest management guru has the quick fix to all your problems (for a small fee)? He brought in this one guy he read about to give us a seminar on the best way to hire people. The guru had a method that was guaranteed to work. It involved hiring only those applicants who had a high 'developmental quotient.' You brought the candidate in, sat them down in a quiet room, and asked them a series of questions about their childhood and adolescence. The guru claimed that most people were stuck in the adolescent stage and your goal was to find candidates who had progressed to the adult level, which was difficult to do since very few people had attained that level. You could hire people who were at the pre-adult stage if you sent them to his training seminar to learn how to advance to the next stage. He trained people to identify a person's 'developmental quotient' based on their answers to the interview questions.

"After the seminar my boss pulled me aside and said he wanted to change our selection procedures to the 'DQ' method. I laughed and told him what I thought of the procedure. He said I would either implement the 'DQ' selection system and a training program to increase 'DQ' levels or look for a new job. I knew I should have stood up for what was right and for what I believed in, but I couldn't afford to lose my job at my age with a mortgage to pay. I convinced myself that the new system met the selection standards outlined by my professional association and decided to give it a try.

"It's not a simple thing to make quality beer. It takes a lot of highly qualified people interacting with one another to make sure our plant is operated safely and efficiently and that our beer meets all the regulatory standards for the food and beverage industry. We have engineers, system analysts, computer people, and food scientists working for us along with the brewers. There was a good team spirit in place and people were committed to the company until the new hires started arriving. The older employees did not think the new people were competent. More and more of our older employees became dissatisfied with the way things were going and took jobs with our competitors. We kept hiring their replacements through the 'DQ' system until most of the plant was staffed with very young people hired by this procedure. The new people kept referring to the older workers as 'pre-adolescents'; that didn't help morale.

"I began to feel things were going wrong when I saw one of our new technicians running his hands along the filtered water supply pipes leading into the brew vats. He told me he was checking the pressure in the pipes. I asked if he should be using some type of pressure gauge to do that. He said he was trying to save time and money and he could really sense the pressure. A week later, the pipe burst, causing a shutdown in the whole plant. Everyone was asked to pitch in and help control the damage and repair the system. The older employees worked like dogs; so did the newer ones—until 5:00 P.M., quitting time. They up and left because their shift was over. They didn't feel it was their responsibility to stay until the pipe was fixed. The older employees stayed and worked until the system was back in service.

"It went downhill from there. We're a craft beer and we make a big selling point over not pasteurizing our product to maintain its taste. We have to be very careful with our quality control to ensure that there are no E. coli bacteria in our water supply. We continuously test the water we use, and our engineers are supposed to alert us as soon as they detect anything wrong with the supply. Well, one technician discovered a questionable test result late one Friday but didn't tell anybody about it until the following week. We had to destroy the whole production run, but thankfully none of the bad beer had gotten out of the plant. Perhaps this is why we started receiving so many complaints about the decrease in our beer's quality and why our sales started dropping off.

"I should mention that I began to spend most of my time preparing for court and tribunal hearings. Some of our job candidates found out we were only hiring people between 19 and 34 years old. They filed a complaint with the human rights tribunal that we were discriminating against them. We also had another problem with the 'DQ' system when some female applicants thought some of the 'DQ' questions about their adolescent experiences were too intimate and suggestive. They filed a sexual harassment suit. These cases became so costly we had to hire two lawyers to deal with them. We wound up paying these people hundreds of thousands of dollars when our lawyers brought in external consultants who told us there was no way we could legally defend our system as a valid and reliable selection system. The lawyers told us to cut our losses and settle the suits.

"Of course as the HR director, I took the fall for all these problems and was fired by my boss. It wasn't a big deal as Beaver Beer had lost so much market share by this time that it was headed down the tubes with the bad beer. Luckily, enough people in the industry knew I wasn't responsible for the 'DQ' system, and I was able to get a job with another beer company where they emphasize only the best recruiting and selection practices. As I said, my name is Joe."

WHY RECRUITMENT AND SELECTION MATTER

As you probably guessed, "Joe" does not exist. He is a composite based on several HR managers and their experiences in different organizations. The incidents in the story are based on actual situations. The important work of human resources departments is often overlooked, or if it is recognized, it is not given sufficient credit for the value it adds to an organization. Is the attitude toward human resources in your organization one of, "Aren't they the people who collect job applications and plan the Christmas party?" There is a growing disconnect between organizational management and the people in the organization (Pfeffer and Veiga, 1999). Too often it is only when things go wrong, or accident reports point to "human error," that organizations begin to re-examine the contribution that their employees make not only to the health and safety of the workers and public, but also to the financial success of the company. Pfeffer and Veiga (1999) make the point that today's managers must begin to take seriously the often-heard, yet frequently ignored, adage that people are a company's most important asset.

Our purpose in writing this book is to lay out the "best practices" in finding and hiring people who will contribute to the overall success of an organization. Best practices are valid, reliable, and legally defensible. By definition, these practices are supported by empirical evidence that has been accumulated through accepted scientific procedures. Best practices do not involve "hunches," "guesses," or unproven practices. Best practices involve the ethical treatment of job applicants throughout the recruitment and hiring process. Best practices result from human resources professionals following the accepted standards and principles of professional associations.

Human resources is a very broad field. We are only going to examine the recruitment and selection components of the human resources field (the other books in this series will introduce you to other human resources topics). Recruitment and selection are the means organizations use, for better or for worse, to find and choose employees.

Recruitment is the generation of an applicant pool for a position or job in order to provide the required number of candidates for a subsequent selection or promotion program. Recruitment is done to meet management goals and objectives for the organization as well as current legal requirements (human rights, employment equity, labour law, and other legislation).

Selection is the choice of job candidates from a previously generated applicant pool in a way that will meet management goals and objectives as well as current legal requirements. Selection can involve any of the following functions: hiring at the entry level from applicants external to the organization, promotion or lateral transfer of people within the organization, and movement of current employees into training and development programs.

Effective recruitment and selection practices can mean the difference between an organization's success or failure. Differences in skills among job candidates translate into performance differences on the job that have economic consequences for an organization. Hiring people with the right skills or the highest levels of those skills leads to positive economic outcomes for the organization. Hiring people with the wrong set of skills leads to disaster for both the person and the organization. Effective recruitment and selection practices identify job applicants with the appropriate level of knowledge, skills, abilities, and other requirements needed for successful performance in a job or an organization.

Empirical studies demonstrate that organizations using effective recruitment and selection practices gain a competitive advantage in the marketplace. Best practices in recruitment and selection

- Reduce employee turnover and increase productivity (Koch and Gunter-McGrath, 1996). A one standard deviation increase in the use of sophisticated HR practices decreased turnover by 7 percent and increased sales by $27 000 per employee per year (Huselid, 1995).
- Are responsible for up to 15 percent of a firm's relative profit (Huselid, 1995).
- Correlate with an organization's long-term profitability and productivity ratios (d'Arcimoles, 1997).
- Help to establish employee trust (Whitener, 1997).
- Improve the knowledge, skills, and abilities of an organization's current and future employees, increase their motivation, and help to retain high-quality employees while encouraging poor performers to leave (Jones and Wright, 1992).

Today's workplace must also adapt to increasing global competition, rapid advances in information technology, and changing workforce demographics. Belcourt and McBey (2000) present a detailed discussion of these topics in the context of strategic human resources planning. To remain competitive, organizations must have in place human resource strategies for recruiting, identifying, and selecting employees who will contribute to the overall effectiveness of the organization. With respect to recruitment and selection, the old ways of hiring on the basis of a résumé and a brief interview, or

BOX 1.1 Recruitment and Selection of Transit Workers

One highly visible job in Canadian cities from Victoria to St. John's is that of transit operator. Transit companies and commissions from coast to coast (and as far north as Yellowknife), some large and some small, have the responsibility of providing public transportation to their urban populations. To do this, they must recruit and hire workers of many different skills into positions throughout the organization: senior- and middle-level managers, street supervisors and superintendents, mechanics, cleaners, and many others. Transit experts generally agree that the most critical job is that of transit operator, that is, the person who delivers the front-line service by driving the bus and conveying passengers from place to place. Transit operators also make up the largest employee group in any transit company.

Where does recruitment and selection come in and why are these important to the operation of transit companies? To begin with, the financial health of the transit company depends on attracting and keeping a loyal ridership. These are the management goals of many such companies. Because there are viable alternatives to public transportation, such as private automobiles and cabs, the company must strive to provide the safest and most comfortable ride at a reasonable cost or risk losing riders to other forms of transportation.

What are the major factors that you would consider when deciding whether to take a city bus or a private vehicle to a concert? Which of the following have you identified? A clean and tidy bus? A pleasant, helpful operator? A smooth ride without too much bumping and jostling? A safe, trouble-free trip with no sudden stops or running over curbs? Getting picked up on time? Arriving at your stop on schedule? Many people list these factors when they are asked why they use, or do not use, transit services, and all of these factors are at least to some extent under the control of the operator driving the bus. Furthermore, anyone who takes public transit regularly will know that there are big differences between operators in how well they provide these things. Done well, these services will help meet management goals of attracting and holding the ridership that the company needs to stay in business; done poorly, these services will drive away riders to other forms of transportation.

Now the importance of properly recruiting and selecting transit operators becomes clear. The transit company should choose as new operators those people who have the potential to do the right things and to do them well. So what types of people might the company be looking for? Probably conscientious people who get along well with the general public, people who are safety conscious and do not get stressed when they are stuck in heavy traffic and are running behind schedule. The purpose of recruitment is to advertise the job so that people with high potential for it will be encouraged to apply, as well as to make sure that various groups not traditionally associated with transit operation (e.g., women) will apply for work with the company so that they can be put into the selection system.

The purpose of the selection process is to identify and choose the "right" people from the pool of qualified job applicants that has been provided through recruitment. These "right" people will then help the transit company by meeting the goals and objectives set by management (e.g., for customer service and traffic safety) as well as current legal requirements (e.g., women must be given a fair chance at the job). The selection process is done by various means, including testing and interviewing, as described in later chapters of this book.

on whom you know, do not work in the new economy. Those old practices may also lead an employer astray of new legal requirements. The socioeconomic changes taking place in today's workplace have an impact on human resources recruitment and selection. Today, more than ever before, effective recruitment and selection matter.

GLOBAL COMPETITION

Foreign trade has always been vital to the Canadian economy, dating as far back as the trading of beaver pelts in this country. As more than half of what is now produced in Canada is exported, we are extremely vulnerable to these foreign markets. Selling our products globally creates jobs for us, brings money into the country, helps sustain the purchasing power of the Canadian dollar, and contributes directly to the growth of our country. Our standard of living is at stake here, including the quality and size of our homes, the newness of the vehicles we drive, as well as our ability to purchase other consumer products.

What has changed is the *level of competition* as new players enter international markets and trade barriers between countries are softened. Companies relying mostly on domestic markets are no less vulnerable as foreign-owned businesses set up shop in Canada. In the retail sector, for example, large U.S.-owned nonunionized discount chains such as Costco and Wal-Mart are serious threats to the survival of smaller, unionized, Canadian-owned retailers who must scramble to increase efficiencies and lower costs of goods and labour (Williamson, 1996).

As trade tariffs are removed between countries, foreign-owned manufacturers with branch plants in Canada will move these facilities back home, or to other countries where efficiencies and the availability of lower-cost labour provide greater return on investment. Opponents of the North American Free Trade Agreement (NAFTA), which provides for a free-trade zone between Canada, the United States, and Mexico, are concerned that Canadian jobs will be lost to Mexico, where labour costs are significantly lower. Others have argued that the freer access to U.S. and Mexican markets provided by NAFTA will be a boon to the Canadian economy, resulting in far more jobs being created than are lost. Regardless of which side economic indicators support in the years ahead, Canadians must continually work on improving their competitiveness in providing goods and services domestically and internationally. Within the context of higher costs for human resources in Canada, companies and organizations must find a way of becoming more efficient. This means finding the best, most productive employees.

RAPID ADVANCES IN TECHNOLOGY

Technology refers to the tools, equipment, and machinery used to perform work. Advances in technology over the past decade have been incredible, spurred on by the arrival of and ongoing improvements to the computer. Computers are increasingly evident in the design and manufacture of products (e.g., cars, movies), in provision of services (e.g., automated banking machines), in the manipulation and transfer of data (e.g., the national census, human resource information systems), and in telecommunications (e.g., Internet, electronic conferencing). Uses of advanced technology by Canadian employers are numerous. Technology is affecting every aspect of our lives,

Technology—refers to the tools, equipment, and machinery used to perform work.

from the way we do our banking to way we study and pursue our education. Employers now expect new hires to be computer literate. Employers are also using technology to a greater extent than ever before to recruit and select employees. Employers are making use of technology to help them find the best people to hire.

CHANGING WORKFORCE DEMOGRAPHICS

The demographic makeup of the Canadian labour force is also undergoing significant transformations. The workforce is older, more gender-balanced, more culturally diverse, and more highly educated than at any other time in Canadian history. Consider the following:

- From 1993 to 2015, the ratio of Canadians aged 15–24 to those aged 55–64 will flip from 2:1 to 1:2 (Dumas, 1995).
- Women now represent close to half of the paid workforce, and many of them are mothers of preschool-age children ("The Progress of Women," 1995). Over 58 percent of all women between the ages of 15 and 65 participate in the Canadian labour force (Statistics Canada, 2000).
- Dual-earner couples and single-parent families have become commonplace ("Where Women Stand Now," 1995; Crompton and Geran, 1995).
- Multiculturalism in this country flourishes, with fully 49 percent of the increase in employment among 25–34-year-olds from 1986–91 attributable to recent immigrants (Chui and Devereaux, 1995).
- From 1991 to 1996, 78 percent of new entrants into Canada were from Asia, Central/South America, the Caribbean, and Africa, providing a truly multicultural mosaic. In the period 1971–80, immigrants from these regions comprised 57 percent of all new entrants to Canada (Statistics Canada, 2000).
- Visible minorities comprise 11 percent of the Canadian labour force (Statistics Canada, 2000).
- Over 16 percent of the Canadian population speak neither English nor French as their first language (Statistics Canada, 2000).
- People with disabilities account for a growing proportion of the labour force. Estimates put the figure at 3 percent (Belcourt and McBey, 2000).

DIVERSITY Today, women and nonwhites make up 70 to 80 percent of new entrants into the Canadian labour force. Ethnic groups in Canada possess expertise, skills, knowledge of foreign cultures and business practices, and natural trade links with overseas markets that are of value to employers in today's global economy. Special challenges, but tremendous opportunities, emerge from having a workplace that is increasingly diverse in functional expertise, gender, and culture.

Additionally, there is a growing population of people who have physical or mental challenges. Employers cannot discriminate against existing or potential employees who have disabilities; rather, they must accommodate the employee both in their hiring practices and on the job. Accommodation, as we will see in later chapters, may require an employer to redesign a job to integrate individuals with physical and mental disabilities into the workplace. Employers must hire on the basis of a job applicant possessing the knowledge, skills, and abilities that are necessary to perform a job, not on the basis of an applicant's disability.

EDUCATION   Educational trends are somewhat diverse. While formal educational attainment among workforce entrants is at an all-time high, the skills of these individuals are not well matched to the skills sought by employers (Evers, 1993). During these times of unprecedented educational attainment among Canadian youth, we are, nonetheless, in the midst of an illiteracy crisis with one-fifth of Canadian adults unable to complete a cheque or fill out a job application (Montigny and Jones, 1990). Not surprisingly, the end result is that many individuals enter the labour force with formal educational qualifications, accompanied by high expectations of their workplace, but often lacking the basic skills required to fulfill their jobs.

IMPLICATIONS FOR HR   How do employers ensure that the people they hire will have the knowledge, skills, and abilities that are needed to perform the jobs for which they are being hired? How do employers decide that one candidate has "more" of the required abilities than another? More fundamentally, how do employers know that the knowledge, skills, and abilities that they are seeking in new hires are actually needed for a specific job? How do employers ensure that their hiring policies and procedures will treat candidates from different gender and ethnic groups fairly as part of the recruitment and selection process? How do employers accommodate people with disabilities in both recruitment and selection? These are just a few of the questions that must be addressed by any HR manager or practitioner in setting up a recruitment and selection system.

WORKPLACE ADJUSTMENTS

There are multiple workplace adjustments resulting from the interactive forces of intense global competition, advanced technology, and demographic population shifts. These forces interact in a way that often requires workplace adjustments that have considerable implications for recruitment and selection. The Organisation for Economic Co-operation and Development reported that 25 percent of the enterprises within its member countries, which include Canada, had adopted new approaches to human resource management and organizational practices. These practices included hiring and layoffs, altering hours of

BOX 1.2 What's in a Name?

Recruitment and selection should contribute through the human resources system to the efficiency, effectiveness, and productivity of the larger organization. But to get the most out of their efforts, human resources specialists must determine what it is that recruitment and selection can contribute to the organization. This naming game is complicated by the fact that some people are able to contribute more than others to the organization and to the larger society, thus making it desirable to discriminate between people and put people to work doing the things they are best at. For example, according to Plato, the best soldiers in ancient Greece were those who possessed keen perception, courage, speed, and strength. In any group of people selected at random, there will be some who possess these qualities in good measure and others who do not. Today, human resources managers would refer to these characteristics as worker specifications and would seek to recruit and select people with worker specifications that are best suited to the job.

The first step in recruitment and selection is to name what workers bring to a job that will help the organization the most. This naming of what the employer wants in a new worker can be done in various ways. One approach commonly used is to identify the knowledge, skills, abilities, and other attributes (KSAOs) the best workers bring to the job (with the idea that these KSAOs will be later assessed in job applicants). Another approach is to define the *competencies* workers must have to perform to a level of excellence on the job. A third approach is to identify *critical incidents,* which are examples of especially effective and ineffective behaviour on the job. A fourth approach is to point out the *performance standards* that workers must meet on the job. All of these approaches can be used to describe either worker potential to do the job or the actual contribution a worker is expected to make once in the job. These approaches are not mutually exclusive, and two or more of them may be combined into a single methodology (e.g., a competency model may draw on critical incidents and performance standards). Job analysis methodologies are discussed again in Chapter 4, which describes ways in which industrial psychologists and others can label person and job variables in the recruitment and selection process.

So, what's in a name? As it turns out, a name means a great deal. The proper naming of the person and job variables in the recruitment and selection system is of fundamental importance. The kinds of methods used and results achieved in the recruitment and selection process will depend greatly on the labels used when analyzing the job, regardless of whether those labels are KSAOs, job competencies, critical incidents, performance standards, or all of the above.

---

work, using part-time and contract workers, subcontracting, and outsourcing work, flattening hierarchical structures, more fluid job designs, multitasking, multiskilling, self-managed teams, and multifunctional teams. The adoption of these practices increased with firm size, the rate of technological change, and the degree of international competition ("The Changing Workplace," 1997). Our focus here is on the impact of workplace adjustments on recruitment and selection. Belcourt and McBey (2000) present a much broader discussion on downsizing and restructuring issues in *Strategic Human Resources Planning*.

JOB DISPLACEMENT Labour-saving technology, coupled with disappearing tariffs and intense global competition, have caused the elimination of thousands of manufacturing jobs in Canada. Clothing, tools, appliances, and countless other items once made by Canadians for Canadians are now imported from countries that can make them cheaper. Canadian employers wanting to survive in this world of global trade must trim costs wherever possible to be competitive. In the 1980s it was cheaper to add workers than to add machines; now the cost of labour in Canada is twice the cost of machines (Foot and Stoffman, 1996). Today's organizations are adding machines to replace labour for low-skilled, high-routine jobs. The unskilled, low-entry jobs previously available to people between the ages of 15 and 24 with less than high-school education are fast disappearing. Labour-saving technology is having a similar impact on the service sector—for example, consider the widespread use of automated banking machines and the rapid rise of sales through the Internet. The common denominator throughout manufacturing and service sectors, and across worker and management functions, is that the routine aspects of jobs requiring little skill (i.e., the drudgery) are increasingly being done by technology.

ORGANIZATIONAL RESTRUCTURING   At the same time that technology is reducing the need for labour, organizations must cope with the aging of a large segment of their workforce. In particular, "baby boomers" (those born from 1947 to 1966 and who comprise one-third of the Canadian population) will begin to approach normal retirement in the next 10 years or so. To cope with these changing demographics over the past decade, employers have implemented layoffs and early-retirement incentive packages, and have restructured or downsized their enterprises. Most notably, the traditional organizational structure of a pyramid, where there is a broad base of employees at entry-level positions and fewer employees at each of several higher levels, is being flattened. A pyramidal organizational structure works best when there is a large and continuous flow of new workers into entry-level positions: the 60-year-olds at the top direct the 40-year-olds in the middle, who in turn manage the 20-year-olds at the bottom (Foot and Stoffman, 1996). At the peak of the baby boom (1960) the fertility rate was four children per family. When these boomers grew up and went to work, labour force growth shot up to 3 percent per year in Canada, and our economy created jobs faster than any other industrialized country. But fertility rates dropped significantly from 1967 to 1979, resulting in a much smaller cohort entering the workforce 20 years later, and an annual labour growth rate of half of what it was for the boomers. This in turn has led to too many people in their 40s looking for management positions and too few teens and people in their 20s to fill the lower-level positions vacated by the boomers (Crompton, 1995). In the coming years as aging "boomers" retire, will there be an adequate labour supply to replace them? In a seller's market, there will have to be more emphasis placed on recruiting as more organizations compete to hire fewer qualified candidates.

REDEFINING JOBS In today's information era, workers are required to apply a wider range of skills to an ever-changing series of tasks. Individuals just entering the workforce may face at least three to four career changes in their lifetime. Employers will expect workers to possess the skills and knowledge of two or three traditional employees (Greenbaum, 1996). On the factory floor, jobs are moving targets as they change rapidly. Workers themselves may be asked to move or rotate among positions; to do so they will need to have or be able to acquire multiple, generic skills. This poses special challenges when trying to match people to jobs. Does it make sense to select people on the basis of very specific skills and abilities required by one job? Should employers re-define recruitment and selection in terms of finding people with broader skills or "competencies" that are of value to the organization and cut across many jobs?

Contingent employment— part-time work, tempo-rary work, contract work, or any work where an employee is hired on less than a full-time, perma-nent basis by an employer.

CONTINGENT EMPLOYMENT Part-time work, temporary work, contract work, and self-employment in Canada increased between 1989 and 1994 (Krahn, 1995). Since 1990, full-time jobs (30 or more hours per week) accounted for only one of every four new jobs created; the rest were part-time (Greenspon, 1996). From 1995 to 1999, 19 percent of all people who participated in the labour force did so on a part-time basis (Statistics Canada, 2000). Part-time employment is more heavily concentrated among females and among those between the ages of 15 and 24. It is also higher in the services sector, which grew by 55 percent between 1976 and 1995, compared with only a 2 percent growth rate in goods-producing industries. The services share of total employment rose from 64 to 73 percent over the same period (Krahn, 1995). Interestingly, approximately one-third of the part-time workforce is part-time by choice, perhaps to allow for greater balancing of home and work responsibilities.

Self-employment has grown rapidly, rising from 10.9 percent of the work-force in 1976 to 15.4 percent in 1995 (Little, 1996). This increase has been attrib-uted, in part, to business opportunities arising from large employers downsizing and restructuring, coupled with the adoption of policies pro-moting contracting out and privatization by government. Long-term specific contracts with companies are replacing permanent jobs. In these cases, the company pays a flat fee for the contract and is freed from paying costly bene-fits. What impact does the use of such contingent employment practices have on traditional recruitment and selection?

RECRUITMENT AND SELECTION, HRM, AND THE ORGANIZATION

The above section illustrated that recruitment and selection do not take place in isolation. They are influenced by the events occurring in broader society that affect the organization as a whole. Recruitment and selection also take place in the somewhat narrower context of the organization itself. Recruitment and selection play an important role in the human resources management function. Effective human resources management contributes to organizational survival,

BOX 1.3 The Origins of Recruitment and Selection in Ancient Times

Recruitment and selection began to make sense as societies grew in size and became more complex. In these societies, people began to specialize in the work they performed rather than in doing all the jobs that had to be carried out for their survival. With the rise of specialization, some people became artisans, others labourers, others soldiers, and still others priests and rulers. To survive, a society had to devise ways of identifying those people who would be the best soldiers, clerks, or skilled labourers so that it could be properly defended, administered, and maintained.

One of the earliest indications that society recognized that people differ in their aptitude or ability to do different jobs can be found in Plato's *Republic*. In this book, Plato paints a vivid picture of his society in fourth century B.C. He explains that societies come together for the purpose of meeting needs (food, shelter, clothing) that individuals by themselves cannot satisfy. In doing so, the state achieves greater efficiency of production because workers can specialize in jobs for which they have the most natural aptitude. Plato even recommends that for the most vital job, that of soldier or guardian of the state, the individuals

chosen for this position should possess "suitable natural aptitudes," including psychological characteristics of keen perception and courage combined with physical characteristics of speed and strength.

Internal organization and defence of the state have remained important to societies throughout history. Recruitment and selection, as advocated by Plato, have been used to staff key positions within government and military institutions; for example, Imperial China relied for over 1300 years on a complex system of examinations to select candidates for its civil service (Wang, 1994). Today, the federal government and the military are two of the largest users of advanced recruitment and selection practices in Canada (Cronshaw, 1991). Both the federal civil service and the Canadian Forces invest large amounts of time and money to find the qualified and experienced people that are needed to ensure that the core functions of the government and the military are maintained. To do otherwise, either today or in Plato's time, would be to court disaster by compromising the most fundamental economic, social, and political institutions that hold society together.

---

success, and renewal. This is as true today as it was in Plato's day (see Box 1.3). To appreciate the importance and role of recruitment and selection in today's organization, let's review the function of human resources management within the context of a large organizational system.

The systems model in Figure 1.1 represents a typical private-sector organization that is set up to produce and sell a product or service on the open market.* Systems models are meant to be broad and comprehensive, taking in the full scope of the process or system they represent. **Systems models** reflect the relationships among the various components of the system, showing how they work together to achieve desired outcomes. The model contains some

Systems models—representations of the important relationships among the various components of an organization showing how the constituent parts work together to achieve desired outcomes.

---

*Figure 1.1 presents a general model for profit-making businesses. Organizations in the public sector (e.g., the transit companies described in Box 1.1) work in somewhat the same way, except that they receive their money input from public sources such as income and property tax revenues. Money surpluses that are realized are retained in the organization or are returned to a centralized government office rather than being distributed to individuals as dividends.

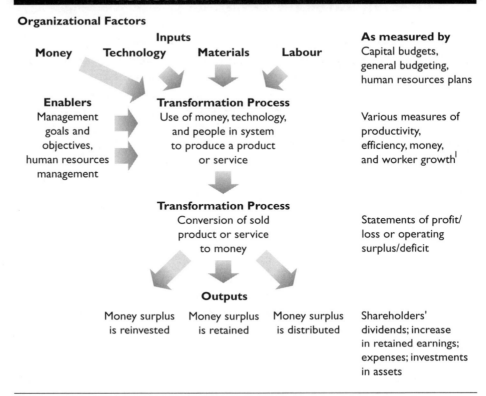

FIGURE 1.1 A GENERAL MODEL FOR ORGANIZATION FUNCTIONING

Organizational Factors

Inputs

Money	Technology	Materials	Labour

As measured by
Capital budgets, general budgeting, human resources plans

Enablers
Management goals and objectives, human resources management

Transformation Process
Use of money, technology, and people in system to produce a product or service

Various measures of productivity, efficiency, money, and worker growth[1]

Transformation Process
Conversion of sold product or service to money

Statements of profit/ loss or operating surplus/deficit

Outputs

Money surplus is reinvested	Money surplus is retained	Money surplus is distributed

Shareholders' dividends; increase in retained earnings; expenses; investments in assets

[1] Includes HR measures such as individual performance ratings, absences, work attitudes, and so on.

typical measures (see right-hand side of Figure 1.1) that are used for planning, process control, coordination of materials and people, and evaluation of financial success. Some of these measures come out of the human resources function, including performance appraisals, individual production records, and attitude surveys. The final output at the bottom of Figure 1.1 is money, rather than the product or service, to emphasize that the organization does not realize its "payoff" until the output is sold.

There are four basic components in the systems model: inputs, transformation processes, outputs, and enablers. Inputs are those things that go into a system to be acted on and combined within the transformation process. For example, car parts purchased from supplier companies are an input to an automotive assembly plant (the assembly plant being the organization system for the purpose of this example). Labour is another input because the assembly plant requires skilled and trained people to operate equipment and maintain the plant. Technology comprises the machines and procedures used in production. Money simply represents the financial contribution that stakeholders (e.g., owner, shareholders) have made to start the business and keep it going.

In the first transformation process, the inputs are taken into the system, converted, and combined to generate a product or service. In our auto plant example, the transformation process is an assembly line whereby materials (car parts, frames, engines) are put together by workers into a completed automobile using the available technology. The automobile rolls off the end of the assembly line as the output of the production system, which is in turn converted by a second transformation process to money at the point of sale. This money is placed in the bank, then tracked by the organizational accounting system. In the case of the car manufacturer, the conversion of the product to money occurs when the cars are sold from the factory to retail car dealers.

If the organizational system as a whole is efficient, effective, and productive enough, then the manufacturer's financial statements will show a profit or surplus, which will move as a money surplus to the bottom level of Figure 1.1. This money surplus can be reinvested in the company to acquire new technology, human resources, or raw materials for the production process; retained by the company as money in the bank; or distributed back to owners and shareholders as dividends. Money distributed back to the business owner or shareholders may be invested in other businesses, which in turn recruit and hire workers through their human resources systems.

Enablers are the most relevant of the four systems components to human resources management and to recruitment and selection. Enablers are closely connected to the transformation process. Enablers contribute to the organizational system by assisting the transformation process to efficiently and effectively combine the inputs in generating outputs. The two enablers in Figure 1.1 are management goals and objectives (to give the necessary direction and coordination to the productive effort), and human resources management practices and policies (to support and enable the integration of the labour input into the production process). There are other enablers (e.g., engineering, accounting) that we have not included in Figure 1.1 to keep the focus on the human resources enabler, which is most relevant to recruitment and selection.

The systems model in Figure 1.1 illustrates two basic principles:

Principle 1: Human resources management must carefully coordinate its activities with the other enablers and with the transformation processes as a whole if the larger organization system is to function properly.

Principle 2: Human resources managers must think in systems terms and have the welfare of the whole organization in mind.

If HR managers fail to recognize the contributions of the other enablers or if they fail to coordinate their efforts with them, senior management may begin to question the added value that human resources brings to the firm. Human resources must be in full touch with the needs of the larger organization. As a staff unit, the role of human resources is to support line units pursuing the central mission of the organization. HR professionals must have an understanding and appreciation of their interdependencies with, and reliance on, other stakeholders throughout the organization. Recruitment and selection must be carried

Enablers—functions or processes that assist in transforming system inputs into outputs.

out in the context of the system, not simply as an isolated function divorced from other aspects of the organization.

The human resources enabler in Figure 1.1 can be broken down into its component parts to examine the path of an individual worker within the organization. As shown at the far-left side of Figure 1.2, the employee first becomes involved with the organization through recruitment and selection. After entering the organization, the newcomer undergoes an orientation period as part of becoming ready to make a long-term productive contribution within the transformation process. The human resources department is responsible for making the employee become as productive as possible and ensuring that the employee properly meshes with the other inputs and enablers in the system. The human resources department will undertake interventions such as training and development, performance evaluation, compensation, and motivation to meet these objectives. Finally, as the worker's time with the organization draws to a close, the HR department may assist in helping the employee exit from the organization through retirement, outplacement, or other means.

As Figure 1.2 shows, recruitment and selection set the stage for other human resources interventions. If recruitment and selection are done properly, the subsequent movement of the worker through the organizational system is made easier and the individual makes a long-term, positive contribution to organizational survival and success. When this happens, human resources management becomes more of an enabler within the organizational system as a whole. Conversely, if the worker enters the organization on a flat trajectory because of poor recruitment and selection, then the entire system, including human resources, is adversely affected. The human resources management function becomes less of an enabler. In today's competitive, ever-changing, and unforgiving business environment, human resources must be seen as an effective enabler or else face a grim (but deserved) fate at the hands of results-oriented senior managers.

FIGURE 1.2 STAGES IN EMPLOYEE TRANSISTION AND INVOLVEMENT IN THE HR MANAGEMENT PROCESS

Entry	Transition	Contribution	Exit
◆ Recruitment ◆ Selection	◆ Newcomer orientation	◆ Training and development ◆ Performance evaluation and management ◆ Compensation ◆ Motivational programs	◆ Voluntary separation ◆ Outplacement ◆ Retirement

RECRUITMENT AND SELECTION AND THE HR PROFESSIONAL

We have emphasized the need for HR staff to be aware of both the external and the internal influences that affect the working environment in which organizations operate. We have also argued that HR staff must not become isolated within the organization. There is another aspect to isolation: HR staff are professionals, who must keep abreast of developments in their field through continuous learning. HR staff are responsible for knowing the latest legal and scientific information with respect to recruitment and selection. They are responsible for implementing policies and procedures that are in accordance with accepted professional standards.

Recruitment and selection activities within human resources management are frequently carried out by in-house human resources staff, sometimes assisted by consultants from management consulting firms. These in-house staff and consultants come to human resources management from various educational backgrounds, which are augmented by practical experience in managing human resources (see Box 1.4).

Many practitioners and consultants involved in human resources management hold membership in one or more professional associations and may be certified or registered with an association or professional licensing body in their area of specialization. Box 1.5 gives some basic information on associations having an interest in recruitment and selection practices in Canada. These

---

BOX 1.4 Several Career Paths into Recruitment and Selection

Ms. L. became interested in human resources management when taking a business program at a community college. After obtaining her college degree, she took eight courses in order to earn a Certificate in Human Resources Management. Since then, Ms. L. has worked as a human resources specialist in a large manufacturing plant, where she has run an assessment centre used by her employer to hire new workers. Ms. L. hopes to eventually move into a senior human resources management position with her present employer or with a similar company in the manufacturing sector.

Mr. R. moved into the field after completing his degree in sociology at university. He started work in the human resources department of an aircraft parts manufacturer and over the following year earned a Human Resources Certificate. Following completion of his human resources program, he accepted a more senior HR position with a new employer. Much of his time is spent in recruitment and selection activities, especially in monitoring the results of an employment equity program put in place by his current employer.

Ms. S. obtained a bachelor's degree in psychology and became interested in personnel psychology. She went on to complete a two-year graduate program in industrial and organizational psychology. Since receiving her master's degree, Ms. S. has worked in the human resources department of a major urban hospital, where her primary duties are testing and interviewing job applicants for various hospital

BOX 1.4 Continued

positions. Her other duties focus on compensation and benefits.

Ms. M. also received a master's degree in industrial and organizational psychology, but continued her studies to get a Ph.D. She works for an internationally based consulting firm, where she designs and implements large-scale recruitment and selection systems for banks, insurance companies, and other financial institutions. She is now a partner with the consulting firm and takes regular overseas assignments to assist clients in Europe and Asia with installation and maintenance of their selection systems.

associations have professional involvement well beyond recruitment and selection. With membership in these associations come certain rights and obligations, including adherence to ethical codes or standards.

Maintaining memberships in professional associations keeps the HR professional from becoming isolated and provides assistance when the practitioner encounters ethical difficulties. Professional associations have developed well-thought-out codes of conduct and behaviour that are designed to protect

BOX 1.5 Links to Professional Associations Involved in Recruitment and Selection

CANADIAN COUNCIL OF HUMAN RESOURCES ASSOCIATIONS (HTTP://WWW.CHRPCANADA.COM)

The CCHRA is a collaborative effort of 10 provincial and specialist human resources associations. Its website provides links to each member organization. The mission of the CCHRA includes establishing national core standards for the human resources profession and being the recognized resource on equivalency for human resources qualifications across Canada.

Membership Qualifications: Practitioners and students join provincial associations, not CCHRA. Membership requirements vary and can be found on each provincial association's website. Generally, provincial associations require completion of education and training as described

under their professional certification requirements; student memberships are normally available for those taking approved courses in a post-secondary or degree program.

Professional Certification Offered: The Certified Human Resources Professional (CHRP) designation recognizes achievement within the human resources field and the holder's distinguished professionalism. To receive this designation, practitioners must complete accredited courses, supervised professional experience in HR, or other requirements as specified by their provincial human resources association (e.g., Human Resources Professional Association of Ontario, HRPAO).

Ethical Guidelines or Standards: CCHRA Code of Ethics.

BOX 1.5 Continued

THE ASSOCIATION OF CANADIAN SEARCH, EMPLOYMENT AND STAFFING SERVICES (ACSESS) (HTTP://WWW.ACSESS.ORG)

ACSESS resulted from the merger of the Association of Professional Placement Agencies & Consultants and the Employment & Staffing Services Association of Canada. Its mission is

> providing services to, and communicating with, members of the employment, recruitment and staffing services industry; assuming a leadership role in industry licensing and regulation; coordinating educational programs and conferences; assisting in the development of required standards of professional performance; promoting best business practices, and adherence to both the spirit and letter of all applicable employment legislation and regulations; and developing pertinent statistics for the purpose of identifying economic and socio-economic trends.

Membership Qualifications: ACSESS does not accept membership from individuals. Corporate membership in the association is open to any independent organization in Canada engaged in the business of providing staffing services to its customers.

Professional Certification Offered: ACSESS provides and administers the CPC Certification Program. Candidates who meet core requirements, which include post-secondary education, length of service in the industry, compliance with the Code of Ethics and testing requirements, may use the designation CPC (Certified Personnel Consultant).

Code of Ethics: Association's Code of Ethics and Standards.

CANADIAN PSYCHOLOGICAL ASSOCIATION (INCLUDING THE CANADIAN SOCIETY FOR INDUSTRIAL AND ORGANIZATIONAL PSYCHOLOGY) (HTTP://WWW.CPA.CA)

The CPA is a national organization that represents all aspects of psychology, including industrial and organizational psychology and psychological testing and assessment. Psychologists, particularly practitioners, may also be members of provincial psychological associations. The CPA website contains links to provincial associations, provincial regulatory bodies, and psychology programs at Canadian universities.

The Canadian Society of Industrial and Organizational Psychology is composed of CPA members and other professionals with a particular interest in personnel psychology and organizational behaviour. More information on CSIOP can be found at http://www.sscl.uwo.ca/psychology/csiop/.

Membership Qualifications: Master's or Ph.D. degree in psychology.

Professional Certification Offered: Neither CPA nor CSIOP offer professional designations. Psychology is regulated at the provincial level through legislation. In order to use the designation "psychologist," an individual must be "registered" with a provincial regulatory body after meeting their educational, supervised practice, and other requirements.

Ethical Guidelines or Standards: Canadian Code of Ethics for Psychologists; Standards for Educational and Psychological Testing.

both the HR professionals and their clients. These codes help the professional to act in a manner that will be accepted by others in the profession. Whenever possible, we will use these codes to guide our discussion on recruitment and selection practices, as should any HR professional.

Ethics—the determination of right and wrong; the standards of appropriate conduct or behaviour for members of a profession: what those members may or may not do.

Ethics are the means by which we distinguish what is right from what is wrong, what is moral from what is immoral, what may be done from what may not be done. Of course, the laws of our country also tell us what is or is not permissible by imposing penalties, such as fines or imprisonment, on violators. Ethics is a difficult subject because it deals with the large grey area between those behaviours that society punishes as illegal and those that everyone readily agrees are noble and upright. A careful consideration of ethics is important because human resources management requires the balancing of the rights and interests of management with those of workers, as well as the rights and interests of the human resources professional with those of the larger society (see Box 1.6).

BOX 1.6 Looking for Common Ground: Ethical Codes

The professional associations described in Box 1.5 have ethical codes that apply to their members. In all codes, members are required to obey the laws of the country, avoid conflicts of interest, and remain current in their fields of expertise. In addition, these ethics codes outline other obligations that their members have to clients, management, and workers, as well as to the larger society. One of the principles from the Code of Ethics for the Human Resources Professionals Association of Ontario (HRPAO) states that their members shall "demonstrate commitment to such values as respect for human dignity and human rights and promote human development in the workplace, within the profession and society as a whole." The ACSESS Code of Ethics and Standards describes responsibilities that their members have to the public, the profession, other members, and to the client. The code states, "We will ensure that our clients, candidates and employees are aware of our duty to abide by this Code of Ethics and will undertake to bring any potential infringements before the appropriate Association body." Finally, the Canadian Code of Ethics for Psychologists, written by the Canadian Psychological Association (CPA), presents the following four ethical principles, which provide

a guide for individual ethical decision making: respect for the dignity of persons, responsible caring, integrity in relationships, and responsibility to society.

All of these ethical codes place constraints on what their members may and may not do when practising human resources management, including recruitment and selection. However, ethical decision making is not always clear-cut; often decisions must be made in the grey areas of ethics where reasonable people differ in what they consider to be right and wrong. To complicate matters even more, an action that is considered ethical under one code might be deemed unethical under another. These inconsistencies can and do occur because the HRPAO, ACSESS, and CPA ethical codes differ in content, scope, and emphasis. The bottom line to this discussion is that ethics is a complex matter and has the potential to be the Achilles' heel of many a promising human resources career. Professionals practising recruitment and selection should read carefully, then discuss with colleagues, the ethical codes that apply to them and their work.

Each association's code of ethics may be accessed through the website listed for it in Box 1.5.

Two examples of ethical dilemmas in recruitment and selection will help to illustrate why ethics are so important and why a professional may need assistance in deciding how to behave. In the first ethical dilemma, put yourself in the position of a management consultant who is asked by a large employer to design and implement a system to select workers for a manufacturing plant. The plant is unionized, and there is a history of poor union–management relations. Management informs you that it intends to break the union and, as a part of this effort, you are to come up with a selection system that will screen out all new job applicants having pro-union attitudes. The idea is to skew the workforce toward management so that the union can be broken in a future decertification vote. What's more, you are to keep the purpose of the selection system a secret and are asked by management to sign a contract in which you promise not to reveal its intentions to the union, the labour board, or any other outsiders. Where do your loyalties lie? Whose interests should you serve? Is it wrong for you, as the management consultant, to accept a fee to do what management is asking?

For the second ethical dilemma, imagine that you are a human resources manager who is considering the use of a selection system. You know that it will do a good job at selecting the best workers, but it also screens out members of visible minorities at a rate much greater than that for the white majority. Should you use this system or try to find another that does not screen out so many members of visible-minority groups? What if the new system does not do as good a job at selecting the best workers? Should you favour societal goals of increasing visible-minority representation in the workforce or the interests of your company?

These two ethical dilemmas raise difficult questions that cut to the very core of ethics. But such questions are unavoidable because ethics are central to any group representing itself as a professional association. Fortunately, professional human resources associations in Canada have written codes and standards to provide guidance on ethical matters to their members (see Box 1.6). Violations of these codes and standards result in professional censure, embarrassment, and, in the most serious cases, removal from the profession. Membership in the profession is based on adherence to its ethics and professional standards. Membership in the professional association is a public guarantee that the member operates in accordance with accepted principles. Naturally, these codes should factor heavily into the recruitment and selection work done by human resources professionals and described in this book.

A PREVIEW OF THIS BOOK

The remaining chapters of this book present a detailed treatment of the science and practice of recruitment and selection in Canada. In Chapter 2, we look at the legal and legislative context for recruitment and selection in Canada.

Recruitment and selection practices have been seriously affected by human rights and employment equity over the past 20 years; Chapter 2 discusses important implications of these trends for the present and future practice of recruitment and selection.

Chapter 3 lays down a conceptual platform for a later discussion of the techniques and methods of recruitment and selection in Canada. It describes how the scientific method has been adapted to recruitment and selection. It also presents an introduction to psychometric measurement, which is at the heart of assessing individual differences among job candidates. This third chapter is crucial; human resources management, if it is to meet the legal requirements set out in Chapter 2, must adhere to policies and practices that are supported by empirical evidence. A basic understanding of the scientific method and psychometric issues such as reliability and validity are necessary for any informed discussion of recruitment and selection.

Chapter 4 discusses job analysis, which is the means by which job and person variables are identified for the purpose of recruitment and selection. In fact, job analysis provides the essential information for all of the recruitment and selection activities described in Chapters 5 through 10 of the book. Taken together, then, the material in Chapters 2, 3, and 4 provides a solid foundation of legal and scientific principles, as well as detailed job information, on which to build effective recruitment and selection systems.

The next six chapters of the book (5 through 10) discuss how recruitment and selection are done. Chapter 5 presents a new discussion on the issue of "competencies": how they differ, if they do, from skills and abilities, and what role they should play in the selection process.

Chapter 6 deals with the job performance end of the recruitment and selection function, showing how performance of individual workers can be measured as a criterion against which to evaluate the success of recruitment and selection efforts. We also present several methods that can be used to measure job performance.

Chapter 7 discusses recruitment strategies that can be used to attract a qualified applicant pool in preparation for selection; it includes information on recent developments on how the Internet is transforming recruiting. Chapters 8 and 9 examine different selection methods that can be used in screening the applicant pool to find the most qualified workers, including work samples, assessment centres, and psychological tests. Chapter 8 also presents a selection model that is built on the principles identified in Chapters 3, 4, and 6, while Chapter 9 includes an expanded section on the use of personality tests in selection, as well as recent topics such as emotional intelligence. Chapter 10 discusses the employment interview, with an emphasis on structured interviews as highly effective selection tools. Chapter 11 concludes the text with a review of the strategies that are used to combine information from different selection methods as part of making selection decisions. It also discusses utility analysis as a means of evaluating the effectiveness of selection systems.

BOX 1.7 Human Resources and the Internet

One of the most significant developments in recent years has been the growth of the Internet. This resource has made available to students and practitioners a vast array of resources and information related to every aspect of recruitment and selection. It is impossible to list every HR resource that is available on the Internet. We suggest that as you read through this text you type in key terms or phrases from the text into your favourite search engine. We recommend that you use several different search engines as each may give you different results. We have listed specific websites throughout the text that are related to the topic being discussed.

There are four general sites that we would like to draw to your attention. These sites can serve as gateways to many other related sites and topics. Two of these have already been listed in Box 1.5:

CSIOP: http://www.sscl.uwo.ca/psychology/csiop/
CCHRA: http://www.chrpcanada.com

The remaining two are U.S. sites. The first is for the Society for Industrial and Organizational Psychology:

SIOP: http://www.siop.org/

The second is the Human Resources Internet Guide, which provides information and links to almost every HR topic, including information on a variety of selection tests. One caution when using this site: the legal information and legal references are based on U.S. law and may not necessarily apply to Canada. The address is:

http://www.hr-guide.com/

SUMMARY

This chapter describes the larger socioeconomic context for recruitment and selection in Canada. Essentially, effective recruitment and selection are important because they contribute to organizational productivity and worker growth. Recruitment and selection practices, which have found a place in organization practices for thousands of years, play an essential role in contemporary organizations. Effective human resource management, including recruitment and selection, must be carried out within the context of an organizational system, as well as that of the external environment. In both cases, the HR professional must not become isolated. In recognition of this, professional associations and groups exist to help HR professionals and their clients through ethical codes and standards of practice.

KEY TERMS

Contingent employment, p. 12
Enablers, p. 15
Ethics, p. 20

Systems models, p. 13
Technology, p. 7

EXERCISES

1. Identify the primary socio-economic, demographic, and technological changes affecting the workplace, and provide examples of how each type of change is having an impact on human resources recruitment and selection.

2. Think of a job you have held and briefly sketch out two profiles. The first profile is that of the 95th percentile job performer—that is, the person you have worked with who would be better than 95 out of a 100 of his or her co-workers. What was that person like? What skills and abilities did he or she have? Then sketch out a second profile of the 5th percentile job performer—the person who was only as good as the bottom 5 percent of his or her co-workers. Compare the profiles and discuss how use of recruitment and selection might be helpful in choosing the 95th rather than 5th percentile performer. How much difference would it make to have the 95th rather than the 5th percentile performer on the job? If you were the employer, would these differences be of sufficient value for you to invest the necessary money into recruitment and selection in order to get the 95th percentile performer?

3. As a class or in small groups, discuss the two scenarios raised in the ethics section of this chapter. Decide what the human resources professional should do in each instance, and provide an ethical justification for your decision.

4. Sketch out your preferred career track in human resources management. What professional associations would you join and what activities would you engage in? Where do recruitment and selection fit in the mix of activities that you have planned for yourself?

5. Explore one of the websites listed in this chapter. Print a copy of the homepage and present a description of the site to your classmates. Describe some of the information available on the site. Follow one of the links from that site and describe another site relevant to recruitment and selection.

CASE

The Toyota (Cambridge, Ontario) plant exemplifies the changing workplace requirements described in this chapter and their impact on human resources practices. Toyota is a Japanese company that competes in the global marketplace. It has production facilities in many countries where labour costs are high; yet it strives to maintain a very efficient workforce. One reason for Toyota's ability to be an effective producer is its use of empirically proven recruitment and selection practices.

Toyota's recruitment and selection practices are designed to find the best possible people for it to hire, whether the job being staffed is on the shop floor or at the executive level. In 1996, Toyota received thousands of applications for 1200 blue-collar positions. As part of its hiring procedure, Toyota took prospective employees through a rigorous, comprehensive, multi-stage assessment process. According to Sandie Halyk, assistant general manager for human resources, Toyota "wants people who take pride in their work and are able to work well with others. If you're not comfortable working for a team, you won't be comfortable working here." The selection process involved realistic job previews, paper-and-pencil cognitive ability and personality assessments, tests of fine and gross motor coordination, work samples, and structured employment interviews. The work sample alone entailed a six-hour manufacturing assembly exercise that involved individual and group problem solving. Group leaders and first-line supervisors were active participants in the panel selection interview. For those "making the grade," references were checked, and health and fitness tests undertaken by those given conditional offers of employment. The process was designed to "find out if you're able to identify problems and do something about them, and to ensure a good fit between the company and the new employee."

Source: Keenan (1996).

DISCUSSION QUESTIONS

We will review the components of Toyota's selection procedures later in this text. For now, we would like you to discuss the following points.

1. Is Toyota's elaborate selection system justified? What are appropriate criteria for assessing its effectiveness?

2. Toyota received over 40 000 applications for the 1200 positions. Is this an effective approach? What is the cost associated with reviewing all of these applications? How do you reduce the number of applicants to a reasonable number that can be run through the selection system?

3. What are some of the cultural issues that might arise with a Japanese-managed auto plant located in Ontario?

4. Provide examples of how technology might be used to facilitate and improve the recruitment and selection used by Toyota.

5. What criteria should Toyota use in selecting "team players"?

REFERENCES

Belcourt, M.L., and K.J. McBey. 2000. *Strategic Human Resources Planning.* Toronto: Nelson.

"The Changing Workplace and Public Policy." 1997. *Applied Research Bulletin.* Ottawa: Human Resources Development Canada. http://www.hrdc-drhc.gc.ca/arb/publications/bulletin/vol3n2/v3n2toce.shtm.

Chui, T., and M.S. Devereaux. 1995. "Canada's Newest Workers." *Perspectives on Labour and Income* 7, no. 1: 17–23. Statistics Canada, 75-001E.

Crompton, S. 1995. "Employment Prospects for High-School Graduates." *Perspectives on Labour and Income* 7, no. 3: 8–13. Statistics Canada, 75-001E.

Crompton, S., and S.L. Geran. 1995. "Women as Main Wage Earners." *Perspectives on Labour and Income* 7, no. 4: 26–29. Statistics Canada, 75-001E.

Cronshaw, S.F. 1991. *Industrial Psychology in Canada.* Waterloo, ON: North Waterloo Academic Press.

d'Arcimoles, C.-H. 1997. "Human Resource Policies and Company Performance: A Quantitative Approach Using Longitudinal Data." *Organizational Studies* 18: 857–74.

Dumas, J. 1995. "Greying of the Workforce: Report on a Symposium." *Perspectives on Labour and Income* 7, no. 1: 34. Statistics Canada, 75-001E.

Evers, F.T. 1993. "Making the Match: How Ontario's Employers Can Help Graduates Develop Exactly the Right Skills Portfolios They'll Need as Tomorrow's Corporate Managers." *Challenges* (Fall): 8–9.

Foot, D.K., and D.K. Stoffman. 1996. *Boom, Bust and Echo: How to Profit from the Coming Demographic Shift.* Toronto: Macfarlane Walter and Ross.

Greenbaum, P.J. 1996. "Canada's Hiring Trends: Where Will Canadian Jobs Come From in the Next Millennium?" *HR Today* (July). Canadian Institute of Professional Management, Ottawa, Ontario.

Greenspon, E. 1996. "Economy Changing Far Faster than People." *The Globe and Mail* (April 20): A1.

Huselid, M.A. 1995. "The Impact of Human Resource Management Practices on Turnover, Productivity, and Corporate Financial Performance." *Academy of Management Journal* 38: 635–72.

Jones, G.R., and P.M. Wright. 1992. "An Economic Approach to Conceptualizing the Utility of Human Resource Management Practices." In K.R. Rowland and G. Ferris, eds., *Research in Personnel and Human Resources Management*, vol. 10. Greenwich, CT: JAI Press.

Keenan, G. 1996. "Toyota's Hunt for 1,200 Team Players." *The Globe and Mail* (January 5): B7.

Koch, M.J., and R. Gunter-McGrath. 1996. "Improving Labor Productivity: Human Resource Management Policies Do Matter." *Strategic Management Journal* 17: 335–54.

Krahn, H. 1995. "Non-Standard Work on the Rise." *Perspectives on Labour and Income* 7, no. 4: 35–42. Statistics Canada, 75-001E.

Little, B. 1996. "Lone Wolves Who Are Turning Grey." *The Globe and Mail* (April 22): A8.

Montigny, G., and S. Jones. 1990. "Overview of Literacy Skills in Canada." *Perspectives on Labour and Income* 2 (Winter): 32–39.

Pfeffer, J., and J.F. Veiga. 1999. "Putting People First for Organizational Success." *Academy of Management Executive* 13: 37–48.

"The Progress of Women." 1995. *The Globe and Mail* (August 11): A10.

Rampton, G., I. Turnbull, and A. Doran. 1996. *Human Resources Management Systems*. Scarborough, ON: Nelson Canada.

Statistics Canada. 2000. "Labour, Employment and Unemployment." http://www.statcan.ca/english/Pgdb/People/labour.htm.

Wang, Z.M. 1994. "Culture, Economic Reform, and the Role of Industrial and Organizational Psychology in China." In H.C. Triandis, M.D. Dunnette, and L.M. Hough, eds., *Handbook of Industrial and Organizational Psychology*, vol. 4. 2nd ed. Palo Alto, CA: Consulting Psychologists Press, Chapter 14.

"Where Women Stand Now." 1995. *The Globe and Mail* (August 12): A6.

Whitener, E.M. 1997. "The Impact of Human Resource Activities on Employee Trust." *Human Resource Management Review* 7: 389–404.

Williamson, R. 1996. "Food Fights Put Squeeze on Workers." *The Globe and Mail* (June 7): B4.

2

LEGAL ISSUES

CHAPTER GOALS

This chapter presents an overview of the legal issues that affect the practice of recruitment and selection in Canada.

After reading this chapter you should

- understand the major legal issues affecting recruitment and selection;
- know how relevant human rights and employment equity legislation and policies affect recruitment and selection;
- understand how legal concerns translate into recruitment and selection;
- know the key legal concepts that have had an impact on recruitment and selection in this country; and
- be able to use the basic concepts and principles discussed in the chapter in the development of recruitment and selection systems that meet legal requirements.

This chapter is organized into three parts. Part I describes the key legislation and legal means that affect recruitment and selection practices in Canada, including a review of existing legislation. Part II discusses the important legal concepts that have emerged from this existing legislation. These legal concepts require recruitment and selection programs to be nondiscriminatory with respect to hiring members of designated groups. Part III provides some practical guidance on what to do, and what not to do, in recruitment and selection to meet legal obligations.

We have taken many of the examples presented in this chapter from Canadian federal human rights, employment equity, employment standards, or labour laws for two reasons. First, provincial and municipal jurisdictions often draw on federal law when drafting their own legislation and programs. Examining federal laws provides a common framework for understanding what is happening in these other jurisdictions. Second, the laws and practices vary across jurisdictions. We encourage you to become familiar with the human rights, employment equity, employment standards, and labour laws that apply to your provincial, territorial, and municipal jurisdictions.

Part I: A Basic Background in Legal Means for Nondiscriminatory Recruitment and Selection

Discrimination—in employment, discrimination refers to any refusal to employ or to continue to employ any person, or to adversely affect any current employee, on the basis of that individual's membership in a protected group. All Canadian jurisdictions prohibit discrimination at least on the basis of race or colour, religion or creed, age, sex, marital status, and physical or mental disability.

Four legal means affect Canadian employment practices in recruitment and selection: (1) constitutional law; (2) human rights law; (3) employment equity; and (4) labour law, employment standards, and related legislation. *Constitutional law* is the supreme law of Canada. It has a pervasive impact on employment practices, as it does on all spheres of Canadian society. *Human rights* legislation across Canada prohibits **discrimination** in both employment and the provision of goods and services (e.g., rental housing, service in restaurants). This legislation generally establishes human rights commissions or tribunals to deal with complaints, including those involving employment discrimination. *Employment equity* programs are administrative mechanisms set up in many Canadian organizations, frequently as a response to employment equity legislation by federal, provincial, or municipal governments. Employment equity programs have a major impact on employment systems, including recruitment and selection. Employment equity programs are intended to promote the entry and retention of people from designated groups (including women, visible minorities, Aboriginal peoples, and people with disabilites). *Labour law, employment standards, and related legislation* grant certain employment rights to both employers and employees, but also impose a wide range of employment responsibilities and obligations. Some of this legislation may have a direct impact on recruitment and selection practices in the jurisdiction where it is in force. Box 2.1 illustrates some of the differences among these four legal means.

BOX 2.1 Not All Legal Means Are the Same

The four legal means discussed in this chapter have varied historical roots and they address needs of different stakeholder groups in society. *Constitutional law*, which has its origins in the British North America Act of 1867, spells out the division of powers between the federal and provincial governments, as well as the rights and freedoms that Canadians enjoy under governments at all levels. All citizens are stakeholders under constitutional law, and its provisions directly or indirectly affect all of us.

Human rights legislation (federal and provincial) exists in Canada partly in response to international conventions declared by the United Nations and partly because of domestic pressure to eliminate discrimination in the workplace and in other areas such as housing and provision of services. Human rights acts prohibit discrimination on protected grounds such as race or sex, and the legislation is restrictive in that its provisions have no force beyond the protected groups.

Employment equity legislation and programs have evolved in Canada as a response both to affirmative action programs in the United States and to pressures within our own country to increase workforce diversity. Employment equity addresses the concerns of designated groups (visible minorities, women, Aboriginal people, and people with disabilities) and has no force or effect beyond these stakeholder groups.

Labour laws in the federal and provincial jurisdictions across Canada are a response to a long history of labour union activity undertaken to improve worker job security, wages, hours, working conditions, and benefits (Dessler and Duffy, 1984). These laws provide mechanisms for collective bargaining and union certification and rules for a "fair fight" between management and union, as well as protecting the public interest (Dessler and Duffy, 1984). Of course, the stakeholders under this legislation are unionized workers covered by collective agreements and managers in unionized workplaces.

Employment standards, both federal and provincial, trace their origins back to the British North America Act

and reflect societal norms about the respective rights and responsibilities of employers and their employees, whether these employees are unionized or not. Employment standards covered in legislation across Canada include statutory school-leaving age, minimum age for employment, minimum wages, vacations and leave, holidays with pay, and termination of employment. All workers in Canada, and their managers, are stakeholders in this legislation.

Other legislation, including regulation of workers in the federal government, results from unique conditions in those specific sectors and is restricted to addressing the needs of those stakeholders. As a general rule, human rights and employment equity address the problem of discrimination, whereas the remainder of the legal means (labour law, employment standards, and related legislation) provide mechanisms to resolve procedural or contractual disagreements between specific stakeholders named in the legislation. (Examples of the latter would be promotion based on the merit principle for federal government employees under the Public Service Employment Act passed by Parliament, seniority rights in collective agreements for employees of Crown corporations, or other types of contractual and legal obligations between employer and employee in either the private or public sectors.) However, even this basic distinction between anti-discrimination legislation and procedural/contract enforcement legislation can blur in practice. For example, equal pay between men and women for work of equal value, which is a discrimination issue, comes under human rights acts in some provinces and employment standards legislation in others (Stone and Meltz, 1988).

This chapter only hints at the complexity of the legal issues involved in recruitment and selection practices. As a starting point, human resources professionals must understand the origins, purpose, and stakeholders of each legal means if they are going to manage recruitment and selection activities in compliance with the law. They need to keep up with legislative changes on a continuing basis.

Means One: Constitutional Law

The Constitution of Canada consists of a series of acts and orders passed since 1867 by the British and Canadian parliaments (Simon, 1988). These separate acts and orders begin with the British North America Act of 1867 and end with the Constitution Act of 1982. Sections 1 to 34 of Part 1 of the Constitution Act of 1982 are called the Canadian Charter of Rights and Freedoms. The Constitution, taken as a whole, serves as the supreme law of Canada, as stated in Subsection 52(1) of the Constitution Act of 1982:

> 52. (1) The Constitution of Canada is the supreme law of Canada and any law that is inconsistent with the provisions of the Constitution is, to the extent of the inconsistency, of no force or effect.

All laws in Canada that come into force in a dispute between a private person and a branch of government (whether legislative, executive, or administrative) fall under the Constitution (Simon, 1988). The Constitution has precedence over all the other legal means discussed in this chapter.

A section of the Constitution often cited in employment law is Section 15 of the Canadian Charter of Rights and Freedoms. Section 15 lays out the principle of equality rights:

[handwritten note: powerful statement]

> 15. (1) Every individual is equal before and under the law and has the right to the equal protection and equal benefit of the law without discrimination and, in particular, without discrimination based on race, national or ethnic origin, colour, religion, sex, age or mental or physical disability.

> (2) Subsection (1) does not preclude any law, program or activity that has as its object the amelioration of conditions of disadvantaged individuals or groups including those that are disadvantaged because of race, national or ethnic origin, colour, religion, sex, age or mental or physical disability.

The discrimination provision in Subsection (1) of the Charter resembles provisions found in human rights legislation across Canada. Subsection (2) makes it clear that programs, such as employment equity, which may favour individuals or designated group as a means to overcoming past disadvantages, are not, in themselves, discriminatory and barred by Subsection (1).

As a practical matter, constitutional law does not directly affect everyday recruitment and selection activities. Constitutional law becomes an issue only when recruitment or selection practices are challenged in a human rights tribunal or court. Nevertheless, constitutional law has a pervasive, indirect impact on employment practices by setting limits and conditions on what federal, provincial, and municipal governments and courts can legally do to alter employment policies and practices. The interpretation of constitutional law through legislation and jurisprudence has an indirect, but substantial, influence on all aspects of the practice of human resources management—from the development of an organization's human resources policy to the conduct of an employment interview.

MEANS TWO: HUMAN RIGHTS

Each province and territory, as well as the federal government, has established a human rights act or code that prohibits discrimination in employment or in the provision of goods and services. The Canadian Human Rights Act contains the following section (Canadian Human Rights Commission, 1989):

> *8. It is a discriminatory practice, directly or indirectly,*
>
> *(a) to refuse to employ or continue to employ any individual, or*
> *(b) in the course of employment, to differentiate adversely in relation to an employee, on a prohibited ground of discrimination.*

The Canadian Human Rights Act applies to federal government departments, Crown corporations and agencies, and businesses under federal jurisdiction, including banks, airlines, railways, the CBC, and Canada Post (Canadian Human Rights Commission, 1994).

Section 8 of the Canadian Human Rights Act refers to "a prohibited ground of discrimination." Under this act, the following are grounds on which discrimination is prohibited (Canadian Human Rights Commission, 1994):

- race
- national or ethnic origin
- colour
- religion
- age
- sex (including pregnancy and childbirth)
- marital status
- family status
- mental or physical disability (including previous or present drug or alcohol dependence)
- pardoned conviction
- sexual orientation

The prohibited grounds of discrimination vary somewhat between jurisdictions. Table 2.1 compares prohibited grounds of discrimination across federal, provincial, and territorial jurisdictions. Table 2.1 lists 19 prohibited

TABLE 2.1 PROHIBITED GROUNDS OF EMPLOYMENT DISCRIMINATION IN JURISDICTIONS ACROSS CANADA

Prohibited Grounds	Federal	British Columbia	Alberta	Saskatchewan	Manitoba	Ontario	Quebec	New Brunswick	Prince Edward Island	Nova Scotia	Newfoundland	Northwest Territories	Yukon
Race or colour	◆	◆	◆	◆	◆	◆	◆	◆	◆	◆	◆	◆	◆
Religion or creed	◆	◆	◆	◆	◆	◆	◆	◆	◆	◆	◆	◆	◆
Age	◆	◆	◆	◆	◆	◆	◆	◆	◆	◆	◆	◆	◆
Sex (incl. pregnancy or childbirth)	◆	◆	◆	◆	◆	◆	◆	◆	◆	◆	◆	◆	◆
Marital status	◆	◆	◆	◆	◆	◆	◆	◆	◆	◆	◆	◆	◆
Physical/Mental handicap or disability	◆	◆	◆	◆	◆	◆	◆	◆	◆	◆	◆	◆	◆
Sexual orientation	◆	◆		◆	◆	◆	◆			◆	◆		◆
National or ethnic origin (incl. linguistic background)	◆			◆	◆	◆	◆	◆	◆	◆	◆	◆	◆
Family status	◆	◆	◆	◆	◆	◆	◆			◆		◆	◆
Dependence on alcohol or drug	◆	◆	◆	◆	◆	◆			◆	◆	◆		
Ancestry or place of origin		◆	◆	◆	◆		◆					◆	◆
Political belief		◆			◆		◆	◆	◆	◆			◆
Based on association					◆	◆		◆	◆	◆			◆
Pardoned conviction	◆					◆	◆				◆		
Record of criminal conviction		◆					◆						◆
Source of income			◆	◆	◆					◆			
Assignment, attachment, or seizure of pay											◆		
Social condition/origin							◆				◆		
Language						◆	◆						

Source: Canadian Human Rights Commission. Reproduced with permission of the Minister of Supply and Services Canada, 1993. (Adapted to include 1996 information.)

grounds of employment discrimination found across these jurisdictions. There are, however, only six prohibited grounds of employment discrimination on which all jurisdictions agree: race or colour, religion or creed, age, sex, marital status, and physical/mental handicap or disability.

Human rights legislation in all jurisdictions is enforced through human rights commissions or tribunals that have the legislated power to undertake actions that may be necessary to eliminate discrimination. The Canadian Human Rights Act empowers the Canadian Human Rights Commission to investigate complaints, develop and deliver public information programs, undertake or sponsor research programs, liaise with other human rights commissions, and review federal legislation for conformity with the Canadian Human Rights Act. The commission has a full-time, paid staff to carry out its mandate.

The Canadian Human Rights Commission spends much of its time investigating human rights complaints. Human rights protection is predicated on the idea that individuals who believe that they are victims of discriminatory practices bear the responsibility of filing complaints with the commission. In the case of workplace disputes, a complaint would be filed after discussions with the employer failed to resolve the matter. The commission's procedure for investigating complaints is shown in Steps 4–8 in Box 2.2. Applicants who believe that they have suffered discrimination in recruitment or selection can lodge a complaint the human rights commission that has jurisdiction over the employer.

BOX 2.2 Filing a Complaint under the Canadian Human Rights Act

1. First, the individual who believes he or she has been discriminated against should tell the people involved and attempt to resolve the problem on the spot.

2. If Step 1 does not succeed, seek assistance from someone named under the organization's human rights policy.

3. File a company or union grievance against the practice believed discriminatory.

4. If Steps 1–3 do not work, the individual may file a complaint with the Canadian Human Rights Commission.

5. If the complaint fulfills certain conditions (e.g., it is not trivial, frivolous, vexatious, or made in bad faith), the commission may assign an investigator to examine the complaint.

6. After the report from the investigator is filed, the commission may appoint a conciliator, who will attempt to bring about the settlement of the complaint. The commission must then either approve or reject the settlement.

7. After the complaint is filed, the commission may refer the complaint to a human rights tribunal composed of not more than three members. The tribunal then investigates the complaint in a quasi-legal hearing. Both the complainant and the employer are permitted representation by legal counsel in this hearing. The tribunal will either dismiss the complaint or, if the employer is found to have discriminated, levy penalties (e.g., rehiring, financial compensation).

8. A review tribunal may be set up to hear an appeal if one of the parties is not satisfied with the decision under Step 7.

9. If either party is dissatisfied with the decision of the review tribunal, the complaint may go to the federal court system, in some instances ending at the Supreme Court of Canada.

Means Three: Employment Equity

Employment equity— refers to the elimination of discriminatory practices that prevent the entry or retention of members from designated groups in the workplace, and to the elimination of unequal treatment in the workplace related to membership in a designated group.

Employment equity legislation at the federal, provincial, or municipal level requires organizations that come under their jurisdiction to set up and operate employment equity programs. These programs involve any human resource activities introduced into an organization to ensure equality for all employees in all aspects of employment, including recruiting, hiring, compensation, and training (Weiner, 1993). Organizations may voluntarily adopt employment equity programs in the absence of employment equity legislation. The purpose of employment equity legislation is stated in the Employment Equity Act passed by the Canadian Parliament in 1986:

> *2. The purpose of this Act is to achieve equality in the work place so that no person shall be denied employment opportunities or benefits for reasons unrelated to ability and, in the fulfilment of that goal, to correct the conditions of disadvantage in employment experienced by women, aboriginal peoples, persons with disabilities and persons who are, because of their race or colour, in a visible minority in Canada by giving effect to the principle that employment equity means more than treating persons in the same way but also requires special measures and the accommodation of differences.*

The intent of the act is to address past systemic discrimination in employment systems that have disadvantaged members of the designated groups. The act provides for a review of practices that may constitute systemic barriers to the employment of members from designated groups and for establishing measures to eliminate any of the barriers. The federal Employment Equity Act of 1986 describes this process:

> *Employer's duty*
>
> *4. An employer shall, in consultation with such persons as have been designated by the employees to act as their representatives or, where a bargaining agent represents the employees, in consultation with the bargaining agent, implement employment equity by*
>
> *(a) identifying and eliminating each of the employer's employment practices, not otherwise authorized by a law, that results in employment barriers against persons in designated groups; and*
>
> *(b) instituting such positive policies and practices and making such reasonable accommodation as will ensure that persons in designated groups achieve a degree of representation in the various positions of employment with the employer that is at least proportionate to their representation*

(i) in the work force, or

(ii) in those segments of the work force that are identified by qualification, eligibility or geography and from which the employer may reasonably be expected to draw or promote employees.

The development and implementation of an employment equity (EE) plan typically involves at least the following steps:

1. Obtain support of senior management for the EE effort.
2. Conduct a survey to determine the present representation of designated groups in the organization's internal workforce.
3. Set future representation targets for designated groups based on availability of qualified workers in the labour market.
4. Remove systemic employment barriers to increase representation for designated groups in the internal workforce.
5. Monitor the changing composition of the internal workforce over time.
6. Make necessary changes to the EE intervention to bring designated group representation up to future targets.

EE programs often require an employer to undertake an extensive overhaul of the organization's recruitment and selection system. In comparison, a human rights commission may only require an employer to take action to remedy a specific complaint. Both human rights and employment equity legislation have the same ultimate aim: to eliminate discrimination in the workplace against disadvantaged groups and to improve their positions in employment systems.

Employment equity legislation is often a contentious issue, subject to the political process. As times change, employment equity legislation may be delivered through different mechanisms, may be strengthened or weakened, or may even be discontinued altogether. For example, in 1995 the Ontario government repealed the Employment Equity Act passed by the previous NDP government and said that it would implement an "equal-opportunity plan" together with business, labour, and community groups to replace the repealed legislation. The government claimed that the plan would better promote hiring and promotion policies based on merit (Scotland, 1995).

Means Four: Labour Law, Employment Standards, and Related Legislation

Federal and provincial labour laws stipulate the rights of employees to organize trade unions and to bargain collective agreements with employers. Provincial labour relations acts and the Canada Labour Code establish labour relations boards to oversee union certifications and handle complaints about unfair labour practices. Collective agreements, which are legally binding and enforceable documents, cover unionized employees. Collective agreements set out the conditions under which job changes must occur and have a major impact on "internal selection" or "internal movement" of workers—for example, promotion, lateral transfer, and demotion (Belcourt and McBey, 2000). Because "closed-shop" agreements, under which only union members may work for the organization, are legal in Canada, some unions have considerable control over external recruiting, even running their own hiring halls from which the employer must hire workers. While collective agreements do restrict the freedom of the employer, unions, on the whole, tend to be more cooperative than adversarial in terms of HR practices such as selection (Jackson and Schuler, 1995).

Federal and provincial employment standards laws regulate minimum age of employment, hours of work, minimum wages, statutory holidays, vacations, work leaves, and termination of employment (Human Resources Development Canada, 1995–96). These laws have little impact on recruitment and selection practices, with the possible exception of termination, which might be considered "deselection" of people already in the organization's workforce.

Federal and provincial governments also have specialized legislation governing labour relations and setting employment standards for its own public service employees. Both the federal Public Service Employment Act and the Parliamentary Employment and Staff Relations Act illustrate the impact of this legislation on recruitment and selection. The Public Service Employment Act designates the Public Service Commission of Canada as the central staffing agency for the federal government. This act gives candidates from the general public, as well as some public service employees, the right to request an investigation if they believe that their qualifications were not properly assessed as part of a hiring competition for a public service position (Public Service Commission of Canada, undated). The Public Service Commission resolves complaints through mediation and conciliation or through the direct intervention of the commission or a deputy head (Public Service Commission of Canada, 1994–95). Candidates may also lodge appeals against personnel selection processes used by the Public Service Commission. (An important appeal involving the use of psychological testing in the federal public service is summarized in Box 2.3.) The Parliamentary Employment and Staff Relations Act provides a mechanism for collective bargaining between the federal government as employer and the various unions certified to represent federal workers. This legislation is administered by the Public Service Staff Relations Board (PSSRB), which is empowered to hear complaints under the act and arbitrate collective bargaining disputes (Public Service Staff Relations Board, 1994–95). PSSRB decisions that address promotion practices covered in collective agreements between the federal government and public sector unions affect recruitment and selection practices in the public sector.

BOX 2.3 Psychological Testing in the Federal Government

In 1986, an appeal board of the Public Service Commission (PSC) heard the complaints of job applicants for the job of collections enforcement clerk with the federal taxation department *(Maloley et al. v. Department of National Revenue (Taxation)*, 1986). Four individuals who were not hired alleged that the GIT 320 (a paper-and-pencil test of cognitive ability) in use at the time for screening job applicants was (1) not properly validated; (2) had an unjustifiably high cutoff score; and (3) was gender-biased. Expert witnesses, including several top industrial psychologists, testified on the technical merits of the test at the invitation of either the complainants or the commission. Based on this evidence, the appeal board concluded that the GIT 320 had been validated (using a method called validity generalization, which is discussed later in this book). The two other allegations were dismissed because (1) the PSC had demonstrated the test cutoff score was reasonable and not

excessively high under the circumstances and (2) the test was neither biased nor unfair to women. All three allegations about the test were dismissed and the PSC continued to use the GIT 320 in its selection work.

The *Maloley* decision is especially informative because it involves allegations of two distinct types: (1) the first two allegations claimed that the GIT 320 violated procedural rules in the PSC selection system based on the merit principle; and (2) the third allegation claimed the test was discriminatory against women. Here we see an internal appeal board, which normally would deal with procedural and technical matters only, ruling on discrimination issues customarily the prerogative of human rights commissions. This suggests that, in at least some instances, there is a blurring of the divisions separating the four legal means discussed in this chapter. Legal issues in recruitment and selection are made even more complicated as a result.

Table 2.2 summarizes the impact of the four legal means on three aspects of recruitment and selection. The impact of federal and provincial legislation is pervasive and must be kept in mind when developing recruitment and selection systems.

TABLE 2.2 JURISDICTIONAL COVERAGE OF ASPECTS OF RECRUITMENT AND SELECTION IN CANADA

DOES THE JURISDICTION COVER ...

Legal means	Entry-level job applicants?	Incumbent employees in promotion and transfer?	Incumbent employees in training and development?
Constitutional law	YES	YES	YES
Human rights legislation	YES	YES	YES
Employment equity legislation and programs	YES	YES	YES
Labour law, employment standards, and related legislation	OCCASIONALLY	SOMETIMES	SOMETIMES

Part II: Key Legal Concepts in Recruitment and Selection

Direct Discrimination

In the 1985 Supreme Court of Canada decision, *O'Malley v. Simpsons-Sears* (CHRR, D/3106, 24772), Justice McIntyre defined direct discrimination in an employment setting as follows:

> *Direct discrimination occurs in this connection where an employer adopts a practice or rule which on its face discriminates on a prohibited ground. For example, "No Catholics or no women or no blacks employed here." There is, of course, no disagreement in the case at bar that direct discrimination of that nature would contravene the Act.*

The application of this definition to human resources practice is quite simple. If direct discrimination occurs, then the burden is on the employer to show that the rule is valid in application to all the members of the affected group. An employer who is hiring steelworkers for foundry work involving heavy lifting in a dirty environment may believe that this job is unsuited to women and specifies that no women will be hired. This is a clear instance of direct discrimination under the McIntyre ruling. If a female applicant were to complain about the blatant nature of this discrimination, the employer would have to prove to a human rights investigator that all women lack the ability to do the work—that is, that no women could perform the work successfully. If even one woman can do the job, the employer's use of the "no women allowed" rule will be struck down by a human rights tribunal or court. In all but rare circumstances, it is impossible to justify direct discrimination.

As part of recruitment and selection, no statement may be made in advertising a job that would prohibit or restrict members of a protected group from seeking that job. A statement, for example, in any job advertisement or posting that the employer is seeking "single males" constitutes direct discrimination and is illegal. During the selection process itself, application forms and interviews are potential sources of direct discrimination. As a result, some human rights commissions have published guidelines for questions asked by employers on employment application forms and at employment interviews. An excerpt from these guidelines published by the Canadian Human Rights Commission is given in Table 2.3. These guidelines provide practical and detailed advice on how to avoid direct discrimination in many common selection situations and should be carefully heeded by employers. The complete guide is available on the Canadian Human Rights Commission's website at: http://www.chrc-ccdp.ca/publications/screen-preselection.asp.

TABLE 2.3 GUIDELINES TO SCREENING AND SELECTION IN EMPLOYMENT

SUBJECT	AVOID ASKING	PREFERRED
NAME	about name change; whether it was changed by court order, marriage, or other reason maiden name	
ADDRESS	for addresses outside Canada	ask place and duration of current or recent address
AGE	for birth certificates, baptismal records, or about age in general	ask applicants if they are eligible to work under Canadian laws regarding age restrictions
SEX	males or females to fill in different applications about pregnancy, child-bearing plans, or child-care arrangements	can ask applicant if the the attendance require-ments can be met
MARITAL STATUS	whether applicant is single, married, divorced, engaged, separated, widowed, or living common-law	if transfer or travel is part of the job, the applicant can be asked if he or she can meet these require-ments
FAMILY STATUS	number of children or dependents about child-care arrangements	can ask if the applicant would be able to work the required hours and, where applicable, overtime
NATIONAL OR ETHNIC ORIGIN	about birthplace, nationality of ancestors, spouse, or other relatives whether born in Canada for proof of citizenship	since those who are entitled to work in Canada must be citizens, permanent residents, or holders of valid work permits, appli-cants can be asked if they are legally entitled to work in Canada
MILITARY SERVICE	about military service in other countries	inquiry about Canadian military service where employment preference is given to veterans by law

TABLE 2.3 (continued)		
SUBJECT	**AVOID ASKING**	**PREFERRED**
LANGUAGE	mother tongue where language skills obtained	ask if applicant understands, reads, writes, or speaks languages required for the job
RACE OR COLOUR	any question about race or colour, including colour of eyes, skin, or hair	
PHOTOGRAPHS	for photo to be attached to applications or sent to interviewer before interview	
RELIGION	about religious affiliation, church membership, frequency of church attendance, if applicant will work a specific religious holiday, or for references from clergy or religious leader	explain the required work shift, asking if such a schedule poses problems for the applicant
DISABILITY	for listing of all disabilities, limitations, or health problems whether applicant drinks or uses drugs whether applicant has ever received psychiatric care or been hospitalized for emotional problems whether applicant has received workers' compensation	ask if applicant has any condition that could affect ability to do the job ask if the applicant has any condition that should be considered in selection
MEDICAL INFORMATION	if currently under physician's care, name of family doctor if receiving counselling or therapy	
PARDONED CONVICTION	whether an applicant has ever been convicted if an applicant has ever been arrested whether an applicant has a criminal record	if bonding is a job requirement ask if applicant is eligible
SEXUAL ORIENTATION	about the applicant's sexual orientation	

Source: Excerpted from Canadian Human Rights Commission. Reproduced with permission of the Minister of Supply and Services Canada, 1993.

Direct discrimination is much less frequent in Canadian workplaces than it once was. Discriminatory job advertising in major daily newspapers is now quite rare, as the media may also be held accountable for running such types of ads. Direct discrimination, however, does exist to some extent in selection practices to make continued vigilance necessary. These instances generally occur in those occupations where gender-based stereotyping persists. Despite many efforts, people still think of certain occupations as being either "female" or "male"—for example, only women make good nurses, only men make good construction workers. Direct discrimination occurs when this stereotyping carries over into the workplace and influences recruiting and selection practices. Hopefully, such gender-based stereotyping will occur much less often in the future than in the past.

ADVERSE EFFECT DISCRIMINATION

In the *O'Malley v. Simpsons-Sears* decision, Justice McIntyre also defined **adverse effect discrimination**—sometimes also referred to as indirect discrimination—as arising where (CHRR, D/3106, 24772):

> ... *an employer for genuine business reasons adopts a rule or standard which is on its face neutral, and which will apply equally to all employees, but which has a discriminatory effect upon a prohibited ground on one employee or group of employees in that it imposes, because of some special characteristic of the employee or group, obligations, penalties, or restrictive conditions not imposed on other members of the work group.... An employment rule honestly made for sound economic or business reasons, equally applicable to all to whom it is intended to apply, may yet be discriminatory if it affects a person or group of persons differently from others to whom it may apply.*

Adverse effect discrimination—refers to a situation where an employer, in good faith, adopts a policy or practice that has an unintended, negative impact on members of a protected group.

Adverse effect discrimination occurs in recruitment and selection when an employer, in good faith, adopts a policy or practice that has an unintended, negative impact on members of a protected group. In recruiting, employers often ask current employees for the names of friends or relatives who might be suitable for a position. A human resources manager might solicit shop-floor employees for names of potential candidates to fill a welder's apprentice position. After receiving all the names, the HR manager chooses the best candidate according to a set of objective criteria. How does this recruiting strategy lead to adverse effect discrimination? If the shop-floor employees were all white males, almost all of the candidates put forward by the current employees will be white males. The recruitment practice will likely lead to the outcome of hiring a white male, to the exclusion of women or visible minorities. The HR manager may have believed that the strategy was a sound and effective business practice for identifying suitable candidates for the position. The manager did not intend to exclude members of any protected group from consideration and asked all the existing employees to nominate potential job candidates. Nevertheless, this recruitment strategy results in adverse effect discrimination by imposing on women and visible minorities penalties or restrictive conditions not imposed on white males: they are less likely to be nominated for the job, and less likely to be hired regardless of their qualifications. Women and visible minorities, two groups protected under human rights legislation, are negatively affected by the supposedly neutral recruiting practice.

In selection, adverse effect discrimination often involves the use of a practice or use of an employment test. Suppose the HR manager, in the above example, corrected the flawed recruiting practice and subsequently obtained an applicant pool that included a proportion of women and visible minorities consistent with their representation in the general population. The HR manager decides to use a mechanical comprehension test to select applicants as a welder's apprentice. Performance on the mechanical comprehension test predicts success as a welder's apprentice and will identify those applicants who are most likely to contribute to the company's overall productivity. How does this selection strategy lead to adverse effect discrimination? Women tend to score lower, on average, on mechanical comprehension tests than do men. If the same test cutoff score were used for men and women or if applicants were offered jobs in order of their test scores (from highest to lowest), proportionately fewer women than men would be hired for the job. The use of the mechanical comprehension test would impose on women, as a group protected under human rights legislation, a penalty not imposed on men. Even though the test is applied equally to women and men, the test affects women, in a negative sense, to a greater extent than men. Even though the test predicts performance for welders' apprentices and there was no intention to discriminate against women, a human rights complaint may be launched against the employer on the grounds that use of the test had an adverse effect on women as a group and, thus, discriminated against them on that basis. Any employment rule, practice, or policy that has a negative effect on a group protected under human rights legislation, no matter how well intentioned by the employer, constitutes adverse effect discrimination.

ADVERSE IMPACT

Adverse impact—occurs when the selection rate for a protected group is lower than that for the relevant comparison group.

The concept of **adverse impact** is closely related to adverse effect discrimination. At times, *adverse impact* and *adverse effect* are used synonymously (Weiner, 1993). In terms of recruitment and selection, the concept of adverse impact has a narrower definition:

> *Adverse impact occurs when the selection rate for a protected group is lower than that for the relevant comparison group (which has the higher selection rate).*

In our example of adverse effect discrimination, the mechanical comprehension test also had an adverse impact on women in that proportionately fewer women than men would be selected for the job.

Adverse impact is based on statistical evidence showing that proportionately fewer of the protected group are selected using a selection device (such as an employment test or interview) or that fewer members of the protected group pass through the selection system taken as a whole. Establishing adverse impact in selection can be very complex (Vining, McPhillips, and Boardman, 1986). One rough-and-ready rule that is frequently used to establish adverse impact in selection is the *four-fifths* rule. According to this rule, adverse impact is established where the selection rate for the protected group is less than four-fifths that of the comparison group. Table 2.4 demonstrates a situation in which a mechanical comprehension test had adverse impact on women according to the four-fifths rule. Despite its widespread adoption in Canada, the four-fifths rule has serious limitations on both rational and statistical grounds (Vining, McPhillips, and Boardman, 1986).

TABLE 2.4 EXAMPLE OF THE FOUR-FIFTHS RULE IN DETERMINING ADVERSE IMPACT ON WOMEN

SELECTION BASED ON MECHANICAL COMPREHENSION TEST

	Total applicant pool (A)	Number of people made job offers (B)	Selection rate (ratio of B/A)
Women	10	1	.10
Men	100	15	.15

Minimum selection rate of women according to the four-fifths rule must be $4/5 \times .15 = .12$

Because the selection rate of women (.10) is less than the minimum selection rate under the four-fifths rule (.12), we conclude that the mechanical comprehension test had adverse impact.

DISCRIMINATION IS DISCRIMINATION

Many people have had difficulty in differentiating direct discrimination from adverse effect discrimination since the outcomes in both cases are the same: members of a protected group are subject to discrimination, although in one case the discrimination is unintentional. In a recent Supreme Court of Canada decision—*British Columbia (Public Service Employee Relations Comm.) v. B.C.G.E.U.; CHRR, D/275, 54*—Justice McLachlin argued that while one could differentiate between the two forms of discrimination, the distinction had little importance since the principal concern of the Court in human rights cases was the effect of an impugned law. According to Justice McLachlin:

> *The conventional analysis [of distinguishing between direct discrimination and adverse effect discrimination] was helpful in the interpretation of the early human rights statutes, and indeed represented a significant step forward in that it recognized for the first time the harm of adverse effect discrimination. The distinction it drew between the available remedies may also have reflected the apparent differences between direct and adverse effect discrimination. However well this approach may have served us in the past, many commentators have suggested that it ill-serves the purpose of contemporary human rights legislation. I agree. In my view, the complexity and unnecessary artificiality of aspects of the conventional analysis attest to the desirability of now simplifying the guidelines that structure the interpretation of human rights legislation in Canada.*

While this decision is a landmark ruling, it is too soon to know its full impact on recruitment and selection policies and practices. It does, however, appear to undermine use of the four-fifths rule as a defence to discrimination. Justice McLachlin wrote that leaving a "neutral" practice in place, even if its adverse effects were felt only by a small number of people, was questionable. The policy or practice is itself discriminatory because it treats some individuals differently from others on the basis of a prohibited ground; the size of the "affected group" is irrelevant. This suggests that the Court would not approve a selection practice that met the four-fifths rule. Her ruling also laid out a unified approach for establishing whether performance standards for a job are discriminatory and reinforced the concept of individual accommodation in the workplace. These issues are addressed in the following sections.

BONA FIDE OCCUPATIONAL REQUIREMENT

Bona fide occupational requirement (BFOR)—a procedure used to defend a discriminatory employment practice or policy on the grounds that the policy or practice was adopted in an honest and good-faith belief that it was reasonably necessary to assure the efficient and economical performance of the job without endangering employees or the general public.

Most human rights acts in Canada allow an employer to defend a discriminatory policy or practice as a **bona fide occupational requirement (BFOR)** if there is a good reason for it based on the employer's need to "engage and retain efficient employees" (Canadian Human Rights Commission, 1988: i). The Canadian Human Rights Act states that (Canadian Human Rights Commission, 1989):

> *15. It is not a discriminatory practice if*
>
> *(a) any refusal, exclusion, suspension, limitation, specification or preference in relation to any employment is established by an employer to be based on a bona fide occupational requirement; ...*

Justice McIntyre clarified the definition of the BFOR in the 1982 Supreme Court of Canada decision *Ontario Human Rights Commission et al. v. the Borough of Etobicoke* as follows (CHRR, D/783, 6894):

> *To be a bona fide occupational qualification and requirement, a limitation, such as a mandatory retirement at a fixed age, must be imposed honestly, in good faith, and in the sincerely held belief that such limitation is imposed in the interests of adequate performance of the work involved with all reasonable dispatch, safety and economy, and not for ulterior or extraneous reasons aimed at objectives which could defeat the purpose of the Code. In addition, it must be related in an objective sense to the performance of the employment concerned, in that it is reasonably necessary to assure the efficient and economical performance of the job without endangering the employee, his fellow employees and the general public.*

Justice McIntyre went on to point out that the above definition of the BFOR contains both a subjective and an objective element. The subjective element refers to the employer's state of mind when setting the rule or policy. That is, the limitation levelled on a protected group through a restrictive rule or policy must be imposed in good faith (i.e., without discriminatory intent). The objective element refers to scientific and other evidence that the employer can present to support the use of the restrictive rule or policy. For example, when an employment test has adverse impact on a protected group, such objective evidence would include validation studies demonstrating that the scores on the employment test predict subsequent job performance for those hired. This type of evidence was used in the successful defence of an employment test in Ontario (*Persad v. Sudbury Regional Police Force* [1993]).

More recently, Justice McLachlin, in writing for the Supreme Court of Canada in *British Columbia (Public Service Employee Relations Comm.) v. B.C.G.E.U.* (CHRR, D/275, 54), set out a new, "unified approach" to defining a BFOR for cases of both direct and adverse effect discrimination:

> *Having considered the various alternatives, I propose the following three-step test for determining whether a prima facie discriminatory standard is a BFOR. An employer may justify the impugned standard by establishing on the balance of probabilities:*
>
> *(1) that the employer adopted the standard for a purpose rationally connected to the performance of the job;*
>
> *(2) that the employer adopted the particular standard in an honest and good faith belief that it was necessary to the fulfilment of that legitimate work-related purpose; and*

(3) that the standard is reasonably necessary to the accomplishment of that legitimate work-related purpose. To show that the standard is reasonably necessary, it must be demonstrated that it is impossible to accommodate individual employees sharing the characteristics of the claimant without imposing undue hardship upon the employer.

The "standard" referred to in this decision is the BC government's use of aerobics tests to assess forest firefighters against a minimum test score set for the "maximal oxygen uptake." This standard was believed to be necessary for firefighters to meet the physical demands required in fighting forest fires. All candidates had to meet the same minimum test score. The Court found that the standard had a *prima facie* discriminatory effect on women. Women have, on average, a lower aerobic capacity than men and had difficulty achieving the minimum test score that had been set for the test. Fewer women, therefore, would be hired under the standard. The Court held that the BC government had met the first two steps of the unified approach by adopting the standard in an honest and good-faith belief that the standard was job-related and was linked to successful job performance. It failed, however, to demonstrate to the Court's satisfaction that the minimum performance standard set on the aerobics tests was reasonably necessary to the accomplishment of the legitimate work-related purpose for which it had been adopted. The employer had not demonstrated that women required the same minimum level of aerobic capacity as men to perform the job safely and efficiently; nor had the employer shown that it was impossible to accommodate women candidates without imposing undue hardship upon itself. The employer failed to demonstrate that the aerobics standard was a BFOR under the new "unified" definition and so could not successfully defend the use of the test for assessing the fitness of forest firefighters. All selection practices that come under human rights scrutiny in the future will be asked to meet this new definition of a BFOR.

REASONABLE ACCOMMODATION

The concept of reasonable **accommodation** is incorporated into the concept of a bona fide occupational requirement. Where discrimination has occurred, the employer is under a duty to accommodate the complainant, short of undue hardship. For example, an employer who administers a standardized employment test in selection may have to demonstrate that administration instructions were appropriately modified to allow persons with mental or physical disabilities a fair chance to demonstrate their ability. The Supreme Court of Canada, in *O'Malley v. Simpsons-Sears* (1985), placed the employer under a burden to take reasonable steps to accommodate the complainant, with hardship occurring at the point where a policy or practice (such as modifying a

Accommodation—refers to the duty of an employer to put in place modifications to discriminatory employment practices or procedures to meet the needs of members of a protected group being affected by the employment practice or procedure. As part of a BFOR defence, an employer must demonstrate that such accommodation is impossible to achieve without incurring undue hardship in terms of the organization's expense or operations.

selection procedure) causes undue interference in the operation of the business or unsupportable expense to the employer. The Supreme Court of Canada, in *Central Alberta Dairy Pool v. Alberta (Human Rights Commission)* (1990), noted some factors that are relevant to assessing whether an employer has reasonably accommodated an individual or group protected under human rights legislation. Included among these factors that place the employer under a greater or lesser burden of accommodation are the following:

- the financial cost to the employer as a result of making the accommodation;
- disruption of an existing collective agreement;
- the impact of lowered morale on other employees;
- flexibility of workforce and facilities;
- the magnitude of risk for workers and the general public when safety is compromised.

INDIVIDUAL ACCOMMODATION

The concept of individual accommodation follows that of reasonable accommodation. In the *Bhinder v. CN Rail* (1985) decision, the Supreme Court of Canada found that once an employment policy or practice has been established as a BFOR, there is no need for the employer to accommodate to the special circumstances of the individual. For example, let us suppose that an individual with arthritis has asked for reasonable accommodation to this disability and wants to complete a realistic work sample in place of the usual standardized manual dexterity test required of job applicants. Under the *Bhinder* decision, the employer would not be under a burden to grant the applicant's request. As stated in that decision, the BFOR refers

> ... to a requirement for the occupation, not a requirement limited to an individual. It must apply to all members of the employee group concerned because it is a requirement of general application concerning the safety of employees. The employee must meet the requirement in order to hold the employment. It is, by its nature, not susceptible to individual application.

However, the *Central Alberta Dairy Pool* decision changed that basis of accommodation to an individual one. In the aftermath of the *Pool* decision, it is likely that the employer using the manual dexterity test will be required to accommodate the arthritic job candidate, even if that person is the only candidate with that disability applying for the job. The employer might accommodate such a candidate by using a realistic work sample or job tryout in place of the standardized test.

BOX 2.4 Accommodation May Be Expensive but Not Being Accommodating May Be Costlier

Accommodation on the job, while laudable, is not sufficient to accommodate those with a disability seeking employment or entry into a new position. Accommodation, at an individual level, also applies to the hiring process. Before an employer may rightfully conclude that an applicant's test score reflects a skill deficiency rather than the disability, the employer must accommodate the disability as part of the selection process.

Two decisions of the Canadian Human Rights Tribunal clearly state the need for accommodation with respect to tests used to hire employees with disabilities. In *Andrews v. Treasury Board and Department of Transport* (1994), discussed in this chapter, the tribunal held that a hearing test administered to applicants to the Coast Guard College discriminated against a hearing-impaired applicant because "the test was flawed and the pass scores were established at unrealistic levels. Therefore, the test itself does not satisfy the requirements of the BFOR defence."

More recently, the Canadian Human Rights Tribunal in *Green v. Public Service Commission* (1998) held that the Modern Language Aptitude Test, a test of aptitude for learning a second language, discriminated against an applicant who had a learning disability. The disability, dyslexia affecting auditory processing functioning, interfered with auditory discrimination and rote auditory memory and sequencing skills. The Public Service Commission took Ms. Green's test results as indicating a "negative prognosis" to acquire a new language. The test requires a person to listen to obscure languages (e.g., Kurdish) and then answer questions based on relating sounds on the tapes to symbols, among other exercises. The intent of using obscure languages is to provide a level playing field for all candidates by not giving any one of the candidates an advantage by using a language that they might know. In this case, Ms. Green claimed to be at a severe disadvantage because she relied on contextual information to make sense out of auditory sounds. An expert in the field

of learning disabilities substantiated Ms. Green's claim. Ms. Green, on the basis of her test score, was denied access to a French-language training program and a promotion into a bilingual management position.

The Canadian Human Rights Tribunal ruled that Ms. Green must be given the management position without further testing. In coming to that conclusion, the tribunal had followed Supreme Court of Canada decisions, including *Andrews v. Treasury Board and Department of Transport*, which established the principle that an employer had to accommodate employees with disabilities to the point of undue hardship.

The Public Service Commission appealed the tribunal's decision to the Federal Court of Canada. The Appeal Court recently upheld the tribunal's decision. Justice François Lemieux, writing for the court, stated that the test dwelled on Ms. Green's disability and did not take into account evidence that showed she had a higher-than-average aptitude to learn French and that her skills, determination, and visual processing ability more than made up for her disability.

The Appeal Court awarded Ms. Green $170 000 plus interest, $5000 in special compensation, and compensation for the lost pension and benefits she would have received in the management position. It also ordered the government to admit her to a French-language training program, to give Ms. Green the promotion she should have received 13 years earlier (the complaint originated in 1987), and, upon her successful completion of a management training program, a further promotion to an executive-level position without holding a competition.

Sources:
Andrews v. Treasury Board and Department of Transport. Canadian Human Rights Tribunal decision rendered September 1994 (T. D. 18/94).
Green v. PSAC, Treasury Board and Human Resources Development Canada. Canadian Human Rights Tribunal decision rendered June 26, 1998 (T. D. 6/98).
J. Tibbets and C. Grey, "Judge Slams PS Language Aptitude Testing," *Ottawa Citizen* (June 10, 2000): A1, A9.

The decision of the Canadian Human Rights Tribunal in *Canada (Attorney General) v. Thwaites* (1993) clarified the application of the principles in the *Central Alberta Dairy Pool* case as follows (26–27):

> *In respect of the BFOR defence provided for in Section 15(a) of the CHRA, the Supreme Court of Canada initially held in Bhinder v. C.N. in 1985 that consideration of a BFOR was to be without regard to the particular circumstances or abilities of the individual in question. In the short span of five years, the majority of the Court in Alberta Human Rights Commission v. Central Alberta Dairy Pool, [1990] 2 S.C.R. 489 reversed its position and held that in cases of adverse effect discrimination, the employer cannot resort to the BFOR defence at all. In such cases, there is now a positive duty on employers to accommodate the needs of employees disparately affected by a neutral rule unless to do so would create undue hardship for the employer. Put another way, the employer must establish that the application of the neutral rule or practice to the individual was reasonably necessary in that allowing for individual accommodation within the general application of the rule or practice would result in undue hardship. No longer, in such cases, can an employer justify its practice as a BFOR in relation to safety of employees in a general way and maintain that its discriminatory effect on certain groups of individuals is totally irrelevant.*

Clearly, employers can no longer apply a BFOR as a general practice or policy and by so doing disproportionately exclude members of a protected group, especially in the case of mental or physical disability. To establish a BFOR, the employer must successfully argue that accommodating the needs of the adversely affected individual would produce undue economic or administrative hardship for the organization. Justice McLachlin raised the requirements for establishing the BFOR in the *British Columbia (Public Service Employee Relations Comm.) v. B.C.G.E.U.* case. Employers must now demonstrate that it is *impossible* to accommodate individual employees who are members of the protected group without imposing undue hardship on the employer. As stated by Justice McLachlin:

> *Employers designing workplace standards owe an obligation to be aware of both the differences between individuals, and differences that characterize groups of individuals. They must build conceptions of equality into workplace standards. By enacting human*

rights statutes and providing that they are applicable to the work-place, the legislatures have determined that the standards governing the performance of work should be designed to reflect all members of society, in so far as this is reasonably possible. Courts and tribunals must bear this in mind when confronted with a claim of employment-related discrimination. To the extent that a standard unnecessarily fails to reflect the differences among individuals, it runs afoul of the prohibitions contained in the various human rights statutes and must be replaced. The standard itself is required to provide for individual accommodation, if reasonably possible. A standard that allows for such accommodation may be only slightly different from the existing standard but it is a different standard nonetheless.

REASONABLE ALTERNATIVE

The concept of reasonable alternative is also closely related to the BFOR. Under the burden of reasonable alternative, the employer must show that no reasonable or practical substitute exists for the discriminatory practice. For example, where the employer uses a cognitive ability test that has adverse impact on members of visible minorities, a tribunal may require that employer to show that no other valid selection predictor (e.g., a different employment test or a structured interview) is available that has less adverse impact. The concept of reasonable alternative can involve important elements of individual accommodation as well. As stated in the Canadian Human Rights Tribunal decision of *Andrews v. Treasury Board and Department of Transport* (1994, 92):

> *As one component to the BFOR defence, an employer must usually explain why, as a practical alternative to a blanket rule, it was not possible to assess individually the risk presented by the individual employee.*

For example, an employer who administers a manual dexterity test to all job applicants may have to show a tribunal why it was not possible to provide a practical work sample test as a reasonable alternative to assess the ability of one particular disabled applicant to do the job. Indeed, following *British Columbia (Public Service Employee Relations Comm.) v. B.C.G.E.U.*, an employer will now be required to address the following questions posed by Justice McLachlin with respect to searching for reasonable alternatives:

> *Some of the important questions that may be asked in the course of the analysis include:*
>
> *(a) Has the employer investigated alternative approaches that do not have a discriminatory effect, such as individual testing against a more individually sensitive standard?*

(b) If alternative standards were investigated and found to be capable of fulfilling the employer's purpose, why were they not implemented?

(c) Is it necessary to have all employees meet the single standard for the employer to accomplish its legitimate purpose or could standards reflective of group or individual differences and capabilities be established?

(d) Is there a way to do the job that is less discriminatory while still accomplishing the employer's legitimate purpose?

(e) Is the standard properly designed to ensure that the desired qualification is met without placing an undue burden on those to whom the standard applies?

(f) Have other parties who are obliged to assist in the search for possible accommodation fulfilled their roles? As Sopinka J. noted in Renaud, supra, at pp. 992–96, the task of determining how to accommodate individual differences may also place burdens on the employee and, if there is a collective agreement, a union.

SUFFICIENT RISK

The notion of risk is important to the concepts of BFOR, reasonable and individual accommodation, and reasonable alternative. That is, the employer is obliged to accommodate workers, including job applicants, and provide reasonable alternatives up to, but not beyond, a certain level of risk. Tribunals and courts have restricted the application of the risk criterion to those situations in which workplace safety is at issue. For example, an airline company may set a visual acuity standard for pilots, requiring that all candidates have uncorrected 20/20 full-colour vision, and defend this standard on the grounds that public safety would be compromised without it.

One of the key questions that tribunals and courts have dealt with lately is whether the criterion of risk should be defined as "acceptable risk," "significant risk," "**sufficient risk**," or some other level. Although the issue is still being debated, one Federal Appeal Court decision, *Canada (Human Rights Commission) and Husband v. Canada (Armed Forces)* in 1994 established that the appropriate risk criterion applying to a BFOR is whether accommodating an employee with a particular characteristic would create "sufficient risk" to justify rejecting that individual for employment. Sufficient risk was a criterion first suggested in the 1982 Supreme Court decision *Ontario Human Rights Commission et al. v. The Borough of Etobicoke* (1982) and was reaffirmed by the Court in the *Husband v. Canada* decision as follows (CHRR, D/301, 68):

> *A BFOR will be established if there is a "sufficient risk of employee failure" to warrant the retention of an otherwise discriminatory*

Sufficient risk—as part of a BFOR defence, an employer may argue that an occupational requirement that discriminates against a protected group is reasonably necessary to ensure that work will be performed successfully and in a manner that will not pose harm or danger to employees or the public.

employment qualification (Etobicoke at p. 210 [D/784, para. 6896]). Thus, whether or not an occupational requirement is "reasonably necessary" is dependent, at least in part, on whether members of the group alleging discrimination pose a sufficient risk of harm to themselves or others in the event of employee failure.

Justice Robertson, in this same decision, further defined sufficient risk as follows (CHRR, D/304, 77):

In my opinion, the proper standard, outlined in Dairy Pool, supra, embraces a "substantial" increase in safety risk within tolerable limits.

Justice Robertson goes on to describe some of the following factors that impact on risk assessment for BFORs:

- the nature of the employment (e.g., teacher versus airline pilot in the case of visual impairment);
- the likelihood of employee failure, stated in empirical, rather than speculative, terms;
- whether risk of employee failure is restricted to health and safety considerations;
- the seriousness of the harm arising from employee failure.

The sufficient risk criterion is well above a minimal or nominal risk. A minimal or nominal risk criterion would, for example, suggest that a person with muscular dystrophy should not be hired because that person might be injured in a fall (an organizational policy that many human rights authorities would argue reinforces a stereotype about the physically disabled, rather than being supportable by fact). On the other hand, a severe vision disability in an airline pilot would be well above minimal or nominal risk, because a plane crash caused or contributed to by that disability could kill hundreds of people. In that instance, risk resulting from the disability might well be sufficient to justify the otherwise discriminatory action of refusing to offer the disabled person a job.

LEGAL CONCEPTS APPLIED TO RECRUITMENT AND SELECTION

Two human rights decisions illustrate the application of the above principles to employers' recruitment or selection systems (see Table 2.5). In both decisions, each employer's system was found wanting and the court or tribunal awarded damages or remedies to the complainant.

The first decision is that of *Action Travail des Femmes v. Canadian National* (1984). Here a women's group in Quebec lodged a complaint with the

TABLE 2.5 LEGAL PRINCIPLES IN TWO KEY LEGAL DECISIONS

LEGAL CONCEPT		LEGAL DECISION	
		Action Travail des Femmes v. Canadian National (1984)	Andrews v. Treasury Board and Department of Transport (1994)
1.	Direct discrimination	X	
2.	Adverse effect discrimination	X	X
3.	Adverse impact	X	X
4.	Bona fide occupational requirement	X	X
5.	Reasonable accommodation	X	
6.	Individual accommodation	X	
7.	Reasonable alternative	X	
8.	Sufficient risk	X	

Canadian Human Rights Commission aimed at CN's recruitment and selection practices in the St. Lawrence region. Action Travail des Femmes alleged that CN's practices disproportionately excluded women from nontraditional jobs, including those of trade apprentice, brakeman, and coach cleaner, all of which were male dominated. Furthermore, they alleged that the employment practices in question were not bona fide occupational requirements. One selection predictor that came under scrutiny by the tribunal was the Bennett Mechanical Comprehension Test, which was used to select people for entry-level positions. The Bennett is known to have adverse impact against women, and, in addition, CN had not validated it for the jobs in question. As a result, the tribunal ordered CN to stop using the test. In addition, the tribunal ordered CN to cease a number of other discriminatory recruitment and selection practices. The tribunal also ordered CN to begin a special hiring program with the goal of increasing the representation of women in nontraditional jobs in that company. This decision was widely noted at the time and has since influenced recruitment and hiring practices in Canada.

The second decision is that of *Andrews v. Treasury Board and Department of Transport* (1994). In that decision, a Canadian Human Rights tribunal criticized a practical hearing test developed to assess a hearing-impaired applicant to the Canadian Coast Guard College. The test, which was administered in place of a maximum hearing loss standard for Canadian Coast Guard officers, was designed at a cost of over $100 000 and consisted of 14 different subtests administered to the applicant on the bridge of an operating Coast Guard ship. The subtest scenarios were administered by Coast Guard staff, who in turn supervised crew members of the ship serving as role players. The applicant's responses to the subtest scenarios were recorded and then compared against predetermined test standards. Andrews subsequently failed the test, was declined admission to the college, and filed a complaint with the Canadian Human Rights Commission. When testifying about the test during the tribunal hearings, expert witnesses criticized it on various grounds, including incomplete technical development, lack of reliability and validity, administration under insufficiently standardized conditions, and absence of norm data against which to compare and interpret the applicant's scores. The tribunal concluded that the practical hearing test was discriminatory and granted monetary compensation to the complainant Andrews.

In the *Andrews v. Treasury Board and Department of Transport* decision, the tribunal cited all the legal principles previously discussed in this chapter (see Table 2.5). The complainant Andrews lodged his complaint against the Coast Guard on the grounds of physical disability (hearing impairment) and also alleged both direct discrimination and adverse effect discrimination. The application of the hearing loss standard had the effect of producing adverse impact against hearing-disabled persons. The tribunal found that the Coast Guard had discriminated against Andrews by refusing him entry to the Coast Guard College and then considered whether the Coast Guard had successfully argued a BFOR defence. The tribunal accepted the subjective element of the BFOR (that the Coast Guard had set the limitation honestly, in good faith, and in sincerity that the limitation was necessary), but rejected the Coast Guard argument that they had established the objective element of the BFOR. Importantly, the tribunal found that the Coast Guard had not established the practical hearing test as a BFOR because of the numerous technical problems associated with it. What is more, the tribunal found that Andrews could have been reasonably and individually accommodated by use of a less expensive

BOX 2.5 Cultural Bias in Selection Testing

Much of the legislation and policy discussed in this chapter draws heavily on other countries, especially the United States. Nowhere is this truer than for human rights and employment equity, which are called "equal employment opportunity" and "affirmative action" in the United States. In fact, many Canadian tribunals and courts cite American cases as precedents when making their human rights decisions. In addition, many of the same issues and concerns about recruitment and selection in this country are mirrored in the United States. For example, an article in the *U.S. News & World Report* describes the political upheaval in Chicago over results of a promotional examination for city police officers (Glastris, 1994). Despite a cost of over $5 million paid to consultants to develop a bias-free promotional system, the multiple-choice tests used in the promotion competition still had adverse impact against African-Americans and Hispanics. As a result, fewer members of these groups were promoted than were whites, and city politicians were quick to line up on both sides of the controversy. Chicago is a microcosm reflecting wider societal concerns in the United States and Canada over employment testing. The debate over adverse impact and cultural bias in selection testing continues to rage intensely on both sides of the border and is likely to do so for years to come.

and simpler test, which would have been a reasonable alternative to the practical hearing test. Finally, the nature of Andrews's disability did not pose sufficient risk to the safe performance of a Coast Guard navigational officer to justify denying him the job.

Again, Table 2.5 provides a summary of the legal concepts that apply to these two human rights decisions. A comparison between the decisions, which were made 10 years apart, illustrates that at least four important legal concepts (those of reasonable accommodation, individual accommodation, reasonable alternative, and sufficient risk) assumed greater importance in the 1990s than in the 1980s. The *British Columbia (Public Service Employee Relations Comm.) v. B.C.G.E.U.* decision will likely place even greater emphasis on these four legal concepts in the next decade. Because of the rapidly evolving character of legal issues in Canadian human resources management, practitioners and HR specialists must continually upgrade their knowledge and skills in this area.

PART III: SOME PRACTICAL GUIDELINES IN NONDISCRIMINATORY RECRUITMENT AND SELECTION

The first two parts of this chapter provided a historical and conceptual backdrop for legal issues in recruitment and selection in Canada. This third part presents some practical guidelines for developing nondiscriminatory recruitment and selection practices and for reviewing and improving those practices already in place. The guidelines presented here are exactly that—guidelines; they are not meant to be applied in a mechanical fashion. The guidelines point to the right direction, and help to identify typical problem areas, in recruitment and selection systems. The guidelines should stimulate critical discussion and appraisal of those systems with an eye to improvement. There are no easy answers to many of the problems discussed in this chapter; the issues are simply too complex. HR managers may need to draw on the expert help of legal and professional consultants in dealing with many of these complex issues, particularly when there is insufficient time or expertise to deal with them in-house.

KEY PRACTICAL CONSIDERATIONS IN NONDISCRIMINATORY RECRUITMENT

Recruitment is a complex human resources activity. This can make it difficult to develop nondiscriminatory recruitment practices for protected group members (in the case of human rights legislation) or designated group members (in the case of employment equity). The scope of practices that must be considered is more manageable if the success or failure of recruitment is traced back to two main causes: (1) the effectiveness or ineffectiveness of the organization in contacting and communicating with target group members; and (2) the positive or negative perceptions that target group members hold about the organization. (It is irrelevant whether those perceptions existed before the target group members were recruited or developed during the recruiting process.)

People will not apply for a job if they are unaware that the job or organization exists or that the organization is recruiting. Getting the word out is not enough—job seekers must have a positive perception of the organization, as well as of their chances of getting the job, before they will apply. That perception is formed in at least two ways: (1) at the time the organization makes the initial contact through its recruiting outreach; or (2) through knowledge gained about the organization and its practices via third parties (e.g., friends, family, or news media).

Boxes 2.6 and 2.7 present a summary of effective and ineffective recruiting practices. They provide some practical guidance on what to do and what not to do when setting up and running recruitment programs that will meet legal requirements.

BOX 2.6 Practices for Nondiscriminatory Recruiting

Effective

- In employment offices, post in a conspicuous spot complete, objective, and specific information on all available jobs
- Advertise job openings in media that are read, viewed, or listened to by protected or designated group members
- Train employment clerical staff and recruitment officers in outreach recruiting
- Use opportunities to visually present protected or designated group members in positive employment roles (e.g., brochures and posters in employment office waiting area)
- Establish networks with community groups from which protected or designated group members are drawn
- Set and advertise objectively determined selection criteria for the job

- Base selection criteria on bona fide occupational requirements

Ineffective

- Permit receptionists and recruiters in employment offices to "pre-screen" applicants on the basis of informal criteria (e.g., appearance, dress)
- Rely on word-of-mouth advertising

- Post job advertisements only in-house

- Rely solely on seniority when promoting employees

- Allow each recruiter to use and communicate idiosyncratic criteria for selecting among job applicants

- Categorize and stream job applicants based on stereotyped assumptions about protected or designated group membership (e.g., that women are not physically strong enough for certain work)

BOX 2.7 Recruiting Perceptions

Practices That Promote Positive Recruiting Perceptions

- Include role models from protected or designated groups in job advertising.
- Implement management practices and policies that recognize and deal with special challenges or difficulties faced by protected or designated groups (e.g., wheelchair ramps for the physically disabled).
- Communicate and demonstrate commitment of senior management to outreach recruiting.
- Actively challenge negative myths and stereotypes about protected or designated group members (e.g., through training programs).
- Bring organizational policies and procedures into line with human rights and employment equity legislation.
- Reward supervisors and managers with the pay and promotion system for success in advancing human rights and employment equity goals.
- Build outreach recruiting into departmental and organizational business plans.
- Set specific and measurable recruiting targets against which managers can work.
- Present protected and designated group members in positive roles within organization newspapers and magazines.

- Offer training and development programs to protected and designated group members to address their specific needs in adapting and progressing within the organization.
- Modify working conditions as needed to accommodate protected and designated group members.

Practices That Promote Negative Recruiting Perceptions

- Permit sexual, racial, or other forms of harassment in the organization.
- Show lack of interest by senior management in improving recruitment practices.
- Allow negative myths and stereotypes to persist regarding the capabilities of protected and designated group members.
- Leave outreach recruiting unrewarded by the pay and promotion system.
- Leave outreach recruiting outside of departmental and organizational business plans.
- Tell managers to "do your best" in recruiting protected and designated group members rather than providing them with specific numerical targets.

A LEGAL REQUIREMENTS MODEL

The legal concepts discussed earlier in this chapter are summarized and related to each other in the legal requirements model for selection presented in Figure 2.1. This model is intended as a general guide to assist HR specialists in deciding whether a selection system is legally defensible with respect to the important legal concepts that apply to selection. The legal requirements model is meant only to clarify the application of *legal* concepts in recruitment and selection. The procedures contained in the table are consistent with good professional practice in selection; however, this model is not designed to address professional practice per se. Professional principles in selection are emphasized, wherever appropriate, throughout this book.

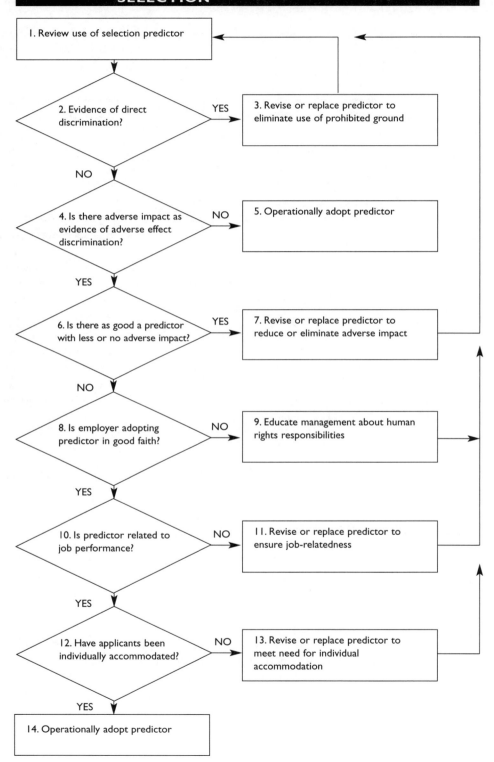

FIGURE 2.1 A LEGAL REQUIREMENTS MODEL FOR SELECTION

1. Review use of selection predictor

2. Evidence of direct discrimination? — YES → 3. Revise or replace predictor to eliminate use of prohibited ground

NO

4. Is there adverse impact as evidence of adverse effect discrimination? — NO → 5. Operationally adopt predictor

YES

6. Is there as good a predictor with less or no adverse impact? — YES → 7. Revise or replace predictor to reduce or eliminate adverse impact

NO

8. Is employer adopting predictor in good faith? — NO → 9. Educate management about human rights responsibilities

YES

10. Is predictor related to job performance? — NO → 11. Revise or replace predictor to ensure job-relatedness

YES

12. Have applicants been individually accommodated? — NO → 13. Revise or replace predictor to meet need for individual accommodation

YES

14. Operationally adopt predictor

The model in Figure 2.1 is set up in a series of steps that can be followed in reviewing a selection process before it is implemented. To use the model, start at Step 1, "Review use of selection predictor" and move down the page through the diamond-shaped figures. In each of these figures, answer either YES or NO to the question, then move along to the next step of the model based on the answer to the preceding question. For example, if the answer to the question in Step 2, "Evidence of direct discrimination," is NO, then move immediately to Step 4. If the answer is YES, then move to Step 3. The diamond-shaped figures all represent points at which a decision must be made; the boxes represent actions that should be taken.

Although there are no practical differences in the outcomes from direct and adverse effect discrimination, it is still important to recognize the type of discrimination. Knowing the origin of the discrimination will help to put in place procedures for eliminating it. Steps 2 and 3 in the model address the possibility of direct discrimination in a selection predictor; steps 4–14 address the possibility of adverse effect discrimination. Direct discrimination is less likely to occur (as compared with adverse effect discrimination) when professional human resources managers, test developers, and psychologists are involved in developing selection systems. For example, the human resources professionals would probably not trigger a direct discrimination complaint by setting an age standard for a job, such as only hiring airline pilots who are below age 50. Rather, they would likely develop a test or other assessment, such as a work sample, that measures job-related skills of visual acuity or colour vision in place of the age standard. The test, however, may well result in adverse impact against the protected group and trigger an adverse effect complaint. Human resources professionals will most likely move directly from Step 1 to Step 4 in the model since they will rarely have to justify direct discrimination.

To give you a better idea of how the legal requirements model works, we will discuss each of the steps in more detail and relate it to concepts discussed earlier in the chapter.

Step 1. Review use of selection predictor. Obtain a copy of the predictor (e.g., structured interview pattern or psychological test) and related research documents such as research manuals, articles from the scientific literature, and in-house studies. These materials should contain information related to adverse impact, reliability, validity, and utility. This information is needed to answer later questions in the model such as "Does the predictor have adverse impact?" "Is there an equally good alternate predictor without adverse impact?"

Step 2. Evidence of direct discrimination? By definition, direct discrimination involves the general exclusion of a group or class of people protected under human rights legislation. This scenario is getting rarer in selection, although employers should still be sensitive to the possibility of it happening. If evidence of direct discrimination is found, Pentney (1986) presents two preconditions that the employer must meet to justify the general exclusion rule as a BFOR:

1. Show that the bona fide occupational requirement which it seeks to invoke is reasonably necessary to the essence of its business; and

2. Show a factual basis for believing that all or substantially all persons within the class would be unable to perform the job safely and efficiently, or that it is impossible or impractical to test persons individually.

In selection terms, taking into account the recent Supreme Court of Canada ruling in *British Columbia (Public Service Employee Relations Comm.) v. B.C.G.E.U.*, these preconditions would translate into

- the need to show that the exclusion is related to job performance or safety;
- a burden to demonstrate that *all* of those people in the class excluded by the selection standard are incapable of performing the job or present a sufficient safety risk;
- a burden to show that individual testing of class members affected by the rule is impossible or impractical, and that there are no reasonable alternatives to that testing; and
- a burden to show that every attempt has been made to accommodate the unique capabilities and inherent worth and dignity of every individual, up to the point of undue hardship.

One area where direct discrimination might still happen with some regularity is in the area of physical or mental disability. For example, a hospital employer might screen out from the hiring process all people with HIV or AIDS. The concern of the employer would probably centre on the safety of patients during use of invasive techniques (such as injections by syringe). If the hospital did intentionally exclude all persons with HIV/AIDS during selection, then the employer would have to show through the use of objective data that (1) people with HIV/AIDS are a sufficient safety risk; (2) all persons with HIV/AIDS present a safety risk; (3) individual testing of applicants with HIV/AIDS is impossible or impractical; and (4) that these individuals cannot be accommodated without imposing undue hardship on the employer.

Step 3. Revise or replace predictor to eliminate use of prohibited ground. This action is recommended if there is evidence of direct discrimination. The revision might be relatively limited in scope (e.g., dropping an interview question that asks applicants about their family responsibilities) or extensive (e.g., dropping a requirement that all applicants test negative for HIV/AIDS). Sometimes, where standards of age, height, or weight are dropped, performance tests may be developed to replace them, but these tests cannot simply serve as proxies for the standards being dropped. They must not have an adverse effect on protected groups. After the selection predictor is revised, it is a good idea to review it again for evidence of direct discrimination (see the arrow connecting Box 3 to Box 1 in Figure 2.1).

Step 4. Is there adverse impact as evidence of adverse effect discrimination? Assume that an age requirement is dropped in favour of a performance test of physical agility for a given job; the concern now shifts from one of direct discrimination to that of possible adverse effect discrimination. At this juncture, the possibility of adverse impact should be investigated.

Step 5. Operationally adopt predictor. If the conditions in Steps 2 and 4 are met (i.e., both direct and indirect discrimination can be ruled out), then the selection predictor is legally defensible and can be adopted for use.

Step 6. Is there as good a predictor with less or no adverse impact? This step captures the legal idea that under the burden of reasonable accommodation, the employer must show that no reasonable or practical alternative exists to the discriminatory practice. If no alternative can be found, then move on to Step 8; if alternatives are available, then go to Step 7 and begin the review process again.

Step 7. Revise or replace predictor to reduce or eliminate adverse impact. Investigate alternative predictors to those having adverse impact. Consider various factors, including whether the alternative has adequate reliability and validity, to justify its use in place of the predictor with adverse impact.

Step 8. Is the employer adopting the predictor in good faith? Evaluate the attitude of management toward human rights in employment. The intentional use of selection tools or recruitment practices that are known to have adverse impact on protected groups is evidence of lack of good faith. There is no difference between choosing tools or procedures with known adverse effects and directly refusing to hire members of protected groups. A manager may wish to exclude women from a given job but masks this blatantly discriminatory attitude behind a recruitment and selection system that is as neutral in appearance as possible but nonetheless achieves the effect of excluding the unwanted group members. These types of situations place the HR professional in a serious ethical bind and should prompt him or her to move to Step 9.

Step 9. Educate management about their human rights responsibilities. The intent of human rights legislation is clear: Everyone should have the opportunity to compete for the jobs available on an equal footing and on the basis of objective qualifications, regardless of group membership or employer stereotyping about what members of particular groups can and cannot do. If this message has not gotten through to management, then the HR professional has the primary responsibility for providing the necessary education.

Step 10. Is the predictor related to job performance? If the predictor has adverse effect, the employer should establish that the predictor is job-related. Usually this can be done by validating the predictor using the strategies and techniques discussed in subsequent chapters of this book.

Step 11. Revise or replace predictor to ensure job-relatedness. If the predictor is not job related, find or develop one that is.

Step 12. Have applicants been individually accommodated? The BFOR now also places the employer under the burden of individual accommodation during recruitment and selection of those protected group members who have special needs. Further, the employer must accommodate to the point of undue hardship or sufficient risk.

Step 13. *Revise or replace predictor to meet the need for individual accommodation.* Revisions are sometimes straightforward and inexpensive (e.g., providing a large-print copy of an employment test to a visually impaired job applicant). The employer should also develop and communicate HR policies concerning the provision of individual accommodations to the physically and mentally disabled and to everyone in the organization who is involved in recruitment and selection.

Step 14. *Operationally adopt predictor.* If the requirement for individual accommodation has been met, adopt the selection predictor; it is likely to be legally defensible. In going through Steps 9 to 14, the employer has met the requirements of the unified approach to establishing a BFOR as specified in *British Columbia (Public Service Employees Relations Comm.) v. B.C.G.E.U.*

Box 2.8 Human Rights and the Internet

The following are Internet addresses for Canadian and provincial human rights tribunals and commissions along with those for some other valuable human rights resources. On each site you will find links to other related sites and to lists of decisions or publications that can be found on the site. For example, the "Publications" link on the Canada Human Rights Commission site will provide you access to a list of recent reports, guides, and other materials that you can read directly from the site, print, or download. By this means, you can obtain a copy of the *Guide to Screening and Selection in Employment.* HR managers and others who engage in recruitment and selection should make a habit of reviewing recent information, including new decisions posted on these sites.

Human Rights Boards/Tribunals:

Canada	http://www.chrt-tcdp.gc.ca/
British Columbia	http://www.bchrt.gov.bc.ca/
Quebec (French)	http://www2.lexum.umontreal.ca/qctdp/fr/
Quebec (English)	http://www2.lexum.umontreal.ca/qctdp/en/

Human Rights Commissions:

Canada	http://www.chrc-ccdp.ca/
Alberta	http://www.albertahumanrights.ab.ca/
British Columbia	http://www.bchrc.gov.bc.ca/
Manitoba	http://www.gov.mb.ca/hrc/
New Brunswick	http://www.gov.nb.ca/hrc-cdp/e/
Newfoundland	http://www.gov.nf.ca/hrc/
Nova Scotia	http://www.gov.ns.ca/humanrights/
Ontario	http://www.ohrc.on.ca/
Prince Edward Island	http://www.isn.net/peihrc/
Quebec	http://www.cdpdj.qc.ca/
Saskatchewan	http://www.gov.sk.ca/shrc/

Valuable Human Rights Resources on the Internet:
Canadian Human Rights Reporter (CHRR)
http://cdn-hr-reporter.ca/

Human Rights Research and Education Centre (Ottawa)
http://www.uottawa.ca/hrrec/

Human Rights Resources on the Internet (AAAS)
http://shr.aaas.org/dhr.htm

Virtual Canadian Law Library
http://www.droit.umontreal.ca/doc/biblio/en/index.html

The legal requirements model illustrates the many complex decisions and tradeoffs that must be made to make selection systems as legally defensible as possible. HR specialists must have the knowledge and time to collect and interpret the technical data that are essential to establishing the legal defensibility of a selection system. The model presented here works best when these data are available. It should be used in an open discussion format where managers can question and challenge each other's assumptions about what constitutes a legally defensible selection predictor. Even then, the legal issues are complex enough that managers may hold differing opinions about whether a predictor is legally defensible. In those cases, legal consultation should be obtained. Nevertheless, the application of this model to practical selection problems should lead to more defensible selection systems over the long run.

SUMMARY

The Canadian workforce has always been ethnically heterogeneous, and now it is becoming increasingly diverse with regard to race, gender, and disabilities. Given that recruitment and selection are crucially important human resources activities for achieving diversity, human rights and employment equity are here to stay. As well, a large segment of the Canadian workforce is unionized, which means that labour codes and related legislation will affect recruitment and selection practices in many Canadian organizations. Legal issues in recruitment and selection are complex and take a great deal of time, study, and experience to master. What is more, the legal scene changes constantly and rapidly as new legislation, legislative amendments, human rights policies, and tribunal or court decisions are introduced. This requires practitioners in recruitment and selection to regularly update their knowledge and skills in legal issues. The legal scene will continue to grow and develop in the future as members of protected groups seek fuller participation in the Canadian labour market and as employers and employees (unionized and nonunionized) renegotiate their relationships through labour law and employment standards.

KEY TERMS

Accommodation, p. 48

Adverse effect discrimination, p. 43

Adverse impact, p. 44

Bona fide occupational requirement (BFOR), p. 46

Discrimination, p. 30

Employment equity, p. 36

Sufficient risk, p. 53

EXERCISES

1. Go to a local business and ask for a copy of their application form. Access the homepage for the Canadian Human Rights Commission on the Web and then find their guidelines on questions permitted on application forms or else refer to Table 2.3 in this chapter. How well does the employer do? Are there any improvements to their application form that you could recommend?

2. Locate the *Canadian Human Rights Reporter (CHRR)* in your college or university library. Find a recent decision published in the *CHRR* that involves recruitment or selection. Which of the principles discussed in this chapter come into play in the decision? What are the implications when human resources professionals design recruitment or selection systems in Canada?

3. In small groups, use the legal requirements model to evaluate a selection predictor as described in a human resources trade magazine or discussed in the later chapters of this book. Report the group findings back to the class. What conclusions did the groups draw about the legal defensibility of the predictor? If the groups disagreed in their conclusions, why did this happen? Can the class reach consensus about whether the predictor is legally defensible? If not, what are the implications for human resources practice?

4. In the *British Columbia (Public Service Employees Relations Comm.) v. B.C.G.E.U.* case, a lower appeals court had suggested that accommodating women by permitting them to meet a lower aerobic standard than men would constitute "reverse discrimination." The Supreme Court of Canada disagreed and stated that "the essence of equality is to be treated according to one's own merit, capabilities and circumstances. True equality requires that differences be accommodated ... A different aerobic standard capable of identifying women who could perform the job safely and efficiently therefore does not necessarily imply discrimination against men. 'Reverse' discrimination would only result if, for example, an aerobic standard representing a minimum threshold for all forest firefighters was held to be inapplicable to men simply because they were men." What are your views on "reverse" discrimination? Do you agree with the views expressed by the Appeals Court or the Supreme Court?

5. There is considerable evidence showing that smokers are less productive than nonsmokers. Costs to organizations, besides those related to medical care, health, and life insurance, include absenteeism and loss of on-the-job time. Estimates place time loss per day due to smoking at 35 minutes a day, or 18.2 lost days per year per

employee who smokes. In addition, smokers are absent three more days per year than other employees. Estimates place the cost of smoking to an employer at around $4500 per smoker per year (Belcourt and McBey, 2000). These data suggest that it is in an employer's best interests to hire only nonsmokers or to fire smokers who cannot overcome their addiction. Would such policies, hiring only nonsmokers and firing smokers, be acceptable under human rights legislation in your province? Are smokers a "protected" group? How would you defend these policies to an investigator from a human rights commission?

6. You may recall hearing about females being fired from U.S. television news anchor positions because they were too old. Clearly this practice would be contrary to all human rights codes in Canada. However, one area of discrimination that is less clear is "lookism," in which a person is chosen for a job on the basis of his or her "looks" rather than his or her other qualifications. Individuals, particularly females, who are overweight tend to receive fewer job offers than others, even in cases where their appearance has no possible bearing on their work performance or where they are not involved in dealing with clients or customers. Can an employer in Canada, or in your jurisdiction, choose not to hire someone on the basis of their "looks" or for being overweight? Do job applicants so denied have protection under your province's human rights provisions?

CASE

Ms. Smith works as a clerk/typist in a government department that is undergoing downsizing. Ms. Smith, who is severely hearing-impaired, has been a productive employee in her department for the last five years. Her performance has always been above average. Ms. Smith has received notice that her position is being eliminated as part of the downsizing. Under her union's contract she must be given preference for any government job that becomes available and for which she is qualified. Ms. Smith has been invited to apply for a term position in another government department, which is converting archival data from paper to an electronic database. To qualify for the position, Ms. Smith will have to pass an interview, a timed typing test, an accuracy test that involves accuracy in transcribing information from a computer screen, and another accuracy test that involves following written instructions to enter written records into the computer database. These are the same tests that all candidates for the position had to pass to become eligible for the jobs.

Ms. Smith was interviewed one week prior to being administered the three skill tests. The interview protocol followed a standardized form used by all government departments. The three skill tests were administered to groups of nine applicants each. The applicants were seated at desks with computers, which were arranged in three rows of three desks each. The instructions for the tests were given verbally by the test administrator. Ms. Smith was provided with the services of a sign language interpreter during the testing and interview sessions.

Ms. Smith passed the interview but failed the skill tests. Her scores are presented in Table C1 along with the minimum scores that had to be obtained on each test to receive a job offer. Based on her performance on the tests, Ms. Smith did not receive an offer for the job and was laid off when her current job ended. Ms. Smith now believes that she was the victim of discrimination based on her physical disability; she claims that during the interview many references were made to her disability and that the interviewer always addressed questions to the sign language interpreter and never made eye contact with her. She feels that she was at a disadvantage in taking the skills tests.

Her prospective employer claims that had she passed the tests she would have been hired and her disability would have been accommodated. The employer argues that the testing standards were reasonably necessary for the efficient performance of the work. The standards in Table C1 are being justified as bona fide occupational requirements (BFORs). Ms. Smith has now filed a complaint with her provincial human rights commission.

Table C1	Ms. Smith's Scores Relative to Standards Needed to Pass Each Test	
	Standards	**Smith**
Interview	30 out of 50 points	36
Typing test	50 words per minute with 5 errors or less	36 wpm
		5 errors
Accuracy—Following Instructions	7 out of 10	5.5
Accuracy—Transcribing	7 out of 10	5

DISCUSSION QUESTIONS

1. Should Ms. Smith have received a job offer? Why or why not? (In answering this and the following questions, base your arguments on the court cases presented in this chapter.)

2. Was Ms. Smith the victim of discrimination because of her disability?

3. Did she receive appropriate accommodation?

4. Are the employer's standards defensible as a BFOR?

5. Based on the material presented in this chapter, do you think the Human Rights Commission will support her claim of discrimination?

6. If you were the employer's legal counsel, how would you defend the employer at a human rights tribunal that is called to hear Ms. Smith's complaint? What would you advise your client to do with respect to the charge?

REFERENCES

Belcourt, M., and K.J. McBey. 2000. *Strategic Human Resources Planning.* Toronto: Nelson.

Canadian Human Rights Commission. 1988. *Bona Fide Requirement Policy.* Ottawa: Canadian Human Rights Commission.

———. 1989. *Office Consolidation: Canadian Human Rights Act.* Ottawa: Minister of Supply and Services Canada.

———. 1994. *Filing a Complaint with the Canadian Human Rights Commission.* Ottawa: Minister of Supply and Services Canada.

———. Undated. *A Guide to Screening and Selection in Employment.* Ottawa.

Cronshaw, S.F. 1986. "The Status of Employment Testing in Canada: A Review and Evaluation of Theory and Professional Practice." *Canadian Psychology* 27: 183–95.

———. 1991. *Industrial Psychology in Canada.* Waterloo, ON: North Waterloo Academic Press.

———. 1995. "Human Rights and Employment Testing." Presented at the annual conference of the Canadian Psychological Association in Charlottetown, PEI.

Dessler, G., and J.F. Duffy. 1984. *Personnel Management.* 2nd ed. Scarborough, ON: Prentice-Hall.

Glastris, P. 1994. "The Thin White Line: City Agencies Struggle to Mix Standardized Testing and Racial Balance." *U.S. News & World Report* (August 15): 53–54.

Human Resources Development Canada. 1995–96. *Employment Standards Legislation in Canada.* Ottawa.

Jackson, S.E., and R.S. Schuler. 1995. "Understanding Human Resource Management in the Context of Organizations and Their Environments." *Annual Review of Psychology* 46: 237–64.

Pentney, W. 1986. "The BFOR Defence since Etobicoke." *Canadian Human Rights Reporter,* vol. 7, C/86-1.

Public Service Commission of Canada. 1994–95. *Annual Report.* Ottawa.

———. Undated. *Investigations: An Overview.* Ottawa: Public Service Commission of Canada, Appeals and Investigations Branch.

Public Service Staff Relations Board. 1994–95. *Parliamentary Employment and Staff Relations Act: Ninth Annual Report of the Public Service Staff Relations Board.* Ottawa.

Scotland, R. 1995. "Ontario Introduces Bill to Repeal 'Quotas': Aims to Restore 'Merit Principle.'" *The Financial Post* (October 12): 4.

Simon, P.L.S. 1988. *Employment Law: The New Basics*. Don Mills, ON: CCH Canadian Limited.

Stone, T.H., and N.M. Meltz. 1988. *Human Resources Management in Canada*. 2nd ed. Toronto: Holt, Rinehart and Winston.

Tibbetts, J., and C. Grey. 2000. "Judge Slams PS Language Aptitude Testing." *Ottawa Citizen* (June 10): A1, A9.

Vining, A.R., D.C. McPhillips, and A.E. Boardman. 1986. "Use of Statistical Evidence in Employment Discrimination Litigation." *The Canadian Bar Review* 64: 660–702.

Weiner, N. 1993. *Employment Equity: Making It Work*. Toronto: Butterworths.

3

SCIENTIFIC METHODS

CHAPTER GOALS

This chapter develops the idea that personnel recruitment and selection strategies based on information obtained through scientific methods are more likely to benefit an organization than decisions based on impressions or intuition. The chapter starts with an introduction to scientific methodology and goes on to examine basic measurement concepts that underlie contemporary recruitment and selection practices. This chapter is an excellent review for those who have had previous courses on research methods and psychological measurement. For others, it is an overview of research terms and methods.

After reading this chapter you should

- appreciate the difference between information discovered through scientific and non-scientific ways of knowing;

- understand the scientific method and several different types of research strategies;

- understand the important role that measurement plays in the scientific process and in describing differences between individuals;

- know what a correlation coefficient is, along with a few other basic statistical concepts used in personnel selection;

- recognize the importance and necessity of establishing the reliability and validity of measures used in personnel selection;

- identify common strategies that are used to provide evidence on the reliability and validity of measures used in personnel selection; and

- appreciate the requirement for measures used in personnel selection to evaluate applicants fairly and in an unbiased fashion.

THE RECRUITMENT AND SELECTION PROCESS

In most employment situations, there are many applicants for each available job. The employer's goal is to hire an applicant who possesses the knowledge, skills, abilities, or other attributes required to successfully perform the job being filled. The employer makes a guess about which applicant will perform the job most effectively. This basic decision, which is made hundreds of times each day throughout Canada, is the end result of a complex process. Correct guesses by the employer have positive benefits for the organization and the employee; bad guesses not only affect the productivity and profitability of the company but may also have negative emotional consequences for the poorly performing employee.

As part of making this decision, the employer must have a good idea of both the duties that will be performed as part of the job and the level of performance required for job success. The employer must identify the knowledge, skills, abilities, or other attributes (KSAOs) that are required for job success and measure or assess KSAOs within individual job applicants. Hiring someone through an assessment of job-related attributes is based on an inference: higher levels of attributes are linked to higher levels of job performance.

THE HIRING PROCESS

Every employer who makes a hiring decision follows a hiring process, even though the managers may not realize they are doing so. When a position becomes vacant, or is newly created, the employer has a general idea of the duties to be performed as part of the job. These duties are included in an advertisement used to recruit candidates for the position. This job advertisement may also state broad educational or experiential requirements expected from the candidates. Applicants submit résumés and, after a preliminary screening, a few may be interviewed. Based on review of the applicant's file, work references, and impressions formed during the interview, the employer makes a decision to hire one of the candidates. This decision may reflect the employer's experience, a gut feeling or intuition about a certain candidate, or simply personal preference. The employer has an *idea* of the type of person who will do well in the job or in the organization and looks for an applicant who matches this idealized employee. In any event, the employer is making a guess about which applicant will do well in the job based on information collected from the job applicant. Unfortunately, all too often the employer's guess reveals more about the biases of the employer than it does about either the requirements for the job or the qualifications and abilities of the applicants. Bad guesses may lead not only to lower productivity but also to legal difficulties. This brief overview of how things are too often done in Canadian organizations should not be mistaken for how they ought to be done. The information presented in this book illustrates acceptable recruitment and selection practices.

BUILDING A FOUNDATION

The chapters in this book explore in depth the topics that make up the typical recruitment and selection process. To move beyond a guess, a selection system must be built on a sound scientific foundation. In buying a house, you may not need to know how to lay a foundation, but you must be able to tell whether the house's foundation is solid. Often, human resources managers are asked to adopt selection systems; this chapter provides the tools needed to determine if a selection system or procedure rests on solid footings. The concepts and procedures developed in this *tools* chapter are applied throughout this book. By necessity, this chapter presents only the most basic information related to research methodology and measurement. For a more extensive discussion of this chapter's topics we highly recommend the companion book in this series, *Research, Measurement, and Evaluation of Human Resources* (Saks, 2000).

DIFFERENT WAYS OF KNOWING

There are several ways in which we can acquire information about people, places, things, or events. These different methods fall into four broad categories. While the three non-scientific methods of tenacity, authority, and rationalization provide us with information, the scientific method produces the most accurate information. This is due to the fundamental difference between scientific and non-scientific methods: science is self-correcting. Information that is acquired through a scientific process can be "falsified"; that is, the information, if incorrect, can be disproved through objective, empirical means. If we believe that a "developmental quotient" is somehow related to better job performance, we have to state that relationship in such a way that it can be tested and disproved if that relationship does not exist. The following sections provide greater detail on these different ways of knowing, including the process of "falsification."

NON-SCIENTIFIC METHODS

METHOD OF TENACITY Often we accept as fact statements that have been made repeatedly over an extended period of time. If we continue to believe that something is true, it becomes true. For example, believing that "women are not suited to be police officers" may lead to selection policies that exclude women from that occupation. This belief may have more to do with stereotypes or traditional roles assigned to women than with their actual ability or skill to do the job. A few years ago, Al Campanis, who was an executive with the Los Angeles Dodgers baseball team, demonstrated how knowledge based on tenacity influenced personnel decisions. He had been invited to the TV show *Nightline* to discuss the employment of blacks and other minorities in front-office positions. Campanis expressed the view that blacks did not have the "necessities" for appointment to executive positions in professional baseball. The statement not only led to Campanis's resignation but also had a negative impact on a multi-million-dollar industry. More recently in Canada, two Reform Party members of Parliament expressed the view that an employer should have the right to move homosexual and black employees "to the back of the shop" or even to fire them to accommodate clients' prejudices. Both members were suspended from their party for making those remarks ("The Reform Party's Days," 1996). Tenacity produces the poorest-quality information. As we discussed in Chapter 2, personnel and other staffing decisions based on this type of information may well have serious legal and financial consequences for an organization.

METHOD OF AUTHORITY We often accept as true statements made by people in positions of authority or sources we consider infallible. These may include our own or others' experience, values, and norms derived from a culture or religious system, or statements made by "experts" such as editorial writers for *Report on Business* or the *Financial Post*. People in organizations frequently seek out authorities for insight into how to manage. Autobiographies of the latest corporate hero are examined for guidance; thousands of dollars are spent sending staff to training seminars conducted by the latest corporate guru. If you accepted Al Campanis as a leading authority on staffing baseball organizations, you probably would not hire many blacks to fill nonplaying positions.

Corporate cultures define truth as well. If you worked for IBM in years past, you might have believed that wearing a white shirt and tie each day improved creativity and productivity; if you worked for Apple Computers, you might have believed just the opposite. Once established, truth based on authority is difficult to change. In recent years, IBM and other companies have tried to move away from a "white shirt" image through "casual Fridays" and other activities; but many other organizations still believe that wearing formal business attire leads to more effective performance. The problem here is that truth based on authority is not absolute; it depends on both the authority and the acceptance of the authority by the believer. The authority may take a

BOX 3.1 Glass Ceilings, Organizational Prejudice, and Managerial Attitudes

"Glass ceilings" refers to the invisible barriers that prevent women from advancing upward in organizations. It reflects an attitude that "women don't belong in top-level executive positions." Despite increasing levels of education and corporate experience, women have difficulty advancing to senior organizational and professional positions. According to *Worklife Report*, a recent study by the International Labor Organization, called *Breaking through the Glass Ceiling: Women and Management*, found that women have made progress in overcoming the prejudice and stereotypical attitudes that prevent them from top organizational positions. Women now represent over 20 percent of senior management positions in Canada, an increase from 4 percent in the early 1970s. Women managers still tend to be clustered in certain occupations that employ large numbers of women such as health and community services. Women now represent a significant portion of top positions in the fields of personnel and labour relations. In the United States, nearly 60 percent of managers in these fields are women. The career paths open to women, such as human resource management, are less likely to lead to top-level positions. The study concluded that social attitudes and prejudices contributed to the segregation of women into specific occupations.

The glass ceiling effect is another example of unscientific thinking that may prevent organizations from hiring or promoting the best person for the job.

Source: "'Glass Ceiling' Separates Women from Top," *Worklife Report* 11 (1997): 15.

different position on what is "truth" as easily as changing the colour of a shirt. Also, not all people accept or recognize the same authority; one person's management expert may be another person's fool.

METHOD OF RATIONALIZATION   This method, also known as the *a priori method*, refers to knowledge developed through the process of reasoning, independent from observation. An individual begins with an initial set of assumptions (which are accepted as true without the benefit of observation or experimentation) and uses these initial assumptions to derive new statements or truths. Mathematicians and philosophers develop a set of initial or *a priori* assumptions and apply the process of logic to deduce new knowledge. Of course, the derived knowledge is only true within the context of the initial *a priori* assumptions. Different starting assumptions lead to different conclusions. If you believed that (a) blacks do not have the "necessities" to be baseball executives and (b) good executives are critical to an organization's success, you could easily reason that blacks should not be hired as baseball executives. If you started with the assumptions that (a) race is irrelevant to performance as a baseball executive and (b) good executives are critical to an organization's success, you would come to the conclusion that the best executive should be hired, regardless of race. Each of these conclusions is correct within the context of its assumptions. The starting assumptions serve as the authority for the new knowledge.

INTUITION   Often human resources decisions are made through intuition; a manager hires someone because of a *good feeling* about the applicant. Intuition is a form of rationalization based on vague or fuzzy, unstated assumptions and a deductive process that may not always be logical. As with other forms of rationalization, once the initial source of knowledge is accepted, so must the derived information. There is no means to challenge the correctness of decisions based on intuition. Increasingly, today's executives are making decisions through intuition. Forty percent of managers who held significant positions in 60 major organizations used intuition or gut feelings as part of their decision-making process. Most of these managers believed that their intuition was built on their accumulated successes and failures in work and in life. These managers are using intuition to make personnel or people-related decisions involving hiring, training, promotion, and performance evaluation (Burke and Miller, 1999). With such prevalent reliance on intuition, it is not surprising, then, when U.S. companies report that good decision-making skills are used only about 12 percent of the time. As a result, many consultants and companies have initiated practices designed to enhance intuitive decision-making skills by having managers understand how experiential learning affects their decision making.

SCIENTIFIC KNOWLEDGE

Human resources decisions affect the lives of individuals and organizations. Those decisions must be as accurate as possible. Science produces the highest-quality information; it accepts as true only the information that can withstand continued challenges to its accuracy. Science is self-correcting. Information is checked for accuracy with methods that are objective; this means that scientific methods can be examined, critiqued, and used by others. Conclusions based on badly designed, biased, or flawed experiments become corrected through public examination by other investigators of a study's methods, data, and conclusions. Because of these features, scientific knowledge is constantly undergoing revision. Even in the space of a few years, previously accepted truths may become outmoded through new discoveries.

CHARACTERISTICS OF SCIENCE   The quality of scientific knowledge reflects the nature of the scientific process. Science is characterized by several essential features (Whitehead, 1967):

- *Science is concerned with reality*—objects and events exist apart from an observer.
- *Science accepts causality*—the universe, including human behaviour, is based on a set of orderly relations, which can be described, predicted, and explained.
- *Science is empirical*—reliable knowledge about the universe is obtained through observation of objects and events. While reasoning is required as

part of the scientific process, it alone does not produce new knowledge; it is used to organize the observed objects and events.

- *Science is public*—observations are subject to error; therefore, scientific knowledge must be made available to others for criticism and review. Approaching all knowledge with a degree of skepticism helps to establish its truthfulness or falsity.

- *Science provides method*—science employs specific rules and procedures in the quest for new knowledge. A hallmark is the inclusion of controls built into the procedure, which serve to check or verify the truthfulness of the newly discovered knowledge.

THE SCIENTIFIC APPROACH

The scientific approach includes a number of methods that can be used to generate knowledge. Regardless of any special features, a scientific method follows a common strategy. Kerlinger (1986) outlined four general steps in this process.

STATEMENT OF THE PROBLEM

This is often the most difficult, yet the most important, part of the process. This step involves taking a generally vague idea or feeling and transforming it into a statement that captures the issues at hand. For example, people may have very strong feelings about the appropriateness of selecting women for police SWAT teams. The reason for their beliefs may be captured by the statement "Women are not suited for roles on police SWAT teams." Once the idea is expressed, it can be pursued to the next stage. Simply expressing the idea does not make it true, as may be the case with non-scientific methods. The statement must be capable of being tested and proven false if the idea is incorrect.

HYPOTHESIS

A **hypothesis** is a proposition about the relation between two or more events, objects, people, or phenomena. It is an attempt to redefine the problem in terms that are amenable to objective investigation. It is a prediction about relations that can be tested. Many hypotheses are presented as "If X happens, then Y results" types of statements. Believing that women are not suited for police SWAT teams might lead you to propose that the aggressiveness required to subdue criminals is related to gender. This belief is expressed in the following hypothesis:

Hypothesis—a proposition about the relation between two or more events, objects, people, or phenomena.

H_1: *There is a relationship between gender and aggression.*

REASONING AND DEDUCTION

While hypothesis H_1 can be examined empirically, more precision is achieved by deducing the consequences of the hypothesis. Based on experience, previous knowledge, or empirical work, we may expect to find higher levels of aggression in males. This reasoning leads to a change in the initial hypothesis:

H_2: *Males are more aggressive than females.*

The reasoning/deductive process may lead to examination of new or different problems. If aggressiveness is needed for success in SWAT team roles and women are less aggressive than men, placing women in SWAT units should lead to lower levels of success. This prediction is expressed in a new hypothesis:

H_3: *If women are placed in SWAT units, the level of success will decrease.*

Of course, all these hypotheses remain conjecture subject to verification.

OBSERVATION/TEST/EXPERIMENT

Up to this point, the scientific approach is similar to the non-scientific methods of knowing in that all the activity, so far, has emphasized reasoning. Reasoning is only part of the scientific process; it is not the final step. The relationship specified in the hypothesis must be tested empirically. The most critical step is to gather empirical evidence that is relevant to the hypothetical relationship.

OPERATIONAL DEFINITIONS In science, *empirical* means that an event is capable of being experienced, that it can be observed or measured, either directly or indirectly. Many hypotheses involve relationships between abstract events. While it is fairly easy to categorize humans into groups of males and females, it is more problematic to define *success*. Before any testing can take place, abstract constructs, like success, must be defined in a manner that allows observation and measurement. This is done through use of **operational definitions**, which define abstract constructs in terms of specific procedures and measures. Operational definitions are very specific to the study in which they are used and may differ between studies. SWAT team success could be defined as the rating assigned by a supervisor to a SWAT unit after its participation in a training exercise, or the number of medals or awards given to members of the unit over a period of time; it could also be defined in many other ways. Operational definitions may differ in the degree to which they represent, or capture the essence of, the abstract construct. Medals and awards made to members of a SWAT team may have little relevance to success in subduing criminals (e.g., members may be given awards to mark the number of years of service in the unit). In this case the operational definition is affected by processes that are irrelevant to the construct. The degree to which this occurs

Operational definitions— define abstract constructs in terms of specific procedures and measures.

is called *construct–irrelevant variance*. The supervisor's rating of the team performance following training may be relevant to the construct but it may not present a complete measure of the team's performance. The degree to which the operational definition fails to capture important aspects of the construct is termed *construct underrepresentation*. The validity of operational definitions is an important concern in any scientific investigation. It is also of equal importance when measurements are used to make inferences about constructs such as "success" or "cognitive ability."

VARIABLES   The events, objects, people, or phenomena referenced in hypothetical propositions must vary in amount, degree, or kind. Such **variables** must have at least one defined characteristic that has at least two values. The variable of gender has two values—male and female. There must be at least two values associated with the variable of SWAT team success; the exact number of values depends on how it is operationally defined. In terms of a rating definition for success, a two-value pass/fail system could be used, as could a five-point letter-grade system of A, B, C, D, or F, a 100-point system, or one of many others.

Variables—events, objects, people, or phenomena that vary in amount, degree, or kind with respect to certain aspects.

RESEARCH PLAN   Once the variables relevant to the hypothesis are defined, a *research plan* is developed. A research plan, or research design, lays out the framework for making measurements or observations on the variables. The research plan specifies the strategy used in collecting data; it identifies the subjects or participants, the environment in which they will be measured, the frequency with which they will be measured, and any interventions or manipulations that the investigator will introduce into the environment. One way in which research designs vary is the degree of control given to the investigator.

OBSERVATIONAL STUDIES   In *observational studies*, the researcher exercises very little control or manipulation of variables; the investigator records naturally occurring behaviours and establishes patterns of relationships between different aspects of the observed behaviour. A police force assigns women to SWAT teams, but there are still SWAT units to which women have not been assigned. Comparing the performance ratings given to these two types of SWAT teams provides a test of H_3. If units with mixed teams had lower performance ratings, we might conclude that the hypothesis is correct. Unfortunately, the lack of control allows alternative conclusions to be drawn. The performance of the SWAT team may have more to do with the ability of the teams' leaders and senior officers than with the gender composition of the team. The ability and experience of the mixed team's officers may have been less than those commanding the all-male unit. Although there is a relationship between the presence of women and team performance, the lack of control over other variables makes it very difficult to attribute the lower performance rating to the presence of women on the SWAT team or to the leadership of the units.

CORRELATIONAL STUDIES   Correlational studies, a class of observational studies, are perhaps the most common design used in personnel selection research—for example, to establish the validity of a selection instrument. The goal of this type of research is to understand patterns of relationships among a set of variables. What is the relationship between the presence of women on a SWAT team and the team's performance? One purpose of correlational studies is to predict one variable from another or from a set of several variables. If we have several SWAT teams that have different numbers of women as members and the team's performance increases as does the number of women on the team, the two variables—number of women and team performance—are said to be positively correlated, as indicated by a correlation coefficient (see page 89). We could then use our knowledge of the number of women on a team to make a prediction about any team's performance through developing a regression equation (see page 91). To say that two variables are related or that one variable predicts another does not mean, nor does it imply, that the change in the first variable has caused the change in the other. As in any observational study, the lack of control over the variables prevents this type of statement from being made. The SWAT team's performance may be due to more effective leaders in the teams that, coincidentally, have more women members.

EXPERIMENTAL DESIGNS   In *experimentation*, the researcher actively manipulates variables and controls different aspects of the environment to exclude alternative explanations for the observed events. To test H_3, an investigator finds two SWAT teams that are similar in terms of performance capability; the investigator then assigns members and officers to each of the teams in a way that equates the ability and experience within each unit. One team is assigned only males while the second is assigned males and females. This is the only difference between the two units. Each team is rated under identical training conditions. If the mixed team receives lower ratings, there is more justification for attributing the cause of the poor performance to the composition of the unit. The control procedures lead to greater confidence in making cause-and-effect statements.

QUASI-EXPERIMENTAL DESIGNS   Unfortunately, many situations do not lend themselves to experimentation on the grounds of either practicality or ethical considerations. In these instances, investigators fall back on less-intrusive strategies. In practice, applied research falls somewhere between the two extremes of pure observation and pure experimentation. In most studies, it is possible to implement some control and to manipulate variables to reduce the number of alternative explanations. In *quasi-experimental* research, we do not have the ability to randomly assign people to the different conditions, or groups. We can, however, manipulate variables that may have an effect on outcomes. It is highly unlikely that any police force would allow a researcher to randomly assign police officers to SWAT teams. The researcher works with teams that are already in place, similar to those in an observational study. The inability to randomly assign members to teams allows for the possibility that the units differ on a number of factors, in addition to gender, which might produce differences on the outcome measure. As in experimentation, the researcher manipulates, controls, and measures these conditions as part of comparing the performance of both teams. Both units might undergo a set of standardized exercises, (e.g., a simulated attack or a hostage rescue operation). While differences between the performance of the two teams could be due to factors other than the teams' gender composition, the quasi-experimental design reduces the number of alternative explanations. Quasi-experimental research strategies are often used to evaluate the results of personnel selection and recruitment efforts.

THE NULL HYPOTHESIS Testing hypotheses is somewhat more involved than described above. Would any decrease in performance of the mixed team, no matter how small, be accepted as proof of H_3? Could the difference in performance ratings be due to chance or to errors in measurement, rather than to

BOX 3.2 Comparison of Research Designs

RESEARCH DESIGN	ADVANTAGES	DISADVANTAGES
Observational/Correlational Designs—provide researchers with little, if any, control or manipulation of variables; the investigator records naturally occurring behaviours and establishes patterns of relationships among different variables.	Research takes place in a natural setting; results are applicable to other environments and populations.	No manipulation of variables; no control of the research environment; no random assignment of people to conditions or groups; design does not eliminate possibility of alternate explanations for results; does not allow researcher to draw cause-and-effect conclusions from the results.
Quasi-Experimental Designs—allow researchers to manipulate and control variables in applied research settings where random assignment of people to different conditions or groups is not possible.	Allow manipulation and control of variables in an applied setting; allow study of behaviour in naturally occurring groups; research takes place in a natural setting; results are applicable to other environments and populations.	No random assignment of people to conditions or groups; in most cases, design does not eliminate possibility of alternate explanations for results; normally, does not allow researchers to draw cause-and-effect conclusions from the results.
Experimental Designs—allow researchers to manipulate and control variables as well as the environment in which the research takes place. These designs provide for the random assignment of people to different conditions or groups.	Allow manipulation and control of variables normally in a laboratory setting; allow the random assignment of people to conditions or groups; design eliminates possibility of alternative explanations for results; allow researcher to make cause-and-effect conclusions from the results.	Research normally takes place in an artificial environment; results may not be applicable to other environments or populations.

actual differences in performance? To assess this possibility, researchers actually test a *null hypothesis,* H_0, which proposes that there will be no difference or no relationship in the data collected across different conditions. The null hypothesis that corresponds to H_3 would be:

H_0: *If women are placed in SWAT units, the level of success will not decrease.*

In other words, the performance of the mixed-gender crew will be the same as the all-male crew, with the exception of slight variation due to chance factors such as measurement error.

STATISTICAL SIGNIFICANCE If the null hypothesis is rejected, the alternative hypothesis, in this case H_3, is assumed to be true. Statistical procedures are used to evaluate the likelihood that a difference across groups occurs by chance. In general, the larger a difference between two groups on some measurement, the less likely that difference is attributable to chance. As part of the research plan, the investigator specifies the size of an empirical difference that is used to reject the null hypothesis and to accept the alternative. If there is only one chance in 20 (a probability of .05) that a difference of such size could have occurred by chance, the difference is said to be *statistically significant*; that is, the difference is probably *not* due to chance. A statistically significant result does not automatically mean that the research hypothesis is accepted. The researcher must also show that alternative explanations for the results are unlikely, a task that is more easily accomplished with a well-designed experiment.

DRAWING CONCLUSIONS The results of a study, whether positive or negative with respect to the research hypothesis, have implications for both theory and application. In either case, we draw conclusions, based on the empirical evidence, about the initial problem. While there is an end to any one study, the research process is ongoing. The results and conclusions from one study are integrated into a larger body of knowledge. There is always a probability that a research hypothesis should *not* have been accepted. With repeated research over time, evidence accumulates on the appropriateness of the findings from any one study. Similarly, theories and proposed solutions to problems evolve with the knowledge obtained from new studies.

THE NATURE OF MEASUREMENT

Measurement—the assignment of numbers to aspects of events, objects, people, or phenomena according to a set of rules or conventions.

Measurement plays an important role in the scientific process. Hypothesizing that higher levels of cognitive ability are related to higher levels of job performance implies that both cognitive ability and job performance can be measured. **Measurement** is the assignment of numbers to *aspects* of objects or events according to a set of rules or conventions. The act of measuring an abstract construct such as cognitive ability does not differ from measuring more concrete ones such as job performance.

The starting point in measurement is to define the construct that is to be measured. What do cognitive ability and job performance mean? Defining *cognitive ability* as "knowing how to use words and numbers" might produce a different set of measurements than defining it as "knowing how to get things done." Both of these definitions are legitimate ways of defining cognitive ability, yet each emphasizes different *aspects* of the cognitive ability concept. Similarly, *job performance* could be defined to emphasize either quality or quantity aspects. The next step is to select or to develop a set of operations or measurement procedures that will assign numbers to the different objects to reflect the degree of the aspect inherent in the object. The fundamental assumption in measurement is that relations among numbers assigned to the aspects convey information about relations among the objects themselves.

SCALES OF MEASUREMENT

Most people agree that there are four basic sets of rules by which numbers may be assigned to aspects of objects. Each set of rules constitutes a **measurement scale**, or level of measurement. From the lowest to highest level, these four measurement scales are *nominal, ordinal, interval,* and *ratio*.

Measurement scale—a set of rules by which numbers may be assigned to aspects of events, objects, people, or phenomena.

NOMINAL SCALES   A nominal scale simply uses numbers to assign labels to aspects of objects, for example, categorizing people on the basis of sex by assigning 1 to males and 2 to females. The numbers do not convey any information about the people or objects, or relations between them, except to identify the class or group to which the person or object belongs. The values of the assigned numbers are arbitrary. The number 2 could have been assigned to males and 1 to females, or 16 and 27, or any other two numbers. The higher-valued numbers do not imply that members of a group have more of the aspect being measured. The numbers simply denote that the groups, not the objects or people within the groups, are different from one another. Although classification schemes can be quite complex, the only requirement for a nominal scale is that all members of the same class or group be given the same number, that all members or objects be assigned to a group, and that no two different groups be given the same number.

ORDINAL SCALES   An ordinal scale uses numbers to rank-order people or objects in terms of a selected aspect. A human resources manager might interview four job applicants—Ms. A, Mr. B, Ms. C, and Mr. D—and decide that in terms of knowing how to get things done, Ms. A is the best candidate, followed, in order, by Ms. C, Mr. D, and Mr. B. This order is maintained by assigning the numbers 4, 3, 2, and 1 to Ms. A, Ms. C, Mr. D, and Mr. B, respectively. In this case, a higher number reflects a higher rank order. This initial number assignment is arbitrary; rank 1 could just as easily have been assigned to the best candidate, as long as the remaining numbers were assigned in a consistent fashion to reflect the applicant's degree of know-how. The rank ordering implies that Ms. A has more know-how than any of the other three applicants, that Ms. C has more than Mr. D or Mr. B, and that Mr. D has more know-how than Mr. B. More specifically, if Ms. A is superior to Ms. C and Ms. C is superior to Mr. D, then Ms. A must also be superior to Mr. D. Ordinal numbers convey information about order relationships, and nothing more.

Using an ordinal measure is much like using a measuring stick made out of elastic; rank 1 is assigned to the person or object having the highest property and then the stick is pulled as much as needed until rank 2 coincides with the second-highest. No matter how much or how little the stick is pulled, the order of the numbers is maintained. Because of this elasticity, ordinal rankings do not convey any information on the magnitude of the difference between the people or objects being measured. The difference in know-how between Ms. C and Mr. D may be very large or very small; the ranking simply means that Ms. C has more of it. Differences between the rank numbers are also meaningless; for example, the difference between Ms. C's and Mr. D's ranks (3 − 2 = 1) may represent a very large difference in know-how, while the same difference between Mr. D's and Mr. B's ranks (2 − 1 = 1) may represent only a very slight difference. Similarly, comparisons cannot be made between rank orders obtained

---

BOX 3.3 Rank and Rancour

Every year *Maclean's* magazine ranks Canadian universities, comparing schools grouped into three categories: Primarily Undergraduate, Comprehensive, and Medical/Doctoral. The special November issue that contains the rankings is the highest-selling issue of the magazine. It also produces fear and loathing among university administrators whose universities do not fare well in the ratings or whose school has slipped a few points in the rankings from the previous year. Certainly, the rankings create a great deal of buzz on campus with student newspapers prominently featuring their school's ranking, for better or worse.

How meaningful are these rankings? Academics and statisticians have questioned the methods used by *Maclean's* staff to compile the ratings, and, to be fair, *Maclean's* has tried to improve the process through which it generates the rankings for each school. Nonetheless, as a performance measure, the rankings suffer from all the problems inherent in ordinal data. The rankings may lead prospective students to believe that there are meaningful differences among the universities in each category when in fact the difference in quality between the highest- and lowest-ranked school may be inconsequential. The rankings may lead the public to believe that the lower-ranked schools are of poor quality when they are providing their students with an excellent education.

The *Maclean's* rankings also illustrate the point that you cannot compare rankings outside the group in which the ranking has been made. Rankings are relative values. The university ranked Number 1 in the Comprehensive category is not necessarily superior to the Number 3 school in the Primarily Undergraduate group; the reverse could, in fact, be true.

Human resources managers use performance measures (numbers) to evaluate personnel and to make selection decisions. The HR specialist must understand the limitations of the data they are working with if they are to make decisions in the long-term interest of their organization.

from different groups. The human resources manager's assistant might have interviewed and rated, from top down, three other job candidates, Mr. X, Ms. Y, and Mr. Z. It is quite possible that Mr. B, the lowest-rated candidate in the first group, is far superior to Mr. X, the top-rated candidate in the second group. Rank orders apply only within the group on which they were made.

INTERVAL SCALES   An interval scale assigns numbers to reflect not only rank order but also the degree of the property being measured. Differences between interval scale values reflect differences in magnitude of the property. An interval scale requires equal distances or units between measured values. Here, the measuring stick is made out of a rigid substance with constant units between each measurement division; the distance between numbers cannot be stretched to give the second-most property the rank of 2 or the third-most, 3. Instead, the property of one person or object being measured is assigned a number from the measuring stick, which reflects the number of constant units between it and the same property of a different person or object.

While there is much discussion over how to construct an interval scale, assume that the human resources manager had one available and used it properly to assign numbers to reflect each applicant's degree of know-how. Each applicant received a rating from a 10-point scale where a value of 10 means that a candidate is perfect and 1 that the candidate is unsuited for the job. The manager assigned Ms. A, Ms. C, Mr. D, and Mr. B scores of 8, 4, 3, and 2, respectively. The differences between assigned numbers represent differences in each candidate's degree of know-how. Ms. A has four more units of know-how than Ms. C ($8 - 4 = 4$), while Ms. C has one more unit than Mr. D ($4 - 3 = 1$) and two more than Mr. B ($4 - 2 = 2$). The assigned numbers do not tell anything about the actual amount or magnitude of each applicant's know-how, only that each has so many units as measured by the specific interval scale. The numbers on the scale are arbitrary; another scale, starting at 11 and ending at 38, might have produced values of 32, 20, 17, and 14, respectively, for the four candidates. Nonetheless, the differences in assigned values still represent the same differences in candidates' degree of know-how. However, in terms of the scale values, Ms. A now has 12 more units of know-how than Ms. C ($32 - 20 = 12$). All that's happened here is to take the rigid measuring stick and divide it into smaller units with the starting point called 11 rather than 1. Three units on the new measuring stick equal one on the old. This is the same situation as using either a Fahrenheit or Celsius scale to measure temperature: on one the freezing point for water is called 32, on the other it is labelled 0, but they both report the *same* degree of temperature.

Interval scales allow comparisons across groups. If the assistant manager had assigned values of 9, 3, and 1 from the 10-point scale to Mr. X, Ms. Y, and Mr. Z, those applicants could be compared with the other four (assuming that the assistant manager assigned values the same way as did the manager). Likewise, temperatures in Halifax, Montreal, Toronto, Calgary, and Vancouver could be represented by Celsius scale values and compared with those for London, Paris, Amsterdam, and Rome.

The comparisons made with interval measures are limited to assessing differences between the interval scale values. Because interval scales have arbitrary starting points, ratios formed between interval measures are meaningless. Forming a ratio of Ms. A's to Ms. C's scores on the 10-point scale (8 to 4) suggests that Ms. A has twice as much know-how; comparing them on the other scale (32 to 20) shows a different relation. In both cases, the comparison is inappropriate. This is similar to arguing that a temperature of 30°C is twice as hot as one of 15°C, or that one of 80°F is twice as hot as 40°F.

RATIO SCALES Ratio scales require that the measurement scale used to assign values to properties have equal units and that the starting or zero point on the measurement scale represent the total absence of the property being measured. In other words, regardless of the number of divisions on the rigid measuring stick, the values on the stick must be assigned in a way that a zero on the measuring stick represents the condition where no degree of the measured property is present. In this way, all ratio scales have the same starting value and all scale values are referenced to the true absence of the property. If the human resources manager had a scale with a true zero point, a value that could be assigned to a candidate with absolutely no cognitive ability, then ratios formed between values assigned to different candidates would take on meaning. Additionally, the ratio would not be affected by the number of divisions on the scale. With a true zero point, the first scale might assign values of 6 and 3 to Ms. A and Ms. C, respectively; on the other, their assigned values might be 18 and 9. Each scale suggests that Ms. A has twice as much know-how as Ms. C; the relationship holds regardless of the size of the intervals on each scale. A ratio of the scale values gives a direct estimate of the ratio of the magnitude of the property.

MEASURING INDIVIDUAL DIFFERENCES FOR SELECTION

For personnel selection, the purpose of measurement is to describe differences among individuals with respect to those constructs that are important to the task at hand. Defining cognitive ability as knowing how to get things done implies that some people have more know-how than others and that numbers can be systematically assigned to represent each person's degree of know-how. Measurement quantifies characteristics of individuals who belong to a specific group or population. Personnel selection generally focuses on quantifying differences between individual job applicants on the basis of their job-related knowledge, skill level, intellectual abilities, personality attributes, and their likelihood to maximize organizational desires or goals. These characteristics remain, for the most part, relatively stable (Ackerman and Humphreys, 1990).

Methods of Measurement

In the above examples, the human resources manager assigned a number to indicate a person's degree of know-how. The manager is assigning a value to a self-report or self-disclosure made by the applicant. There are other methods that the manager could have used to measure know-how (Sackett and Larson, 1990).

Behavioural observation occurs when someone measures behaviours that are produced by someone else. Behavioural observation may be either direct or indirect. In the first case, an individual is observed and the quality, frequency, or intensity of some aspect of overt behaviour is recorded. For example, the human resources manager might count the number of times a job applicant pauses in mid-sentence during a job interview. Indirect observation focuses on the products of the behaviour rather than on the behaviour itself. A human resources manager might ask applicants for a secretarial position to type a sample document; the number of errors made or the number of words typed per minute by each applicant is an indirect measure of one aspect of their behaviour.

Self-report measures involve individuals responding to a series of questions, or items, that require them to report on their own characteristics. Interviews and questionnaires constitute self-report measures. Self-reports may serve as (1) substitutes for factual information that can be verified (e.g., asking an individual to report his or her age); (2) a means to assess constructs that may not be easily observed (e.g., having an individual answer a series of questions related to attitudes, values, intentions, and beliefs); or (3) ways in which to measure an individual's perception of events or other people (e.g., asking an employee to rate the abilities required to perform a given task). Self-reports may consist of responses to single items or to a series of related items, in which case an individual's score is derived from the set of items.

Reports about others involve an individual describing the characteristics of another person. For example, employees may complete a survey that asks them to rate how well a series of items describe their supervisor. In another instance, the human resources manager might draw up a report on a job applicant based on an individual's performance during a job interview.

Unobtrusive measures involve the analysis of archives, records, documents, or other physical evidence to make inferences about characteristics of interest. These physical traces are used as proxies for actual behaviour or for internal states of individuals. For example, an increase in employee absenteeism following the hiring of a new supervisor might indicate that problems exist between the supervisor and employees.

Each of these different types of measures has strengths and weaknesses. There is no such thing as a perfect measure. However, it is important that the measure being used capture the essence of the characteristic or aspect under consideration. The measure must also assign values to the different characteristics in a fairly consistent manner.

THE NATURE OF OBSERVED SCORES

Many human characteristics that play an important role in personnel selection remain stable over time. Therefore, the same human resources manager should assign the same score to an applicant on two different occasions, or two different managers should assign the same score to the applicant at the same time. However, this does not generally happen because the assigned scores reflect not only the characteristic being measured, but also error. The difference in the two scores is attributed to error that varies randomly over time. For example, the second interview with some applicants may have taken place in a noisy environment, causing the manager to miss vital information needed to assign *degree of know-how* scores. Hardly any human characteristic is measured without error. Measurement models deal with errors in different ways. The classical measurement model (Nunnally and Bernstein, 1994), which has had a major impact on personnel research, assumes that any observed score, X, is a combination of a **true score**, T, and an **error score**, e, such that:

$$X = T + e$$

> **True score**—the average score that an individual would earn on an infinite number of administrations of the same test or parallel versions of the same test.
>
> **Error score or measurement error**—the hypothetical difference between an observed score and a true score.

This model assumes that the characteristic being measured is stable and that the only reason an observed score changes from one measurement to another is due to random error. Error scores are independent of the characteristic being measured; errors are attributable to the measurement process, not to the individual. That is, the magnitude of error scores is unrelated to the magnitude of the characteristic being measured. The error score for an applicant with a very high level of know-how could be very large, or very small; that same situation would hold for any level of know-how. The model also assumes that true scores and error scores combine in a simple additive manner. We will return to this point a bit later after a brief introduction to some statistical concepts that will aid that discussion. If you are familiar with basic statistical concepts you may want to skip ahead to the section on reliability.

CORRELATION AND REGRESSION

BASIC STATISTICS If a human resources manager interviewed only a few job applicants, it is possible to directly compare the applicants on the basis of their assigned scores. What if there were a very large number of applicants? How would the manager keep track of all the scores? One way is to use statistical procedures to describe important information contained in the set of applicant scores (Kerlinger, 1986). The manager could compute the *mean* or average score. The mean represents the most typical or "average" score that might be expected within a group of scores; it is the one score that best represents the set of scores. Not every applicant has a score that is similar to the mean score. It is also useful to know how different, on average, any one score is from the mean score and from any other score. The *variance* gives this information. The more the observed scores differ from each other and from the mean, the higher the variance; scores that are tightly clustered around a mean score will have a smaller variance.

Often in reporting scores the *standard deviation* is used rather than the variance. The standard deviation is the square root of the variance; it is more convenient to use since it presents information in terms of the actual measurement scale. Knowing both the mean and the variance allows the manager to know the score that an average applicant should attain, and how much variability to expect in applicant scores. If most applicant scores fall within one standard deviation from the mean, then someone with a score that exceeds three standard deviations might be considered an exceptional applicant. For example, if the mean were 50 and the size of the standard deviation were 10, most applicant scores normally would fall between 40 and 60. Scores greater than 80 would be exceptional and indicate that an applicant received a very high rating compared with the average applicant; on the other hand, scores less than 20 would indicate that the applicant fared poorly.

CORRELATION   Measures of central tendency and variability are quite useful in summarizing a large set of observations. However, in many areas of personnel selection, the relationship between two variables is of considerable interest. The human resources manager is interested in the relationship between cognitive ability and job performance—that is, the degree to which the variation in cognitive ability is associated with the variation in job performance, or the degree to which the variation in job performance can be predicted from the variation in cognitive ability.

A *correlation coefficient* is a statistic that presents information on the extent of the relationship between two variables. To establish this correlation, the manager must have two scores for each applicant, one for cognitive ability and the other for job performance. In the case of job applicants, the manager could establish a know-how score based on the interview or through some other test that was administered to each applicant. But the manager would not have a job performance score since this can only be obtained once the applicants are hired. The manager has two options: (1) the applicants are hired and their job performance is evaluated after a period of time; the performance score of each new employee is then paired with the know-how score obtained at the time of application; or (2) a group of existing employees with known job performance scores could be put through the interview process to determine their degree of know-how with both scores paired for each employee. These two approaches provide *predictive* and *concurrent* evidence, respectively, that may be used in establishing the validity of inferences about job performance made from the test scores. Validation strategies are reviewed later in this chapter.

Table 3.1 presents hypothetical data obtained from existing workers. Each pair of scores for each employee is graphed on a scatterplot where each axis represents a variable. In Figure 3.1 these data points are enclosed with an ellipse to show the relationship between the two variables. In this case the ellipse tends to tilt upward as both cognitive ability and job performance scores increase. This orientation of the ellipse suggests a linear, positive relationship between

TABLE 3.1	MEASURING A RELATIONSHIP BETWEEN COGNITIVE ABILITY AND JOB PERFORMANCE		
EMPLOYEE X	COGNITIVE ABILITY, Y	JOB PERFORMANCE, Y	PREDICTED JOB PERFORMANCE, Y'
Mr. E	10	7	6.91
Ms. F	4	5	5.11
Mr. G	5	4	5.41
Mr. H	8	6	6.31
Mr. I	2	4	4.51
Ms. J	6	5	5.71
Mr. K	7	5	6.01
Mr. L	3	6	4.81
Ms. M	8	7	6.31
Mr. N	6	8	5.71

For the above data:

$r = 0.56$

$r^2 = 0.31$

$Y' = 0.30 X + 3.91$

cognitive ability scores and job performance scores. High cognitive ability scores are associated with high job performance scores. If the ellipse had tilted downward at the high end of the job performance axis and upward at the low end, it would have suggested a linear, negative relationship, that high cognitive ability scores are associated with low job performance scores.

CORRELATION COEFFICIENTS While the scatterplot gives a good visual indication of the relationship between the two variables, its usefulness becomes limited as the size of the data set increases. The information in a scatterplot is summarized through an index, r, the correlation coefficient. A correlation coefficient indicates both the *size* and *direction* of a linear relationship between two variables. For the data in Table 3.1, $r = 0.56$. Direction indicates the nature of the linear relationship between the two variables. A positive or direct relationship of the type presented in Table 3.1 is signified by a plus sign. Negative or indirect relationships are indicated by minus signs; for example, $r = -0.56$ indicates a situation in which high cognitive ability scores predicted low job performance scores. The strength or size of the relationship is indicated by the value of the correlation coefficient. A correlation of $r = 1.00$ indicates a perfect positive, linear relationship between two variables, while $r = -1.00$ indicates a perfect negative, linear relationship. Correlations of $r = 0.00$ signify that there

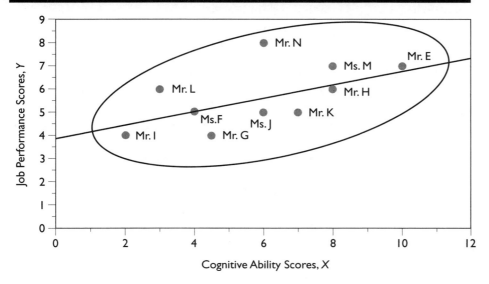

FIGURE 3.1 COGNITIVE ABILITY AND JOB PERFORMANCE—I

is no linear relationship between the two variables under study. With correlations approaching $r = 0.00$, one variable cannot be used to predict the score on the second variable; knowing the status of the first variable or characteristic does not help you know anything about the status of the second. The more closely the correlation coefficient approaches a value of either plus or minus 1.00, the more accurately one variable predicts the other.

COEFFICIENT OF DETERMINATION   Another index that gives an indication of the strength of a relationship between two variables is r^2, the *coefficient of determination*. This value represents the proportion of variability in one variable that is associated with variability in another. It is the proportion of variability that can be accounted for in one variable by knowing something about a different variable. For Table 3.1, about 31 percent (i.e., $r^2 = 0.56 \times 0.56 = 0.31$) of the variance in job performance ratings can be accounted for by knowing the applicants' cognitive ability scores. Looking at this from a different direction, about 69 percent of the variability in job performance ratings is not related to cognitive ability scores. Both r and r^2 give an indication of the size of a relationship.

SIMPLE REGRESSION   The relationship between two variables can also be expressed in terms of a straight line. Remember that a correlation expresses the degree and direction of a linear relationship between two variables. The correlation coefficient is used to derive an equation for a straight line that best fits the data points contained in the scatterplot. This is a *regression line*. The diagonal line in Figure 3.1's scatterplot is the regression line that provides the best fit to the data contained in the ellipse. In regression, one variable is used to predict another. The independent or *predictor variable* is plotted along the X-axis of the scatterplot with the dependent or *criterion variable* plotted along the Y-axis. The equation used to generate the straight line is:

$$Y' = bX + c$$

This equation states that a predicted job performance score, Y', is equal to an individual's cognitive ability score, X, multiplied by b, the regression coefficient, plus c, a constant. The regression coefficient, b, represents the slope of the straight line, and the constant, c, represents the intercept, where the line crosses the Y-axis. For the hypothetical data in Table 3.1, $b = 0.30$, and $c = 3.91$; these values are used to generate a predicted job performance score, Y', for each applicant. These Y' values are also presented in Table 3.1. Notice that the predicted values differ from the actual values; for Mr. E, the difference is relatively small (6.91 v. 7.00) but relatively large for Mr. N (5.71 v. 8.00). The regression line produces the smallest error between predicted and actual values of the criterion variable.

MULTIPLE REGRESSION Many practical situations involve more than two variables. The human resources manager may have not only information about cognitive ability and job performance but also other information obtained from letters of reference and the application form. Each one of these sources of information, on its own, may predict job performance scores to some degree. The set of predictors can be combined into one equation to indicate the extent to which the set, taken as a whole, is related to the criterion variable. The mathematical procedure to compute this equation, while more complicated than the case of two variables, follows the same logic as that for simple regression. Both simple and multiple regression techniques are used to combine information to make human resources decisions.

RELIABILITY

Hardly any human characteristic is measured in an error-free manner. The act of measuring produces a score that measures both the true score and an error component. **Reliability** is the degree to which observed scores are free from random measurement errors. Reliability is an indication of the stability or dependability of a set of measurements (Kerlinger, 1986). Reliability refers to the consistency of a set of measurements when a testing procedure is repeated on a population of individuals or groups (American Educational Research Association [AERA], American Psychological Association [APA], and National Council on Measurement in Education [NCME], 1999). Think of an employer who requires each employee to punch a time clock upon arrival at work. Mr. X, Ms. Y, and Mr. Z, without fail, arrive at work each morning at 8:55 A.M., 8:56

Reliability—the degree to which observed scores are free from random measurement errors. Reliability is an indication of the stability or dependability of a set of measurements over repeated applications of the measurement procedure.

A.M., and 8:57 A.M., respectively. If, on each day, the time clock stamped these same times, exactly, on each employee's time card, the time clock would be considered extremely reliable. The observed score—the time stamped on the time card—is the same as the true score, the time the employees arrived at work; no degree of error has been added to the measurement. On the other hand, if the clock stamped times of 9:03 A.M., 9:00 A.M., and 9:00 A.M. for Mr. X, Ms. Y, and Mr. Z, the measurement would include an error component. Mr. X's time is off by eight minutes, Ms. Y's by four minutes, and Mr. Z's by three minutes. The time clock is not accurate, or reliable, in reporting the time people arrived for work. In this case, the error appears to be random or unsystematic; the occurrence or degree of the error does not appear to be predictable.

Errors may also be systematic; that is, the errors may be made in a consistent, or predictable, fashion. If the time clock were five minutes fast, it would report the three arrival times as 9:00 A.M., 9:01 A.M., and 9:02 A.M. The clock is still reliable in reporting the arrival times of the three employees, but it is systematically adding five minutes to each worker's time. The observed scores are reliable, but they do not represent the true arrival times. In other words, while the observed scores are accurate, they are not a valid indication of whether the employees started work on time. Systematic errors do not affect the accuracy of the measurements but rather the meaning, or interpretation, of those measurements.

INTERPRETING RELIABILITY COEFFICIENTS

Another way to think of reliability is in terms of the variability of a set of scores. If the measuring instrument is not very accurate—that is, if it adds large random error components to true scores—then the variance of the measured scores should be much larger than the variance of the true scores. Reliability can be thought of as the ratio of true score variance, Var(T), to observed score variance, Var(X) (AERA et al., 1999); this can be expressed as the following equation:

$$r_{xx} = \frac{\text{Var } (T)}{\text{Var } (X)}$$

where r_{xx} is the reliability coefficient, the degree that observed scores, which are made on the same stable characteristic, correlate with one another. In this case, r^2 represents the proportion of variance in the observed scores that is attributed to true differences on the measured characteristic. For the arrival times in our example, Var(T) = 1.0; for the reported times, Var(X) = 3.0, with r_{xx} = 0.33. Only 10 percent of the variability in the reported arrival times, $(r_{xx})^2$, is attributable to the true arrival time; the remaining 90 percent of the variability is attributable to the inaccuracy of the time clock. When the time clock is systematically fast by five minutes—Var(X) =1.0, giving an r_{xx} = 1.00—the systematic error did not affect the reliability coefficient; the scores are very reliable, but they do not tell anything about the time people actually arrived at work.

MEASUREMENT ERROR   Measurement error can be thought of as the hypothetical difference between an individual's observed score on any particular measurement and the individual's true score. Measurement error, whether systematic or random, reduces the usefulness of any set of measures or the results from any test. It reduces the confidence that we can place in the score the measure assigns to any particular individual. Does the score accurately represent the individual's knowledge or ability or is it so fraught with error that we cannot use it to make meaningful decisions? Information on the degree of error present in any set of measurements must be considered when using the measurements to make employment decisions. In our example, the manager must consider the possible major sources of the error, the size of the error, and the degree to which the observed scores would reoccur in another setting or with other employees. The *standard error of measurement* is a statistical index that summarizes information related to measurement error. This index is estimated from observed scores obtained over a group of individuals. It reflects how an individual's score would vary, on average, over repeated observations that were made under identical conditions.

FACTORS AFFECTING RELIABILITY

The factors that introduce error into any set of measurements can be organized into three broad categories.

TEMPORARY INDIVIDUAL CHARACTERISTICS   Following his interview with the human resources manager, Mr. B is assigned a relatively low score for know-how, which is assumed to be stable over time. If Mr. B were sick on the day of the interview, or extremely anxious or tired, his know-how score might reflect a larger-than-normal error component. On another occasion when Mr. B is in better shape, he is interviewed again and given a higher know-how score. The difference in the two scores is attributed to the difference in Mr. B's state of well-being, rather than to a change in know-how. Mr. B's ill health negatively affected his performance during the initial interview, leading to a lower score. Factors such as health, motivation, fatigue, and emotional state introduce temporary, unsystematic errors into the measurement process.

LACK OF STANDARDIZATION   Changing the conditions under which measurements are made introduces error into the measurement process. Ms. A, Mr. B, Ms. C, and Mr. D are asked different questions during their interviews. Ms. A is interviewed over lunch in a very comfortable restaurant while the other candidates are interviewed in a very austere conference room. Mr. B is given a few minutes to answer each question, but others are given as long as they need.

The manager displays a lack of interest in Mr. B during the interview, but reacts very positively to Ms. A. These are just a few of the ways that lack of standardization can enter into the measurement process.

CHANCE Factors unique to a specific procedure introduce error into the set of measurements. Luck of the draw may have done in Mr. B during his interview. His know-how score is based on how he answered a specific set of questions. Mr. B did poorly on the questions he was asked, but he might have done extremely well on any others. Mr. D had no prior experience with interviews while Ms. A knew what to expect from previous experience. Ms. C was distracted and did not understand a critical question.

METHODS OF ESTIMATING RELIABILITY

To measure reliability, we have to estimate the degree of variability in a set of scores that is caused by measurement error. We can obtain this estimate by using two different, but parallel, measures of the characteristic or attribute. Over the same set of people, both measures should report the same score for each individual. This score will represent the true score plus measurement error. Both measures reflect the same true score; discrepancies between the two sets of scores suggest the presence of measurement error. The correlation coefficient based on the scores from both measures gives an estimate of r_{xx}, the reliability coefficient. It is extremely difficult, if not impossible, to obtain two parallel measures of the same characteristic; therefore, several strategies have been developed as approximations of parallel measures.

TEST AND RETEST The identical measurement procedure is used to assess the same characteristic over the same group of people on two different occasions. The human resources manager invites the job applicants back for a second interview. They are asked the same questions in the same order. The correlation of their first and second interview scores estimates the reliability of the know-how scores. High correlations suggest high levels of reliability.

ALTERNATE FORMS Having a person take the same interview twice may lead to a false estimate of the reliability of the interview process. The candidates may recall their original answers to the interview questions; they may also have thought of better answers after the first interview and give the improved answers on the second opportunity. To prevent the intrusion of effects from the first interview, the manager asks the applicants alternate questions during the second interview. The correlation between both know-how scores again estimates reliability, with high correlations once more indicating strong reliability.

INTERNAL CONSISTENCY Both test–retest and alternate forms procedures require two sets of measurements made on different occasions. In the case of interviews, it is quite costly in time and money to put all the candidates through a second interview procedure. Besides, isn't each question in the interview directed at measuring know-how? Why not consider any two questions in the interview to be an example of a test–retest situation, and determine the correlation between scores given to each item in that pair? This is the logic behind establishing reliability through internal consistency. Rather than select any particular pair of items, the correlations between the scores of all possible pairs of items are calculated and then averaged. This average estimates the internal consistency, the degree to which all the questions in the set are measuring the same thing. These estimates are sometimes called *alpha* coefficients, or *Cronbach's alpha*, after the formula used to produce the estimate. *Split-half reliability* is a special case of internal consistency where all the items are first divided into two arbitrary groups. For example, all the even-numbered items may form one group with the odd-numbered items placed into the second. The correlation over each person's average scores in the two groups is used as the reliability estimate.

INTER-RATER RELIABILITY Measurement in personnel selection is often based on the subjective assessment, or rating, of one individual by another. The human resources manager's assessment of know-how based on the interview is a subjective measurement. How likely would the rating assigned by one judge be assigned by other judges? The correlation between these two judgments estimates the reliability of their assessments. The manager and the assistant manager independently rate each applicant's interview; a high correlation between their two scores suggests that their scores are reliable measures of know-how. Sometimes, this index is referred to as *classification consistency* or *inter-rater agreement*. This distinction is purely semantic.

CHOOSING AN INDEX OF RELIABILITY Measures of test–retest reliability, alternate forms reliability, and internal consistency are special cases of a more general type of index called a generalizability coefficient. These three measures, however, provide slightly different views of a measure's reliability. Each is limited and does not convey all the relevant information that might be needed. The specific requirements of a situation may dictate which index is chosen. As well, it remains within the professional judgment of the human resources specialist to choose an appropriate index of reliability and to determine the level of reliability that is acceptable for use of a specific measure. Before using any measurement to make decisions about employees, the HR specialist must consider the consequences of the decisions based on the measure. The need for accuracy increases with the seriousness of the consequences for the employee (AERA et al., 1999).

VALIDITY

It is important and necessary to demonstrate that a measure is reliable; it is also necessary to show that the measure captures the essence of the characteristic or attribute. Often, validity is incorrectly thought of as indicating the worth or goodness of a test or other measurement procedure. **Validity** simply refers to the legitimacy or correctness of the inferences that are drawn from a set of measurements or other specified procedures (Cronbach, 1971). During an employment interview, a human resources manager measures the height of each applicant with a metal measuring tape. These height measurements are likely to be very reliable. What if the manager assumes that taller applicants have more job know-how and hires the tallest people? Are the inferences drawn from the physical height measures valid statements of job know-how? In other words, can the manager make a legitimate inference about know-how from the height data? Could Al Campanis make a legitimate inference about baseball front-office know-how from skin colour?

Before using any set of measurements, it is essential to demonstrate that the measurements lead to valid inferences about the characteristic or construct under study. It is relatively easy to demonstrate that the metal tape provides valid measures of physical height. The metal tape measure can be scaled to an actual physical standard that is used to define a unit of length. The standard exists apart from the measurement process. In the case of length, the standard is a bar of plutonium maintained under specific atmospheric conditions in government laboratories. It is more difficult to demonstrate the validity of inferences made from many psychological measurements because they deal more with abstract constructs, such as cognitive ability or know-how. As discussed earlier in this chapter, the measures may not represent important aspects of a construct (construct underrepresentation) or they may be influenced by aspects of the process that are unrelated to the construct (construct-irrelevant variance). In most of these cases, independent physical standards for the construct do not exist, making validation more difficult, but not impossible. Validation rests on evidence accumulated through a variety of sources and a theoretical foundation that supports specific interpretations of the measurements.

Validity—the degree to which accumulated evidence and theory support specific interpretations of test scores in the context of the test's proposed use.

VALIDATION STRATEGIES

Validity is a unitary concept (Binning and Barrett, 1989; AERA et al., 1999). Different, but interrelated, strategies are commonly used to assess the accuracy of inferences based on measurements or tests used in the workplace. Sometimes the different strategies are mistakenly viewed as representing different types of validity. To overcome this misinterpretation, older terms such as construct validity, content validity, and criterion-related validity are no longer used. Both construct and content validity are validation strategies that provide *evidence based on test content*, while criterion-related validity provides *evidence based on relations to other variables*. While these traditional terms are still used in the older literature on validity, our presentation is based on the recent *Standards for Educational and Psychological Testing* (AERA et al., 1999).

One major document that HR specialists and personnel psychologists rely on is *Principles for the Validation and Use of Personnel Selection Procedures*

(Society for Industrial and Organizational Psychology, Inc., 1987). This document, which is currently under revision and predates the new version of the *Standards for Educational and Psychological Testing*, uses the traditional terms of content, construct, and criterion-related validity in its presentation of validation strategies. Our presentation of validation strategies is not exhaustive; we will examine only those sources of evidence for validity that are likely to be encountered in employment situations. You may want to refer to both the *Standards* and the *Principles* for a more thorough discussion of validity issues.

Figure 3.2 illustrates different sources of evidence for validity using the know-how data collected by the human resources manager. The manager initially hypothesized that higher levels of cognitive ability were related to higher levels of job performance; this relationship is represented by Line A. This relationship is based on theoretical and logical analyses of expert opinion and empirical data that show, in this case, that cognitive ability is linked to job performance. Both cognitive ability and job performance are abstract constructs, which we operationally defined, respectively, as know-how scores based on the employment interview and a job performance score derived from an assessment of an employee's work. Figure 3.2 also presents the relationships between these two constructs and their two measurements; these different relationships help to illustrate two different validation strategies.

EVIDENCE BASED ON TEST CONTENT This type of validity evidence comes from analyzing the relationship between a test's content and the construct the test is intended to measure. Each construct has a set of associated behaviours or events; these include not only test questions but also tasks, themes, and procedures for administering and scoring the test, among others. In any measurement

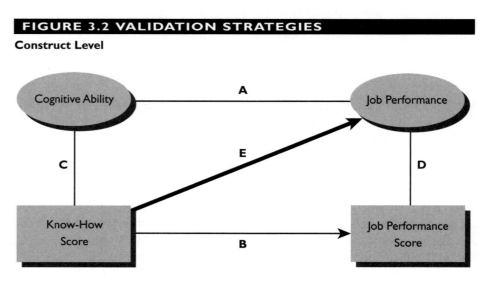

FIGURE 3.2 VALIDATION STRATEGIES

Construct Level

Measurement Level

situation, only a relatively small handful of these behaviours are measured. Evidence of validity based on test content can consist of either empirical or logical analyses of how well the contents of the test, and the interpretation of the test scores, represent the construct. For example, 10 questions are used to test your knowledge of the content of this chapter. Based on the number of correct answers, your professor makes an inference about your *knowledge of scientific methods*. Is the inference justified? That is, do the 10 questions measure knowledge of scientific methods and does the score based on those questions represent your degree of knowledge of scientific methods? Evidence for the validity of your professor's test may be based on the consensus of a group of experts that the behaviours being measured do, in fact, fairly represent the behaviours associated with the construct. It is a judgmental process. Evidence of the validity of the 10 questions used to measure knowledge of scientific methods could be established by a review of those questions by several experts on scientific methods. The agreement of these subject-matter experts (SMEs) that the questions fairly represented the information contained in this chapter constitutes evidence of validity based on the test contents.

The job performance construct shown in Figure 3.2 may represent a large number of tasks that have been identified through one of the job analysis procedures we discuss in Chapter 4. SMEs next identify those tasks that are the most important, the most frequently performed, or the most critical to successful job performance. An HR specialist can take that information and turn it into a test that samples those job tasks. Chapter 10 provides examples of situational or patterned behaviour interviews that are linked to tasks performed on the job. In Figure 3.2, the relationship represented by Line D represents an inference based on a measure of job performance about the job performance construct; Line C illustrates an inference based on a score from the know-how measure to the cognitive ability construct.

The issue here is the degree to which valid inferences can be made about the cognitive ability and job performance constructs from their respective measures. If Ms. C has a higher know-how score than Mr. B, can we make the inference that Ms. C has more cognitive ability than Mr. B? If Mr. B has a higher job performance score than Ms. C, can we make the inference that Mr. B performs better on the job? In other words, do the two measures, know-how and job performance scores, measure the two constructs, cognitive ability and job performance, that they purport to measure? Answers to these questions are based on logical analysis, expert opinion, and the convergence of the measures with other accepted measures of the construct. This last type of evidence is really an example of evidence based on a relation to another variable.

EVIDENCE BASED ON RELATIONS TO OTHER VARIABLES This type of evidence is based on an analysis of the relationship between test scores and other variables that are external to the test. For example, a relatively high correlation between the know-how test and the Wonderlic Personnel Test, a measure of cognitive ability, and a relatively low correlation between the know-how test and the 16-PF, a measure of personality, would be evidence for its validity. In personnel selection, a test score is usually correlated with a score from a performance criterion rather than one from another test.

A criterion is an outcome measure; it assesses the degree of success or failure associated with some decision. Job applicants are selected for employment; over time, some of the applicants perform at a higher level than do others. Measures of job performance are criterion measures. In selecting job applicants, one goal is to hire only those applicants who will perform at very high levels. But the applicants have to be hired before job performance can be measured. Is there another variable that is correlated with job performance that can be measured prior to hiring the applicant? Can we use information from this pre-employment measure to make valid inferences about how an individual will perform once in the job? How accurately do test scores predict criterion performance? The goal of establishing *test-criterion relationships* is to address questions like these. The usefulness of test-criterion relationship data rests on the reliability of the measures of the test and the criterion and on the validity of the inferences drawn from those measures about their respective constructs.

In Figure 3.2, Line B expresses a test-criterion relationship. Know-how scores, based on the pre-employment interview, are used to predict job performance scores. The arrow on the line indicates that a prediction is being made from one measure to the other. Evidence for validity based on a test-criterion relationship involves establishing a correlation between two measures. However, both those measures must validly represent their respective constructs. While test-criterion relationships focus on the observable measures, the relationship that is of primary interest is represented in Figure 3.2 by Line E. What the human resources manager really wants to do is predict, or make an inference about, the job performance construct from the know-how scores. Similar to Lines C and D, Line E represents a relationship between a measure and a construct. This relationship, like those of Lines C and D, is established through validity evidence based on test content. If the test contains many aspects of the job performance construct, such as a work sample test, the test score itself may provide direct evidence for the relationship expressed in Line E. For example, typists may be hired based on how well they perform on a typing test, a sample of the performance they will be required to do on the job. The score on the test directly predicts job performance.

In most cases the relationship of Line E is established indirectly. In Figure 3.2, we want to make inferences from the know-how test scores to the job performance construct. We can only establish that relationship indirectly. First, we must show that both the predictor (the know-how scores) and the criterion (the job performance scores) are valid measures of their respective constructs (Line C and Line D) *and* that a strong relationship exists between the predictor and criterion measures (Line D). We must also establish the theoretical or logical relationship between the two constructs (Line A). Showing that these four relationships (Lines A, B, C, and D) exist provides evidence for the existence of

Line E. Unfortunately, many test-criterion relationship studies suffer from a failure to demonstrate that the criterion measure is a valid measure of the job performance construct.

PREDICTIVE EVIDENCE FOR TEST-CRITERION RELATIONSHIPS *Predictive* and *concurrent* strategies are popular methods used to provide evidence for test-criterion relationships. Predictive evidence is obtained through research designs that establish a correlation between predictor scores (know-how scores) obtained before an applicant is hired and criteria (performance scores) obtained at a later time, usually after an applicant is employed. If all those who apply are hired, both variables can be measured, but at a substantial cost. Many applicants will be hired with the knowledge that they will likely fail on the job. This not only is expensive for the organization but causes a great deal of emotional distress for those applicants who fail.

This procedure also raises serious legal and ethical considerations about the rights of job applicants and the obligations of people who make hiring decisions. To circumvent these problems, a variation on this procedure requires that hiring decisions be made without using information from the predictor measure; the hiring decisions are made according to existing procedures while the validity of the new predictor is established. The human resources manager places all the applicants through the interview and collects know-how scores, but the hiring decision is based solely on information contained in the applicants' résumés and references. Job performance information is then collected from the group of hired applicants and correlated with their know-how scores. If the correlation is high, the know-how score may be used to select future job applicants. The high correlation is evidence in support of the position that accurate inferences can be made about job performance from the know-how scores. But there is a problem with this strategy as well. Validity concerns the correctness of inferences made from a set of measurements. Does the validity coefficient, which is based on only those applicants who were hired, apply to all applicants? This will only be the case if the hired applicants fairly represent the total pool of applicants; the only way this can happen is if those hired were randomly selected from the larger pool. Therefore, those who are hired on the basis of the existing selection system will likely differ from those not hired on at least one characteristic, whether or not that characteristic is related to job success.

CONCURRENT EVIDENCE FOR TEST-CRITERION RELATIONSHIPS Concurrent evidence is obtained through research designs that establish a correlation between predictor and criteria scores from information that is collected at approximately the same time from a specific group of workers. The human resources manager interviews all current employees and assigns each a know-how score; at the same time, each worker is also assigned a job performance score. While concurrent evidence may be easier to collect, these strategies, too, are problematic. The group of existing workers used to develop the validity evidence are likely to be older, more experienced, and certainly more successful than those who apply for jobs. Unsuccessful or unproductive workers most likely are not part of the validation study as they probably were let go or transferred to other positions. The primary concern here is whether a validity coefficient based on only successful applicants can be used as evidence to validate decisions based on predictor scores from a pool of both successful and unsuccessful job candidates. An additional concern is the same one expressed with predictive strategies: does the validity coefficient computed on one group of workers apply to the pool of applicants? The current workers, who are asked to complete a battery of selection tests, may approach the whole exercise with a different attitude and level of motivation than job applicants. These differences may affect selection instruments, particularly those like personality and integrity tests that rely on the test-taker's cooperation in responding truthfully. Statistically, validity coefficients based on concurrent evidence will likely

BOX 3.4 Validity

Validation studies require relatively large numbers of hires. This is a challenge for many Canadian organizations, particularly small businesses, that do not hire many people. Several validation techniques are suited for use with small samples (Sackett and Arvey, 1993):

- Build a database by combining *similar* jobs *across* organizations or companies, with special care taken to ensure comparability of performance measures.
- Accumulate selection scores and performance measures *over time*, as workers leave and are replaced.
- Generalize to your particular case the mean (average) predictive validity for a test as found for jobs similar to the one to which you wish to generalize (i.e., *validity generalization*).
- Generalize to your case the *specific* validity of the test as previously established for a similar job in another setting (i.e., *validity transportability*).

Frequently, however, a *content sampling* strategy may be necessary. The steps for this process are

1. Tasks (or activities) of the target position are identified by job experts.

2. Job experts infer, on a task-by-task basis, the required knowledge, skills, abilities, and other attributes (KSAOs).

3. Job experts independently rate the relevance of each KSAO for each task.

4. Assessment items (e.g., test questions, situational exercises, interview questions) are developed to measure the most relevant KSAOs.

5. Job experts provide independent ratings of the degree to which each assessment item is linked to the KSAOs.

6. Job experts evaluate the relationship between performance on each of the selection assessments and job success.

7. A scoring scheme is developed for the selection assessments.

The case for the validity of the selection system is then argued on the basis of an explicit systematic linking of the selection assessments (interview questions, test items, situational exercises) to the position requirements (KSAOs), as established by job experts.

underestimate the true validity of using the predictor to make decisions within the pool of applicants.

VALIDITY GENERALIZATION   Suppose in attempting to establish the validity of the know-how interview as a predictor of specific job performance in the organization, the human resources manager discovered that there were many other studies that also investigated measures of cognitive ability as predictors of similar job performance. Could the manager somehow combine all the information provided by these other correlation coefficients to obtain an estimate of the true validity of cognitive ability as a predictor of job performance in the new employment setting? These other validity coefficients were obtained under vastly different measurement conditions and from employees who differ dramatically across these studies on a number of characteristics. Most likely the value of the individual validity coefficients will be very inconsistent across all of these other studies. In other words, can the manager estimate the validity of know-how scores as a predictor of job performance in the manager's work setting from the validity of inferences based on other measures of cognitive ability found in other work settings with other groups of workers?

> **Validity generalization—** the application of validity evidence, obtained through meta-analysis of data obtained from many situations, to other situations that are similar to those on which the meta-analysis is based.

Starting in the mid-1970s, Schmidt and Hunter (1977), in conjunction with several colleagues, challenged the idea that a validity coefficient was specific to the context or environment in which it was measured. They used a procedure known as *meta-analysis* to combine validity coefficients for similar predictor and criterion measures reported by different validity studies. Schmidt and Hunter argued that the relative inconsistency in validity coefficients across studies could be attributed to statistical artifacts such as the range of scores in each study, the reliability of the criterion measures, and sample size (i.e., the number of people in the validity study). In combining the data, meta-analysis weights the results from each separate validity study according to its sample. On the whole, the smaller the study size, the less accurate the results. Validity studies usually involve relatively small study sizes since most organizations do not hire large numbers of people. Schmidt and Hunter demonstrated that, once the effects associated with study size and the other artifacts were removed, the validity between a predictor and a criterion remained relatively stable within similar occupations. For example, the human resources manager could use the know-how interview scores to make predictions about job performance if other validity studies had linked cognitive ability to job performance for similar jobs and if the know-how scores were a valid measure of cognitive ability.

Should the HR specialist rely on validity generalization evidence or conduct a new validity study on-site? The answer is not straightforward. If the meta-analysis database is large and adequately represents the type of job to which it will be generalized in the local situation, there is a strong case for using the validity generalization data. On the other hand, if the database is small, the results inconsistent, and there is little in common between the specific job and those included in the meta-analysis, then a local validity study should be carried out. If conducted properly with an adequate sample size, the local study may provide more useful information than the validity generalization data. A study carried out on the specific job in the local environment will also provide a means of corroborating questionable validity generalization data (AERA et al., 1999).

FACTORS AFFECTING VALIDITY COEFFICIENTS

RANGE RESTRICTION   When measurements are made on a subgroup that is more homogeneous than the larger group from which it is selected, validity coefficients obtained on the subgroup are likely to be smaller than those obtained from the larger group. This reduction in the size of the validity coefficient due to the selection process is called *range restriction*. Selection results in a more homogeneous group. The applicant pool reviewed by the human resources manager contains a broad range of know-how. The people selected for employment are more likely to fall in the upper range of know-how; the existing workers are also more likely to have levels of know-how more similar to one another than to the applicant pool. The range of know-how scores for the hired workers is narrower or more restricted than the scores of all the applicants. Statistically, the magnitude of correlation coefficients, including validity coefficients, decreases as the similarity or homogeneity of characteristics being measured increases. There are several statistical procedures that correct for range restriction and provide an estimate of what the validity coefficient is likely to be in the larger group.

MEASUREMENT ERROR   The reliability of a measure places an upper limit on validity. Mathematically, the size of a validity coefficient cannot exceed the reliability of the measures used to obtain the data. Validity coefficients obtained from perfectly reliable measures of the predictor and criterion will be higher than those obtained with less-than-perfect measures. The decrease in magnitude of the validity coefficient associated with measurement error of the predictor, the criterion, or both, is called *attenuation*. As with range restriction, there are statistical procedures that provide an estimate of what the validity coefficient would be if it had been obtained by using measures that were perfectly reliable (i.e., $r_{xx} = 1.00$).

SAMPLING ERROR   Criterion-related validity coefficients are obtained from people who have been hired and are used to assess the accuracy of inferences that are made about individual applicants. The validity coefficient based on a sample is an estimate of what the coefficient is in the entire population; usually, it is impractical or impossible to measure the validity coefficient directly in the population. Estimates of the validity within a population may vary considerably between samples; estimates from small samples are likely to be quite variable.

The statistical procedures that are used to compensate for range restriction, attenuation, and problems related to sampling will almost always produce higher estimates of validity than the uncorrected coefficients. When correction procedures are used, both the corrected and uncorrected validity coefficients should be reported along with a justification for the use of the correction.

BIAS AND FAIRNESS

BIAS

In discussing reliability, we noted that measurement errors could be made in a consistent, or predictable, fashion. In the time clock example, five minutes were added to each worker's arrival time. What if the clock had added five minutes only to the arrival times of female employees? The observed scores are still reliable, but now they validly represent the true arrival times for male employees, but not females. The clock is biased in measuring arrival times of female employees. **Bias** refers to systematic errors in measurement, or inferences made from measurements, that are related to different identifiable group membership characteristics such as age, sex, or race (AERA et al., 1999). For example, the human resources manager assigns higher know-how scores to females, when in fact there are no differences in cognitive ability between men and women. Inferences, or predictions, drawn from the biased measurements are themselves biased.

Bias—refers to systematic errors in measurement, or inferences made from measurements, that are related to different identifiable group membership characteristics such as age, sex, or race.

Figure 3.3 illustrates a hypothetical situation in which the cognitive ability scores of females are higher, on average, than those for the males, reflecting some type of systematic error. This is the same scatterplot given in Figure 3.1 (page 91), but with the data for Ms. F and Mr. E, and Ms. J and Mr. H, reversed. Therefore, it will have the same regression line as given in Table 3.1 on page 90. Now Ms. F's job performance score is predicted to be 6.91 versus 5.11 previously; Ms. J's is predicted to be 6.31 versus 5.71. The regression line, using the biased cognitive ability measure as a predictor, overestimates the likely job performance of the female employees and underestimates that of males. If this regression line were used to make hiring decisions (e.g., "We want employees who will obtain performance scores of 6 or better, so hire only applicants with cognitive ability scores of 8 or higher"), the predictions of successful job performance would be biased in favour of the female applicants. This type of bias is known as *differential prediction*; that is, the predicted, average performance score of a subgroup, in this case males or females, is systematically higher or lower

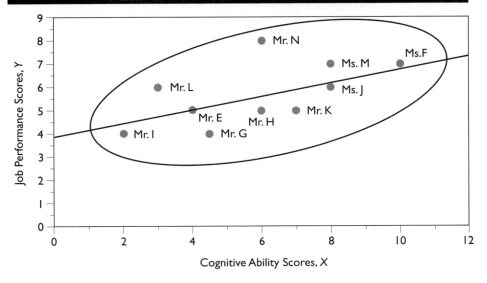

FIGURE 3.3 COGNITIVE ABILITY AND JOB PERFORMANCE—II

than the average score predicted for the group as a whole. This situation results in a larger proportion of the lower-scoring group being rejected on the basis of their test scores even though they would have performed successfully had they been hired. This condition results from a less-than-perfect correlation between the predictor and criterion measures. One way to overcome this type of bias is to generate separate regression lines (that is, separate prediction formulas) for males and females (AERA et al., 1999). In Canadian federal organizations, separate prediction formulas are often used in selecting job applicants from anglophone and francophone linguistic groups. In U.S. federal organizations, the use of different selection rules for different identifiable subgroups (often referred to as subgroup norming) is prohibited by U.S. federal law.

There are other, more complicated, types of bias that might occur in a set of measurements (Sackett and Wilk, 1994). Items on a test may elicit a variety of responses other than what was intended, or some items on a test may have different meanings for members of different subgroups. For example, the Bennett Test of Mechanical Comprehension contains pictures related to the use of different tools and machines that tend to be used mostly by males. Males are more likely to recognize these tools and their proper use and perform well on the test. On the other hand, females with good mechanical comprehension may not do as well on the test because of their lack of familiarity with specific tools pictured on the Bennett Test. The result is that the test may underestimate the true mechanical ability of female job applicants. The statistical procedures needed to establish bias are often complicated and difficult to carry out. Nonetheless, the question of bias can be answered through empirical and objective procedures.

FAIRNESS

The concept of **fairness** in measurement refers to the value judgments people make about the decisions or outcomes that are based on measurements. An unbiased measure or test may still be viewed as being unfair either by society as a whole or by different groups within it. Canada is a bilingual country composed of French- and English-language groups. Suppose a completely unbiased cognitive ability test were used to select people for the Canadian civil service and that all the francophone applicants scored well above the highest-scoring anglophone. Such cognitive ability scores would predict that francophones do better on the job than anglophones; only francophones would be hired for the civil service. This outcome would very likely be judged as unfair by English-speaking Canadians even though it would be the empirically correct decision. Canadians might expect their civil service to represent both official language groups. In fact, political considerations might require that the civil service be proportional to the two linguistic groups.

Issues of fairness cannot be determined statistically or empirically. Fairness involves perceptions. An organization may believe it is fair to select qualified females in place of higher-ranking males in order to increase the number of women in the organization; on the other hand, the higher-ranking males who were passed over might not agree. The *Principles for the Validation and Use of Personnel Selection Procedures* (Society for Industrial and Organizational Psychology, 1987) states this about fairness:

> *Fairness is a social rather than a psychometric concept. Its definition depends on what one considers to be fair. Fairness has no single meaning, and, therefore, no single statistical or psychometric definition. Fairness or lack of fairness is not a property of the selection procedure, but rather a joint function of the procedure, the job, the population, and how the scores from it are used.*

Fairness is an even more complex topic than bias. Achieving fairness often requires compromise between conflicting interests (Gottfredson, 1994; Sackett and Wilk, 1994). This is particularly so in the case where, for whatever reason, there may be persistent differences in average test scores between different groups in the population but those differences do not necessarily indicate test bias. A test score predicts the same level of performance for members of all groups, but the average test score for one group is lower than another group's, leading to the exclusion of a larger proportion of the group with the lower average score. Lowering the selection standards to include more applicants from this group in order to make the workforce more representative of the general population may come at the cost of reduced productivity.

Does an organization have an obligation to make the enterprise as profitable as possible on behalf of its owners, or should it meet the objectives of society by providing equal employment opportunities for members of

Fairness—is the principle that every test taker should be assessed in an equitable manner.

BOX 3.5 Different Views of Fairness

Any discussion of fairness quickly becomes complicated as there are several ways of defining this concept. *The Standards for Educational and Psychological Testing* provide five definitions (AERA et al., 1999).

1. *Fairness as Lack of Bias*—a test or testing procedure is considered fair if it does not produce any systematic effects that are related to different identifiable group membership characteristics such as age, sex, or race.

2. *Fairness as Equitable Treatment in the Testing Process*—all examinees should be treated equitably throughout the testing process. They should experience the same or comparable procedures in the testing itself, in how the tests are scored, and in how the test scores are used.

3. *Fairness as Opportunity to Learn*—all examinees should have had an equal opportunity to learn the material covered in achievement tests. The opportunity to learn is relevant to some uses and interpretations of achievement tests.

[Comment: There is general consensus among professionals that these three conditions should be met in establishing the fairness of a test.]

4. *Fairness as Equality in Outcomes of Testing*—requires that the passing rates be comparable across iden-

tifiable group membership characteristics such as age, sex, or race. That is, the same percentage of applicants from each identifiable group should "pass" the test or score above the cutoff that might be used to make hiring decisions.

[Comment: This view of fairness is mostly rejected in the professional literature. Professionals would argue that examinees of equal standing with respect to the ability or skill being measured should, on average, earn the same test score regardless of group membership.]

5. *Fairness in Selection and Prediction*—often requires a compromise between the perspective that equates fairness with lack of bias and the perspective that focuses on testing outcomes. A selection test might be considered fair if the same test score predicts the same performance level for members of all groups, but it might be considered unfair if average test scores differ across groups. The fairness of the test should, in this situation, be evaluated relative to fairness of other, nontest, alternatives that could be used in place of the test.

[Comment: This situation is the one most often encountered in personnel selection. It generally requires a compromise between the two perspectives to achieve a resolution.]

different population groups? There are no easy answers to this question. In cases such as this, one resolution is to compare the fairness of the test in question with the fairness of an alternative that might be used in place of the test (AERA et al., 1999).

In addition to the concerns about the impact of tests on different groups, fairness issues also include the reaction of applicants to testing and personnel selection decisions. It is important from business, ethical, and legal standpoints to have tests that are scientifically sound; it is also important to have procedures that are perceived as fair. From a business perspective, the adverse reactions to selection tests and procedures may impair the ability of an organization to recruit and hire the best applicants, thereby reducing the utility of the recruitment and selection process. The perceived fairness of selection procedures used by a major telecommunications company influenced the views of prospective employees on the attractiveness of the company as a place to work, their intentions to recommend the company to others, and their intentions to accept a job (Oliver, 1998).

From an ethical view, the perceived fairness of the testing procedures may negatively affect the unsuccessful candidates. From a legal perspective, the perception of unfairness may lead unsuccessful applicants to pursue discrimination charges against the prospective employer in various legal arenas (Gilliland, 1993). Serious consideration should be given to the perception of a test or selection procedure from the applicant's perspective prior to its adoption. This does not mean that an employer should discard scientifically valid procedures because they may be perceived as unfair; there is far more risk for an organization that makes employment decisions on the basis of unproven methods. In the final analysis, fairness is a question of balance.

INTEGRATING VALIDITY EVIDENCE

An argument for the validity of interpretations from a selection test or procedure rests on the integration of scientific evidence obtained through a variety of sources. It includes information that is collected from the existing scientific literature as well as data newly collected as part of the validation effort. Both existing data and theory are used to support the proposition that test scores allow accurate inferences to be made about a candidate's future job performance. The technical quality of the testing procedure (e.g., careful test development, test reliability, standardized test administration and scoring procedures, and test fairness) must also be considered along with other validity evidence. All of this evidence must support the proposed use of the information obtained through the testing procedure if that test is to be used as part of the selection process.

SUMMARY

Science produces information that is based on accepting as true only that objective information that can withstand continued attempts to cast doubt on its accuracy. The accuracy of scientific statements is examined empirically through methods that can be observed, critiqued, and used by others. Scientific information is dynamic and constantly evolving. One goal of personnel selection is to use scientifically derived information to predict which job applicants will do well on the job. Scientific procedures allow for the measurement of important human characteristics that may be related to job performance. The reliability and validity of the information used as part of personnel selection procedures must be established empirically. The methods used to establish reliability and validity can be quite complex and require a good statistical background. As a scientific process, any personnel selection system must be able to withstand attempts to cast doubt on its ability to select the best people for the job in a fair and unbiased manner.

KEY TERMS

Bias, p. 105

Error score or measurement error, p. 88

Fairness, p. 107

Hypothesis, p. 77

Measurement, p. 82

Measurement scale, p. 83

Operational definitions, p. 78

Reliability, p. 92

True score, p. 88

Validity generalization, p. 103

Validity, p. 97

Variables, p. 79

EXERCISES

1. Measure the length of your classroom without using a measuring tape or ruler. Describe the standard of measurement you chose to use. What are the difficulties inherent in using a standard such as the one you chose?

2. Have at least three different people measure the length of the room using your standard of measurement. How similar are their measurements? What does this imply about the accuracy of your measure? What does this imply about the accuracy of the observers?

3. Choose a specific job held by one of the people in your group. After discussing the job, choose one characteristic that you think is crucial to performing that job. How would you measure both the characteristic and job performance?

Use Figure 3.2 to help you specify the conceptual and measurement levels. How would you establish the validity of your characteristic as a predictor of job performance?

4. Does an organization have an obligation to make the enterprise as profitable as possible on behalf of its owners, or does it have an obligation to meet the objectives of society by providing equal employment opportunities for members from different population groups?

5. A significant portion of this chapter has dealt with tests and testing procedures. In later chapters we will explore the use of different types of employment tests that have good reputations for reliability and validity. Access to these tests is restricted for obvious reasons.

They can only be administered by qualified examiners, unlike the types of "IQ" and "personality" tests that you may come across in newspapers or magazines. While these tests are fun to take, they may have questionable reliability and validity.

Many sites on the Internet are devoted to tests, some serious and some for fun. One of the better sites is Queendom Mind and Body at www.queendom.com. This site offers an array of tests including IQ, personality, and emotional intelligence. All of the tests are free and can be taken online and are immediately scored. Unlike some of the other sites, it offers statistical information on the reliability of almost all of its tests and on the validity of some. Most of the reliability data are based on measures of internal consistency.

As part of this exercise we will ask you to take the Classical IQ Test, the Emotional IQ Test, and the Extroversion/Introversion Inventory. Queendom.com will provide you with a report containing your scores and inferences from your scores about how you fare on the three constructs. Please download copies of each report as well as the statistical data provided for each test. Your instructor will arrange for you to anonymously record your scores from these tests so that data may be accumulated over the whole class for the following exercises. We will also ask you to record your sex and your cumulative grade point average or percentage (if you

don't know this last item, an estimate will do).

a. *Test–Retest Reliability.* Wait at least one week after taking the three tests and then retake all three. Once all the data from the class are compiled, your instructor will compute the correlation between the first and second administration of the three tests.

- Are each of the tests reliable? (Tests with reliability coefficients greater than 0.70 are generally considered to have acceptable reliability.)

- How does the test–retest reliability compare with the reliability values presented online?

- What do you think the reasons may be for any differences?

- What factors may have led you to perform differently on each of the two testing occasions?

b. *Validity.* Examine the content of each test; that is, examine the nature of the test questions (you are allowed to download a copy of each test).

- Do you think that the contents of each test reflect the essential nature of the construct it attempts to measure?

- Based on other empirical and theoretical evidence, we would not expect there to be a strong relationship between Classical IQ (a measure of cognitive ability) and

Extroversion/Introversion (a measure of personality). Emotional Intelligence has been presented as a construct, which is different from both cognitive ability and personality. There should be very low correlations among the test scores from these three tests. A high correlation between Emotional Intelligence and Extroversion/Introversion might suggest that both tests are measures of the same construct. Your instructor will correlate the three test scores for the class using data from the first test administration. What is the relationship between the three test scores?

- Cognitive ability is associated with academic performance. The Classical IQ Test measures cognitive ability and your cumulative grade point average (GPA) is an estimate of your academic performance. GPA is a criterion. What is the correlation between Classical IQ and GPA for your class, as reported by your instructor? Does this correlation indicate that you may make accurate inferences about academic performance from your IQ test scores? Is there a strong correlation between the Emotional IQ scores and GPA? between Extroversion/Introversion? If so, what do you think these correlations suggest?

c. *Bias.* You or your instructor will have to analyze the class data separately for males and females. Compare the mean score for each group across the three tests. Compute the correlations among the three tests for men and women.

- Do you obtain similar results for males and females?

- Are any of the three tests biased?

d. *Fairness.* Do you believe that each of these three tests is fair? How would you react if you were given any of these three tests when you applied for your next job?

CASE

A story in the *Daily Commercial News* ("Will EQ," 1998) reported that a growing number of Canadian companies are using measures of emotional intelligence (EQ) as part of the screening devices administered to job applicants. These companies are looking for a measure to tap into emotions. They are seeking candidates who have the ability to inspire colleagues, to handle customers, and to be a positive influence in the office. One of the more popular measures of emotional intelligence is the Bar-On Emotional Quotient Inventory (EQ-i), which is distributed by Multi-Health Systems of Toronto. Steven Stein, president of Multi-Health Systems, is quoted in the article as saying that IQ has to do with solving math problems and that verbal ability has its place but emotional skills are much more valuable for success in the workplace. Can a measure of emotional intelligence predict job success? Lorne Sulsky, an industrial-organizational psychologist at the University of Calgary is skeptical because the concept is too fuzzy and EQ tests are too imprecise to be reliable. Sulsky asks, "Why should there be a relationship between job performance and EQ?"

DISCUSSION QUESTIONS

What do you think? Do the data that you collected in Exercise 5 help you to answer this question? Should there be a relationship between job performance and EQ? Can you support your answer with any empirical data? How can the construct of EQ be improved? Is it too broad? Is EQ simply another aspect of personality? If you were going to use EQ as part of your selection system, discuss the steps that you would take to ensure that you were able to make reliable and accurate inferences about job performance in your work situation.

REFERENCES

Ackerman, P.L., and L.G. Humphreys. 1990. "Individual Differences Theory in Industrial and Organizational Psychology." In M.D. Dunnette and L.M. Hough, eds., *Handbook of Industrial and Organizational Psychology*, vol. 1. 2nd ed. Palo Alto: Consulting Psychologists Press, 223–82.

American Educational Research Association, American Psychological Association, and National Council on Measurement in Education. 1999. *Standards for Educational and Psychological Testing*. Washington, DC: American Educational Research Association.

Binning, J.F., and G.V. Barrett. 1989. "Validity of Personnel Decisions: A Conceptual Analysis of the Inferential and Evidential Bases." *Journal of Applied Psychology* 74: 478–94.

Burke, L.A., and M.K. Miller. 1999. "Taking the Mystery out of Intuitive Decision Making." *The Academy of Management Executive* 13: 91–99.

Cronbach, L.J. 1971. "Test Validation." In R.L. Thorndike, ed., *Educational Measurement*, 2nd ed. Washington, DC: American Council of Education.

Gilliland, S.W. 1993. "The Perceived Fairness of Selection Systems: An Organizational Justice Perspective." *Academy of Management Review* 18: 694–734.

" 'Glass Ceiling' Separates Women from Top." 1997. *Worklife Report* 11: 15.

Gottfredson, L.S. 1994. "The Science and Politics of Race-Norming." *American Psychologist* 49: 955–63.

Kerlinger, F.N. 1986. *Foundations of Behavioral Research*, 3rd ed. New York: Holt, Rinehart and Winston.

Nunnally, J.C., and I.H. Bernstein. 1994. *Psychometric Theory*, 3rd ed. New York: McGraw-Hill.

Oliver, D.H. 1998. "Exploring Applicant Reactions to Selection Processes from an Organizational Justice Perspective." *Dissertation Abstracts International: Section B: The Sciences and Engineering* 59(2-B): 0902.

"The Reform Party's Days of Discontent." 1996. *Maclean's* (May 20): 21–22.

Sackett, P.R., and R.D. Arvey. 1993. "Selection in Small N Settings." In N. Schmitt, W.C. Borman, and Associates, eds. *Personnel Selection in Organizations*. San Francisco: Jossey-Bass, 418–47.

Sackett, P.R., and J.R. Larson, Jr. 1990. "Research Strategies and Tactics in Industrial and Organizational Psychology." In M.D. Dunnette and L.M. Hough, eds., *Handbook of Industrial and Organizational Psychology*, vol. 1. 2nd ed. Palo Alto: Consulting Psychologists Press, 419–90.

Sackett, P.R., and S.L. Wilk. 1994. "Within-Group Norming and Other Forms of Score Adjustment in Pre-employment Testing." *American Psychologist* 49: 929–54.

Saks, A.M. 2000. *Research, Measurement, and Evaluation of Human Resources*. Toronto: Nelson.

Schmidt, F.L., and J.E. Hunter. 1977. "Development of a General Solution to the Problem of Validity Generalization." *Journal of Applied Psychology* 62: 529–40.

Society for Industrial and Organizational Psychology, Inc. 1987. *Principles for the Validation and Use of Personnel Selection Procedures*, 3rd ed. College Park, MD: Author.

Whitehead, A.N. 1967. *Science and the Modern World*. New York: Free Press.

"Will EQ Gradually Replace IQ in Screening Candidates for Jobs?" 1998. *Daily Commercial News*, 71, S2, A14.

4

ORGANIZATION AND
JOB ANALYSIS

CHAPTER GOALS

This chapter begins with a discussion of organizational analysis and its relevance to the recruitment and selection of employees and ends with a discussion of several **job analysis** techniques.

Job analysis—the process of collecting information about jobs.

After reading this chapter you should

- be able to describe the purposes of organizational analysis and its relation to human resources recruitment and selection;

- understand organizational structures and the evolution of organizations from hierarchical to vertical process-based structures;

- be familiar with three levels of analysis in any organization;

- recognize some useful tools for conducting organizational, process, and job analyses;

- be able to describe guidelines for conducting analyses employing a variety of job analysis techniques; and

- recognize processes for identifying personnel specifications to be used in recruitment and selection of human resources.

ORGANIZATION ANALYSIS: A MACRO PERSPECTIVE ON RECRUITMENT AND SELECTION NEEDS

Canadian organizations have faced growing challenges to productivity and survival during the past two decades. Contributing factors include government deregulation, increasing global competition, free trade, rapidly changing technology, and consumers who have come to expect more for their money. One result has been the explosion of schemes for improving organizational performance. From the quality audits and quality circles of the late 1970s through the total-quality philosophy of the 1980s and 1990s, quality improvement programs have taken firm hold in Canadian organizations. Unfortunately, as many organizational consultants have discovered, "piecemeal approaches that are assumed to be *the* answer are as dangerous as no response at all" (Rummler and Brache, 1990, 2).

Inefficient improvement programs, including those in human resources recruitment and selection, can be avoided if the organization is viewed as a **dynamic system**. Function rather than structure is critical to the organizational systems model, and the organization is defined as a set of interactive functions rather than a collection of discrete departments. This model proposes that the organization exists to fulfill its **strategic goals**; it is made up of subsystems (e.g., departments and functions) that produce outputs contributing to the achievement of those goals.

The Ste. Thérèse auto assembly plant in Quebec is an example of a complex dynamic system. It "builds Pontiac Firebird, coupes and convertibles ... from the ground up" (GM of Canada, 2000, 1). The **subsystems** that taken together make up the Ste. Thérèse plant would include industrial and plant engineering, plant safety, quality control, assembly, materials procurement and distribution, human resources, and plant administration and maintenance. No single one of these components makes up the total organization, nor does the plant simply comprise the total collection of these subsystems. That is, were the departments allowed to function in relative isolation, management would be left with suboptimal organizational performance—it is the interactions and connections between each of the subsystems that make a healthy operating system.

Human behaviour drives operating systems while simultaneously placing constraints on how those systems function. Because individuals are responsible for system operation at every level, and human behaviour varies with individuals and situations, organizational effectiveness can be directly linked to the effectiveness of subsystems and the individuals employed within them (Katz and Kahn, 1978). A dynamic system view leads the analyst to focus on the organization's overall strategic goal when intervening within any part of the system or its components. The key objective of this approach is to generate effective performance at all levels, and recruiting and selecting the right people for the work is an important step in creating a well-oiled system.

Dynamic system—a way of viewing an organization as a collection of interacting functions and processes that operate to achieve an overall strategic goal.

Strategic goal—summarizes the company's relationship with the ultimate customer (i.e., the consumer who buys the final product or service) and defines the outcomes that the organization must achieve to be successful.

Subsystem—a component of an organization that produces a deliverable (service or product) to an internal or external customer.

The recruitment and selection functions of human resources departments make two major contributions to the organization. First, they exist to maximize the probability of making accurate selection decisions about applicants, thus placing individual performers within each operating subsystem of the organization. Second, in participating in these placement decisions, they directly influence the level of functioning of every other subsystem in the organization. Human resources departments are often actively involved in quality-of-work-life issues. Although the debate on the nature of the relationship between job performance and job satisfaction has yet to be settled, good work performance tends to lead to enhanced quality of worklife as indicated by the amount of job satisfaction experienced by individual employees (e.g., Wanous, 1974). Additionally, job satisfaction is moderately correlated with absenteeism; thus, it is to the benefit of the organization and the individual job incumbents to select those who are likely to perform successfully. In order for recruitment and selection specialists to make the best possible decisions, an organizational analysis should provide the backdrop for all human resources initiatives.

THE PURPOSE OF ORGANIZATION ANALYSIS

Organization analysis, the study of the organizational system and its components (subsystems), serves the following functions:

1. Identification of an organization's overall goals.
2. Description of the environmental constraints in which the organization operates.
3. Definition of the functions of and relationships between organizational components.
4. Assessment of the capabilities of the system and its components relative to the strategic goals.
5. Identification of gaps in the system that must be addressed in order to promote optimal system functioning.

Information obtained through organizational analysis can provide a valuable context for the operation of human resources programs. When the guiding principles of the organization are laid out as goals, and the environment in which the organization operates is defined, recruitment and selection processes can effectively contribute to the long-term survival of the organization. That is, human resources recruitment and selection programs don't function solely to attract people to fill positions; **human capital** is assessed in an organization analysis as an essential component of system capabilities and is addressed on a systemwide level when gaps are evident. The following sections address how organization analyses are conducted and how the information gained is used to address system needs.

Organization analysis—the study of the organizational system and its components (subsystems).

Human capital—the competence and opportunity brought to an organization by its people, which is viewed as an essential component of system capabilities.

CHARTING ORGANIZATIONAL RELATIONSHIPS

The traditional view of organizations is evident in the organizational chart. Typically, such charts show a top-down view of the departments and positions that make up organizations. Figure 4.1 presents a generic organizational chart. The CEO is placed at the top; a collection of senior managers report directly to the top and each senior manager may be responsible for one or more departments. Within each of these departments exists a manager to whom function or area supervisors report. Each supervisor is responsible for many employees. This view of the organization tends to promote chart management rather than the management of critical **processes** and human performance systems (Rummler and Brache, 1990). Furthermore, jobs get done and data on department functioning look good, but the company financials may suffer and innovations that contribute to continuous company improvement are stifled. It is a structural view of the organization that fails to capture the functional links between the departments and between individuals within those departments.

Hierarchical charts have dominated organization design since the onset of the Industrial Revolution. Weber (1947) concluded that top-down authority protected the organization from abuse of power and thus improved both organizational functioning and individual employee well-being. Organizational theory held that the "people actually doing the work have neither the time nor

Processes—the means by which an organization produces outputs.

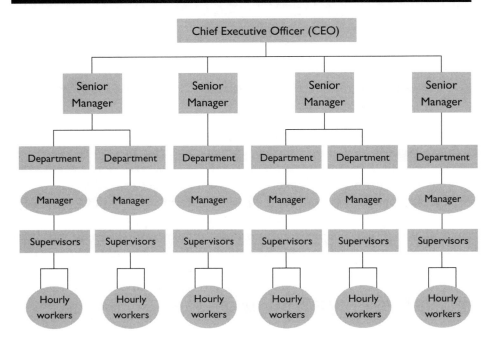

FIGURE 4.1 CONVENTIONAL ORGANIZATIONAL CHART WITH VERTICAL DELINEATION OF POSITIONS

the inclination to monitor and control it and ... they lack the depth and breadth of knowledge required to make decisions about it" (Hammer and Champy, 1993, 53).

The vertical view of the organization, in which authority flows from the top down, is becoming a liability. Kiechel (1993) identified trends in organizational design that are rapidly accelerating. Three of these trends have the potential to significantly influence job analyses and recruitment and selection of human resources:

- The average company will become smaller, employing fewer people.
- The traditional hierarchical organization will give way to a variety of organizational forms, the network of specialists foremost among these.
- Work itself will be redefined: constant learning, more high-order thinking, less nine-to-five. (39)

In addition to these trends, newer types of structures including team-based and matrix organizations are evolving, adding yet more complexity to the mix. *Team-based* work environments group employees together as process teams to produce their deliverables. The automobile industry has become well known for its team approach to making cars. Individuals no longer work alone on discrete tasks, but interact as part of a team to build a car or its major components. *Matrix* organizations add a third dimension to the horizontal-vertical chart. In a matrix, employees typically report functionally to a discipline head and structurally to a department or project head. An engineer working on a bridge-building project could, for example, report functionally to an engineering chief and get day-to-day supervision from a project manager on the bridge-building job. In the global economy move toward knowledge-based work, organizational structures can be expected to continue evolving to meet new needs.

As the Canadian marketplace becomes more competitive and technology continues to evolve, many organizations have responded by reengineering their structures. *Downsizing* and *rightsizing* characterized the reengineering movement of the '80s and '90s. As an article in *Fortune* magazine noted, "corporate restructuring fever has held pitch for over a decade now—some 400,000 hapless folks got the boot during 1995 [in the United States] alone" (Labich, 1996, 65). Data from Statistics Canada show that the total Canadian labour force grew by 4.2 percent from 1990 to 1995 and by another 6.5 percent between 1995 and 1999. Unemployment figures, however, increased by 22.2 percent during the 1990–95 period and have only just begun to decline to reach early 1990s' rates (Statistics Canada, 2000). Furthermore, although public demand for products and services has continued to grow, fewer people are now employed in goods manufacturing, primary industries, construction, and trades and more are employed in service industries including the ever growing Web-based sector. It is in this context that organizations are more often seeking employees who can bring, along with their particular skills and job expertise, the ability to adapt and grow within a constantly changing world (Longo,

1995). One organizational consulting group (Deloitte and Touche, 1995) asserts that:

> *In a world of ever-shorter product cycles and nimble global competitors who can quickly copy new technology innovations, it's the three T's—talent, training and teamwork—that win. There's only one differentiable element in global competition anymore—who's got the better people. (1)*

Empowerment of employees and a process-based view of organizational performance means that individuals are now placed in positions where decision making and control over job processes are within their daily work experiences. Organizations are getting leaner and smarter, and the role of recruitment and selection programs is changing alongside. The shift from task-based to process-based thinking is placing new pressures on human resources specialists to "move beyond valid job-based predictors because the work to be done changes constantly" (Cascio, 1995, 932).

The implementation of new technology can dramatically shift the fundamental nature of jobs. Makers of pulp, paper, and other textiles, for example, have seen their roles move from a hands-on art to one of a hands-off setting and monitoring of machinery that produces the product. Modified job analysis procedures that capture redefined forms of work are needed to complement, and perhaps in some cases replace, task-based job analysis techniques (Kiechel, 1993; May, 1996).

A dynamic systems view of the organization (e.g., Gilbert, 1978; Katz and Kahn, 1978; Rummler and Brache, 1990), charting the functional relationships that exist between departments, will facilitate analysis of the changing face of organizations as they move onward in the twenty-first century. Figure 4.2 shows how the functional relationships within departments of an organization and between the organization and its external customers can be charted using a total performance system approach (Brethower, 1982). The overall organization is functionally described as an input–processing–output system, with human activities implicit in each component. Similarly, each department or function is viewed as a processing system with its own inputs, outputs, and receiving systems. Inputs into the system (e.g., information, human capital, and tools) are processed via machines and human performance, with the support of management systems and specific production methods. Internal quality-control feedback consists of ongoing measurement and charting of system performance, usually related to the quality of the products and services generated in the processing system and the human performance that generates them. Each processing subsystem produces outputs that serve as inputs into other subsystems within the organization. All of this occurs in an environmental context that supports the organization by requiring and purchasing its services and products.

FIGURE 4.2 TOTAL PERFORMANCE DIAGRAM OF A SYSTEM AND SUBSYSTEMS

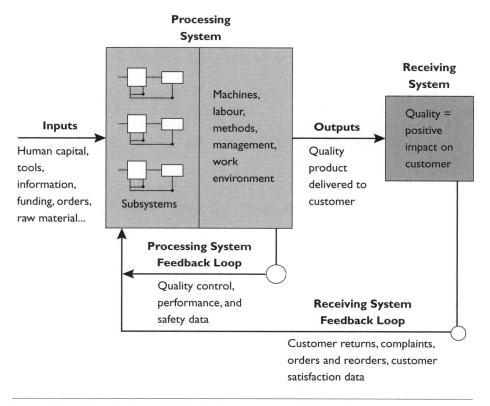

Source: Adapted from Brethower (1982); cf. Redmon and Agnew (1991) and Redmon and Wilk (1991).

Consider Tom's Landscaping Service, a small company that provides lawn and garden care and landscaping services to homes and small businesses (Devries, 1995). Suppose that Tom has hired a consultant to complete an analysis of his organization. The consultant produced total performance diagrams similar to those depicted in Figure 4.2. Tom's Landscaping Service delivers completed services to its receiving system, the external customers, through its subsystem functions that interact to produce quality outcomes. The *sales* subsystem of Tom's produces sales orders by contacting potential customers identified through market data, following up on referrals from previous and current customers, and responding to new customer requests. Thus, salespeople work within their own processing subsystem to produce outputs (service orders) that are received by operations—accurate orders are required by operations in order to deliver a final quality output to the client. Clearly, interactions between functions and departments are equally as important as the activities that go on within departments.

THREE LEVELS OF ANALYSIS

Organizations comprise three levels: the organizational or strategic level, the process or subsystem level, and the job level (Gilbert, 1978; Rummler and Brache, 1990). An organizational system is defined by the sum of the interactions between its subsystems. One overall mission defines the purpose of the organization and each subsystem is justified by how its objectives contribute to the achievement of that mission (Churchman, 1979). Subsystem outputs comprise the total of all products and services contributed by each job within a subsystem. Each of the three levels of analysis can be functionally charted using the total performance system approach (Brethower, 1982), and each are considered subsequently in detail.

LEVEL I: THE ORGANIZATION LEVEL

The focus at the organizational level is the company's relationship with the ultimate customer (i.e., the consumer who buys the final product or service), which is summarized in a strategic goal. The strategic goal for Tom's Landscaping Service is "to provide top service (no complaints from customers about the workers' care of their lawns) on a dependable basis at a reasonable price. They may not always be able to charge less than the larger companies but they would provide higher quality service and dependability than their larger counterparts could" (Devries, 1995, 78). Tom's is a comprehensive strategic goal that describes not only the specific output (service) but also includes a statement of quality (top quality) and competitiveness in the marketplace (reasonable rates). An organization analysis pinpoints factors at this level that directly influence performance toward the goal and, thus, the satisfaction of the ultimate customer. Analysis at the organizational level considers four components (Gilbert, 1978; Rummler and Brache, 1990):

1. Organizational missions and goals define the crucial outputs of the organization that are necessary to ensure survival.

2. Standards and measures of organizational productivity are used to define exemplary performance contributing to those outputs and to track system results.

3. Organizational culture and structure are concerned with the reward systems operating in the organization and how those rewards flow through the organization to influence performance.

4. Deployment of human capital and other resources considers how resources are dispersed throughout the system and how this influences progress toward or away from the strategic goal.

The resulting *big picture* provides the reference point for all processes, jobs, and activities that occur within organizational subsystems. Conducting business at process and job levels, while ignoring this referent, can jeopardize the organization's long-term survival. An organization's overall performance may be poor, while performance at process and job levels appears healthy, because of management's focus on processes and people without viewing them in the larger organizational context (Rummler and Brache, 1990). Under these conditions, processes and jobs are managed as individual entities, linked only by reporting relationships rather than by one common goal. The selection and placement process within a healthy organization will link recruitment, hiring, placement, and promotion decisions within the context of the strategic goals of the organization.

Latham and Sue-Chan (1998) predict that a major strategic focus in employee selection in the twenty-first century, one that will distinguish high-performing from under-performing organizations, is the linkage between superordinate (organization level) goals and contributing short-term and proximal goals. Definition of these goals will be essential "before one can predict who is likely to perform effectively" (15).

MEASUREMENT AND RELEVANCE TO RECRUITMENT AND SELECTION Strategy-driven organizations view themselves as functional entities. Zemke and Gunkler (1982) assert that there are three prerequisites for treating an organization as an entity. First, a measurement system that tracks organizational results and provides information regarding individual and subsystem performance is in place. Second, a feedback system is needed for making organizational performance and outcome information available at all levels, including those of subsystems and individuals. Information flows both up and down in this type of organization. Finally, the organization must establish contingent relationships between organizational results and rewards for individual behaviour. Thus, the organization assuming a dynamic systems vantage establishes links between behaviour and results and between results and the values and expectations of those in the receiving system—the ultimate customers. The strategic goal functions as the rule that explicitly states the link between system results and its impact on the receiving system (e.g., to deliver quality service at affordable prices). The strategy-driven organization directs the performance of individuals and subsystems accordingly. Because the dynamic system strives for constant improvement within a rapidly changing market and culture, it is insufficient to define the strategic goal at one point in time and take steps toward achieving it. Instead, an overall strategic goal is defined, implementation steps are identified and carried out, performance and outputs are measured, and goals are refined based on the impact data.

Where does the human resources recruitment and selection process fit into this define–implement–test–refine cycle? When data from internal and external feedback sources indicate that the desired organizational performance is not occurring, the analyst seeks to determine if the source of the problem is a deficiency in job design, information, tools or raw materials; selection, placement or training; or incentives for motivating human performance (Brethower,

1982; Gilbert, 1978). While human resources subsystems can vary in the extent of their size and power within organizations, they typically exert some influence over a major source of organizational performance.

When designing and implementing recruitment and selection programs to fill jobs within specific subsystems, human resources specialists must always link their own subsystem goals to the overall organizational goal. Losing sight of the goal can result in less-than-optimal recruitment and selection policies and practice. Interestingly, a 1998 Human Resources Practices Survey found that although the largest (Fortune 1000) employers continue to rely heavily on their people to "fuel growth and sustain competitive advantage" (Deloitte and Touche, 1999, 1) there was a weak link between the HR function and customers. These results were surprising given the customer focus in current business strategizing. Clearly there is a role here for the HR specialist to have an impact on organizational performance by developing systems for recruiting and hiring that are aligned with customer-focused organizational goals.

LEVEL II: THE PROCESS LEVEL

Processes are the means by which an organization produces outputs to fulfill its strategic goals. A process is "a collection of activities that takes one or more kinds of input and creates an output that is of value to the customer" (Hammer and Champy, 1993, 35). Customers can be those in internal receiving systems or they can be the ultimate customers that purchase the product or service. At this level, the focus is on the interrelationships between components of the organization. Processes do not occur within single departmental structures; they are input–throughput–output systems that are best described by what gets done and how. The systems analyst focuses on strategic goals even when intervening at the process level. All interventions, including those in human resources selection, are guided by their relationship to the overall goal. With function in mind, the analyst asks "What is the process?" and "What does the process accomplish?" All subsystem processes in the organization have process goals that are specific to them. In a healthy system, accomplishment of those goals contributes to the overall strategic goal. Similar to strategic goals, subsystem goals are stated in terms of accomplishments, overall objectives, control, and numbers or measures.

An important criterion for useful subsystem goals is reconciliation (Gilbert, 1978); that is, is the goal reconcilable with other system goals, or does it conflict with them? A good subsystem goal is compatible with the goals of all other subsystems in the organization and with the overall strategic goal. Attainment of any of the subgoals does not have adverse impact on the achievement of desired subsystem or strategic results. The strategic goal of Tom's Landscaping Service is to provide top-quality service on a dependable basis at a reasonable rate. If, for example, the goal of *sales* is to generate as many customer orders as possible and the goal of *operations* is to complete the job in a timely manner, then the achievement of Tom's strategic goal is in jeopardy. The goal of the sales subsystem is in conflict both with the operations subsystem and with the overall organizational goal that specifies quality service at reasonable rates. Further, the operations subsystem goal will also be in conflict with the overall strategic goal if some quality criterion is not specified. A reconcilable subsystem goal might state that "sales will generate X number of orders per time period, given data from operations specifying their current workload and job completion projections." A reconcilable operations objective would be "to complete jobs in a timely manner while remaining within quality specifications." Achievement of these subsystem goals will then contribute to attaining the overall goal of the organization.

Processes in any organization follow normal business activities but are difficult to detect and trace if a structural view of the organization is taken. Hammer and Champy (1993) suggest that processes go unmanaged because of the traditional structural approach to defining organizations. People are put in charge of managing departments, but rarely is anyone put in charge of managing a process from beginning to end. They further suggest that processes should be given names that express their beginning and end. Thus, the product development process should be called "concept to prototype" (118). Similarly, the human resources process could be called "recruitment to promotion." Identifying the process in terms of its logical beginning and end permits the analyst to chart the process as it plays out in the organization. The next section describes how processes are traced using a functional approach rather than a structural one.

PROCESS MAPPING   Process mapping can be a useful intermediate step between organization analysis and job analysis and can help the HR practitioner to better understand the nature of the job under scrutiny. It permits the analysts, often a cross-functional team, to assess how different functions are involved in a single process. This information can be used by the team to improve processes and by human resources specialists to guide recruitment and selection initiatives. Process mapping serves a function similar to organizational charting in that it provides a picture of the way work gets done (Hammer and Champy, 1993; Rummler and Brache, 1990). Process mapping is best completed by a team of individuals representing all areas that participate in the process. Two general steps in process mapping are (Hammer and Champy, 1993; Rummler and Brache, 1990):

1. Identify all functions, departments, and specialty areas involved in the process.
2. Trace the process through all its steps from initial inputs to the final output.

Once the process has been mapped, the team can see how different functions, departments, and personnel are involved in producing the final output. Gaps in the system, if they exist, become evident as missing or extra steps readily stand out (Rummler and Brache, 1990; Scholtes, 1988). Next, an *ideal process* map can be produced to be used as a guide for process improvement. In the ideal map (i.e., what the process would look like in the perfect-case scenario), the team identifies all functions, departments, or work areas that should be involved in the process and the most effective links between these areas are drawn. The ideal map can provide objective guidance to support recruitment and selection strategies. Human resource deficiencies and surpluses are made evident when the map of the current process is compared with that of the ideal process. Those who have considerable experience with process mapping will realize that human resources deficiencies and surpluses are not always readily evident. It may take the team several iterations of mapping and observing work flow to pinpoint areas of shortage and surplus.

Suppose that in response to internal quality control data and customer complaints, Tom's Landscaping Service (Devries, 1995) put together a cross-functional team to map the *order-to-delivery* process. Figure 4.3 shows the map that the team generated. This map shows the functions involved from the start to the end of this process. Starting with the customer, the order is generated and a service order invoice is completed in sales. If this order is cleared through finances, it is passed on to operations; if it is not, the order is returned to sales so the terms can be clarified with the customer. An order received by operations results in a site visit by the operations manager, who determines the

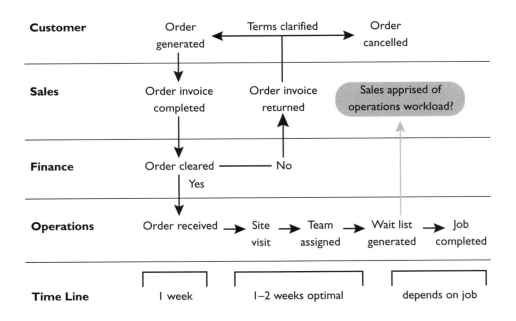

FIGURE 4.3 PROCESS MAP FOR TOM'S LANDSCAPING SERVICE FOR THE PROCESS "SERVICE ORDER TO JOB COMPLETION"

exact nature of the job. A team of landscapers is assigned to the job based on the information gathered at the site visit. The team leader then places the order on a wait list and jobs are completed in turn.

This process map highlighted a critical gap in the system: There were more orders coming in than the operations teams could handle in a timely manner. The cross-functional team concluded that there were two possible solutions. Sales could be apprised of the workload in operations and turn down orders accordingly. This solution would mean that an additional line on the process map would connect the operations back with the sales, indicating that sales would receive the wait-list data from operations. It would also mean that those customers would give their business to another firm. Or, additional personnel could be hired so that jobs would not sit on wait lists prompting customers to complain or to go elsewhere for service. Tom's financial advisers would then be consulted to confirm whether it makes good business sense to purchase the extra equipment necessary and to hire additional landscapers to handle the extra business. If so, the human resources process *recruitment to placement* would be invoked to seek out new individuals to be hired by Tom's.

IMPACT OF PROCESS-LEVEL REQUIREMENTS ON INDIVIDUAL AND ORGANIZATIONAL PERFORMANCE   More Canadian employees than ever are members of "process teams," and individuals are less likely than ever to be linked to an easily identifiable collection of discrete job tasks. According to Hammer and Champy (1993):

> *A task-oriented, traditional company hires people and expects them to follow the rules. Companies that have reengineered don't want employees who can follow rules; they want people who will make their own rules. As management invests teams with the responsibility of completing an entire process, it must also give them the authority to make the decisions needed to get it done.* (70)

The implications of this changing view of organizational performance for the recruitment and selection subsystems are far reaching. They include the need for valid predictors of the behaviours required under a process model of job performance, and these predictors must be acceptable from a human rights perspective (see Chapter 2). It is no longer sufficient to assess a candidate's education, experience, and skills. The prospective employee's ability to make good decisions and to generate usable ideas, to work in a team environment, and to work under conditions of minimal supervision are becoming equally important in the reengineered organization (Cascio, 1995; Hammer and Champy, 1993). We will explore these issues further in considering analysis at the job level of an organization.

BOX 4.1 Process Mapping in a Dot.Com Firm

Work processes are the means by which organizations produce their products and services. Imagine a process called "estimating," in which a team of people must determine how much their service is going to cost their customer. The team typically uses historical company data, lessons learned from previous jobs, and customer specifications to develop a number—one that won't be so high it will drive the potential customer to the competitor or so low that the company will not make a profit.

It is commonplace in organizations striving to maintain their competitive edges and improve quality to ask employees, managers, and executives to develop process maps. Process mapping enables the organization to clearly specify how work gets done, where the gaps and redundancies are, and how profit is made (or lost). Imagine that you are a member of an estimating team in a dot.com firm that develops websites for Canadian upstart companies. Your boss has named you as the team leader for redesigning the estimating process. What are the steps you would take? Process mapping in this case begins with establishing a need for change and ends with recognizing accomplishments. Here are five steps to effective process mapping:

1. Define the business need.
2. Map the "is" process and develop the "should be" process.
3. Implement the new process and measure its effect.
4. Analyze the data and adjust the process as necessary.
5. Recognize and celebrate achievements of the process and implementation teams.

To start, your team compares outcomes on previous estimates (the figure the job was sold at) to job outcomes (the figure at which the work was actually performed) to iden-tify the existence and magnitude of failed estimates. The team, comprising representatives from each department or function involved in the estimating process, then develops the current (or "is") map, which identifies each of the steps in the process. Once the steps are named, your team then identifies the owners of each step and traces the path the estimate takes from conception to completion. The next step is to develop the ideal (or "should be") map, which defines how the process would flow best. In the best-case scenario, your manager identifies the parameters of the solution—that is, what barriers the team is allowed to break down to produce the best flow and what sacred ground the team is not permitted to disrupt in developing the solution.

Now for the hard part! Step 3 involves implementing the new process. People may be asked to stop doing some of the things they have always done, start doing things they never have done, or do some things differently. As the team leader, you may need to coach or ask for management support in coaching employees on the change process and the impact on their job duties. Remember, people typically resist change, especially when they were not involved in developing the solution. Rolling out the new process, then, is best done with the involvement of all those who will be impacted by the change. They should be asked to review the new process, comment on its pros and cons, and offer suggestions for how to make the new process work.

How will you know if the new process is effective? Measure its impact! Compare the "as sold price" with the "work completed at price" on jobs using the process. An effective process will result in an increased accuracy of estimates. Your team may need to adjust parts of the process as it is tested on new jobs, but make sure you are reacting to objective measures of results. Finally, rejoice in the success of a job well done. Recognize the accomplishments of the team developing the solution and all of those enabling it to work in real time on real jobs.

Level III: The Job Level

A **job** is defined as a collection of positions that are similar in their significant duties (e.g., supermarket cashier, anesthetist); a **position** consists of a collection of duties assigned to individuals in an organization at a given time (Cascio, 1982; Harvey, 1991). Jobs and positions are among the basic building blocks of any organization, and selection of individuals to fill these positions has a significant impact on the success of the organization.

The unit of analysis at the job level is human performance and events that affect it. In the early part of the twentieth century, this meant that people performed a set of tasks that were specifically related to a job. The view of efficiency experts such as Frederick Taylor was that job tasks should be highly organized and distributed among specialized workers (Haber, 1964). Operations research focused on identifying problems, designing models for testing, and deriving solutions to work problems based on these job models. Human behaviour was considered to be a constant and employees were paid to produce an output under a given set of operational constraints. Organizational culture and the modern business environment have learned from their early attempts, and human behaviour is now considered to be an important variable in determining system functioning. Employees are now paid to think and make decisions as well as to produce outputs.

Individual employees and managers are the means by which processes function, whether poorly or effectively. Among the variables that are critical to performance at the job level are recruitment, selection, and promotion of individual employees, assessment and communication of job responsibilities, development and application of standards for performance, and implementation of feedback and reward systems and training programs (Rummler and Brache, 1990). Analysis at the job level involves identifying the goals and the major responsibilities of a job.

IDENTIFICATION AND MEASUREMENT OF JOB-LEVEL REQUIREMENTS Jobs can be mapped and analyzed just as organizations and processes can be mapped, and jobs have major objectives to be accomplished. At this level, objectives are defined in terms of the major responsibilities of the job. The requirements for success on the job are described as the levels of performance and the quality of relevant outputs that are achieved in relation to specified standards. Figure 4.4 shows the contribution of individual job outputs to subsystem outputs. Each individual within the processing system is responsible for one or more job responsibilities and tasks. Those tasks collectively produce the results that are generated by the processing system. Feedback loops within the processing system tell each individual how he or she is performing relative to specified standards.

Job—a collection of positions that are similar in their significant duties.

Position—a collection of duties assigned to individuals in an organization at a given time.

FIGURE 4.4 CONTRIBUTION OF INDIVIDUAL JOB OUTPUTS TO SUBSYSTEM OUTPUTS

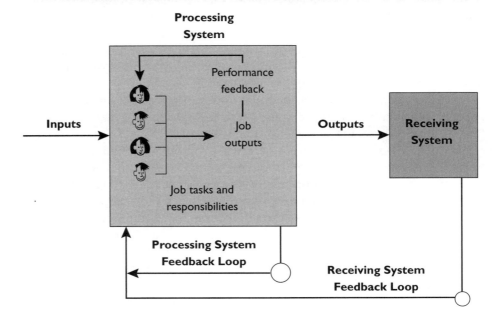

Daniels (1994) defines feedback as "information about performance that allows an individual to adjust his or her performance" (99). He cites internal feedback deficiencies as "a major contributor to virtually all problems of low performance" (100). For performance feedback to be useful, objectives for individual behaviours and results must be consistent with and contribute to process and organizational-level goals (Gilbert, 1978; Rummler and Brache, 1990), and both positive and constructive information is flowed back to the performer (Wilk Braksick, 2000). In a high-performance organization, job objectives are linked to process goals, subsystem process goals are aligned with the overall strategic goal of the organization, and strategic goals are linked to receiving-system (customer) values and expectations.

Although job-level objectives are more specific than subsystem goals, they are not necessarily easier to identify. The variables identified by Kiechel (1993) relevant to the recruitment and selection functions at the process level also affect job-level variables. Because companies are downsizing, organizations are shifting toward flatter and less hierarchical structures, work itself is being redefined, and jobs are becoming more complex. Thus, the analyst looking to identify major responsibilities and tasks inherent to specific jobs will often find that a functional rather than a structural approach better serves the purpose. The following sections describe some common means for analyzing the content of jobs and consider job analysis in the changing culture of the world of work.

Job Analysis

Job analysis refers to the process of collecting information about jobs "by any method for any purpose" (Ash, 1988). The information collected from a job analysis can be used toward several ends (e.g., classifying and describing jobs, developing employee appraisal systems, designing jobs, and developing training programs). In the context of employee recruitment and selection, the results of the analysis specify the requirements of the job that are subsequently used to establish employee selection programs. Harvey (1991) contends that

> it is critical that the term job analysis be applied only to procedures that collect information describing verifiable job behaviors and activities; it should not be used to denote the wide assortment of procedures that make inferences about people or otherwise apply job analysis data (e.g., to infer personal traits that might be necessary for successful job performance). (73)

Job analysis techniques generally fall into two categories: work-oriented and worker-oriented (Harvey, 1991; McCormick, 1979; McCormick and Jeanneret, 1991; McCormick, Jeanneret, and Mecham, 1972). In **work-oriented** job analysis, the emphasis is on work outcomes and description of the various tasks performed to accomplish those outcomes. These methods produce "descriptions of job content that have a dominant association with, and typically characterize, the *technological* aspects of jobs and commonly reflect what is achieved by the worker" (McCormick et al., 1972, 348). The descriptions of tasks or job duties generated via work-oriented methods are typically characterized by their frequency of occurrence or the amount of time spent on them, the importance to the job outcome, and the difficulty inherent in executing them (e.g., Gael, 1983; Ghorpade, 1988). Because task inventories generated via work-oriented techniques are developed for specific jobs, or occupational areas, the results are highly specific and may have little or no relationship with the content of jobs in other fields (McCormick and Jeanneret, 1991).

Work-oriented—job analysis techniques that emphasize work outcomes and descriptions of the various tasks performed to accomplish those outcomes.

Alternatively, **worker-oriented** job analysis methods focus on general aspects of jobs that describe perceptual, interpersonal, sensory, cognitive, and physical activities. Worker-oriented methods generate descriptions "that tend more to characterize the generalized human behaviors involved; if not directly, then by strong inference" (McCormick et al., 1972, 348). These techniques are not limited to describing specific jobs; they are generic in nature and the results can be applied to a wide spectrum of task-dissimilar jobs (Harvey, 1991; McCormick, 1979; McCormick and Jeanneret, 1991; McCormick et al., 1972). Changes from a task- to process-based way of thinking highlight the usefulness of worker-oriented job analysis procedures in meeting the new demands placed on human resources specialists.

Worker-oriented—job analysis methods that focus on general aspects of jobs that describe perceptual, interpersonal, sensory, cognitive, and physical activities.

Employment/worker specifications—the knowledge, skills, abilities, and other attributes necessary for a new incumbent to do well on the job.

KSAOs—the knowledge, skills, abilities, and other attributes necessary for a new incumbent to do well on the job; also referred to as employment or worker specifications.

Whether work- or worker-oriented, Harvey (1991) proposes three criteria that should characterize any job analysis method: First, the goal of job analysis should always be the description of observable work behaviours and analysis of their products. Second, the results of a job analysis should describe the work behaviour "*independent of the personal characteristics or attributes of the employees who perform the job*" (75). Positions in an organization exist independently of the incumbents who fill those positions; in job analysis it is the job (i.e., the collection of positions) that is being analyzed, not the performance of the individual incumbents. **Worker specifications** (i.e., the knowledge, skills, abilities, and other attributes—or **KSAOs**) necessary to perform successfully on the job are inferred in a separate process using the results of a job analysis. Finally, the analysis must be verifiable and replicable. That is, the organization must be able to produce evidence of both the validity and the reliability of each step in the job analysis process.

Although there are no laws that specifically require a job analysis prior to implementing recruitment and selection programs, employment decisions must be based on job-related information (Sparks, 1988). Job analysis is a legally acceptable way of determining job relatedness, and has been endorsed in U.S. case law. In 1975 the United States Supreme Court made a precedent-setting decision when it criticized the Albermarle Paper Company for its failure to use a job analysis to demonstrate the job relatedness of its selection procedures (*Albermarle Paper Co. v. Moody*). According to Harvey (1991), "Albermarle established job analysis as something that virtually *must* be done to defend challenged employment practices" (120). Additionally, even though the *Uniform Guidelines on Employee Selection* (1978) are not law, the U.S. courts have granted them significant status in guiding administrative interpretations of the job analysis–job relatedness link (Levine, 1983; Sparks, 1988). The *Uniform Guidelines* represent a joint agreement between several U.S. government departments and agencies (Equal Employment Opportunity Commission, Civil Service Commission, Department of Labor, and Department of Justice) outlining professional standards for employee selection procedures.

Although these legal precedents and guidelines originate in the United States, Canadian human rights commissions and courts will continue to recognize them as professional standards unless it is established that Canadian legal precedent and professional practice deviate substantially from those of the United States (Cronshaw, 1988). Furthermore, the Industrial-Organizational Psychology section of the Canadian Psychological Association has adopted the principles outlined in the *Uniform Guidelines* for developing equitable selection systems for use in Canada (Latham and Sue-Chan, 1998). Thus, job analysis not only aids the organization in determining what KSAOs should be included in its selection measures, it is an essential step in protecting the organization should its selection procedures be challenged in court (Ash, 1988; Levine, Thomas, and Sistrunk, 1988). In fact, the 1995 Employment Equity Act (Human Resources Development Canada, 1996) specifies the obligations of employers and directs them to identify and remove barriers against equitable representa-

BOX 4.2 Employment Equity and Its Relationship to Job Analysis

Employment equity is a human rights initiative aimed at reducing and eliminating unfair discrimination and to increasing the representation of designated groups (including women, visible minorities, Aboriginal people, and people with disabilities) in the Canadian workplace. A recent banner case in British Columbia highlights the usefulness of a good job analysis in specifying criteria for employment. Newly established physical fitness requirements developed by the BC government for forest firefighters employed through the Forest Ministry were found, by the Supreme Court of Canada in 1999, to unfairly discriminate against women (see Chapter 2). The claimant was a female firefighter who had performed her job satisfactorily for three years prior to the new aerobic test standards and who was dismissed from her job after failing the minimum test requirement. She filed a grievance.

The test in question required that fully equipped firefighters complete a run, a rowing exercise, and an equipment-dragging exercise within time limits and that they meet a minimum standard for aerobic performance during the test. The government argued that these requirements are necessary for the safety of the job incumbent and the public and are essential to effective service delivery. The Supreme Court disagreed and found that the employer was

unable to demonstrate that the new standard was adopted based on job-relatedness information, or that the standard is reasonably necessary for the adequate performance of the job. The firefighter was reinstated to her job with back pay.

How could a job analysis have helped the government determine whether or not and how it should implement new performance standards for the selection and retention of employees? Did the government, as the employer, gather thorough background information? Did they interview a representative cross-section of incumbents? Did they observe incumbents as they performed job duties or review historical performance evaluation documents? Did they ensure that they used valid analysis methods for determining the KSAOs for successful performance?

The court found that although the employer hired job analysis experts to develop a fair test, the experts used flawed methodologies. Hence, the analysis did not demonstrate that the aerobic standard was necessary to identify incumbents who could perform their firefighting duties safely and effectively. The purpose of a good job analysis in this case should have been to ensure that the results would identify only those specifications that were bona fide occupational requirements and would be free of discrimination on prohibited grounds such as the sex of the incumbent.

---

tion of protected groups. A good job analysis ensures that accurate information on skill, effort, responsibility, and working conditions are specified, reducing the likelihood of impediments to equitable employment access for all Canadians.

THE JOB ANALYSIS PROCESS

Although the various existing job analysis techniques differ in the assumptions they make about work, they follow the same logical process when applied to the recruitment and selection of human resources. First, work activities are described in terms of the work processes or worker behaviours that characterize the job. Next, machines, tools, equipment, and work aids are defined in relation to the materials produced, services rendered, and worker knowledge applied to those ends. The job context is characterized in terms of physical working conditions, work schedules, social context and organizational culture, and financial and nonfinancial incentives for performance. Finally, personnel specifications are inferred by linking the job requirements identified in the analysis with the education, experience, skills, and personal attributes required for successful job performance (McCormick, 1979).

GETTING STARTED: GATHERING JOB-RELATED INFORMATION

In preparing for a job analysis, the first step should be to collect existing information describing the target job. The analyst mines information from organizational charts, legal requirements (e.g., the job *clinical psychologist* may be governed through legal statutes at the provincial level), job descriptions, union regulations, and previous data from related jobs. In addition, job-related information can be found in the National Occupational Classification (NOC) system (Human Resources Development Canada, 2000). The NOC systematically describes occupations in the Canadian labour market based on extensive occupational research and is now available online (http://www.worklogic.com:81/noc/NOCView.htm). Boxes 4.3 and 4.4 present the NOC descriptions for Veterinarians and Visual Artists, respectively. Such information, when gathered and studied in advance will prove invaluable for organizing and conducting the ensuing analysis.

Alternative sources to the NOC include the Canadian Classification Dictionary of Occupations (CCDO) (Citizenship and Immigration Canada, 1997) and the Dictionary of Occupational Titles (DOT) (National Academy of Sciences, Committee on Occupational Classification and Analysis, 1981). The CCDO, designed in 1971 by Employment and Immigration Canada, was widely used by human resources professionals in Canada. Although some find the CCDO easier to use, it was abandoned in 1992 because its design was no longer able to accurately reflect the contemporary Canadian labour market. Human Resources Development Canada replaced the CCDO with the NOC (Citizenship and Immigration Canada, 1997).

Similarly, the DOT (available online at http://www.oalj.dol.gov/libdot.htm) is being replaced with a new system of gathering and disseminating job analysis data underway in the United States. O*NET, the Occupational Information Network, is an electronic database developed by the U.S. Department of Labor to replace the Dictionary of Occupational Titles (DOT). The occupational/skill descriptors "serve as a solid, but flexible foundation for vendors and others to develop sophisticated occupational and career information systems" (DOL Office of Policy and Research, 2000, 1). O*NET was first released for public use in the fall of 1998 and is available online at http://www.doleta.gov/programs/onet/. The database grows as information becomes available on more occupations, and the U.S. Department of Labor encourages organizations to use the new database in place of the DOT, which was last updated in 1991.

BOX 4.3 Occupational Description for Veterinarians

Veterinarians prevent, diagnose, and treat diseases and disorders in animals and advise clients on the feeding, hygiene, housing, and general care of animals. Veterinarians work in private practice or may be employed by animal clinics and laboratories, government, or industry.

EXAMPLES OF TITLES CLASSIFIED IN THIS GROUP

Small-animal veterinary specialist, Veterinarian,

Veterinary inspector, Veterinary pathologist,

Veterinary physiologist, Zoo veterinarian

MAIN DUTIES

Veterinarians perform some or all of the following duties:

- Diagnose diseases or abnormal conditions in animals through physical examinations or laboratory tests.

- Treat sick or injured animals by prescribing medication, setting bones, dressing wounds, or performing surgery.

- Inoculate animals to prevent diseases.

- Advise clients on feeding, housing, breeding, hygiene, and general care of animals.

- May supervise animal health technologists and animal care workers.

- May be responsible for overall operation of animal hospital, clinic, or mobile service to farms.

- May conduct veterinary research.

- May enforce government regulations in disease control and food production including animal or animal-based food inspection.

PHYSICAL ACTIVITIES

For some occupations in this group, Strength 3 (Medium) may also apply.

EMPLOYMENT REQUIREMENTS

- Two to four years of pre-veterinary university studies or, in Quebec, completion of a college program in health science and

- A four-year university degree in veterinary medicine and

- Completion of national certification examinations are required.

- Provincial licensure is required.

- In Quebec, membership in the professional corporation for veterinarians is mandatory.

- Entry into research positions may require post-graduate study.

SIMILAR OCCUPATIONS CLASSIFIED ELSEWHERE

Animal Health Technologists (3213)

Biologists and Related Scientists (2121)

Source: Human Resources Development Canada, National Occupational Classification. Reproduced with the permission of the Minister of Public Works and Government Services Canada, 2000.

In addition to occupational databases, attention should be given to determining which techniques will be employed for gathering job information. Gael (1988) notes that, depending on the objective of the job analysis, some techniques are better suited than others for providing job information.

Analyses typically involve a series of steps, often beginning with interviews or observations that provide the information to construct a task inventory or to complete a structured questionnaire. Ideally, the job analyst employs a combination of strategies to arrive at a comprehensive and accurate description of the job in question (Cascio, 1982; Harvey, 1991), although analysts operating within the very real constraints of time and funding often use a single method. Each analysis method contributes slightly different information, and, by using a combination of methods, potential gaps in the results are minimized.

SURVEY OF JOB ANALYSIS TECHNIQUES

The following discussion is intended as an overview of common job analysis methods and their major strengths and weaknesses. We also include in each overview a brief description of the method that is normally used to derive employee specifications from the job analysis data. You should consult the references for each method for detailed descriptions of how to conduct job analyses before using the different techniques.

INTERVIEWS

The **interview** is perhaps the most commonly used technique for gathering job facts and establishing the tasks and behaviours that define a job. This method involves questioning individuals or small groups of employees and supervisors about the work that gets done. The interview may be structured or unstructured, although for job analysis purposes, a structured format is recommended. The results of a job analysis interview may stand on their own, as in a formal integrated report, when there are few incumbents working within a small geographical area. Or, they may provide the necessary information for completing a task inventory, structured questionnaire, or other analytic technique (Gael, 1983, 1988).

> **Interview**—a job analysis method that involves questioning individuals or small groups of employees and supervisors about the work that gets done.

Because it is such an important step in most job analyses, the interview should be well planned and carefully conducted. McCormick (1979) and others (Fine, Holt, and Hutchinson, 1974; Gael, 1988; Gatewood and Feild, 1998; Levine, 1983) offer many valuable guidelines for conducting interviews. Adhering to these criteria will help both the interviewer and the person being interviewed remain at ease and will result in useful job information.

1. **Announce the job analysis well ahead of the interview date.** The impending job analysis and its purpose should be well known among employees and management.

2. **Participation in interviews should be voluntary, and employees should be interviewed only with the permission of their supervisors.** The job analyst avoids creating friction within the organization and is sensitive to the use of coercion in obtaining information. In general, when analysis interviews are free from organizational politics, they can be completed in a timely manner with valid, uncontaminated results.

3. **Interviews should be conducted in a private location free from status earmarks.** It would be unwise, for example, to conduct interviews with hourly workers in the company president's office. The job analyst is a nonpartisan party whose primary objective is to accurately describe the content of jobs; interviewees should feel comfortable and able to provide truthful information about their work and the conditions under which it is done.

4. **Open the interview by establishing rapport with the employee and explaining the purpose of the interview.** Interviews are often associated with anxiety-provoking events such as job and promotion applications and even disciplinary action. The experienced interviewer takes time at the outset to create a nonthreatening environment and alleviate any fears that interviewees might have.

5. **Ask open-ended questions, using language that is easy to understand, and allow ample time for the employee's responses.** Most people, given

the opportunity, will talk in great detail about the work they do. The good analyst avoids rushing or intimidating people, does not talk down to them, and takes a genuine interest in the interviewee's responses.

6. **Guide the session without being authoritative or overbearing.** Keep the interview on topic and avoid discussions concerning worker–management relations and other unrelated topics. When discussions become tangential, the analyst can bring them back on track by summarizing relevant details and referring to the interview outline.

7. **Explain to the employees that records of the interviews will identify them only by confidential codes.** The names of interviewees and other personal information should be protected. When confidentiality is ensured, more accurate information will be obtained.

The job analyst should record the incumbent's or supervisor's responses by taking notes or by tape recording the interview. Trying to remember what was said following the interview is difficult at best and likely to produce inaccurate information. Recall that the purpose of the interview is to obtain information about the work that the employee does; thus, questions should elicit information describing important job tasks, physical activities involved in the job, environmental conditions (physical and social) under which the work occurs, and typical work incidents.

An interview outline prompts the interviewer to ask important questions about the job to all interviewees. The interviewer may start out asking: "What are the main things that you do in your job?" Based on the response, and on the interviewer's previous knowledge of the job, the interviewer then probes for more detail (Gael, 1988; Ghorpade, 1988). The tasks that make up each job area are identified and the result of the interview should be a clear description of critical job domains and their related elements. Interview outlines can vary from presenting a few informal prompts to listing very structured questions to be addressed in a specific order. In general, the more specific the interview outline is, the more reliable will be the information obtained from interviewees.

While there are no hard-and-fast rules concerning how many people should be interviewed, the job analyst is wise to demonstrate that the collection of incumbents interviewed is representative of the employees whose job the analysis reflects. For example, when conducting a job analysis for meeting planning consultants employed in a large travel company, the analyst may obtain a stratified sample that reflects the proportion of males and females in the position. Other demographic variables such as race and ethnicity, age, physical disabilities and abilities, and native language would also be considered in a representative sample of interviewees. Representativeness is important for two reasons. First, interviewing a range of employees will generate more accurate information concerning the job. Second, if the job analysis is challenged in court, the analyst must be able to defend the procedure. A charge of unfair discrimination will be hard to defend if the analyst cannot demonstrate that the job analysis results were obtained from a sample representative of those who actually do the work (Thompson and Thompson, 1982).

Supervisors should always be included in the pool of interview respondents, as they have a unique perspective of how jobs are performed and the standards for acceptable performance.

One advantage of the interview method is that the job is described by those who know it best: the employees who do the work and their immediate supervisors. And, although interviews should be well structured, they enable interviewees to contribute information that may be overlooked by other analysis techniques.

There are, however, certain disadvantages to job analysis interviews. First, they can be expensive and time consuming and may be impractical for jobs with a large number of incumbents. Interviews take a great deal of time to conduct and may require a substantial number of interviewees to be truly representative of the job incumbent pool. Individual interviews are more time consuming and more expensive to conduct than group interviews, but the benefits of individual interviews can outweigh the relative costs. Individual employees, free from immediate social controls, are likely to respond with greater openness than those interviewed in a group. Thus, the information obtained from the individual interview may be more accurate than that obtained from the same people interviewed together. A second disadvantage of this technique is that workers may be prone to distorting the information they provide about their jobs, particularly if they believe that the results will influence their pay (Cascio, 1982). This distortion can be overcome by making the purpose of the interview clear and by interviewing multiple incumbents and supervisors.

DIRECT OBSERVATION

Martinko (1988) makes the case that "the most effective way to determine what effective job incumbents do is to observe their behavior" (419). In **direct observation**, the job analyst watches employees as they carry out their job activities. This allows the analyst to come into direct contact with the job; thus the data are obtained firsthand as contrasted with the "more remote types of information generated by questionnaires and surveys" (Martinko, 1988, 419).

Direct observation is most useful when the job analysis involves easily observable activities (Cascio, 1982). Analyzing the job "poet" through direct observation would likely produce little of value, whereas the job of "landscaper" lends itself more readily to direct observation. Before conducting direct observations, the analyst will already have learned about the job by studying existing documents. Next, the job analyst determines the nature of the job by asking: "Does the job involve easily observable activities?" and "Is the work environment one in which unobtrusive observations can be made?" If the answer to both questions is "Yes," then direct observation may be a viable analysis method.

In direct observation, systematic observations of employee activities are made and data can be recorded either in narrative format or using a customized checklist or worksheet (Cascio, 1982; Martinko, 1988). Different jobs and environments will require different observation methods. A landscaper's

Direct observation—a job analysis method in which the analyst watches employees as they carry out their job activities, allowing the analyst to come into direct contact with the job and gather firsthand information.

job, one that does not occur within a complex social context, might best be observed and recorded by using a tally sheet such as that shown in Figure 4.5. The job of residential counsellor, in which the job tasks are heavily influenced by dynamic social conditions, will require a recording format that enables the observer to identify important activities and the conditions under which they occur. An example of a recording sheet used in observing residential counsellors at work can be found in Figure 4.6. The form enables the observer to collect information about the job by defining the conditions under which a particular activity occurs and listing the tools and aids employed in the activity. Both recording formats permit the observer to record valuable qualitative and quantitative data.

FIGURE 4.5 FREQUENCY TALLY SHEET

Observation Record for Landscaper   Date: _15–03–00_ Start time: _10:30 am_ End time: _11:07 am_

Observer: _Keltie_   Employee ID: _734_

Tasks (planting trees)	Check if done	Time spent
1. Measure area and mark spot	x	5 min
2. Dig hole	x	16 min
3. Move shrubbery	—	—
4. Lift trees (manually)	x	< 1 min
5. Lift trees (winched)	—	—
6. Fill hole	x	7 min
7. Rake area	x	5 min

FIGURE 4.6 FORM FOR RECORDING WORK ACTIVITIES OF RESIDENTIAL COUNSELLORS IN A COMMUNITY GROUP HOME

Observation Record for Residential Counsellor

Employee ID: _735_   Observer: _Faiz_   Date: _15 Feb 2000_

Condition	Activity	Tools	Time
Resident arrives home from school	Counsellor helps resident remove snow clothes	No special tools	5 min
Physiotherapy program	Counsellor leads resident through exercises	Walker, leg splints, physiotherapy program instructions	20 min
After meal	Medication delivery to residents	Med recording forms, medication instructions	15 min

In preparing for observations, the analyst might ask: "How many observations are enough?" or "How long should observations be?" These questions are addressed in planning the job analysis observations, and, once again, there is no rule book one can turn to for the answers. As with the individual and group interviews, a representative sample of workers is needed. If the organization or department is small (e.g., Modern Builders with only three employees in the job "electrician"), samples from all workers can be obtained. If, however, the organization or department is large (e.g., New World Residential Centres with 10 homes employing over 120 residential counsellors), a sample of workers consisting of at least 10 to 15 percent of the staff can be observed (McPhail, Jeanneret, McCormick, and Mecham, 1991). Observation times should be stratified so that all shifts are covered, and all work conditions are observed, ensuring that important patterns in worker activities are evident and extraneous information is eliminated. When observing at New World Residential Centres, for example, an analyst would want to observe morning, afternoon, and evening shifts during weekdays and weekends, as activities during these periods can change substantially. Similarly, when observing shift workers in a manufacturing plant, activities may change during peak and down times and shift and day considerations will influence the observation schedule.

There are a variety of technological aids available to the observer. Audio and video recording, for example, can facilitate the observation process. Each has its advantages and disadvantages. Audiotapes can augment observer notes with important verbal behaviour of the worker, but they are rarely useful observation tools on their own. Important information may be lost because of poor recording quality and background noise, or because many of the behaviours of interest may be nonverbal (Martinko, 1988). Video recording provides a permanent product of the verbal and nonverbal components of the observation session, which the analyst can review in private for later data collection. When the work area is small and a camera can be placed unobtrusively, videotaping is an option to consider. But, while it may be easier to make unobtrusive observations in some settings using a videotape, the video cannot follow workers around in large work areas without someone at the controls. Another disadvantage, reactivity to observation, may be greater during videotaped sessions than during observation sessions employing live observers. Martinko (1988) also concludes that videotaping can be expensive and may require a skilled technician to produce quality tapes.

The analyst conducting direct observation sessions should be aware that regardless of the observation technique employed, his or her presence may change the behaviour of the employees. Imagine yourself at work; a strange individual with a clipboard begins to write down everything you do. Knowing you are being watched, you may respond by doing your work according to what you think the observer is looking for rather than doing it as you would in the normal day-to-day routine. This effect can be minimized when the analyst blends into the surroundings (e.g., by choosing an unobtrusive observation position) and when the employees have been informed of the purpose of the observations and are only observed with their explicit permission.

In addition to direct observation, the job analyst may ask incumbents to monitor their own work behaviour (Harvey, 1991; Martinko, 1988). Martinko (1988) describes several advantages that self-monitoring may have over other observation procedures. First, it is less time consuming and less expensive because the job incumbents observe and record their own behaviour. Second, self-monitoring can be used when the conditions of work do not easily facilitate direct observation by another person as in potentially dangerous or sensitive work. Finally, self-monitoring can provide information on otherwise unobservable cognitive and intellectual processes involved in the job. The potential shortcomings of self-monitoring are that incumbents may not be reliable observers of their own behaviour, the self-monitoring task is an additional duty to be completed above the normal workload, and some amount of training may be required in order to generate valid and reliable results from self-generated data.

After interview, observational, or self-monitoring data are collected, the analyst uses the resulting notes and tally sheets to identify critical task statements, which are used to generate employee specifications. The analyst objectively describes the critical components of the job in terms of (1) the actions performed, (2) the person, data, or things affected by the actions, (3) the intended outcome or product of the action, and (4) the materials, tools, and procedures used in performing the action. Once the task statements are identified, they are further described in terms of the KSAOs required to perform the job successfully. Gatewood and Feild (1998) proposed these definitions of knowledge, skills, and abilities in order to make inferences concerning employee specifications for a job:

> *Knowledge*: A body of information, usually of a factual or procedural nature, that makes for successful performance of a task.
>
> *Skill*: An individual's level of proficiency or competency in performing a specific task. Level of competency is typically expressed in numerical terms.
>
> *Ability*: A more general, enduring trait or capability an individual possesses at the time he or she first begins to perform a task. (347)

Other attributes (the "O" in KSAO) include personality traits and other individual characteristics (see Box 4.5) integral to job performance. It is good practice to have the incumbents or other subject-matter experts (SMEs) rate the importance of the KSAOs associated with each task after the final inventory is generated, as it is the KSAOs that will be ultimately sampled with the subsequent selection measures. KSAOs are rated with respect to their necessity to the job, whether they are required upon entry to the job, the difficulty inherent

Knowledge—a body of information, usually of a factual or procedural nature, that makes for successful performance of a task.

Skill—an individual's level of proficiency or competency in performing a specific task. Level of competency is typically expressed in numerical terms.

Ability—a more general, enduring trait or capability an individual possesses at the time he or she first begins to perform a task.

BOX 4.5 Is Loyalty a Reasonable Employment Specification?

There's no doubt that the labour market is filled with candidates who are on the move more than ever before. The knowledge economy has generated mobile jobs for mobile people and this means that employers are faced with the problem of how to retain skilled personnel. The following nontechnical requirements for jobs could be found in the careers section of any major newspaper or online employment service.

- You are an effective communicator, both verbally and in writing.
- You possess good organizational and interpersonal skills.
- Negotiation skills would be an asset.
- You are strategically orientated.
- You are open-minded and have wide-ranging interests.
- You are a fast learner and enjoy cross-training.
- Must be able to adapt to a fast-growing, multicultural, and challenging environment.
- You are committed to being a team player and growing with the organization.

How can a job analyst ensure that these are essential KSAOs that would stand up to a legal challenge? Are they requirements the incumbent must have or be able to achieve within a reasonable time on the job? Organizations need not only to select technically skilled people but also to find those who will function well in a team environment and display commitment to the organization.

Canadian employers in the public and private sectors invest in the training of their personnel with the goal of developing employees who will contribute to their financial success. But how do they ensure that their human capital assets will stay with them? One method is to select employees with traits that are suggestive of commitment and longevity. Another is to design the organization so that employees want to stay. Both are reasonable means of ensuring retention of desired workers.

It is reasonable to expect people to function effectively on teams in many work environments. Is it also reasonable to expect them, as a condition of employment, to commit to a long-term career with the organization? In order to hire committed individuals, the job analyst would likely use a worker-oriented methodology that focuses on the general human behaviours and traits related to the work. But commitment is also a matter of person–organization fit and is a function of both what the organization does to select employees and the conditions of work it provides with a view to retaining desired employees. Thus, selection based on a good job analysis is not the sole means of ensuring retention. The organization and its management must be committed to cultivating a desirable culture that provides employees with the motivation to stay that goes beyond working for a paycheque.

---

in obtaining them (i.e., the experience or education that is required), and the frequency with which they are performed. Table 4.1 presents a sample task statement with its component KSAOs described.

STRUCTURED JOB ANALYSIS QUESTIONNAIRES AND INVENTORIES

Structured job analysis questionnaires and inventories require workers and other subject-matter experts to respond to written questions about their jobs. Respondents are asked to make judgments about activities and tasks, tools and equipment, and working conditions involved in the job. These can be off-the-shelf

Structured job analysis questionnaires and inventories—job analysis methods that require workers and other subject-matter experts to respond to written questions about the activities and tasks, tools and equipment, and working conditions involved in their jobs.

TABLE 4.1 TASK STATEMENT AND COMPONENT KSAOS FOR THE JOB "MEETING PLANNER"

Task Statement

Summarizes information in report form from potential hotel and air- and ground-transportation vendors in order to convey information to clients and facilitate comparisons between vendor offers and bids for service using meeting and travel reference guides.

Knowledge

K1. Knowledge of service offers from vendors.

K2. Knowledge of negotiated goods and services agreements from vendors.

K3. Knowledge of facility and travel reference guides.

K4. Knowledge of vendor pricing structures and policies.

Skills

S1. Skill in typing 40 words per minute without error.

Abilities

A1. Ability to use *Meeting Facilities Guide*.

A2. Ability to use *Official Airlines Guide*.

A3. Ability to use *S.A.B.R.E.* and *Apollo* airline reservation systems.

A4. Ability to compile information from several sources.

A5. Ability to record information through writing, Dictaphone, or word processor.

questionnaires and inventories that are amenable for use in a variety of jobs, such as the worker-oriented Position Analysis Questionnaire (PAQ) (McCormick, Jeanneret, and Mecham, 1989), or they can be developed by the analyst for the specific job and organization in question using the critical incident technique (Flanagan, 1954), functional job analysis (Fine et al., 1974; Fine and Wiley, 1971), or other inventory methods.

Position analysis questionnaire (PAQ)—a structured job analysis questionnaire that focuses on the general behaviours that make up a job, organizing 195 job elements into six dimensions.

POSITION ANALYSIS QUESTIONNAIRE (PAQ)   The **PAQ** is a structured job analysis questionnaire that focuses on the general behaviours that make up a job. It assumes that all jobs can be characterized in terms of a limited number of human abilities. The PAQ includes 195 items, called job elements; the first 187 describe general work activities, and the remaining items relate to compensation. The job elements are organized into six dimensions:

1. *Information input* assesses the sources of information a worker uses on the job.
2. *Mental processes* statements refer to the types of reasoning, decision-making, planning, and information-processing behaviours used by the employee.
3. *Work output* items relate to the physical activities engaged in and the tools used by the worker.
4. *Relationships* with other persons measure the types of interpersonal relationships inherent in the job.

5. *Job context* elements measure the physical and social environment in which the work takes place.

6. *Other job characteristics* measure other conditions of work not falling into the other five categories (McCormick et al., 1989).

Each of the six dimensions is subdivided into sections made up of items related to particular job facets (i.e., components of job dimensions). Facets of information input, for example, include visual sources of job information, non-visual sources of job information, sensory and perceptual processes, and estimation activities. Items used to assess visual sources of job information ask respondents to rate the extent to which they use written, quantitative, and pictorial materials, visual displays, mechanical devices, and so on. With this method, the job analyst reviews background job information, conducts extensive interviews with incumbents, observes the job, and rates the extent to which each item of the questionnaire applies to the target job (McPhail et al., 1991). Each item is rated using a specified response scale. For example, the response scale accompanying the facet "visual sources of job information" is:

Extent of Use
0   Does not apply
1   Nominal/very infrequent
2   Occasional
3   Moderate
4   Considerable
5   Very substantial
(McCormick et al., 1989, 3)

"Extent of use" measures the degree to which an item is used by the worker. The five other scales employed are: importance to this job, amount of time (spent doing something), possibility of occurrence (of physical hazards on the job), applicability (of an item to the job), and other special codes used for a small number of job elements (McCormick et al., 1989).

The PAQ can be completed by trained job analysts, personnel professionals, or job incumbents and supervisors, although trained job analysts produce the most accurate and reliable results in the least amount of time (McPhail et al., 1991). Researchers have concluded that the quality of job information obtained via the PAQ is partially dependent on the readability of the instrument. Ash and Edgell (1975) assessed the readability of the PAQ using four indexes. These authors concluded that the PAQ requires at least a college-level reading ability for both the directions and the questionnaire items, and that "the questionnaire as presently constituted probably should not be routinely given to job incumbents and supervisors except in those areas requiring much higher levels of education than 10–12 years" (766). The authors of the *Position Analysis Questionnaire: Job Analysis Manual* (McPhail et al., 1991) recognize that although some organizations have obtained useful job information from having incumbents and supervisors complete the questionnaire, some of the items have unique definitions that may not be readily apparent to those employees.

The job analyst begins the PAQ process by reviewing available information about the job, and by observing the work, the work environment, and the equipment used on the job. Job description questionnaires administered to a large sample of employees may also be used to gather information. Finally, interviews with a sample of incumbents and supervisors provide the detailed information required to accurately complete the PAQ. An interview guide can be found in the PAQ manual (McPhail et al., 1991) and is recommended for use by novice job analysts. The authors warn that the interview should not be conducted "as an oral administration of the PAQ. The analyst's goal in the interview is to gain enough information about the job to enable him or her to respond to all of the PAQ items at some later time" (McPhail et al., 1991, 12). When complete information about the job is obtained, the job analyst assigns ratings to each of the PAQ items; one PAQ answer sheet is completed for each individual interviewed.

Because the PAQ is a standardized job analysis tool, data from single or multiple positions may be used (McCormick, Mecham, and Jeanneret, 1977; Mecham, McCormick, and Jeanneret, 1977). Ratings from the 195 PAQ items are sent to PAQ Services, Inc. for computer processing, where job dimension scores and estimates of required aptitudes to perform the job are derived based on statistically determined relationships. Attribute profiles were generated during the development of the PAQ using a sample of industrial psychologists who rated the relevance of 76 human attributes (e.g., verbal comprehension, movement detection) to each of the job elements assessed by the instrument (McCormick, 1979). For employee selection purposes, the final analysis of PAQ data identifies individual attributes that serve as employee specifications, which can subsequently be used for selecting new employees.

There are several advantages to using the PAQ. First, it can be used with a small number of incumbents yet generates valid results, and it is standardized, thereby permitting easy comparisons between jobs. Second, it is a straightforward process to get from PAQ results to selection procedures. Finally, the PAQ has been rated as one of the most cost-efficient job analysis methods (Levine, Ash, and Bennett, 1980). The primary disadvantages are (1) that because it is a worker-oriented technique, the PAQ does not quantify what work actually gets done on the job (Gatewood and Feild, 1998; McCormick, 1979) and (2) the reading level of the PAQ is too difficult for many lower-level workers. Considering the change in the world of work, from task- to process-based modes of thinking, this first disadvantage may well be an advantage. However, because the required reading level is high and the content of the PAQ is best suited to blue-collar–type jobs, the people occupying those jobs are unlikely to be able understand the questions (Cascio, 1998). Furthermore, important task differences between jobs may not be picked up because of the PAQ's focus on behaviours and the emphasis on overlooking the context within which the work occurs (hence the homemaker job ends up looking similar to that of a police officer).

The interview, direct observation, and self-monitoring methods define task statement. The PAQ does not generate task statements; instead, SMEs rate the criticality to the job of those PAQ items that received the highest ratings for the "extent of use" category. In particular, the SMEs note whether the PAQ attribute is essential for new hires to possess at the time of their hiring. If so, the attribute is included as a KSAO to be used in employee selection. More information on the PAQ can be found on the PAQ website at http://www.paq.com/.

TWO NEW ALTERNATIVES TO THE PAQ   Two recently available alternatives to the PAQ are Harvey's common metric questionnaire (CMQ) (Personnel Systems and Technologies Corporation, 2000; Harvey, 1993) and Saville and Holdsworth's Work Profiling System (WPS). The **common metric questionnaire (CMQ)** is a structured, off-the-shelf job analysis questionnaire that captures important context variables. It promises up-to-date job analysis information corresponding to what people actually do at work and a database describing jobs in terms of observable aspects of the work rather than subjective ratings systems (Personnel Systems and Technologies Corporation, 2000). The reading level is appropriate for lower-level jobs and the content appears to be appropriate for both lower- and higher-level jobs. The CMQ asks questions in five sections pertaining to background information, contacts with people, decision making, physical and mechanical activities, and work setting:

1. **Background**: 41 questions about work requirements such as travel, seasonality, and licensure requirements.

2. **Contacts with People**: 62 questions regarding level of supervision, degree of internal and external contacts, and meeting requirements.

3. **Decision Making**: 80 questions focusing on relevant occupational knowledge and skill, language and sensory requirements, and managerial and business decision making.

4. **Physical and Mechanical Activities**: 53 items about physical activities and equipment, machinery, and tools.

5. **Work Setting**: 47 items that focus on environmental conditions and other job characteristics (HR-Guide.Com, 2000).

The CMQ has been field tested on 4552 positions representing over 900 occupations. Job descriptions produced by the CMQ correlate strongly with descriptions found in the DOT ($0.80 < r < 0.90$) (Harvey, 1993). More information on the CMQ can be found at http://www.pstc.com/analyzejob/index.html.

The **work profiling system (WPS)** is a job analysis method that consists of three versions applicable to managerial, service, and technical occupations. The WPS is a computer-administered structured questionnaire that can be completed and scored online in the workplace (http://www.shlusa.com/products/WPS/wps.htm). It measures ability and personality attributes including hearing skills, sight, taste, smell, touch, body coordination, verbal skills, number skills, complex management skills, personality, and team role

Common metric questionnaire (CMQ)—a structured off-the-shelf job analysis questionnaire that has a reading level appropriate for lower-level jobs and content appropriate for both lower- and higher-level jobs.

Work profiling system (WPS)—a computer-administered structured questionnaire that measures ability and personality attributes required for effective performance.

(HR-Guide.Com, 2000). WPS defines the KSAOs required for effective performance and generates employment specifications based on the highest-ranking survey items across respondents. Another advantage to using the WPS is that it "builds an organizational map of related jobs and job families, providing critical information for selecting jobs for rotation, cross-training and teams" (SHL Group, 1999).

Task Inventories

Task inventories—work-oriented surveys that break down jobs into their component tasks.

Task inventories are work-oriented surveys that break down jobs into their component tasks. A well-constructed survey permits workers to define their jobs in relation to a subset of tasks appearing on the inventory (Christal and Weissmuller, 1988). Drauden (1988) indicates that certain task inventory methods were developed in response to the *Uniform Guidelines* criteria for job analysis. According to these criteria, job analysis should assess: (1) the duties performed, (2) the level of difficulty of job duties, (3) the job context, and, (4) criticality of duties to the job. An inventory comprises task statements that are objectively based descriptions of what gets done on a job. Tasks are worker activities that result in an outcome that serves some specified purpose (Levine, 1983; McCormick and Jeanneret, 1991). These inventories are typically developed for specific jobs or occupations in contrast to worker-oriented methods that permit application of instruments to a wide variety of unrelated jobs.

Functional job analysis—a job analysis method that distinguishes between what a worker does and what is accomplished.

Functional Job Analysis Fine and his colleagues (Fine, 1988; Fine et al., 1974) distinguish between what a worker does and what is accomplished in the **functional job analysis** (FJA) method. They define task statements as "verbal formulations of activities that make it possible to describe what workers do *and* what gets done so that recruitment, selection and payment can be efficiently and equitably carried out" (Fine et al., 1974, 4).

In FJA, well-written task statements clearly describe what an employee does so that an individual unfamiliar with the job should be able to read and understand each task statement. Task statements contain four elements: (1) a verb describing the action that is performed; (2) an object of the verb that describes to whom or what the action is done; (3) a description of tools, equipment, work aids, and processes required for successful completion of the task; and (4) an expected output describing the result of the action (Fine et al., 1974; Levine, 1983). Taken together, task statements describe all the essential components of the job. Although recommendations vary for the optimal number of task statements that define a job—from as little as 6 to 12 (Gatewood and Feild, 1998) to as many as 30 to 100 (Levine, 1983)—one is well advised to keep in mind the purpose of generating task statements: When conducting a job analysis to support a human resources selection program, the task statements should be specific enough to be useful in pinpointing employment specifications, but not so specific as to be cumbersome. Generally, 20 to 30 task statements are sufficient for this purpose.

Task statements should be carefully edited for inclusion in the task inventory. Fine and his colleagues (1974) suggest that

> the most effective way of testing whether or not Task Statements communicate is for a group of analysts to compare their understandings of the tasks and to reach an agreement on their meaning. The broader the range of experience represented by the editing group, the more likely the Task Statements are to be complete, accurate, and clearly stated, and the less likely the information in them is to be dismissed as merely a matter of opinion. Group editing can increase the objectivity of tasks analysis and, therefore, the reliability of Task Statements. (9)

Once the inventory is made (see Figure 4.7 for an example), it is distributed to a sample of job incumbents and other experts, who are asked to rate the tasks on several scales including: (1) data, people, and things, which describe the way in which the worker interacts with sources of information, other people, and the physical environment; (2) worker function orientation, which describes the extent of the worker's involvement with data, people, and things; (3) scale of worker instructions, which describes the amount of control a worker has over the specific methods of task performance; and (4) general educational development scales, which assess the abilities required in the areas of

TABLE 4.2 MODEL FOR TASK STATEMENTS DESCRIBING RESPONSIBILITIES OF RESIDENTIAL COUNSELLORS EMPLOYED IN A COMMUNITY GROUP HOME

Who performs what? (verb)	To whom or what? (object)	To produce or achieve what? (output)	Using what tools, aids, equipment, and processes?
Counsellor observes and records frequency of behaviours	group home resident	to determine cause of undesirable behaviours	using record sheets, customized data forms, videotapes, live observation
Counsellor meets with, talks to, describes data to, answers questions	parents and group home staff and management	to explain results of analysis and describe proposed intervention	using data collected during observations, mediator techniques

Source: Adapted from Fine, Holt, and Hutchinson (1974).

reasoning, mathematics, and language (Fine, 1973; Fine et al., 1974; Gatewood and Feild, 1998). Workers are then asked to rate tasks on the inventory according to whether or not they perform the task and, if desired, to indicate the frequency, criticality, and importance of the task to the job.

Fine (1988) notes that the usefulness of the latter three ratings is dubious. "The critical issue is really whether the task needs to be performed to get the work done. If it is necessary, then it is important and critical, and frequency does not matter" (1029). A worker in a nuclear power facility may, for example, be required to enter and conduct rescues in radiologically contaminated confined spaces. While the rescue operation is rarely, if ever, necessary in the life of a job, it is essential that certain workers be able to perform to stringent standards at any given time and is thus a critical component in employee selection.

FIGURE 4.7 EXAMPLE OF TASK STATEMENTS APPEARING ON A TASK ANALYSIS INVENTORY TO ASSESS THE JOB "MEETING PLANNER"

Job tasks	Frequency of performance	Criticality of performance	Difficulty of execution	Importance for new hire
Researches pricing structure of potential hotel meeting facilities in order to determine the sites that are within the negotiable price range of the client	[ ]	[ ]	[ ]	[ ]
Prepares reports for clients summarizing hotel, air- and ground-transportation vendor offers.	[ ]	[ ]	[ ]	[ ]

Frequency	Criticality	Difficulty	New Hire
1 = never	1 = not at all critical	1 = not at all difficult	1 = not at all important
2 = seldom	2 = somewhat critical	2 = somewhat difficult	2 = somewhat important
3 = occasionally	3 = moderately critical	3 = moderately difficult	3 = moderately important
4 = frequently	4 = very critical	4 = very difficult	4 = very important
5 = most of the time	5 = extremely critical	5 = extremely difficult	5 = extremely important

Once a task inventory is completed by the incumbent sample, the results can be summarized according to the mean rating each item received. McCormick (1979) points out that there is no easy formula for determining job requirements from task inventories. Gatewood and Feild (1998) suggest that the analyst set a cutoff point for mean ratings (e.g., 3 on a 5-point scale) and for standard deviations (e.g., 1), which are computed for each item scored by the respondents. Items with a mean rating of > 3 and a standard deviation of < 1 would, according to this rule, be included in the list of job requirements. Finally, they suggest that at least 75 percent of employees indicate that they perform the task. Thus, any task statements receiving a score of 3 or higher, a standard deviation of 1.0 or less (lower standard deviations are associated with more agreement among raters) and that at least 75 percent of employees engage in are included in the final task inventory that describes the job. The final inventory determines the content of the measures to be used in the new selection program.

It is good practice to have the incumbents rate the KSAOs associated with each task after the final inventory is generated, as it is the KSAOs that will be ultimately sampled with the subsequent selection measures. Recall, KSAOs are rated with respect to their necessity to the job, whether they are required on entry to the job, the difficulty inherent in obtaining them (i.e., the experience or education that is required), and the frequency with which they are performed.

Task inventories are advantageous in that they are efficient to use with large numbers of employees and are easily translated to quantifiable measures. On the other hand, they can be time consuming to develop and thus can be expensive. Motivating incumbents to participate in the rating process may also be a problem with long inventories (Cascio, 1982). When the task inventory procedure and analysis are well planned, the results can be extremely valuable in developing human resources selection programs.

CRITICAL INCIDENT TECHNIQUE **Critical incidences** are examples of effective and ineffective work behaviours that are related to superior or inferior performance. The **critical incident technique**, which generates behaviourally focused descriptions of work activities, was originally developed as a training needs assessment and performance appraisal tool (Bownas and Bernardin, 1988). Ghorpade (1988) notes that it is also commonly employed as a means of generating employee specifications based on critical job behaviours.

The first step in this method is to gather a panel of job experts, usually consisting of people with several years' experience, who have had the opportunity to observe both poor and exemplary workers on the job. The job of the panel is to gather critical incidents. Flanagan (1954) defined an incident as an observable human activity that is sufficiently complete to facilitate inferences and predictions about the person performing the act. Panel members describe incidents, including the antecedents to the activity, a complete description of the behaviour, the results of the behaviour, and whether the results were

Critical incidences—examples of effective and ineffective work behaviours that are related to superior or inferior performance.

Critical incident technique—job analysis method that generates behaviourally focused descriptions of work activities.

within the control of the worker. After the incidents are gathered, they are translated into dimensions that are expressed as KSAOs. The incidents represent real behaviours of both exemplary and inferior workers; thus it is assumed that they provide a logical basis for determining employee specifications (Ghorpade, 1988).

WORKER TRAITS INVENTORIES

Worker traits inventories are not job analysis techniques according to strict criteria (Harvey, 1991). Recall Harvey's strong assertion that the term job analysis "should *not* be used to denote the wide assortment of procedures that make inferences about people or otherwise *apply* job analysis data (e.g., to infer personal traits that might be necessary for successful job performance)" (73). These methods are mentioned here because they are widely used to infer employee specifications from job analysis data, and are commonly included in the job analysis literature.

THRESHOLD TRAITS ANALYSIS SYSTEM
The **threshold traits analysis system** (Lopez, 1988) is designed to identify worker **traits** that are relevant to the target job. This method assumes that work behaviours encompass the position function, the worker traits, and the resulting job performance. According to Lopez (1988), a trait is "a set of observable characteristics that distinguishes one person from another" (881). Supervisors, incumbents, and other subject-matter experts rate the job according to the relevancy of 33 worker traits (e.g., stamina, perception, oral expression, adaptability to pressure, and tolerance). Traits are also rated with respect to the level of trait possession necessary to perform the job, and the practicality of expecting potential incumbents to possess the traits upon hiring.

FLEISHMAN JOB ANALYSIS SURVEY (F-JAS)
The **Fleishman job analysis survey** (F-JAS) (Fleishman, 1992), formerly known as the ability requirements scale (ARS), was developed as a system for identifying employee characteristics that influence job performance. It assumes that job tasks differ with respect to the abilities required to perform them successfully, and that all jobs can be classified according to ability requirements. Fleishman and his colleagues (Fleishman and Mumford, 1988; Fleishman and Quaintance, 1984) used factor analysis to identify a collection of 52 ability categories. Categories range from oral comprehension to multilimb coordination to night vision. Administration of the F-JAS requires that 20 or more subject-matter experts, including job incumbents, supervisors, and others, be presented with a job description or task list. The experts are asked to rate the extent to which each ability is required for the job. Ratings on the ability scales are then averaged to identify the overall ability requirements essential to the job (Fleishman and Mumford, 1988).

Worker traits inventories—methods used to infer employee specifications from job analysis data; commonly included in the job analysis literature.

Threshold traits analysis system—an inventory designed to identify worker traits that are relevant to the target job; assumes that work behaviours encompass the position function, the worker traits, and the resulting job performance.

Trait—an observable characteristic that distinguishes one person from another.

Fleishman job analysis survey—a system for identifying employee characteristics that influence job performance; assumes that job tasks differ with respect to the abilities required to perform them successfully.

JOB ELEMENT METHOD   A third worker trait technique is the **job element method** (JEM), which attempts to distinguish between superior and inferior workers on the basis of job-related abilities. Elements describe the range of employee specifications commonly called KSAOs (Primoff and Eyde, 1988). The JEM procedure requires supervisors and other subject-matter experts to generate a list of elements required for job performance. Elements (e.g., accuracy for a grocery store cashier) are broken down into sub-elements (e.g., ability to determine cost of items, press register keys, and make change) that exhaustively describe the job (Primoff and Eyde, 1988). The expert panel is subsequently asked to rate the elements and sub-elements on four scales: (1) *barely acceptable* measures whether or not minimally acceptable employees possess the ability; (2) *superior* asks whether the ability distinguishes superior workers from others; (3) *trouble likely if not considered* asks whether or not the ability can be safely ignored in selecting employees; and (4) *practical* asks whether or not workers can be expected to have an ability.

> **Job element method**—a worker trait technique that attempts to distinguish between superior and inferior workers on the basis of job-related abilities.

One advantage of worker trait inventories is that they are designed to identify traits or KSAOs that are predictive of job success. The identification of these KSAOs is made by SMEs, who are the individuals most familiar with the job or occupation. The F-JAS in particular stands out as a standardized approach, based on a solid theoretical foundation, for rating the KSAOs critical to performance on the job.

RATING JOB ANALYSIS METHODS

Much research has considered the efficacy of various job and worker trait analysis techniques for generating employee specifications. Levine and his colleagues (Levine, Ash, Hall, and Sistrunk, 1983) assessed seven job analysis methods for their effectiveness for a variety of organizational purposes and for their practicality. Job analysis experts were asked to rate the threshold traits analysis, ability requirements scales (F-JAS), position analysis questionnaire, critical incident technique, functional job analysis, and the job elements method, all of which have been discussed in this chapter. Additionally, they assessed the task inventory with the Comprehensive Occupational Data Analysis Program (TI/CODAP). For purposes of identifying personnel requirements and specifications, the seven methods rated in the following order: (1–5) threshold traits analysis, job elements method, functional job analysis, ability requirements scales, and position analysis questionnaire; (6–7) TI/CODAP and critical incident technique. The first five ratings were not significantly different from each other, meaning that they were rated as equally acceptable for identifying personnel requirements. All five were rated significantly higher than the TI/CODAP and the critical incident technique.

Since job analyses must meet legal requirements if challenged in court, respondents were asked to rate each of the job analysis methods in terms of how well they stand up to legal and quasi-legal requirements. TI/CODAP and functional job analysis ranked highest, followed closely by the PAQ. The job elements method, critical incident technique, threshold traits analysis, and the ability requirements scales ranked fourth through seventh respectively. Hence, the highest-ranking method for meeting legal requirements scored as one of the least-preferred methods for identifying personnel requirements and specifications. Functional job analysis was highly ranked by job analysis experts on both of these important aspects of use.

Regarding practicality, Levine and colleagues (1983) assessed the versatility, standardization, user acceptability, amount of training required for use, operational practicality, sample size requirements, off-the-shelf usability, reliability, cost of use, quality of outcome, and amount of time required for completion for each of seven job analysis methods. The PAQ received consistently high ratings (i.e., above 3 on a 5-point scale) on all items except the amount of training required. Functional job analysis was next, with high ratings on all scales with the exception of training, cost, and time to completion. In terms of overall practicality scores, these methods were followed by the JEM, the threshold traits analysis, ability requirements scales, and TI/CODAP. The critical incident technique received the overall lowest ratings on practicality measures. The TI/CODAP and PAQ rated highest for reliability, followed by functional job analysis.

Other researchers have assessed job analysis techniques to determine whether or not different results are produced when different subject-matter experts are used. Mullins and Kimbrough (1988) found that different groups of SMEs produced different job analysis outcomes using the critical incident technique. They also determined that performance levels of SMEs influenced analysis outcomes. These results are inconsistent with previous studies that found no difference in job analysis outcomes relative to performance levels. The authors suggest that the complexity of the job may mediate the performance level–analysis outcome relationship. In a similar study, Schmitt and Cohen (1989) found that when using a task inventory, people with different occupational experience produced different outcomes, as did males and females. No difference was found for experts of different races.

Job analysis researchers have also questioned the relationship between the amount of information analysts are given about a job and the quality of analysis outcomes (Harvey and Lozada-Larsen, 1988). They concluded that differential accuracy of analysis results is a function of the amount of information provided for the analysts. Specifically, analysts having the job title and job description were more accurate in their analyses than those given only the job title. The authors make an important conclusion that should be considered when preparing for a job analysis:

> Our results indicate that the amount of job descriptive information available to raters has a significant effect on job analysis accuracy. Raters with more detailed job information are consistently more accurate that those given only a job title. (460)

THE EVOLUTION AND FUTURE OF JOB ANALYSIS

In the world of work, jobs are rapidly evolving due to changing technology and organizational practices. For many workers, this means that the tasks performed today may be radically different from those required a few months from today. Skill requirements for employees may be increased or decreased depending on the type of technology employed (Methot and Phillips-Grant, 1998). Task and job instability create a growing need for hiring people with an already-learned set of skills and the ability to make decisions and adapt to changing organizational demands. As a result, human resources professionals may increasingly find the need to combine organization, process, and job analysis techniques in novel ways, while remaining within acceptable legal limits in making recruitment and selection decisions. In addition to the techniques discussed here, personality is becoming a frequent consideration in personnel selection. The methods for determining the personality requirements of jobs and the best methods for identifying them, however, are still in their infancy (Raymark, Schmitt, and Guion, 1997).

BOX 4.6 Job Analysis on the Internet

The following Web addresses provide useful resources to help students and professionals learn about and conduct job analyses. The sites provide information on the methods and uses of job analysis as well as links to relevant sites. The most comprehensive site, HR-Guide.Com, also provides links for users to research legal issues, tips for conducting job analyses, and FAQs, along with up-to-date descriptions of commonly used interview, observation, and structured questionnaire methods.

The official websites for the NOC, DOT, and O*NET are sources of standard occupational dictionaries and employment specifications. The NOC site, for example, contains a search engine enabling the user to retrieve information by searching job titles, aptitudes, interests, and other work characteristics. Sites for specific job analysis tools enable users to review the tools and learn about their application, scoring, and commercially available services.

GENERAL INFORMATION SITES

HR Guide.Com (contains links to Web-based resources for HR professionals and students):
http://www.hr-guide.com/jobanalysis.htm

Harvey's Job Analysis and Personality Research Site:
http://harvey.psyc.vt.edu/

American Institutes for Research; Occupational Classification Systems Review List:
http://www.air-dc.org/ssa/air_ocs2.html

American Institutes for Research; Information on Critical Incident Technique:
http://www.air.org/about/critical.html

SITES FOR JOB CLASSIFICATION SYSTEMS

DOT: http://www.oalj.dol.gov/libdot.htm

O*NET: http://www.doleta.gov/programs/onet/

NOC: http://www.worklogic.com:81/noc/

SITES FOR JOB ANALYSIS TOOLS

PAQ: http://www.paq.com/

CODAP: http://www.codap.com/index.html

CMQ: http://www.pstc.com/cmq/index.html

WPS: http://www.shlusa.com/products/WPS/wps.htm

Cronshaw (1998) proposes that job analysis methodologies for use in dynamic environments be prescriptive of how work should be organized, be interactionist and systems-based, and vividly portray "the unique skills, adaptations, and competencies each individual worker expresses in his/her specific work context, as a complement to the present methods emphasizing generalized person and work constructs" (9). No such methodology incorporating these features currently exists, although Cronshaw presents them as important areas for both theoretical and applied development. This position is supported by Latham and Sue-Chan (1998), who argue that new job analysis techniques will need to identify skills and abilities required in a one- to three-year strategic outlook because worker adaptability is a growing requirement for organizational success.

Approaches to job analysis are evolving as the world of work changes. Longo (1995) argues that one side effect of reengineering and flattening organizations is the disappearance of the job as a stable collection of tasks. In the context of these changes, May (1996) addressed some current issues surrounding ways that job analysis remains of value to organizations as a relevant descriptive tool. She states:

> *Traditionally, job analysis provides detailed information regarding tasks and activities performed in a specific job. Often this information is used to document job boundaries and assign tasks and responsibilities. The resulting products, namely job descriptions and job specifications, are then used to inform human resource functions such as selection and performance management. Job analysis captures the content of jobs as they are described at one point in time. What happens to the usefulness of this technique when the content of jobs changes, sometimes frequently? (1)*

Not only do jobs change frequently in the modern market, but approaches to defining work and jobs are also evolving rapidly. Post-job, or "dejobbed," organizations have resulted as new technology in reengineering and quality management has taken hold. The post-job organization is one that hires people to work well and adaptively, not to fit a job slot. In such an organization, responsibilities are assigned based on the demands of current projects rather than on the basis of previous work patterns (Longo, 1995). In this type of organization, traditional work-based approaches to job analysis are clearly not adequate for determining who will "work well." According to Kichuk and Weisner (1998), the flattening of organizations and the redefinition of jobs have resulted in an increasing use of work teams. They propose personality measures as useful tools not only for identifying people who can stand up to the demands of the job, but also for finding individuals who will work well within particular teams.

Kiechel (1993) confirms that the nature of work is being redefined. This means that the "shelf-life of job analysis results is only as long as the duration of the current job configurations" (May, 1996, 1). Organizations that survive this trend will do so if they adjust their practices accordingly. Core competencies for employment in many sectors will include "behavioural definitions of adaptability, ability to create and acquire information, team playing in a mosaic of cultures, and the ability to work with people" at a distance through audio, video, and Web-based systems (Latham and Sue-Chan, 1998, 16). Human resources practitioners are responding by looking for new ways to select incumbents based on work-related competencies in addition to specific job knowledge and skills. May (1996) aptly concludes that

> *Job analysis will continue to be useful if: 1) organizations consist of jobs that are structured around specific tasks and are relatively stable, 2) organizations are collecting data for the purpose of legal compliance and defensibility, and 3) organizations can use modified approaches to job analysis to capture new forms of work.* (1)

Trends in job analysis reflect the shift from structurally based to process-based views of work and organizations. These trends, as summarized by May (1996) include

- obtaining job information from customers, technical experts, and those who design work, as well as from job incumbents and supervisors;
- describing how the work or job is expected to change in the future and the KSAOs that will be required for the new work;
- focusing on collections of tasks or work functions rather than on specific and isolated tasks;
- using tools borrowed from other areas of organizational practice, such as flowcharting and process charting, to capture the dynamics of work as it occurs in the organizational context.

Kiechel (1993) notes that "the average number of employees per company increased until the 1970s, it has been decreasing since then" (40). He contends that we are moving toward modular corporations that are pared down to core competencies. This view, combined with May's (1996) discussion of the evolution toward rapidly changing jobs and organizations that demand flexibility of their workers, suggests that the need for new approaches to job analysis is now an organizational reality. In order to recruit, select, and promote flexible workers who are able to make their own rules and adjust to the changing demands of work, human resources specialists are faced with the ever-increasing need to adjust their methods to ensure that people are hired based on the needs of the organization while remaining within legal boundaries. Chapter 5 continues this discussion with a presentation of work-related competence as an alternative to traditional job analysis.

BOX 4.7 Information Technology and Employee Recruitment and Selection

Recruiting and selecting employees for work in technological work environments is a growing concern for HR professionals in many sectors. The use of automated systems in production and service delivery means that more companies are selecting employees based on outdated employment specifications. Those companies wishing to keep up with the competition in an increasingly aggressive marketplace are required to make substantial investments in computer-based systems and to develop new methods for identifying employees. Selecting workers who have the requisite skills and the ability to quickly learn new systems introduced into the workplace is essential. Without an appropriately skilled workforce, the anticipated efficiency gains and the money invested in them will be lost. This problem is faced daily by Canadian companies, in both public and private settings and on a local and national level.

Problems in recruiting, selecting, and maintaining a skilled workforce are compounded by the growing number of jobs requiring technologically skilled employees, the shortage of new graduates and trained personnel, and outdated recruitment and selection systems. Job analysis data can be used to specify the KSAOs essential to the high-tech workplace and are needed to

- help organizations specify competitive salary ranges;

- manage the number of employees recruited and selected to enable high quality and timely delivery of products and services;

- establish training and advancement programs; and

- create career growth programs to maintain the right level of skill rather than lose selection and training dollars on migrating employees.

Organizations are also being challenged by an employable workforce demanding more flexibility in terms of variable work hours, telecommuting, and job sharing. HR professionals need to weigh the benefit of hiring new employees versus training existing incumbents. When establishing new selection, training, and advancement systems, the organization faces both direct and indirect costs. Direct costs include funding new job analyses, changing job descriptions to match organizational realities, and administrating new systems. Indirect costs include opportunities lost when current systems are inadequate for recruiting, selecting, and retaining skilled employees. Conversely, the cost of developing and administering new systems is lost when workers migrate to other employers, taking with them their newly developed skills. The goal of the HR professional in this situation is to identify ways to attract, select, and maintain the right people to do the work and fit with the organizational culture.

SUMMARY

This chapter began with a discussion of organizational analysis and its relevance to employee recruitment and selection and ended with a discussion and survey of several job analysis methodologies. As the workplace rapidly changes with the introduction of new technologies and global competition, human resources professionals will need to combine organizational, process, and job analysis techniques to produce effective employee selection programs. Recall that organizational analysis is a way of assessing the organization's ability to meet its strategic goals. The organization is made up of subsystems, teams, and individuals—it is ultimately the performance of collections of individual performers that results in corporate success or failure. When conducting an organizational analysis, the analyst charts relationships and describes them in hierarchical, process, team-based, matrix, or other structural terms.

At the organizational level, objectives for success are defined relative to delivery of products or services to paying customers. At the process level, the analyst describes the means by which the organization produces its deliverables. At the job level, the analyst describes collections of positions that are similar in their significant duties, which when taken together contribute to process outputs. Job analysts must link job requirements to organization functioning; organization and process analyses help them to do this, thereby optimizing their recruitment and selection systems.

Job analysis is a process of collecting information about jobs and encompasses many methods, which fall into two broad categories: work-oriented and worker-oriented. Work-oriented methods result in specific descriptions of work outcomes and tasks performed to accomplish them. Worker-oriented methods produce descriptions of worker traits and characteristics necessary for successful performance. There is no one right way of conducting a job analysis; all methods follow a logical process for defining employment or worker specifications (KSAOs). While job analysis is not a legal requirement for determining KSAOs and selecting employees, the employer must demonstrate job-relatedness of selection criteria if challenged in court.

Regardless of the method used, a good job analysis begins with collection of background information. Gathering job descriptions defined in the NOC, CCDO, DOT, or O*NET is a recommended first step. It is also good practice for the analyst to employ a combination of methods, typically beginning with interviews or observations of employees on the job. The resulting information can then be used to construct a task inventory or provide a backdrop for completing structured questionnaires. Employment specifications are generated by identifying the most frequently occurring activities or requirements in interviews and observations or by identifying those items in an inventory or questionnaire receiving the highest ratings of criticality.

A wide variety of techniques are available for analyzing jobs. While some focus primarily on the work that gets done, others focus on generic human behaviours that are relevant to all work. Deciding which of these techniques to use is based on the goal of the analysis, the resources available to the analyst, and the needs of the organization. No one method will be completely acceptable for all selection needs in an organization. Job analysts must themselves be adaptable in the methods they apply. Employing a process analysis to the needs of the human resources functions in an organization can help the analyst make wise choices concerning which tools best serve the current needs of the system. This chapter demonstrates how human resources functions should tie their process goals to those of the overall organization. Conducting job analyses against a backdrop of process and organization analyses can enhance the effectiveness of the human resources function.

KEY TERMS

Ability, p. 142

Common metric questionnaire (CMQ), p. 147

Critical incidences, p. 151

Critical incident technique, p. 151

Direct observation, p. 139

Dynamic system, p. 116

Employment/worker specifications, p. 132

Fleishman job analysis survey, p. 152

Functional job analysis, p. 148

Human capital, p. 117

Interview, p. 137

Job, p. 129

Job analysis, p. 115

Job element method, p. 153

Knowledge, p. 142

KSAOs, p. 132

Organization analysis, p. 117

Position analysis questionnaire (PAQ), p. 144

Position, p. 129

Processes, p. 118

Skill, p. 142

Strategic goal, p. 116

Structured job analysis questionnaires and inventories, p. 143

Subsystem, p. 116

Task inventories, p. 148

Threshold traits analysis system, p. 152

Trait, p. 152

Worker traits inventories, p. 152

Worker-oriented, p. 131

Work-oriented, p. 131

Work profiling system (WPS), p. 147

EXERCISES

1. Visit a local store, restaurant, or other retail or service organization in your community and observe the service delivery process. Make a customer service process map from your observations. The map should include information on what happens from the time customers enter the establishment until they pay for their product or service and leave. Label the organizational divisions that are responsible for different stages of the customers' experiences and the products and services each of those divisions provides. Next, identify any gaps in the service system and draw a second process map of what the ideal service flow would look like.

2. Prepare a brief outline for conducting a job analysis interview. Use the outline to interview an incumbent or supervisor. You may choose to interview a parent or sibling about his or her work, a co-worker or supervisor from your workplace, or a classmate. Make careful notes during the interview and write up a point-form summary of the major job tasks as described by the interviewee.

3. Choose an occupation that interests you and retrieve the description of that job from the NOC, DOT, and O*NET websites. Compare the results from the three sources. Note their similarities and differences. Provide a brief critique regarding the ease or difficulty of retrieving information from each system.

CASE

Stan is the proud owner of East Side Eatery. He has owned the place for the past five years, and until recently it has been a financial success. Stan tells you that his number one concern is customer satisfaction. With Stan, you get more than you pay for. "Here we surpass customer expectations. Our goal is to provide great food, great service, and a unique environment in which to dine. Complimentary wine for those who have a reservation and have to wait. Anything extra that is not specified in the menu is a perk to most of my patrons," exclaims Stan. He tells you that the motto of all the employees is "We aim to please."

You used to frequent Stan's eatery and have always been satisfied with the food, but it's been four months since you've eaten in this restaurant, and now you are remembering why. The service here is poor, at best. You've been waiting over 20 minutes and you had a reservation, but no complimentary glass of wine has been offered. Once you are finally seated at a table (which looks as though someone squeezed it in at the last moment), it is another five minutes before you get your menu. Ten minutes after you get your menu, your waiter returns to take your order. You are interested in the special—boneless chicken—but the waiter can give you no information on how it is prepared. Obviously, you stick to an old standby rather than risk the mystery chicken.

When your meal finally does arrive (20 minutes after you ordered it), you are impressed with the food. Even the salad is good here. It is aesthetic in appearance, with a plethora of unusual vegetables and not a speck of iceberg lettuce to be found. As you munch on your salad, you watch the employees as they "work." Most of them are laughing and talking a bit too loudly for the atmosphere. Food is placed on a counter from the kitchen but often sits there for five minutes or more before it is picked up. Patrons have to request beverage refills and tables are only cleared as they are needed, not as customers leave.

Stan has told you that he has specified the behaviours that he wants to see his employees display: "Greet every customer within 10 seconds of entering the restaurant. Those who have reservations and have to wait should be offered free drinks. When the waitresses or waiters are busy, the hostess or host will provide drink refills, menus, and any other assistance. The people who bus the tables can also fill in to assist the waitpersons. Here we all work together to make this one of the best eateries in town. Can't ask for much more than that, can you? Since the employees' performance is specified I don't need to hire a manager for everyone already knows what to do."

Source: Devries (1995, 66).

DISCUSSION QUESTION

1. Make a customer service process map from the information provided in this case. The map should include information on what happens from the time customers enter the restaurant until they pay for their meals and leave. Label the organizational divisions that are responsible for different stages of the customers' experiences and the products and services each of those divisions provides. Next, identify any gaps in the service system and draw a second process map of what the ideal service flow would look like according to Stan's descriptions.

REFERENCES

Albermarle Paper Co. v. Moody. 1975. 422 U.S. 405.

Ash, R.A. 1988. "Job Analysis in the World of Work." In S. Gael, ed., *The Job Analysis Handbook for Business, Industry and Government*, vol. I. New York: John Wiley and Sons, 3–13.

Ash, R.A., and S.L. Edgell. 1975. "A Note on the Readability of the Position Analysis Questionnaire (PAQ)." *Journal of Applied Psychology* 60: 765–66.

Bownas, D.A., and H.J. Bernardin. 1988. "Critical Incident Technique." In S. Gael, ed., *The Job Analysis Handbook for Business, Industry and Government*, vol. II. New York: John Wiley and Sons, 1120–37.

Brethower, D.M. 1982. "Total Performance Systems." In R.M. O'Brien, A.M. Dickinson, and M. Rosow, eds., *Industrial Behavior Modification*. New York: Pergamon Press.

Cascio, W.F. 1982. *Applied Psychology in Personnel Management*. 2nd ed.

Reston, VA: Reston Publishing Company, Inc.

————. 1995. "Whither Industrial and Organizational Psychology in a Changing World of Work?" *American Psychologist* 50: 928–39.

————. 1998. "Disadvantages of the Position Analysis Questionnaire." *Applied Psychology in Human Resources Management* 20: 145.

Christal, R.E., and J.J. Weissmuller. 1988. "Job-Task Inventory Analysis." In S. Gael, ed., *The Job Analysis Handbook for Business, Industry and Government*, vol. II. New York: John Wiley and Sons, 1036–50.

Churchman, C.W. 1979. *The Systems Approach*. New York: Dell.

Citizenship and Immigration Canada. 1997. *Regulations Amending the Immigration Regulations*. [Online]. Available: http://www.cic.gc.ca/manuals/english/ompercent2Dweb/1997/ip/ip97percent2D17app.html.

Cronshaw, S.F. 1988. "Future Directions for Industrial Psychology in Canada." *Canadian Psychology* 29: 30–43.

Cronshaw, S. F. 1998. "Job Analysis: Changing Nature of Work." *Canadian Psychology* 39: 5–13.

Daniels, A.C. 1994. *Bringing Out the Best in People*. New York: McGraw-Hill.

Deloitte and Touche LLP. 1995. *U.S. Manufacturers Need Top Talent to Meet Challenge of Global Competition*. [Online]. Available: http://www.dttus.com/dttus/hot/hotlist.htm.

Deloitte and Touche. 1999. *Hyper-Employment Challenges HR Departments: Survey of Fortune 1000 Companies Finds*. [Online]. Available: http://www.dttus.com/us/news/99march/hyperemp.htm.

Devries, J. 1995. "The Effects of Systems-Centered versus Individual-Centered Training on the Analysis of Organizational Problems." Unpublished doctoral dissertation, Western Michigan University.

DOL Office of Policy and Research. 2000. *O*NET Project*. [Online]. Available: http://www.doleta.gov/programs/onet/.

Drauden, G.M. 1988. "Task Inventory Analysis in Industry and the Public Sector." In S. Gael, ed., *The Job Analysis Handbook for Business, Industry and Government*, vol. II. New York: John Wiley and Sons, 1051–71.

Fine, S.A. 1973. "Functional Job Analysis Scales: A Desk Aid." *Methods for Manpower Analysis No. 7*. Kalamazoo, MI: The W.E. Upjohn Institute for Employment Research.

———. 1988. "Functional Job Analysis." In S. Gael, ed., *The Job Analysis Handbook for Business, Industry and Government*, vol. II. New York: John Wiley and Sons, 1019–35.

Fine, S.A., A.M. Holt, and M.F. Hutchinson. 1974. "Functional Job Analysis: How to Standardize Task Statements." *Methods for Manpower Analysis No. 9*. Kalamazoo, MI: The W.E. Upjohn Institute for Employment Research.

Fine, S.A., and W.W. Wiley. 1971. *An Introduction to Functional Job Analysis*. Washington, DC: Upjohn.

Flanagan, J.C. 1954. "The Critical Incident Technique." *Psychological Bulletin* 51: 327–58.

Fleishman, E.A. 1992. *The Fleishman Job Analysis System*. Palo Alto, CA: Consulting Psychologists Press.

Fleishman, E.A., and M.D. Mumford. 1988. "Ability Requirement Scales." In S. Gael, ed., *The Job Analysis Handbook for Business, Industry and Government*, vol. I. New York: John Wiley and Sons, 917–35.

Fleishman, E.A., and M.K. Quaintance. 1984. *Taxonomies of Human Performance: The Description of Human Tasks*. Orlando, FL: Academic Press.

Gael, S. 1983. *Job Analysis: A Guide to Assessing Work Activities*. San Francisco, CA: Jossey-Bass Limited.

———. 1988. "Interviews, Questionnaires, and Checklists." In S. Gael, ed., *The Job Analysis Handbook for Business, Industry and Government*, vol. I. New York: John Wiley and Sons, 391–418.

Gatewood, R.D., and H.S. Feild. 1998. *Human Resources Selection*. Orlando, FL: Harcourt Brace and Co.

Ghorpade, J.V. 1988. *Job Analysis: A Handbook for the Human Resource Director*. Englewood Cliffs, NJ: Prentice Hall.

Gilbert, T.F. 1978. *Human Competence: Engineering Worthy Performance*. New York: McGraw-Hill.

GM of Canada. 2000. *GM of Canada Operations*. [Online]. Available: http://www.gmcanada. com/ english/about/hist_can_op.html.

Haber, S. 1964. *Efficiency and Uplift: Scientific Management in the Progressive Era, 1890–1920*. Chicago: The University of Chicago Press.

Hammer, M., and J. Champy. 1993. *Reengineering the Corporation*. New York: HarperBusiness.

Harvey, R.J. 1993. *Research Monograph: The Development of the CMQ*. Monograph describing the development and field-testing of the Common Metric Questionnaire (CMQ). [Online]. Available: http://harvey.psyc.vt.edu/ja_reports. htm.

Harvey, R.J. 1991. "Job Analysis." In M.D. Dunnette and L.M. Hough, eds., *Handbook of Industrial and Organizational Psychology*, vol. I. Palo Alto, CA: Consulting Psychologists Press, Inc., 71–163.

Harvey, R. J., and S.R. Lozada-Larsen. 1988. "Influence of Amount of Job Descriptive Information on Job Analysis Rating Accuracy." *Journal of Applied Psychology* 73: 457–61.

HR-Guide.Com. 2000. *Classification Systems Used as Basis for or Resulting from Job Analyses*. [Online]. Available: http://www.hr-guide.com/data/ G012.htm.

Human Resources Development Canada. 1996. *An Act Respecting Employment Equity*. [Online]. Available: http://info.load-otea.hrdc-drhc.gc.ca/~weeweb/billc64e.htm.

Human Resources Development Canada. 2000. *National Occupational Classification*. [Online]. Available: http://www.worklogic.com:81/noc/ home.html.

Katz, D., and R.L. Kahn. 1978. *The Social Psychology of Organizations*. New York: Wiley.

Kichuk, S.L., and W.H. Weisner. 1998. "Work Teams: Selecting Members for Optimal Performance." *Canadian Psychology* 39: 23–32.

Kiechel, W., III. 1993. "How We Will Work in the Year 2000." *Fortune* (May 17): 38–52.

Labich, K. 1996. "How to Fire People and Still Sleep at Night." *Fortune* 133(11): 65–72.

Latham, G.P., and C. Sue-Chan. 1998. "Selecting Employees in the 21st Century: Predicting the Contribution of I-O Psychology to Canada." *Canadian Psychology* 39: 14–22.

Levine, E.L. 1983. *Everything You Always Wanted to Know About Job Analysis*. Tampa, FL: Mariner Publishing Company, Inc.

Levine, E.L., R.A. Ash, and N. Bennett. 1980. "Exploratory Comparative Study of Four Job Analysis Methods." *Journal of Applied Psychology* 65: 524–35.

Levine, E.L., R.A. Ash, H. Hall, and F. Sistrunk. 1983. "Evaluation of Job Analysis Methods by Experienced Job Analysts." *Academy of Management Journal* 26: 339–48.

Levine, E.L., J.N. Thomas, and F. Sistrunk. 1988. "Selecting a Job Analysis Approach." In S. Gael, ed., *The Job Analysis Handbook for Business, Industry and Government*, vol. I. New York: John Wiley and Sons, 339–52.

Longo, S.C. 1995. "After Reengineering —'Dejobbing'?" *CPA Journal* 65: 63.

Lopez, F.M. 1988. "Threshold Traits Analysis System." In S. Gael, ed., *The Job Analysis Handbook for Business, Industry and Government*, vol. I. New York: John Wiley and Sons, 880–901.

Martinko, M.J. 1988. "Observing the Work." In S. Gael, ed., *The Job Analysis Handbook for Business, Industry and Government*, vol. I. New York: John Wiley and Sons, 419–31.

May, K.E. 1996. "Work in the 21st Century: Implications for Job Analysis." *The Industrial Psychologist*. [Online]. Available: http://cmit. unomaha. edu/tip/TIPApr96/ may.htm.

McCormick, E.J. 1979. *Job Analysis: Methods and Applications*. New York: AMACOM.

McCormick, E.J., and P.R. Jeanneret. 1991. "Position Analysis Questionnaire (PAQ)." In S. Gael, ed., *The Job Analysis Handbook for Business, Industry and Government*, vol. II. New York: John Wiley and Sons, 825–42.

McCormick, E.J., P.R. Jeanneret, and R.C. Mecham. 1972. "A Study of Job Characteristics and Job Dimensions as Based on the Position Analysis Questionnaire (PAQ)." *Journal of Applied Psychology* 56: 347–67.

McCormick, E.J., P.R. Jeanneret, and R.C. Mecham. 1989. *Position Analysis Questionnaire*. Palo Alto, CA: Consulting Psychologists Press, Inc.

McCormick, E.J., R.C. Mecham, and P.R. Jeanneret. 1977. *Technical Manual for the Position Analysis Questionnaire (PAQ) (System II)*. Logan, UT: PAQ Services, Inc.

McPhail, S.M., P.R. Jeanneret, E.J. McCormick, and R.C. Mecham. 1991. *Position Analysis Questionnaire: Job Analysis Manual*. Rev. ed. Palo Alto, CA: Consulting Psychologists Press, Inc.

Mecham, R.C., E.J. McCormick, and P.R. Jeanneret. 1977. *Users Manual for the Position Analysis Questionnaire (PAQ) (System II)*. Logan, UT: PAQ Services, Inc.

Methot, L.L. and K. Phillips-Grant. 1998. "Technological Advances in the Canadian Workplace: An I-O Perspective." *Canadian Psychology* 39: 133–41.

Mullins, W.C., and W.W. Kimbrough. 1988. "Group Composition as a Determinant of Job Analysis Outcomes." *Journal of Applied Psychology* 73: 657–64.

National Academy of Sciences, Committee on Occupational Classification and Analysis. 1981. *Dictionary of Occupational Titles (DOT)*. Washington, DC: U.S. Department of Commerce.

Personnel Systems and Technologies Corporation. 2000. *Solve Strategic HR Problems with the Common-Metric System*. [Online]. Available: http://www.pstc.com/cmq/ index.html.

Primoff, E.S., and L.D. Eyde. 1988. "Job Element Analysis." In S. Gael, ed., *The Job Analysis Handbook for Business, Industry and Government*, vol. I. New York: John Wiley and Sons, 807–24.

Raymark, P.H., M.J. Schmit, and R.M. Guion. 1997. "Identifying Potentially Useful Personality Constructs For Employee Selection." *Personnel Psychology* 50: 723–36.

Redmon, W.K., and J.L. Agnew. 1991. "Organizational Behavior Analysis in the U.S.: A View from the Private Sector." In P.A. Lamal, ed., *Behavior Analysis of Societies and Cultural Practices*. Washington. DC: Hemisphere.

Redmon, W.K., and L.A. Wilk. 1991. "Organizational Behavior Analysis in the U.S.: Public Sector Organizations." In P. A. Lamal, ed., *Behavior Analysis of Societies and Cultural Practices*. Washington, DC: Hemisphere.

Rummler, G.A., and A.P. Brache. 1990. *Improving Performance: How to Manage* the White Space on the Organization *Chart*. San Francisco, CA: Jossey-Bass.

Schmitt, N., and S.A. Cohen. 1989. "Internal Analyses of Task Ratings by Job Incumbents." *Journal of Applied Psychology* 74: 96–104.

Scholtes, P.R. 1988. *The Team Handbook*. Madison, WI: Joiner Associates, Inc.

SHL Group. 1999. *Job Analysis Tools: WPS*. [Online]. Available: http://www.shlusa.com/products/WPS/wps.htm.

Sparks, C.P. 1988. "Legal Basis for Job Analysis." In S. Gael, ed., *The Job Analysis Handbook for Business, Industry and Government*, vol. I. New York: John Wiley and Sons, 37–47.

Statistics Canada. 2000. *Canada at a Glance: Labour Market*. [Online]. Available: http://www.statcan.ca/Documents/English/Faq/Glance/labour.htm.

Thompson, D.E., and T.A. Thompson. 1982. "Court Standards for Job Analysis in Test Validation." *Personnel Psychology* 35: 872–73.

Uniform Guidelines on Employee Selection Procedures. 1978. *Federal Register* 43: 38290–315.

Wanous, J.P. 1974. "A Causal-Correlational Analysis of the Job Satisfaction and Performance Relationship." *Journal of Applied Psychology* 59: 139–244.

Weber, M. 1947. *The Theory of Social and Economic Organization*. Trans. A.M. Henderson and T. Parsons. New York: Oxford University Press.

Wilk Braksick, L. 2000. *Unlock Behavior, Unleash Profits*. New York: McGraw-Hill.

Zemke, R.E., and J.W. Gunkler. 1982. "Organization-Wide Intervention." In L.W. Fredericksen, ed., *Handbook of Organizational Management*. New York: Wiley.

5

THE ROLE OF COMPETENCIES AND JOB PERFORMANCE IN SELECTING EMPLOYEES

CHAPTER GOALS

This chapter explores recent developments in competency-based human resources systems as an alternative to the traditional job analyses discussed in Chapter 4. It provides an introduction to job-related performance as an integral part of the recruitment and selection process. It links job performance not only to individual competencies but also to organization goals and values.

After reading this chapter you should

- understand what competencies are;
- understand the role competencies play in recruitment and selection;
- be able to distinguish competency-based human resources models from those based on job analysis;
- know how to identify competencies;
- be able to distinguish core competencies from specific and unique competencies;

- understand the need to validate competency-based systems;
- appreciate the important role played by job performance in selection and assessment; and
- know how organizational goals influence both individual and group performance.

THE ROLE OF COMPETENCIES IN RECRUITMENT AND SELECTION

Today's workplace is in the midst of unprecedented change as it struggles to adapt to increasing global competition, rapid advances in information technology, and changing workforce demographics. Emerging from this turbulence are worker requirements unlike any we have seen in the past. With much of the routine aspects of work now done by machines, jobs have been re-defined, with a greater emphasis given to the management of technology. In this post-industrial information era, workers are required to apply a wider range of skills to an ever-changing series of tasks. Individuals just entering the workforce will face at least three to four career changes in their lifetime. Workers will be expected to possess the skills and knowledge of two or three traditional employees (Greenbaum, 1996). On the factory floor, jobs change rapidly, and workers constantly rotate among positions, acquiring multiple and generic skills. Today's workplace poses special challenges when trying to match people to jobs.

Recruitment and selection are guided by the knowledge, skills, abilities, and other characteristics (KSAOs) considered important for the work to be performed. As we saw in Chapter 4, KSAOs are traditionally determined through

---

BOX 5.1 Competency-Based Professions

Competency-based approaches have been adopted not only by organizations but also by professional organizations. Competency models have been used to identify successful professional performance for
- dentists
- engineers
- management accountants
- managers
- nurses
- occupational therapists
- organizational development practitioners/consultants
- pediatricians
- physicians
- police officers
- psychologists
- speech therapists

Recently, the Canadian Council of Human Resources Associations developed a competency-based model for human resources specialists. Details on the competencies that human resources specialists are expected to possess are available at the CCHRA website http://chrpcanada.com.

a job analysis; but traditional methods of job analysis may no longer be adequate. Jobs may change before a job analysis has been completed. Today, many human resources specialists and corporations are emphasizing generic skills or competencies that may be required for success among many jobs rather than those specific to one job.

TRADITIONAL JOB ANALYSIS

Traditional job analysis gives detailed information about the tasks and activities performed in a specific job. The job descriptions and job specifications are written from the job analysis and are used to inform recruitment and selection activities. However, traditional job analysis captures the content of jobs as described at one point in time and may be inadequate for jobs that change frequently. The more frequently jobs change, the less value there is to taking a snapshot of the job, as it will soon have to be repeated. Furthermore, given the decreased specialization and shifting of shared work assignments typical of today's work, traditional methods of job analysis may not be appropriate (Morgan and Smith, 1996). That is, they are simply inconsistent with the new management practices of cross-training assignments, job and task rotation, self-managed teams, and increased responsibility at all organizational levels (May, 1996).

Organizations often create entirely new positions. For example, AFG Glass Industries Ltd. (Canada) needed to recruit and select for a newly created position of corporate communications adviser. No job description existed for this position, nor was there a similar position within the organization to turn to for information. The director of human resources and the chief executive officer, to whom the communications adviser would directly report, were asked to list the expected outcomes for the position and then to identify the specific behaviours necessary to achieve each outcome. Next, the personal characteristics considered relevant to performing the job were inferred from these behaviours. This information was incorporated into a job description listing the job specifications. This job description was cross-referenced to job descriptions of similarly titled positions within other organizations to ensure that important common activities had not been overlooked. Finally, the information obtained through this procedure was used in staffing the position.

EMERGING IMPORTANCE OF GENERIC SKILLS

In recent years there has been considerable concern over the mismatch between the skills sought by employers and the skills of students graduating from our high schools, colleges, and universities. The Corporate Higher Education Forum, a nonprofit group of Canadian educators and business leaders, sponsored research into identifying the set of **generic skills** required to meet current and future job demands in the context of changing organizations. Employers identified the following 18 skills as highly desirable in new graduates:

Generic skills—individual skills that are not related to specific jobs but that are believed to be prerequisites for effective performance in any job.

- problem solving
- decision making
- planning/organizing
- time management
- risk taking
- oral communication
- written communication
- listening
- interpersonal skills
- managing conflict
- leadership/influence
- coordinating
- creativity/innovation
- visioning
- ability to conceptualize
- learning
- personal strengths
- technical skills

These 18 skills represent the skill areas widely perceived to be prerequisites for effective job performance across industry, function, and level. Statistical techniques were used to group these 18 skills into four primary groupings, or "competencies" (Evers and Rush, 1996):

1. *Mobilizing innovation and change:* conceptualizing as well as setting in motion ways of initiating and managing change that involve significant departures from the current mode.

2. *Managing people and tasks:* accomplishing the tasks at hand by planning, organizing, coordinating, and controlling both resources and people.

3. *Communicating:* interacting effectively with a variety of individuals and groups to facilitate the gathering, integrating, and conveying of information in many forms (e.g., verbal, written).

4. *Managing self:* constantly developing practices and internalizing routines for maximizing one's ability to deal with the uncertainty of an ever-changing environment.

These types of generic skills may be important regardless of level, function, or type of organization. Many of these same generic skills, which have also been labelled "core proficiencies" or "core competencies," are required for entry-level positions. These include the ability to use resources such as time and money effectively (self-management), good interpersonal skills, the ability to work well in teams, the ability to work well with culturally diverse individuals (managing others), and the ability to use technological systems (Camara, 1994; Offerman and Gowling, 1993). Clearly, individual assessments for positions at all levels and functions in an organization may need to include an array of generic skills or competencies. Increasingly, human resources specialists across North America are using competencies as the basis of their recruitment, selection, and performance appraisal systems.

COMPETENCY-BASED RECRUITMENT AND SELECTION

The New York City–based Colgate-Palmolive Company has operations in nearly 200 countries throughout the world, including Canada. It recruits and hires people from around the world. Its workforce consists of people from different cultures and different backgrounds. In order to remain a successful and competitive global enterprise, Colgate must be capable of sustaining organizational excellence. Colgate has chosen to do this through its selection process, which is based on identifying and communicating Colgate's values, vision, and strategic goals. Colgate accomplished this by setting up *competency-development teams*, which identified the skills and experiences that were required for each job level within each function. For example, a team composed of financial officers from various Colgate operations identified the skills and experiences needed to perform successfully as an associate accountant, senior accountant, or supervisor of accounting. These skills and experiences, or competencies, are then used to select people, identify their training needs, and assess their performance (Anfuso, 1995). In effect, Colgate integrates its strategic goals with individual performance through the recruitment and selection process. It seeks to hire people who have the competencies needed to perform at a successful level to maintain Colgate's organizational excellence.

When Colgate or other companies go to the marketplace to recruit and hire, they know what they are looking for in terms of competencies as well as what they expect in the way of performance from the people they hire. Job applicants may only have a vague, general idea about the job for which they've applied and the competencies that it requires. This idea may be shaped by a job description in a want ad, word of mouth, or by an expectation associated with a job title (e.g., senior accountant). As part of the recruitment and hiring process, applicants want to learn more specific information about their prospective job. They want to know the set of duties, behaviours, or tasks that they will be asked to perform if they are hired, and they want to know what competencies they must have to perform those duties. They also want to know the performance level that will be needed to maintain organizational excellence and how that performance will be measured. Employers must be able to answer these questions if they are to compete successfully in the labour market and to recruit and select the most appropriate job candidates.

Colgate's goal is to hire top-performing employees who will maintain organizational excellence. Before Colgate's competency-development teams could identify the skills and experiences, they had to know the behaviours performed in different jobs. Based on their knowledge gained through experience in the job, and assisted by human resources professionals, the members of the competency-development teams defined a set of behaviours and established the level of performance required for organizational excellence. Once the behaviours were established, the knowledge, skills, abilities, and other characteristics or experiences (KSAOs) related to those behaviours could be identified. This is the same situation as presented in Chapter 3 where a human resources manager links cognitive ability to higher levels of job performance (see Figure 3.2, Line A, p. 98). The competency-development team (subject-matter experts) is actually carrying out a job analysis based on organizational goals.

What Is a "Competency"?

Definitions of "competency" tend to reflect either individual or specific organizational concerns. While various definitions of competency may differ, they generally contain three elements. First, most suggest that competencies are the KSAOs that underlie effective or successful job performance; second, the KSAOs must be observable or measurable; and third, the KSAOs must distinguish among superior and other performers. Competencies, then, are measurable attributes that distinguish outstanding performers from others in a defined job context.

Competencies—may be thought of as groups of related behaviours that are needed for successful job performance in an organization.

Competencies have also been defined as groups of related behaviours, rather than the KSAOs, that are needed for successful job performance in an organization. Similarly, they have been defined as the behaviours that superior performers in an organization exhibit more consistently than others do. The competencies are then used to identify the KSAOs that distinguish superior performers from others. There are no practical differences between these two definitions of competency. Each requires the identification of KSAOs from behaviours displayed by superior performers. In one definition, the KSAOs are labelled "competencies" and in the other the term is applied to the behaviours. In both cases, we are concerned with identifying and measuring the KSAOs that underlie the successful performance.

Competency-Based Human Resources Models

The selection procedures outlined in Chapter 4 are organized around jobs. Human resources specialists use the information obtained through these traditional job analytic techniques to identify a set of job tasks from which they make inferences about the KSAOs needed to perform those job-related tasks. Competency-based selection systems, such as the one used by Colgate-Palmolive, take the view that employees must be capable of moving between jobs and carrying out the associated tasks for different positions (Reitsma, 1993). In the competency-based approach, the human resources specialist attempts to identify those KSAOs that distinguish superior performers from others, regardless of the specific job, and that will allow an organization to achieve its strategic goals. By selecting people who possess KSAOs that lead to superior performance, organizations are attempting to establish a closer connection between organizational success and individual performance.

Identifying Competencies

There are several procedures for identifying competencies. These methods generally start with the identification of target groups of workers. The groups must include both high and low performers for each job included in the group. The HR specialist observes the workers doing their jobs and interviews both the workers and/or their supervisors to obtain as much information as possible on how the workers actually perform their jobs. The HR specialist reviews all of the data to identify patterns of behaviour that separate superior from average performers. Finally, the HR specialist, assisted by subject-matter experts, identifies those competencies and related KSAOs that are linked to superior performance.

This general procedure is shown in Figure 5.1. The starting point is the organizational context, as defined through its mission, vision, and values statements, which suggest expectations for a specific position, for example, a senior manager. An organization whose mission is to produce for its customers quality goods on time every time while making a profit might expect senior

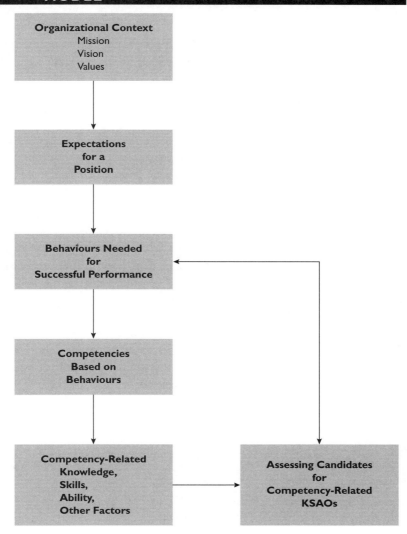

FIGURE 5.1 COMPETENCY-BASED HUMAN RESOURCES MODEL

managers to implement a specific managerial philosophy and to identify and develop managerial talent, among other things. These expectations might require the senior manager to undertake specific behaviours such as communicating the new philosophy to subordinates and monitoring their performance. Based on these and other essential behaviours, the HR specialist and subject-matter experts might identify communication and management as two competencies that are important to accomplishing the company's goals. Communication might require the senior manager to have excellent written and oral communication skills as well as an ability to listen to others. The management competency might involve knowing how to build work teams and how to monitor performance. Once the critical KSAOs have been identified, the selection system assesses whether any applicants for the position possess the required characteristics. The final component in the system is maintaining an ongoing evaluation to ensure that the KSAOs are predicting effective job behaviours.

BOX 5.2 The Job Competence Assessment Method

McBer and Company, now a part of the Hay Group, uses the job competence assessment method (JCAM) to identify competencies (Dubois, 1993). The method consists of three basic steps:

1. Convene a group of subject-matter experts (SMEs) to:
   - identify the major job components or tasks that must be performed to produce desired outputs;
   - develop a comprehensive list of knowledge, skills (technical and nontechnical), and thought patterns related to both average and superior performance of the major job components;
   - identify behavioural indicators for each of the KSAOs, which job incumbents then rate for importance to superior job performance; and
   - identify superior and average performers based on the KSAOs.

2. Use critical behaviour interviews to investigate the attributes of both the superior and average performers:
   - Job incumbents, whose level of performance is unknown to the interviewer, describe work situations in which they were effective and ineffective.

   - The interviews are taped and later coded and analyzed with the aid of a list of characteristics produced in the first stage.
   - The analysis produces two sets of competencies: (1) minimum competencies that apply to both average and superior performers, and (2) major competencies that apply only to superior performers.

3. The final stage validates the competency model. There are three possible validation methods:
   - Replicate the original research results with another sample of average and superior performers. This new model is then compared with the original one that was based on the superior performers.
   - Use research procedures that are different from those used in the original study to identify the competencies.
   - Have independent SMEs, or "jurors" who hold expert knowledge, present their best professional opinion on the original model. These jurors must include both internal and external experts.

Some organizations use a slightly different approach than the one outlined in Figure 5.1. Rather than identify the behaviours that are related to successful performance, they begin by identifying the competencies. The HR specialist and subject-matter experts specify those competencies they believe are related to organizational excellence and then determine the KSAOs that job applicants must have. This is the approach British Petroleum uses to select employees for its global workforce (Moravec and Tucker, 1992). This approach often makes use of a competency dictionary as a means of identifying the relevant competencies.

Competency dictionaries (e.g., Slivinski et al., 1996) are generic lists of standardized competencies that have been developed over time across many occupations. They are generic in the sense that they have not been tailored to any particular company or position. The dictionary presents a narrative description of a broad competency category followed by several related indicators. Box 5.3 presents typical definitions for the communication and management competencies.

Competency dictionaries—generic lists of standardized competencies that have been developed over time and across many occupations.

Competencies generally included in these dictionaries are

- Achievement
- Business orientation

BOX 5.3 Examples of Standard Competencies

COMMUNICATION COMPETENCY
- Communicating orally
- Communicating in writing
- Listening to others
- Selling the message

Communication involves communicating ideas and information orally and/or in writing in a way that ensures the messages are easily understood by others; listening to and understanding the comments and questions of others; marketing key points effectively to a target audience; and speaking and writing in a logical, well-ordered way.

MANAGEMENT COMPETENCY
- Results oriented
- Supportive
- Team building
- Recruiting and developing talent
- Coaching/mentoring

- Monitoring performance
- Providing feedback
- Valuing diversity

Management involves orienting a team toward high productivity; communicating performance expectations; keeping team members focused on goals; keeping people motivated through help and encouragement; facilitating the implementation of change; creating a positive climate for a well-functioning and effective work group; developing others through personal attention and effort; empowering team members to contribute to decision making and to make decisions on their own; delegating responsibility to team members; recruiting and assigning team members for optimum effectiveness; providing performance feedback to facilitate team member performance; enhancing the development of team members who show the potential for advancement in the organization; and facilitating and capitalizing on workplace diversity.

- Client/customer service orientation
- Communication
- Interpersonal relations
- Leadership
- Learning
- Management
- Organizing
- Problem solving
- Self-management
- Technical/operational

The HR specialist and the subject-matter experts review the generic competencies and identify those they believe are relevant to the organization. This shortcut procedure saves time and money but may not be as valid as following the procedure laid out in Figure 5.1. Simply selecting competencies from a generic competency dictionary may fail to capture those that are not in the dictionary but are critical for successful job performance.

COMPETENCY CATEGORIES

Core competencies are those characteristics that apply to every member of the organization regardless of their position, function, or level of responsibility within the organization. Core competencies hold for every position in the organization. Core competencies support the organization's mission. Core competencies are what an organization or individual does or should do best; they are key strengths that organizations and individuals posses and demonstrate (Lahti, 1999). The Royal Canadian Mounted Police (RCMP) identified eight core competencies that every member, from the commissioner to the newest recruit, is expected to exhibit in the performance of his or her duties. The RCMP core competencies are leadership; thinking skills; organization and planning; service orientation and delivery; personal effectiveness and flexibility; motivation; interpersonal relations; and communication.

Role or specific competencies are characteristics shared by different positions within an organization. Any position may require the person in that position to play a number of roles. Each role may require the job incumbent to demonstrate different competencies. A vice-president at the Widget Corporation may take on the role of financial adviser to the president. This role might require competency in business orientation, which includes understanding and applying financial data in ways that further the goals of the organization. Business orientation, however, may not be required from all employees in the organization, only those taking on the role of financial adviser.

Unique or distinctive competencies are characteristics that apply only to specific positions within the organization. These are competencies that are

Core competencies—characteristics that every member of an organization, regardless of position, function, or level of responsibility within the organization, is expected to possess.

Role or specific competencies—characteristics shared by different positions within an organization. Only those members of an organization in these positions are expected to possess these competencies.

Unique or distinctive competencies—characteristics that apply only to specific positions within the organization. Only those people in the position are expected to possess these competencies.

associated with a position in addition to core and role competencies. For example, two vice-presidents at Widget Corporation have to demonstrate the core competency of leadership and the role competency of business orientation, but only the vice-president in charge of media relations must have competency in communications. This last competency is unique to only one of the two positions.

LEVELS OF PROFICIENCY

Although all individuals in an organization are expected to exhibit all of the core competencies, they are not expected to do so to the same degree. Individuals may possess different levels of core, role, and unique competencies. Each competency may require a different level of proficiency depending on the organizational level of the individual (Trainor, 1997). As employees take on more responsibility in an organization, they may be required to become more proficient with respect to any competency if they are to perform effectively. Table 5.1 presents examples of some behavioural indicators for communication that might occur at different levels in an organization. As can be seen, the level of proficiency increases with organizational level. A corporate vice-president would be expected to have a greater proficiency in communication than a sales representative. Those at the higher levels are expected to be capable of expressing the behavioural demands at one level before moving on to a higher-ranking position. An organization, such as Colgate-Palmolive, identifies the behavioural indicators associated with competencies at each

TABLE 5.1 PROFICIENCY IN COMMUNICATION AT DIFFERENT ORGANIZATIONAL LEVELS	
ORGANIZATIONAL LEVEL	**BEHAVIOURAL INDICATORS**
Sales Representative	• Writes and speaks using clear and meaningful language • Comprehends written and verbal instructions
Immediate Supervisor	• Delivers information in a timely manner to ensure that others have the needed facts • Communicates effectively with other work units
General Manager	• Structures communication to meet the needs of the audience • Presents complex information in a clear, concise, and credible manner
Corporate Vice-President	• Represents the organization with tact and diplomacy both internally and externally • Articulates and promotes the interests of the organization

organizational level and uses these for evaluation and training purposes (Anfuso, 1995).

COMPETENCY-BASED SELECTION SYSTEMS

Six or seven competencies generally account for most differences between average and superior job performance within a specific position. These key competencies form a "template" for use in recruiting and selection (Mitrani, Dalziel, and Fitts, 1992). Before any "templates" can be used, the organization must answer an important question: What level of competency should be expected among the job applicants? Keep in mind that the information on the competencies has been obtained from experienced workers. Few, if any, new recruits may be able to demonstrate behaviours that are derived from superior, experienced personnel.

Spencer and Spencer (1993) proposed that organizations identify *threshold* and *differentiating* competencies. **Threshold competencies** are those essential characteristics that all job incumbents must have in order to perform the job at a minimal level of proficiency. **Differentiating competencies** distinguish superior from average performers. This suggests a recruitment and selection strategy of looking for those applicants with the highest levels of the competency and not hiring anyone who does not posses the competency at a threshold level. We will return to this issue later in our discussion of decision-making strategies for selection.

An increasing number of Canadian organizations have realized the economic benefits that result when they select employees who have the competencies or characteristics that predict excellent or superior performance of goal-related job behaviours. The Ontario Lottery Corporation, the Ontario Ministry of the Solicitor General and Correctional Services, Goodyear Canada, Guardian Insurance Company of Canada, the Royal Canadian Mounted Police, and University Hospitals of Alberta have all implemented core competency strategies that link performance measurement with recruiting and staffing processes. Developing measurable processes is crucial to the success of the recruitment and selection function. At some point, a human resources manager must determine whether a job applicant possesses the required competencies; at another point, the human resources manager must measure job performance associated with the competencies to ensure the validity of the competency-based hiring strategy.

VALIDATING COMPETENCY-BASED SELECTION SYSTEMS

A substantial number of professional and business articles have been written on competency-based models; however, most of these articles offer only theoretical or anecdotal descriptions of competencies. These articles are short on details describing the process used to establish the competencies or how they

Threshold competencies—essential characteristics that all job incumbents must have in order to perform the job at a minimal level of proficiency.

Differentiating competencies—those characteristics that can be used to distinguish superior from average performers.

were assessed as part of a selection process. Rarely do any of these articles present data showing the impact of competency-based selection on job or organizational performance. Research is needed to compare the bottom-line effectiveness of traditional selection systems based on job analysis with that of competency-based systems. There is a need to validate competency–job performance relationships and not to accept their validity and superiority without benefit of research. Klein (1996) called for empirical research on the reliability and validity of competency-based systems to avoid litigation. This is well-founded advice, particularly in view of the legal requirements that apply to selection, as outlined in Chapter 2.

To validate a competency-based selection system, the human resources manager must measure the level of competencies possessed by any job applicant. Chapters 8, 9, and 10 examine the different techniques that have been developed over the years to make these assessments, both those that are routinely used (résumés, interviews) and those that are less familiar (employment tests). Often overlooked by human resources managers is the need to measure performance as well. As the Canadian companies noted earlier recognize, performance measurement is an integral part of the recruiting and selection system. Chapter 8 provides a model showing this integration. Before proceeding further with this chapter, you may want to skip ahead to Chapter 8 and review Figure 8.3, which presents this integrated model. In the remainder of this chapter, we will review the role played by job performance in recruitment and selection.

JOB PERFORMANCE

In Chapter 2, we saw the need to establish performance standards as bona fide occupational requirements in order for a selection system to meet legal requirements. In Chapter 3, we said that both the construct of job performance and measures of job performance played essential roles in validating selection systems. In Chapter 4, we discussed ways of identifying critical tasks and behaviours that comprised job performance in any given job, as well as the KSAOs that were related to performance of those tasks and behaviours. In the first part of this chapter, we saw that the identification of different levels of performance was integral to identifying competencies and validating competency-based selection systems. But just what is "job performance," and what part of job performance should we measure?

Today's organizations and companies take job performance and its measurement seriously. They use it as a way to emphasize and reinforce their core competencies and to identify top-performing employees. Performance measurement is used to transform companies into results-oriented organizations. It provides a means of identifying employees who need improvement and development ("Best Practices," 2000). Measuring performance is easier said

Job performance—behaviour, the observable things people do, that is relevant to accomplishing the goals of an organization.

Criteria—measures of job performance that attempt to capture individual differences among employees with respect to job-related behaviours.

than done. The organization, or its human resources manager, must decide what performance to measure and the level of performance needed to attain organizational excellence. **Job performance** is behaviour, the observable things people do, that is relevant to accomplishing the goals of an organization. As we've seen in the last chapter on job analysis, rarely if ever do jobs involve the performance of only one specific behaviour. Also, individuals may perform at different levels of proficiency across job-related tasks or competencies. Measures of job performance that attempt to capture these differences are called **criteria** (Austin and Villanova, 1992). They are the performance standards for judging success or failure on the job.

Choosing a criterion or performance measure may be rather complex. Suppose you are the human resources specialist in charge of selecting petroleum engineers for British Petroleum. You are responsible for recruiting and selecting men and women who will perform successfully as engineers. Do you recruit and select people on the basis of their job-related technical skills, or do you also consider competencies such as leadership, business awareness, planning and organizational ability, communication and interpersonal skills, initiative, and problem-solving ability? British Petroleum identified all of these competencies, through job and organizational analysis, as related to success. What, then, constitutes successful performance by a petroleum engineer? What if someone is judged to be a success as a leader but a failure in the technical aspects of engineering, or vice versa? Are any of these competencies more important than others? Should we combine performance across all competencies or always consider each competency separately? These are some of the criterion-related issues that must be addressed when an organization develops an integrated selection and recruitment system. How these questions are answered establishes not only how we define and measure job-related performance but also who the organization will recruit and hire.

BOX 5.4 Linking Competencies and Job Performance to Selection

- Core competencies are instrumental in achieving success for all members of the organization. Role or unique competencies are relevant to success in a particular job family, role, or process.
- Competencies must be defined in terms of observable behaviours.
- Job performance is behaviour related to achieving an organization's goals.
- Both competencies and job performance must be capable of being measured.

- Competencies used in recruitment and selection must be related to successful job performance; that is, the competencies used to select employees must be valid predictors of job performance.
- In measuring or appraising employee performance, an organization must be committed to providing opportunities for the continuous improvement of employees to allow their progression to a higher level of proficiency.

THE CRITERION PROBLEM

The usefulness of selection measures is assessed by how well they predict performance. Typically, a supervisor's rating of the employee's performance is used for this purpose. Hard measures of performance, such as dollar sales, units produced, and absenteeism data, are less frequently available. Performance measures need to capture the contributions workers make as they move from one assignment to another, and from team to team. Frequently, they will have to come from multiple sources (e.g., peers, customers, supervisors). In validating selection measures, we will need to decide whether we wish to predict a few aspects of performance or some overall composite measure of performance. If the former, then we need to determine which aspects of performance contribute most to the success of the organization. If the latter, then we must find a method for combining the performance data that we obtain from different sources.

Most efforts directed at improving selection systems have focused on the measurement of job-related KSAOs or competencies. Until recently, relatively less thought has been given to improving the measurement of job performance. Most organizations rely on criterion-related validity studies to defend the appropriateness of their selection systems before human rights and other tribunals. No matter how accurately the organization measures KSAOs or competencies, the criterion-related validity will still be low without improvement in performance measurement. There remains a need to use valid criterion measures and to develop a better understanding of what constitutes job performance (Austin and Villanova, 1992). Fortunately, more companies and human resources managers are beginning to appreciate the linkage between selection and performance measurement ("Best Practices," 2000). Performance measures, however, are still too often chosen because the pressure of getting things done leads to choosing the most convenient measure at hand and hoping it will turn out all right.

The criterion problem is really one of defining what is meant by performance and choosing a measure or set of measures that best capture the essence of that complex job-related performance. Without a clear understanding of what constitutes job performance, the best measurement systems will never be able to effectively measure performance at work. We need first to define job performance before we can attempt to assess it (Sulsky and Keown, 1998).

Successful companies like Body Shop Canada and Coors Brewing recognize the important role that performance measurement plays in developing strategies for effective recruitment and selection. Rather than simply choosing a measure and hoping it works, the first step is to specify the job performance in terms of measurable behaviours; the next step is to find valid measures of those behaviours. The criterion or performance measure must be a valid indicator of job performance as determined by job and organizational analysis. There is an important difference in contemporary approaches to establishing criteria. Companies such as Sun Microsystems not only are looking to hire people who have the competencies needed for successful job performance, they also link the required performance to organizational goals and values. Desired job-related behaviours and outcomes are those that secure organizational goals. Increasingly, companies are looking for a fit between the person and the organization; this search for a person–organization fit often drives the company's recruitment process. (We will discuss the person–organizational fit in more detail in Chapter 7.)

ORGANIZATIONAL GOALS: LINKING INDIVIDUAL PERFORMANCE AND AGGREGATE PRODUCTIVITY

Individuals affect productivity through behaviours that directly contribute to the organization's goals. In the case of British Petroleum, technical skills, leadership qualities, business awareness, planning and organizational ability, communication and interpersonal skills, initiative, and problem-solving ability were linked to organizational effectiveness. These competencies also specify performance dimensions. Competencies and **performance dimensions** are similar in that both are identified through job or organizational analysis and bring together a set of KSAOs that are required for successful job performance within an organization (Lahti, 1999). In fact, some researchers and practitioners define competencies as performance dimensions or clusters of behaviours related to work performance that are reasonably stable over time (Klein, 1996, Thornton, 1992).

Performance dimensions—sets of related behaviours that are derived from an organization's goals and linked to successful job performance.

Performance factors or dimensions are related to achieving an organization's goals. Differences between workers at British Petroleum on any or all of these performance dimensions will result in different levels of individual productivity. Recruiting and selecting workers who excel on these job dimensions leads to organizational productivity at British Petroleum. Organizational productivity is influenced to a considerable degree by such factors as organizational culture and climate; management practices including performance evaluation and reward schemes; individual attitudes and values; and consensus about organizational goals that may exist between the individual and the supervisor and the supervisor and the manager. The level of organizational productivity may depend on the degree to which employees, supervisors, and managers share the same attitudes, values, and goals (Vancouver and Schmitt, 1991). Obviously, the differences across organizations, reflected in their goals and values, will lead to different levels of organizational productivity.

ORGANIZATIONAL GOALS

The measurement of productivity is closely tied to the goals and values of the organization. Different subgroups or individuals within an organization may not share the same goals or values. For example, managers may view productivity increases as a means to their own advancement, while a worker may believe that increased productivity will only lead to demands for more productivity. Often, employees at all levels are unaware of the organization's goals. Organizational goals must be clearly stated and linked to specific individual performance. An organization should measure employee behaviour that is directed toward accomplishing its goals and not simply measure some aspect of employee behaviour because the behaviour is easy to measure. Once relevant goals have been defined, the next step is to define the set of behaviours that are necessary for reaching the goals. As we discussed in Chapter 4, organizational analysis provides the human resources specialist with a set of tools that can be used to assess the work environment in terms of the characteristics of the organization, while job analysis provides information about a specific job. Both must be used together to identify appropriate criteria for measuring job performance in a specific organizational environment.

IDENTIFYING APPROPRIATE CRITERIA: ORGANIZATIONAL GOALS AND VALUES

SPECIFYING THE JOB PERFORMANCE DOMAIN

As we've seen, British Petroleum identified seven specific competencies or performance dimensions that were essential to its organizational effectiveness. A different company with different goals (e.g., Ontario Lottery Corporation) would have different performance dimensions and different performance measurement systems or criteria. A multimillion-dollar project designed to develop an integrated selection, classification, and performance evaluation system for use with the U.S. Army (Project A) suggests that the job dimensions defined through different organizational goals may have a common underlying structure (Campbell, 1990).

Job performance is behaviour (i.e., the observable things people do) that is related to accomplishing the goals of an organization. Job behaviours can be grouped into job performance dimensions. The **job performance domain** is a name given to the set of those job performance dimensions—that is, behaviours that are relevant to the goals of the organization, or the unit, in which a person works. The goals pursued by an organization are value judgments on the part of those empowered to make them. Goals are defined for employees who hold specific positions within the organization. Individual performance must contribute to achieving the organizational goals. The activities or behaviours needed to accomplish goals may vary considerably from job to job, or across levels in organizations. It becomes a matter of *expert* judgment whether particular actions or behaviours are relevant for particular goals. Performance is *not* the consequence or result of action; it is the action itself (Campbell, 1990).

Job performance domain—the set of job performance dimensions (i.e., behaviours) that are relevant to the goals of the organization, or the unit, in which a person works.

This is the concept of the performance domain presented in Figure 3.2, p. 98. This concept is consistent with the competency-based human resources model presented in Figure 5.1, which directly links criteria performance (behaviours needed for successful job performance) to values and goals, and the competencies needed to maintain organizational effectiveness.

THE JOB PERFORMANCE DOMAIN

The need to define job performance is a necessary first step to its effective measurement. One of the most significant developments has been the attempt by John Campbell and his associates to specify a theory of work performance (Campbell, McCloy, Oppler, and Sager, 1993). The behaviours that people are expected to do as part of their job appear to fall into eight *job dimensions* or job components, which together specify the job performance domain. The relationship of these job dimensions to the competencies we discussed previously is quite apparent. These eight job dimensions, as identified by Campbell (1990), are as follows:

1. **Job-specific task proficiency** reflects the degree to which an individual can perform technical tasks that make up the content of the job. A petroleum engineer and an accountant must perform different behaviours as part of their specific jobs. Within jobs, individuals may vary in their level of competence. One engineer may be more technically proficient than another, just as one accountant may be more technically proficient than some other accountants.

2. **Nonjob-specific task proficiency** reflects the degree to which individuals can perform tasks or behaviours that are not specific to any one job. Both the engineer and accountant may have to have a good understanding of the business environment in which their company operates.

3. **Written and oral communication task proficiency** is the degree to which an individual can write or speak, independent of the correctness of the subject matter. Both the engineer and accountant make oral reports to people they deal with on the job; both also make written reports on the work they perform.

4. **Demonstrating effort** reflects the degree to which individuals are committed to performing all job tasks, to working at a high level of intensity, and to working under adverse conditions. How willing are the engineer or accountant to work overtime to complete a project? Do they begin their workdays earlier than expected? Can they be relied on to give the same level of effort day in and day out? Do they show initiative?

5. **Maintaining personal discipline** characterizes the extent to which negative behaviours are avoided. Does either the engineer or accountant drink on the job? Do they follow the appropriate laws, regulations, or codes that govern their professions? Do they show up for scheduled assignments?

6. **Facilitating peer and team performance** is the degree to which an individual supports co-workers, helps them with job problems, and keeps them working as a team to achieve their goals. Is the engineer or accountant available to give the others a helping hand? Does either offer new trainees the benefit of their experience? Do they keep their colleagues focused on completing the work team's goals?

7. **Supervision/leadership** includes behaviours that are directed at influencing the performance of subordinates through interpersonal means. Does either the engineer or accountant set goals and performance standards for people they direct? Do they use whatever influence is at their disposal, including authority to reward and punish, to shape the behaviour of subordinates?

8. **Management/administration** includes all other performance behaviours involved in management that are distinct from supervision. Do the engineer and accountant contact clients and arrange appointments? Do they schedule work in the most efficient manner? Do they complete all the paper work related to a project?

Job-specific task proficiency, demonstrating effort, and maintaining personal discipline are likely to be major performance components of every job (Campbell, 1990); however, not all eight dimensions have to be present in every job. Few, if any, management skills are required by an assembly line worker in an auto plant; on the other hand, the seven performance dimensions identified by British Petroleum fit nicely into this framework. The pattern of differences in these eight dimensions can be used to classify jobs and is consistent with the job classification schemes used by the U.S. *Dictionary of Occupational Titles*, the *Canadian Classification Dictionary of Occupations*, and the *National Occupational Classification* system (Internet: http://www.hrdc-drhc.gc.ca).

What determines individual differences on these eight job performance components? That is, why does one petroleum engineer perform more efficiently than another? Using data gathered as part of Project A, Campbell and his associates (McCloy, Campbell, and Cudeck, 1994) showed that these job dimensions are influenced by three factors: declarative knowledge, procedural knowledge and skill, and motivation. *Declarative knowledge* is knowledge about facts and things including knowledge of rules, regulations, and goals. *Procedural knowledge and skill* are attained when declarative knowledge, knowing what to do, is combined with knowing how to do it. One petroleum engineer knows all about drilling techniques but lacks the appropriate skills to perform successfully on an oil rig. Procedural knowledge and skill include cognitive, psychomotor, physical, perceptual, interpersonal, and self-management skills. *Motivation* is defined in terms of choice to perform, level of effort, and persistence of effort. Job performance is some combination of these three factors; performance cannot occur unless there is both a choice to perform at some level and at least a minimal amount of knowledge and skill.

Contextual Performance

Contextual
performance—the activities or behaviours that are not part of a worker's formal job description but that remain important for organizational effectiveness.

Campbell's job dimensions specify what people do as part of their jobs. Borman and Motowidlo (1993) make the point that work performance extends beyond performing tasks that are related to job dimensions. Employees are called on to perform activities that are not part of their formal job duties; they are, however, part of the context in which those job duties are performed. **Contextual performance** involves activities or behaviours that are not part of a worker's formal job description but that remain important for organizational effectiveness.

While job performance is closely related to underlying knowledge, skills, and abilities, contextual performance supports the organizational, social, and psychological environment in which the job is performed. Contextual activities are not related to a specific job or role but extend to all jobs in an organization. Contextual performance often reflects organizational values. For example, many Canadian companies actively support worthwhile causes as part of their desire to be good corporate citizens and may expect their employees to contribute time or money to these projects. The United Way campaign is one fundraising activity that enjoys strong corporate support. Volunteer fundraising activities on the part of employees are not related to specific jobs but may advance the goals of the organization.

Contextual performance appears to fall into five major categories (Borman and Motowidlo, 1993):

1. Persisting with enthusiasm and extra effort as necessary to complete one's own task activities successfully.
2. Volunteering to carry out task activities that are not formally part of one's own job.
3. Helping and cooperating with others.
4. Following organizational rules and procedures.
5. Endorsing, supporting, and defending organizational objectives.

Contextual performance is related to organizational citizenship behaviour (OCB). OCB is individual behaviour that is discretionary, that is not directly recognized by a formal reward system, and that, overall, promotes the effective functioning of the organization. The difference between these two concepts is that OCB is considered to be beyond the role requirements of a job and, thus, not rewarded. Contextual performance, on the other hand, is not required to perform specific job tasks, but it is behaviour, much like core competencies, that an organization wishes all of its employees to exhibit. Contextual performance is regarded as part of an employee's role in an organization and is often rewarded through pay increases or promotion (Organ, 1997).

In many ways, the contextual performance dimensions appear to be extensions of the eight job performance dimensions included in Campbell's model (Campbell, Gasser, and Oswald, 1996). For example, "persisting with enthusiasm and extra effort" appears to be related to "demonstrating effort"; volunteering to carry out tasks not part of one's job" and "helping and cooperating with others" to "facilitating peer and team performance"; "following organizational rules and procedures" to "maintaining personal discipline"; and "endorsing, supporting, and defending organizational objectives" to "supervision/leadership." The primary difference is that Campbell's job dimensions relate to specific jobs, while contextual performance relates to the broader organizational roles taken on by an employee without reference to specific job-related tasks.

Contextual performance activities may represent important criteria for jobs in many organizations because of their relationship to organizational effectiveness. Contextual performance dimensions may not all have the same degree of relevance or importance across organizations. Organizations are likely to emphasize those that are most compatible with their values and goals. Contextual performance is not a substitute for job performance; it represents *additional* factors that may be considered in developing personnel selection criteria. Contextual performance by itself does not get the job done; in evaluating staff, managers place more emphasis on task performance than on contextual performance (Conway, 1999).

An increasing number of North American companies such as Apple Computer, GE, Honeywell, and 3M assess how well employees fit the organization in addition to how well they can do the job (Bowen, Ledford, and Nathan, 1991). Organizational fit between an employee's organizational culture and the desired environment predicts an employee's contextual performance (Goodman and Svyantek, 1999).

The expansion of the job performance domain to include contextual performance has important implications for personnel selection. Contextual performance and task performance may have different sets of predictors. Contextual performance appears to be linked to different aspects of personality and motivation. When opportunities for advancement within an organization are limited, employees may perform contextual acts because they are conscientious; however, when there are opportunities for advancement, employees may engage in contextual acts because they are ambitious (Hogan, Rybicki, Motowidlo, and Borman, 1998). Personality improves the ability to predict contextual performance among sales and service representatives (McManus and Kelly, 1999). The increasing emphasis is on organizational citizenship behaviour and contextual performance as performance dimensions may require the addition of personality measures as part of the selection process. We will return to the use of personality in selection in Chapter 9. You may want to read that chapter now to gain a better understanding of some of the issues related to these types of measures.

SUMMARY

Organizations must compete in a global environment that is often unpredictable and unstable. Organizations have to change quickly in order to survive.

To meet these demands, organizations are placing more emphasis on the competencies of individual workers rather than on the specific tasks that those workers will perform. All employees are expected to possess core competencies that are related to the organization's mission or goals, as well as role or unique competencies, which are related to successful performance in a specific position or job. This emphasis on competencies has taken place in the absence of an agreed-upon definition of what constitutes a "competency" and of an agreed-upon methodology for identifying competencies. Competency–job performance relationships must be valid and must meet legal requirements, just as more traditional selection systems.

One key to validating selection systems, whether competency-based or the more traditional type, is to understand the nature of the job performance that is being predicted by the competencies or KSAOs. Job performance is also linked to an organization's mission, values, and goals. One useful approach to understanding job performance is to categorize jobs in terms of their requirements with respect to eight performance dimensions, and to understand how the context or environment in which the job is performed affects the performance of the job. Understanding the factors that underlie job performance is necessary to its measurement.

KEY TERMS

Competencies, p. 172

Competency dictionaries, p. 175

Contextual performance, p. 186

Core competencies, p. 176

Criteria, p. 180

Differentiating competencies, p. 178

Generic skills, p. 169

Job performance, p. 180

Job performance domain, p.183

Performance dimensions, p. 182

Role or specific competencies, p. 176

Threshold competencies, p. 178

Unique or distinctive competencies, p. 176

EXERCISES

[Note: These exercises can be carried out for any occupation, but teaching is used since it is an occupation with which student analysts will have some familiarity and that will allow these exercises to be completed in class. Another occupation can be used to serve as the basis for a field project.]

As consumers, students are concerned about the quality of instruction they receive in the classroom. Over time, colleges and universities have developed teaching evaluations to assess teaching performance. These forms ask rather specific questions—for example, "Does the instructor have mastery over the material?"—but often fail to address significant issues related to good teaching. For this exercise:

1. Use the model presented in Figure 5.1 to determine the competencies related to teaching. Your subject-matter experts should include both professors and students. Keep in mind that you are focusing on teaching only, and not other aspects of the performance domain for the job of professor or instructor such as research or counselling activities. Do this exercise in groups of five and compare the competencies identified by the different groups. Are the groups using different labels for the same set of behaviours?

2. As an alternative, you may start with the 12 competencies presented in the section on competency dictionaries (on pages 175–76). Develop a broader definition for each competency and then with the aid of subject-matter experts, shorten the list to those competencies you believe are related to teaching. Again, compare competencies identified by different groups. Are they the same?

3. Have half of the groups use the procedure outlined in Exercise 1 and the remaining groups use that in Exercise 2. Do both procedures lead to the same set of competencies? Did the competency dictionary produce more standardization of competencies across the groups using that procedure?

4. Rather than begin with a competency dictionary, start your procedure using the dimensions that make up Campbell's job performance domain. Identify those that are essential to effective teaching and proceed to derive the specific behaviours related to each dimension. Do the same with the contextual performance dimensions listed in this chapter.

5. Using the specific behaviours that you identified as part of establishing your competencies or job dimensions, specify the KSAOs that are critical to successful teaching performance.

CASE

Polaris Systems is an aerospace company that designs and manufactures subsystems for communications satellites. It grew from a very small start-up to a large company in a very short period of time. As a small company it had always had an entrepreneurial and risk-taking approach. Unit heads always did the hiring; in fact, it never had a human resources department as such. As the company expanded, it developed a very competitive culture. People were loyal to their unit and not to the company. Units began to fight among themselves and would do things like holding up supplies and inventory needed by another unit to do its work.

Polaris Systems had a good product and was able to survive on its strengths. It took over DogStar Computers and integrated DogStar's operations and employees into its own plant. Even more competition resulted. Eventually, Polaris Systems began to lose orders. It could not meet its delivery deadlines. Production fell as internal competition increased. Profits decreased and Polaris began having cash flow problems. It started laying off workers, and some of its most valuable talent began to leave. Polaris Systems' stock became undervalued and it was acquired by Centauri, Inc.

Centauri's mission was to deliver quality products, on time, every time, to satisfied customers. This philosophy drove its entire operation. When it took over Polaris, it recognized that there was a serious internal problem that was affecting productivity and profitability. It undertook a series of organizational development exercises to deal with the existing staff at Polaris. It also brought in its crack corporate human resources team to develop a strategy for restaffing the plant.

DISCUSSION QUESTIONS

1. Discuss the various factors affecting the loss of productivity at Polaris.

2. What additional information should the human resources team seek before developing its plan?

3. The HR team believes that because of the rapidly changing nature of the industry, a competency approach should be used in selecting new hires. Develop a plan for identifying the core competencies that should be used to select employees who will be most successful.

4. What are the core competencies that the HR team should use as part of the selection process? Identify the behaviours related to those competencies.

5. The HR team recognizes that it will have to validate its selection strategy. Using the information in Chapter 3, develop a validation plan to identify the appropriate criterion measures.

REFERENCES

Anfuso, D. 1995. "Colgate's Global HR Unites under One Strategy." *Personnel Administrator* 74: 44–52.

Austin, J.T. and P. Villanova. 1992. "The Criterion Problem: 1917–1992." *Journal of Applied Psychology* 77: 836–74.

"Best Practices in Performance Appraisals." 2000. *HR Focus* 2: 8.

Borman, W.C., and S.J. Motowidlo. 1993. "Expanding the Performance Domain to Include Elements of Contextual Performance." In N. Schmitt, W.C. Borman, and Associates, eds.,

Personnel Selection in Organizations. San Francisco, CA: Jossey-Bass, 71–98.

Bowen, D.E., G.E. Ledford Jr., and B.R. Nathan. 1991. "Hiring for the Organization, Not the Job." *Academy of Management Executive* 5: 35–51.

Camara, W.J. 1994. "Skill Standards, Assessment and Certification: One-Stop Shopping for Employers?" *The Industrial-Organizational Psychologist* 32 (1): 41–49.

Campbell, J.P. 1990. "Modelling the Performance Prediction Problem in Industrial and Organizational Psychology." In M.D. Dunnette and L.M. Hough, eds., *The Handbook of Industrial and Organizational Psychology*, vol. 1. 2nd ed. San Diego: Consulting Psychologists Press, 687–732.

Campbell, J.P., M.B. Gasser, and F.L. Oswald. 1996. "The Substantive of Job Performance Variability." In K.R. Murphy, ed., *Individual Differences and Behavior in Organizations*. San Francisco: Jossey-Bass, 258-299.

Campbell, J.P., R.A. McCloy, S.H. Oppler, and C.E. Sager. 1993. "A Theory of Performance." In N. Schmitt, W.C. Borman, and Associates, *Personnel Selection in Organizations*. San Francisco, CA: Jossey-Bass.

Conway, J.M. 1999. "Distinguishing Contextual Performance from Task Performance for Managerial Jobs." *Journal of Applied Psychology* 84: 3–13.

Dubois, D. 1993. *Competency-Based Performance: A Strategy for Organizational Change*. Boston, MA: HRD Press.

Evers, F.T., and J.C. Rush. 1996. "The Bases of Competence: Skill Development during the Transition from University to Work." *Management Learning* 27 (3): 275–99.

Goodman, S.A., and D.J. Svyantek. 1999. "Person–Organization Fit and Contextual Performance: Do Shared Values Matter?" *Journal of Vocational Behavior* 55: 254–75

Greenbaum, P.J. 1996. "Canada's Hiring Trends: Where Will Canadian Jobs Come from in the Next Millennium?" *HR Today* (July). Canadian Institute of Professional Management, Ottawa, Ontario.

Hogan, J., S.L. Rybicki, S.J. Motowidlo, and W.C. Borman. 1998. "Relations between Contextual Performance, Personality, and Occupational Advancement." *Human Performance* 11: 189–207.

Klein, A.L. 1996. "Validity and Reliability for Competency-Based Systems: Reducing Litigation Risks." *Compensation and Benefits Review* 28: 31–37.

Lahti, R.K. 1999. "Identifying and Integrating Individual Level and Organizational Level Core Competencies." *Journal of Business and Psychology* 14: 59–75.

May, K.E. 1996. "Work in the 21st Century: Implications for Job Analysis." *The Industrial Organizational Psychologist* 33 (4): 98–100.

McCloy, R.A., J.P. Campbell, and R. Cudeck. 1994. "Confirmatory Test of a Model of Performance Determinants. *Journal of Applied Psychology* 79: 493–505.

McManus, M.A., and M.L. Kelly. 1999. "Personality Measures and Biodata: Evidence Regarding their Incremental Predictive Value in the Life Insurance Industry." *Personnel Psychology* 52: 137–48

Mitrani, A., M. Dalziel, and D. Fitts. 1992. *Competency-Based Human Resource Management: Value-Driven*

Strategies for Recruitment, Development and Reward. London: Kogan Page Ltd.

Moravec, M., and R. Tucker. 1992. "Job Descriptions for the 21st Century." *Personnel Administrator* 71: 37–44.

Morgan, R.B., and J.E. Smith. 1996. *Staffing the New Workplace: Selecting and Promoting for Quality Improvement*. Milwaukee, WI: ASQC Quality Press.

Offerman, L.R., and M.K. Gowling. 1993. "Personnel Selection in the Future: The Impact of Changing Demographics and the Nature of Work." In N. Schmitt and W.C. Borman and Associates, *Personnel Selection in Organizations*. San Francisco: Jossey-Bass, 385–417.

Organ, D.W. 1997. "Organizational Citizenship Behavior: It's Construct Clean-up Time." *Human Performance* 10: 85–97.

Reitsma, S.J. 1993. *The Canadian Corporate Response to Globalization*. Report no. 10693. Ottawa: Conference Board of Canada.

Slivinski, L., E. Donoghue, M. Chadwick, F.A. Ducharme, D.W.

Gavin, A. Lorimer, R. McSheffrey, J. Miles, and G. Morry. 1996. *The Wholistic Competency Profile: A Model*. Ottawa: Staffing Policy and Program Development Directorate, Public Service Commission of Canada

Spencer, L.M., and S.M. Spencer. 1993. *Competence at Work*. New York: Wiley.

Sulsky, L.M., and J.L. Keown. 1998. "Performance Appraisal in the Changing World of Work: Implications for the Meaning and Measurement of Work Performance." *Canadian Psychology* 39: 52–59.

Thornton, G.C. 1992. *Assessment Centers in Human Resource Management*. Reading, MA: Addison-Wesley.

Trainor, N.L. 1997. "Five Levels of Competency." *Canadian HR Reporter* 10: 12–13.

Vancouver, J.B., and N.W. Schmitt. 1991. "An Exploratory Analysis of the Person–Organization Fit: Organizational Goal Congruence." *Personnel Psychology* 44: 333–52.

6

PERFORMANCE
MEASUREMENT:
THE ROLE OF CRITERIA
IN SELECTING EMPLOYEES

CHAPTER GOALS

This chapter provides the foundation for the measurement of job-related performance as an integral part of the recruitment and selection process. Measures of job performance are used as criteria in selecting new employees and as a means of evaluating current employees. The chapter discusses issues related to the measurement of job performance and the identification of criteria. It reviews several performance measurement and appraisal techniques.

After reading this chapter you should

- understand the importance of developing and using scientifically sound measures of job performance in selection and assessment;
- understand the relationship between individual performance measures, criteria, and performance dimensions related to a job;
- appreciate the technical aspects of measuring job performance;
- be familiar with the strengths and weaknesses of different types of performance rating systems; and

- understand the features that a performance appraisal system should have in place to satisfy human rights concerns.

CRITERION MEASUREMENT

In previous chapters we discussed the need to validate selection measures to establish that they are meeting legal requirements. We also need to establish validity to assure ourselves that the people we are hiring will be the "best" or most "productive." Improvements in selection procedures can lead to substantial increases in productivity. For example, in sales occupations replacement of invalid selection procedures with valid procedures produces an average increase in sales of $60 000 per employee for each year that employee stays on the job (Farrell and Hakstian, 2000). To evaluate the effectiveness of selection systems, we must find a way to measure those behaviours we identify as being important for job success. As we saw in Chapter 3, and as we shall see in Chapter 8, criterion measurement plays an essential part in recruitment and selection. Measuring performance is easier said than done; criterion measurement is a complex and technical process.

EFFECTIVE PERFORMANCE MEASURES

Once job and organization analyses have identified the major performance dimensions, the next step is to measure employee performance on those dimensions. How will we measure job task proficiency, supervision, or helping and cooperating with others? We can think of these job dimensions as labels that are constructed to describe different aspects of job performance. Before we can measure any job dimension, we have to define that dimension in terms of specific, measurable activities or behaviours. For example, supervision includes giving orders to subordinates, accomplishing organizational goals, and teaching employees the proper way to do a job, among many other things. One person may be better at "giving orders to subordinates" than "teaching subordinates"; our view on that person's supervisory performance will depend on which of these behaviours we include in our measure of supervisory performance. Smith (1976) established general guidelines to help identify effective and appropriate performance measures.

RELEVANCY *Relevancy* requires that a criterion measure be a valid measure of the performance dimension in question. Suppose we develop a measure of sales representatives' performance based on an overall rating assigned by a supervisor. This measure might be relevant to sales performance in that it captures behaviours related to service orientation, communication, and interpersonal relations. The measure may be deficient in not measuring competencies such as achievement, business orientation, self-discipline, and organizing, which may also be related to success in sales. Additionally, the measure may be influenced by problem solving, learning, and management, competencies that are not critical for success in this particular job. As a criterion measure, a supervisor's rating may be contaminated in that it is measuring things other than the sales representative's performance. **Criterion relevance** is the degree to which the criterion measure captures behaviours or competencies that constitute job performance. **Criterion deficiency** refers to those job performance behaviours or competencies that are not measured by the criterion. **Criterion contamination** is the degree to which the criterion measure is influenced by, or measures, behaviours or competencies that are not part of job performance. These three aspects of criterion measurement are illustrated in Table 6.1.

RELIABILITY   *Reliability* involves agreement between different evaluations, at different periods of time, and with different, although apparently similar, measures; that is, the criterion measure must meet scientific and professional standards of reliability. Reliability is the degree to which observed scores are free from random measurement errors (i.e., the dependability or stability of the measure). Criterion or performance measures are subject to the same errors as any other kind of measurement. There is no such thing as error-free criterion measurement; some criteria, however, are more reliable than others. Reliable criterion measures will tend to produce similar scores when the same behaviour is measured on more than one occasion. The reliability of any criterion measure must be established, as part of its use in a personnel selection system, through the procedures discussed in Chapter 3.

Criterion relevance—the degree to which the criterion measure captures behaviours or competencies that constitute job performance.

Criterion deficiency—refers to those job performance behaviours or competencies that are not measured by the criterion.

Criterion contamination—the degree to which the criterion measure is influenced by, or measures, behaviours or competencies that are not part of job performance.

TABLE 6.1	ILLUSTRATION OF CRITERION RELEVANCY FOR PERFORMANCE IN A SALES REPRESENTATIVE POSITION
Unmeasured Competencies — Relevant to Sales Performance	CRITERION DEFICIENCY Achievement Business Orientation Self-Management Organizing
Measured Competencies — Relevant to Sales Performance	CRITERION RELEVANCE Service Orientation Communication Interpersonal Relations
Measured Competencies — Not Relevant to Sales Performance	CRITERION CONTAMINATION Problem Solving Learning Management

Practicality—the degree to which a criterion measure is available, plausible, and acceptable to organizational decision makers.

PRACTICALITY Practicality means that the criterion measure must be available, plausible, and acceptable to organizational decision makers. The supervisor's rating of the sales representative's performance must mean something to those responsible for evaluating the sales representative. It must also be a number that can be readily obtained from the supervisor with little cost in time or money. It should also be a plausible indicator of individual performance. That is, the criterion measure must have meaning and credibility for those who will use the measurements in making decisions. There is a danger of being seduced by practicality and choosing criteria that, while readily available, do not meet standards of validity and reliability. These two requirements cannot be traded off in favour of practicality.

DEVELOPING CRITERION MEASURES

Several issues must be considered as part of the process of developing a criterion or a set of criterion measures. The resolution of these issues influences which measures are selected as criteria and when measurements are made.

MULTIPLE, GLOBAL, OR COMPOSITE CRITERIA

THE ULTIMATE CRITERION The first issue is one that has generated a great deal of controversy over the years; namely, how many criteria should be measured? In large part this controversy arises through misunderstanding of the job performance domain. At one time, criterion research was dominated by a concern to find the ultimate criterion for a given job. The **ultimate criterion** is the concept of a single criterion measure that could reflect overall job success. The idea of an ultimate criterion implies that job performance is a unitary concept, that one measure could be found that assessed a person's overall job performance. Even Thorndike (1949), who developed the idea, recognized that an ultimate criterion would rarely, if ever, be found in practice: "A really complete ultimate criterion is multiple and complex in almost every case. Such a criterion is ultimate in the sense that we cannot look beyond it for any higher or further standard in terms of which to judge the outcomes of a particular personnel program" (121). Unfortunately, many who followed Thorndike did not heed his advice and wasted considerable time trying to find ultimate measures of job performance. It is unlikely that you will ever find one measure that will tell you everything about performance in a specific job.

Ultimate criterion—the concept that a single criterion measure reflects overall job success.

GLOBAL VERSUS MULTIPLE CRITERIA Job analysis procedures used by most organizations are inductive: the job analyst infers the dimensions that make up the overall job performance domain from specific empirical data. Other approaches, such as those used by Colgate-Palmolive or British Petroleum, deduce performance dimensions from organizational goals with the help of job analysis data. As we have seen, British Petroleum identified technical skills, leadership qualities, business awareness, planning and organizational ability, communication and interpersonal skills, initiative, and problem-solving ability as important job dimensions and assessed potential employees on each dimension. If there is a need to compare the relative performance of petroleum engineers, is it appropriate to combine the scores on each dimension into an overall composite score, or should a new criterion be developed to measure overall, global performance?

Many practitioners, heavily influenced by the controversy surrounding the search for the ultimate criterion, would answer "No." They would emphasize that the multidimensionality of job performance requires the use of multiple, independent criteria to measure performance. They would say that independent criteria, reflecting independent performance dimensions, should not be combined into an overall composite measure of job performance. Combining *leadership qualities* and *initiative* to understand the engineer's performance would be, to use Smith's (1976) analogy, like adding toothpicks to olives to understand a martini. Furthermore, they would not believe it was appropriate to obtain a separate, overall measure of performance because such a global criterion measure would lose the rich information contained in the multiple performance dimensions.

More recently, this position has changed. The choice of a criterion measure should be determined by its intended purpose: "If you need to solve a very specific problem (e.g., too many customer complaints about product quality), then a more specific criterion is needed. If there is more than one specific problem, then more than one specific criterion is called for. But in most situations, a global measure will serve quite well" (Guion, 1987, 205).

COMPOSITE VERSUS MULTIPLE CRITERIA   We have emphasized the multidimensionality of job performance and the requirement of assessing those different dimensions through multiple criterion measures. Nonetheless, there may be times when a single, all-inclusive criterion measure is needed as part of making employment decisions and no global criterion measure is available. Not everyone agrees that it is inappropriate to combine individual criterion measures into a single composite (Landy, 1989). There seems to be general agreement on how to proceed. Since performance measures will be used for a variety of purposes, it makes sense to collect each criterion measure separately or in its multiple, uncollapsed form. That information can be combined to compute a composite criterion as needed for different administrative decisions.

The weights assigned to the separate performance measures in creating a composite measure should reflect the priority of the different performance dimensions as set by the organization's goals. Implicit in this position is a recognition that the priority of organizational goals may change over time. If separate performance measures have been maintained, it is a relatively straightforward exercise to recompute the composite to reflect the new organizational, and economic, realities. Caution should be taken; creating a composite averages performance across all the performance dimensions. Performance on one dimension may be so critical that deficiencies cannot be made up by excellent performance on other dimensions. In this case, a composite criterion is inappropriate.

CONSISTENCY OF JOB PERFORMANCE

In discussing reliability as a requirement for criterion measurement, we assumed that the employee's behaviour was more or less consistent at the time the observations were made. Of course, people's job performance may change over time. This is a substantially different issue from the random, daily fluctuations in performance. Changing performance levels may affect criterion measurements.

TRAINING VERSUS JOB PROFICIENCY CRITERIA   Do you obtain the same criterion results if you measure performance very soon after a person is placed in a job as opposed to several months or years later? Generally, early performance in a job involves informal learning or systematic training. Workers are continually evaluated during training or probationary periods. Performance measures taken during early training will be very different from those taken later when workers are more proficient. Criterion measurements taken during training periods may produce validity coefficients that overestimate the selection system's ability to predict later job proficiency (Ghiselli, 1966). Nonetheless, the convenience of short-term performance measures, rather than their relevance to long-term performance, dictates their use as criteria. Training criteria remain very popular performance measures.

TYPICAL VERSUS MAXIMUM JOB PERFORMANCE   Maximum performance occurs in situations where individuals are aware that they are being observed or evaluated, or where they are under instructions to do their best. Their performance is measured over a short time period when their attention remains focused on performing at their highest level. Typical performance is the opposite of maximum performance, in which individuals are not aware that their performance is being observed and evaluated, in which they are not consciously attempting to perform to the best of their ability, and in which performance is monitored over an extended period of time. There is very little relationship between performance under typical and maximum performance situations, for either inexperienced or experienced workers. Performance measures taken during training are measures of maximum performance and may be inappropriate if a selection system is to predict long-term typical performance. Motivational factors play a larger role in typical, everyday performance. In maximum performance, motivation is probably at high levels for everyone; in typical performance situations in the actual work setting, motivation is likely to differ among individuals (Sackett, Zedeck, and Fogli, 1988).

DYNAMIC VERSUS STABLE CRITERIA Employee performance appears to decrease over time regardless of the employee's experience or ability. These changes may reflect the effects of many personal, situational, and temporal factors. Early job performance may be limited only by ability and experience since every new employee is motivated to do well, while later job performance may be influenced more by motivation (Deadrick and Madigan, 1990).

SUMMARY Early job performance, which may occur under more rigorous scrutiny than later performance, is ability-driven and is a better estimate of what individuals can maximally achieve rather than how they will typically perform on the job. Performance will decrease over time, generally reflecting changes in motivation. Training criteria are acceptable performance measures for estimating maximum performance, but will overestimate typical performance. To be safe, several performance measures should be taken at different times when validating selection systems.

JOB PERFORMANCE CRITERIA

It is very unlikely that any two workers doing the same job will perform at exactly the same level. Factors such as knowledge, skill, and motivation are likely to cause variation in job performance within and between workers. Most likely, any two petroleum engineers hired by British Petroleum would not perform at the same level on all of the critical job dimensions; nor is it likely that any one engineer would perform at the same level on all dimensions. Every employee has strengths and weaknesses. How do we actually measure these differences in performance between employees on the relevant job dimensions? What do we actually use as the criterion data necessary for validating selection systems? The remainder of this chapter reviews some of the more common criterion measures and measurement techniques.

If you have previously studied performance appraisal, you will recognize many of the methods presented in the following sections. Performance appraisals or evaluations often provide the answers to the above questions. Despite their importance, performance appraisals tend to be resisted by both employees and their supervisors. As one anonymous wag has said, "Performance appraisals are given by someone who does not want to give them to those who don't want to get them." One reason performance appraisal is stressful for both employees and their supervisors is that most performance measures are based on a judgmental process subject to many sources of error and bias. Some performance measures are better than others and have a better chance of being accepted by both workers and their supervisors.

A 1997 survey by the Watson Wyatt consulting group, as reported in *The Canadian Manager* (Davis and Landa, 1999), revealed the following information about Canadian workers' experience with performance appraisals:

- 60 percent of employees understood how their performance was evaluated.
- 57 percent thought that their performance was rated fairly.
- 47 percent reported that their managers set clear goals and assignments.
- 42 percent reported that they received regular, timely performance reviews.
- 39 percent thought that their performance review helped to improve their job performance.
- 37 percent reported that their supervisor regularly talked with them about their performance.
- 19 percent reported a direct linkage between their pay and their performance.

The different criteria that have been used to measure job performance are grouped into broad categories as part of the following presentation.

OBJECTIVE MEASURES: PRODUCTION, SALES, AND PERSONNEL DATA

Objective performance measures—or hard criteria, are production, sales, and personnel data used in assessing individual job performance.

Objective production, sales, and personnel data, also known as *hard criteria* or ancillary measures, are often used as performance measures. These data are produced by the workers in doing their jobs, or are related to observable characteristics or behaviours of the workers. They are called **objective performance measures** because they represent the actual number of things produced or number of sales made. The assigned number does not depend on the subjective judgment of another person. The number of audits completed by an accountant at Colgate-Palmolive is known for any given period; the quality of those audits may be reflected in the number of errors detected by a higher-level review. In this case, both the quantity and quality (number that are error-free) of audits are objective measures related to the actual job performance of the accountant. If the quality of the audit rested on the judgment or perception of the accountant's supervisor that the audits met acceptable, professional standards, quality would then constitute a subjective measure. Production or sales measures generally involve quantity, quality, and trainability, which is the amount of time needed to reach a specific performance level. Box 6.1 lists examples of production and sales criteria.

PERSONNEL DATA Using personnel data as criteria involves the use of objective measures that are not directly related to actual production or sales but that convey information about workplace behaviour. Criteria derived from personnel data tend to be global in nature and may tell more about contextual performance than the worker's actual performance on specific job dimensions. Personnel data may be better measures of organizational behaviours than of job performance. Absence data are routinely collected and stored in each worker's file and are often used as criteria. Absence measures likely tell more about employee rule-following behaviour than how well they perform their jobs (i.e.,

BOX 6.1 Examples of Objective Measures of Job Performance*

PRODUCTION OR SALES MEASURES

Quantity

- Number of items produced
- Volume of sales
- Time to completion
- Number of calls processed each day
- Average size of sales orders
- Words typed per minute
- Speed of production

Quality

- Number of errors
- Dollar cost of errors
- Number of customer complaints
- Number of spelling and grammatical mistakes
- Degree of deviation from a standard
- Number of cancelled contracts

Trainability

- Time to reach standard
- Rate of increase in production
- Rate of sales growth

PERSONNEL DATA

Absenteeism

- Number of sick days used
- Number of unscheduled days off work
- Number of times late for work

Tenure

- Length of time in job
- Voluntary turnover rate
- Involuntary turnover rate

Rate of Advancement

- Number of promotions
- Percent increase in salary
- Length of time to first promotion

Accidents

- Number of accidents
- Cost of accidents
- Number of days lost to accidents
- Number of safety violations

*These are measures that have been used over time; inclusion on this list does not necessarily mean that these are the best objective measures of individual or group performance.

---

when they do show up for work). In addition to absence data, information on job tenure, rate of advancement or promotion within the organization, salary history, and accident history have been used as criteria. Box 6.1 also presents examples of personnel data used as criteria. Criteria should be selected because they are reliable, relevant, and practical. While most objective measures may meet the test of practicality, they may not necessarily be reliable or relevant. While quantity may be measured with a fair degree of accuracy, the consistency of the information may depend on the time of the measurement or the duration over which it was taken.

CONTAMINATION AND DEFICIENCY OF OBJECTIVE MEASURES   Objective measures may be influenced by factors beyond a worker's control. Insurance companies use the total dollar value of insurance sold in a month to measure an agent's performance. One agent may sell more insurance in a month than another because one's territory includes a compact city district populated by upper-income professionals, while the other's includes a sparsely populated rural county of low-income farm workers. Both the opportunity to make sales and the amount of insurance sold may have more to do with the sales territory than the sales ability of either of the agents. The total dollar value of insurance sold may not measure how safely the agents drove to their territories, the oral communication skills needed to explain the complex insurance policies, or how accurately they completed the necessary paperwork to initiate the policy and to bill for its premiums.

Successful performance of these other job dimensions may have as much to do with the long-term success of the insurance company as the dollar sales volume. Using personnel data, such as absenteeism, turnover, rate of advancement, salary history, and accidents, as criteria leaves an organization open to criticism of criterion deficiency or contamination. The practicality and convenience of objective data do not justify their use. Before production, sales, or personnel data can be used as criteria, their reliability and validity as measures of job performance dimensions must be established.

SUBJECTIVE MEASURES: RATING SYSTEMS

It is relatively easier to find objective measures for jobs that involve people in the actual production of goods and services. As a person's job becomes removed from actual production or sales work, it becomes more difficult to associate objective measures to the employee's performance. Upper-level jobs in an organization may involve more administration, leadership, team building, and decision making, dimensions that are not easily measured in objective terms. The issues of criterion relevance, deficiency, and contamination become even more serious. How should Colgate-Palmolive evaluate the

---

BOX 6.2 Some Potential Constraints on Individual Performance

Lack of supplies/materials	High stress levels in workplace
Lack of needed staff	Change in policies, procedures, and/or regulations
Absenteeism of critical personnel	Peer pressure to limit production
Failure to receive material/assemblies from other units	Poor communication of goals and objectives
Poor working conditions	Lack of necessary equipment
Inadequate physical facilities	Inadequate training of new hires
Poor leadership	Too many inexperienced staff in unit
Excessive bureaucracy	Lack of support staff
Unpredictable workloads	Budget restrictions/cost-saving measures
Overextended staff	

performance of the accountant's supervisor? Most likely, the supervisor's own manager, peers, and perhaps even subordinates will be asked to rate, or judge, the supervisor's performance on relevant job dimensions. Without a doubt, performance ratings are the most frequently used criterion measure.

Recent evidence suggests that, when used as performance criteria, **subjective performance measures** may provide better estimates of a selection system's validity than objective measures. Farrell and Hakstian (2000) compared the effectiveness of typical selection measures (cognitive ability, interviews, personality, etc.) in predicting either objective or subjective criteria that had been used to evaluate performance in sales occupations. They used meta-analytic procedures to integrate results across 59 empirical performance appraisal studies. On average, a combination of predictors (e.g., a cognitive ability test and a biographical inventory, or a job knowledge test and a personality test) led to higher validity coefficients when subjective criteria ($r = .65$) were used as performance measures compared with objective criteria ($r = .51$). The choice of criteria may lead an HR manager to come to different conclusions about the effectiveness of a selection system.

Subjective performance measures—ratings or rankings made by supervisors, peers, or others that are used in assessing individual job performance.

RATING ERRORS A rating system is simply a procedure that is used to quantify an opinion or judgment. A rating system must satisfy all the measurement requirements we discussed in Chapter 3. As with any measurement system, ratings are open to error. Leniency, central tendency, and severity errors are types of errors made by judges who restrict their ratings to only one part of the rating scale. Some raters may assign only extreme ratings; some may give only very positive ratings **(leniency)** while others give only very negative ones **(severity)**; others may judge all performance to be average and not assign extreme ratings in either direction **(central tendency)**.

Most students can identify teachers who have a reputation for giving mostly A's or F's (extreme ratings) or those who pass everyone with a C. Leniency errors are common in performance appraisal as many supervisors try to keep on good terms with their employees or think that a higher-than-deserved rating might motivate them to do better. If the employee's compensation is linked to the performance appraisal, the supervisor may not wish to be the person responsible for denying the raise. Supervisors may also believe that high ratings for everyone in their work group will reflect positively on their managerial skills (Bowman, 1999).

Halo errors occur when the rating a judge first assigned to a particularly important dimension influences the judge's ratings over several job dimensions. After assigning a very high rating on "leadership," a rater may feel that the same score is warranted for "effort," particularly since the judge may have little experience with the employee on this dimension. Halo errors are often the result of the following type of thinking: "If I rated her excellent on Leadership, she must be excellent on Effort as well. Besides, if I give her a low rating on effort, or say I have no basis for judging her effort, my boss who will review this assessment may think I'm not doing my job. So, I know she's excellent on

Leniency errors—rating errors in which a rater tends to assign only positive ratings regardless of the true level of performance.
Severity errors—rating errors in which a rater tends to make only negative ratings regardless of the true level of performance.
Central tendency errors—rating errors in which a rater tends to assign only average ratings regardless of the true level of performance.
Halo errors—occur when a rater uses a rating assigned to one job dimension to rate several other dimensions regardless of the true level of performance on those dimensions.

Leadership; she's probably excellent on Effort. I'll give her an Excellent rating on Effort." A similar effect can occur when a manager's negative perception or observation of the employee on one job dimension or competency spills over to another dimension. That is, the "black mark" on one dimensions colours the whole appraisal. These types of rating errors introduce the personal biases of the raters into the measurement process and reduce the likelihood that the assigned ratings are appropriate measures of the performance under review.

What impact do rating errors have on the accuracy of a performance rating? Surprisingly, the answer may be "Not much." Rating errors are largely unrelated to direct measures of the accuracy of the ratings. Using a meta-analysis approach, Murphy and Balzer (1989) computed accuracy scores and measures of the three common types of error discussed above. There was little, if any, correlation between the two sets of measures. The relationships that did emerge, particularly for halo errors, were paradoxical in that rater errors appeared to contribute to rating accuracy! Along these lines, Nathan and Tippins (1990) demonstrated that the validity of selection tests increased when more halo seemed to be present in performance ratings; this was contrary to common assumptions that the presence of rating error would lead to decreases in validity. Murphy and Cleveland (1995) suggest that this "paradox" is not really a paradox but rather a reflection of the inadequate ways in which rating errors have been operationalized.

REDUCING RATING ERRORS Over the years many different aspects of both raters and rating systems have been examined in an attempt to reduce rating errors. While rating errors can never be eliminated, they can be reduced. Rating errors can be reduced by (1) defining the performance domain; (2) adopting a well-constructed rating system; and (3) training the raters in using the rating system. Reducing rating errors may have unintended effects. The procedures used to reduce rating errors may also reduce rating accuracy. Trained raters appear to be so focused on avoiding rating errors that they stop using whatever strategy they were using before training. Rather than devising strategies to reduce rating errors, a better approach may be to develop programs to increase rating accuracy (Murphy and Cleveland, 1995). Frame-of-reference training is one method of improving rating accuracy, but before discussing rater training programs, we will briefly review different types of rating systems.

RELATIVE RATING SYSTEMS

Relative rating systems— compare the overall performance of one employee with that of others to establish a rank order of employee performance.

Relative rating systems, also known as comparative rating systems for obvious reasons, compare the overall performance of one employee with that of others to establish a rank order of performance. With the exception of the relative percentile method, these techniques provide global assessments as the rater compares overall performance rather than performance on each job dimension. The use of a single overall rating avoids the problems with rating errors over the set of dimensions. The tradeoff for avoiding these errors is the loss of performance information on specific job dimensions. As we discussed previously, global criteria may not always be the most appropriate to use.

There are three traditional relative rating systems: rank order, paired comparison, and forced distribution methods, as well as the more recent relative percentile method.

RANK ORDER   In rank ordering, the rater arranges the employees in order of their perceived overall performance level. For a group of 10 workers, the best performer would be assigned rank 1 and the worst, rank 10. There are two problems with this procedure. Raters may have a good idea of who are the best and worst performers but often have difficulty discriminating—that is, assigning ranks—between the remaining employees. Second, because the system is relative, it does not tell whether any or all of the workers are performing above or below acceptable levels. In other words, an employee may be rated the third-best accountant but, in absolute terms, may not meet acceptable performance standards.

PAIRED COMPARISONS   In this method, the rater compares the overall performance of each worker with that of every other worker who must be evaluated. In rating four employees, their supervisor compares every possible pair of workers: Employee 1 versus Employee 2, Employee 1 versus Employee 3, and so on. The workers are then ranked on the basis of the number of times they were selected as the top-rated performer over all the comparisons. One problem with the procedure is the large number of comparisons that often have to be made. With four workers, a supervisor must make six comparisons; for 10 workers, the number of paired comparisons increases to 45. Making a large number of paired comparisons becomes tedious, leaving some raters to rush through the procedure. While this technique does guarantee that all employees being rated are given due consideration, it still does not provide information on absolute performance levels.

FORCED DISTRIBUTION   This system attempts to provide absolute information within a relative rating context. Rather than rank workers from top to bottom, the system sets up a limited number of categories that are tied to performance standards. For example, the rater may be given a scale with the categories excellent, above average, average, below average, and poor to evaluate each worker overall or on specific job dimensions. So far, this procedure resembles that used by an absolute graphic rating scale procedure; the difference is that the rater is forced to place a predetermined number or percentage of workers into each of the rating categories.

Generally, raters assign workers to categories on the basis of a normal frequency distribution, which assumes most workers to be average with only a few judged excellent or poor. This technique is quite good at controlling leniency, central tendency, and severity errors; however, it does not reduce halo effects. Often raters oppose systems like this, which require them to label a given percentage of their subordinates into extreme categories, on the grounds that this distorts the true state of affairs. They may feel that the number of poor or excellent performers working for them does not match the quota the system has allocated to those categories. Forced systems work best when only gross discriminations are required between workers.

RELATIVE PERCENTILE METHOD (RPM)   The RPM is a new and improved comparative rating system (Goffin, Gellatly, Paunonen, Jackson, and Meyer, 1996). The system overcomes one of the major shortcomings of other comparative rating systems by allowing raters to compare individuals on job performance dimensions that have been derived through job analytic procedures. The system can also be used to make overall performance ratings. The RPM requires raters to use a 101-point scale (0 to 100), with a score of 50 representing *average* performance. For each performance dimension, or for the global comparison, a rater uses the 101-point scale to assess each ratee relative to one another. The rating scale anchors each rater's comparisons to an absolute standard and, thus, allows meaningful comparisons among ratings obtained from different raters. The RPM appears to be a very promising relative rating procedure. It appears to produce validity estimates and levels of accuracy that surpass those obtained with some absolute rating scales (Goffin et al., 1996; Wagner and Goffin, 1997).

ABSOLUTE RATING SYSTEMS

Absolute rating systems—
compare the performance
of one worker with an
absolute standard of per-
formance; they can be
used to assess perfor-
mance on one dimension
or to provide an overall
assessment.

Absolute rating systems compare the performance of one worker with an absolute standard of performance. These methods provide either an overall assessment of performance or assessments on specific job dimensions. A rating scale is developed for each dimension that is to be evaluated. Over the years, a variety of formats have been developed to assess performance in absolute terms. While these rating scales may have important qualitative differences, they usually lead to the same administrative decisions. One rating system may provide more effective feedback, while supervisors are more likely to favour another and support its use. The ratings assigned to employees by either rating system are likely to be highly correlated, once measurement errors are taken into account. The particular ratings scale format may not make much difference in the relative order of scores derived for each employee. However, different rating formats may not have the same degree of validity or meet relevant legal requirements (Greene, Bernardin, and Abbott, 1985). A review of several of the more popular ratings formats follows.

GRAPHIC RATING SCALES   Graphic rating scales can be produced to assess an employee on any job dimension. The scale usually consists of the name of the job component or dimension, a brief definition of the dimension, a scale with equal intervals between the numbers placed on the scale, verbal labels or anchors attached to the numerical scale, and instructions for making a response. Figure 6.1 presents samples of relatively good and poor scales that have been designed to rate effort. The presence or absence of these elements helps to distinguish between these two samples. The poor scale presented in Figure 6.1(a) does not provide the rater with a definition of effort. It is left for each rater to define this term in a different way, leaving open the possibility that the definitions are so variable that the raters will not be assessing the same dimension. The good example in Figure 6.1(b) provides a definition of the performance dimension. There is no guarantee that the raters will not use other interpretations of effort in making their ratings (or that this is the best way to define effort), but at least they have had to consider the standardized definition. The poor example contains very general anchors at each end of the scale but provides no information on what constitutes high or low effort. Again each rater may use a different reference point to characterize the effort of the person being rated. The anchors in the good example provide benchmarks to help understand the differences between various degrees of effort. Finally, the poor example allows the rater such latitude in making a response that the person in

FIGURE 6.1 EXAMPLES OF RATING SCALES

(a) Effort
Low   High

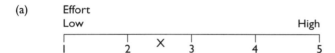

1   2   X   3   4   5

(b) Effort — Consider the amount of energy brought to the job. Will subordinate personal convenience to complete work in a professional manner.

1	2	③	4	5
Poor	Below Average	Average	Above Average	Excellent

(c) Effort — Reflects the degree to which individuals are committed to performing all job tasks, to working at a high level of intensity, and to continue working under adverse conditions.

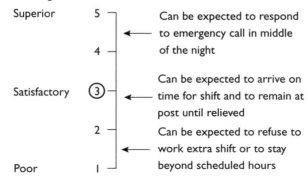

Superior   5 — ←— Can be expected to respond to emergency call in middle of the night

4 —

Satisfactory   ③ — ←— Can be expected to arrive on time for shift and to remain at post until relieved

2 — ←— Can be expected to refuse to work extra shift or to stay beyond scheduled hours

Poor   1 —

charge of reviewing the completed assessments may have difficulty knowing what rating was given. In the poor example, does the x indicate a rating of 2 or 3? In the good example, there is no doubt about which response was intended.

TRAIT-BASED RATING SCALES   Trait-based rating scales are graphic rating scales that ask the rater to focus on specific characteristics of the person being reviewed. The rater judges the extent to which a worker possesses traits such as dependability, leadership, friendliness, and so on. In most cases the traits are either very poorly defined or extremely vague. Furthermore, the traits under assessment rarely are chosen because they are job-related. The failure to demonstrate the relevance of the chosen traits to job dimensions is a fatal flaw, which makes such appraisal systems next to worthless. Nonetheless, trait-based performance measurement systems continue to be used. Partly, this is due to the ease with which such a scale can be concocted, and the apparent cost savings of using one general performance measure across all jobs that are being evaluated. Organizations that use such systems in decision making run the risk of justifying the validity of such performance ratings in costly litigation before various tribunals.

CHECKLISTS   Checklists present the rater with a list of statements that may describe either work behaviours or personality traits. Sometimes the list is restricted to behavioural statements only. The rater goes through the list and identifies those statements that apply to the employee being evaluated. With behavioural checklists, the rater is describing what the worker does. Since some behaviours may be more valuable to an organization, weights can be assigned to the different statements. Generally, the weights are developed through a job analysis or by people who are very familiar with the job. The rating for an individual is obtained by adding the weights of those statements that have been identified for that person. This approach is known as the method of summated ratings.

A second checklist method is the forced-choice procedure, in which a rater is given several statements and is asked to select one that most or least typifies the employee. By forcing the rater to choose from among a group of all positive or all negative statements, the format tends to reduce leniency, central tendency, and severity errors. On the whole, raters detest using the forced-choice procedure, particularly when they believe that several statements apply equally well to the worker. A further limitation of the forced-choice procedure is its failure to provide an easily understood performance measure that can be interpreted in terms of job dimensions. One purpose of any evaluation is to provide workers with feedback on their performance, to identify strengths and weaknesses. This is difficult to do if either the rater or the person being measured does not readily understand the performance measure.

CRITICAL INCIDENT METHODS   Critical incident methods require raters to observe the job behaviour of an employee and to record those behaviours displayed by the worker that are critical to effective or ineffective performance. The technique forces the rater to concentrate on the behaviour, not traits or characteristics, of the worker. The critical incidents are identified through interviews with people knowledgeable about the specific job. The critical incidents are then given to an observer who checks off those that are displayed by the worker while performing the job. This method is essentially the same as a summated checklist method. Box 6.3 contains a series of critical incidents for a security dispatcher related to the job dimensions of job-specific task proficiency, demonstration of effort, and personal discipline. These critical incidents were collected as part of a job analysis for the security dispatcher position at a Canadian university. The dispatcher's supervisor would mark off those behaviours present in the dispatcher's job performance.

One drawback of this type of system is its very nature of focusing on specific behaviours. Workers may do those activities that can be easily recorded or documented. It may also lead to supervisors micromanaging employees by looking for employee mistakes rather than accomplishments, since employees are assumed to be competent (Bowman, 1999). This is like a parent noticing only a child's mistakes and never complimenting good behaviour.

MIXED STANDARD RATING SCALES Mixed standard rating scales are variations on critical incident checklists. Three critical incidents, similar to those presented in Box 6.3, are selected for each job dimension being reviewed. The items represent excellent, average, and poor performance, respectively. The items are randomly presented on a checklist without labelling the job dimensions, and raters are asked to indicate whether the employee's behaviour is better, worse, or the same as the behaviour presented in the statement. A score is assigned to each job dimension on the basis of the pattern of ratings for each dimension. For example, if a security dispatcher were judged to perform better than that given in the statement, he or she would be given a score of 7, while a dispatcher judged to perform worse on all three statements would be given a score of 1. Other weights would be assigned to the remaining possible patterns.

BOX 6.3 Critical Incidents for a Security Dispatcher

JOB-SPECIFIC TASK PROFICIENCY
- Properly secures lost and found articles
- Controls visitor access to buildings
- Monitors multiple surveillance devices

DEMONSTRATION OF EFFORT
- Reports early for shift to hear debriefing from preceding shift

- Remains at post until relieved
- Volunteers for overtime when needed

PERSONAL DISCIPLINE
- Follows safety procedures
- Does not take unauthorized breaks
- Maintains proper demeanour during stressful situations

While the mixed standard rating scale does reduce rating errors, it tends to introduce another: many raters make logically inconsistent responses to the set of three statements within each dimension. The time needed to construct mixed standard rating scales, coupled with the inconsistent responding of those who use it, argue against its wide-scale use. It can be very useful, however, in those organizations willing to spend time and money improving the scales to eliminate the inconsistent responding.

BEHAVIOURALLY ANCHORED RATING SCALES (BARS) Behaviourally anchored rating scales use empirically derived critical incident job behaviours to anchor the values placed on a rating scale. Although this procedure sounds simple, it is actually quite complex and time-consuming. An example of a BARS designed to measure effort is presented in Figure 6.1(c). To construct this scale, a group of workers most familiar with the job use a critical incident procedure to identify specific job dimensions. A second, independent group generates behavioural examples of excellent, average, and poor performance on each dimension identified by the first group. A third group is given the dimensions identified by the first group and the behavioural items generated by the second and asked to match items to dimensions. This step is called *retranslation* and represents an attempt to establish the content validity of the items. A fourth group then takes the valid items and assigns each a value from the measurement scale that represents its level of performance. Items with low variability in assigned scale values are retained for the scale. The resultant scale is tested and refined before being adopted for general use (Smith and Kendall, 1963).

Box 6.4 shows the resulting behavioural anchors developed for the competency of communication. The definition for communication is identical to the one given in Box 5.3. Since the competencies have already been identified, the first step in the procedure may be skipped. This definition is presented to subject-matter experts (SMEs) who are asked to generate behavioural examples for each competency under review. The behavioural examples are matched to a competency, retranslated, and rated. Behavioural examples with similar ratings are grouped together, edited, and refined to form the anchors for a competency. In Box 6.4, statements such as "Makes interesting and informative presentations" and "Explains complicated points in different ways to ensure understanding" both would have been assigned similarly high ratings by SMEs. A rating scale like this could then be used to evaluate an employee's level of proficiency with respect to communication. Scales like this could be constructed for all competencies that were related to successful job performance. A procedure very similar to this one was used to develop scales for eight core competencies that were then used in evaluating the performance of RCMP members who applied for promotion (Catano, Campbell, and Darr, 2000).

BARS is the Rolls Royce of rating scales (and perhaps as costly). It has the advantage of being, arguably, the best rating procedure in use today. It integrates job analytic information directly to the performance appraisal measure.

BOX 6.4 Behavioural Anchors Used to Assess Communication Competency

COMMUNICATION

- Communicating Orally
- Communicating in Writing
- Listening to Others
- Selling the Message

Communication involves communicating ideas and information orally and/or in writing in a way that ensures the messages are easily understood by others; listening to and understanding the comments and questions of others; marketing key points effectively to a target audience; and speaking and writing in a logical, well-ordered way.

5. Excellent
Makes interesting and informative presentations; explains complicated points in different ways to ensure understanding; written reports are concise, understandable and lead to defendable and convincing conclusions; actively listens to others to ensure understanding of what they said; uses humour to capture and maintain attention of audience; makes effective use of nonverbal communication; provides feedback to ensure comprehension of messages that are received.

4. Above Average
Written and oral communication exhibit excellent grammar and vocabulary; maintains eye contact with audience during oral presentations; speaks with confidence and authority; written and oral presentations are well organized; gets to the point in oral presentations; accurately summarizes positions taken during group discussions; listens carefully to opinions and concerns of others.

3. Average
Performs well in a structured setting; actively participates in group discussions; presents unpopular positions in a nonthreatening manner and acknowledges opposing points of view; asks for feedback from audience; makes presentations in a clear and concise manner.

2. Below Average
Oral presentations are factual and accurate but lose the attention of the audience; presentations are overly long; leaves out important points in both oral and written reports; performs other tasks while listening to people and does not hear what was said; needs to repeat points to get them across to an audience; does not make an effort to obtain feedback from audience.

1. Unsatisfactory
Has difficulty establishing a relationship with the audience; uses inappropriate grammar and vocabulary; responds inappropriately to what has been said; does not make an effort to ensure that presentation was understood; ideas are presented in a disorganized manner; written communication is brief and incomplete.

It also involves a large number of people in the development of the measure. Generally, these people—supervisors and workers—support the process and become committed to its success.

BEHAVIOUR OBSERVATION SCALES (BOS)   Behaviour observation scales are very similar to BARS in that the starting point is an analysis of critical job incidents by those knowledgeable about the job to establish performance dimensions (Latham and Wexley, 1981). Once the list of behaviours that represent different job dimensions is constructed, supervisors are asked to monitor the frequency with which employees exhibit each behaviour over a standardized time period. Next, the frequency data are reviewed through an *item analysis* where the response to each item is correlated to a performance score for a dimension. This performance score is obtained by summing all the items that belong to a particular dimension. Only those items that attain high correlations with the total score are retained for the performance appraisal measure. This procedure assures a high degree of internal consistency for each dimension.

An example of a BOS scale used in evaluating the performance of a security dispatcher is presented in Table 6.2. Several differences are apparent in comparison to a BARS designed to measure the same dimension. First, there is no attempt to integrate the critical incidents into one overall scale. Second, there are no behavioural anchors attached to the scale; rather, the rater judges the frequency with which each employee displays the critical behaviours. Latham and Wexley (1981) recommend using a five-point scale where the numbers are defined in terms of frequencies; for example, they would assign the value 1 if the worker displayed the critical behaviour 0–64 percent of the time, 2 for 65–74 percent, 3 for 75–84 percent, 4 for 85–94 percent, and 5 for 95–100 percent. In this way, the rater assesses the frequency of engaging in actual critical behaviours as opposed to rating the employee in terms of a behavioural expectation that the worker might not have had an opportunity to perform.

TABLE 6.2 BEHAVIOURAL OBSERVATION SCALE USED TO EVALUATE A SECURITY DISPATCHER

JOB-SPECIFIC TASK PROFICIENCY

Properly secures lost and found articles	Almost Never	1	2	3	4	5	Almost Always
Controls visitor access to buildings	Almost Never	1	2	3	4	5	Almost Always
Monitors multiple surveillance devices	Almost Never	1	2	3	4	5	Almost Always
Ensures confidentiality and security of information	Almost Never	1	2	3	4	5	Almost Always
Activates appropriate emergency response teams as needed	Almost Never	1	2	3	4	5	Almost Always

Total Score _____

6–16	17–19	20–21	22–23	24–25*
Very Poor	Unsatisfactory	Satisfactory	Excellent	Superior

* Management sets performance standards

BOS generally take less time and money to develop than BARS. The BOS development procedure requires participation of supervisors and workers leading to their greater acceptance of the system. Nonetheless, there are some weaknesses to this procedure. One major problem lies with the rating scale. A rating of 1 suggests poor performance since the critical behaviour is displayed less than 65 percent of the time. Consider using this scale to rate the hitting and fielding performance of a major league baseball player. A ball player who hits the ball 30 percent of the time is called a millionaire; the BOS would classify him as a failure. A major leaguer who successfully fielded the ball 85 percent of the time would soon be out of a job; the BOS would classify his performance as excellent.

The frequency with which a behaviour occurs may have different interpretations depending on the behaviour. Frequency measures also do not capture the importance or criticality of the behaviour. The captain of the *Titanic* almost always missed hitting icebergs. Another very serious problem with the BOS is that the demands it makes on human memory may exceed the available capacity. Raters may not be able to remember accurately the specific behavioural information required by the BOS and may end up making global judgments (Murphy and Cleveland, 1995).

MANAGEMENT BY OBJECTIVES (MBO) Management by objectives is a performance measurement system that emphasizes completion of goals that are defined in terms of objective criteria such as quantity produced or savings realized. It is a results-based system. MBO starts with the identification of organizational goals or objectives and uses these to specify goals for each employee's job performance. Before any goals can be set, the job-related behaviours must first be identified through a job analysis. The employee plays an important role in this process. Once both the employee and supervisor understand the job, both meet to develop a mutually agreeable set of goals that are outputs of the employee's job. Once the goals are established, the supervisor uses them to evaluate the employee's performance. Over the review period there are several meetings between employee and supervisor to review progress. At the end of the review period, there is a final meeting to assess whether the employee met the established goals and to set the goals for the next review period.

Strengths of this system involve the linkage between organizational and individual goals, frequent analysis and discussion of the employees' progress toward meeting the goals, and immediate feedback about performance. The employees know, from the objective criteria, whether they are performing up to expectations. Because the system is based on objective or hard criteria, the system suffers from all the problems inherent in the use of that type of performance measure. In addition, the process can be as time-consuming as a BARS procedure to develop, with managers at different levels in the organization having conflicting views on what constitute appropriate goals. The process may stifle creativity because of its emphasis on short-term results. It leads to the emphasis on personal goals, which may impede the development of teamwork (Bowman, 1999).

PERCEIVED FAIRNESS AND SATISFACTION OF RATING SYSTEMS

An important consideration in the choice of a rating system is not only the validity and reliability of the system, but also its acceptance by those it will be used to evaluate. Acceptance of the rating system by those subject to evaluation by the system is critical to the system's successful implementation and continued use (Hedge and Teachout, 2000). Rating systems that are perceived to be fair and those that produce a high degree of satisfaction among the ratees are more likely to find acceptance. Both the BOS and BARS produce greater degrees of satisfaction and perceived fairness than trait scales. The BOS also reflects a greater degree of procedural justice. Managers do not view trait scales as an acceptable measurement instrument, particularly when they are used to assess their own performance by other managers (Latham and Seijts, 1997).

IMPROVING RATINGS THROUGH TRAINING AND ACCOUNTABILITY

RATER TRAINING Training raters in the use of the rating system helps to reduce rating errors and to increase the reliability of the measurements (Day and Sulsky, 1995). A training program for raters ensures that all the raters are operating from a common frame of reference. **Frame-of-reference (FOR) training** seeks to ensure that raters have the same understanding of the rating system's instructions; that they have the same interpretation of the performance dimensions that are to be evaluated; and that they know how to use the rating system's measurement scale. FOR training improves the accuracy of ratings and provides information that assessors use long after the training ends (Sulsky and Keown, 1998).

Training programs can also include information on the types of rating errors that occur and how to avoid them. Some programs include information on how to improve observation of work behaviour. Although training programs can become quite elaborate, involving role-playing and use of demonstration videotapes, many rater-training sessions consist of workshops built around explanation of the rating system accompanied by practice rating sessions.

RATER ACCOUNTABILITY Apart from training, the factor that has the most impact on rating accuracy is rater accountability. In 1996, the Alberta Court of Queen's Bench ordered Purolator Courier Ltd. to pay a former employee $100 000 in a wrongful dismissal suit that centred on the appropriateness of the employee's performance evaluation (Gibb-Clark, 1996). Rating accuracy increases when raters are called on to explain or to justify the ratings they make. Accountability can be built into a system by requiring the rater to provide the employee who is being rated with feedback from the appraisal. Many supervisors are uncomfortable doing this, particularly when the feedback is negative. However, if feedback is not given, the employee can neither benefit

Frame-of-reference (FOR) training—a procedure used to "calibrate" raters by ensuring that they have the same understanding of a rating system's instructions; that they have the same interpretation of the performance dimensions that are to be evaluated; and that they know how to use the rating system's measurement scale.

from the appraisal by improving performance nor challenge evaluations that are suspect. In the Purolator Courier case, the trial judge was most concerned that the employee had not been given assistance to meet increased expectations.

Most organizations that undertake performance appraisals require both the rater and the employee to review, and to sign, the completed rating form. Employees, however, cannot be forced to sign rating forms with which they disagree. Accountability is also established by building into the rating system a mechanism for the formal review of all performance appraisals. By monitoring all evaluations, a review panel can assess whether any one rater's assessments appear to significantly deviate from those obtained from the other raters. Knowing that their ratings will be reviewed can lead raters to play it safe by giving everyone an acceptable evaluation (i.e., making a central tendency error). On the other hand, raters under this type of system can usually justify any extreme ratings they give to employees. Organizations that cannot justify their performance evaluations may suffer both public and financial embarrassment.

WHO DOES THE RATING?

SUPERVISOR RATINGS   Most workplace assessments are traditionally carried out by an immediate supervisor or manager. In recent years, organizations have started to recognize that this may not be the best practice. They have started to obtain ratings from other co-workers and subordinates. Some organizations also ask the worker to perform an appraisal of their own performance. Each of these groups provides information about the employee's performance from a different perspective and some may not see the total scope of the employee's job performance (Murphy and Cleveland, 1995).

PEER RATINGS   Co-workers tend to provide more lenient reviews than supervisors. As part of a class project, suppose the professor requires each member of the group to evaluate each other with respect to certain criteria related to the project. Would you assign a very lenient grade in the expectation that the other students will evaluate you similarly, or would you assign a grade that reflects your honest judgment of how others contributed to the project? If you knew your grade was based on this peer evaluation, would group performance be enhanced or hindered? Self-comparisons with other members of a work group do have an impact on peer performance evaluations and may lead to tensions within the work group and ultimately affect both individual and group performance (Saveedra and Kwin, 1993). Most organizations avoid involving co-workers in the assessment process out of this fear that doing so will lead to hostility between co-workers, increased competitiveness among the co-workers, and a breakdown in team functioning. Nonetheless, evaluations from co-workers or peers can be quite reliable and valid sources of information about an employee's job performance.

SUBORDINATE RATINGS Ratings by subordinates of their supervisor are relatively rare, although some large companies such as Ford Motor Company (Bernardin and Beatty, 1984) do obtain such ratings as part of reviewing managerial performance. Subordinate ratings, however, are very common in universities where a professor's teaching performance is evaluated through student evaluations, and where faculty routinely evaluate the performance of their supervisors (department heads, deans, presidents). Student evaluations of teaching performance are used by a professor's peers in evaluating that professor for promotion or tenure. While the students would be in a good position to observe teaching effectiveness, they might not be the best persons to evaluate the professor's research productivity or administrative work on committees.

There are two related concerns about subordinate ratings; either the subordinates will give lenient ratings to influence their own treatment ("If I rate my professor highly, I'm more likely to get a good grade") or the supervisor will attempt to manipulate the subordinate ratings through altering performance expectations ("I'll give them an easy test so they all pass and, perhaps they'll remember this gift when they evaluate my teaching").

SELF-RATINGS What if your professor asked you to evaluate your own performance on the group project? How would your evaluation compare with those of other students in your group and of your professor? Generally, self-appraisals are the most lenient of all. That is, while people tend to give ratings that accurately reflect differences in their performance on different job dimensions, the ratings they give themselves tend to be higher than ratings given to them by others. More and more companies, including most of the Fortune 500 firms, are including self-assessments as part of their performance appraisal systems. These self-ratings are typically used along with ratings obtained from other sources as part of a 360-degree feedback process.

Self-ratings and those made by an employee's manager will disagree substantially. The extent of the disagreement does not only extend to the appropriate rating that should be applied but also to fundamental differences in how the employee and supervisor view the job dimensions underlying the rating scales (Cheung, 1999). That is, if both were evaluating the competency of communication, the employee and supervisor would most likely have different views of what that competency included. Employees and managers have different perceptions of whether job factors are under the control of the employee. When employees perform less than their best they tend to attribute this to external factors beyond their control. On the other hand, their supervisor tends to attribute the less-than-stellar performance to internal factors under the employee's control. These differences in perception are another factor in the discrepancy between self- and supervisory ratings (Bernardin, 1992).

CLIENT OR CUSTOMER RATINGS An increasing number of organizations ask customers or clients to rate the performance of employees with whom they have interacted. For example, Sun Life of Canada asks customers to rate the performance of salespeople in terms of the service they provided to the customer. Other companies such as Ford, and Honda's Acura division also obtain information from an employee's internal clients. Internal clients include anyone who is dependent on the employee's work output. For example, the manager of an engineering division might be asked to evaluate the human resources manager in charge of recruiting engineers for the division. Both internal and external customers can provide very useful information about the effectiveness of an employee or a team of employees (Belcourt, Sherman, Bohlander, and Snell, 1996). This information provides a unique view of the employee's performance from individuals who are directly involved with the employee, but who at the same time are neither subordinate nor superior to the employee.

360-DEGREE FEEDBACK   The 360-degree feedback procedure uses information obtained from supervisors, peers, subordinates, self-ratings, and clients or customers to provide the employee with feedback for development and training purposes. The intent of the process is to provide employees with feedback about their performance from numerous independent sources to give the employees as complete a picture as possible about their performance (Sulsky and Keown, 1998). As noted above, the information provided by these different sources is likely to disagree to some extent. Self-ratings tend to be higher than those provided by others and show less congruence with other's ratings. There is a relatively high correlation between peer and supervisor ratings but only modest correlations between self–peer and self–supervisor ratings (Harris and Schaubroeck, 1988). That is, supervisors and peers are more likely to agree on a rating they apply to someone else than that person is likely to agree with either of them (Furnham and Stringfield, 1998). The difference in information suggests that no one evaluation is the right one.

There is no clear evidence why the assessments from different sources disagree. Harris and Schaubroeck (1988) suggested that ego-defensiveness and attributional differences produced the discrepancies. Sulsky and Keown (1998) note some other possibilities for these differences:

- quality differences in the ratings across sources
- individual performance variability across different contexts (e.g., being friendlier to customers than to peers)
- different conceptions of work performance across rating sources

During the mid-1990s many companies embraced 360-degree feedback and saw it as an essential tool in developing managers. Many organizations that adopted this procedure had no clear idea of what they wanted to achieve through its use or which competencies they wished to evaluate. Experience over the past years suggests that the success of this procedure depends on the organizational culture in which it is embedded. It does not do well in a "command and control" environment (McCurry, 1999). Because 360-degree feedback

BOX 6.5 Performance Measurement—A Different View

In recent times, different organizations have adopted a total quality management (TQM) philosophy. It may surprise some that the advocates of TQM disapprove of individual performance appraisals. The TQM approach emphasizes outputs from a production system that are the product of a complex interaction between basic materials, resources, tools, work methods, and people. The TQM philosophy asserts that it is impossible to distinguish an individual's performance from that of others or from the work team as a whole, and, even if you could, such measures would be useless because they do not capture important things such as the customer and the continuous improvement of processes. These criticisms can be summarized in five main points:

1. Performance appraisal assumes that the individual is the major cause of important performance differences.
    - A manager receives a number of complaints about a salesperson's performance in handling credit card transactions. The manager assumes that the behaviour of the salesperson is at issue rather than investigating problems with the credit card system.
2. There is little, if any, research on group, unit, or team performance.
    - Most people in organizations work as parts of teams. Team performance should be assessed to provide group feedback to all members of the team.
3. Supervisors play too prominent a role in measuring and motivating performance.

- Within a TQM context, feedback on performance should come from the work system. Feedback from customers and clients is considered more valid than supervisory feedback in a TQM system. Peer appraisals are also important as they relate to an individual's impact on teamwork.

4. Most performance appraisal research is based on simple tasks.
    - Performance appraisals assume stability in jobs over time, low interdependence among people performing tasks, and low interdependence among different tasks being performed. Very few jobs meet these requirements; increased complexity, interdependence, and rapid change characterize work performed by individuals in organizations.
5. Performance appraisal does not focus on continuous improvement of work methods, procedures, or systems.
    - In a TQM system, all employees and the organization itself must focus on continuous improvement of processes to improve quality. The selection process is assumed to have ensured that the organization has workers who have a basic level of ability and that they will be motivated to work if treated well and given responsibility. Finding a solution to systemic problems that have blocked improvement in quality are taken to be more important than improving individual performance.

Source: Berwald (1992).

includes peer appraisals, it is also prone to all the disadvantages associated with peer ratings.

NONTRADITIONAL METHODS FOR MEASURING PERFORMANCE

Following a decline in use during the 1970s, ratings have regained popularity with the development of rating systems that focus on behaviours related to the job's performance domain. New performance measurement systems developed over the past several years, however, offer alternative methods for obtaining criteria data. In most cases, these procedures are adapted from techniques used in personnel selection. Figure 6.2 illustrates the relationship between these different types of criterion categories and the eight performance

FIGURE 6.2 CRITERION MEASURES RELATED TO CAMPBELL'S PERFORMANCE DIMENSIONS

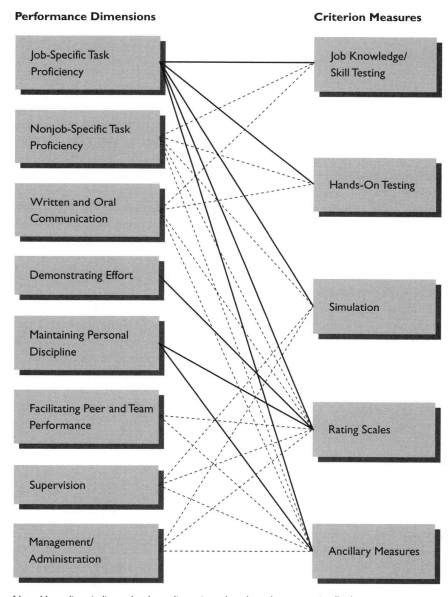

Performance Dimensions

Job-Specific Task Proficiency

Nonjob-Specific Task Proficiency

Written and Oral Communication

Demonstrating Effort

Maintaining Personal Discipline

Facilitating Peer and Team Performance

Supervision

Management/ Administration

Criterion Measures

Job Knowledge/ Skill Testing

Hands-On Testing

Simulation

Rating Scales

Ancillary Measures

Note: Heavy lines indicate the three dimensions thought to be present in all jobs.

dimensions defined by Campbell (1990). The lines connecting dimensions and categories, based on empirical evidence, suggest that ratings have been used for every performance dimension. The alternative measures presented in Figure 6.2 are briefly described here.

Job knowledge/skill testing—in performance appraisal, a procedure that is based on an assessment of an employee's knowledge or skills required to achieve a desired outcome.

JOB KNOWLEDGE/SKILL TESTING

Job knowledge or skill testing procedures include paper-and-pencil tests as well as "walk-through" procedures, which require an individual to demonstrate knowledge or general skills such as manipulating controls or equipment to achieve a desired outcome. These types of measures reflect a worker's requisite skill or knowledge to perform a task; they do not indicate the worker's proficiency or what the worker will or can do. Since these measures are "tests," the same issues arise as when they are used as predictors; particularly, they must not lead to adverse impact against subgroups. These procedures and issues will be discussed in later chapters.

Hands-on testing—in performance appraisal, a procedure in which raters assess workers as they perform one or more tasks associated with their job.

Simulation—in performance appraisal, a procedure in which raters assess workers as they perform one or more tasks associated with their job in a setting that emulates salient features of the job and the work environment.

HANDS-ON TESTING AND SIMULATION

There are two categories containing related techniques but differing in the degree to which they attempt to reproduce actual critical work behaviours. In **hands-on testing**, workers perform one or more tasks associated with their job. The testing may take place either through formal observation of normal job tasks or off-site, where the worker is asked to perform using normal job equipment and techniques. This latter case is really a type of work samples test where the employee is asked to produce a sample of job-related behaviour. Similarly, **simulations** attempt to duplicate salient features of the work site and to measure job proficiency under realistic conditions (Murphy, 1989). As part of the RCMP's promotion procedures, constables must successfully complete a paper-and-pencil, job situation exercise that simulates conditions they encounter on the job.

Work samples testing and simulation have been used primarily as predictor measures rather than criteria or, in the case of simulation, as a training method (e.g., flight simulators). When used to measure performance, hands-on methods appear to produce reliable scores on critical job-related tasks. These new evaluation procedures are generally complex, expensive to develop, and demanding to administer, raising the issue of their practicality in most situations. Nonetheless, they may have immense potential for use in validation research.

HUMAN RIGHTS AND PERFORMANCE APPRAISAL

Ever since *Griggs* v. *Duke Power Co.* (1971), personnel practices in the United States and Canada have been increasingly subject to review by judiciary or human rights tribunals. Although the Canadian legal precedents have occurred more recently, they have been influenced by U.S. case law (Cronshaw, 1986, 1988). Reviews of U.S. decisions related to criterion-related validity studies and performance measurement systems emphasize that the defensibility of criterion measures rests on the ability to demonstrate that performance measures are job-related (Barrett and Kernan, 1987). This point was emphasized in the recent Supreme Court of Canada decision with respect to the use of criterion measures in selecting forest firefighters in British Columbia (*British Columbia (Public Service Employee Relations Commission) v. BCGSEU*, 1999). The court ruled that a standard—that is, a criterion—must be reasonably related to the accomplishment of work-related purposes (see Chapter 2, p. 51).

The absence of a job or work analysis as part of criterion development will likely cast suspicion on any performance measurement system subject to judicial review (Landy, 1989). In *B.L. Mears v. Ontario Hydro* (1984), a tribunal under the Ontario Human Rights Commission decided that black employees were unfairly ranked for layoffs, compared with white employees, through the use of vague and undefined criteria (e.g., productivity, safety, quality of work, attendance, and seniority). Additionally, the ranking system was informal as no written records of productivity or quality of work were kept. In reviewing U.S. court decisions involving performance appraisal systems, Barrett and Kernan (1987) also note the requirement for written documentation regarding performance measurements. They go on to advise employers to maintain a review mechanism through which employees can appeal performance assessments they believe to be unfair or discriminatory.

Increased critical examination of performance measurement practices by Canadian human rights commissions and courts will mean strict adherence to accepted professional standards of criterion development (Cronshaw, 1988). These standards will include those that apply in the United States unless it can be shown that professional standards in Canada seriously deviate from those in the United States, or that Canadian legislation or case law has established practices that vary from U.S. standards. At present neither of these conditions hold. The most explicit statement on criteria is contained in the "Uniform Guidelines" (1978), which were jointly developed by the U.S. Equal Employment Opportunity Commission, Civil Service Commission, Department of Labor, and Department of Justice ("Uniform Guidelines," 1978, 38300-01):

> *Whatever criteria are used should represent important or crucial work behavior(s) or work outcomes ... The bases for the selection of the criterion measures should be provided, together with references to the evidence considered in making the selection of criterion measures. A full description of all criteria on which data were collected and means by which they were observed, recorded, evaluated, and quantified should be provided. If rating techniques are used as criterion measures, the appraisal form(s) and instructions to the raters should be provided as part of the validation evidence or should be explicitly described and available. All steps taken to insure that criterion measures are free from factors which would*

unfairly alter the scores of members of any group should be described.

The research presented in this chapter, standards of professional practice, and reviews of legal decisions suggest that the following steps must be included in a performance measurement system that will satisfy human rights requirements:

1. Conduct a job and organization analysis to describe the job performance domain and competencies that are necessary for successful completion of the organization's goals.

2. Select criteria that are valid, reliable, and practical measures of the job performance dimensions or competencies. Document the development of the criteria and measurement scales as well as their validity.

3. Identify the performance standards, goals, or expected results that will be used to evaluate employees on the selected criteria. These standards should be made known to employees in understandable terms at the beginning of the review period. These standards must be work-related and bona fide occupational requirements.

4. Train people in the use of the performance measurement system, particularly when they will be called on to make judgments about employee performance. This training should include a review of the criteria, the measurement scales, and the standards.

5. Provide written instructions to all assessors on the proper use of the measurement system, particularly if the system involves the use of rating procedures.

6. Provide feedback from the performance evaluation to the employees. Assist those employees who receive poor evaluations to improve their performance. Raters should be trained in the effective use of feedback.

7. Establish a formal review mechanism, which has responsibility for the appraisal system and for any appeals arising from the evaluation process.

8. Document all steps in the development of the appraisal system and its use, as well as all decisions affecting employees that result from using the performance measurement data.

SUMMARY

Any criteria chosen for use must be valid, reliable, practical, and capable of withstanding legal challenge. A construct validation strategy such as that outlined by Campbell (1990) will help to satisfy legal requirements. Once job-related performance dimensions or competencies have been identified, the type of criterion measure that most validly represents each performance dimension or competency should be selected. Most likely there will be different measures for different performance dimensions or competencies. There is no evidence to suggest that any one type of measure is inherently more sound than any other; in particular, rating systems, if properly developed, will provide data that are as reliable as other types of measures.

Current research suggests that training criteria are acceptable performance measures for estimating maximum performance. However, to obtain a better understanding of possible changes in validities over time, repeated measures of performance should be taken over time. Data from the various criterion measures should be collected in an uncollapsed form and formed into composites when necessary. The weighting of composites should reflect the priority assigned by the organization to the different goal-related behaviours. All the procedures used in establishing the performance dimensions or competencies, their measures, and data collection and analysis should be documented.

KEY TERMS

Absolute rating systems, p. 206

Central tendency errors, p. 203

Criterion deficiency, p. 195

Criterion contamination, p. 195

Criterion relevance, p. 195

Frame-of-reference training, p. 214

Halo errors, p. 203

Hands-on testing, p. 220

Job knowledge/skill testing, p. 220

Leniency errors, p. 203

Objective performance measures, p. 200

Practicality, p. 196

Relative rating systems, p. 204

Severity errors, p. 203

Simulation, p. 220

Subjective performance measures, p. 203

Ultimate criterion, p. 196

EXERCISES

[Note: These exercises build on the set of exercises in Chapter 5. While the exercises here focus on teaching performance, any activity may substituted for teaching. Use whatever occupation you chose in Chapter 5 for the following exercises.]

Many of the forms used by colleges and universities to assess teaching performance suffer from all the defects of graphic rating scales. For this exercise:

1. Obtain a copy of the teaching assessment form used by your institution and critique it using the information presented in this chapter.

2. Use a set of competencies you identified in one of Chapter 5's exercises. (If you did not do this exercise, use the following major activities: Lecture Preparation and Organization; Communication Skills; Use of Examples and Exercises; Use of Audiovisual Materials/ PowerPoint/Internet; Grading; Course-Related Advising and Feedback; Interaction with Students.) Identify the major behaviours and/or KSAOs for each dimension or competency. (You may already have done this if you completed Exercises 4 and 5 in Chapter 5.)

3. For each job dimension or competency, construct a behaviourally anchored rating scale of the type shown in Figure 6.1(c). You do not have to follow all the steps required to construct a BARS, but you should at least have your subject-matter experts rate the different behaviours for their importance. Shaw, Schneier, and Beatty (1991) present useful information for constructing a BARS.

4. Compare your scale with the one used in your institution. Which one would you prefer to use? Which would your professor prefer? Why?

5 Box 6.5 presented some arguments used by proponents of TQM in arguing against the need for individual performance appraisals. What are your views on this matter? Do you believe that individual performance feedback will have no impact on improving performance?

CASE

As part of restructuring, a television network decided to close one of its local stations in Cape Breton. Several different unions represented the employees at the station. Employees were given severance packages or opportunities to transfer to the network's Halifax station if they were qualified for any available positions. Two electronic news-gathering (ENG) camera operators received layoff notices and requested transfer to Halifax, where two ENG positions were open. Two ENG operators—two ENG positions to fill. No problem? Not quite. A recent hire at the Halifax station also applied for one of the two positions. Under the terms of the ENG operator's collective agreement, during any restructuring the employer had the right to fill positions with employees deemed to be the best performers.

The network had never employed any type of performance assessments with its unionized employees and was at a loss as to how to determine which two of the three were the best, other than through their supervisors' opinions.

The collective agreement, however, called for an "objective" assessment. The network's HR director recalled that a few years previously their Toronto station had to prepare for compliance with pay equity legislation and had developed a rating system to evaluate all their Toronto employees, from secretaries to on-air news anchors. The survey was a graphic rating scale very similar to the type shown in Figure 6.1(b). It listed twelve traits or characteristics, including "effort," as shown in Figure 6.1(b). The twelve traits were very general characteristics such as "knowledge," "willingness to learn," and so on. The HR director asked two different managers who had worked with the three employees to use the form to rate the employees' performance. The new hire received the highest rating and was offered a position. The two potential transfers received low ratings and neither was offered a position.

Under the terms of the collective agreement, the two laid-off employees had the right to grieve the decision and their union carried the case to arbitration. The arbitration panel was composed of a neutral chairperson, who was mutually selected by the other two members of the panel, one of whom was appointed by the employer and the other by the union. In presenting its case to the arbitration panel, the union's lawyer decided to call an expert in human resources to comment on the performance measure that had been used to assess the employees. After hearing the expert's opinion, which was not challenged by the employer, the arbitration panel threw out the decision based on the performance measure and declared that the two laid-off employees must be offered the two vacant positions.

DISCUSSION QUESTIONS

1. What did the expert most likely tell the arbitration panel?

2. If you were that expert, what would you tell the arbitration panel? Be as detailed as possible and call upon all the material that has been covered in previous chapters.

3. Do you think an "off-the-shelf" measure that was designed for one purpose can be used to assess performance in another context?

4. After rejecting the performance measure, the arbitration panel itself was charged with assessing which of the three employees were the best performers. What would you advise the panel to do in this situation? How should they evaluate the employees' performance?

REFERENCES

Barrett, G.V., and M.C. Kernan. 1987. "Performance Appraisal and Terminations: A Review of Court Decisions since Brito v. Zia with Implication for Personnel Practices." *Personnel Psychology* 40: 489–503.

Belcourt, M., A.W. Sherman Jr., G.W. Bohlander, and S.A. Snell. 1996. *Managing Human Resources*. Toronto: Nelson Canada.

Bernardin, H.J. 1992. "An 'Analytic' Framework for Customer-Based Performance Content Development and Appraisal." *Human Resources Management Review* 2: 81–102.

Bernardin, H.J., and R. Beatty. 1984. *Performance Appraisal: Assessing Human Behavior at Work*. Boston: Kent-PWS.

Berwald, M.C.A. June 1992. *A Practitioner's View of the Utility of Performance Appraisal Research within a Total Quality Management Work Environment*. Paper presented at the annual meeting of the Canadian Psychological Association, Quebec City.

B.L. Mears, Gifford Walker, George Wills, Hollis Trotman, Thomas Atherly, Hubert Telphia and Leon Francis v. Ontario Hydro and Jack Watson, A. Watkiss, T. Ouelette and Mossis Loveness. 1984. Canadian Human Rights Reporter, 5, D/3433 (Ontario Human Rights Commission Board of Inquiry, December 1983).

Bowman, J.S. 1999. "Performance Appraisal: Verisimilitude Trumps Veracity." *Public Personnel Management* 28: 557–76.

British Columbia (Public Service Employee Relations Commission) v. BCGSEU. Supreme Court of Canada decision rendered September 9, 1999.

Campbell, J.P. 1990. "Modelling the Performance Prediction Problem in Industrial and Organizational Psychology." In M.D. Dunnette and L.M. Hough, eds., *The Handbook of Industrial and Organizational Psychology*, vol. 1. 2nd ed. San Diego: Consulting Psychologists Press, 687–732.

Catano, V.M., C.A. Campbell, and W. Darr. April 2000. *The RCMP Promotion System: Performance Appraisal of Behavior-Based Competencies*. Paper presented at the annual meeting of the Society for Industrial and Organizational Psychology, New Orleans.

Cheung, G.W. 1999. "Multifaceted Conceptions of Self–Other Ratings Disagreement." *Personnel Psychology* 52: 1–36.

Cronshaw, S.F. 1986. "The Status of Employment Testing in Canada: A Review and Evaluation of Theory and Professional Practice." *Canadian Psychology* 27: 183–95.

Cronshaw, S.F. 1988. "Future Directions for Industrial Psychology in Canada." *Canadian Psychology* 29: 30–43.

Davis, T., and M. Landa. 1999. "A Contrary Look at Employee Performance Appraisal." *The Canadian Manager* 24: 18–19.

Day, D.V., and L.M. Sulsky. 1995. "Effects of Frame-of-Reference Training and Ratee Information Configuration on Memory Organization and Rater Accuracy." *Journal of Applied Psychology* 80: 156–67.

Deadrick, D.L., and R.M. Madigan. 1990. "Dynamic Criteria Revisited: A Longitudinal Study of Performance Stability and Predictive Validity." *Personnel Psychology* 43: 717–44.

Farrell, S., and R. Hakstian. June 2000. *A Meta-Analytic Review of the Effectiveness of Personnel Selection Procedures and Training Interventions in Sales Occupations*. Paper presented at the annual meeting of the Canadian Psychological Association, Ottawa.

Furnham, A., and P. Stringfield. 1998. "Congruence in Job-Performance Ratings: A Study of 360-Degree Feedback Examining Self, Manager,

Peers, and Consultant Ratings." *Human Relations* 51: 517–30.

Ghiselli, E.E. 1966. *The Validity of Occupational Aptitude Tests*. New York: Wiley.

Gibb-Clark, M. 1996. "Court Orders Purolator to Pay Fired Employee." *The Globe and Mail* (May 4): B3.

Goffin,R.D., I.R. Gellatly, S.V. Paunonen, D.N. Jackson, and J.P. Meyer. 1996. "Criterion Validation of Two Approaches to Performance Appraisal: The Behavioral Observation Scale and the Relative Percentile Method." *Journal of Business and Psychology* 11: 23–33.

Greene, L., H.J. Bernardin, and J. Abbott. 1985. "A Comparison of Rating Formats after Correction for Attenuation." *Educational and Psychological Measurement* 45: 503–15.

Griggs v. Duke Power. 1971. 401 U.S. 424.

Guion, R.M. 1987. "Changing Views for Personnel Selection Research." *Personnel Psychology* 40: 199–213.

Harris, M.M., and J. Schaubroeck. 1988. "A Meta-Analysis of Self–Supervisor, Self–Peer, and Peer–Supervisor Ratings." *Personnel Psychology* 41: 43–62.

Hedge, J.W., and M.S. Teachout. 2000. "Exploring the Concept of Acceptability as a Criterion for Evaluating Performance Measures." *Group & Organizational Management* 25: 22–44.

Landy, F.L. 1989. *Psychology of Work Behavior*, 4th ed. Pacific Grove, CA: Brooks/Cole.

Latham, G.P., and G.H. Seijts. 1997. "The Effect of Appraisal Instrument on Managerial Perceptions of Fairness and Satisfaction with Appraisals from Peers." *Canadian Journal of Behavioural Science* 29: 278–82.

Latham, G.P., and K.N. Wexley. 1981. *Increasing Productivity through Performance Appraisal*. Reading, MA: Addison-Wesley.

McCurry, P. 1999. "New Angle on 360-Degree Feedback." *Director* 53: 36.

Murphy, K.R. 1989. "Dimensions of Job Performance." In R.F. Dillon and J.W. Pelligrino, eds., *Testing: Theoretical and Applied Perspectives*. New York: Praeger, 218–47.

Murphy, K.R., and W.K. Balzer. 1989. "Rater Errors and Rating Accuracy." *Journal of Applied Psychology* 74: 619–24.

Murphy, K.R., and J.N. Cleveland. 1995. *Understanding Performance Appraisal: Social, Organizational, and Goal-Based Perspectives*. Thousand Oaks, CA: Sage.

Nathan, B.R., and N. Tippins. 1990. "The Consequences of Halo 'Error' in Performance Ratings: A Field Study of the Moderating Effects of Halo on Test Validation Results." *Journal of Applied Psychology* 75: 290–96.

Saavedra, R., and S. Kwin. 1993. "Peer Evaluation in Self-Managing Work Groups." *Journal of Applied Psychology* 78: 450–62.

Sackett, P.R., S. Zedeck, and L. Fogli. 1988. "Relations between Measures of Typical and Maximum Job Performance." *Journal of Applied Psychology* 73: 482–86.

Shaw, D.G., C.E. Schneier, and R.W. Beatty. 1991. "Managing Performance with a Behaviorally Based Appraisal System." In J. Jones, B.D. Steffy, and D.W Bray, eds., *Applying Psychology in Business: The Handbook for Managers and Human Resource Professionals*. New York: Lexington Books, 314–25.

Smith, P.C. 1976. "Behaviours, Results, and Organizational Effectiveness: The Problem of Criteria." In M.D. Dunnette, ed., *Handbook of Industrial* and *Organizational Psychology*. Chicago: Rand McNally, 745–76.

Smith, P.C., and L.M. Kendall. 1963. "Retranslation of Expectations: An Approach to the Construction of Unambiguous Anchors for Rating Scales." *Journal of Applied Psychology* 47: 149–55.

Sulsky, L.M., and J.L. Keown. 1998. "Performance Appraisal in the Changing World of Work: Implications for the Meaning and Measurement of Work Performance." *Canadian Psychology* 39: 52–59.

Thorndike, R.L. 1949. *Personnel Selection: Test and Measurement Technique*. New York: Wiley.

"Uniform Guidelines on Employee Selection Procedures." 1978. *Federal Register* 43: 38290–315.

Wagner, S.H., and R.D. Goffin. 1997. "Differences in Accuracy of Individual and Comparative Performance Appraisal Methods." *Organizational Behavior and Human Decision Processes* 70: 95–103.

7

....

RECRUITMENT: IDENTIFYING, CONTACTING, AND ATTRACTING THE TALENT POOL

CHAPTER GOALS

This chapter reviews the role played by recruitment in human resources planning. We present this topic from the perspective of both the job seeker and the employing organization.

After reading this chapter you should

- understand the link between recruitment and selection;

- appreciate the strategies used by job seekers to investigate jobs and organizations;

- understand how a job seeker's interests and values influence job search strategies;

- appreciate how job candidates use characteristics of the job and organization in choosing among jobs;

- know the role that accurate expectations play to improve the fit between a person and an organization;

....

- know why a realistic job preview may benefit both the job seeker and the organization;
- be aware of the internal and external factors that influence an organization's recruitment strategy;
- understand the linkage of recruitment to job and organization analysis;
- be able to design and implement a recruitment action plan;
- be aware of the different methods that can be used to recruit internal and external job applicants; and
- understand the increasingly important role played by the Internet in recruiting.

THE ORGANIZATION AND JOB FROM THE CANDIDATE'S PERSPECTIVE

Figure 7.1 presents a simplified view of the human resources management system, which serves as the framework for our discussion. In this model, recruitment is an outcome of human resources planning. The decision to recruit candidates for jobs in an organization is based on (1) an assessment of the internal and external factors affecting the organization; (2) an organization analysis based on those factors; and (3) a job analysis that identifies worker behaviours and characteristics that will identify candidates who are qualified for the position. The ultimate goal of a job-related selection system is to bring people into the organization who will perform at above-average levels and who will increase the productivity of the organization.

Only within the last 20 years has recruitment received serious attention for the important role it plays in the selection process. Previously, recruitment was simply a means of attracting a large enough pool of candidates from which the organization could select the best qualified (Guion, 1976). Hardly any consideration was given to the possibility that candidates were using the recruiting process to select the organization. Job applicants are not passive organisms. During the recruitment and selection process, they form opinions about the organization, the selection process, the people they meet, and the desirability of working in the organization. Because of their experience, many candidates conclude that they do not want to work in a particular organization, or that they will not fit in; they may also form other attitudes, which last through their early work experience (Rynes, 1993). In the long run such **self-selecting out** may be in the interests of both the applicant and the organization, if that decision is based on accurate information and a realistic perception of the job and the organization. On the other hand, if these early decisions are based on inaccurate information, both the candidate and the organization may be worse off.

In many ways recruitment is the first step in the selection process. People apply for jobs in organizations on the basis of their interest in the job, and their belief that they have the required knowledge, skills, abilities, and other talents

Self-selecting out— occurs during the recruitment and selection process when candidates form an opinion that they do not want to work in the organization for which they are being recruited.

FIGURE 7.1 RECRUITMENT AS PART OF THE HR PLANNING PROCESS

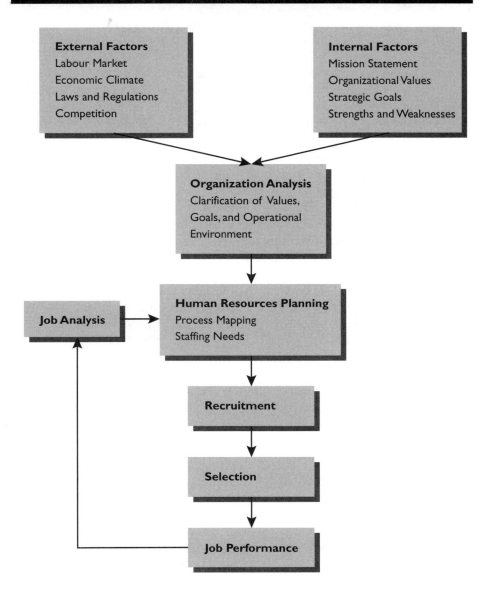

needed to do the job well. They also hope that the organization will provide a hospitable environment in which to spend the better part of their working day. Obviously, this is an idealized view of the world; in bad economic times, when jobs are at a premium, people may change their perceptions of jobs and organizations, as well as their willingness to work in either. In hard economic times, people may value the security of having a job and the income it provides above everything else. Security and income, although important considerations, are not always the most influential factors in attracting applicants to jobs or organizations.

Investigating the Organization

Individuals become job applicants after forming an opinion on the desirability of working in a particular job within a specific organization (Schwab, Rynes, and Aldag, 1987). The strategies and information that people use in arriving at such decisions are by no means clear. Some people undertake extensive searches before applying for a job with an organization. They consult a variety of published documents for information about the organization, including annual reports and stories about the company and its employees in newspapers and business periodicals. With the advances of technology, many of these documents can be located quite readily through computer searches of CD-ROM databases or through access to archives located on the company's home-page on the Internet. In addition, many Internet employment-related websites offer profiles on companies that use their site. For example, Monster.ca (http://www.monster.ca) provides information on who the company is, its major products or services, the number of people it employs, its location, and current employment opportunities. It also lists contact information in the form of website addresses. Job applicants also seek out employees of the organization or friends or acquaintances who have experience in it to obtain personal views on what it is like to work for the company and what the employees are like as co-workers. Often, the nature of supervision in the organization and the reputation of the company are important concerns to the candidate.

It is unlikely that any candidate, no matter how thorough his or her search for information, will get a complete picture of what life is like in the organization. One of the characteristics of the recruitment process is a mutual search for information about each other by the candidate and the organization. At some point an individual forms an impression of the organization and decides to apply for a job. Many well-qualified individuals may not pursue jobs based on their impression that they and the organization are incompatible. Of course, some individuals are more concerned with finding any job and make no effort to find out information about the organization beforehand.

Investigating the Job

Candidates investigate the job as well as the organization. The likelihood of job candidates accepting an offer of employment is closely associated with the perceived attributes of the position and the work environment. Box 7.1 presents a summary of job attributes that candidates consider as part of their job search. The relative importance of these attributes depends on a person's age, sex, career interests, and previous work experience (London and Stumpf, 1982). Pay and the nature of the work to be done as part of the job rank consistently near the top in importance for all job seekers. They tend to rate vacant positions as less attractive when help-wanted advertisements contain minimal information about both the attributes of the position and the pay associated with it (Yeuse and Highhouse, 1998). Applicants for managerial and professional positions emphasize opportunities for advancement and promotion,

BOX 7.1 Influential Job Attributes

ALL CANDIDATES

Pay

Nature of work

Opportunities for knowledge and skill development

Recognition

Good interpersonal relations with co-workers

WHITE-COLLAR JOB CANDIDATES

Opportunity for advancement

Opportunity for promotion

Geographic location of work

Responsibility

Opportunity to be creative

BLUE-COLLAR JOB CANDIDATES

Job security

(The order of listing does not imply order of importance, which may depend on many other factors.)

Source: Adapted from Heneman et al. (1989), and London and Stumpf (1982).

while blue-collar candidates are more concerned with job security (Heneman, Schwab, Fossum, and Dyer, 1989).

In today's rapidly changing workplace with a highly educated workforce, jobs providing autonomy, decision-making authority, and opportunities for self-development win out over those that lack these attributes. Moreover, with the increase in dual-career couples, single-parent families, and female representation in the workforce, organizations that offer special accommodations and flexible work arrangements gain competitive advantages in recruiting (see Box 7.2). For positions requiring geographical relocation of

BOX 7.2 Questions for Campus Recruiters

College and university students are a prime source of applicants for many organizations. Each year companies send recruiters onto campuses across the country seeking candidates for positions with their organizations. Today's students are asking a much broader range of questions than their predecessors. In addition to questions about salary and working hours, students are asking questions about the corporate culture and seek to maintain a balance between work and family. Here are some typical questions that campus recruiters report being asked that reflect these new concerns (Shellenberger, 1999):

- How long do you work in a day? In a week?
- Is this job going to suck the life out of me?

- How do people work together?
- How are people treated?
- Is the work environment friendly and supportive?
- How much pressure is there to achieve your projects?
- How much freedom is there to extend a deadline?
- How does the company view work–life balance?
- May I talk to a working mother who is one of your employees?
- What is your parental leave policy?
- Do you allow flexible work scheduling to accommodate family needs?
- Will I get called about work issues at home?

candidates, employers that assist working spouses to secure local employment gain further advantage. Ultimately, the values and interests of the job applicant influence the relative importance of these different attributes. Unfortunately, many candidates fail to take the last step in their investigation: an examination of their own interests, values, and talents.

INTERESTS AND VALUES

Interests and values—an individual's likes and dislikes and the importance or priorities attached to those likes and dislikes.

A person's **interests and values** determine whether that individual applies for a specific job. People who dislike sitting in an office all day are unlikely to apply for jobs as accountants, even if they have the appropriate qualifications. Such people, however, might pursue jobs as managers of wildlife preserves, even though they do not meet all of the requirements. Interests and values are strong factors in guiding career or job choice decisions.

Interests and values do not indicate whether a person is qualified for a job. Interests and values only suggest the type of work a person may find satisfying. Nonetheless, the degree of satisfaction with a job is one of the many factors that influence job turnover, especially in good economic times when jobs are plentiful (Carsten and Spector, 1987).

VOCATIONAL COUNSELLING Most new job seekers are unsure of their interests and career goals. Vocational guidance counsellors assist job seekers in identifying groups of jobs that are compatible with their values and interests. One technique that guidance counsellors use as part of this process is to have the person complete a value or interest inventory. These are self-report measures that require individuals to complete a systematic series of questions about their likes and dislikes. The scores from these measures are compared with normative data that have been collected from actual incumbents in many different types of jobs and professions. The individuals are advised of those occupations where job incumbents hold interests similar to their own.

Interest inventories— questionnaires that ask people to report their likes and dislikes with respect to issues, topics, or occupations.

Interest Inventories

Many of the measures that are used to assess vocational interest are based on vocational theories developed by Holland (1973). According to Holland, six major themes can be used to classify both vocational interests and related jobs. Holland proposed that in North America most people can be categorized in terms of some combination of six basic personality types:

- *Realistic* types perceive themselves as having mechanical and athletic ability but lacking ability in human relations; they tend to value money, power, and status; they prefer working in technical and skilled occupations such as farmer, and metal or machine worker.

- *Investigative* types perceive themselves as scholarly, intellectually self-confident, and possessing mathematical and scientific ability but lacking in leadership; they tend to value scientific and intellectual activities; they prefer working in scientific occupations such as chemist, engineer, and medical technologist.

- *Artistic* types perceive themselves as expressive, nonconforming, original, introspective, independent, and disorderly; they tend to value artistic and musical activities and aesthetic qualities; they prefer working in artistic, literary, and musical occupations such as photographer, writer, and music teacher.

- *Social* types perceive themselves as liking to help others, understanding of others, having teaching ability, and lacking mechanical and scientific ability; they tend to value social activities and problems; they prefer working in educational and social welfare occupations such as a member of the clergy, social worker, and counsellor.

- *Enterprising* types perceive themselves as aggressive, popular, self-confident, sociable, possessing leadership but not scientific abilities; they tend to value political and economic achievement; they prefer working in sales and managerial occupations such as sales person, buyer, and office manager.

- *Conventional* types perceive themselves as conforming, orderly, and having clerical and numerical ability; they tend to value business and economic achievement; they prefer working in office and clerical occupations such as accountant and bookkeeper.

Holland proposed that occupational environments are dominated by a given type of person and thus the environments can also be categorized by combinations of these six RIASEC types. People search for environments that are compatible with their own values and interests and let them exercise their skills and abilities on problems that they find satisfying. Ultimately, the person's work performance is determined by an interaction of personality and environment, with the best performance occurring when there is a match between both. For example, an individual who is categorized as a conventional type is more likely to be satisfied working as an accountant in an occupational environment dominated by conventional types than as a photographer working in an artistic environment. An interest inventory does not assess the individual with respect to the knowledge, skills, or abilities that are needed to work as an accountant or a photographer; it only assesses the compatibility of interests.

Holland's theory is much more complex than what can be presented here, with most interests and occupations related to a combination of the six basic types. Holland's theory, on the whole, has received a good deal of empirical support. For example, RIASEC types, measured while college students were still in school, predicted their employment status a year after graduation. The graduates were, in fact, employed in occupations and environments that were consistent with their RIASEC types. While other factors such as personality played a role in predicting employment outcomes, the fit among RIASEC types and work environments helped to explain the students' job choices (DeFruyt and Mervielde, 1999). Holland's theory has influenced the work of professionals in the areas of educational, occupational, and career counselling.

BOX 7.3 Commonly Used Interest Inventories

Canadian Occupational Interest Inventory

General Occupational Interest Inventory

Jackson Vocational Interest Survey

Kuder Preference Record, Vocational

Minnesota Importance Questionnaire

Self-Directed Search

Sixteen Personality Factor Questionnaire

Strong Interest Inventory

Vocational Preference Inventory

Interest inventories, those based on Holland's theory or on others (see Box 7.3), are useful tools in the hands of a trained vocational counsellor; they identify lines of work or occupations that individuals may never have considered. Interest inventories are most useful when the individual responds openly and honestly. They are of little value if an individual fakes answers to convince the counsellor or someone else that he or she should, or should not, pursue a certain career.

IDENTIFYING KNOWLEDGE, SKILLS, ABILITIES, AND COMPETENCIES

Potential job applicants must also have a good idea of the knowledge, skills, abilities, and other attributes (KSAOs) as well as the competencies they possess and their compatibility to those required for the job they are seeking. Job advertisements and other recruiting materials generally give the individual guidance about the needed KSAOs and competencies; candidates must decide on their own whether they meet those qualifications. Many job applicants do not have an accurate perception of their own strengths and weaknesses; neither do they know how to present vital information to prospective employers. People apply to many jobs for which they are not qualified.

Employers take several steps, based on the candidates' applications and résumés, to screen out individuals who do not meet the basic job requirements. Vocational guidance counsellors can help job seekers, both new and experienced, avoid futile applications by helping them to identify their abilities, skills, and other talents. Many of the tests used by employers to identify knowledge, skills, and personality types are also available for use by qualified counsellors. Vocational counsellors have a good understanding of the level of abilities, skills, or competencies needed in certain jobs and can help candidates determine whether their applications for those jobs have a realistic chance of meeting with success. They can also assist job seekers in presenting themselves to prospective employers by helping them to write letters and résumés that are well organized and that will create a favourable impression of the candidate. Many of the services offered by vocational counsellors can be obtained over the Internet (see Box 7.4).

BOX 7.4 Job Search on the Internet

One of the most useful tools in conducting a job search is the Internet. There are hundreds of sites related to work and occupations. One of the best is the site operated by Human Resources Development Canada (HRDC). The URL for this site is http://www.hrdc-drhc.gc.ca/. The first step is to choose your language of choice and then proceed to the next page, which lists the services provided by HRDC. Choosing the "Work/Jobs" button will lead you to a wealth of information not only about jobs available across Canada but also about effective job search strategies including information on preparing a résumé and interview hints. There are links to every HRDC centre throughout Canada and a list of available jobs in each province and territory. There are also links to other employment sites such as Ask the Headhunter (http://www.asktheheadhunter.com/), Monster Board Canada (http://www.monster.ca/), and Career Mosaic Canada (http://canada.careermosaic.com/). These sites also offer considerable information on preparing and searching for a job.

The HRDC site also has an interactive feature called Work Search at http://worksearch.gc.ca/cgi-bin/start.pl. This site takes potential job seekers through a job search process. It starts with getting to "Know Yourself." A series of exercises, questionnaires, and inventories help you to:

- identify your skills
- explore your interests
- assess your aptitudes
- identify your learning style
- make decisions in choosing among jobs
- understand the style of supervision that you prefer
- identify your communication skills

Other modules take you through the process of looking for work and exploring careers. One of the best things anyone can do is to spend some time at the HRDC website before they begin their job search. It will be time well invested.

INTENSITY OF THE JOB SEARCH

Job seekers pursue employment with different levels of intensity. Some take a very casual, passive approach and apply only for those positions that meet their ideals. They may not do a very thorough or systematic job search, simply relying on formal advertisements or job announcements. They do not take the time to find out anything about the organization, the job, or themselves. They do not make an effort to use resources such as vocational counsellors to assist in the **job search**. Other applicants spend several hours a day job hunting by examining all possible sources of information, including social networks, news groups on the Internet, and friends and relatives. They apply for any position that falls within their area of interest. These applicants also investigate the organization and have a good perception of the job and their own strengths and weaknesses. The more intense the job search, the more likely an individual will find a job placement (Zadny and James, 1977).

> **Job search**—the strategies, techniques, and practices an individual uses in looking for a job.

Two factors, financial need and self-esteem, influence job search intensity. Individuals with greater financial need pursue jobs with greater intensity. Studies done on unemployment compensation systems consistently show that higher unemployment benefits, as well as lengthier benefit periods, are related to longer periods of unemployment. The higher benefit levels may reduce the financial consequences of unemployment and allow job seekers to hold out for a better job (Schwab et al., 1987). Regardless of financial considerations, some people are achievement-oriented; being unemployed lowers their self-esteem and self-worth. Having a job is an important part of their identity. Whatever the reasons, the intensity of the job search effort increases the likelihood of attracting job offers and of finding a job (Schwab et al., 1987).

The intensity of the job search is also influenced by the size of the organization in which a job seeker prefers to work. Job seekers appear to tailor their job search to match the recruiting strategies used by large or small organizations. Large firms, particularly when recruiting college or university graduates, tend to have more formal and bureaucratic recruiting practices, while smaller firms rely on more informal methods. Large firms tend to start recruiting earlier and to use trained recruiters and campus placement offices. They also are more likely to base their decisions on a candidate's objective qualifications and the results of employment tests. Smaller firms tend to rely more on traditional sources such as advertising and internal referrals to fill their positions and to base their decisions on an interview. Students who prefer a large firm start their job search earlier and make use of recruiting sources, such as the campus placement office, that are used by larger firms. Students who prefer smaller firms are less intense in their search efforts and rely on traditional sources of information about jobs (Barber and Wesson, 1999).

JOB CHOICE MODELS

Successful job searches end with offers of employment. The successful applicant may be in the enviable position of having to choose between several offers. How do job applicants make such decisions, and more importantly, what are the implications of these decision strategies for recruitment efforts?

BOX 7.5 A Job Search Strategy

1. Determine your values and interests.

2. Determine your knowledge, skills, abilities, and other talents.

3. Determine the jobs or occupation in which you are interested and for which you qualify.

4. Begin an intensive and systematic search for jobs in your designated occupations.

5. Thoroughly investigate all available jobs uncovered by your search.

6. Thoroughly investigate the organizations in which those jobs are available.

7. Determine if there is a fit between yourself, the job, and the organization.

8. Pursue all available jobs where there is a fit.

Box 7.1 presents several job attributes that job applicants believe are important. How does an applicant compare these attributes when deciding between competing offers? If an applicant wants to find a job that provides both excellent pay and opportunity for advancement, which job will the applicant choose when Job A provides excellent pay but no opportunity for advancement and Job B provides opportunity for advancement but poor pay?

EXPECTANCY THEORY

Expectancy theory (Vroom, 1964) is a widely studied theory of work motivation that has also been used as a framework to study how job candidates make job choices. The theory proposes that a job candidate's decision to join an organization is based on the candidate's belief about the likelihood that a job will bring with it valued attributes. The theory proposes that candidates will choose the job with the highest expected value. This score is based on adding together the perceived value for each attribute, weighted by its likelihood. If the score for Job A is higher than for Job B, the candidate will choose Job A.

Expectancy theorists disagree on whether candidates evaluate all job attributes or only a limited number. Regardless of the number of attributes involved, expectancy models differ in assuming whether candidates evaluate job attributes sequentially or simultaneously. They also differ in assuming whether candidates attempt to find a job that maximizes the expected value, or whether candidates accept a job as soon as they find one that meets a minimum expected value (Schwab et al., 1987). On the whole, expectancy models provide a reasonably good framework for understanding job choice decisions (Wanous and Colella, 1989).

Box 7.6 An Illustration of Expectancy Theory

VALUES FOR JOB ATTRIBUTES

Suppose that job candidates assign values that range from −5 to +5 to different job attributes. Candidate X assigns a value of +5 to pay and +3 to opportunity for advancement. [Note: In reality there are more than two attributes to evaluate for any position.]

LIKELIHOOD OF OBTAINING THE DESIRED OUTCOME

Candidate X believes there is an 80 percent chance that Job A will provide excellent pay but only a 60 percent chance of opportunity for advancement. In evaluating Job B, Candidate X comes to expect a 40 percent chance of excellent pay and an 80 percent chance of advancement.

WEIGHTED EXPECTANCY SCORE

For Job A, Weighted Expectancy Score = [(+5 × .80) + (+3 × .60)] = 4.8
For Job B, Weighted Expectancy Score = [(+5 × .40) + (+3 × .80)] = 4.4

DECISION

Expectancy theory predicts that the candidate will pursue the job with the highest score when all the attributes, weighted by their perceived value and likelihood, are added together. Therefore, Candidate X should choose Job A.

Job Search/Job Choice

Job choice—a decision strategy that a job candidate uses in making a choice among competing job offers.

The job search/job choice model (Soelberg, 1967) proposes that candidates follow four steps in making a **job choice** decision. The four steps in Soelberg's model integrate many of the points already discussed in this chapter:

1. The candidate identifies an occupation based on his or her values and perceived qualifications.

2. The candidate plans a job search.

3. During the job search and job choice stage, a candidate examines all possible job choices until one is found that meets the candidate's minimum standards on a selected number of job attributes. Each attribute is examined sequentially; high scores on one attribute do not compensate for low scores on another. If one attribute is perceived to be deficient, the job is not accepted. (In expectancy models, high scores on one attribute compensate for low scores on another since all scores are added together.) Once a minimally acceptable job is found, the candidate attempts to find at least one other minimally acceptable job before making a choice.

4. Before making a commitment to accept a job, the candidate attempts to verify the information used in making the initial job choice decision.

While the job search/job choice model is very appealing, there is insufficient empirical evidence on which to judge its soundness (Wanous and Colella, 1989).

Image Matching

Tom's (1971) image matching theory proposes that job candidates compare their own self-image with their image of an organization and choose to work for the organization whose perceived image closely matches their own. This approach is very similar to Holland's argument that candidates seek occupational environments that are congruent with their interests. For example, a computer designer, whose self-image is that of a laid-back, easy-going person, would be less likely to take a job at IBM (which might be perceived as a straight-laced, buttoned-down organization) and more likely to take a job at Apple Computers (which might be perceived as a more informal, easy-going organization). Whether these perceptions are correct is irrelevant; what matters is the match between the candidate's perception of self and the organization.

Like job search/job choice theory, Tom's model has generated very little research on which to judge its soundness. The few studies that have investigated this theory tend to support its premise (Wanous and Colella, 1989). It remains an interesting alternative by proposing that candidates make job choices through a simultaneous comparison of organizations rather than through a comparison of job attributes, and that they make choices on the basis of an image match rather than seeking the best job.

IMPLICATIONS FOR RECRUITMENT

REDUCING INFORMATION OVERLOAD All of the job choice models require the job candidate to handle and process large amounts of information about jobs and organizations. Candidates may experience information overload and try to cope with this situation by either ignoring additional information or by only paying attention to selected pieces of information. Either way, important information about the job and organization is lost. Job candidates can only base their decisions on information that they have retained. This limitation offers suggestions on how organizations should present information to job candidates.

ACCURACY AND CONSISTENCY OF INFORMATION Organizations must recognize that candidates have a limited capacity to retain information. It is of no benefit to present candidates with an extensive amount of information when most of it will be lost in a very short time. Organizations should limit their information flow to a reasonable level while at the same time making sure that the candidate becomes aware of important features of the job and its environment. The information that a candidate receives from an organization should be consistent. Candidates may use the behaviour of organization representatives as signals or indicators about the organization's climate, efficiency, and attitude toward employees (Schwab et al., 1987). While the organization cannot control the message a candidate receives about it from external sources, it can ensure that all information and materials received from the organization and its representatives are accurate and consistent. This does not mean that a company should insist that only positive information be presented about itself. As we will discuss shortly, it may be more desirable in the long run to convey accurate information, even if some of that material is negative.

REPETITION Job seekers often distort information they receive to make it support decisions they make or want to make. Information theory suggests that repetition is an effective communication strategy to ensure that important information is accurately received. Important information should be presented to the candidate by several different information sources. The sources chosen to present important information on job and organizational attributes must be seen by the candidate as reliable and credible. These sources represent the organization and are used by the candidate to form an image of it. Organizations must give serious consideration not only to the content of information presented to candidates but also to the context in which it is presented. The organization must take extreme care in preparing recruiting materials, selecting advertising media, and choosing the recruiters who will interact with job applicants.

IMAGE ADVERTISING In making a job choice, candidates evaluate the organization as well as the job. As part of an initial job search, job seekers may not even consider applying for jobs in organizations that have a negative image.

Job seekers may decide against smaller companies with little or poor public visibility. To counteract such perceptions, or to create an accurate perception, organizations often initiate activities designed to enhance their image and reputation. **Image advertising** seeks to raise the profile of organizations in a positive manner to attract interest from job seekers (Magnus, 1985). A good example of image advertising is the "No life like it" advertising campaign used by the Canadian Forces to create a positive image about the military lifestyle. The campaign is directed at attracting the attention and interest of individuals who might not normally consider a military career because of misperceptions.

An organization that is having trouble attracting qualified candidates should investigate how it is perceived by job candidates and take corrective action, if necessary. One of the difficulties here is identifying the components that influence an organization's image as different individuals may hold different images of the same company. Job seekers and company executives may hold very different perceptions of the organization's image. Smithers, Highhouse, Zickar, Thornsteinson, Stierwalt, and Slaughter (1999) present a method for assessing a company's "employment image" or the image that job seekers hold about the company as an employer. This concept is similar to that of organizational attractiveness. Identifying the applicant's perceptions through this methodology will help to ensure a better fit between the applicant and the organization. Image advertising must present an accurate and consistent picture of the organization. Image advertising that creates misperceptions will lead to mismatches in the fit between person and organization. Image advertising should be designed to improve the attractiveness of the organization on the basis of an accurate representation of its characteristics.

THE PERSON–ORGANIZATION FIT

Up to this point we have discussed the job search and job choice process from the job candidate's perspective. Obviously, there is another player involved in this process. No matter how desirable or compatible a job and organization appear to the candidate, it is all for naught unless the candidate receives an offer of employment. While the candidate seeks to learn as much as possible about the job and organization, the organization, through its representatives, is seeking to learn as much as it can about the candidate. At the same time, both the candidate and the organization are trying to appear as attractive as possible to each other. The organization wants to have a choice of top candidates, while the candidate wants to have a choice of job offers. The job candidate and the organization are each trying to determine if the other is the right fit.

The attraction-selection-attrition model developed by Schneider (1987; Schneider, Goldstein, and Smith, 1995) provides a good illustration of the **person–organization fit** process. This model rests on the mutual attraction

Image advertising— advertising designed to raise an organization's profile in a positive manner in order to attract interest from job seekers.

Person–organization fit— a process through which a job applicant and an organization reach a mutual decision that the candidate is the right choice for the organization and the organization is the right choice for the candidate.

between a job candidate and an organization, which is represented by the people involved in the recruiting and selection process. Job candidates view organizations as being an attractive place to work based on their perception of the level of compatibility between their own characteristics and those of the organization, that is, the recruiter. The organization selects those people who it believes have the characteristics and attributes it finds desirable. Once job seekers are hired and begin to work in the organization, they assess the fit between themselves and their work environment. If there is a match, they remain on the job; if there is a mismatch, they leave.

One of the significant factors that new hires consider in assessing their fit within the organization is their view of the people in the organization. Managers within a company tend to have very similar personality attributes (Schneider, Smith, Taylor, and Fleenor, 1998). This is similar to Holland's theory that people within a specific occupation tend to have similar attributes. New hires who perceive a lack of congruence between themselves and their supervisors express less commitment to the company and more intentions to leave (Van Vianen, 2000). In addition, the degree of similarity between an organization's culture and a job applicant's value preferences predicts their turnover. The lower the degree of similarity, the more likely an employee will leave an organization within the first year of employment with the company (Vandenberghe, 1999).

The company's recruiter makes two assessments during the recruiting process. The first concerns whether the job applicant has the knowledge, skills, abilities, or competencies required by the job. The second concerns whether the recruiter perceives the candidate to fit the organization. The recruiter's perception that the applicant fits the job appears to be based mainly on an assessment of the candidate's skill and experience derived from information gathered during the recruiting process. The recruiter's perception of a person–organization fit is mostly based on an assessment of the candidate's personality and values. Both the perception of person–job fit and of person–organization fit predict whether the company will make a job offer. The perception of a poor person–organization fit, however, will reduce the likelihood that a person with a good job fit will receive a job offer. Recruiters form and use perceptions of a candidate's organizational fit as part of the hiring process (Kristof-Brown, 1998).

The assessment of fit and the decision of the company to make an offer and the candidate to accept it are based on the exchange of information that takes place over the recruitment process. If the job candidate does not make an adequate investigation of the job or organization, or if the organization does not represent itself accurately through the people involved in recruiting and selection, the probability of a person–organization mismatch increases. Mismatches can be quite costly in terms of absenteeism, low productivity, and turnover. A major goal of any recruitment campaign should be to improve the chance of making a good fit between candidates and the organization.

Communication and Perception

Based on information that was available or obtained during the recruitment process, the candidate and the organization form a perception of each other. If the perceptions of both are positive ("This is the right candidate," "This is the right job for me"), a job offer is made and accepted. If the perceptions of one do not match those of the other, a job offer is either not made, or if made, not accepted. Figure 7.2 presents the possible outcomes from this process. In all cases, there is a possibility that the perceptions formed by both the candidate and the organization are wrong. Candidates, particularly, develop overly positive perceptions of the organization (Wanous and Colella, 1989).

Perceptions are based on communication. During the recruiting process both the candidate and the organization try to control the flow of information from one to the other. One party may not wish to share some information with the other. An organization may fear losing top-quality candidates by revealing that it is not the perfect workplace; candidates may fear losing a job offer by admitting they do not plan to stay with the organization for a long period of time. Both may misrepresent their attributes or characteristics. An organization may exaggerate the chances for promotion to attract a candidate; candidates may exaggerate their experience. Both the organization and the candidate evaluate each other during the recruitment process (Rynes, 1993).

Inaccurate, incomplete, or distorted information leads to misperceptions and inaccurate decisions. A primary goal of recruitment should be to increase the accuracy of the perceptions that each party holds about the other.

FIGURE 7.2 MATCHING THE CANDIDATE'S AND ORGANIZATION'S PERCEPTIONS: JOB OFFER OUTCOMES

		Candidate's Perception of the Organization	
		Positive	Negative
Organization's Perception of the Candidate	Positive	Job offer made by organization and accepted by candidate.	Job offer made by organization and rejected by candidate.
	Negative	Job offer not made by organization but would have been accepted by candidate.	Job offer not made by organization and would not have been accepted by candidate.

ACCURATE EXPECTATIONS

By developing a systematic job search strategy, job candidates will come into contact with information on jobs and organizations. Many of the initial expectations that candidates develop are based on the accuracy of this preliminary information, as well as the more extensive information that accumulates during the recruiting process. For example, accuracy of information received from the recruiting source and the organization directly influenced the length of time that Canadian students stayed in seasonal jobs as well as their commitment to the organization and their job satisfaction (Saks, 1994). Candidates actively evaluate the merits of any message they receive (Wanous and Colella, 1989). Organizations, however, have no control over whether candidates search for any information, or which information they select and use in forming an opinion about the job or organization. Newcomers in an organization often develop overly high expectations about the job and organization. These initial expectations may substantially influence the long-term relationship between the candidate and the organization (Buckley, Fedor, Marvin, Veres, Wise, and Carraher, 1998). Organizations do, however, have control over the accuracy and the completeness of the information they present when recruiting job candidates. During the United States' war with Iraq, many military personnel who were recruited into the U.S. reserve forces were shocked and outraged to learn that they were liable for combat duty; they claimed that they had never been made aware of such a possibility before signing on (Buckley, Fedor, and Marvin, 1994).

Courts in both Canada and the United States have held employers accountable for the accuracy of information they present to job candidates as part of the recruiting process. False promises and misrepresentations made in recruiting candidates to work for a company may result in a damage award. Employees who believe that they were misled about the nature of their working conditions or their working environment are likely to take legal action against their employers to the extent that they are injured through reliance on the false or misleading statements (Buckley et al., 1994). As part of orienting newcomers into an organization, a company may wish to initiate a set of procedures that are designed to lower the expectations of the new hire to more realistic and accurate perceptions of the organization, apart from that individual's specific job (Buckley et al., 1998).

CREATING ACCURATE EXPECTATIONS

Four factors play an influential role in creating accurate expectations that candidates hold about prospective jobs: (1) the source of the information, (2) the media used to deliver the information, (3) the content of the information, and (4) the nature of the job candidates who receive the information (Popovich and Wanous, 1982).

SOURCE OF INFORMATION In describing a job or position, the organization should present information to job candidates that accurately describes the job and its context. As discussed in previous chapters, the best way to obtain this information is through organization and job analysis. The information obtained through these means serves as a good basis for recruiting materials and other information presented to job candidates. Year-end reports, shareholder reports, technical manuals, and other documents are also good sources of accurate information. In particular, annual reports offer insight into the mission, values, and goals of the organization.

COMMUNICATION MEDIA There is an extensive array of media that organizations can use to contact job seekers. We will take a more detailed look at some of the more prominent recruitment media, and their effectiveness, later in this chapter. In choosing recruitment media, organizations should consider the effect of the communication channel itself on the recruitment process. Both Wanous and Colella (1989) and Rynes (1991) summarize empirical research on the effectiveness of recruiting media. Those reviews suggest that media differ in effectiveness in relation to the criteria used to measure the effectiveness. Job applicants who are recruited through referrals from people in the organization are less likely to quit than job candidates who are recruited through newspaper advertisements; on the other hand, job applicants who walk in off the street may perform at higher levels than referrals.

At present, there is little theoretical understanding of the relationship between recruitment sources and organizational outcome measures, thus limiting the usefulness of this empirical information in constructing recruitment programs. Perhaps the best advice is to use a broad approach and to use as many different types of communication media as the organization can afford, including newer technologies such as job postings on the Internet or an organization's homepage on the World Wide Web. These newer technologies offer the potential for quick, two-way interaction between job candidates and the organization that may be very effective in promoting accurate communication (Wanous and Colella, 1989).

CONTENT OF INFORMATION The content of information provided throughout the recruitment process is the most important factor in creating accurate job expectations (Breaugh and Billings, 1988). Breaugh and Billings propose that the content of the recruitment message should be

- Accurate—job candidates should be given both positive and negative information about the job and the organization.
- Specific—job candidates should be given detailed information that will allow them to make an informed decision.
- Broad—job candidates should be given information about a wide range of job and organizational attributes, not only information related to a narrow range of topics.

- Credible—job candidates must believe that the information they receive is reliable and accurate.

- Important—job candidates should be given information that is important to their decision making, which they are unlikely to receive through other means.

NATURE OF THE JOB CANDIDATES The organization must know something about the audience that will receive the information. This includes knowledge of the social and demographic characteristics of the target group. For example, the written materials used as part of the recruitment process should be readable by the potential job applicants. Written recruiting materials that require a college or university reading level might not be understood by job candidates with less education; this could create a problem if the job only requires a high-school education. Conversely, materials written at a lower level might present the wrong image when trying to attract college and university graduates. In the case of recruiting people with very specialized expertise, the recruitment materials may contain specialized terms that will only be understood by people with the appropriate background. In this way, they act to screen out inappropriate applicants.

In addition to being understood, the content of the message should be presented in a manner compatible with its intended audience. The materials should encourage interest in the job and company on the part of the candidate. This is more likely to happen if the material addresses the needs and interests of its target group.

The organization should also know the sources of information that its target audience is likely to use. Professionals who are looking for a job may use the services of a private employment agency, or search job advertisements in professional newsletters or journals. Blue-collar job seekers may rely on classified ads in the local newspaper or the services of Human Resources Canada Centres (HRCC; these were formerly called Canada Employment Centres). Cost is always a factor in determining choice of media; nonetheless, limited job advertising compromises an employer's ability to mount a defence against charges of discriminatory hiring practices. If the organization only recruits carpenters by placing job ads in male-oriented magazines, it runs the risk of not attracting female applicants and of not hiring female carpenters. Female carpenters could argue that the recruiting process was designed to limit female applications by not advertising the position in media of interest to female carpenters. If a lawsuit by female carpenters were successful on these grounds, the organization might be liable for substantial damages.

REALISTIC JOB PREVIEWS

Recruitment programs can be designed to increase the accuracy of the expectations that job candidates hold about the job and the organization. One such

Realistic job preview—a procedure designed to reduce turnover and increase satisfaction among newcomers to an organization by providing job candidates with accurate information about the job and the organization.

program, **realistic job previews** (RJPs), is very effective in improving the fit between the job candidate and the organization. The primary goal of RJPs is to reduce turnover among newcomers to an organization by providing job candidates with accurate information about the job and the organization (Wanous, 1980). Other hoped-for outcomes of the RJP are (1) that the job candidates will develop realistic perceptions of what it is like to work in the organization; (2) that they will view the organization in a more credible light; and (3) that, if they accept the job offer, they will be more satisfied with their job and committed to the organization. Extensive research shows that RJPs accomplish their goals. RJPs given before an applicant is hired do reduce job turnover and lead to increased job satisfaction (Phillips, 1998).

Rather than have a candidate accept a job on the basis of unrealistic expectations, only to quit after discovering a mismatch with the organization, RJPs give the candidate an accurate preview of the job before the job offer is accepted (e.g., weekend work, limited promotional opportunities). In this way, candidates who discover a mismatch self-select out, or remove themselves from the competition, saving themselves the aggravation of having made a bad decision and the organization the cost of hiring and training them. There are some concerns, however, that the realism also discourages very qualified candidates from accepting job offers from the organization (Rynes, 1991).

The more exposure a job applicant has to a job, the more likely it is that the applicant may overemphasize the negative aspects of the job and refuse a job offer; this aspect of RJPs may prove problematic in extremely competitive job markets (Meglino, Ravlin, and DeNisi, 1997). The negative information in the RJP does influence the job applicant's decision and may have a greater adverse impact on the best-qualified applicants (Bretz and Judge, 1998), requiring greater compensation to attract them to the position (Saks, Wiesner, and Summers, 1996).

The Canadian Forces (CF) use RJPs as part of its recruitment program. The program was designed to reduce early attrition of new recruits by improving the person–job fit; the RJP is carried out throughout the Canadian Forces as a matter of policy. The RJP is embedded in a comprehensive counselling system designed to match the goals, interests, and abilities of applicants to the characteristics and conditions of service associated with specific trades in the Forces (Wilson, 1980). By using advertising media and recruiting visits to schools and public places such as shopping malls, the Canadian Forces raise the interest of potential applicants in the military as a career and attract them to recruiting centres. The applicant is met by a recruiting officer who presents the candidate with brochures and information on the CF and determines initial suitability of the candidate for a career in the CF. Applicants who pass this first screen then view an orientation video, which depicts the careers of two actual candidates from recruitment through basic and trades training, and on to their first job postings. The video provides a realistic preview of life in the Forces in general and includes information on both the positive and negative aspects of military life. For example, it may portray the personal and social support

BOX 7.7 Developing and Implementing Realistic Job Previews in a Recruitment Program

1. Initiate RJPs to avoid future problems, not current problems.

2. The diagnosis of organizational problems that prompt the introduction of an RJP does not have to be highly structured.

3. An RJP should evaluate or judge conditions as well as simply describe them.

4. RJPs should concentrate on a few major issues and make in-depth presentations on those items rather than try to cover every possible issue.

5. Proportional to what the job is really like, RJPs should include moderately negative information but not extremely negative information.

6. RJPs should include the presentation of audiovisual materials.

7. The people appearing in RJP materials should be actual employees rather than actors.

8. The RJP should take place relatively early in the recruitment process.

9. The RJP should be implemented as a matter of policy and not left to the wishes of individuals handling the recruiting.

10. The results of any evaluation of an RJP program should be made available to any interested parties, including competitors.

Source: Based on Wanous (1989).

offered to members of the CF and their families as well as the hazards and physical demands of military duty (Ellis and Angus, 1985).

Following the orientation video, the candidate meets with a military career counsellor and has an opportunity to raise any questions or concerns stimulated by the video. At this point, the candidate must make a decision about whether to continue the process by completing an application form and a series of ability and aptitude tests. Candidates are next shown up to five trade/lifestyle videos for entry-level positions for which they qualified through ability and aptitude testing. These videos are based on interviews with personnel from each trade they represent; they contain both verbal descriptions and live action footage of what it is like to work in that trade in a military environment. The speakers not only provide a description of what the trade is like but also express their views about their work. Following these videos, the candidate meets once again with a military career counsellor to review all aspects of the different trades and the military lifestyle. If the candidate remains interested in one of the selected trades, if there is an appropriate vacancy in that specialty, and if the candidate has passed a series of employment tests and interviews, the candidate is given an offer to enroll in the Canadian Forces (Ellis and Angus, 1985). This offer is made conditional on the candidate's meeting appropriate medical and physical requirements.

RJPs remain one of the most intriguing aspects of the recruiting process. Notwithstanding the methodological flaws in RJP research (Rynes, 1991), RJPs lead to accurate expectations on the part of job candidates, to reductions in turnover, and to improvements in job satisfaction (Phillips, 1998). Today's increasingly educated workers have higher expectations about their workplace and their jobs. They expect greater opportunities for skill development and empowerment (i.e., input into decision making). Many of these expectations may be unrealistic. Realistic job previews may be a valuable tool in helping to lower these expectations to more reasonable levels; as such, they are likely to be used on a wider scale. Greater use of RJPs is also consistent with recent attempts by organizations to improve communications and strengthen bonds of trust with their members. One could argue that a realistic job preview is necessary if an organization wishes to behave ethically and to treat all applicants fairly.

EXPECTATION-LOWERING PROCEDURE

There is one more step an organization can take to ensure accurate expectations once job applicants become new hires. Many companies have new hires go through an orientation procedure to learn about the policies and practices of the company. The inclusion of material designed to lower expectations as part of this orientation will also lead to a reduction in some of the negative outcomes experienced by new hires. These expectancy-lowering procedures (ELPs) focus on the expectations of the new hires rather than on specific aspects of the job or organization, which are typically included in an RJP.

An ELP workshop would present information showing (1) how important it is to have realistic expectations at the start of a job and how expectations are formed, (2) how unrealistically high expectations are related to negative organizational outcomes, and (3) how unrealistically high expectations that remain unfulfilled lead to dissatisfaction with work and turnover. Buckley et al. (1998) demonstrated that an ELP such as this led to less dissatisfaction and turnover and recommended that organizations use it as a complement to RJPs.

RECRUITMENT STRATEGY

The first part of this chapter presented an overview of the job recruitment process from the perspective of both the job candidate and the organization. The remaining sections of this chapter focus on the more practical aspects of the recruiting process. Recruitment takes place in a human resources context, which is influenced by both internal and external factors as well as the more immediate needs of the job and the organization. Figure 7.1 illustrates the role that these factors play in recruiting. These factors raise a number of issues that must be addressed when developing a recruitment strategy in the context of an organization's strategic planning. A sustainable competitive advantage is achieved through people, starting with *recruiting* the best.

BOX 7.8 Brain Drain or Brain Trickle?

Business leaders, particularly those in the high-tech industries, have raised the issue of a "brain drain" of the best and brightest Canadian professionals from Canada to the United States, and have advocated lower taxes as one means of stemming the drain and competing for talented people. Is there a critical shortage of highly skilled employees in knowledge industry occupations?

A recent Statistics Canada report sheds some light on this situation. It says that the "brain drain" of highly skilled Canadians to the United States remains small in comparison with historical data and in relation to the supply of workers in sensitive occupations, and that it is more than offset by a huge "brain gain"—the immigration of knowledge workers into Canada from the rest of the world.

Statistics Canada reported that during the 1990s, between 22 000 and 35 000 Canadians moved to the United States each year, including 10 000 who held university degrees. This loss was more than offset by the entry into Canada each year of over 39 000 degree-holders, 11 000 of whom held Master's or Ph.D. degrees.

The major losses to the United States were, in order, physicians (0.78%), natural scientists (0.39%), nurses (0.33%), engineers (0.27%), post-secondary teachers (0.13%), managerial workers (0.12%), and computer scientists (0.07%). The figures in parentheses represent the loss of workers expressed as a percentage of the supply of workers in the occupation.

The empirical data suggest that the "brain drain" is more of a "brain trickle." They also suggest that companies experiencing difficulties in attracting qualified applicants reexamine their recruitment policies and practices.

The full Statistics Canada report is available at: http://www.statcan.ca/english/indepth/81-003/feature/eq2000_v06n3_a01_hi.htm

RECRUITMENT AND ORGANIZATIONAL STRATEGY

Linking recruitment to organizational strategy involves expanding standardized and formalized job descriptions to reflect the broader and more changeable strategic requirements of the organization (Snow and Snell, 1993). The knowledge, skills, abilities, competencies, and other requirements for the work to be performed must be derived from both the technological and cultural requirements of the company's strategy. For example, the Guelph, Ontario, plant of Asea Brown Bovari (ABB), manufacturer of electrical power transformers, adopted a participative team-oriented workplace. They recruited individuals to serve as "team leaders" (replacing the role of "foremen"). The position requirements called for individuals who, in addition to having the expertise to provide technical support, had good interpersonal skills and were comfortable working in a participatory, team-oriented culture. These qualities were assessed largely through behaviour-based interviews and personality inventories. In the move to this team-based structure, considerable effort went into explicitly linking individual and team performance to the overall mission of the plant. This was done to help employees attain a better sense of where they fit within the organization.

As an alternative to recruiting and offering full-time employment to individuals with a specific set of skills that match an organization's current strategy, companies may seek employment relationships that enhance their ability to quickly change strategy as circumstances require by hiring workers contingent on their anticipated needs. Specifically, they may recruit individuals with the skills and abilities to complement a particular strategy, but hire them under a short-term contract. Should the organization's strategy change, calling for a different mix of human resources, the organization could then recruit individuals with the new attributes, allowing the earlier short-term contracts to lapse (Snow and Snell, 1993). In addition to using such "contingent" workers, organizations may make increasing use of part-time employees and outsourcing. All of these arrangements are dependent on the nature of the existing labour market. A further consideration is whether such arrangements lead to an organization attracting and retaining the best possible employees.

EXTERNAL FACTORS

All recruitment is influenced by two factors over which the organization has little control: (1) the labour market, and (2) the legal environment (Rynes, 1991).

LABOUR MARKETS AND RECRUITING Organizations must develop a recruiting campaign that makes sense in the context of a specific labour market. Labour markets impose different constraints than do economic conditions. The overall nature of the economy may influence an organization's decision to hire or not to hire, but once a decision to hire is made, the nature of the labour market determines how extensively the organization will have to search to fill the job with a qualified candidate. Toyota Canada was in the enviable position of having more than 50 000 people apply for 1200 positions that were being created as part of an expansion at its Cambridge, Ontario, plant. The jobs paid $20 per hour plus benefits in a geographic area that had an 8.3 percent rate of unemployment. Toyota had 11 000 applications on file before it had run a single advertisement or posted the jobs with Human Resources Canada Centres (Keenan, 1996).

When qualified labour is scarce, the organization must broaden its recruiting beyond its normal target population. This includes going beyond normal recruiting channels to attract applicants it might not seek in more favourable times. For example, if there is a shortage of chartered accountants, the organization may take a look at hiring finance majors with a background in accounting whom they believe will develop into the position with some additional training. The organization may also recruit outside its normal territory, emphasizing those geographic regions with high unemployment rates or low economic growth. In favourable labour markets, the organization may only advertise the accounting position in one or two professional journals. In a poor market, it may decide to use a variety of media to attract as many qualified applicants as possible. With poor labour markets, the organization may make the job more attractive by improving salary and benefits, training and educational opportunities, and working conditions. In poor markets, the organization may spend additional resources to overcome the shortage of qualified applicants and to increase the attractiveness of the organization and the job as a place of employment. These considerations become even more important when the organization must compete with its rivals for scarce human resources. Recruiting when the labour market is poor is an expensive proposition.

Part-Time Labour Markets and Recruiting

In response to today's global economy, more and more companies are employing low-wage, entry-level workers on a part-time basis. Temporary or contingent jobs have shown tremendous growth over the last decade. Nearly two million people go to work each day in North America on a part-time basis. North American retailing giants such as Sears, Wal-Mart, and K-Mart have made part-time work their industry norm.

Recruiting and retaining the best part-time workers present unique problems to companies choosing to go this route. Workers who receive lower pay and benefits are less likely to feel committed to their organization or to go out of their way to get the job done. Many part-time workers are unskilled and poorly educated. Companies such as Whirlpool have responded to the need to recruit part-time workers by restructuring their pay and benefits as well as providing training and educational opportunities for them. Others, such as Taco Bell, have attempted to restructure the work environment to meet the needs of their part-time employees (Greengard, 1995).

Increasingly, temporary work is serving as a training ground for more permanent positions. A recent survey found that over two-thirds of temporary workers reported that they gained new skills while in their temporary positions. On the other hand, ever greater numbers of skilled professionals and retired workers are taking jobs on a part-time or contract basis (Flynn, 1995). Organizations that depend on part-time workers will need to develop recruiting methods to attract and retain contingent employees.

OUTSOURCING Outsourcing is the practice of contracting with an outside agent to take over specified human resource functions, specifically, recruitment. Companies that need workers on a temporary or short-term basis often turn to temporary help agencies to provide them with contingent workers. In these cases, the workers are employees of the temporary help firm, not of the organization in which they do their work. The employee is actually "leased" from the outside firm. The individual is employed by the outside agency but assigned to a position with the client organization. The outside firm assumes all payroll responsibilities (pay and benefits), but charges the client administration and placement costs, usually prorated to salary. If the client chooses to hire the individual to a full-time permanent position, then additional fees are paid to the personnel agency. Some Canadian banks now meet part of their staffing needs through these arrangements. Client organizations benefit from increased workforce flexibility and savings in administrative costs. They also get to see the worker on the job over a period of time before any decisions to hire directly are made.

Investigations in both Canada (Galt, 1992) and the United States (Castro, 1993) suggest that some temporary help agencies may be willing to accommodate their client organizations' requests that the agency not send blacks, people with accents, or unattractive women. Often, the client organizations have the mistaken notion that since they are not the legal employer, they are immune to charges of discrimination and free from any employment equity obligations. By allowing temporary workers on their premises and directing their work, the client organization can be subject to discrimination claims, unless it can show that the assignment based on group membership was a bona fide occupational requirement (Ryan and Schmit, 1996).

THE LEGAL ENVIRONMENT   Any organizational recruitment program must comply with the legal and regulatory requirements that apply to its operation. Chapter 2 presented some of the landmark cases and legislation that govern employment in Canada. In the United States, employment laws and regulations are assumed to affect both recruitment practices and outcomes (Rynes, 1991). It is likely that Canadian employment legislation has similar effects on recruitment in Canadian organizations. The most important considerations are employment equity and pay equity legislation. Any recruitment campaign that intentionally or unintentionally excludes members of groups that are protected under human rights legislation runs the risk of being declared discriminatory, with the organization subject to penalties and fines. The best defence against charges of **systemic discrimination** is to document that every attempt has been made to attract members from the protected groups.

In Canada, employment equity legislation seeks to eliminate discrimination in the workplace for women, people with disabilities, Native people, and visible minorities. Organizations may be called on, particularly if they wish to do business with the federal government, to demonstrate that they have actively sought to recruit members from these four groups. Good faith recruitment efforts mean that the organization must use a variety of communication channels to get its message to members of different groups and to present its recruiting message in a way that interests different audiences. The recruitment effort must make members from these groups feel welcome within the organization, even when they are working there on a temporary basis. Organizations perceived as hostile to workplace diversity will see the effectiveness of their recruitment efforts significantly compromised, and the quality of their overall applicant pool adversely affected.

Many Canadian communities have made an effort to recruit women and visible minorities for employment as police officers. Most of these efforts have been relatively unsuccessful. In this regard, Afro-Canadian police applicants often perceive a lack of fit between their attitudes and the demands of modern policing that is related to racial prejudice on the part of serving police officers and the community (Perrott, 1999). To help overcome these types of barriers,

Systemic discrimination—in employment, the intentional or unintentional exclusion of members of groups that are protected under human rights legislation through recruiting, selection, or other personnel practices or policies.

women, visible minorities, Aboriginal people, and people with physical challenges should participate as front-line recruiters to help send a clear message of equal employment opportunities and of welcoming women and members of visible-minority groups.

INTERNAL FACTORS

While it is clear that different organizations take different approaches to recruiting new employees, very little is known about how organizational characteristics produce differences in recruiting practices, processes, or outcomes. Partly, this is the result of most research focusing on job seekers rather than the employing organizations (Rynes, 1991). There are many possible organizational characteristics that could influence a job seeker's perception of the organization during the job search phase (e.g., the type of industry, size of the organization, profitability, growth, and financial trends). These characteristics may influence both the number and the quality of applicants who apply for a position with the organization. They may also influence how the organization recruits candidates and how competitive the organization is in making offers to the best applicants (Rynes, 1991).

BUSINESS PLAN   A company's business plan has a major impact on its recruiting strategy. An organization's **business plan** includes a statement of its mission and philosophy, a recognition of its strengths and weaknesses, and a statement of its goals and objectives for competing in its economic environment. A business plan addresses those aspects of the external environment that affect how the organization does business. An organization's business plan influences the degree to which the organization fills vacancies with internal or external applicants (Rynes, 1991). Rarely do organizations fill entry-level positions with internal candidates; however, it is quite common to bring someone in from the outside to fill a vacant position.

> **Business plan**—an organization's statement of its mission and philosophy, a recognition of its strengths and weaknesses, and a statement of its goals and objectives for competing in its economic environment.

Organizations differ in their approach to staffing these positions. Some insist, as a matter of organizational policy, that internal candidates be given preference as a means of motivating employees (recall that advancement is a recruiting factor) and ensuring that the successful candidate knows and shares the organization's philosophy, values, and goals. In some cases, collective agreements with employees may require that internal applicants be given first consideration for positions for which they are qualified. Other organizations insist that external candidates be given preference for jobs in order to expose the company to new ideas and to new ways of doing business. Still other organizations may insist that the best candidate be given the job offer, regardless of whether they are an internal or external applicant.

JOB LEVEL AND TYPE   Both the type of occupation and the nature of the industry in which it is involved may influence an organization's recruiting strategy (Rynes, 1991). In some industries or occupations people are recruited in a particular way, not so much because that method is very effective, but because it is the norm. It is how recruiting is done for that type of work, and how it is expected to be done. For certain executive-level positions, vacancies are never advertised but given to a consulting company to carry out an executive search. Such "headhunting" firms generally have a list of potential executive candidates that they have developed over time through contacts in many different organizations. The search firm knows the organization and works to find a match with one of its candidates. Rarely, if ever, are such firms used to recruit production or service workers; vacancies for these types of positions are filled from candidates who respond to local newspaper advertisements or job postings with Human Resources Canada Centres, or who are referred by other employees, as was the case with the 55 000 applicants for the production jobs at Toyota Canada (Keenan, 1996).

ORGANIZATION AND JOB ANALYSES

Job and organization characteristics play a major role in the recruitment process. Chapter 4 described procedures that allow organizations to identify these characteristics. Organization analysis provides an organization with a means of clarifying its values and goals and of assessing the internal and external environments in which it operates. Job analysis provides the organization with an understanding of the expectations, behaviours, and tasks that are associated with a specific job. Job analysis also provides the organization with an understanding of the knowledge, skill, ability, competencies, or other talents that are needed to perform the job successfully. Both organization and job analyses provide information that helps to increase the person–organization fit. The information produced by these analyses helps the organization's human resources team produce a recruitment strategy.

TRANSLATING ORGANIZATION ANALYSIS DATA INTO THE RECRUITING STRATEGY
There are major differences in how organizations recruit personnel. Recruiting strategies reflect the organization's culture, values, and goals, as does all the information provided to job applicants. These materials, which should accurately represent the organization's culture, values, and goals, also influence who is recruited. As we saw previously, Colgate-Palmolive and British Petroleum recruit applicants who match their goals and values. IBM Canada also ties its recruiting initiatives to achieving organizational goals. In 1995, it hired about 800 new employees based on achieving its objectives of growth, customer satisfaction, and a high-performance culture. Different organizational goals lead to different recruitment strategies. Similarly, an organization's philosophy and values influence whether it actively seeks to recruit women and members of minorities, or whether its approach to employment equity is one of minimal compliance. Organization analysis helps to clarify these issues.

In developing recruiting strategies, one must decide whether to concentrate recruiting efforts on internal or external candidates. Organization analysis reveals the likelihood of finding suitable internal candidates and the extent to which qualified internal candidates can fill the job openings by providing an inventory of skills and abilities that exist within the company as well as indicating the potential for advancement among current employees. In conjunction with job analysis, this information gives a good indication of the likelihood of finding the right internal people for the job and the need for external recruiting. Unfortunately, relatively few companies inventory their employees' skills and abilities; such inventories are expensive to develop and to maintain.

TRANSLATING JOB ANALYSIS DATA INTO RECRUITING MATERIALS One of the most important pieces of information candidates rely on throughout the recruiting process is a description of the job and worker requirements. Recruiting information should give applicants a clear idea of the duties and tasks that form part of the job and the resources that they will need to do the job. It is very difficult to recruit job applicants without knowing the essential characteristics of the position or the requirements of the workers. Job descriptions that are up-to-date and based on a job analysis lead to accurate expectations on the part of the job candidate. Box 7.9 presents a job description for a security dispatcher at a university, which was derived from a critical incident job analysis.

Both applicants and recruiters should have a clear idea of the qualifications needed by people in the position. Often recruiters are told to seek the

---

BOX 7.9 Job Description of a University Security Dispatcher

The Security Dispatcher plays a vital role as part of the Campus Security team. The Security Dispatcher receives, analyzes, and collects vital information from various devices such as emergency telephone lines and surveillance equipment. The Security Dispatcher facilitates and coordinates appropriate responses between university and emergency response teams such as Campus Security, fire department, Metro Police, and others. The Security Dispatcher works in conjunction with the Manager of University Security, the Warrant Officer in charge of Commissionaires, and the Assistant Director of Residence Security.

The Security Dispatcher provides general information, processes requests for assistance (help desk and telephone calls), monitors all surveillance equipment, operates and organizes all recording and communications equipment, and records all incidents, complaints, and information requests in the shift log. The Security Dispatcher is respon-

sible for proper storage and distribution of security equipment. The Security Dispatcher is also responsible for recording, storing, and returning lost and found items.

The Security Dispatcher has a strong team commitment and is responsible for providing guidance and leadership for all veteran and new team members. The Security Dispatcher performs all responsibilities and duties in a polite and efficient manner, particularly when dealing with the public. Also, the Security Dispatcher remains knowledgeable on all policies and duties related to the position.

Previous work experience, first-aid courses, and any type of security training is highly desirable. In view of the above-mentioned responsibilities, the Security Dispatcher must possess a sense of integrity, good written and oral communication skills, general knowledge of campus layout and services, and a general understanding of the role campus Security plays within a university environment.

"best person" for the job, instead of being told to find the "best-qualified person" for the job. Perhaps the best applicant for the security dispatcher's position is a graduate of the police academy who has worked for several years as a desk sergeant with the city police. Without knowing exactly what the security dispatcher did, the university could spend a lot of money hiring someone who was overqualified for the position.

HUMAN RESOURCES PLANNING

Human resources planning—the process of developing and implementing plans and programs to ensure that the right number and type of individuals are available at the right time and place to fill organizational needs.

Human resources planning "is a process of developing and implementing plans and programs to ensure that the right number and type of individuals are available at the right time and place to fill organizational needs" (Dolan and Schuler, 1994, 90). This planning process is based on analysis of the organization's business plan, resulting in a forecast of the number and type of employees required to meet the plan's objectives. Through organization and job analyses, the planning process identifies the human resources needed to carry out the business plan, both those resources that exist within the organization and those that must be secured through a recruiting program. Human resources planning develops an action plan to eliminate any discrepancy between the supply of and demand for human resources. With respect to the recruitment process, human resources planning must provide answers to the following questions:

- Based on our business plan, how many positions will we need to staff?
- Based on the job analysis, what is the nature of the position that must be filled?
- Based on the job analysis, what qualifications (knowledge, skills, abilities, experience) must job candidates possess to do the job successfully?
- Based on organization analysis, what percentage of the positions can, or should, be staffed with internal candidates?
- Based on the labour market, is there an available supply of qualified external candidates?
- Based on the labour market, how extensively will we have to search for qualified applicants? Will we have to search beyond our normal geographic boundaries? Will we have to take special measures to locate our target applicant population? What sources or methods should we use to reach the potential applicants?
- Based on legal considerations, what are our goals with respect to employment equity?
- Based on the business plan, organization analysis, and job analysis, what information and materials will we present to job candidates?

Answers to these questions form the organization's recruiting strategy (i.e., its plan for staffing the organization). The human resources management team must also have a plan for implementing the strategy.

RECRUITMENT ACTION PLAN

TIMING OF RECRUITMENT INITIATIVES In many organizations, recruiting occurs in response to need. An employee leaves for one reason or another and, if the position is retained, must be replaced either through internal or external hiring. In cases like this, there is little organizational control over timing. Delays in hiring may lead to delays in production, with unrealistic demands placed on the remaining employees. The recruitment goal is to hire someone qualified to do the work as soon as possible, even if hiring at a later date may have found someone who was better qualified for the position. In other organizations, where there is a systematic turnover of employees, recruiting may follow a well-defined pattern. This pattern occurs most often in large organizations, which recruit heavily from among college and university graduates (Barber and Wesson, 1999). The availability of such graduates in the spring of each year often determines when organizations implement their recruiting strategy; it influences when they send information to campus employment centres, place advertisements in campus newspapers, visit the schools, meet with the potential applicants, extend invitations to visit the organization, and make their job offers. Figure 7.3 represents a typical time line for these activities. If an organization is late in recruiting, top candidates may have already accepted offers from the competition. To remain competitive, the organization must synchronize its recruiting to when the best candidates are available. This means that the human resources team must have a good working knowledge of the labour market.

In competing for qualified candidates, particularly when supply is weak, organizations are starting to incorporate in their recruiting strategies knowledge of how job candidates evaluate jobs and make choices. There is evidence to suggest that job seekers prefer early job offers as a way of reducing anxiety and uncertainty about other offers; there is also evidence to suggest that more-qualified candidates generate offers earlier and more easily than less-qualified candidates (Rynes, 1991). If this is so, then organizations may have to begin recruiting as early as possible if they want to hire the most-qualified candidates. Instead of waiting until the spring to recruit college and university graduates, a company may begin the process earlier in order to make job offers before the end of the fall semester. Some organizations are also beginning to pursue college and university students before they enter the job market.

FIGURE 7.3 RECRUITING TIME LINE

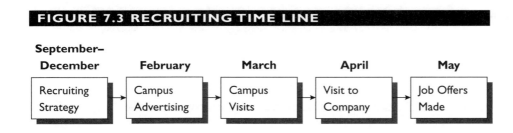

Companies often use summer job placements, internships, or cooperative education as early recruitment programs (Rynes, 1991). These strategies are designed to have candidates accept an early job offer that meets their minimum standards rather than waiting to make a choice between competing offers.

The timing of events within a recruiting program is important. The process outlined in Figure 7.3 can extend over a considerable period of time, with several candidates evaluated for each vacancy. Job candidates do not put a halt to their job search activities while waiting for a decision. An organization that does not provide candidates with timely feedback about their progress through the recruitment and selection process may risk losing top candidates. Job seekers may take lack of contact as a lack of interest and accept an early offer from a less preferred company. Job candidates may not put a halt to job search activities even after accepting an early offer from an organization. They may continue to receive interest from other companies that were late off the mark in recruiting, and if they receive an attractive offer, they may change their

---

BOX 7.10 Elements of a Recruitment Action Plan

1. Develop Recruitment Strategy

Establish selection committee
Review organization's goals and objectives
Establish budget for the recruitment process
Establish time lines for recruitment and selection activities
Review job description for position
Develop selection criteria
Develop profile of "ideal" applicant
Develop job advertisement/recruiting materials

2. Develop the Applicant Pool

Review state of the labour market
Consider employment equity issues
Determine if recruitment will be internal or external
Identify target applicant pool
Identify recruitment methods to be used
Place ad/recruiting materials in agreed-upon media

3. Review the Applicant Pool

Determine whether applicant pool is large enough; if not renew recruitment efforts
Screen job candidates' application forms and résumés

Conduct short screening interview
Select "long list" of candidates for further review

4. Conduct Review of Job Applicants

Selection committee develops shortlist of candidates
Arrange visits of shortlisted candidates to company
Conduct realistic job preview for candidates
Conduct employment tests
Conduct selection interview
Identify leading candidate(s) for position
Complete reference and background checks on leading candidates
Make hiring recommendation
Contingent on offer of employment, arrange for any required medical or physical examinations

5. Evaluate the Recruiting Effort

Review the recruiting process: what went right, what went wrong
Review the outcome of the recruiting process
Review the performance of people who were hired

minds about accepting the first offer. Maintaining contact with the candidate after an offer is accepted helps to forestall such reversals.

LOCATING AND TARGETING THE APPLICANT POOL In an ideal world, an organization could search as broadly as possible until it found the most suitable applicant. However, extensive recruiting is an expensive proposition, which few organizations can afford. It is also questionable whether the benefits of extensive recruiting overcome its associated costs. A more effective plan is to target recruiting efforts on a specific pool of job applicants who have the appropriate knowledge, skills, abilities, competencies, and other talents needed to perform the job. This **applicant pool** may be concentrated in one geographic area or spread widely throughout the country. The human resources team must know where to find the appropriate applicant pool.

Applicant pool—the set of potential candidates who may be interested in, and who are likely to apply for, a specific job.

If a company wants to hire electronics technicians, it makes more sense to concentrate on recruiting graduates from electronics training programs or from areas where there is a concentration of electronics technicians rather than search broadly throughout the country. The human resources team must know which colleges or institutes offer training in electronics; they must know where electronics industries are concentrated. If a company were recruiting experienced miners, it would be more appropriate to target Cape Breton as a source for this applicant pool rather than Metropolitan Toronto. On the other hand, recruiting upper-level executives might require a nationwide search to find the best candidate.

Targeting a specific applicant pool allows the organization to tailor its message to that group, to understand where that applicant pool is likely to be located, and to attract applications from that pool. In limiting its recruiting to a target applicant pool, however, an organization must be careful not to systematically exclude members of protected groups.

RECRUITMENT METHODS

Once the target applicant pool has been identified and located, the human resources team must choose the most appropriate **recruitment methods** for reaching all members of internal and external applicant pools, including members of protected groups. The following sections describe some of the more popular recruiting methods that have been used to contact members of different applicant pools.

Recruitment methods—procedures used in recruiting to reach all members of internal and external applicant pools, including members of protected groups.

INTERNAL CANDIDATES

Internal candidates provide the organization with a known source of labour. Many of the activities carried out as part of human resources planning provide the organization with information about the best-qualified internal applicants.

Job postings—refer to internal advertisements of job vacancies.

JOB POSTINGS **Job postings** refer to internal advertisements of job vacancies. The advertisements can take the form of notices posted on bulletin boards, ads placed in company newsletters, announcements made at staff meetings, or notices circulated through departments. The intent of the posting is to make internal employees aware of the vacancy and to allow them an opportunity to apply for the position. As a matter of policy, some organizations seek to fill positions through internal sources before going to the external market. Other organizations may have agreed, through a collective agreement with employees, to give first consideration to internal candidates for any vacant position that falls under the collective agreement. In these cases, the jobs are posted for a period of time in specified locations. Internal postings generally provide information on the job, its requirements, and compensation associated with the position.

Job postings provide an excellent means of discovering talented people within the organization and providing them with an opportunity for advancement within the organization. Knowing that good performance will be awarded through advancement has a positive effect on employee motivation. Job postings make the vacancy known to all employees; this is an important consideration when implementing employment equity programs throughout different levels of the organization. There are, however, disadvantages to job postings. Internal postings lengthen the time needed to fill the position; external searches generally do not begin until after all internal candidates are first evaluated. Internal candidates who are unsuccessful may become less motivated, or may initiate a job search outside the organization. Placing an internal candidate in a vacant position sets off a sequence of events that brings with it a degree of instability and change: the position the employee leaves must itself be posted and filled. The effects of filling the first position with an internal candidate reverberate through several layers of the organization before the process comes to an end.

Replacement chart—shows each job relative to others in the organization along with the job incumbent and likely internal replacements for the incumbent, including information on the potential replacement's performance and readiness to step into the position.

REPLACEMENT CHARTS Organizations expect that vacancies will occur through death, illness, retirement, resignation, or termination. As part of the human resources planning function, organizations develop a succession plan for filling vacancies with existing employees. Organizations have a good idea of the talent in higher-level positions that can step in to fill a vacancy, either on a short- or long-term basis. **Replacement charts**, like organizational charts, list each job with respect to its position in the organizational structure, particularly its relationship to positions above and below it. The replacement chart lists the incumbent for the position and the likely internal replacements for the incumbent. The chart includes information on the present job performance of each potential successor (e.g., "excellent performer"), an assessment of his or her readiness to step into the position (e.g., "needs more experience in present position"), and a rank ordering of each as the incumbent's replacement.

Replacement charts provide a quick, visual presentation of an organization's human resources, but they give little information beyond that of a candidate's performance and promotability. Replacement charts are limited by the constraints imposed by the organizational chart. Employees are evaluated for positions one level above theirs in the chain of command; they are not evaluated for positions that are horizontal or lateral to theirs.

HUMAN RESOURCES INFORMATION SYSTEMS Human resources planning often involves the creation of a comprehensive computerized database that contains the job analysis information on each position, including information on the required KSAOs. This computerized inventory also contains information on employee competencies and KSAOs, along with their work histories, experiences, and results of performance evaluations. Internal candidates for a vacant position may be found through a computer match of the person's characteristics with those required by the job. The match does not give any indication of interest in the position or motivation to take on the new job. It is simply a first cut of employees who qualify for the position.

NOMINATIONS Nominations are the least systematic internal recruitment method. They occur when someone who knows about a vacancy nominates another employee to fill it. In most cases, supervisors nominate one or more of their employees for a vacant position. Presumably, the supervisor nominates those employees whose KSAOs or competencies match those needed by the job. This process often results in very good employees not being nominated for a position. Supervisors or managers may use the nominating process to rid themselves of a problem employee or someone with whom they have poor interpersonal relations. Nominations also leave the organization open to charges of discriminatory promotion practices. For example, in replacing a manager, the other senior managers who are male may fail to nominate any women for the position. The women employees who were passed over may ask whether the failure to nominate women was due to lack of qualified female employees or to male bias against female managers.

EXTERNAL CANDIDATES

Organizations do not have a dependable supply of external applicants. The sources they use to attract external applicants have to be more creative and varied than those for internal candidates. The following section reviews some of the more common means used to reach external candidates.

JOB ADVERTISEMENTS Organizations spend a considerable part of their recruiting budgets on advertising vacant positions. The advertisements identify who the employer is and include basic information on the job and compensation, the requirements needed for the job, and how to apply (including closing dates for applications). The ad may also contain information on the organization's employment equity program. The ad should not include any statements that could lead to charges of discrimination (e.g., "The ideal applicant will be between 25 and 30 years old"), unless those statements can be supported as bona fide occupational requirements.

Organizations also use job advertisements to enhance their image with potential candidates. Image concerns may dictate the size of the advertisement, where it is placed, and the content of the ad as much as the information needed to attract qualified candidates. Nonetheless, job advertisement campaigns should be designed with the target applicant pool in mind:

- Who are we trying to reach? Who is our target applicant pool?
- How large is the applicant pool and what portion of it do we need to reach to obtain a reasonable number of applicants?
- How many applicants do we need to fill the position with qualified people?
- What type of ad content will attract the target applicant pool's attention?
- What advertising media are likely to reach the target applicant pool?

The answers to most of these questions are very complex and depend on consideration of many factors including the nature of the organization, the job, and the target applicant pool. One of the most important decisions is choosing the media for the advertising campaign.

Newspapers are perhaps the most common media for job advertisements. They offer a quick and flexible means of contacting potential applicants. Newspapers need only two or three days of lead time before an ad is published. The ad can be placed in the classifieds section listing employment opportunities or prominently displayed in another section of the paper. Often managerial and professional positions are advertised in a newspaper's business section. Newspapers have specific geographic distribution areas. An organization can choose to advertise locally in a paper that serves the immediate area of the organization, or it can advertise in papers such as *The Globe and Mail,* which have a national distribution. Of course, the increased distribution comes at an increase in cost. Blue-collar positions tend to be advertised locally, with managerial and professional positions advertised nationally. Newspaper ads run for a very short period of time; they attract the interest of people who are actively searching for a job and who happen to see the advertisement before it disappears.

Professional periodicals and trade journals allow the organization to reach very specialized groups of applicants. Many professional or trade associations publish newsletters or magazines that are distributed to each member. These publications carry job advertisements. The association, and the distribution of its publication, may be international, national, or regional. Publications of this type are the best means of reaching people with specific skills or qualifications. Ads in these types of publications can be quite expensive and often require a long lead time before the ad appears. For example, an advertisement appearing in the March issue of a newsletter may have had an early January deadline for ad copy. With the recent growth of the World Wide Web, many professional and trade associations have reduced the publication lag by placing the job ads that are carried in their publications online as they are received.

Radio and television job advertising, in comparison to print media, has not been used extensively. These media offer the potential to reach large numbers of the target applicant pool. Radio and television advertising directors have detailed demographic information on the audience for specific shows and can place the advertisement during shows likely to be watched or listened to by the target applicant pool. Nonetheless, organizations appear reluctant to use these sources for job advertisements and limit their use to image advertising. The cost of such advertising, particularly on a national scale, may be quite high even for a 15- or 30-second commercial. The short duration of most commercials prevents the inclusion of essential job information.

When radio and television advertising is used, the focus of the ads is to stimulate interest in the organization and to motivate the potential applicant to seek additional information from another recruiting source. This approach is used in the radio and television advertising of the Canadian Forces. While much of the ad content is devoted to image advertising, the ads always end with a phone number or address through which interested people may obtain more detailed information.

Public displays attempt to bring job vacancies to the attention of the target applicant pool through the use of advertisements that range from help wanted notices to display ads placed in buses, subway stations, and trains. Service and retail employers rely on help wanted signs posted in their windows or near service counters to attract job applicants. Most positions advertised through these types of notices are at the entry level and do not require extensive skills or abilities on the part of the applicant. These ads are directed at recruiting employees from among the employer's normal range of customers. Display ads in public transportation stations and vehicles attempt to reach a broader population than help wanted ads, but like those notices, they are also directed at attracting people for low-skill or ability entry-level positions. These ads simply advertise the availability of jobs with an organization and provide those who are interested with a means of contacting the organization to obtain more specific information. Public display ads tend to be low in cost relative to the number of people that they reach. For example, one ad inside a bus may be seen by several thousand commuters over a month's display.

Direct mail advertising attempts to bring the organization's recruiting message directly to members of the target applicant pool. The potential employer sends each person on the mailing list recruiting information about the organization and the job, reaching both those who are actively seeking jobs and those who may become interested through reading the materials. The keys to this type of advertising are the acquisition or development of a mailing list consisting of names and addresses of the target applicant population, the attractiveness of the recruiting materials, and the ease with which follow-up contacts can take place. Often mailing lists can be obtained from various professional associations. In Canada, many rural communities have had trouble in recruiting medical practitioners. In response to this need, several communities have started active recruitment campaigns involving direct contact with potential graduates of medical schools, where the target applicant population is easy to identify and locate (LeBlanc, 1996).

Special recruiting events involve bringing a large number of potential job candidates into contact with an organization that is seeking to fill positions. Two well-established events used successfully to attract job seekers are open houses and job fairs. In an open house, an organization invites potential job applicants within its community to visit the company facilities, to view demonstrations or videos about the company and its products, and to meet the organization's employees informally over refreshments. Open houses work best when an organization has several jobs to fill and when there are tight labour markets. In a job fair, several organizations seeking to hire from the same target applicant pool arrange to recruit in conjunction with an ongoing event. For example, a trade or professional association may invite employers to hold a job fair as part of its annual convention. The employers who pay a fee to participate have access to all the convention delegates, both those who are actively seeking jobs and those who may become interested through meeting an organization's representative. The convention delegates represent the ideal target applicant pool. The job seekers make contact with organizations while the employers meet many prospective employees in a short period of time, at relatively low cost. The disadvantage is information overload, where the candidate is bombarded with too much information from too many organizations.

Employee referral is word-of-mouth advertising that relies on current employees telling their friends and relatives about job vacancies within their company. This is a low- or no-cost method of advertising. It assumes that the employees know other people with skills and abilities similar to their own, that the employees refer people with good work habits and attitudes similar to their own, and that current employees are the best representatives of the organization. In some companies, employees are paid a bonus for each successful referral. The greatest concern with using this method is the probability that it may produce charges of discriminatory hiring practices. In referring friends and relatives, employees are likely to refer individuals from their own ethnic, racial, or gender groups; this could work against meeting employment equity goals.

WALK-INS In the external methods described above, the organization makes every attempt to contact members of the target applicant pool. The recruitment is initiated by the employer. Walk-in recruitment is initiated by the job seeker, who visits an organization's personnel office and requests to fill out an application for employment, even though the company may not have any job vacancies. The *write-in* method is a variation of this approach; rather than visiting the company, job seekers send a copy of their résumés to the company. The company usually holds the applications for a period of time (e.g., three months), in case vacancies do occur. Walk-in and write-in methods are inexpensive ways to fill entry-level positions. In the past, these methods were rarely used to recruit professionals or managers, but with the prevalence of corporate downsizing, where supply exceeds demand, more professional and technical positions are being filled by walk-ins.

EMPLOYMENT AGENCIES **Employment agencies** are independent organizations that attempt to find a match between a person and a job. Their success depends on the willingness of both the job seeker and the organization to use their services. There are three major types of employment agencies.

Human Resources Canada Centres (HRCCs) are publicly funded employment agencies operated throughout the country by Human Resources Development Canada (HRDC). As soon as employers voluntarily notify their local HRCC of job vacancies, the position is posted at the HRCC's Job Information Centre. The posting is also included in the HRDC's National Job Bank (URL: http://jb-ge.hrdc-drhc.gc.ca/job-html/provResE.html), which lists vacancies that are available throughout the country, in case job seekers wish to relocate. Prospective applicants scan the job postings and meet with a job counsellor to determine whether their skills and abilities fit those required by any of the jobs. When matches occur, the counsellor refers the applicant to the company's personnel department, where additional screening takes place. To facilitate matches, the HRCCs offer vocational guidance counselling, and interest, skill, and ability assessment to job seekers. As noted in Box 7.4, many of these services are accessible on the Internet at the national HRDC website: At present, HRCCs charge neither the job seeker nor the employer any fees for their services. The effectiveness of HRCCs is somewhat mixed; most of their job placements are in sales, clerical, and service industries with very few in managerial and professional occupations.

Private employment agencies act in much the same fashion as HRCCs. They provide many of the same services to both job seekers and organizations who are seeking to hire, except they charge a fee for their services. Their primary function is to place people in jobs. Most provinces regulate employment agency fees and prohibit the agency from charging the job seeker for placing them with an employer. Their fees are paid by the employing organization, usually in the form of a commission tied to a percentage of the job candidate's starting salary. The employment agency may use any of the recruiting methods we've discussed, but they tend to rely on walk-ins, newspaper advertising, and lists of potential job seekers compiled over time. Employment agencies tend to have a fair degree of success in finding both skilled and managerial workers.

Executive search firms are private employment agencies that specialize in finding executive talent. Executive search firms charge the organization for their services, whether or not they are successful in filling a position. The major difference between search firms and employment agencies is that search firms rarely advertise positions, although they will do so if requested by their clients. Rather, they seek out candidates who are not actively seeking jobs through an extensive list of contacts that they have developed over time. Their main supply of talent comes from executives who are already employed by other organizations; consequently, these search firms are known as "headhunters."

Employment agencies—independent organizations that attempt to find a match between a person and a job. They may be either public or private enterprises and may provide general or specialized employment services.

BOX 7.11 Executive Search Firms

Why use an executive search firm?

- To obtain suitable candidates who otherwise might not have applied.
- To maintain objectivity.
- To avoid conflicts of interest between parties involved in the search.
- To eliminate administrative burdens related to the search.

What does an executive search firm do?

- Anything, within reason, that the client wants.
- Obtains description from the client of the type of person being sought.
- Develops a profile of suitable applicants.
- Develops and places advertisements, if necessary.
- Contacts potential candidates directly.

- Searches résumé banks.
- Facilitates interview process.
- Conducts reference checks.
- Conducts hiring negotiations.

What does an executive search cost?

- Fees: As a rule of thumb, 30 percent of the candidate's gross starting salary.
- Expenses: As high as 15 percent of gross starting salary.
- Fees and expenses are generally negotiable.
- Hiring is guaranteed: If the new employee does not work out by the end of the first year, a replacement is found without cost.

How long does an executive search take to complete?

- Three to four months.

The major disadvantages of using search firms are their cost and the likelihood that some firms develop specific recruiting philosophies that lead them to look for the same type of executive to fill all positions.

Hiring a search firm does not absolve the company of all responsibilities for the hiring process. A successful search depends on the company working with the search firm and doing its homework about the nature of the position to be filled and the required KSAOs and competencies before the search firm is called on to begin the search. Box 7.12 presents the views of a headhunter on the common mistakes companies make when recruiting executives.

Temporary help agencies are similar to private employment agencies except that they specialize in providing organizations with short-term help. In most cases, the worker remains employed by the temporary help firm, but carries out duties under the direction and control of the temporary help firm's client organization. These agencies provide clients with temporary help, contract workers, and seasonal and overload help in certain specialized areas such as secretarial help, computer experts, labourers, or executives, among others. Temporary help agencies are an example of outsourcing, which we discussed earlier in this chapter. Temporary help agencies rely on inventories of talent pools they have developed over the years and are capable of filling their clients' needs within a reasonable amount of time. However, as discussed previously, the client organizations may be liable for

BOX 7.12 A Headhunter's View of Company Mistakes in Executive Recruiting

Carlos Fernandez-Araoz is a partner with Egon Zehnder International of Switzerland. During a visit to Toronto he discussed with *The Globe and Mail* some common mistakes that companies make when recruiting executives (Church, 1999). According to Mr. Fernandez-Aroaz, these missteps include:

- **Reactive approach**: Companies seek someone with the same qualities as the person they are replacing but without that person's defects.

- **Unrealistic expectations**: Asking for a candidate who can do it all.

- **Evaluating people in absolute terms**: A person may be a "good manager" but under what terms?

- **Accepting people at face value**: Readily believing the information provided by candidates either on résumés or in interviews.

- **Believing references**: Accepting references at their word.

- **The "just-like-me" bias**: Favouring candidates with the same experience and education as current employees.

- **Delegation gaffes**: Letting others do the groundwork such as writing job descriptions.

- **Unstructured interviews**: Basing decisions on loose conversations that cover subjects such as mutual acquaintances and sports events.

- **Ignoring emotional intelligence**: Looking only at hard data such as education, cognitive ability, job history.

- **Political pressures**: Hiring for reasons other than the candidate's qualifications.

any discrimination claims incurred through the control and direction of the temporary employee.

RECRUITING AT EDUCATIONAL INSTITUTIONS   Technical schools, colleges, and universities are common sources of recruits for organizations seeking entry-level technical, professional, and managerial employees. Many schools provide their students with placement services, which assist the recruiting efforts of visiting organizations. Recognizing educational institutions as a good source of target applicants, organizations have well-established campus recruiting programs that involve both campus advertising and campus visits by company recruiters. Campus recruiting is one of the most popular ways in which graduates find their first job. It is also an expensive proposition in terms of both time and money. It becomes even more expensive considering that on average about 50 percent of recruits may leave the organization within the first years of employment (Dolan and Schuler, 1994). Many research studies have tried to identify factors that produce successful recruiting campaigns at educational institutions. At one time, the characteristics of the recruiter were thought to be of utmost importance, but reviews of recent studies on this topic suggest there is little, if any, relationship between recruiter characteristics and the success of a recruiting program (Rynes, 1991). A more likely determinant is the choice of campuses an organization decides to visit (Boudreau and Rynes, 1987).

THE INTERNET/WORLD WIDE WEB In a few short years the Internet has transformed recruiting. Traditionally, a company used one of the means we just described to reach potential job applicants. The company may have placed an advertisement in the print media, made use of referrals and nominations from current employees, or participated in job fairs. Applicants who happened to become aware of the vacancy submitted their résumés by mail or fax, or dropped it off in person. The applications were reviewed by staff in the HR department. Applications from those candidates the staff judged to be qualified were invited for an interview and possible further review through employment tests. Eventually, one of these applicants might be offered a position. The remaining applications were likely discarded, with perhaps a few kept on file. This process could take weeks or months from the initial announcement of the position to an offer.

BOX 7.13 Canadian Job- and Career-Related Internet Websites

GENERAL JOB AND CAREER SITES

Ask The Headhunter	http://www.asktheheadhunter.com/
BrainHunter.com	http://www.brainhunter.com
CanadianCareers.com	http://www.canadiancareers.com
CareerExchange.com	http://www.careerexchange.com
Canada Job Search	http://www.canadajobsearch.com/postings.htm
CareerMosaic Canada	http://careermosaic.com
CareerPath.com	http://www.careerpath.com
HRDC Job Bank	http://jb-ge.hrdc-drhc.gc.ca
Human Resources Development Canada	http://www.hrdc-drhc.gc.ca/
Jobs.com	http://www.jobs.com
JobOptions.com	http://www.joboptions.com
JobShark	http://www.jobshark.com

The Monster Board Canada	http://www.monster.ca
Workopolis.com	http://www.workopolis.com
Work Search	http://worksearch.gc.ca/cgi-bin/start.pl

SITES DESIGNED FOR HIGH-SCHOOL, COLLEGE, AND UNIVERSITY STUDENTS

All Canadian Student Centre	http://geocities.com/collegepark/1338
Canada Prospects	http://www.careerccc.org
College Grad Job Hunter	http://collegegrad.com
HRDC National Youth Internet Site	http://youth.hrdc-drhc.gc.ca/index.html
National Graduate Register	http://www.canadorec.on.ca/services/employment/NGR.HTM
Youth Resources Network of Canada	http://www.youth.gc.ca

The Internet has changed everything. Now a company may place notice of a vacancy on its website or list it with one of the online job or career websites. The job site does a keyword search of résumés in its database and forwards those that match the position requirements to the company. Some sites, such as JobShark.com, alert job seekers who are listed with it by e-mail when a job is posted that exactly matches their qualifications.

Once a company receives the electronic résumés, it begins its review. It may decide to continue its search or to invite a few of the applicants for interviews, after which it may make job offers. The interviews may take place on-site at the company or through videoconferencing if the candidate is outside the company's geographic area. Any employment testing that the company wishes to do may also be carried out online with a human resources consultant. Videoconferencing and online testing are becoming increasingly popular as the Internet has no geographical boundaries. A company may receive applications from far outside its normal territory. The whole process may take just a few days from placing the notice of the vacancy to making an offer.

Internet recruiting takes many forms. A company may simply post job vacancies on its own website—for example, Microsoft, http://www.microsoft.com/jobs/—or list the job with an Internet job search site that represents a large database of job seekers (see Box 7.13). Applications are made online, and most communication takes place through e-mail. Corporations can combine their job listings with a wealth of information about the company, making it easier for candidates to develop an impression of the company's culture and values. Most job search sites also provide job hunting advice to applicants listed in their databases (see Box 7.13).

Large national or international Internet sites (e.g., HRDC (http://www.hrdc-drhc.gc.ca/) may list tens of thousands of jobs. The job seeker usually has the option of limiting the search to specific geographic areas or types of work, occupations, or industries. Some sites are limited to specific regions of the country, for example, Atlantic Canada Careers (http://www.atlanticcanadacareers.com/). Certain sites are specific to an industry or profession; for example, prospective university professors may find out about job postings by checking the Canadian Association of University Teachers' website (http://www.caut.ca/). Increasingly, newspapers and professional journals are placing copies of classified ads for job openings on their websites to run in parallel with the print ads.

Internet recruiting has several advantages for both the employer and the job seeker. The biggest advantage to the company is that it can reach a potentially limitless talent pool at minimal cost and beyond its normal geographic location. It allows the company to provide more information about the position to job seekers than in a typical print ad. New jobs can be posted on a daily basis rather than being at the mercy of a newspaper or journal's publication schedule. Most of all, it provides a quick turnaround in making a hiring decision through searches of thousands of résumés stored in data banks. From the job seeker's perspective, Internet recruiting allows them to apply for many jobs

Internet recruiting—the use of the Internet and World Wide Web to match candidates to jobs through electronic databases that store information on jobs and job candidates.

quickly at minimal cost. When their résumés are posted on a job search website, their applications can be accessed by an unlimited number of employers. Their résumés remain in the database to be reviewed by other companies, should they not receive a job offer. They may modify the résumé at any time. Job seekers receive information on new job openings as they become available.

Internet recruiting is not without its disadvantages. The ease of submitting résumés coupled with the sheer number of websites devoted to jobs and careers means that a company may be flooded with applications. According to the Internet Business Network (Pearsall, 1998), the number of websites related to jobs or careers jumped from 3500 in 1996 to 15 000 in 1997 and was expected to reach 100 000 in 1998. Whatever savings a company makes through Internet recruiting may be eroded by the costs of dealing with the large volume of applications. To deal with this flood of applications, CareerBridge Corp., based in Ottawa, has developed software that allows recruiters to target specific job or career sites and to receive résumés ranked in order according to keywords. While this software reduces recruiting time, it also reduces the "hands-on" review of the résumés by those who are most knowledgeable about the company.

The disadvantages of Internet recruiting for job seekers take a different form. First of all, Internet recruiting and job searching are only available to job seekers who have access to the Internet and the expertise to use computers and related software. This restriction may impede an organization's ability to attract candidates from different population subgroups and meet employment equity goals. Most, if not all, job or career sites require candidates to complete a standardized, online résumé, which limits the type of information that can be included on the form and requires the job seeker to specify keywords under which the résumé is filed in the database. When job seekers send their own résumés directly to employers they often include it as an attachment, which may make the file unreadable when it is received. Most companies expect the file to be sent as either an ASCII file (text only with no formatting) or a Microsoft Word file, which is more or less the business standard.

Perhaps the major concern of job seekers is related to privacy. When a résumé is included in a database, or when it is circulated, it becomes more or less a public document. Often job seekers who are employed do not want their current employer to know they are looking for other work. Some employers now routinely have staff or agencies comb through job or career sites to find out if any of their employees are on the job market. At least one site, Brainhunter.com, keeps any identifying information confidential and only releases it with the permission of the job seeker, thus shutting out the employee's current employer (Vardy, 2000). Nonetheless, corporate recruiters routinely "mine" job sites using sophisticated technology to gather lists of prospects. They also mine news articles and corporate websites for candidates even though those individuals may not be seeking employment elsewhere (Piturro, 2000).

The Web appears to suit all types of jobs. Although managerial and professional jobs appear to be particularly well suited to Internet recruiting, people in these types of positions have concerns about their résumés appearing in databases and having others know that they are "shopping around." Except for a few high-tech firms, most companies have not abandoned more traditional forms of recruiting. Internet recruiting is used as part of a mix of methods to obtain the "best" candidates. With the phenomenal growth of the Internet, this may change very rapidly as more companies start to rely solely on Internet recruiting.

BOX 7.14 An Interview with the JobShark

Matthew von Teichman is the president of JobShark.com, a leading Internet job search firm. He provided the following description of his service in response to several questions we put to him:

JobShark is a career network that provides an effective conduit for job seekers to find "the perfect job" and recruiters to find the perfect employee. JobShark is not like an online classified section (like some of our competitors); we emphasize the matching of a job to a job seeker based on multiple levels of criteria that allow our search engines to find perfect candidates as opposed to anyone who happens to see the job.

The way the system works is that a job seeker will spend 20 minutes on the site in the beginning, filling out their "professional profile." The system will ask for specifics on salary range, education, work experience, work-related skills, and soft skills they may have. After the job seeker has gone through this, they will be set up to receive jobs by e-mail (JAWS) that match the exact criteria they have specified. For a job seeker, it is an ideal situation because they do not have to do the looking—the system will do it for them.

Recruiters pay to post positions on the site and every job they post is categorized using the same forms as the job seekers filled out. Therefore, a recruiter controls the level of the people who see the job. For instance, if a recruiter wants someone who has seven-plus years' experience working with a particular type of accounting system, they can indicate this and JAWS will only e-mail the job to

the people who have that exact experience. It is very targeted.

We've been in operation since April of 1997. JobShark's growth has been astronomical. We are about to complete our second straight year of 400+ percent revenue growth. We have gone from 9000 candidates in 1998 to 45 000 candidates in 1999 to 255 000 candidates now (March 2000). Last year at this time we had an average of 25 companies per month using us, and this month alone we had 155 companies use the service. In terms of jobs posted, we now average 700–900 jobs at any given time where we were averaging 300–400. One of the keys to that number is that a year ago jobs stayed up on the system for an average of 45 days and now they stay up for an average of 10 days. We are filling jobs faster, so the numbers of jobs posted at any given time is not an issue, because they are almost always new jobs. We don't have any data on the number of successful matches. We do know that 90 percent of recruiters are telling us that they are receiving "high-quality candidates" now whereas a year ago that number was more like 50 percent.

We have company profiles on our website to assist job seekers. These profiles are used but not as often as you would think. The big corporate names draw good attention to their profiles but smaller companies do not draw the same traffic. Most of the people who use our site are currently employed and will receive a job by e-mail. They do not spend a lot of time on the site browsing and viewing profiles.

BOX 7.14 Continued

Job seekers have some flexibility with their résumés. We don't require them to post their résumés except when responding to a job notice. Most job seekers are happy to give us their professional profile and wait for a good opportunity before they put their résumés in the system. When they do decide to post their résumés, they can build it according to our template or they can cut and paste it from their own file. The issue with cut and pasting is that any formatting they had from their word processor does not show up on the site so the person must be careful to format it again using the formatting features of a basic text editor. We don't screen résumés for accuracy but we do insist that applicants answer questions from the company that are designed to give the company a better idea of the applicants' qualifications.

Professional profiles and résumés can be updated and removed by the job seeker at any time. Most will remove their professional profiles to stop receiving JAWS e-mails. We also delete inactive accounts of job seekers who are no longer interested in our service.

JobShark is extremely attentive to privacy issues. We are the only company that does not sell any kind of access to our database! People know that we provide a completely confidential way to search for a job and that is why we have so many passive job seekers (those who are currently employed).

Users don't need any special computer tools or software to use JobShark as long as they have a functioning Web browser. We have not had many problems with users who are not computer literate or 'Net savvy because we have designed our system to be as user-friendly as possible. We seldom hear complaints about how to use it.

When we started JobShark, most of the jobs we posted were for companies in the information technology sector, but now we post jobs for all types of industries. Job seekers who use JobShark tend to be well educated, in a middle-income bracket ($35 000–$50 000/year); 65 percent are currently employed, 55 percent are men (a very even split for the Internet), and represent all industries.

I would advise job seekers to use multiple sites if they are unemployed as there is little duplication in job listings across job search sites. If job seekers are currently employed, I would suggest using a site that doesn't require a lot of their time and that makes it really easy to locate and apply for jobs. Companies should be careful to pick a site that offers quality candidates and not to make decisions based on price. There are a lot of free or very cheap services out there that do not offer value and cannot fill jobs with good people. Companies are better off paying for a site that offers some accountability. Recruiters should focus their efforts on those sites that are the most successful.

INTERNAL VERSUS EXTERNAL RECRUITMENT

Table 7.1 summarizes the advantages and disadvantages of different recruitment methods. Internal recruitment has the advantage of dealing with known quantities. Internal job applicants already have realistic expectations of life in the organization. They are, or should be, aware of the organizational goals and values. Likewise, the organization is familiar with the internal applicant's work history and performance record. Internal recruitment is also relatively inexpensive. Most middle-level jobs in an organization are filled through this means. External recruitment, on the other hand, is mostly used to staff jobs at either the entry or executive levels. External recruitment brings needed skills and competencies to an organization and prevents organizations from becoming "inbred." It exposes companies to new people, new ideas, and new ways of doing things. External recruitment may be the only means through

TABLE 7.1 COMPARISON OF INTERNAL AND EXTERNAL RECRUITMENT METHODS

METHODS	ADVANTAGES	DISADVANTAGES
Internal Recruitment		
Job Postings	Inexpensive. Rewards performance. Discovers talent.	Time-consuming. Produces instability. Demoralizing process.
Replacement Charts	Based on known human resources.	Limited by organizational chart and structure.
Information Systems	Known KSAO database linked to job.	Expensive. Rarely used by companies.
Nominations	Based on known human resources.	Random process. May lead to discrimination.
External Recruitment		
Newspaper Ads	Quick and flexible. Specific market.	Expensive. Short lifespan for ads.
Periodicals/Journals	Targets specific groups or skills.	Long lead time for ads. Expensive.
Radio and TV	Mass audience. Targets specific groups. Image advertising.	Very expensive. Short ad duration. Provides little information.
Public Displays	Inexpensive.	Provides little information.
Direct Mail	Targets specific groups and skills. Can provide much information.	Expensive and inefficient. Requires mailing list. Often not read.
Special Events	Useful for filling multiple jobs. Relatively inexpensive. Targets job pool.	Shares job pool with competition. Information overload/stress.
Employee Referrals	Inexpensive.	May lead to discrimination and inbreeding.
Walk-Ins	Inexpensive.	Random process. Inefficient.
Canada Employment Centres	Inexpensive. Job–KSAO fit.	Success limited to certain occupational categories.
Private Employment Agency	Person–job fit.	Expensive.

TABLE 7.1 (continued)		
METHODS	**ADVANTAGES**	**DISADVANTAGES**
Executive Search Firm	Known talent pool.	Very expensive.
Temporary Help Agency	Access to short-term labour pool. Few recruiting demands.	Exposure to risk of discrimination claims. Mostly unskilled and poorly educated talent pool.
Recruiting at Schools	Known talent pool. Pretrained applicants.	Time-consuming. Very expensive.
Internet	Inexpensive. Mass audience. Specific audience.	Random process. Unknown audience.

which employment equity programs succeed. External recruitment can be very time-consuming and expensive.

RECRUITING AND INTERNATIONAL ASSIGNMENTS   With the spread of globalization, Canadian organizations increasingly need to staff foreign operations. Recruiting someone to head a project in another country is very important if a company is to expand its business into foreign markets. Typically, Canadian organizations have recruited internally or domestically for foreign assignments and have paid the recruits up to three times their normal salaries for accepting the foreign posting (Ondrack, 1996). Use of North American expatriates to staff the operations of North American firms overseas, however, has not been successful. Problems associated with family adjustment to new cultures and the manager's lack of personal adjustment to the foreign business environment often lead to failure (Ondrack, 1996).

Canadian firms must do a much better job of identifying, recruiting, and selecting individuals based on those competencies related to success abroad. With the development of the borderless job search websites and résumé data banks, companies may have an easier time finding job applicants from around the world who have the requisite knowledge of the laws and culture of the host country.

EVALUATING RECRUITING EFFORTS

We started this chapter with the proposition that recruitment is simply a means of attracting a large enough pool of candidates from which an organization can select those it believes are the best qualified to fill job vacancies. It is quite obvious that recruiting can be very expensive. Organizations that engage in recruiting should be concerned that their money and time are well spent. They should want to know whether the job advertisements paid off in

Chapter 1 pesented information on the changing nature of the workforce and of work itself. These changes affect the recruitment process. Jobs that provide autonomy, decision-making authority, and opportunities for self-development will more likely attract highly educated employees than jobs that lack these attributes. The increasing number of dual-career couples, single-parent families, and females in the workforce will require organizations to offer special accommodations and flexible work arrangements to gain competitive advantages in recruiting.

These arrangements may include flextime, work-sharing, on-site or subsidized daycare, and teleworking. For positions requiring geographical relocation of candidates, employers that assist the employee's partner to secure local employment will gain further advantage. Finally, organizations perceived as hostile to workplace diversity will see the effectiveness of their recruitment efforts significantly compromised, and the quality of their overall applicant pool adversely affected. These effects will be most noticeable in international recruitment. Women, visible minorities, Aboriginal people, and those with physical challenges should participate as front-line recruiters to help send a clear message of equal employment opportunities.

more applications; whether better-qualified candidates were hired; what it cost to recruit the new employees; whether the new recruits are more productive or have a more positive attitude about the organization; and whether they stay with the organization for a longer period of time.

Unfortunately, many companies do not bother to ask these questions or to evaluate their recruiting efforts. Their primary criteria for judging the success of recruiting appears to be whether the vacant jobs were filled. Very few organizations track the performance and behavioural outcomes of people recruited into the organization or the costs associated with the recruiting campaign, including advertising costs (Rynes and Boudreau, 1986). Without doubt, recruiters will be increasingly required to demonstrate the effectiveness of their programs.

Recruiting should not be taken at face value but evaluated on the basis of specific criteria. Recruiting efforts should be evaluated separately from the selection system. The criterion measures that an organization uses to evaluate its recruiting program should be consistent with the goals that were set for that effort. If the organization wanted to recruit the best possible candidates available, it would be unfair to evaluate the recruiting program on the cost that it took to find those candidates. The appropriate measure would be whether the best possible candidates were hired. If the organization used recruiting to generate a large applicant pool, then an appropriate criterion measure might be the number of applications that were received rather than the quality of the people hired.

There are many different criterion measures that can be used to evaluate recruiting efforts. Box 7.16 lists criterion measures that have been used to investigate the effectiveness of different recruitment methods (Rynes, 1991; Wanous and Colella, 1989). These criteria can be grouped into three broad categories: behavioural measures, performance measures, and attitudinal measures.

BOX 7.16 Examples of Criteria Used to Evaluate Recruiting Methods

BEHAVIOURAL MEASURES

Turnover

    within 6 months

    within 12 months

    within 24 months

Absenteeism

PERFORMANCE MEASURES

Performance Ratings

Sales Quotas

Performance Potential

ATTITUDINAL MEASURES

Job Satisfaction

Job Involvement

Satisfaction with Supervisor

Commitment to Organization

Perceived Accuracy of Job Descriptions

Source: Rynes (1991); Wanous and Colella (1989).

Noticeably absent from Box 7.16 are any measures that are based on cost or an integration of cost and benefits. Human resources professionals will be called on to link their activities to their company's bottom line. Utility analysis, which will be discussed in Chapter 11, provides a mechanism for applying cost–benefit analysis to human resources decisions. Boudreau and Rynes (1985) adapted utility analysis to incorporate the effects of recruitment, including financial and economic factors, and the effects associated with changes in the size and quality of the applicant pool, the number of applicants processed, and the average qualification level of those hired. Improved recruitment altered the benefits that could be expected from improved selection procedures because recruitment produced a more qualified and less diverse applicant pool. Boudreau and Rynes concluded that the most effective procedure was an integrated recruitment–selection strategy. Boudreau (1991) demonstrates the use of utility analysis to evaluate the effectiveness of different recruiting approaches in conjunction with selection models.

Employment equity—policies and practices designed to increase the presence of qualified women, visible minorities, Native people, and people with disabilities in the workforce.

There is one final criterion, **employment equity**, that should be considered as part of evaluating any recruitment efforts. The organization must review whether its recruiting campaign has produced an increased presence of qualified women, visible minorities, Native people, and people with disabilities in its workforce. In the context of Canadian employment equity legislation, as discussed in Chapter 2, recruiting efforts must be judged on this basis as well as the more traditional outcome measures.

SUMMARY

Recruitment is the first step in the personnel selection process, but, unlike other aspects of the personnel process, the actions and decisions of the job seeker play a major role. A recruitment process, no matter how brilliantly conceived, is a failure if it does not attract job applicants. Recruitment campaigns are a success when they understand the recruitment process from the job seeker's point of view. The recruitment process must take into account the strategies that job seekers use to investigate jobs and organizations. The recruitment process should provide job candidates with information they need about the job and the organization to make appropriate job choices.

Recruitment campaigns should be based on the principle of improving the fit between job candidates and the organization. Organizations can help to achieve this by presenting an accurate image of both the job and the organization to job seekers. The organization should use communications in a way that develops accurate expectations and perceptions on the part of job applicants. One method that appears capable of doing this is a realistic job preview.

In developing a recruitment strategy, human resources planners must consider both the internal and external constraints on the organization. All recruitment is influenced by external factors over which the organization has little control (e.g., the labour market and the legal environment), as well as internal factors that it can influence (e.g., its business plan and values). Recruitment strategies and materials, which are grounded in organization and job analysis, establish both realistic expectations among job applicants and the availability of qualified internal and external job candidates. Every recruitment strategy must contain an action plan, which schedules recruiting initiatives and provides a means of identifying and locating the target applicant pool. The action plan must also identify the appropriate methods for contacting the target applicant pool. The action plan should also include a method for evaluating the effectiveness of the recruitment campaign.

KEY TERMS

EXERCISES

1. Choose an organization in your community. Schedule a meeting with its human resources manager (or designate). Using the material in this chapter as a guide, interview the manager on the organization's recruiting efforts (e.g., determine the role that job and organization analysis played in developing the strategy). Ask whether the organization considers how potential applicants would react to the recruiting materials. Prepare a report on the organization's recruiting strategy and its effectiveness.

2. Examine the organization's recruiting program (the one chosen for Exercise 1) from a job candidate's perspective. With the assistance of the human resources manager, locate a recently hired employee; interview that employee with respect to job search strategy, perceptions of the organization and the job, the recruiting process, what influenced their decision to take the job, and whether their views have changed after being in the organization for a period of time. Prepare a report summarizing this interview.

3. Using the information presented in this chapter and the information obtained from your interviews in Exercises 1 and 2, develop a comprehensive recruitment strategy for the organization based on the job of the person whom you interviewed.

4. How did the organization advertise the position? Identify the best ways for reaching the target applicant pool for this job.

5. Prepare an advertisement for the position of the person you interviewed. Compare the costs of running this advertisement in some of the commonly used media discussed in this chapter.

6. Box 7.4 presented information on the HRDC site, Work Search, at http://worksearch.gc.ca/cgi-bin/start.pl. The Work Search site contains exercises that help you assess the degree of fit between yourself and a specific job or organization. These exercises illustrate many of the issues presented in this chapter. Visit the site and complete the "Know Yourself" exercise. Print out your summaries from the "Know Yourself" tutorial and bring them to class. Do they provide an accurate picture of you? What do they suggest in terms of your "fit" to an organization? Is this the type of company or organization you had considered as a work setting? Visit another job search site listed in Box 7.13 that offers advice on your likes and dislikes. Complete their tutorial as well. How does the feedback from the two sites compare?

CASE

When qualified applicants are scarce, recruiting becomes extremely competitive, particularly when two companies go after the same candidate, as often happens in the case of searching for professionals. This case was recently the subject of an Internet discussion.

Recruiting faculty for university positions is not very different from procedures outlined in this chapter, although there are some differences in that the line manager (department chair) normally handles the search rather than a professional recruiter. After interviewing three shortlisted candidates, University X made an offer to one and advised the other two candidates that they were unsuccessful. The successful candidate was given one week to consider the offer. The candidate asked for a week's extension to consider the offer but was granted only an additional three days. At the end of the time period the candidate verbally accepted the offer and was sent a contract to sign. Rather than returning the signed contract, the candidate informed the department chair at University X that he had accepted a position at University Y. He had received the second offer after verbally accepting the first position. The department chair at University Y knew the candidate had verbally accepted University X's offer. Before accepting University Y's offer, the candidate had consulted a respected mentor who advised him to ignore his verbal commitment and to accept University Y's offer. There were no substantial differences in the salaries being offered by each university or in the work that each would expect the candidate to perform. The candidate saw University Y as the more prestigious of the two employers.

DISCUSSION QUESTIONS

1. Did the candidate act in an appropriate manner?

2. What should the candidate have done?

3. What would you have done if you had been in the candidate's position?

4. Did University Y act ethically, knowing that the candidate had verbally accepted an offer?

5. Does a verbal acceptance constitute a legal and binding contract?

6. What should the candidate's mentor have advised him to do?

7. Should University X take any action to enforce the verbal commitment? Should it take any legal action against the candidate or University Y? Why or why not?

8. How can situations like this be avoided?

REFERENCES

Barber, A.E., and M.J. Wesson. 1999. "A Tale of Two Job Markets: Organizational Size and Its Effects on Hiring Practices and Job Search Behavior." *Personnel Psychology* 52: 841–68.

Boudreau, J.W. 1991. "Utility Analysis for Decisions in Human Resource Management." In M.D. Dunnette and L.M. Hough, eds., *Handbook of Industrial and Organizational Psychology*, vol. 2. 2nd ed. Palo Alto, CA: Consulting Psychologists Press. 399–444.

Boudreau, J.W., and S.L. Rynes. 1985. "The Role of Recruitment in Staffing Utility Analysis." *Journal of Applied Psychology* 70: 354–66.

———. 1987. "Giving It the Old College Try." *Personnel Administrator* 32: 78–85.

Breaugh, J.A., and R.S. Billings. 1988. "The Realistic Job Preview: Five Key Elements and Their Importance for Research and Practice." *Journal of Business and Psychology* 2: 291–305

Bretz, R.D., Jr., and T.A. Judge. 1998. "Realistic Job Previews: A Test of the Adverse Self-Selection Hypothesis." *Journal of Applied Psychology* 83: 330–37.

Buckley, M.R., D.B. Fedor, and D.S. Marvin. 1994. "Ethical Considerations in the Recruiting Process: A Preliminary Investigation and Identification of Research Opportunities." *Human Resource Management Review* 4: 35–50.

Buckley, M.R., D.B. Fedor, D.S. Marvin, J.G Veres, D.S. Wise, and S.M. Carraher. 1998. "Investigating Newcomer Expectations and Job-Related Outcomes." *Journal of Applied Psychology* 83: 452–61.

Carsten, J.M., and P.E. Spector. 1987. "Unemployment, Job Satisfaction, and Employee Turnover: A Meta-Analytic Test of the Muchinsky Model. " *Journal of Applied Psychology* 72: 374–81.

Castro, J. 1993. "Disposable Workers." *Time* (March 29): 43–47.

Church, E. 1999. "Headhunter Warns of Matchmaking Missteps." *The Globe and Mail* (October 29): M1.

Cukier, W. 1996. "Job Hunting in Cyberspace." *The Globe and Mail* (April 16): C9.

DeFruyt, F., and I. Mervielde. 1999. "RIASEC Types and Big Five Traits as Predictors of Employment Status and Nature of Employment." *Personnel Psychology* 52: 701–28.

Dolan, S.L., and R.S. Schuler. 1994. *Human Resource Management: The Canadian Dynamic*. Toronto: Nelson Canada.

Ellis, R.T., and R.J. Angus. 1985. *Matching CFCIS Vocational Preference Checklist Items with Probability of Adjustment to Entry-Level CF Trades: A Research Plan*. Technical Note 17/85. Willowdale, ON: Canadian Forces Personnel Applied Research Unit.

Flynn, G. 1995. "Contingent Staffing Requires Serious Strategy." *Personnel Journal* 74 (April): 50–58.

Galt, V. 1992. "Agencies Still Refer Whites Only." *The Globe and Mail* (September 8): B1.

Greengard, S. 1995. "Leveraging a Low-Wage Work Force." *Personnel Journal* 74 (January): 90–102.

Guion, R.M. 1976. "Recruiting, Selection, and Job Placement." In M. Dunnette, ed., *Handbook of Industrial and Organizational Psychology*. Chicago: Rand-McNally, 777–828.

Heneman, H.G., D.P Schwab, J.A. Fossum, and L.D. Dyer. 1989.

Personnel/Human Resource Management. Homewood, IL: Irwin.

Holland, J.L. 1973. *Making Vocational Choices: A Theory of Careers.* Englewood Cliffs, NJ: Prentice-Hall.

Keenan, G. 1996. "Toyota Swamped in Rush for Jobs." *The Globe and Mail* (February 21): A1, A7.

Kristof-Brown, A.L. 1998. "The Goldilocks Pursuit in Organizational Selection: How Recruiters Form and Use Judgments of Person–Organization Fit."*Dissertation Abstracts International Section A: Humanities and Social Sciences* 58(11-A): 4345.

LeBlanc, S. 1996. "Guarantee of Extra Cash Not Luring Doctors to Rural Areas." *The Halifax Mail-Star* (March 1): A1, A2.

London, M., and S.A. Stumpf. 1982. *Managing Careers.* Reading, MA: Addison-Wesley.

Magnus, M. 1985. "Recruitment Ads at Work." *Personnel Journal* 64: 4–63.

Meglino, B.M., E.C. Ravlin, and A.S. DeNisi. 1997. "When Does It Hurt to Tell the Truth? The Effect of Realistic Job Reviews on Employee Recruiting." *Public Personnel Management* 26: 413–22.

Ondrack, D. 1996. "Global Warning." *Human Resources Professional* (May): 27–29.

Pearsall, K. 1998. "Web Recruiting Complicated by Sheer Numbers." *Computing Canada* 24: 11, 14.

Perrott, S.B, 1999. "Visible Minority Applicant Concerns and Assessment of Occupational Role in the Era of Community-Based Policing." *Journal of Community and Applied Social Psychology* 9: 339–53.

Phillips, J.M. 1998. "Effects of Realistic Job Previews on Multiple Organizational Outcomes: A Meta-Analysis." *Academy of Management Journal* 41: 673–90.

Piturro, M. 2000. "The Power Of E-cruiting." *Management Review* 89: 33–37.

Popovich, P., and J.P. Wanous. 1982. "The Realistic Job Preview as a Persuasive Communication." *Academy of Management Review* 7: 570–78.

Ryan, A.M., and M.J. Schmit. 1996. "Calculating EEO Statistics in the Temporary Help Industry. *Personnel Psychology* 49: 167–80.

Rynes, S.L. 1991. "Recruitment, Job Choice, and Post-Hire Consequences." In M.D. Dunnette and L.M. Hough, eds., *Handbook of Industrial and Organizational Psychology,* vol. 2. 2nd ed. Palo Alto, CA: Consulting Psychologists Press, 399–444.

———. 1993. "Who's Selecting Whom? Effects of Selection Practices on Applicant Attitudes and Behaviour." In N. Schmitt, W.C. Borman et al., eds., *Personnel Selection in Organizations.* San Francisco, CA: Jossey-Bass, 240–74.

Rynes, S.L., and J.L. Boudreau. 1986. "College Recruiting in Large Organizations: Practice, Evaluation, and Research Implications." *Personnel Psychology* 39: 729–57.

Saks, A.M. 1994. "A Psychological Process Investigation for the Effects of Recruitment Source and Organization Information on Job Survival." *Journal of Organizational Behavior* 15: 225–44.

Saks, A.M., W.H. Wiesner, and R.J. Summers. 1996. "Effects of Job Previews and Compensation Policy on Applicant Attraction and Job Choice." *Journal of Vocational Behavior* 49: 68–85

Schneider, B. 1987. "The People Make the Place." *Personnel Psychology* 40: 437–53.

Schneider, B., H.W. Goldstein, and D.B. Smith. 1995. "The ASA Framework:

An Update." *Personnel Psychology* 48: 747–73.

Schneider, B., D.B. Smith, S. Taylor, and J. Fleenor. 1998. "Personality and Organization: A Test of Homogeneity of Personality Hypothesis." *Journal of Applied Psychology*, 83: 462–70.

Schwab, D.P., S.L. Rynes, and R.J. Aldag. 1987. "Theories and Research on Job Search and Choice." In K.M. Rowland and G.R. Ferris, eds., *Research in Personnel and Human Resource Management*, vol. 5. Greenwich, CT: JAI Press, 129–66.

Shellenberger, S. 1999. "Employers Polish Their Image to Woo a Demanding New Generation." *The Globe and Mail* (November 26): M2.

Smithers, J.W., S. Highhouse, M.J. Zickar, T.J. Thornstienson, S.L. Stierwalt, and J.E. Slaughter. 1999. "Assessing Company Employment Image: An Example in the Fast Food Industry." *Personnel Psychology* 52: 149–72.

Snow, C.C., and S.A. Snell. 1993. "Staffing as Strategy." In N. Schmitt, W.C. Borman, and Associates, *Personnel Selection in Organizations*. San Francisco: Jossey-Bass, 448–80.

Soelberg, P.O. 1967. "Unprogrammed Decision Making." *Industrial Management Review* 8: 19–29.

Tom, V.R. 1971. "The Role of Personality and Organizational Images in the Recruiting Process." *Organizational Behavior and Human Performance* 6: 573–92.

Vandenberghe, C. 1999. "Organizational Culture, Person–Culture Fit, and Turnover: A Replication in the Health Care Industry." *Journal of Organizational Behavior* 20: 175–84.

Van Vianen, A.E.M. 2000. "Person–Organization Fit: The Match between Newcomers' and Recruiters' Preferences for Organizational Cultures." *Personnel Psychology* 53: 113–50.

Vardy, J. 2000. "Brainhunter.com Stresses Privacy in Net Job Hunt." *Financial Post* (April 19): C8.

Vroom, V.H. 1964. *Work and Motivation*. New York: Wiley.

Wanous, J.P. 1980. *Organizational Entry: Recruitment, Selection, and Socialization of Newcomers*. Reading, MA: Addison-Wesley.

———. 1989. "Installing a Realistic Job Preview: Ten Tough Choices." *Personnel Psychology* 42: 117–33.

Wanous, J.P., and A. Colella. 1989. "Organizational Entry Research: Current Status and Future Directions." In K.M. Rowland and G.R. Ferris, eds., *Research in Personnel and Human Resource Management*, vol. 7. Greenwich, CT: JAI Press, 59–120.

Wilson, F.P. 1980. *Towards a More Systematic Counseling Model for the Canadian Forces*. Working Paper 80–3. Willowdale, ON: Canadian Forces Personnel Applied Research Unit.

Yeuse, P., and S. Highhouse. 1998. "Effects of Attribute Set Size and Pay Ambiguity on Reactions to 'Help Wanted' Advertisements."*Journal of Organizational Behavior* 19: 337–52

Zadny, J.J., and L.F. James. 1977. "A Review of Research on Job Placement." *Rehabilitation Counseling Bulletin* 21: 150–58.

8

SELECTION I: APPLICANT SCREENING AND SELECTION

CHAPTER GOALS

This chapter introduces procedures that provide information for making hiring decisions. It places employment selection in the context of labour markets, the legal environment, and organizational constraints. It establishes organization and job analysis as the foundation for employee selection and reviews some of the common procedures used to screen job applicants: biographical data, application forms, résumés, interviews, and reference checks.

After reading this chapter you should

- understand the role that human resources planning, organization analysis, and job analysis play in selection;

- know the relationship between job analysis and the predictor and criterion measures that are used in selection;

- know the difference between employee screening and employee selection;

- know the advantages and disadvantages of using five common screening devices: biographical data, application forms, résumés, interviews, and reference checks;

- understand the psychometric properties of each of these common screening procedures along with any legal considerations pertinent to their use in making employment decisions; and
- know the importance of considering different aspects of work experience in the screening and selection process.

HR Planning, Organization Analysis, Job Analysis, and Selection

Human resources planning (HRP)—identifies an organization's staffing requirements and develops an action plan for recruiting an adequate supply of qualified job applicants. HRP should be closely linked to the overall strategic planning of the organization.

Human resources planning identifies an organization's staffing requirements and develops an action plan for recruiting an adequate supply of qualified job applicants. Figure 7.1 on p. 231 presented factors that influence this planning process, including organization and job analysis. Once the job applicants are at hand, the organization must decide which individuals, if any, to hire. The goal of the organization is to hire those applicants who are not only capable of performing the job but who will perform at above-average levels. Hiring the best-qualified applicants increases the productivity of the organization (Delaney and Huselid, 1996, 951). Selection involves collecting information from job applicants to discover those who possess the most knowledge, skills, abilities, or other talents linked to successful job performance.

Labour Markets and Selection

A favourable labour market will produce a large number of job applicants and will allow the organization to be more selective in its hiring. On the other hand, unfavourable labour markets may lead the organization to select applicants it might otherwise not consider. Figure 8.1 represents these two market conditions under which a company is trying to fill 10 positions. When there are many job applicants, the organization has the luxury of setting higher selection standards. A smaller proportion of job applicants qualifies for positions in the company. In Figure 8.1(a) approximately 20 percent of 100 applicants meet the minimal requirements that have been established for the position. For the moment, let us assume that offers are made to the highest-ranked candidates in descending order until all 10 positions are filled and that half of all offers are rejected. The **selection ratio** of .20 will produce just enough qualified candidates who accept the offers. Figure 8.1(b) represents an unfavourable market in which there are only 25 applicants. A selection ratio of .20 would not produce a sufficient number of qualified hires. The company could either intensify its recruiting efforts to attract more applicants, as discussed in Chapter 7, or lower the requirements for the position. To obtain 20 candidates who meet the lower standards, the company could set the selection ratio at .80. When unemploy-

Selection ratio—the proportion of applicants for one or more positions who are hired. Fifty applicants for 10 positions would yield a selection ratio of .20 (10/50 = 1/5; or one position for every five applicants).

FIGURE 8.1 THE INFLUENCE OF LABOUR MARKETS ON THE SELECTION PROCESS

Favourable Labour Market

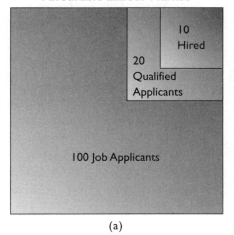

(a)

Unfavourable Labour Market

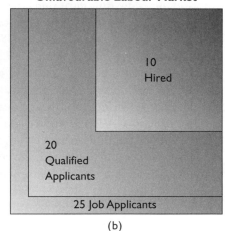

(b)

ment rates are low, employers are forced to compete aggressively for people, particularly for individuals with skill sets that are in high demand (see Box 8.1).

BOX 8.1 No Workers: Desperate Times in the Oil Patch

The Oil and Petroleum industry in the United States, partly spurred on by high crude oil prices, is experiencing an exploration boom that has resulted in a labour shortfall. Many experienced workers left the industry during recent downturns in the oil industry and are no longer available. A 50 percent increase in the number of rigs operating has increased the demand for skilled workers. There simply aren't enough qualified candidates to fill the available positions. This tight labour market has led oil companies to undertake some unusual recruiting tactics.

One oil producer in Oklahoma is so desperate that he tracks prison release dates for parolees; he stands outside the prison gates and asks everyone if they want a job

in the oil patch. In Alaska, rival producers who haven't had to recruit in over 20 years are banding together to provide training to unqualified workers to fill 500 new positions over the next few years. Compounding the shortfall is an aging workforce, many of whose members will soon be retiring. Texas companies are tracking down former employees and offering them jobs. Of course, the operators are prepared to pay high salaries to get the people they need, but they still can't find people. The lack of qualified people is causing delays of as much as one year in drilling new wells in Oklahoma.

Source: Ruble (2000).

Criterion measures— measures of job performance or productivity that attempt to capture individual differences among employees. These performance measures, such as supervisory ratings or absenteeism rates, are used in establishing the validity of screening or selection instruments.

Base rate—a performance standard that is expected from employees; the proportion of all applicants who would be successful if all the applicants for a position had been hired.

Effects of Unfavourable Labour Markets on Selection The performance of the 10 people hired under the unfavourable market conditions is likely to be lower, on average, than that of the 10 hired under favourable conditions. Under the unfavourable labour conditions, more of the applicants who are hired are likely to be unsatisfactory performers. Figure 8.2 illustrates this relationship in the form of a scatterplot. It presents the relationship between a predictor, cognitive ability scores, and a **criterion measure** of job performance for all job applicants. The selection ratio is the proportion of job applicants selected for positions in the company. The **base rate** is a performance standard that is expected from employees. It can be thought of as the proportion of all applicants who would be successful if all the applicants for a position had been hired. Those falling above the base rate criterion are judged to be successful employees. In Figure 8.2, the cutoff score on the predictor, which is used to determine whether a candidate will receive a job offer, has been set to represent a selection ratio (SR) of either .20 (Line A) or .80 (Line B). Job candidates who score above the predictor cutoff and are hired but turn out as "failures" are called *false positives* (their performance falls below the base rate). With a selection ratio of .20, false positives fall into area "a"; when the selection ratio

FIGURE 8.2 THE EFFECT OF REDUCING SELECTION STANDARDS ON JOB PERFORMANCE

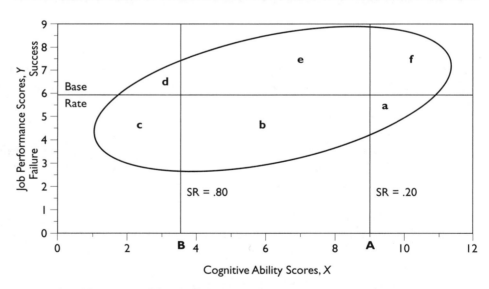

A and B represent Selection Ratios

	A	B
True Positives	f	e + f
False Positives	a	a + b
True Negatives	b + c	c
False Negatives	d + e	d

RECRUITMENT AND SELECTION IN CANADA

is set at .80, the false positives fall into the larger area a + b. Nonetheless, selection still proves beneficial. If all the applicants were hired (i.e., setting the selection ratio at 1.00), there would be even more false positives (area a + b + c). You may want to read the section in Chapter 11 on base rates and false positive errors in decision making before proceeding with the rest of this chapter.

The above discussion is based on the premise that the employer does, in fact, make use of valid selection procedures such as cognitive ability or personality tests (discussed in Chapter 9). Many job applicants do not like taking employment tests. In a tight job market, employers tend to drop these procedures out of fear that they will discourage applicants from applying. They don't want to reduce the size of the applicant pool to one that is even smaller than the available labour supply. A recent poll of 2133 U.S. firms by the American Management Association found that the number of companies using psychological tests dropped from 52 percent in 1998 to 33 percent in 2000 (Armour, 2000). Unfortunately, a decreased reliance on valid predictors will mean that those companies dropping the use of psychological tests will likely increase the number of false positive hires and lower the base rate—that is, to move toward a higher selection ratio and to accept lower performance standards for employees hired from a tight job market.

The Legal Environment and Selection

Selection programs and practices must operate within the legal context described in Chapter 2. Ideally, they do not have adverse impact on members of protected groups (recall that some selection procedures may have an adverse impact on a minority group and yet be "bona fide" if they meet the Supreme Court's stringent test for determining BFORs). Selection programs that intentionally or unintentionally exclude job applicants using characteristics or factors that are protected under human rights legislation run the risk of being declared unfairly discriminatory, and the organization may be subject to penalties and fines. Chapter 2 outlined a procedure to determine whether selection practices withstand legal scrutiny. Recruitment, screening, and selection procedures should yield the best-qualified candidates within the context of agreed-upon **employment equity** programs.

Employment equity—a term coined in the 1986 federal Employment Equity Act referring to policies and initiatives to promote employment opportunities for members of designated minority groups.

Business Plans and Selection

An organization's goals, values, and philosophy influence selection procedures. The business plan identifies the proportion of positions to be filled by internal candidates. Internal candidates may be assessed through different procedures than job applicants from outside the organization. The organization likely has performance data on the internal candidate and may already have used it to develop replacement charts for each position in the organization. However, successful performance in one's current position does not necessarily mean that one will be a good performer at another position within the organization. Specifically, the skills required for success in management positions are different from those required of nonmanagerial positions; requirements for success as a quality control officer are quite distinct from those required of a sales agent. An assessment centre, which we discuss in Chapter 9, is a selection procedure commonly used to evaluate internal candidates for promotion or transfer to other positions in the company. Some organizations require all employees at certain organizational levels to go through an assessment centre as a way of identifying individuals with potential for upper-level managerial positions (Cascio and Ramos, 1986).

SELECTION PROCEDURES AND ORGANIZATIONAL CULTURES Job level and type influence selection just as they do recruitment. An organization may believe that certain selection procedures are inappropriate for one type of job but appropriate for another, although the same assessments predict success equally well for both jobs. Whereas an executive search may involve a review of a candidate's accomplishments and several interviews with people in the candidate's current organization, a search for an entry-level manager might involve candidates taking an extensive series of employment tests in addition to being interviewed. Although the testing may be quite appropriate at the executive level as well, the organization's culture may dictate that such testing is not done beyond the entry level. This could be for any number of reasons, including a belief that legitimate contenders for executive management appointments typically have a "track record" of success in other management positions, where they have already demonstrated an ability to handle cognitively complex tasks in work environments of multiple competing demands. Indeed, in tight labour markets where several organizations are competing for a limited pool of talent, a cognitive ability test may discourage some executive candidates from pursuing employment with that firm.

A recent poll by CareerBuilder, an online career site, found that 12 percent of all job seekers would end an employment interview immediately if asked to take an employment test (Armour, 2000). In part, this negative reaction may reflect a belief that "employment testing" includes such controversial procedures as drug screenings and medical exams (which we will discuss in Chapter 9) in addition to psychological tests of ability and personality. Not surprisingly, applicants' perceptions of selection procedures have become the focus of much research. Applicant perceptions do influence their attitudes, intentions, and behaviour with respect to taking employment with an organization (e.g., Arvey and Sackett, 1993; Elkins and Phillips, 2000; Gilliland, 1994; Herriott, 1989; Landy, Shankster, and Kohler, 1994; Schuler, 1993). In some cases negative perceptions can be overcome by a specific combination of employment tests. For example, Rosse, Miller and Stecher (1994) found that including a cognitive ability test within the selection battery could offset adverse reactions of job applicants to personality assessments, which candidates tend to view negatively (Armour, 2000). Job applicants are likely to be discouraged from pursuing positions where the selection process is perceived as "unfair," either in the way the assessments are administered or in assessment outcomes (see Gilliland, 1993). Clearly, the HR specialist must meet not only technical and legal standards in developing a selection system, but must also be sensitive to organizational culture, labour market conditions, and applicant perceptions and reactions (Smither, Reilly, Millsap, Pearlman, and Stoffey, 1993). This is even more difficult in a tight labour market where the HR specialist is doing everything possible to find qualified candidates for open positions.

ORGANIZATION ANALYSIS, JOB ANALYSIS, AND SELECTION

Organization and job analysis play important roles in developing and evaluating selection systems. They provide the raw data for assessing the internal and external environments in which the organization operates and for understanding the expectations, behaviours, and tasks that make up a specific job. Job analysis data also help identify the knowledge, skills, abilities, or other attributes (KSAOs) required to perform the job in question. The information produced by organization and job analysis provides the basis for designing a selection strategy that is job-related, appropriate to the organizational context, and defensible before the courts.

TRANSLATING ORGANIZATION AND JOB ANALYSIS DATA INTO SELECTION MEASURES

Taking into account the factors discussed above, human resources specialists must develop a procedure for selecting the most appropriate candidates. Selection procedures should be job-related and legally defensible. Selection procedures that follow from a well-conducted job analysis will meet these requirements and lead to hiring decisions that are in the best interests of both the organization and the candidate.

A SELECTION MODEL

Figure 8.3 presents a model of a selection system based on job analysis. In this model, job analysis information is used to identify both the performance domain and the KSAOs or competencies linked to this performance. As discussed previously, job analysis information identifies the tasks and behaviours that make-up a job and, through inference, the KSAOs that contribute to performance of these tasks and behaviours. These inferences are based on empirical evidence demonstrating validity between the job dimensions and KSAO **constructs** in other situations. This relationship between the performance domains and the KSAO constructs is represented by Line A in Figure 8.3.

Construct—an idea or concept constructed or invoked to explain relationships between observations. For example, the construct "extroversion" has been invoked to explain the relationship between "social forthrightness" and sales.

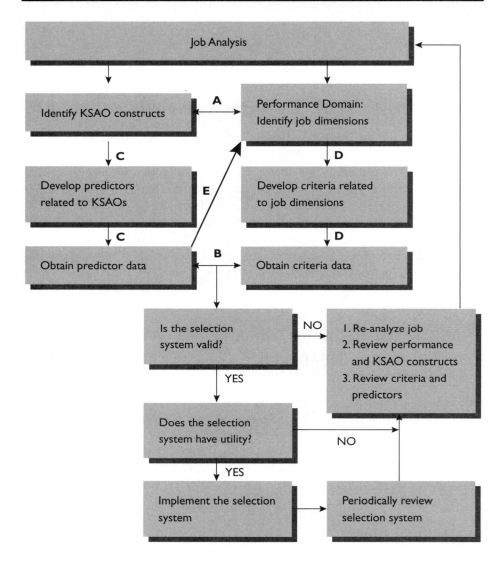

The KSAOs and job dimensions linked by Line A are abstractions; they cannot be measured directly. These constructs must be used to develop predictor and criteria data before they can be used to select job candidates. Chapters 5 and 6 discussed the process of defining the performance domain and developing related criterion measures. Line D represents this process in Figure 8.3. In establishing a selection system, identifying and developing the performance domain and related criteria are just as important to the success of the system as properly developing the predictor side of the model.

Unfortunately, in practice, insufficient attention is given to developing adequate performance measures. Criterion measures may be used because they are available and convenient rather than because they adequately represent the competencies or performance domain of interest (Binning and Barrett, 1989).

The human resources specialist must also translate the KSAO constructs into measurable predictors. The fact that a security dispatcher sends, receives, processes, and analyzes information suggests that an applicant for this position should demonstrate a fair degree of cognitive ability. The fact that a security dispatcher must be capable of operating a variety of electronic equipment suggests that the applicant should have experience operating such equipment. Similarly, if this same position requires the incumbent to remain calm under stressful conditions, applicants should demonstrate a stable personality disposition (e.g., low neuroticism). The human resources specialists must determine how each of these KSAOs will be assessed. With respect to cognitive ability, a general cognitive ability test may be most appropriate. Information about past work history and experience may come from an application form or the candidate's résumé, while information about the candidate's ability to deal with stressful situations may be assessed through a combination of a personality inventory and a situational interview. The predictors that are chosen must be valid measures of the KSAO constructs that have been identified as related to job performance. This relationship is represented by Line C in Figure 8.3. The validity of the predictor measures is established through evidence based on test content, that is, either content or construct validity procedures. Either expert judgment or empirical evidence must support the use of a predictor measure as representative of a KSAO construct.

Keep in mind that the goal of selection is to identify job candidates who have those attributes required for success on the job. On the basis of predictor data obtained through an assessment of job applicants, the human resources team predicts which applicants will be successful in the position. This prediction is represented by Line E in Figure 8.3. In most organizations, this relationship is inferred through establishing a correlation at the measurement level between the predictor and criterion measures, that is, evidence based on relations to other variables. Line B in Figures 8.3 represents criterion-related validity. If the relationship in Line E cannot be established through either criterion-related, content, or construct validity, the human resources team must begin the process again. This may include redoing the job analysis, but more often than not it only involves a review and refinement of the predictor and criterion measures. The work of the human resources team does not end once it establishes the validity of the selection system. The final step is to demonstrate that the selection system has utility—that it results in higher levels of performance and overall productivity than would be the case without such a system. Several methods for assessing utility are described in Chapter 11. Finally, the selection system, once determined as providing utility, must be reviewed periodically as jobs and organizations change.

SELECTION

Selecting individuals for employment is a multi-stage process. Specifically, it starts with human resources planning, in which the organization identifies the number and type of new hires required for meeting its strategic objectives. An analysis of the target positions is then undertaken to make explicit the core competencies or KSAOs the organization is seeking. Once this is done, the organization can determine the most appropriate assessment tools to use in the selection process and where best to target its recruitment efforts (e.g., local, national, international; newspapers, job fairs, conferences, headhunters). The objective at this point is to create the largest qualified pool of applicants possible. As illustrated in Figure 8.2, the larger this pool, the more selective the organization can be (e.g., lowering the selection ratio decreases the number of false positives when using assessment procedures that have established predictive validities). At the same time, the larger the applicant pool, the more resource-intense and costly it is for the organization to process these applications. When unemployment is low and competition for talent high, employers with efficient and effective means of processing applicant files "win out."

The remainder of this chapter introduces various means by which organizations screen applicants, that is, sort the applicant pool into acceptable and unacceptable categories. The tools they use are familiar to everyone who has applied for a job: application forms (including weighted application forms and biographical data), résumés, interviews, and reference checks. Chapter 9 continues with a review of selection testing and Chapter 10 concludes with an in-depth discussion of the employment interview. These procedures, from the most basic to the most sophisticated, must satisfy both psychometric and legal concerns when used to hire employees.

APPLICANT SCREENING

Screening begins after the HR department receives the application. It is the first phase of selection, in which the first "rough cut" of the larger applicant pool is performed. Typically, it involves identifying those candidates who meet the **minimum qualifications** (MQs) established for a position. MQs are often listed as statements of education, experience, and closely related personal attributes required to perform a job satisfactorily that are used as standards to screen applicants (Levine, Maye, Ulm, and Gordon, 1997). Screening procedures, such as those presented here, are designed to cut down the number of job applicants. Candidates who fall short of the minimum standards are eliminated at this point and receive no further consideration. Accordingly, MQs critically affect the entire selection process, and are often closely scrutinized for possible adverse impact against **designated minority group**s. It is essential that these MQs be systematically and carefully established. Levine et al. (1997) provide a clear, step-by-step description of how they developed and validated MQs to

Screening—the first step of the selection process. Involves identifying individuals from the applicant pool who have the minimum qualifications for the target position(s). Candidates "passing" this first hurdle are referred for more extensive assessments.

Minimum qualifications—knowledge, skills, abilities, experiences, and other attributes deemed necessary for minimally acceptable performance in one or more positions. Designed for making the "first cut" in screening job applicants.

Designated minority groups—the four groups designated in the federal government's Employment Equity Act that receive legal "protection" in employment policies and practices because of their underrepresentation in the workplace. The four designated groups are women, Aboriginal people, visible minorities, and people with disabilities.

withstand legal challenge for selected jobs in a large mental health facility. Their procedure is a useful guide for establishing MQs in other situations.

RECRUITMENT, SCREENING, AND SELECTION

Figure 8.4 diagrams the relationship among recruitment, screening, and selection in terms of different questions that are asked at each of these steps. *Recruitment* seeks to find a sufficient number of applicants; *screening* identifies whether those candidates who applied meet minimum requirements; and *selection* reviews each qualified candidate to find those who will be most successful in the job.

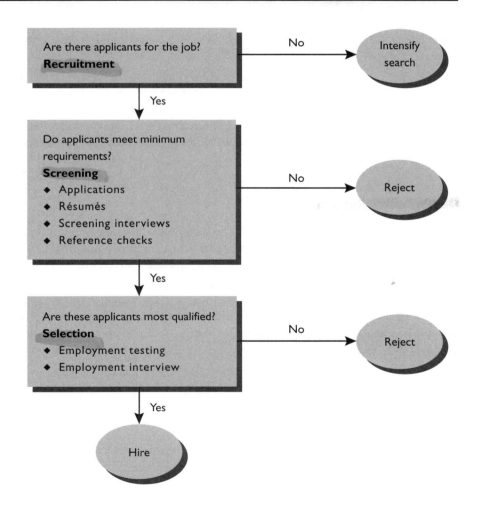

FIGURE 8.4 THE RELATIONSHIP AMONG RECRUITMENT, SCREENING, AND SELECTION

Caution must be exercised when screening job applicants. The screening devices are designed to quickly and inexpensively sort applicants into acceptable and unacceptable categories. Usually, the criteria on which these decisions are made are subjective; the decision maker often has to interpret what an applicant meant when he or she wrote a specific statement or what a person's job experience and training actually are. Screening procedures are open to errors, both **false positives** and **false negatives**. Over the complete selection process, applicants who pass through the initial screening as false positives are likely to be eliminated through more extensive testing. The false negatives, those who met the qualifications but were eliminated, are gone forever. Applicants who find themselves in this position may turn to the courts if they believe the initial screening procedures discriminated on grounds that were unrelated to job performance. Screening instruments that are used without consideration of their psychometric properties and without regard for the legal environment leave employers open to litigation. The next section reviews some of the most common methods used in employment screening.

False Positives—individuals who are predicted to perform successfully for a given position (based on preselection assessment scores), but who do not perform at satisfactory levels when placed on the job.

False Negatives—individuals who are predicted to perform unsuccessfully for a given position (based on preselection assessment scores), but who would perform at satisfactory levels if hired.

SCREENING METHODS

Application forms, résumés, screening interviews, and reference checks are most commonly used in screening. These procedures all seek to predict job performance from past life or work events. Recall that when screening procedures are properly developed they will identify individuals who meet *minimum* qualifications. The following sections examine these screening approaches more closely.

APPLICATION FORMS

Application blank—a form used by job candidates to provide an employer with basic information about their knowledge, skills, education, or other job-related information.

When individuals apply for a job with an employer, they are frequently asked to complete an employment *application form* (sometimes referred to as an **application blank**). Practically all organizations use employment application forms to collect information that will allow them to assess whether the candidate is minimally suitable for the job in question. Application forms consist of a series of questions aimed at securing information on the general suitability of the applicants to the target position. Questions often ask about the applicant's educational background, job experience, special training, and other areas deemed relevant to performance of the job. For example, applicants for a security dispatcher position may be required to have passed a course on CPR (cardiopulmonary resuscitation). Applicants who do not have such training can be identified through a question on the application form and screened out of the competition.

Regardless of the exact format, applications are used to provide a preliminary pre-employment screen, allowing the employer to determine whether the applicant is minimally qualified for the position. If the applicant pool is large compared with the number of positions being filled, employers may choose to be more selective at this stage, assessing and comparing the relative strengths and weaknesses of each candidate. Employers often overlook the fact that before any information on an application form can be used for screening, its job-relatedness should be established through a job analysis. For example, in a court challenge, it must be shown that CPR training is related to the work of a security dispatcher. It is not sufficient to believe that applicants "ought" to have a particular level of education, or to have graduated from a specific type of training program. Where there is adverse impact against members of a designated minority group, whether intentional or otherwise, the standard used to screen applicants must be demonstrably job-related. Because information collected at this stage may be used to restrict or deny employment to women and members of minority groups, the human rights issues must be considered during the development and use of application forms.

HUMAN RIGHTS CONSIDERATIONS Employers cannot ask for information that is prohibited on discriminatory grounds under human rights legislation unless it can be established that the information is a bona fide occupational requirement. Many employers routinely collect information through application forms that will not be used to make a hiring decision, but which is required by the human resources department once the employee is hired. The justification for collecting these data is expediency; if the applicant is hired, the personnel office will already have the necessary personal information on file.

Some employers unwittingly collect information on application forms that will leave them open to charges of discriminatory hiring practices; for example, applicants may be asked their social insurance number, date of birth, sex, marital status, number of dependents, name of next of kin, health status, and so on. Having obtained this information before making a hiring decision, an employer may have to prove that it was not used in making the hiring decision. It is far better to collect this information from applicants only after they have been hired.

Box 8.2 presents an application form that is designed specifically for the position of security dispatcher. This form requests only the most minimal information. There is always the temptation to collect as much background data as possible about a candidate through the application form on the grounds that this may help the human resources manager prepare to interview the candidate. However, once irrelevant information is in hand, there is a temptation to use it in making a decision.

Before putting any item on an application form, the human resources manager should ask the following questions:

- What is the purpose of having the item on the form?
- Is there a better way to obtain the information elicited by the item?
- How will the information be used?

BOX 8.2 Job Application Form: Security Dispatcher

PART I: PERSONAL DATA

Name: _____

Address: _____

City _____ Province _____ Postal Code _____

Home Phone: _____ Work Phone: _____

Are you legally eligible to work in Canada? Yes __ No __

Have you ever been convicted of a criminal offence for which you have not been pardoned? Yes __ No __

Languages Spoken: <u>English</u>: Yes __ No __   <u>French</u>: Yes __ No __
Languages Read: <u>English</u>: Yes __ No __   <u>French</u>: Yes __ No __

Do you wish to work full-time _____ part-time _____?

Have you ever worked for us before? Yes __ No __ If yes, when? _____

If hired, when are you available to begin work? _____

PART II: EDUCATION AND TRAINING

Highest grade or years completed (check all that apply to you):
High school   _____   Diploma received? Yes __ No __
Technical/Trade School   _____   Diploma received? Yes __ No __
Community College   _____   Diploma received? Yes __ No __
University   _____   Degree received? Yes __ No __

Program or areas studied (check all that apply to you):

Security __ Computer __ Clerical __ Management __ Communications __ Electronics __ Criminology __

Public Relations __ Other (please specify) _____

Do you currently possess a valid First-Aid Certificate? Yes __ No __

Do you currently possess a valid CPR Certificate? Yes __ No __

PART III: EMPLOYMENT HISTORY

List in order your last three employers, starting with your most recent employer.

Name and Address: _____

_____

Supervisor's Name and Title: _____

BOX 8.2 Continued

Dates Employed: From _____ To _____

Reasons for leaving: _____

Describe the work you did, including title of job, duties, and responsibilities:

_____

_____

May we contact this employer? Yes __ No __

Name and Address: _____

_____

Supervisor's Name and Title: _____

Dates Employed: From _____ To _____

Reasons for leaving: _____

Describe the work you did, including title of job, duties, and responsibilities:

_____

_____

May we contact this employer? Yes __ No __

Name and Address: _____

_____

Supervisor's Name and Title: _____

Dates Employed: From _____ To _____

Reasons for leaving: _____

Describe the work you did, including title of job, duties, and responsibilities:

_____

_____

May we contact this employer? Yes __ No __

- Does the question conflict with provincial, territorial, or federal human rights guidelines on what can and cannot be asked on an application form? (See Chapter 2.)

- Are responses to the item, if used in making a selection decision, likely to have an adverse impact in screening out members of protected minority groups?

- Is it more appropriate to obtain the information only after making a job offer?

- Has the job-relatedness of the item been established?

In addition to risking lawsuits, employers who include questions on application forms that are likely to discriminate against members of designated minority groups are likely to disadvantage themselves, particularly in tight labour markets. Specifically, applicants who complete application forms containing discriminatory questions tend to view the company as being less attractive. They are less likely to pursue employment with the organization, less likely to accept an offer of employment, and less likely to recommend the organization to a friend (see Saks, Leck, and Saunders, 1995). Moreover, since an application form is used for both selection *and* recruitment, it should be attractively formatted, fair, and "user friendly."

As well as ensuring that the rights and interests of job candidates are respected, employers must take measures to protect their own interests. Specifically, the credentials that the applicants claim to have should be verified.

A case in point is the 1996 elections in Thailand where more than 57 percent of the 2310 candidates for the House of Representatives claimed on their application forms to have at least a college degree, though these credentials were later called into question (Corben, 1997). In anticipation that candidates may misrepresent themselves on an application form, employers should include a statement, which candidates sign and date, stating: "I understand that providing any false, misleading or incomplete information is grounds for immediate discharge from employment" (Solomon, 1998). This requirement should serve to discourage misrepresentation, and provide grounds for dismissal should the candidates be hired and subsequently found to have misrepresented themselves in the application.

WEIGHTED APPLICATION BLANKS

Each item on an application form provides information about the candidate. Only rarely is any one item sufficient to screen out a candidate. Candidates for a staff-lawyer position that involves the actual practice of law would need to have passed the bar exam. That credential would be sufficient to screen out candidates who had graduated from law school but had not been called to the bar. However, an organization might consider hiring such a candidate if the position did not involve actual practice. Many organizations hire lawyers to provide advice or to do research without expecting them to practise law. In this latter case, passing the bar exam is certainly relevant and provides some information for making a screening decision, but it cannot screen out any candidate by itself. That item must be considered in the context of other information obtained from the application blank.

How can information obtained from an application form be objectively combined to make a decision when there is no single item that screens out candidates? Can information from the application form be used to make a prediction about job success or failure? In most cases, the person responsible for making the decision examines the application and makes a subjective decision. Much like a clinical psychologist making a diagnosis, the recruiter or human resources manager examines all the information and comes to a conclusion about a particular applicant based on personal experience and knowledge. There is an alternative to this subjective procedure: the manager develops a scoring key for applicant responses to items on the application form. In the case of lawyers applying for a job, those who have not passed the bar exam might be given a score of 0, while those who have passed are scored 1. Similarly, weights are assigned to the responses given to other items; adding all of the assigned weights together produces a total score on the application form for each job candidate. The weights are not assigned arbitrarily; they reflect the difference between successful and unsuccessful workers on some criterion measure. There are several different methods that can be used to develop the set of weights (Telenson, Alexander, and Barrett, 1983). This alternative is called a **weighted application blank or form**.

Weighted application blank (WAB) or form—methods for quantitatively combining information from application blank items by assigning weights that reflect each item's value in predicting job success.

Like any selection instrument, the weighted application form must exhibit good psychometric properties. Weighted application forms are developed in relation to a criterion measure of performance established for current and previous employees. If an employer were concerned with the level of absenteeism among security dispatchers, number of days absent would serve as a criterion measure. The human resources manager would define the acceptable number of days absent in a year, and then divide the current and previous security dispatchers into two groups, those who fall above and below that value. Then the applications on file for security dispatchers are reviewed, and the frequency of responses for each item on the application form is recorded separately for the low- and high-absenteeism groups. For example, 80 percent of security dispatchers with only a high-school education fall into the good attendance category while the remaining 20 percent with only a high-school education fall into the poor attendance group. The difference between these two percentages, 60 percent (i.e., 80 − 20 = 60), is used to derive a statistical weight that is then applied to answers of "high-school graduate" to the "highest level of education" question. In the case of university graduates, if 60 percent have a low absenteeism rate, with 40 percent having a high rate, a weight based on 20 percent would be applied to "university graduate" answers to this item. This weighting procedure is called the *vertical percentage method*. In this way, applicants who had only a high-school education would be given a higher score (.60) than university graduates (.20).

The *horizontal percentage method* considers the percentage of successful employees in all categories defined by an application form item. If 75 percent of employees with technical/trade diplomas and 70 percent of those with community college degrees fell into the low-absenteeism group, the horizontal percentage method would find the *lowest* common denominator across all four educational response categories. University degree holders would be given a score of 1.00 (i.e., .60/.60); community college graduates, 1.17 (i.e., .70/.60); technical/trade school graduates, 1.25 (i.e., .75/.60); and high-school graduates, 1.67 (i.e., .80/.60). In this way, those with only a high-school degree would get the highest score and those with a university degree, the lowest. Once the weights have been determined using one of the accepted weighting procedures, an overall score is obtained by adding together the weights from all the items. Finally, the overall score is correlated with the criterion measure to determine the validity of the weighted application form.

BENEFITS OF WEIGHTED APPLICATION BLANKS Well-constructed weighted application blanks (WABs) are good predictors of several different types of work behaviour (e.g., absenteeism, accidents, turnover, among others [Cascio, 1976]). Weighted blanks are also easy and economical to use (Lee and Booth, 1974). They are economical in the sense that virtually all organizations require job candidates to complete an employment application as part of their selection process, so the only additional costs are those associated with the scoring of the forms. If well constructed, application forms are unlikely to be perceived as intrusive or threatening, as most job applicants fully expect to complete an application form when seeking employment. Recently, Kettlitz, Zbib and Motwani (1997) used WABs to reduce turnover in the nursing industry. Kaak, Feild, Giles, and Norris (1998) present a step-by-step example of how to use WABs to combat turnover in the hospitality industry (see Box 8.3).

BOX 8.3 Using a Weighted Application Blank to Solve a Turnover Problem

Problem: High turnover rates in large food-service jobs in large hotel chain (85–90 percent). Costs of recruitment, selection and training lost. What to do?

Challenge: Identify applicant attributes that predict employee tenure (e.g., willingness to stick with a job).

Solution: Apply weighted application blank (WAB) technique to employment application data.

Application of WAB employed in a multi-step process:

1. *Collect data.* Collected copies of completed application forms from 10 hotels for all food-service personnel who were hired within past two years.

2. *Identify high- and low-performing groups.* Sorted applicants who met one of two criteria: (a) worker had quit the job within six months or less of employment (short tenure) (166 individuals), or (b) worker had been employed on the job nine months or more (long tenure) (130 individuals). Nine months defined the point at which recruitment, selection, and training costs are recouped.

3. *Select "derivation" and "holdout" group.* Divided high- and low-tenure groups into two additional groups: "weighting group" and "holdout group." Weighting group is the group on which the scoring key is derived. Holdout group is an independent group on which the scoring key is tested.

4. *Select application items.* Omitted from analysis any application items that could be construed as potentially discriminatory against minority group members (six). Thirty-seven application items remained for testing as possible predictors of employee job tenure.

5. *Determine scoring weights.* Application questions with best potential to predict job tenure are those

to which employees from low-tenure and high-tenure groups responded differently. Examined closely the response categories to each of the 37 retained application questions for differential responses by group. Noted the number of short- and long-tenured employees falling into each category of each application question. Specifically, calculated the percentages of long- and short-tenure individuals falling into each category of each question. The greater the difference between the high- and low-tenure groups in the way they responded to any one of the application form items, the higher the prospect that this item will predict job tenure (and hence the higher the weight assigned to this item). In this study, a simple weighting scheme was used—0, 1, or 2—reflecting the extent of group differences. Total score for each application is determined by summing item response weights. Of the 37 application form items tested, long- and short-tenure groups differed on 27.

6. *Test the resulting scoring key.* As the "holdout" group was not used in deriving the weights, it represents an independent group on which to test scoring key derived from the first group. This is referred to as cross-validation. Scoring key is supported if long-tenure employees in this holdout group receive a higher total WAB score than the short-tenure group. Long-tenure employees received a score of 19.4; short-tenure employees received score of 17.5, providing support for the predictive validity of the WAB scoring key.

7. *Set a cutoff score.* A cutoff score is determined by examining distribution of WAB scores for both

---

BOX 8.3 Continued

short- and long-tenure groups and then selecting the WAB score that maximally separates the two groups. The plot revealed an ideal cutoff score of 20, with applicants having scores of 20 or more predicted to be high-tenure employees and those with scores of 19 or fewer predicted to be low-tenure employees. Data showed that individuals with WAB scores of 20 or higher (40 people) had a 58 percent probability of staying on the job for nine months or more, while those scoring 19 or fewer points had only a 32 percent probability of staying on the job for at least nine months.

8. *Project cost savings.* Application of WAB in hiring of 130 new employees into fast-food jobs over a 12-month period across 10 participating hotels results in projected cost savings of approximately $13 000 (associated with increasing tenure rate), hence reducing recruitment, selection, and training costs. Projected savings substantially higher if WAB scoring key is applicable to all hotel chains.

Outcome: Examples of significant determinants of job tenure among fast-food workers at hotel:

- Source of referral to the company
- Number of months of previous customer-service work experience
- Reason for leaving previous job

- Number of previous jobs held
- Length of time at previous address
- Rate of pay desired
- Number of references given
- Length of time in previous position
- Type of employment being sought (part-time versus full-time)

Example of WAB item's response categories and scoring weights:

Item: Type of employment being sought (e.g., part-time versus full-time)

Item response categories

Assigned scoring weights

(A) Full-time position	0
(B) Part-time position	2
(C) Either	1

Conclusions: A weighted analysis of a job applicant's responses to selected job application questions (such as the example above) can produce a statistically significant prediction of the applicant's likelihood of becoming a long-term employee. The WAB technique may be particularly useful for those jobs for which there are a large number of openings, for which turnover is a problem, and for which a standard job application form is used in hiring.

Source: Adapted from Kaak, Feild, Giles, and Norris (1998, 18–24).

CONCERNS ABOUT WEIGHTED APPLICATION BLANKS There are some concerns associated with the use of the WAB technique. First, criterion measures such as turnover, absenteeism, and accident rates that are typically used to validate weighted application forms may not adequately represent a job's complex performance domain. For example, WAB scoring keys are typically derived to predict one specific, often narrow, criterion (e.g., tenure), as opposed to a broader measure of performance. Ghiselli's (1966) analysis of validity data suggests that weighted application forms can also predict training success and overall job proficiency.

Second, it takes data from a large number of employees to obtain percentages that are good stable estimates of the appropriate weights. For example, some would argue that the size of the derivation and **holdout groups**

Holdout group—the sample on which the stability of the regression weight(s) is assessed. The weights are derived from one sample, then tested on a second independent (holdout) sample to assess their stability.

used by Kaak et al. (1998) in their application of WABs to the hospitality industry (see Box 8.3) is much too small to provide for stable, reliable weights. Larger samples might require several years to collect the necessary data; there is the risk that changes in the job, the applicants, or the organization over that period may produce weights that represent neither the first- nor last-hired employees. However, a recent meta-analysis suggests that weighted application forms that include biographical information may have a greater degree of stability than previously thought (Rothstein, Schmidt, Erwin, Owens, and Sparks, 1990).

Finally, while weighted application forms provide the basis for good empirical predictions (Mitchell and Klimoski, 1982), they do not offer any understanding of why those relationships exist (Guion, 1967; Guion, 1998, 603). This approach is sometimes referred to as "dust-bowl empiricism." This criticism becomes less applicable, however, to the extent that the application form items were *rationally* derived from a systematic analysis of the job.

BIOGRAPHICAL DATA

Application forms require job candidates to make a report about their past experiences and accomplishments. As presented in Box 8.2, a typical application form addresses a very narrow range of job-related items. Owens (1976; Owens and Schoenfeldt, 1979) extended this approach to include a much broader range of biographical topics in the **biographical information blank (BIB).** The BIB typically covers a variety of areas, including educational experiences, hobbies, family relations, leisure-time pursuits, personal accomplishments, and early work experiences. Whereas a WAB focuses on more limited, factual, and verifiable information on educational background, training, and work experience, a BIB covers an array of less-verifiable information such as personal interests, attitudes, and values (Gatewood and Feild, 1998, 448).

> **Biographical information blank (BIB)**—a preselection questionnaire in which applicants are asked to provide job-related information on their personal background and life experiences.

Applicants report this information by answering a series of multiple-choice or short-answer questions. Box 8.4 presents an example of a BIB that was developed for use with job candidates for a managerial position. The information obtained from the BIB is scored to produce either a total overall score, or scores for specific sets of items or factors. Like the WAB, the BIB should be validated before being used to select from among job applicants. Compared with the WAB, the BIB provides greater insights into the type of individuals who experience job success, given the content and higher contextual richness of the items.

The life insurance industry has used **biodata** as part of its selection procedures since 1942. The Life Insurance Marketing Research Association (LIMRA), in its role as an industry trade association, has provided biodata selection instruments to the life insurance industry for selecting sales representatives. Since 1942, these biodata instruments have been widely used on literally millions of candidates throughout Canada and the United States. Life insurance sales positions are demanding. Sales agents are not normally provided with

> **Biodata**—biographical data for job applicants that has been gathered from BIBs, application blanks, or other sources.

BOX 8.4 An Example of a Biographical Information Blank

Name _____

Address _____

Number of Dependents _____

How long have you lived at your current address?_____

Do you consider your net worth to be low ____

moderate ____ or high ____ ?

Have you ever been turned down for a loan? Yes ____

No ____

How many credit cards do you have?_____

Highest level of education completed:

High School ____ Vocational School ____ College ____

University ____ Postgraduate ____

What educational degrees do you have? B.A. ____

B.Sc. ____ B.Comm. ____ M.B.A ____ Master's ____

Other _____

What subjects did you major in?_____ _____

What was your grade-point average in university? A ____ B ____ C ____ D ____

Did you graduate with honours? Yes ____ No ____

Did you receive any awards for academic excellence? Yes____No____

Did you receive any scholarships? Yes ____ No ____

List the extracurricular activities you participated in during school:

_____

Did you find school stimulating ____ boring ____ ?

Did you hold a job while attending school? Yes ____ No ____

How did you pay for your post–high-school training? (Check as many as appropriate)

Parents paid ____ Loans ____ Scholarships ____ Paid own way ____

Have you ever held a job where you earned commissions on sales? Yes ____ No ____

If "Yes," were your commissions low ____ moderate ____ high ____ ?

Five years from now, what do you expect your salary to be?_____

Do you enjoy meeting new people? Yes ____ No ____

How many social phone calls do you receive a week? ____

Do people count on you to "cheer up" others? Yes ____ No ____

How many parties do you go to in a year? ____

Do you enjoy talking to people? Yes ____ No ____

Rate your conversational skills:

   Excellent ____ Very Good ____ Good ____ Fair ____ Poor ____

How often do you introduce yourself to other people you don't know?

   Always ____ Sometimes ____ Never ____

Do you enjoy social gatherings? Yes ____ No ____

Do you go to social gatherings out of a sense of duty? Yes ____ No ____

How many times a year do you go out to dinner with friends? ____

BOX 8.4 Continued

Do you enjoy talking to people you don't know? Yes ____ No ____

What nonwork-related social activities are you engaged in?

What are your hobbies?

_____

What sports, recreational, or physical activities do you engage in?

_____

How confident are you in your ability to succeed?

Very Confident ___ Confident ___ Somewhat Confident ___

"leads," but rather are expected to prospect for customers among friends, family, and acquaintances. Rejection rates from among potential clients are high, requiring successful agents who are "thick-skinned" and persevering. First-year attrition rates are high, about 50 percent, and occur before the company can recoup its training costs. The current version of the LIMRA biodata instrument is the "Career Profile," which provides scores on five primary dimensions for individuals with no previous life insurance experience (see McManus and Kelly, 1999):

- *Insurance-related experiences—belief in the value and importance of insurance.* Question types include: Do individuals own the product they will be selling? Does the candidate have a personal insurance sales representative? Individuals whose life experiences show a belief in the value of the product are more likely to be effective sales representatives.

- *Number of friends, relatives, and personal contacts in the industry.* Questions include: Does the individual know any current sales representatives? Does the candidate have any relatives or close friends working in the insurance industry? Individuals who know people in the insurance industry are more likely to be effective sales agents, because they tend to be more aware of the challenges of the position before committing to the job. They know what they are getting into and tend to show greater perseverance in the face of adversity.

- *Recruiting method—knowledge of the position.* This focuses on knowledge of the specific office to which the person is applying rather than general knowledge of the industry. People with greater knowledge of the specific office show lower turnover rates.

- *Establishment—financial and occupational stability.* Question types cover: What is the candidate's financial situation? How many jobs has the candidate held over the past five years? Financial and occupational stability predicts success in the life insurance industry. Past stability and success predict future stability and success.

- *Commitment to present situation—ties to current job situation.* Includes questions like: "What is your employment status?" "How soon would you be available to accept a position?" Individuals with weak ties to their current employer show overall lower success rates as life insurance representatives.

LIMRA, on behalf of the Canadian industry, has developed a BIB for use exclusively in Canada. This biodata instrument conforms to Canadian human rights legislation and is sensitive to the Canadian cultural context.

BIB Dimensions   The BIB, which is also known as a life history or personal history inventory, is based on the view that past behaviour is the best predictor of future behaviour. Understanding how a job applicant behaved in the past through examination of related BIB items allows one to predict that applicant's future interests and capabilities. Statistical analyses of different BIB forms suggests that the BIB items cluster on 13 to 15 major dimensions (Owens, 1976). Although the comparability of dimensions across different BIBs may be questionable (Klimoski, 1993), rational comparison of the different biodata factors suggests that the following eight dimensions may be common to many life event inventories (Owens, 1976):

- School Achievement (academic success and positive academic attitude).
- Higher Educational Achievement (holding a degree from a post-secondary school).
- Drive (motivation to be outstanding, to attain high goals, to achieve).
- Leadership and Group Participation (involvement in organized activities and membership in groups).
- Financial Responsibility (financial status and handling of finances).
- Early Family Responsibility (an "own family" orientation).
- Parental Family Adjustment (happy parental home experience).
- Situational Stability (mid-life occupational stability).

These dimensions appear to be relatively stable and explain why certain applicants may be more successful than others. That is, a relationship between a particular item on the BIB and a criterion measure is not as important to predicting future behaviour as the relationship of the dimension represented by the item and the criterion. Knowing that the applicant is high in *drive* and *financial responsibility* is more important than knowing an applicant's precise goals or financial status. Moreover, it is reasonable to expect that the magnitude of the relationships will vary depending on the BIB dimension and criterion measure pairing, suggesting the use of differential weighting of dimensions based on the criterion being predicted (Morrison, Owens, Glennon, and Albright, 1962).

BIB as a Measure of Personality   An argument can be made that the dimensions underlying biodata or personal histories actually reflect different aspects of the job applicant's personality. In fact, biodata dimensions correlate well with personality-related dimensions of the Strong Interest Inventory (Owens, 1976). As well, life event or personal history inventories have been used to develop measures of personality. The Assessment of Background and Life Experiences (ABLE) measures six different personality constructs through biodata information. A major study conducted for the U.S. Army showed that the ABLE constructs successfully predicted important job-related criteria such as technical proficiency, general soldiering proficiency, effort and leadership, personal discipline, physical fitness, and military bearing (Hough, Eaton, Dunnette, Kamp, and McCloy, 1990).

McBride, Mendoza, and Carraher (1997) developed a 39-item multiple-choice biodata instrument to measure "service orientation" to select candidates for positions in the service industry. Seven dimensions were identified from this instrument, including satisfaction, sociability, agreeableness, resistance to change, responsibility, need for achievement, and need to make a good impression. The composite score of this biodata instrument correlated .65 with criterion ratings of service orientation (performance measure). Chait, Carraher, and Buckley (2000) found that this same 39-item biodata instrument (the Service Orientation Instrument, or SOI) correlated significantly with extroversion ($r = .32$, p. $< .01$), conscientiousness ($r = .28$, p. $< .01$), and openness to experience ($r = .22$, p. $< .01$), three of the core personality factors of the five-factor model of personality (Barrick and Mount, 1991). Moreover, subscales of the SOI correlated highly with corresponding personality scale measures (SOI responsibility and conscientiousness, $r = .74$; SOI sociability and extroversion, $r = .99$; SOI agreeableness and the personality factor "agreeableness," $r = .92$; SOI need for achievement and conscientiousness, $r = .91$). Clearly, the behaviours and experiences captured by a biodata instrument can be considered, in part, manifestations of underlying personality dispositions. Chapter 9 presents a more extensive discussion of the use of personality tests in selection.

VALIDITY OF BIODATA Validation research on biodata produces results similar to that for the WAB. Biodata predicts quite well certain types of job behaviours (e.g., absenteeism, turnover, job proficiency, supervisory effectiveness, and job training) in a wide range of occupations (Asher, 1972; Ghiselli, 1966; Hunter and Hunter, 1984; Maertz, 1999; Rothstein et al., 1990; Stokes and Cooper, 1994; Vinchur, Schippmann, Switzer III, and Roth, 1998). On average, corrected correlations between scores on biodata instruments and job-relevant criteria range from .30 to .40 (Hunter and Hunter, 1984; Reilly and Chao, 1982; Schmitt, Gooding, Noe, and Kirsch, 1984).

Biodata predicted individual differences in within-person performance variability over time for 303 security analysts (Ployhart and Hakel, 1998). The performance of the security analysts was highly variable over time; the degree of performance variability in these analysts could be predicted by biodata. Recognizing that personality may underlie the predictive validity of many biodata instruments, researchers have recently turned their attention to determining whether biodata and personality measures together provide greater prediction of performance criteria than either one used alone. McManus and Kelly (1999) found that the Initial Career Profile (ICP), the biodata instrument developed by LIMRA for life insurance sales agents, predicted 6 percent of the variance in "contextual performance" (measure of effort and personal discipline). When personality measures were added to the prediction model after the ICP, an additional 17 percent of the variance in contextual performance was explained. This result replicates Mael and Hirsch's (1993) finding that the predictive power of an empirically keyed biodata instrument and a set of personality measures is significantly greater than either instrument alone.

In a concurrent validation study of 376 clerical employees, Mount, Witt, and Barrick (2000) found that biodata predictors accounted for substantial incremental variance beyond that accounted for by personality predictors and general mental ability, for three of four performance criteria. Clearly, biodata can predict quite well many different performance criteria, across a variety of jobs. Enhancements in prediction can be obtained by using biodata in combination with other more traditional predictors, such as personality and mental ability tests. The evidence suggests that while biodata and personality measures may correlate positively, they are not "redundant" assessments.

Mael and Ashforth (1995) provide a clear example of how a biodata instrument developed from a theory on organizational identification predicted attrition in new recruits to the U.S. Army. Four biodata factors emerged as significant predictors of attrition over time periods spanning 6 to 24 months: activities involving outdoor work or pastimes; a dependable, nondelinquent lifestyle reflecting socialization to institutional expectations; a general preference for group attachments; and diligent involvement in intellectual pastimes. This research is an excellent example of how theory should precede and guide the development of biodata instruments. Where biodata instruments are well grounded in theory, the empirical relationships established with performance criteria are better understood and more explainable, and provide more promise for cross-sample, cross-organization applications.

ISSUES CONCERNING THE USE OF BIODATA Despite the impressive predictive validity of biodata, there remain concerns over its use for selection purposes. These issues include questions of "legality," "invasiveness," "fakability," and "generalizability." With respect to legality and invasiveness, many BIB items may request personally sensitive information on family background and experiences that borders on violation of local human rights legislation. A case can be made for these types of items provided they are job-related (Cascio, 1976); however, the employer bears the onus of establishing their worth as predictors.

Many other items on a BIB delve into areas that are not protected by legislation, but that raise issues of privacy. For example, job applicants may feel that it is inappropriate to share with a prospective employer information pertaining to their financial status or the number of credit cards they carry. As we discussed earlier, job applicants form perceptions of the organization and its values, which influence their decisions to accept job offers (Rynes, 1993). If a

BIB includes items that give the appearance of unfair discrimination or invasion of privacy, it may have the unintended effect of turning away highly qualified candidates. In one study, potential job applicants who completed application forms with discriminatory items reacted more negatively to the organization than those potential applicants who completed forms with the discriminatory items removed. The potential applicants believed that the organization in the first case was less attractive as a place to work. They indicated that they would be less likely to pursue a job with the company and less likely to accept one if offered. They were also less inclined to recommend the organization to a friend and tended to view the organization as one that treats its employees unfairly (Saks, Leck, and Saunders, 1995).

Both professionals and nonprofessionals perceive certain types of biodata items to be invasive, specifically, those items that are less verifiable, less transparent in purpose, and more personal (Mael, Connerley, and Morath, 1996). Four general topics generate the most apprehension toward biodata items: fear of stigmatization, concern about having applicants recall traumatic events, intimacy, and religion. Avoiding these types of attributes may help to reduce the perceived invasiveness of biodata items.

The perceived acceptability and fairness of BIBs might be context-specific—for example, asking applicants for information on home, spousal, and parental situations; recreation and hobbies; interest in travel and new experiences; and nonwork interests was perceived as more job-relevant, fair, and appropriate when used to select applicants for international postings rather than for domestic positions (Elkins and Phillips, 2000). Personal history questions appear to be more acceptable to job applicants for international assignments because such assignments involve relocation and readjustment of the applicant's entire family. Personal interests, values, stability, and family relations are seen as key to coping with the demands of international assignments (Elkins and Phillips, 2000). Increasing the transparency of purpose of biodata items increases their perceived acceptability (Mael et al., 1996).

In the United States, each item on a BIB must be shown *not* to have an adverse impact on members of protected groups (*State of Connecticut v. Teal* 457 U.S. 440, 1981). Canadian human rights legislation requires that any information used in the hiring process that adversely impacts one or more designated minority groups be "bona fide" (demonstrably job-related). Employers must decide whether the benefits of using a BIB outweigh the potential hazards, or whether it can be replaced by an equally valid but less-intrusive selection instrument. When carefully developed and systematically scored, however, biodata items have less adverse impact on women and other designated minority groups than many other traditional selection measures (Mitchell, 1994). The Canadian insurance industry has shown that having a BIB comply with human rights legislation does not sacrifice its predictive validity. The biodata form developed by LIMRA has been the subject of extensive validation research. Criterion-related studies carried out by LIMRA show that the Canadian biodata form successfully predicts which applicants will stay with the company for at least a year and produce sales in the top half of all agents. LIMRA also estimated the utility of the biodata form; in current dollars, each agent hired through the process returned a net profit of around $25 000.

Managers often express concern that job applicants are less than honest in completing a BIB or life event history, particularly when it comes to reporting negative information. Available evidence on the degree of accuracy in applications is mixed. Cascio (1975) reviewed over 100 biodata inventories completed by job applicants for positions with a Florida police department. He compared the answers that applicants gave to 17 items on the BIB with the actual event. On average, he found an exceptionally high correlation (.94) between the applicant's answer and the true state of affairs. This research suggests that if applicants believe their answers may be verified, they will be more likely to tell the truth. Obviously, this is more likely to happen when the BIB items ask for factual, objective information that can be checked. Indirect biodata items (those for which the respondents report on the opinions they believe others hold about them) show higher validities than items on which respondents report their past experiences and behaviours directly (Lefkowitz, Gebbia, Balsam, and Dunn, 1999). To a lesser degree, higher predictive validities are also associated with more-verifiable and job-relevant items. The higher validities associated with the indirect items, compared with the direct items, may have more to do with their relation to personality factors than their indirect nature. The majority of these indirect items concerned assessments of personality constructs, including "supervisors' views of the respondents' conscientiousness, openness to new ideas, how outgoing, how anxious and ability to 'catch on quickly'" (Lefkowitz et al., 1999).

Some distortion on BIBs should be expected. Specific types of information reported on traditional application forms may be inaccurate in up to 25 percent of cases (Goldstein, 1971). This last figure is consistent with the degree of inaccuracy or misrepresentation, 33 percent, found in application materials supplied by job candidates ("Looking at Job Applications," 1994). Unfortunately, accuracy of application forms and BIBs has not been examined extensively. Moreover, it is not always the case the distortion will adversely affect predictive validities. For example, impression management, which could be accomplished through "distortion of the facts," may well be an asset in certain positions, such as sales (though clearly there would need to be ethical boundaries around what is considered "acceptable" levels of distortion).

As with the WAB, the predictive validity for any one BIB is typically established for a fairly large and specific pool of individuals applying for a specific job. A case in point is LIMRA, whose life history form has been validated on thousands of individuals throughout North America applying for the position of "life insurance sales agent." With very few exceptions, employers cannot purchase a commercially available BIB that will suit their needs. Rather, they will need to develop and validate one on their own. This will require large applicant pools and someone in the human resources department with the technical knowledge to spearhead such a project. Accordingly, despite a respectable track record as a useful predictive tool that has minimal adverse impact, this may explain the scant use of BIBs by North American corporations (see Hammer and Kleiman, 1988; Terpstra and Rozell, 1993; Thacker and Cattaneo, 1992).

There is some recent evidence that suggests a biodata instrument can be used outside of the specific organization for which it was developed (Carlson, Scullen, Schmidt, Rothstein, and Erwin, 1999). The validity of a biodata instrument developed and keyed within a single organization may generalize to other organizations. Specifically, the biodata component of the Managerial Performance Record (MPR), which was developed within a single organization, predicted the rate of managerial progress (e.g., rate of promotion) in 24 other organizations. The MPR predicted the rate of promotional progress across *all* organizations and its validity did not vary much across organizations ($r = .53$, $sd = .05$). There were no differences in the validity of the MPR for males and females, or for managers of all age groups, lengths of company service, and educational levels (Carlson et al., 1999). Similarly, a biodata instrument improved the entry-level selection of graduate trainees in the accounting profession (Harvey-Cook and Taffler, 2000). The biodata form remained valid for applicants selected by the company over the next five years and could be used across a wide range of different firms. This generalizability of biodata forms advocates for a consortium approach to developing and keying biodata instruments that can be used across organizations (Harvey-Cook and Taffler, 2000). Additional evidence for the generalizability of biodata comes from the insurance industry; biodata scoring keys and factor structures remained stable across applicant pools drawn from the United States, the UK, and the Republic of Ireland (Dalessio, Crosby, and McManus, 1996).

Overall, carefully developed and validated BIBs can be a very effective, noninvasive, and defensible means of improving human resources selection decisions. Moreover, recent research shows that BIBs can have similar levels of predictive validity for similar jobs *across* organizations.

Résumés

A résumé is another source of biographical information produced by job applicants. The intent of the résumé is to introduce the job applicant to the organization through a brief, accurate, written self-description. The information contained on most résumés overlaps with the information requested by the employer through application blanks or biographical inventories. One difference is that on the résumé applicants voluntarily provide biographical information about themselves. They believe this information is job-related and that it will lead a potential employer to decide that they meet the minimum job requirements and are worthy of further consideration. A second difference is that job applicants may include information on the résumé that the employer might rather not see. Although it is not as common as it was a few years ago, some job applicants still list information about their citizenship or national origin, height, weight, marital status, or other characteristics that, if used as part of selection, run afoul of employment legislation. It might be extremely difficult for an employer to prove that such prohibited information did not influence an employment decision. Another important difference is that résumés are unstandardized. The uniqueness of each applicant's résumé makes the use of standardized scoring techniques difficult, if not impossible. Nonetheless, all of the psychometric and legal considerations that apply to application forms and biodata apply equally to the use of résumés in selection. Information obtained from the résumé must be job-related and not discriminate against designated minority groups.

FIRST IMPRESSIONS   In addition to providing specific biographical information, the résumé presents a first impression of the applicant. The recruiter or human resources manager may form an image of the applicant based on characteristics of the résumé itself. The résumé's style, neatness, organization, layout of information, and the vocabulary and phrases used throughout convey information about the candidate, in addition to the facts presented within the résumé. In essence, the human resources manager may believe that these characteristics reflect different aspects of the applicant in much the same way as a projective personality test (see Chapter 9).

WRITING A RÉSUMÉ   Many job applicants have difficulty writing a good résumé. Vocational guidance counsellors and employment counsellors often provide help in writing résumés as part of the services they offer. As well, most libraries have many references on writing effective job résumés. There are a few basic points to consider in preparing a résumé. It should include the applicant's name, address, and phone numbers, education and training, employment history, references, and a brief statement of employment goals and objectives. Information on hobbies, interests, and other pursuits should be included only if it is relevant to the career goals. For example, a candidate for a forest ranger position may want to note an interest in hiking.

The résumé should be well organized and laid out to emphasize the different types of information it covers. The type size and style should not discourage someone from reading the résumé. It should be typed or produced with a laser-quality printer. Incorporating features such as unusual fonts, small-point type, excessive italics, or single line spacing, which make the résumé difficult to read, generally guarantees that it will not be read. As electronic submission of résumés is becoming increasingly popular, some career and employment counsellors recommend listing a keyword summary at the beginning of the résumé and using appropriate nouns to match words that the recruiter's computer software is likely to search for (see Box 8.5). Box 8.6 presents a checklist of tips on writing an effective résumé and Box 8.7 presents an example of a standard résumé.

SCREENING RÉSUMÉS   In today's labour market, where many candidates are competing for a limited number of jobs, a voluminous number of résumés make screening more difficult. Organizations have had to develop procedures

BOX 8.5 Using the Internet to Screen Job Candidates

In Chapter 7 we discussed the impact that the Internet has had on recruiting through online job sites such as Workopolis.com and Monster.ca. One disadvantage of such recruiting methods is dealing with the potential flood of applications and résumés. A company using such services may receive over 50 applications a day. Sophisticated software programs are being used to create and manage applicant databases and to screen candidates based on the materials they submit online.

With appropriate software, client companies can access application services such as Cruiter.com, Inc. of Ottawa and screen online applications. Using screening software, a company recruiter can spot an excellent prospect in a matter of minutes. In addition to submitting a résumé, a candidate may be asked to fill out a questionnaire that is specific to a company. The questionnaire attempts to obtain crucial information that may not be addressed by the candidate's résumé. Some companies will only accept an application and résumé if the candidate provides the desired information on the questionnaire. Example questions for an international company might include "Can you travel immediately?" "Do you have a passport?"

The questionnaires used to screen candidates may include multiple-choice questions related to skills or experience (How much experience have you had using a programming language?) or short essays (How would you handle a programming problem that you could not solve by yourself?). Some software programs assign points to answers and only those candidates who meet a minimum score are invited to submit a résumé. Candidates who score high are flagged for action.

Source: Kerr (2000).

---

for efficiently and systematically processing résumés. Wein (1994) reports the following pre-employment screening procedure:

- Think of what the company needs for excellent job performance in terms of its job performance criteria.
- Screen out those résumés that do not include a stated job objective or career goal.
- Read each résumé with reference to the organization's criteria of job performance.
- Check résumés for work experience, chronology, and history.
- Examine surviving résumés for concrete accomplishments and identifiable skills.
- Look at résumés one more time for appearance.

HONESTY AND THE RÉSUMÉ Job applicants should feel free to customize their résumés to include their own unique attributes or experiences. However, it is important to be honest and to avoid exaggeration in presenting qualifications or accomplishments. If facts are checked later and they seem to have been distorted to the applicant's benefit, either job loss or severe embarrassment results. A Toronto-based reference-checking firm, Infocheck Ltd., reports that

BOX 8.6 Tips on Writing an Effective Business Résumé

1. Do a self-assessment—produce a first draft of your résumé by collecting all relevant information about yourself.

2. Analyze and sort out what should and should not be included on your résumé—it should fit comfortably on two pages.

3. Choose a format and type style that is professional in appearance and that is easy to read.

4. Begin your résumé with your name, address, and phone numbers(s)—it is not necessary to include any personal information such as birthdate, marital status, or health.

5. List your education—use reverse chronological order, that is, the most recent first. High school can easily be left off unless it is of particular importance.

6. Use point form (bullets work nicely) and begin each job description with an action verb that describes exactly what you did, for example, *analyzed*, *performed*, *directed*, *produced*, and so forth (try not to use the phrase "responsible for").

7. Be skills-oriented, not duty-oriented. Emphasize what you learned and achieved, and what new skills you gained.

8. Avoid unsubstantiated statements about yourself like "I'm creative, dynamic, a quick learner, a hard worker," and so on. Qualify your statements by backing them up with facts, for example, "Was commended for my creativity in developing a new marketing strategy."

9. Quantify your experiences where possible, for example, "Increased sales by 10 percent," "Handled cash up to $10 000 per shift," "Supervised a team of five," and so on.

10. Include any relevant summer, part-time, and/or volunteer experience, especially if it demonstrates leadership skills or other skills or attributes that may set you apart from the others.

11. Highlight special awards, achievements, scholarships, professional affiliations, memberships, other languages, and so forth. Emphasize your uniqueness.

12. Include extracurricular activities such as sports, hobbies, organizations that you are involved with. This will give you a more well-rounded appearance.

13. Make use of italics, boldface, and so on, to highlight results, accomplishments, and successes.

14. Check and double-check for spelling and grammatical errors—a single mistake on a résumé can put you out of the running.

15. Choose a good-quality paper that will not overpower the résumé in either texture or colour—your best bets for colour are white, cream, buff, vanilla, light grey, and for texture, heavy bond, linen-look, water-stained. As well, several appealing recycled papers are available in various colours and textures.

Source: Business Career Services, Michael G. DeGroote School of Business, McMaster University.

its second annual résumé fraud study shows 33 percent of final candidates lied, compared with 24 percent the previous year ("Résumé Inflation Seen," 1999). The study included 1000 "shortlisted" candidates who already had been through successful interviews or had been referred to prospective employers by search firms. The candidates were applying for jobs ranging from general office help to senior executive positions. Box 8.8 lists some prominent

BOX 8.7 An Example of a Business Résumé

JANE SMITH
595 Main Street West
Hamilton Ontario
Phone: (905) 574-8638; E-mail: jsmith@mcmaster.ca

EDUCATION
MOHAWK COLLEGE—Hamilton, Ontario
Office Administration—Executive Program
- Honours Graduate May 1999
- 4 semester average of A+
- Studies included WordPerfect 7.0, MS Word 97, MS PowerPoint 97, MS Access 97, MS Excel 97, Simply Accounting 5.0, Internet, E-mail, and Records Management

McMASTER UNIVERSITY—Hamilton, Ontario
Social Sciences
- Completed first-year Social Sciences degree in April 1997
- Maintained a Dean's Honour Average of A+
- Studies included English literature, French, gerontology, human geography, and history.

EMPLOYMENT EXPERIENCE
McMASTER UNIVERSITY—Hamilton, Ontario   June 1999 to present
Career Services Assistant—Commerce Career Resource Centre
- Assist Manager with a wide range of activities pertaining to the Commerce Internship Program and with career-related activities for undergraduate business students.
- Interact extensively with students and employers in a professional, efficient, and friendly manner through verbal and written communication.
- Coordinate the registration, monitor the attendance, and prepare course materials for approximately 175 students enrolled in the Commerce internship course 31N0.
- Facilitate the job posting and interview process for the Commerce Internship Program in a timely manner while paying strict attention to detail.

MOHAWK COLLEGE—Hamilton, Ontario
Instructor—Continuing Education
April 1999 to present
- Instruct approximately 15 students in the Keyboarding/Typing for Beginners course one evening per week using KeyboardingPro software.
- Responsible for instructing students in proper keyboarding techniques, marking completed lessons and timings, and troubleshooting computer problems.

Clerk Typist—Office Administration and Business Departments

- Completed typing, printing, and assembly of custom courseware manuals and course outlines.

- Prepared databases and performed merges for large mail-outs using WordPerfect software.

- Handled reception of visitors, transfer of calls, and answering general inquiries.

- Performed general office duties including filing, photocopying, faxing, mail distribution, disk formatting, and supply ordering.

COMPUTER SKILLS
Extensive experience and in-depth training with:

- MS Word 7.0, 97   MS Excel 7.0, 97

- MS Access 7.0, 97   MS PowerPoint 7.0, 97

- WordPerfect 5.1, 7.0, 8.0 Netscape Communicator 4.7

- Windows 3.1, NT, 95, 98 Netscape Calendar

- Simply Accounting 5.0   Basic HTML Programming

- Maximizer DataBase   Keyboarding 65 nwpm

CERTIFICATES AND AWARDS

- **Mohawk College Board of Governors Bronze Medal** for outstanding contribution to the college and community, 1999

- **Nicole Burgion Memorial Bursary** for student displaying initiative and demonstrating excellent analytical, problem-solving, and thinking skills that are complemented by good keyboarding speed, accuracy, and proofreading skills, 1999

- **McGraw-Hill Ryerson Award** for overall academic excellence in Office Administration, 1998

- **The Municipal Chapter of Hamilton IODE Prize** for the student attaining the highest average in a Level I History Course, McMaster University, 1996

- **Fortinos Supermarket Award** for excellence in Environmental Studies, Orchard Park Secondary School, 1994

- **The IODE Stoney Creek Battlefield Chapter Citizenship Award** for proficiency in Canadian Studies, Orchard Park Secondary School, 1994

ACTIVITIES AND INTERESTS

- Participate in jogging, in-line skating, and weight training to stay fit

- Interests include reading, baking, and learning new computer programs

REFERENCES AVAILABLE UPON REQUEST

Canadians whose résumés included misleading statements about their credentials ("Little Stretches," 1996).

In an increasingly competitive labour market, job candidates may be more prone to fudging the truth about their credentials. There is often a fine line between presenting yourself in the best possible light and intentionally misrepresenting your background. Human resource managers must learn how to read between the lines of résumés. Here are some things to look for when examining a résumé:

- unexplained gaps in work or education chronology;
- use of qualifiers such as "knowledge of," "assisted in" to describe work experience;
- listing of schools attended without indicating receipt of a degree or diploma;
- failure to provide names of previous supervisors or references;
- substantial periods in a candidate's work history listed as "self-employed" or "consultant";
- style in place of substance—use of flashy paper or fonts on the résumé.

Such characteristics should serve as a "flag" to examine the résumé closely and to undertake a thorough reference check before proceeding further with the application.

SCREENING INTERVIEWS

In North America, the interview is the most popular selection device; it is used nearly universally (Rowe, Williams, and Day, 1994). The interview, a face-to-face interaction between two people, is designed to allow one of the parties to obtain information about the other. In employment, the employer's representative is called the interviewer while the job applicant is called the interviewee or applicant. This traditional terminology does not convey the complex, dynamic, interactive nature of the interview. It is used only as a matter of convenience to identify each of the parties involved in the interview, since both attempt to obtain information about the other through the interview process. Each, at times, is both an interviewer and an interviewee.

SCREENING FOR ORGANIZATIONAL FIT   In our discussion of recruitment in Chapter 7, we described how job applicants use their initial interview with a recruiter to obtain information about the organization. The interviewer takes the opportunity of this interview to find out information about the applicant that is not apparent from an application form or résumé. The interview has considerable value as a recruiting device and as a means of initiating a social relationship between a job applicant and an organization (Rowe et al., 1994). The selection interview is used to present information, mostly favourable, about the organization as an employer, with the hope of increasing the odds that an applicant will accept a forthcoming job offer. The job applicant uses the occasion of the interview to learn more about the company as an employer and to make inferences about its values and philosophy in deciding whether there is a fit (Gati, 1989).

Without a doubt, interviewing that is done as part of the recruitment process serves as a screening mechanism. Job applicants who do not meet the recruiter's and the organization's standards do not proceed further. Today, organizations such as Goodyear Canada and Guardian Insurance Company of Canada are using the initial screening interview to determine whether job candidates possess competency in core performance areas that have been related to corporate mission statements and strategic plans. As noted previously, Ford Motor Company selects students for sponsorship through universities and technical colleges on the basis of how well the students fit four competency dimensions that were related to successful job performance. These core competencies and performance areas are identified through procedures discussed in Chapter 5. This initial assessment also includes screening based on those values believed necessary to achieving the company's strategic goals. Successful Canadian organizations recognize that selection and performance measurement go hand in hand. Other organizations are not so systematic and resort to highly questionable and untested "interviewing practices" in a desperate attempt to assess as many candidates as quickly as possible in a very tight labour market (see Box 8.9).

IMPROVING THE INTERVIEW—A PREVIEW   For almost as long as it has been used as a selection device, the interview has suffered criticism for poor reliability and validity. However, more recent work by Latham (1989) and Janz (1982) shows that both the reliability and validity of the interview can be substantially improved by structuring job analysis information into interview questions. The work of these two Canadian psychologists on the employment interview is described in more detail in Chapter 10. That chapter examines the use of the interview in the final stages of the selection process as part of

BOX 8.9 Screening with Silly Putty and Unicycles

Screening interviews are normally one-on-one affairs designed to assess whether a candidate meets the minimum qualifications for a job and to allow the candidate and the company to assess their mutual fit. However, screening interviews are taking on a questionable new look in some high-tech companies.

Tech Planet, a California-based company that provides computer services to small businesses, has replaced the screening interview with a weekly lunch. Up to 25 people a week may be invited to have pizza or Chinese food while they mix informally with Tech Planet staff. After lunch the staff vote on which candidates will be invited back for a follow-up with one "No" vote enough to blackball a candidate.

Survivors are invited to a monthly "final hurdle," where they bring an essay describing their next job and how they feel about working with small businesses. They also must bring an inanimate object that they feel best describes them. One candidate brought Silly Putty because, like Silly Putty, she was "energetic yet firm but flexible." At the "final hurdle" candidates work in groups to solve brainteasers and ethical dilemmas and to openly evaluate the strengths and weaknesses of the other competing candidates while sitting around a conference table. The Tech Planet staff then vote on which candidates they wish to hire.

Tech Planet is not alone in adopting such unusual screening procedures. Some recruiters screen candidates for social fit with their company by having them ride a unicycle around an office. Not surprisingly, many personnel selection experts question the merits of such procedures. In Canada, the legal defensibility of such practices would be a primary concern.

Source: Mahar (2000).

deciding which candidates are the most qualified. The remainder of this section reviews the role of the interview in the earlier stages of the selection process as a screening device to decide whether a job applicant meets minimum requirements.

THE TYPICAL SCREENING INTERVIEW Screening interviews typically consist of a series of freewheeling, unstructured questions that are designed to fill in the gaps left on the candidate's application form and résumé. Such traditional interviews take on the qualities of a conversation and often revolve around a set of common questions like those presented in Box 10.1 (e.g., "What is your greatest accomplishment?"). These questions cover the applicant's personal history, attitudes and expectations, and skills and abilities. The information obtained by many of these questions probably would have been better left to a well-constructed application form. Skillful interviewees often have learned how to give socially desirable answers to many of these frequently asked questions. While some distortion is to be expected in the answers an applicant makes during an interview, there is no reason to believe that those inaccuracies, intentional or otherwise, occur with greater frequency than inaccuracies in biodata and résumé information. There is very little direct evidence on the rate or percentage of misinformation that takes place over the course of an interview. As with applications and biodata, when interview questions focus on verifiable events related to past work or educational experiences, accuracy will likely increase.

SCREENING INTERVIEW FORMAT The interviewer often obtains better information from a screening interview by following an interview guide. Following a set of preplanned questions or topics during the interview, in addition to reviewing the applicant's file before the interview begins, will improve the reliability or consistency of information gathered through the interview (Schwab and Henneman, 1969). The format for this type of interview begins with some opening remarks by the interviewer to put the applicant at ease. This generally involves an exchange of pleasantries and personal information, including information on the interviewer's role in the organization. The interviewer states the purpose of the interview and how the information will be used. The interviewer will also mention whether any information presented during the interview will be held in confidence or shared with others. The interviewer will also note whether any notes or recordings will be made during the interview. Following these clarifications, the interview questions concentrate on the applicant's past work history, education and training, and general background. The applicant is given an opportunity to ask questions about the job and company as well as about issues raised during the interview. In closing, the interviewer outlines the time line for the decision process and when applicants are likely to hear the outcome. After the applicant leaves, the interviewer prepares a summary of the interview by completing either a written narrative or a rating form.

DECISIONS BASED ON THE SCREENING INTERVIEW The interviewer is frequently required to make inferences about an applicant's personal qualities, motivation, overall ability, attitude toward work, and potential not only for doing the job but also for fitting into the organizational culture. Organizations that use screening interviews often require the interviewer to rate specific attributes or characteristics of the applicant either in addition to, or instead of, making an overall recommendation. Box 8.10 presents a sample form used to rate applicants following a screening interview. The traits or attributes that interviewers are asked to rate vary among organizations. They range from the very specific (e.g., attitude toward working irregular hours) to the very general (e.g., initiative).

In discussing *realistic job previews* used by the Canadian Forces as part of its recruiting strategy, we noted that applicants first meet with a recruiting officer, who determines their initial suitability for a military career. The recruiter engages in a brief interview with the applicant after reviewing the candidate's application form. Following the screening interview, the recruiter makes a recommendation on the candidate's suitability. No further action is taken on those who are judged unsuitable for the military. Those applicants who pass the screening interview proceed to more-extensive testing as well as the job preview. Microsoft Canada makes similar use of a screening interview to discover computer science graduates whose thinking is fast, flexible, and creative. The Microsoft interview includes questions related to computer science knowledge and brainteaser-type questions about balloons that move in

BOX 8.10 An Example of a Post-Interview Summary

Applicant's Name _____ Date _____

Position _____ Interviewed By_____

Ratings: 0–Unacceptable; 1–Poor; 2–Satisfactory; 3–Good; 4–Excellent

	Rating	Comments
Previous Experience	0 1 2 3 4	
Neatness/Grooming	0 1 2 3 4	
Communicating	0 1 2 3 4	
Interpersonal Skills	0 1 2 3 4	
Adaptability	0 1 2 3 4	
Maturity	0 1 2 3 4	
Emotional Stability	0 1 2 3 4	
Leadership Potential	0 1 2 3 4	
Ability to Work with Others	0 1 2 3 4	
Planning/Organizing	0 1 2 3 4	
Attitude toward Work	0 1 2 3 4	
Realistic Expectations	0 1 2 3 4	
Overall Impression	0 1 2 3 4	

Total Score _____

Recommendation: _____ Unacceptable/Notify applicant of rejection

_____ Applicant is acceptable for

position

If acceptable, arrange for the following:

_____ Employment Testing

_____ Selection Interview

---

mysterious ways. More than the right answer, Microsoft Canada is looking for an ability to think creatively and a display of an inquiring mind. Only about 25 percent of applicants from one of Canada's leading computer science programs make it through the final stages of the screening interview (Carpenter, 1995).

IMPRESSION FORMATION Interviewers use both the verbal and nonverbal behaviour displayed by job applicants in forming an impression of the applicant (Dreher and Sackett, 1983; Rynes and Miller, 1983; Webster, 1982). Similarly, the applicant uses the interviewer's verbal and nonverbal behaviours to form an impression of the interviewer, and the organization, in judging the probability of receiving a job offer and the desirability of accepting it and of working for the organization. Box 8.11 lists common behaviours displayed by applicants during an interview that lead to either positive or negative impressions on the part of the interviewer. While there is no guarantee that presenting all the positive behaviours and avoiding all the negative ones will lead to the next step in the selection process, doing so should increase the likelihood of such an outcome.

VALUE OF THE SCREENING INTERVIEW   Considerable time and energy have been spent on investigating the effectiveness of the interview. In recent years, however, the selection interview has received much more attention than the screening interview. Past reviews of the employment interview (Harris, 1989; Webster, 1982) suggest that it is a useful screening device. Interviewers who screen for production or clerical workers generally develop a stereotype of an acceptable applicant and quickly decide whether the applicant fits that mould. In the remainder of the interview the interviewer seeks information from the applicant either to confirm or to contradict the interviewer's impression. Negative information, particularly when it occurs early in the interview, is difficult to ignore and tends to influence the outcome more than positive information. Training for interviewers may reduce some types of errors that can be made in rating applicants, but there is no evidence that this reduction affects the quality of the overall judgments made by the interviewer.

CAUTIONS   Using the interview as a screening device brings with it the potential for introducing discriminatory practices into the hiring process. Interviews, including those that are highly structured, are conversations between individ-

---

BOX 8.11 Interviewee Behaviours That Influence Interviewer Impressions

APPLICANT BEHAVIOURS THAT INFLUENCE POSITIVE IMPRESSIONS

- Being on time for the interview.
- Being prepared for the interview by having done homework on the company and anticipating common interview questions.
- Making direct eye contact with the interviewer.
- Remaining confident and determined throughout the interview regardless of how the interviewer's cues suggest the interview is going.
- Providing information about strong points when answering questions.
- Answering questions quickly and intelligently.

- Demonstrating interest in the position and organization.

APPLICANT BEHAVIOURS THAT INFLUENCE NEGATIVE IMPRESSIONS

- Presenting poor personal appearance or grooming.
- Displaying an overly aggressive, know-it-all attitude.
- Failing to communicate clearly (e.g., mumbling, poor grammar, use of slang).
- Lacking career goals or career planning.
- Overemphasizing monetary issues.
- Evasiveness or not answering questions completely.
- Lacking maturity, tact, courtesy, or social skills.

uals. Something is said that provokes a response. In opening an interview with small talk or chitchat, interviewers often delve into the personal background of the applicant. They may ask questions about marital status, child-care arrangements, birthplace or birth date, or the applicant's name that relate to national or ethnic origin. Information of this type is clearly prohibited. Should a job applicant who has been asked these questions be turned down, the onus will be on the employing organization to show that the reason was lack of job-related requirements and not discriminatory hiring practices. Interview questions should follow the same rule of thumb as application blanks: Is the information obtained from this question job-related? If you cannot answer yes, don't ask the question.

REFERENCE CHECKS

Job applicants are often asked to provide the names of personal references as well as the names of their supervisors from previous jobs. It is understood that these individuals will be contacted and asked for their views on the applicant. These people may be asked to verify information presented by the applicant or to make judgments about the traits, characteristics, and behaviours of the applicant. Consequently, the term **reference check** may be applied to vastly different procedures, which have different levels of reliability and validity.

Reference check—information gathered about a job candidate from that applicant's supervisors, co-workers, clients, or other "referees." The information is usually collected from the referees through telephone interviews.

In assessing the worth of reference checks, it is necessary to keep in mind the specific procedure that was actually used. Regardless of the specifics, reference checks normally take place *last* in the screening process; references are sought only for those applicants who have survived the previous screens. Reference checking is typically done last to protect the confidentiality of the candidates (who may not have informed their current employers that they are seeking alternative employment) and because it can be labour-intensive if done properly.

POPULARITY AND VALIDITY OF PERSONAL REFERENCES   Along with biodata, the résumé, and the interview, references are the most commonly used screening devices. Unlike biodata, reference checks do not enjoy a good reputation and add little of value to the screening process (Baxter, Brock, Hill, and Rozelle, 1981). One of the most comprehensive investigations into references (Goheen and Mosel, 1959; Mosel and Goheen, 1958; 1959) suggested that ratings based on references from the applicant's past supervisors did not predict performance ratings given by the applicant's current supervisor. Nor did the references identify information that would have led to judging the applicant unsuitable for the position. In effect, the information in the reference was more of a statement about the referee, the person writing the reference, rather than the applicant. Unfortunately, the validity of personal references has not improved over time. Canadian human resources consultants now routinely warn corporate clients to be leery of making hiring decisions on the basis of personal references (Kabay, 1993; Solomon, 1998). Predictions about future job success based on references have not been overly successful. Hunter and Hunter (1984) showed that the validity of reference checks ranged from as low as .16 for promotion criteria to a high of .26 for supervisor rating criteria.

REASONS FOR POOR VALIDITY OF PERSONAL REFERENCES There appear to be several reasons for the low validity of reference checks. In the case of personal references, it is highly unlikely that a job applicant will knowingly offer the name of someone who will provide a bad reference. (Doing so might be more of a statement about the cognitive ability of the applicant!) Most applicants are fairly confident about the type of reference they will be given. Applicants should not hesitate to ask intended referees if they would provide positive comments before listing their names on an application form. It is in the applicant's best interests to do this. The result, however, is a set of uniformly positive recommendations for each applicant. The lack of variability in the references limits their use in discriminating between candidates; this is an example of range restriction, discussed in Chapter 3, which leads to low **validity coefficients**. This is one reason why even the slightest negative information contained in a reference may be sufficient to eliminate an applicant from the job competition (Knouse, 1983). Negative information is simply not expected in a reference.

Employers seek to screen out job applicants who have poor work behaviours or who have problematic backgrounds and often use reference checks to obtain such information. While it is understandable that applicants will use the most favourable references, why are reference checks with previous employers equally ineffective as screening measures? Consider the following two situations:

- An unproductive employee whom you supervise has applied for a job with another company. You receive a call asking for your judgment on the employee. While you may wish to be honest and helpful, you do not want to say anything that will prevent the other company from taking the employee off your hands. The result is that while you truthfully answer any questions you are asked, you do not volunteer any negative information, hoping that your problem employee will be hired away. However, if you are asked specifically about problem behaviours and you intentionally mislead the reference checker or cover up the problems, you might be liable for any economic losses suffered by the new employer after hiring your problem employee (Leavitt, 1992).

- You receive a call checking on a former employee who resigned rather than face dismissal over allegations of sexual harassment. No charges were brought against the employee. If you are completely honest and express your concerns over the employee's behaviour while working for you, the former employee may not receive a job offer. The former employee then learns of your remarks and sues you and your company for slander, defamation, and the lost opportunity of a new job. While you may be able to defend yourself against the lawsuit, you will have substantial legal fees.

Validity coefficient—the correlation between assessment scores and job performance measures.

In the United States, several states have laws that make former employers liable for any statements that wrongfully prevent job applicants from receiving offers from another employer.

Given these liabilities, many Canadian employers are hesitant about making any strong, negative statements about current or former employees, even though reference checking is easier to carry out in Canada than in the United States (McFarland, 1996; "Most Employers Use," 1995). According to Gatewood and Feild (1998, 420), the predictive validity of reference checks is enhanced when:

- the reference check is completed by an applicant's previous immediate supervisor;
- the referee has had adequate time to observe the applicant;
- the applicant is the same gender, ethnicity, and nationality as the supervisor on the previous job; and
- the old and new jobs are similar in content.

TELEPHONE REFERENCE CHECKS   Many employers are also reluctant to provide references in writing, preferring instead to do so over the phone. The telephone reference is perhaps the most common way in which Canadian employers check references. Many have also resorted to using forms that obtain standardized information on all potential employees. Regrettably, most of the questions asked as part of these reference checks ask for judgments on the part of the referee rather than focusing on objective information and suffer the same problems as more general letters of reference. Typical questions asked about the job applicant in telephone checks usually include some of the following:

- How long have you known the applicant? In what capacity?
- What sort of employee is the applicant?
- Does the candidate show initiative?
- How did the applicant get along with other employees, supervisors, clients?
- Did the applicant meet deadlines? Get work done on time?
- Was the applicant punctual? Were there attendance problems?
- Were you satisfied with the applicant's performance?
- Why did the applicant leave your company?
- Is there anything you feel I should know about this candidate?
- Would you rehire the applicant?

ASKING THE RIGHT QUESTIONS   In many cases, the right questions are not asked, and many that are asked may not have any relevance to the job under consideration. Also, reference checks often fail to ask for confirmation of specific information provided by job candidates in their application materials. The referee should be asked to compare the candidate with other employees—for example, "If your worst employee is given a rating of 1 and your best a rating of 10, what rating would you give to this candidate?" Referees should be probed for more information on the candidate when their answers are not forthcoming or appear to be too qualified or general. Ask for specifics and have them describe examples of the candidate's behaviour—for example, "Describe a situation in which the candidate performed exceptionally well or exceptionally poorly." Many of the techniques discussed in Chapter 10 for developing structured or behaviour-based interview questions for employment interviews can be adapted for use in reference checking. As in the case of interviewing, asking specific, behaviour-based questions related to job performance is likely to increase the accuracy of the information obtained through the reference check.

IS THE REFEREE COMPETENT TO ASSESS?   There are implicit assumptions made when a former supervisor or a personal reference is called upon for information about a job candidate; namely, that the referees themselves are competent to make the assessment and are sufficiently knowledgeable about the candidate to provide accurate information. These are not always well-founded assumptions. A former supervisor may not have been in a position long enough to learn much about the employee's behaviour; there is also no guarantee that the supervisor is capable of discriminating poor job behaviour from excellent. When these assumptions are met, the reference information is likely to have a higher degree of accuracy. In effect, the reference checker must also know something about the referees to establish the credibility of their references. This is why greater value is placed on references from people who are known to those evaluating the reference information.

BACKGROUND CHECKS   Reference checks are on safer ground when they concentrate on verifying information obtained from the applicant's biodata, résumé, or interview. An article in *Canadian Banker* magazine reported that recent surveys indicated that about one-third of all résumés included false-hoods related to level of education, length of time in previous job, and level of responsibility. The article advised its readers that the best defence against such misrepresentation is a careful check of the information provided by the candidate during the hiring process ("Looking at Job Applications," 1994). Although some observers believe that lying is not an extensive problem in Canada (McFarland, 1996), it is still a good procedure to carry out reference checks. When the candidate knows that the information from these sources will be checked, the accuracy of that information is likely to increase. Box 8.12 provides a "checklist" of guidelines for conducting a thorough and legally defensible background reference check.

FIELD INVESTIGATIONS   In most cases, checking information is limited to phone calls to supervisors and personal references. However, a very extensive search of an applicant's background may take place for some occupations or positions. Applicants for sensitive government jobs or with security services such as the RCMP undergo field investigations that involve interviews with people who know the applicant, including former employers and co-workers; credit checks; review of police files, court records; educational records; and any other available documentation. Background checks of this sort are very expensive, but in most cases they provide an accurate description of the applicant and any problem areas that might affect job performance. Field investigations are used by corporations before they make top-level managerial appointments. Most organizations are not equipped to do such costly and elaborate investigations of potential new employees. Increasingly they are turning to a growing number of firms that specialize in this activity (Fuchsberg, 1990). A major concern with such field investigations is their invasion of the applicant's privacy. There is always the possibility that the background check will uncover information that

---

BOX 8.12 Reference Checklist

Obtain Waivers: Have candidates sign a comprehensive waiver granting the employer or its agents express permission to contact references and anyone else who might be familiar with the candidate's past job performance.

Check Three References: Check at least three references. Multiple references are preferable, allowing prospective employers to look for consistency and to show that they exercised care in hiring.

Ask for Different Types of References: Best references typically come from former supervisors. Peers and subordinates are also excellent references. Collecting references from supervisors, peers, and subordinates provides for varying perspectives on the candidate.

Ask about Past Job Performance: Ask questions that relate directly to job performance.

Ask Questions on Recent Job Performance: The reference check should cover the preceding five- to-seven-year period.

Avoid Personal References: References from personal friends and family tend to be a waste of time. Insist that candidates provide references who can comment on direct observation of past job performance.

Verify all Licences and Degrees: One of the most common deceptions on résumés and job applications is claiming to hold a degree that was never conferred or a licence never issued. Don't take a document or a copy of it at face value. Call the licensing bureau/board or the registrar's office of the university/college.

Check References by Telephone: Thorough reference checking includes listening carefully to responses: a person's tone of voice can change the meaning of a response considerably. Talking directly to the referee also allows for follow-up questions.

Avoid "Closed" Questions: Avoid questions that can be answered with a simple "yes" or "No."

Use Qualified Professionals or Trained Staff to Check References: People who check references must be trained to listen for the underlying meaning of statements. Whether handled internally or by an outside agency, reference checking should be thorough, professional, and legal. Never be satisfied with a response such as "She was the best employee we ever had." Follow up with the question: "Could you give examples that show why her performance was so outstanding?"

Avoid Invasive/Discriminatory Questions: Never ask questions about race, age, religion, or national origin.

Source: Adapted from Barada (1996).

is unrelated to job performance but disqualifies the candidate because of employer disapproval for the employee's actions or beliefs.

WORK EXPERIENCE Screening job applicants through review of résumés, preliminary interview, or reference checking emphasizes a candidate's credentials, including their formal training and work experiences. Formal credentials (e.g., licence, diploma, or degree) and the work experiences of the candidate are identified and verified. Indeed, in many cases, candidates without some specified minimum level of formal training, education, or work experience do not get any further than the résumé review stage of the screening and selection process. While there are widely agreed-upon, easily verifiable indicators of formal training and educational achievements, this is not the case with work experience.

Work experience refers to "events that are experienced by an individual that relate to the performance of some job" (Quinones, Ford and Teachout, 1995, 890). There are many aspects to work experience, including length of time on a job, time with an organization, or number of times a specific task has been performed. (See Quinones et al., 1995; Rowe, 1988; and Tesluk and Jacobs, 1998, for a more complete breakdown of different ways to conceptualize and measure work experience.) For example, in hiring a car salesperson, we might consider the time candidates spent working for other car dealerships, the time spent specifically as a car salesperson, or the number of vehicles sold. It is likely that the number of previous car sales is the most relevant measure of work experience in making a hiring decision. These are all *quantitative* measures of work experience.

On the other hand, *qualitative* measures allow us to probe into the nature, level, diversity, and complexity of a candidate's work experiences. For example, what is the demographic profile of the customers served by the applicant (age, gender, ethnicity, socioeconomic background)? How much autonomy in negotiating car sales did the candidate have in the previous job? What was the complexity of the job (e.g., number of car models, amount of staff assistance, use of technology/computers, etc.)? Qualitative assessments of work experience are generally done during the screening interview but can also be inferred to a certain extent through the résumé.

Clearly, work experience has many dimensions. Depending on the work environment in which the person is employed, one manager may have 15 years of work experience, while another may have one year of work experience repeated 15 times! The former manager may have worked in a challenging, dynamic, growth-oriented organization, while the other may have worked in a stable, predictable, unchallenging work environment. In assessing work experience, you will want to evaluate both quantitative and qualitative aspects of work experience. However, in the initial sorting of résumés, the temptation may be to simply make quick cuts of those with the least years of previous work experience. However, those with fewer years of work experience may have had "richer" experiences and developed more competencies than the candidates with longer work histories. Ford, Quinones, Sego, and Speer-Sorra (1992) demonstrated that two individuals with equal job and organizational tenure can differ considerably in the level of challenge and complexity encountered in their assignments and tasks. This is why, when conducting screening interviews and reference checks, the HR manager should probe with behavioural questions that tap job-relevant competencies.

A number of studies have found a significant and positive relationship between work experience and performance. Some have shown job tenure to be related to job performance through increases in job knowledge and competencies (Borman, Hanson, Oppler, Pulakos, and White, 1991; Schmidt, Hunter, and Outerbridge, 1986). Vance, Coovert, MacCallum, and Hedge (1989) reported that length of time spent as an engine mechanic predicted performance on three different sets of tasks. Three meta-analyses (quantitative reviews) of the relationship between work experience and job performance showed mean correlations ranging from .18 to .32, with work experience defined in terms of job tenure (Hunter and Hunter, 1984; McDaniel, Schmidt, and Hunter, 1988; Quinones et al., 1995). These mean correlations were considerably higher, $r =$ .41, when work experience was defined in terms such as "number of times performing a task" or "level of task difficulty." Finally, work experience has higher correlations with hard (e.g., work samples) as opposed to soft (e.g., ratings) measures of performance: mean $r = .39$ versus mean $r = .24$ (Quinones et al., 1995). This suggests that HR practitioners should carefully consider work experience when making screening or selection decisions. Specifically, the practitioner needs to identify the kind (quantitative and qualitative) of work experience that is most relevant to the work to be performed in the new job and then to fine-tune the screening and selection process to ensure that those aspects of work experience are adequately assessed.

EVALUATING SCREENING EFFECTIVENESS

Biographical data (including both weighted and traditional application blanks), résumés, screening interviews, and reference checks are perhaps the most frequently used methods of obtaining information used in the hiring process. The psychometric properties of these procedures vary greatly. One difficulty in making any definitive conclusions about their overall worth is the lack of standardization in the way these predictors are measured across organizations. As shown in subsequent chapters of this book, standardized assessment tools for personality, cognitive ability, and skills sets have been used on a variety of samples in a variety of organizations, and validated against common criteria, such as supervisory ratings. However, historically, the process and methods of collecting and integrating information from biodata, reference checks, and screening interviews have been unique to each employing organization. This makes it difficult to aggregate validity findings across studies and to derive definitive conclusions on the worthiness of these tools. However, biodata instruments are now being developed for application across organizations and there is greater use of standardization of screening interviews, allowing for greater integration and summary of effect sizes reported across samples.

BIODATA

Research supports the validity of biographical data in screening job applicants. Rothstein et al. (1990) place biodata second only to cognitive ability as a valid predictor of job proficiency, supporting Reilly and Chao's (1982) earlier position that the validity of biodata was on a par with that of employment tests. Asher and Sciarrino (1974) reported that the validity coefficients for biodata exceeded .50 in six of the 11 studies they reviewed. A more recent quantitative meta-analysis puts the average validity coefficient at .37 (Hunter and Hunter, 1984). Well-constructed biographical inventories that are based on a job analysis provide data that can be used to make valid inferences about an applicant's future job proficiency.

RÉSUMÉS

Few validation studies have been done directly on the résumé itself. Rather, studies report the validity of inferences based on information typically found on a résumé. Hunter and Hunter's (1984) meta-analysis showed that information of the type included on a résumé had relatively low validity in predicting future job success. Experience had the highest validity (.18), followed by academic achievement (.11) and education (.10). Nonetheless, a résumé and its accompanying cover letter remain the primary means by which many job applicants introduce themselves to an organization and create an impression of their fit to the job and to the company.

SCREENING INTERVIEWS

There is considerable research on the validity of interviews in employee selection. Meta-analyses report the validity for unstructured employment interviews, the type mostly used in screening, as ranging from .14 (Hunter and Hunter, 1984) to .20 (Wiesner and Cronshaw, 1988). Even at .20, the validity of the interview is still substantially low in comparison with other types of selection procedures. It is likely that an interview will always play a role in hiring regardless of its validity. Employers will always want to meet the prospective employee face-to-face before making a job offer. Chapter 10 presents ways of substantially improving the interview by relating it to job analysis information. The improvements to the interview discussed in Chapter 10 should be incorporated into screening interviews as well as selection interviews. Properly developed interview questions have the potential for being excellent screening devices. The reality is that, as presently done, most screening interviews cannot be justified in terms of their predictive validity. Nonetheless, they will likely continue as a basis for deciding the acceptability of job applicants.

REFERENCE CHECKS

In general, references are not particularly valuable as selection devices (Muchinsky, 1979). Meta-analyses place the validity for references at either .14 (Reilly and Chao, 1982) or .26 (Hunter and Hunter, 1984). This is in the same range as the unstructured employment interview. While references do have some predictive value, as do unstructured interviews, that value is low, particularly when compared with biodata and the types of employment tests discussed in Chapter 9. Reference checks appear most useful in screening out individuals who may be particularly weak or problematic candidates.

WORK EXPERIENCE

Work experience is usually considered at many different stages of the recruitment and selection process; typically, it is measured in terms of (time) tenure in a job or organization. This is a crude measure of work experience as there are many different facets to work experience. The aspect of work experience considered in screening and selection should be aligned with the specific criterion measure of performance the employer wishes to predict. Recent research shows that "amount" measures of work experience (e.g., number of times performing a task) correlate most strongly with "hard" measures of performance.

UTILITY ANALYSIS

One reason for the popularity of screening devices is their cost and ease of use. They are relatively inexpensive, administered quickly, and easy to interpret. With the exception of weighted application blanks and biographical inventories, there are few, if any, development costs associated with these devices. Those using the devices typically do not have any special training to administer or interpret the data. However, these low costs must be compared with the potential for inaccuracy. The cost of *false positives* screened into the organization through these procedures can be quite high, particularly in smaller firms where hiring a poor performer can be crippling to morale and overall productivity. While there are no reports of formal utility analysis of screening devices available, biodata instruments would likely show a net benefit to the organization. When properly developed and administered, use of biodata forms in HR screening is highly cost-effective (Anderson and Shackleton, 1990).

LEGAL CONSIDERATIONS

All of the selection tools reviewed in this chapter have the potential for running afoul of privacy and human rights legislation, leading to charges of discriminatory hiring practices. Before any of them are used as part of a selection system, they must be reviewed carefully to eliminate questions prohibited under human rights legislation. Alternatively, it must be established that the prohibited information is a bona fide occupational requirement.

Summary

Organizations need to be staffed with people who will not only be capable of doing the work for which they are hired, but who will also do that work in a productive manner. While the role of recruiting is primarily to secure an adequate supply of qualified job applicants, the role of selection is to identify the most-qualified candidates. Like recruitment, the selection process is influenced by factors such as the labour market, the legal environment, and the organization's philosophy and values, which all influence the size and richness of the applicant pool. If selection is to be successful, it must be embedded in organization and job analysis, predict relevant job performance criteria, be legally defensible, and be perceived as "acceptable" (fair) to job candidates.

Screening, which is often the first stage in recruiting, categorizes job applicants as either acceptable or unacceptable with respect to job requirements. Selection gives greater emphasis to identifying the *degree* to which applicants will be successful. In screening, organizations commonly rely on the application form or biodata, the résumé, the preliminary screening interview, and reference checks. Candidates who pass these screening assessments go on for further, more in-depth assessments. As part of the selection process, these screening devices must meet the same psychometric and legal standards required of other more extensive and expensive selection procedures.

Screening devices yield predictions about future job performance based on past behaviour, interests, and experiences. When biodata and interview questions focus on *verifiable* information, their predictive validity is enhanced. Information gathered through application blanks or biodata forms can provide a good prediction of job performance if the instruments are rationally developed and derived systematically from the knowledge, skills, ability, and key competency requirements of the target position. Traditional, unstructured screening interviews are poor predictors but can be substantially improved by the inclusion of structured questions derived from a job analysis. Reference checks appear to offer little value to the screening process, other than in screening out the most undesirable candidates. As these screening devices all have the potential for violating human rights legislation, great care must be taken with their use.

Key Terms

Application blank, p. 296

Base rate, p. 288

Biographical information blank (BIB), p. 304

Biodata, p. 304

Construct, p. 291

Criterion measures, p. 288

Designated minority group, p. 294

Employment equity, p. 289

False negatives, p. 296

False positives, p. 296

Holdout group, p. 303

Human resources planning (HRP), p. 286

Minimum qualifications, p. 294

Reference check, p. 323

Screening, p. 294

Selection ratio, p. 286

Validity coefficient, p. 324

Weighted application blank (WAB), p. 300

EXERCISES

1. Obtain employment application blanks from five different organizations. Determine whether the organization falls under federal or provincial jurisdiction. Do the application blanks request information that is prohibited (see Table 2.1, p. 34)? Use Table 2.1 to prepare a table showing the nature of the violations.

2. Prepare your own personal résumé using the résumé presented in this chapter as a model. Exchange your résumé with one of your classmates. Critique each other's document in terms of organization, clarity of information, style, and presentation. Write a short paragraph describing the impressions you formed from reading your classmate's résumé.

3. Develop an interview guide for doing a screening interview that lists the questions that *cannot* be asked because the information relates to prohibited grounds of discrimination (see Table 2.1).

4. Develop a set of questions based on the security dispatcher's job description that can be used to screen applicants for that position.

5. Identify the people who should provide references for applicants for the security dispatcher position. Develop a set of questions to ask those references.

6. Box 8.9 describes the screening process used by Tech Planet, a California-based provider of computer services for small businesses. Evaluate this screening and selection program, drawing on the material from this and earlier chapters. Your critique should consider issues of perceived credibility (acceptability), fairness, validity, legal defensibility, and ethics.

7. Think of the key activities of a job that you have held (part-time or full-time). From these key activities, list a number of biodata items that you believe could be helpful in predicting success in this job. A brief rationale should accompany each item. Develop a one-page biodata questionnaire, by phrasing each item in question format.

CASE

In this chapter we discussed three primary screening methods—the application blank, the résumé, and the interview—and some problems related to each. For example, job applicants may have a tendency to "enhance" their résumés (see Box 8.8 for examples of prominent Canadians who have done this).

Margie Mosher, the personnel manager for Allied Domecq PLC, a British holding company that owns Dunkin' Donuts and Baskin-Robbins Ice Cream, among other companies, has said that she was minutes away from hiring a company manager who had a "phenomenal résumé" when a background check revealed the candidate had no graduate degree, had been stripped of professional accreditation, and had a criminal record (Butler, 2000). Other companies are not as fortunate. Recently, many companies have ceased doing background checks in response to a tight labour market and the need to fill positions quickly. Competition to fill positions at the senior manager level and in the high-tech industry have led many personnel managers to overlook suspicious job applications. One car dealership in New Jersey lost millions of dollars, which was later discovered to have been stolen by a sales manager who had spent six years in prison for robbery. Nonetheless, managers do not want to lose a hot prospect by delaying a job offer till a background check has been completed.

Source: Adapted from Butler (2000).

DISCUSSION QUESTIONS

1. Should background checks be mandatory for all jobs or only for certain jobs? Explain your reasoning.
2. Describe a procedure that could be used for doing background checks in a tight labour market.
3. Should background checks be made before a candidate receives a job offer? If so, how do you prevent obtaining information that may be used to discriminate against the candidate (see Table 2.1)?
4. How can the Internet be used to do background checks and to speed up the process? Are there any risks in this process?
5. Explain why background checks may be an invasion of a job applicant's right to privacy.
6. If you discover that a job applicant has a criminal record, can you disqualify the candidate solely on that ground and without fear of violating the candidate's human rights?
7. What is the value of an "Ivy League" degree on a résumé? Would a degree from an "elite" school influence your hiring decision if everything else were equal among candidates?

8. What should you do if you discover someone has fudged his or her application form or résumé or lied during the screening interview? Does it matter how big the lie is?

REFERENCES

Anderson, N., and V. Shackleton. 1990. "Staff Selection Decision Making in the 1990s." *Management Decision* 28: 5–8.

Armour, S. 2000. "Test? Forget the Test—You're Hired." *USA Today* (August 8): B1.

Arvey, R.D., and P.R. Sackett. 1993. "Fairness in Selection: Current Developments and Perspectives. In N. Schmitt and W. Borman, eds., *Personnel Selection in Organizations.* San Francisco: Jossey-Bass, 171–202.

Asher, J.J. 1972. "The Biographical Item: Can It Be Improved?" *Personnel Psychology* 25: 251–69.

Asher, J.J., and J.A. Sciarrino. 1974. "Realistic Work Samples Tests: A Review." *Personnel Psychology* 27: 519–23.

Barada, P.W. 1996. "Reference Checking Is More Important than Ever." *HR Magazine* 41 (11): 49

Barrick, M.R., and M.K. Mount, 1991. "The Big Five Personality Dimensions and Job Performance: A Meta-Analysis." *Personnel Psycology* 44: 1–26.

Baxter, J.C., B. Brock, P.C. Hill, and R.M. Rozelle. 1981. "Letters of Recommendation: A Question of Value." *Journal of Applied Psychology* 66: 296–301.

Binning, J.F., and G.V. Barrett. 1989. "Validity of Personnel Decisions: A Conceptual Analysis of the Inferential and Evidential Bases." *Journal of Applied Psychology* 74: 478–94.

Borman, W.C., M.A. Hanson, S.H. Oppler, E.D. Pulakos, and L.A. Whilte. 1991. "Job Behavior, Performance, and Effectiveness." In M.D. Dunnette and L.M. Hough, eds., *Handbook of Industrial and Organizational Psychology*, vol. 2. 2nd ed. San Diego: Consulting Psychologists Press, 271–326.

Butler, C. 2000. "Employers Learn Background Checks Worth the Effort." *The Globe and Mail* (March 29): M2.

Carlson, K.D., S.E. Scullen, F.L. Schmidt, H. Rothstein, and F. Erwin. 1999. "Generalizable Biographical Data Validity Can Be Achieved without Multi-Organizational Development and Keying." *Personnel Psychology* 52 (3): 731–55.

Carpenter, R. 1995. "Geek Logic." *Canadian Business* 68: 57–58.

Cascio, W.F. 1975. "Accuracy of Verifiable Biographical Information Blank Response." *Journal of Applied Psychology* 60: 767–69.

———. 1976. "Turnover, Biographical Data, and Fair Employment Practice." *Journal of Applied Psychology* 61: 576–80.

Cascio, W.F., and R.A. Ramos. 1986. "Development and Application of a

New Method for Assessing Job Performance in Behavioral/Economic Terms." *Journal of Applied Psychology* 71: 20–28.

Chait, H.N., S.M. Carraher, and R.M. Buckley. 2000. "Measuring Service Orientation with Biodata." *Journal of Managerial Issues* 12 (1): 109–20.

Corben, R. 1997. "Why Some Thais Embellish on Degrees." *Asian Wall Street Journal Weekly* 19 (March 24): 13.

Dalessio, A.T., M.M. Crosby, and M.A. McManus. 1996. "Stability of Biodata Keys and Dimensions across English-Speaking Countries: A Test of the Cross-Situational Hypothesis." *Journal of Business and Psychology* 10 (3): 289–96.

Delaney, J., and M.A. Huselid. 1996. "The Impact of Human Resources Management Practices on Perceptions of Organizational Performance." *Academy of Management Journal* 39: 949–69.

Dreher, G.F., and P.R. Sackett. 1983. *Perspectives on Selection and Staffing.* Homewood, IL: Irwin.

Elkins, T.J., and J.S. Phillips. 2000. "Job Context, Selection Decision Outcome, and Perceived Fairness of Selection Tests: Biodata as an Illustrative Case." *Journal of Applied Psychology* 85 (3): 479–84.

Ford, J.K., M.A. Quinones, D.J. Sego, and J. Speer-Sorra. 1992. "Factors Affecting the Opportunity to Perform Trained Tasks on the Job." *Personnel Psychology* 45: 511–27.

Fuchsberg, G. 1990. "More Employers Check Credit Histories of Job Seekers to Judge Their Character." *The Wall Street Journal* (May 30): B1, B3.

Gati, I. 1989. "Person–Environment Fit Research: Problems and Prospects." *Journal of Vocational Behavior* 35: 181–93.

Gatewood, R.D., and H.S. Feild. 1998. *Human Resource Selection.* Orlando, FL: Harcourt Brace and Company.

Ghiselli, E.E. 1966. *The Validity of Occupational Aptitude Tests.* New York: Wiley.

Gilliland, S.W. 1993. "The Perceived Fairness of Selection Systems: An Organizational Justice Perspective." *Academy of Management Review* 18: 694–734.

———. 1994. "Effects of Procedural and Distributive Justice on Reactions to a Selection System." *Journal of Applied Psychology* 79: 691–701.

Goheen, H.W., and J.N. Mosel. 1959. "Validity of the Employment Recommendation Questionnaire, II. Comparison with Field Investigations." *Personnel Psychology* 12: 297–302.

Goldstein, I.L. 1971. "The Application Blank: How Honest are the Responses?" *Journal of Applied Psychology* 71: 3–8.

Guion, R.M. 1967. "Personnel Selection." *Annual Review of Psychology* 18: 105–216.

———. 1998. *Assessment, Measurement and Prediction for Personnel Decisions.* London: Lawrence Erlbaum Associates.

Hammer, E.G., and L.S. Kleiman. 1988. "Getting to Know You." *Personnel Administrator* 34: 86–92.

Harris, M.M. 1989. "Reconstructing the Employment Interview: A Review of Recent Literature and Suggestions for Future Research." *Personnel Psychology* 42: 691–726.

Harvey-Cook, J.E., and R.J. Taffler. 2000. "Biodata in Professional Entry-Level Selection: Statistical Scoring of Common Format Applications." *Journal of Occupational and Organizational Psychology* 73 (1): 631–64.

Herriott, P. 1989. "Selection as a Social Process." In M. Smith and I. Robertson, eds., *Advances in Selection and Assessment*. Chichester, England: Wiley, 171–87.

Hough, L.M., N.K. Eaton, M.D. Dunnette, J.D. Kamp, and R.A McCloy. 1990. "Criterion-Related Validities of Personality Constructs and the Effect of Response Distortion on Those Validities." *Journal of Applied Psychology* 75: 581–95.

Hunter, J.E., and R.F. Hunter. 1984. "Validity and Utility of Alternative Predictors of Job Performance." *Psychological Bulletin* 96: 72–98.

Janz, T. 1982. "Initial Comparisons of Patterned Behaviour Description Interviews versus Unstructured Interviews." *Journal of Applied Psychology* 67: 577–80.

Kaak, S.R., H.S. Feild, W.F. Giles, and D.R. Norris. 1998. "The Weighted Application Blank." *Cornell Hotel and Restaurant Administration Quarterly* 39 (2) (April): 18–24.

Kabay, M. 1993. "It Pays to Be Paranoid When You're Hiring." *Computing Canada* (April 26): 21.

Kerr, A. 2000. "Sophisticated Software Does the Job for On-Line Recruiters: The More Complex Programs Manage Everything from Posting Positions to Pre-Screening Applicants and Keeping Tabs on Future Prospects." *The Globe and Mail* (June 30).

Kettlitz, G.R., I. Zbib, and J. Motwani. 1997. "Reducing Nurse Aide Turnover through the Use of Weighted Applications Blank Procedure." *Health Care Manager* 16 (2): 41–47.

Klimoski, R.J. 1993. "Predictor Constructs and Their Measurement." In N. Schmitt and W.C. Borman, eds., *Personnel Selection in Organizations*. San Francisco: Jossey-Bass, 99–134.

Knouse, S.B. 1983. "The Letter of Recommendation: Specificity and Favorability of Information." *Personnel Psychology* 36: 331–42.

Landy, F.J., L.J. Shankster, and S.S. Kohler. 1994. "Personnel Selection and Placement." *Annual Review of Psychology* 45: 261–96.

Latham, G.P. 1989. "The Reliability, Validity, and Practicality of the Situational Interview." In R.W. Eder and G.R. Ferris, eds., *The Employment Interview: Theory, Research, and Practice*. Newbury Park, CA: Sage, 169–82.

Leavitt, H. 1992. "Should Companies Be Hesitant to Give Ex-Employees References?" *The Toronto Star* (July 20): C3.

Lee, R., and J.M. Booth. 1974. "A Utility Analysis of a Weighted Application Blank Designed to Predict Turnover from Clerical Employees." *Journal of Applied Psychology* 59: 516–18.

Lefkowitz, J., M.I. Gebbia, T. Balsam, and L. Dunn. 1999. "Dimensions of Biodata Items and Their Relationships to Item Validity." *Journal of Occupational and Organizational Psychology* 72 (3): 331–50.

Levine, E.L., D.M. Maye, A. Ulm, and T.R. Gordon. 1997. "A Methodology for Developing and Validating Minimum Qualifications (MQs)." *Personnel Psychology* 50: 1009–23.

"Little Stretches." 1996. *The Halifax Daily News* (April 5): 17.

"Looking at Job Applications? Remember—It's Hirer Beware." 1994. *Canadian Banker* 101 (May/June): 10.

Mael, F.A., and B.E. Ashforth. 1995. "Loyal from Day One: Biodata, Organizational Identification, and Turnover among Newcomers." *Personnel Psychology* 48: 309–33.

Mael, F.A., M. Connerley, and R.A. Morath. 1996. "None of Your

Business: Parameters of Biodata Invasiveness." *Personnel Psychology* 49: 613–50.

Mael, F.A. and A.C. Hirsch. 1993. "Rainforest Empiricism and Quasi-Rationality: Two Approaches to Objective Biodata." *Personnel Psychology* 44: 719–38.

Maertz, C.P., Jr. 1999. "Biographical Predictors of Turnover among Mexican Workers: An Empirical Study." *International Journal of Management* 16 (1): 112–19.

Mahar, K. 2000. "High-Tech Job Interviews Can Be Fun and Games." *The Globe and Mail* (June 9): M2.

McBride, A.A., J.L. Mendoza, and S.M. Carraher. 1997. "The Development of a Biodata Instrument to Measure Service-Orientation." *Psychological Reports* 81: 1395–407.

McDaniel, M.A., F.L. Schmidt, and J.E. Hunter. 1988. "Job Experience Correlates of Job Performance." *Journal of Applied Psychology* 73: 327–30.

McFarland, J. 1996. "Firms Should Spot Rigged Résumés." *The Globe and Mail* (March 1): B7.

McManus, M.A., and M.L. Kelly. 1999. "Personality Measures and Biodata: Evidence Regarding Their Incremental Predictive Value in the Life Insurance Industry," *Personnel Psychology* 52 (1): 137–48.

Mendoza, J.L., M.R. Buckley, L.F. Schoenfeldt, and C.E. Carraher. 1998. "Validation of an Instrument to Measure Service-Orientation." *Journal of Quality Management* 3: 211–24.

Mitchell, T.W. 1994. "The Utility of Biodata." In Garnett S. Stokes, Michael D. Mumford, and William A. Owens, eds., *Biodata Handbook*. Palo Alto, CA: CPP Books, 492–93.

Mitchell, T.W., and R.J. Klimoski. 1982. "Is It Rational to Be Empirical? A Test of Methods for Scoring Biographical Data." *Journal of Applied Psychology* 67: 411–18.

Morrison, R.F., W.A. Owens, J.R. Glennon, and L.E. Albright. 1962. "Factored Life History Antecedents of Industrial Research Performance." *Journal of Applied Psychology* 46: 281–84.

Mosel, J.N., and H.W. Goheen. 1958. "The Validity of the Employment Recommendation Questionnaire in Personnel Selection: I. Skilled Traders." *Personnel Psychology* 11: 481–90.

———. 1959. "The Validity of the Employment Recommendation Questionnaire: III. Validity of Different Types of References." *Personnel Psychology* 12: 469–77.

"Most Employers Use Reference Checks, But Many Fear Defamation Liability." 1995. *Canadian HR Reporter* (March 13): 5.

Mount, M.K., L.W. Witt, and M.R. Barrick. 2000. "Incremental Validity of Empirically Keyed Biodata Scales over GMA and the Five Factor Personality Constructs." *Personnel Psychology* 53 (2): 299–323.

Muchinsky, P.M. 1979. "The Use of Reference Reports in Personnel Selection." *Journal of Occupational Psychology* 52: 287–97.

Murphy, K.M. 1986. "When Your Top Choice Turns You Down: Effects of Rejected Offers on the Utility of Selection Tests." *Psychological Bulletin* 99: 133–38.

Owens, W.A. 1976. "Biographical Data." In M.D. Dunnette, ed., *Handbook of Industrial and Organizational Psychology*. 1st ed. Chicago: Rand-McNally, 609–50.

Owens, W.A., and L.F. Schoenfeldt. 1979. "Toward a Classification of Persons." *Journal of Applied Psychology* 65: 569–607.

Payne, T., N. Anderson, and T. Smith. 1992. "Assessment Centres, Selection Systems and Cost-Effectiveness: An Evaluative Case Study." *Personnel Review* 21: 48–56.

Ployhart, R.E., and M.D. Hakel. 1998. "The Substantive Nature of Performance Variability: Predicting Interindivdual Differences in Intraindividual Performance." *Personnel Psychology* 51 (4): 859–901.

Quinones, M.A., J.K. Ford, and M.S. Teachout. 1995. "The Experience between Work Experience and Job Performance: A Conceptual and Meta-Analytic Review." *Personnel Psychology* 48: 887–910.

Reilly, R.R., and G.T. Chao. 1982. "Validity and Fairness of Some Alternative Employee Selection Procedures." *Personnel Psychology* 35: 1–62.

"Résumé Inflation Seen on the Rise." 1999. *The Globe and Mail* (December 13).

Rosse, J.G., J.L. Miller, and M.D. Stecher. 1994. "A Field Study of Job Applicants' Reactions to Personality and Cognitive Ability Testing." *Journal of Applied Psychology* 79: 987–92.

Rothstein, H.R., F.L. Schmidt, F.W. Erwin, W.A. Owens, and C.P. Sparks. 1990. "Biographical Data in Employment Selection: Can Validities Be Made Generalizable?" *Journal of Applied Psychology* 75: 175–84.

Rowe, P.M. 1988. "The Nature of Work Experience." *Canadian Psychology* 29: 109–15.

Rowe, P.M., M.C. Williams, and A.L. Day. 1994. "Selection Procedures in North America." *International Journal of Selection and Assessment* 2: 74–79.

Ruble, R. 2000. "U.S. Oil Firms Short of Workers: Some Producers Take Desperate Measures as Soaring Crude Prices Spur Drilling Plans." *Associated Press Newswire* (May 23).

Rynes, S.L. 1993. "Who's Selecting Whom? Effects of Selection Practices on Applicant Attitudes and Behavior." In N. Schmitt et al., eds., *Personnel Selection in Organizations* San Francisco, CA: Jossey-Bass, 240–74.

Rynes, S.L., and H.E. Miller. 1983. "Recruiter and Job Influences on Candidates for Employment." *Journal of Applied Psychology* 68: 147–54.

Saks, A.M., J.D. Leck., and D.M. Saunders. 1995. "Effects of Application Blanks and Employment Equity on Applicant Reactions and Job Pursuit Intentions." *Journal of Organizational Behavior* 16: 415–30.

Schmidt, F.L., J.E. Hunter, and A.N. Outerbridge. 1986. "Impact of Job Experience and Ability on Job Knowledge, Work Sample Performance, and Supervisory Ratings of Job Performance." *Journal of Applied Psychology* 71: 432–39.

Schmitt, N., R.Z. Gooding, R.A. Noe, and M. Kirsch. 1984. "Meta-Analysis of Validity Studies Published between 1964 and 1982 and the Investigation of Study Characteristics." *Personnel Psychology* 37: 407–22.

Schuler, H. 1993. "Social Validity of Selection Situations: A Concept and Some Empirical Results." In H. Schuler, J.L. Farr, and M. Smith, eds., *Personnel Selection and Assessment: Individual and Organizational Perspectives*. Hillside, NJ: Erlbaum, 11–26.

Schwab D.P., and G.G. Henneman III. 1969. "Relationship between Interview Structure and Interviewer Reliability in an Employment Situation." *Journal of Applied Psychology* 53: 214–17.

Smither, J.W., R.R. Reilly, R.E. Millsap, K. Pearlman, and R.W. Stoffey. 1993. "Applicant Reactions to Selection Procedures." *Personnel Psychology* 46: 49–76

Solomon, B., 1998. "Too Good to Be True?" *Management Review* 87 (4) (April): 27.

State of Connecticut v. Teal 457 U.S. 440, 1981.

Stokes, G.S., and L.A. Cooper. 1994. "Selection Using Biodata: Old Notions Revisited." In G.S. Stokes, M.D. Mumford, and W.A. Owens, eds., *Biodata Handbook*. Mahwah, NJ: Erlbaum, 103–38.

Telenson, P.A., R.A. Alexander, and G.V. Barrett. 1983. "Scoring the Biographical Information Blank: A Comparison of Three Weighting Techniques." *Applied Psychological Measurement* 7: 73–80.

Terpstra, D.E., and E.J. Rozell. 1993. "The Relationship of Staffing Practices to Organizational Level Measures of Performance." *Personnel Psychology* 46: 27–48.

Tesluk, P.E., and R.R. Jacobs. 1998. "Toward an Integrated Model of Work Experience." *Personnel Psychology* 51: 321–55.

Thacker, J.W., and R.J. Cattaneo. 1992. "Survey of Personnel Practices in Canadian Organizations: A Summary Report to Respondents." Working Paper W92-04, Faculty of Business, University of Windsor.

Vance, R.L., M.D. Coovert, R.C. MacCallum, and J.W. Hedge. 1989. "Construct Models of Task Performance." *Journal of Applied Psychology* 74: 447–55.

Vinchur, A.J., J.S. Schippmann, F.S. Switzer III, and P.L. Roth. 1998. "A Meta-Analytic Review of Predictors of Job Performance for Salespeople." *Journal of Applied Psychology* 83 (4): 586–97.

Webster, E.C. 1982. "The Employment Interview: A Social Judgment Process." Schomberg, ON: S.I.P. Publications.

Wein, J. 1994. "Rifling through Résumés." *Incentive* 168: 96–97.

Wiesner, W.H., and S.R. Cronshaw. 1988. "A Meta-Analytic Investigation of the Impact of Interview Format and Degree of Structure on the Validity of the Employment Interview." *Journal of Occupational Psychology* 61: 275–90.

9

SELECTION II: TESTING

CHAPTER GOALS

This chapter introduces the use of testing in personnel selection. It presents background material on the technical, ethical, and legal requirements governing the use of employment tests, along with a description of different testing procedures.

After reading this chapter you should

- have a good understanding of psychological tests and their use in selection;
- be familiar with the professional and legal standards that govern the use of employment tests;
- know the advantages and disadvantages of using some of the more popular selection testing procedures, including personality and ability testing;
- be aware of controversial testing methods related to honesty or integrity, physical fitness, and drug use;
- appreciate the potential of work samples, simulations, and assessment centres as selection procedures; and
- understand how both test validity and test utility can be used to evaluate testing effectiveness.

APPLICANT TESTING

PSYCHOLOGICAL TESTING

We have all been tested at one time or another. You will most likely be tested on your knowledge of this chapter's contents. You may be given a set of questions related to material in this chapter; based on your answers to those questions, your instructor will assign a number to you, which reflects your knowledge and understanding of the chapter material. In preparing for the test you probably read the material, attended lectures, took notes, discussed the material with classmates, went to the library to read material on reserve, and questioned your instructor on it. All these activities or behaviours should lead to increased understanding of the material. The test you are given is simply a means of obtaining a sample of these behaviours under controlled conditions. A psychological test is nothing more than a standardized procedure used to obtain a sample of a person's behaviour and to describe that behaviour with the aid of some measurement scale (Cronbach, 1990). Psychological testing is one of the oldest and most common methods used to quantify how individuals differ with respect to some variable of interest.

USE OF TESTS   Psychological tests are used for many different purposes in a variety of settings. In schools, psychological tests may be used to determine levels of academic ability, achievement, or interest. In counselling centres, tests may be used to assist in identifying different strengths and weaknesses of clients and may involve assessment of personality, attitudes, or values. In clinical settings, psychological tests are used to assist a psychologist in making a diagnosis of the suspected difficulty or problem being experienced by the client. In hospital settings, neuropsychological tests are often used to assess different types of brain damage. In business or organizational settings, psychological tests are used to hire people, to classify those selected into the most appropriate positions, to assist in promotion of people, and to identify needs for training. The focus of this chapter will be limited primarily to the use of psychological tests in organizational settings as part of the selection process.

EMPLOYMENT TESTING   In most hiring situations, there are more applicants than there are positions to be filled. The employer's goal is to select those candidates who best possess the knowledge, skills, abilities, or other attributes and competencies (KSAOs) that lead to successful job performance. As we discussed in previous chapters, these KSAOs must be related to job performance criteria that have been identified through a job analysis. The employer believes that applicants differ with respect to essential KSAOs and wishes to measure these individual differences to meet the goal of hiring the best-qualified people for the job. The central requirement for any selection tests or assessment procedures is that they "accurately assess the individual's performance or capacity to perform the essential components of the job in question safely, efficiently, and reliably" (Canadian Human Rights Commission [CHRC], 1985, 11).

In Chapter 3 we discussed the process of measurement and quantification of such individual characteristics. If "knowing how to get things done" is important for job success, the employer must be able to measure know-how in a reliable and valid manner that meets the requirements imposed by relevant labour legislation and wins approval from external agencies, such as the CHRC, which may have jurisdiction over hiring decisions.

TESTING STANDARDS   Occasionally in newspapers, magazines, or on the Internet (see Chapter 3) you may come across an article that asks you to test or rate your career interests, personality, compatibility with a partner, or some other topic. You may be asked to complete a series of multiple-choice questions, and, based on your score, you are placed into a particular category that defines your personality type or interest. Rarely, if ever, do these popular tests have any value. These tests are usually created for the purpose of the article, mostly entertainment. The development of a reliable and valid test takes considerable time and effort, which can be undermined by the widespread publication of the test in the popular media. The only tests with any value in terms of hiring decisions are those that meet accepted professional standards for their development and use.

In Chapter 3, we established some fundamental measurement principles. We expect tests to assign numbers to the construct that is being assessed in a *reliable* and *valid* manner. We also expect tests to be *fair and unbiased*, and to have *utility* (see Chapter 11 for a discussion of utility concepts). Psychological tests vary in the degree to which they meet these four standards. These technical or psychometric properties of a psychological test should be established before a test is used as a decision-making tool. The development and construction of a psychological test is a major undertaking, which is governed by several sets of technical guidelines.

PROFESSIONAL GUIDELINES   The Canadian Psychological Association (1987) has published *Guidelines for Educational and Psychological Testing*. Its U.S. counterpart is the *Standards for Educational and Psychological Testing* published by the American Psychological Association in association with two other organizations (see Chapter 3). These documents present the professional consensus on the appropriate procedures for constructing and evaluating tests, for using and administering tests, and for interpreting test results. The *Guidelines* and *Standards* apply to all tests, including those used for personnel selection.

There are also supplementary guidelines that apply specifically to the use of tests as part of the personnel selection process; the most influential of these is the *Principles for the Validation and Use of Personnel Selection Procedures*, published by the Society for Industrial and Organizational Psychology (1987). Another document, the *Uniform Guidelines on Employee Selection Procedures* (1978), was developed by the U.S. Equal Employment Opportunity

Commission, the U.S. Department of Justice, and the U.S. Department of Labor for use in evaluating personnel selection programs that fall under the regulations of the U.S. federal government. The *Uniform Guidelines* have played a prominent role in court challenges that have alleged discrimination in the selection process. While the U.S.-based *Uniform Guidelines*, *Standards*, and *Principles for Validation* have no legal standing in Canada, they are often cited as representing best practice and professional consensus; they are used by different provincial and federal agencies in assessing selection programs.

CODE OF ETHICS In addition to these documents, which regulate the technical aspects of test development and use, are ethical standards, which regulate the behaviour of psychologists using the tests. The *Canadian Code of Ethics for Psychologists* (Canadian Psychological Association, 1986) specifies four principles on which ethical behaviour is based:

1. Respect for dignity of persons
2. Responsible caring
3. Integrity in relationships
4. Responsibility to society

The ethical standards related to each of these principles apply to all testing carried out by psychologists. These ethical standards cover such issues as confidentiality of test results, informed consent, and the competence of those administering and interpreting the test results. The foremost concern is to protect the welfare and dignity of those being tested. A consumer or client may bring any concerns over a psychologist's use of tests, including selection tests, to appropriate regulatory bodies.

WHO CAN TEST? The availability of standardized tests and computerized scoring and interpretation systems often tempts unqualified people to administer tests and to interpret results from them. Proficiency in psychological testing requires a considerable degree of training and experience. Reputable test publishers require purchasers to establish their expertise in using a test before purchasing it. These safeguards help protect the public against misuse of tests and information collected through testing (Simner, 1994).

CAUTIONS

Well-designed tests provide information on different aspects of an individual, including their personality, thinking or reasoning ability, and motivation, among many others. The standards described in the preceding section were developed by professional associations to protect the welfare and rights of individuals who are being tested. These rights, which must be respected, include the following:

1. *Informed Consent*—Job applicants must be told why they are being tested; they must be informed in clear language that the test results may be provided to the prospective employer and that those results may be used in making employment decisions. Applicants should also be given general information, preferably in advance, about the types of tests that they will be asked to take, the testing process, the intended use of the test, scoring procedures, testing policy, and procedures for protecting the confidentiality of the test results. The extent of the general information provided should be consistent with any restrictions that are necessary to obtain valid responses.

2. *Access to Test Results*—Job applicants are entitled to receive feedback on their test performance and on any decisions that are based on those tests, unless this right has been waived by the applicant or if it is prohibited by law or court order. This information should be provided in nontechnical language that can be understood by the job applicants. Such feedback must be put into a proper context by explaining the purpose of the test and the results of the test relative to other applicants. Care must be taken in providing this feedback as this information may have negative implications about the applicant's ability, knowledge, or personality. Care must also be taken to avoid use of labels or terms that may stigmatize the applicant. Providing feedback can be a very stressful situation and is best done by a qualified psychologist or another human resources specialist who is sensitive to the possible consequences of the feedback. Unfortunately, job applicants rarely receive feedback about how they did on employment tests (Camara and Schneider, 1994).

3. *Privacy and Confidentiality*—Job applicants reveal information about themselves during the job selection process. There is no justification for obtaining any information that is not job-related. Applicants have a right to privacy; information that is provided by job applicants must be held in confidence. As part of gathering information, whether through application forms, interviews, or tests, job applicants must be informed about how that information will be used and who will have access to it *before* they provide the information. The limits of confidentiality must be explained to the job applicants. Care must be taken to safeguard the use of any information collected during the selection process. This information should be released only to persons with a legitimate, professional interest in the applicant. Failure to respect the applicant's privacy may leave the employing organization open to legal action.

Workplace privacy is a significant and growing issue. Ontario's Privacy Commissioner recently recommended that the province establish provincial standards for employee testing; municipal and provincial employees in Ontario have a right of access to and protection of their own personal information, including that obtained through employment testing, under existing freedom-of-information and protection-of-privacy legislation (Ontario Commissioner's Report, 1994).

4. *Language and Culture*—Job applicants have the right to be tested in a language in which they are fluent. In Chapter 3 we discussed how bias can influence measurements. Bias refers to systematic measurement errors that are related to aspects of group membership. Language and culture are two important ways of identifying groups. Canada is both bilingual and multicultural. There is no guarantee that a test developed in one language or in one culture will produce meaningful results when administered to people from different linguistic or cultural backgrounds. It is not sufficient simply to translate a test into another language. The reliability and validity of the test in the new language must be established. Similarly, administering the test to applicants who do not have good command of the language in which the test is written will also lead to test bias; the test results will be confounded with their language comprehension. Both the Public Service Commission of Canada's Personnel Psychology Centre and the Canadian Forces rely on various employment tests in making hiring decisions. Both of these organizations undertake extensive research to ensure that equivalent forms of all testing materials are available in both English and French.

OTHER CONSIDERATIONS: DISABILITY   Chapter 2 drew attention to the legal and human rights concerns that apply to selection procedures. A disabling condition cannot be used to screen out applicants unless it can be demonstrated that the ability in question is a *bona fide* occupational requirement. Employers are expected to make reasonable accommodation to meet the needs of employees or applicants with disabilities who meet job requirements. In Canada, the employment of people with disabilities falls under either provincial or federal human rights legislation. In the United States, this situation is covered by the Americans with Disabilities Act of 1990. Disabling conditions must be considered as part of selection testing. For example, some paper-and-pencil ability tests have time limits; a person with limited mobility of their hands or arms might have difficulty completing the test in the allowed time, leading to an ability score that falls below the level set for the job. It is impossible to state whether the low score is a true reflection of the tested ability rather than a test of the disability. In this case, provision should be made for either using a test that is not time-based or allowing for verbal responses, which are recorded by machine. The guiding principle should be that the test is given to the applicant in a way that accommodates the disability even at the expense of changing standardized testing procedures. We will explore the issue of accommodation in testing in more detail later in this chapter.

TESTING METHODS USED IN SELECTION

The first large-scale use of tests to select or classify Canadian employees occurred during World War II. Tests were constructed to screen people for military service and for entry into different training programs (e.g., airplane pilots—Prociuk [1988]). Over the years, thousands of Canadians have been tested for a variety of purposes. Unfortunately, many people remain skeptical about the benefits of testing. People often become upset over testing, particularly that done in the schools, and the decisions that are based on test results. These concerns also arise in the use of employment tests. Although it is quite easy to demonstrate the financial benefits that can be gained through the use of employment tests, only about one-third of Canadian companies use tests to select employees (Cronshaw, 1986).

RELIABILITY AND VALIDITY ISSUES

The technical guidelines and professional standards described above often act to deter companies from adopting employment tests. Many companies continue to rely on the application form, résumés, letters of reference, and interviews to select employees. Organizations may falsely believe that these selection procedures are exempt from requirements to demonstrate reliability, validity, and fairness. Human resources managers often justify not using employment tests by noting that the reliability of a test may be affected by items that may be misunderstood, by lack of uniform testing conditions, by variation in instructions, by lack of rapport between a candidate and the test administrator, and by improper test items. But how does this differ from a typical selection interview where interview questions are misunderstood, where there is lack of uniformity and standardization in interviews, where there is variation in the introduction given to candidates at the start of the interview, where there is often a lack of rapport between the candidate and the interviewer, and where improper questions are often asked?

USING TESTS DEVELOPED IN THE UNITED STATES

There is no need for any organization to develop its own employment tests; unless the KSAOs required for the job are so unique, one or more of the over 1000 commercially available tests are likely to be suitable for use in most situations. Usually these tests have well-known psychometric properties that are extensively documented in technical manuals. However, most of these tests have been developed and validated on workers in the United States, thereby raising the question of whether expensive validity studies must be done in Canada before those tests can be properly used to select Canadian workers.

Fortunately, validity generalization procedures like those described in Chapter 3 have established that test validities from U.S. workers generalize across the border, lessening the need to reestablish their validity in Canada (Getkake, Hausdorf, and Cronshaw, 1992). Tests that are valid for an occupational category in the United States should also be valid for the same occupational category in Canada. Just as with any other selection device, the information obtained through tests should not be used in isolation. It should be compared with information obtained from other sources. Information obtained from several valid tests and measures that are measuring the same construct should converge.

BOX 9.1 Points to Consider in Selecting a Test

1. Determine the knowledge, skills, abilities, or other qualities that have been related to job success through a job analysis.

2. Consult an information resource on testing to identify tests that are relevant to your job needs. Obtain information from several sources including test publishers or developers and human resources consultants knowledgeable about testing.

3. Obtain information on several tests related to what you want to measure. Read through the materials provided by the test developers. Reject out of hand any test for which the publisher or developer presents unclear or incomplete information.

4. Read the technical documentation to become familiar with how and when the test was developed and used. Does the technical documentation provide information on the test's reliability and validity? Does it address the issue of test fairness? Does it include normative data based on sex, age, and ethnicity that is comparable to your intended test takers? Does it include references for independent investigations of the test's psychometric properties? Eliminate from consideration any tests whose documentation does not allow you to answer yes to these questions.

5. Read the independent evaluations of the tests that you are considering adopting. Does the indepen-

dent evidence support the claims of the test developers? Is the test valid and reliable? Eliminate those tests that are not supported by this evidence.

6. Examine a specimen set from each of the remaining tests. Most publishers will sell a package that includes a copy of the test, instructions, test manual, answer sheets, and sample score report at a reasonable cost. Are the test format and reading level appropriate for the intended test takers? Is the test available in languages other than English? Can the test accommodate test takers with special needs? Is the content of the test appropriate for the intended test takers? Eliminate those tests that you do not feel are appropriate.

7. Determine the skill level needed to purchase the test, to administer the test, and to interpret test scores correctly. Do you have the appropriate level of expertise? Does someone else in your organization meet the test's requirements? If not, can you contract out for the services of a qualified psychologist or human resources professional who does?

8. Select and use only those tests that are psychometrically sound, that meet the needs of your intended test takers, and that you have the necessary skills to administer, score, and interpret correctly.

CHOOSING A TEST

Box 9.1 presents some points that should be considered in selecting commercially available employment tests. These points reflect the technical considerations discussed above. Anyone who has the responsibility for choosing employment tests should be knowledgeable about the various standards and technical documents related to the use of tests. The remainder of this chapter presents an introduction to the wide variety of employment tests used in

---

BOX 9.2 Examples of Psychological Tests Used to Select Employees

PERSONALITY TESTS
California Psychological Inventory
Guilford-Zimmerman Temperament Survey
Hogan Personality Inventory
Jackson Personality Inventory
NEO-FFI and NEO-PI-R
Sixteen Personality Factor Questionnaire (16PF)
Work Profile Questionnaire (WPQ)

HONESTY/INTEGRITY TESTS
Hogan Personality Inventory-Reliability Scale
London House Personnel Selection Inventory
PDI Employment Inventory
Reid Report
Stanton Survey

TESTS OF EMOTIONAL INTELLIGENCE
Bar-On Emotional Quotient Inventory (EQi)
Emotional Competence Inventory (ECI)
Multifactor Emotional Intelligence Scale (MEIS)
Work Profile Questionnaire-emotional intelligence (WPQei)

VOCATIONAL INTEREST INVENTORIES
Jackson Vocational Interest Survey
Kuder Preference and Interest Scales
Occupational Preference Inventory
Self-Directed Search
Strong Interest Inventory
Vocational Preference Inventory

COGNITIVE ABILITY TESTS
Otis-Lennon Mental Ability Test
Stanford-Binet Intelligence Scale
Watson-Glaser Critical Thinking Appraisal
Wechsler Adult Intelligence Scale (WAIS)
Wonderlic Personnel Test

APTITUDE TESTS
Comprehensive Ability Battery (CAB)
Differential Aptitude Tests (DAT)
General Aptitude Test Battery (GATB)
Minnesota Clerical Tests

PSYCHOMOTOR TESTS
General Aptitude Test Battery (GATB)
    Subtest 8—Motor Coordination
    Subtests 9 and 10—Manual Dexterity
    Subtests 11 and 12—Finger Dexterity
O'Connor Tweezer Dexterity Test
Purdue Peg Board Test
Stromberg Dexterity Test

PHYSICAL ABILITY AND SENSORY/PERCEPTUAL ABILITY TESTS
Dynamometer Grip Strength Test
Ishihara Test for Colour Blindness
Visual Skills Test

BOX 9.3 Buyer Beware

There are many personality tests that are commercially available and that have been used in personnel selection. We have included in Box 9.2 some of the more commonly used measures of personality, without comment on their validity or reliability. Many commercially available tests do not have credible supporting material on their reliability or validity or on how they assess faking and social desirability responding. Often, employers do not know where to begin in evaluating the merits of a personality test and in many cases end up paying large sums of money for no return.

Box 9.1 provides guidelines for choosing a test that should help an employer in making a choice among different personality tests. Most important, before purchasing a personality test, have someone trained in testing issues review the test's technical manual. The lack of a technical manual by itself tells you that there are no supporting data on the tests reliability and validity. It is not good enough to accept on faith testimonials from the test publisher that the supporting research has been done and is available. It is essential to ask for the technical manual.

Canadian organizations. Box 9.2 lists some of the more common tests used to select employees.

PERSONALITY TESTS

In making hiring decisions, it is not unusual to hear a manager argue in support of one applicant over another because, "She is the right type of aggressive person we're looking for to sell cars," or "He is a very pleasant, outgoing person, the type that will do well as a receptionist." Generally, these sorts of comments are made following a job interview when the manager has formed an impression of what the applicant is like as a person. The manager is stating a personal opinion, or "gut feeling," that the individual's characteristics or traits qualify the applicant for the job. This is the belief that some aspects of what we call personality are related to job success. Indeed, given a choice, most managers would welcome employees who are hard-working and well-motivated, accept higher levels of initiative, fit into existing work groups, show initiative, and are committed to the continuous development of their skills. Most managers and employees believe characteristics like these define the most effective employees (Hogan, Hogan, and Roberts, 1996). Although these characteristics may be very appealing in an employee, more often than not a manager may not succeed in hiring people with these characteristics, or if they do, the person may not turn out to be an effective employee.

There are two reasons for these failures. First, the specific personality traits or characteristics that formed the manager's opinion of the applicant may not be job-related; they may represent only the manager's opinion that they are necessary for effective job performance and may not have been derived through a job analysis. Personality traits or characteristics must be linked to a job or occupation through the same procedures that we use to link other knowledge, skills, abilities, and competencies. Second, the manager's assessment of the applicant's personality may not be objective, reliable, or valid; it is only an opinion. In the next sections we define personality, examine several measurement issues, and review personality as a predictor of job performance.

DEFINING PERSONALITY One of the major difficulties in using personality for selection purposes is the lack of agreement about its definition. **Personality** is generally defined as a set of characteristics or properties that influence, or help to explain, an individual's behaviour (Hall and Lindzey, 1970).

Different personality theories may propose different ways in which people vary (e.g., aggressiveness, pleasantness). These variables are called personality *traits*. **Personality traits** are thought to be stable over time and measurable. Thus, if two people differ in aggressiveness or pleasantness, appropriate measurements can be developed to reflect those differences. Traits can be distinguished from personality *states*, which are more transitory or temporary characteristics.

One applicant may be very nervous and anxious during a job interview but calm otherwise; another applicant may always be anxious. In the first case, anxiety is a state, but in the second it is a trait. Sets, collections, or patterns of traits and states can be used to define a personality *type*. Personality tests attempt to measure traits and/or states and from these measures derive some indication of the type of individual being assessed. A person whose behaviour reflects traits of extreme competitiveness, achievement, aggressiveness, haste, impatience, restlessness, hyperalertness, explosiveness of speech, tenseness of facial musculature, and feelings of being under the pressure of time and under the challenge of responsibility might be said to have a Type A personality (Jenkins, Zyzanski, and Rosenman, 1979).

Self-report inventories are the most frequently used technique in assessing personality for selection purposes. A **self-report inventory** consists of sets of short, written statements related to various traits. The individual answers by agreeing or disagreeing with each item using a rating scale much like those presented in Chapter 6. Some items included in the inventory might relate to aggressiveness, competitiveness, need for achievement, or whatever trait is of interest. Different self-report inventories may measure different traits. A score for each trait is determined by combining the ratings for those items that belong to a specific trait. These scores can be compared with normative data that already exist for the inventory. Patterns of scores across the measured traits are often used to derive statements about personality types. Self-report inventories are also called *objective techniques* because of their scoring methodology. Box 9.4 presents some items* that could be used to assess Time Urgency, a trait related to Type A personality, as part of an objective, self-report inventory.

Personality—a set of characteristics or properties that influence, or help to explain, an individual's behaviour.

Personality traits—stable, measurable characteristics that help explain ways in which people vary.

Self-report inventory—short, written statements related to various personality traits.

---

*These items, and other examples presented throughout the chapter, have been created for illustrative purposes; they are not actual inventory items.

BOX 9.4 Time Urgency

Instructions: For each statement choose the response that best reflects your behaviour, feelings, or attitudes: 1. Strongly Disagree; 2. Disagree; 3. Neither Agree nor Disagree; 4. Agree; 5. Strongly Agree.

I constantly interrupt other people when they are speaking.

I always do several tasks at the same time.

I get very frustrated when people do not get to the point.

I hate standing in lines.

People waste too much time on routine daily chores.

One criticism of self-report inventories is that they are prone to *faking* and *social desirability*. Faking occurs when individuals respond to inventory questions with answers that do not reflect their true beliefs or feelings. Social desirability is a form of faking where individuals choose responses they believe will present them in a socially desirable way or in a positive light. For example, a woman may believe that men and women are equally aggressive but states that men are more aggressive than females because she believes that this is what she is expected to say, and not saying it may create a negative impression. There is no doubt that individuals can distort their responses on self-report inventories in desired directions (Hough, 1998; Ones and Viswesvaran, 1998). What is less clear is the impact of such distortions on employment decisions based on personality inventories.

The major concern in using self-report inventories as part of personnel selection is that job applicants who distort their responses in a socially desirable manner will improve their chances of being hired (Ellington, Sackett, and Hough, 1999; Hough, 1998; Rosse, Steecher, Miller, and Levin, 1998). Response distortion may cause a change in the rank ordering of applicants at the upper end of a distribution of personality scores, leading to a loss of the best-qualified candidates (Zickar and Drasgow, 1996).

Not everyone agrees that faking and socially desirable responding have an impact on personality-based selection (Barrick and Mount, 1991; Ones and Viswesvaran, 1998). Ones and Viswesvaran (1998), using meta-analytic data, argue that socially desirable responding does not affect the validity of personality inventories that are used in work settings and go so far as to call the whole issue a "red herring." They argue that individuals are responding to items to present an identity and that individuals behave in a manner that is consistent with that identity. That is, individuals who view themselves as conscientious will portray themselves in a manner consistent with their identity when asked to complete a personality inventory. Recently, Alliger and Dwight (2000) challenged the methodological soundness of the past meta-analyses leading to Ones and Viswesvaran's position. Their own meta-analysis showed that fakers could indeed fake their way through a selection process involving self-report measures. Their suggestion that it is premature to make any conclusions about the impact of response distortion on self-report measures without additional empirical evidence is perhaps good advice to follow.

While strategies have been developed to "correct" for response distortion, adjusting individual scores may lead to different hiring decisions unless all scores are adjusted, including those where there is no evidence of faking. Such correction procedures may be difficult to defend in a courtroom (Rosse et al., 1998). Perhaps the best way to deal with faking is to warn job applicants that faking can be detected and that it will be taken into consideration when making hiring decisions about the applicants. In addition, the results from a self-report inventory should not be viewed in isolation but in conjunction with a careful review of a candidate's complete file for evidence of distortion (Rosse et al., 1998).

PERSONALITY AS A PREDICTOR OF JOB PERFORMANCE   Historically, personality tests were not thought to be good predictors of job performance. Guion (1965; Guion and Gottier, 1965) reviewed the technical and ethical problems associated with personality testing and concluded that there was insufficient evidence to justify the use of personality tests in most situations as a basis for making employment decisions about people. Guion was very concerned that personality testing invaded the privacy of job applicants and that they asked applicants to provide much information about themselves that was not clearly job-related. With few exceptions, this view prevailed until the 1990s, when both meta-analytic and new empirical studies suggested that personality testing could predict certain aspects of job performance. These studies grouped related personality characteristics into a smaller number of personality dimensions and then linked those broader dimensions to job performance. Personality dimensions that were chosen on the basis of a job analysis were better predictors of job performance (Barrick and Mount, 1991; Hough, Eaton, Dunnette, Kamp, and McCloy, 1990; McHenry, Hough, Toquam, Hanson, and Ashworth, 1990; Salgado, 1997, 1998; Tett, Jackson, and Rothstein, 1991). This body of research demonstrates convincingly that personality characteristics can be used successfully as part of a personnel selection system, provided that the personality measure meets acceptable standards and the personality dimensions are linked to job performance through a job analysis.

The Society for Human Resource Management reports that over 20 percent of its members use personality tests for new as well as existing hires. Business and industry are increasingly concerned about whether their hires will fit into the organization in terms of such factors as being a team player, working well with little supervision, or being too controlling ("Personality Tests," 1999).

THE BIG FIVE   These more recent studies, which led to the change in views on the usefulness of personality in selection, have been heavily influenced by the argument that the many hundreds of different personality traits could be

BOX 9.5 The Big Five Personality Dimensions

Conscientiousness is a general tendency to work hard and to be loyal; to give a full day's work each day and to do one's best to perform well—following instructions and accepting organization goals, policies, and rules—even with little or no supervision. It is an approach to work characterized by industriousness, purposiveness, persistence, consistency, and punctuality. It also includes paying attention to every aspect of a task, including attention to details that might be easily overlooked.

Emotional stability reflects a calm, relaxed approach to situations, events, or people. It includes an emotionally controlled response to changes in the work environment or to emergency situations. It is an emotionally mature approach to potentially stressful situations reflecting tolerance, optimism, and a general sense of challenge rather than of crisis, and maturity in considering advice or criticism from others.

Openness to experience reflects a preference for situations in which one can develop new things, ideas, or solutions to problems through creativity or insight. It includes trying new or innovative approaches to tasks or situations. It is a preference for original or unique ways of thinking about things. It is concerned with newness, originality, or creativity.

Agreeableness reflects a desire or willingness to work with others to achieve a common purpose and to be part of a group. It also includes a tendency to be a caring person in relation to other people, to be considerate and understanding, and to have genuine concern for the well-being of others; it is an awareness of the feelings and interests of others. It is the ability to work cooperatively and collaboratively either as part of a group or in the service of others. It is involved in assisting clients and customers as a regular function of one's work, or assisting co-workers to meet deadlines or to achieve work goals.

Extroversion reflects a tendency to be outgoing in association with other people, to seek and enjoy the company of others, to be gregarious, to interact easily and well with others, and to be likable and warmly approachable. It involves enjoying the company of others and a concern for their interests; it implies sociableness whether work is involved or not. Extroversion refers to being comfortable and friendly in virtually any sort of situation involving others.

summarized under five categories or dimensions (Digman, 1990). These Big Five dimensions are conscientiousness, emotional stability, openness to experience, agreeableness, and extroversion. Box 9.5 presents definitions for each of these dimensions and examples of the traits associated with them.

Barrick and Mount found that each of the Big Five dimensions could predict at least one aspect of job performance with some degree of accuracy, while conscientiousness predicted several different aspects of job or training performance at moderate levels. Recall that Campbell (1990a) believed that "demonstrating effort" and "maintaining personal discipline" were major performance components of every job (see Chapter 5). It is quite easy to see, from the definition given in Box 9.5, how conscientiousness could predict each of these two job dimensions.

The other four Big Five personality dimensions vary in ability to predict job success by occupational group. For example, extroversion predicts performance in occupations involving social interaction such as sales occupations

(McManus and Kelly, 1999), while openness to experience and extroversion predict training readiness and training success (Barrick and Mount, 1991). Moreover, conscientiousness and extroversion together predict job performance for managers in highly autonomous positions (Barrick and Mount, 1993). Agreeableness and emotional stability, in addition to conscientiousness, play an important role in predicting performance in jobs that involve interpersonal interactions (Mount, Barrick, and Stewart, 1998).

SELECTING FOR WORK TEAMS In many Canadian organizations, employees are selected to be part of a work team, either on a permanent basis or as the demands of a project dictate. We need to know how to select members of teams to maximize team performance. Unfortunately, there is a paucity of research on this issue. Personality measures may have the potential to identify those individuals who are capable of working as part of a team and to identify the most desirable combination of people to ensure a good working relationship among team members, resulting in an optimal personality profile for the team (Kichuk and Wiesner, 1998).

Kichuk and Wiesner (1996) conducted one of the few studies to examine the relationship between the Big Five personality factors and team performance. They asked teams of engineering students to design and construct a model bridge using limited resources. Teams whose members were more homogeneous in conscientiousness tended to do better than those teams whose members differed more. Extroversion predicted team member satisfaction, which is necessary for team longevity. Successful teams had higher levels of extroversion, emotional stability, and agreeableness than did those judged to be unsuccessful. Openness to experience was not related to any aspect of team performance. While these results are preliminary, they do demonstrate the potential of using personality measures to construct work teams.

BROAD VERSUS NARROW TRAITS Not everyone agrees on the Big Five method of categorizing the vast array of personality traits; some argue the need for a few dimensions in addition to the Big Five (e.g., Hough et al., 1990). Some researchers (e.g., Tett et al., 1991; Paunonen, Rothstein, and Jackson, 1999) argue that narrower, specific personality traits are the best predictors of performance and that the reason previous research has not confirmed this is related to the lack of use of personality-related job analyses and psychometrically sound personality measures.

Others have been equally outspoken on behalf of the position that "broader and richer personality traits will have higher predictive validity than narrower traits" (Ones and Viswesvaran, 1996). The only empirical evidence relevant to this debate is a study by Ashton (1998) showing that two specific personality traits provided better prediction of workplace delinquency in entry-level employees than a broad-based integrity test. Borman and Motowidlo (1997) come at this issue from another direction by suggesting that the success of broad personality factors in predicting overall job performance is due to their linkage to contextual performance, which supervisors tend to include in their assessment of overall performance. The important point is not whether there are five, six, or more dimensions, but that Big Five–type personality models reduce the problem of terminological confusion and make personality testing more useful in industrial and organizational contexts, particularly personnel selection (Hogan et al., 1996).

POLYGRAPH AND HONESTY (INTEGRITY) TESTING   As discussed in Chapter 5, the Big Five personality dimensions are also related to contextual performance and organizational citizenship behaviour. A manager's desire to find honest, hard-working team players may not be related so much to the specific job that individuals will do but rather to how well they will fit into the organization. Contextual performance involves activities that do not belong to a worker's specific job but are, nevertheless, activities that are considered important for organizational effectiveness.

In many cases, organizational effectiveness may be limited by employee theft or misuse of the organization's property or proprietary information, or other forms of dishonesty. The costs associated with such counterproductive behaviour were $2.3 billion in the Canadian retail sector for 1999, an increase of 21 percent from 1997. The average amount stolen by employees, $450, is now more than triple the average amount, $116, lost through customer theft. In 1999, Dylex Ltd., a major Canadian retail chain, was forced to take a $25 million writedown, partly because of employee theft (Strauss, 2000). In response to this problem, many retailers have established "loss prevention" departments; they have emphasized employee training and workplace improvements as well as installing procedures for controlling inventory. Many organizations have also initiated programs designed to select people who are not only capable of doing the job but who, in addition, are honest, reliable, or of high integrity.

Honesty or integrity are personality traits and can be measured. Over the years, a number of techniques have been used in an attempt to identify these traits. Polygraph testing, otherwise known as a lie detector, was once used extensively to check on employee honesty and to screen job applicants. The polygraph test is based on the assumption that measurable, physiological changes occur when people lie, and that no matter how hard they try to control their responses, changes take place in heart rate, breathing, blood pressure, and so on.

Although lie detectors enjoy a reputation among the public for actually being able to detect lies, the empirical evidence shows that there are many unresolved issues about their reliability and validity. Polygraph results are mostly related to the skill of the polygraph operator, many of whom are poorly trained. Relatively few jurisdictions in either the United States or Canada have any licensing requirements for polygraph operators. Polygraph results are not accepted as evidence in any North American courtroom. Many legislatures, including the U.S. Congress, which passed the 1988 Employee Polygraph

Protection Act, have banned the use of polygraph testing as part of most pre-employment screening procedures (Jones, 1991). In Canada, Ontario has taken the lead in prohibiting the use of mandatory polygraph tests under its Employment Standards Act. Polygraph testing has no place in any selection program. HR specialists who adopt such a practice do so at their, and their company's, peril.

INTEGRITY OR HONESTY TESTING The restrictions placed on polygraph testing have led to an increase in the use of paper-and-pencil **honesty or integrity tests**. These tests are personality-based measures (Sackett, Burris, and Callahan, 1989). They can easily be incorporated into a selection system; they are inexpensive and typically inoffensive to most applicants. There are no legislative restrictions on their use; however, they must meet the same professional and scientific standards as any other type of employment test.

Honesty or integrity— self-report inventories designed to assess employee honesty and reliability.

There are two general types of integrity tests. *Covert tests* are subtests or scales that are included within a general personality inventory; for example, the Reliability Scale of the Hogan Personality Inventory (Hogan and Hogan, 1989) is commonly used to assess employee honesty and reliability. *Overt honesty tests*, such as the Reid Report, ask very direct questions about the individual's attitude toward theft and other forms of dishonesty, as well as the person's prior involvement in theft or other illegal activities. Applicants may not be aware that their integrity is being assessed with a covert honesty test when they complete a personality inventory. There is no doubt about the purpose of an overt test, and this is likely the reason that overt tests are more susceptible to faking than those embedded in personality inventories (Alliger, Lilienfeld, and Mitchell, 1996).

BOX 9.6 CSIS and Polygraph Testing

Polygraph testing continues to be used by some employers to test honesty and integrity. Among this group of employers is the Canadian Security Intelligence Service (CSIS). According to *The Globe and Mail*, the Security Intelligence Review Committee (SIRC), which acts as a watchdog for CSIS, has repeatedly asked CSIS to stop using polygraph testing. SIRC has expressed grave doubts about the accuracy of such testing, noting that even its defenders allow that the results are wrong 10 percent of the time or more.

Dr. Brian Lynch, a former chief psychologist for CSIS, reported that polygraph testing was used on all new CSIS recruits: "It was driven by the police community originally, historically and still primarily. It does not have the academic substance. It doesn't enjoy the kind of reliability that is inherent in most psychological tests." Dr. Lynch, who is now a senior adviser to the Public Service Commission of Canada, called for CSIS to abolish polygraph testing because it was unreliable and had lost scientific credibility. A CSIS spokesman refused a request from *The Globe and Mail* for an interview.

Source: A. Mitrovica, "CSIS Urged to End Polygraph Testing," *The Globe and Mail* (June 12, 2000): A5.

Honesty tests are an increasingly popular method of screening out potentially dishonest employees. Dishonest applicants may be discouraged from applying for jobs when they know they will be tested for honesty. In the case of white-collar crime, personality-based integrity tests may be the best measure of psychological differences between white-collar criminals and honest employees (Collins and Schmidt, 1993). After a chain of home improvement centres in Great Britain started using an honesty test as part of its selection procedures, inventory shrinkage dropped from 4 percent to less than 2.5 percent (Temple, 1992).

A review of over 180 studies that involved 25 different measures of honesty or integrity tests and a wide range of performance measures found integrity tests successfully predict a wide range of dysfunctional job behaviours, including absenteeism, tardiness, violence, and substance abuse (Ones, Viswesvaran, and Schmidt, 1993). A more recent and exhaustive review of psychological studies and law review articles on integrity tests, along with an

BOX 9.7 Integrity at the Checkout Counter

Sobey's of Stellarton, Nova Scotia, operates a chain of food stores throughout Canada under several names. Sobey's use of the Reid Report illustrates some of the pitfalls and negative publicity that may accompany integrity testing. The case involves a job applicant who failed the Reid Report. This applicant had worked for Sobey's for six years and had resigned her job to stay home and take care of her children for a year. When she applied for a position with the company, she was required to take the Reid Report, which had been introduced during her absence.

Sobey's policy was to hire only those applicants who passed the integrity test. The incident made local and national headlines and was the subject of a television feature on the CBC. It also led to a great deal of discussion about the worth of integrity tests. The applicant asked how she could have been rejected for failing the integrity test when she had worked without complaint for Sobey's for six years. The rejected applicant filed a complaint about use of the test with the Nova Scotia Human Rights Commission; resolution of the complaint is still pending.

Sobey's was not alone in sharing the media spotlight over using integrity tests. A few years earlier, one of its main competitors, Loblaw's Real Canadian Superstore sub-

sidiary began using the Reid Report in its Vancouver operations. The British Columbia Civil Liberties Union became aware of the practice and publicly denounced the use of the test. It also called for legislation banning the practice as an invasion of privacy.

Even successful applicants may react negatively to an integrity test and the company using it. David Lindsay (1998) wrote about his experience with an integrity test in *This Magazine*. He found the experience to be invasive and insulting. He failed to see the relevance of questions such as "I like to take chances" and "I am afraid of fire." Neither did he see the value of answering questions such as "What drugs have you taken and how often?" He claims that he and his co-workers had all lied to achieve high "honesty" ratings: "Each of us had falsified a low-risk profile, feigning caution, docility, obedience and inviolable, angelic truthfulness. We had denied all illegal activity, labour sympathies, and feelings of bitterness and alienation."

Mr. Lindsay doubts that a quality such as honesty can be measured quantitatively. Sobey's, on the other hand, continues to see the merit in integrity testing and has not been deterred by the negative publicity arising from their assessing the honesty of job applicants. What do you think?

examination of professional and legislative investigations of integrity tests, came to similar conclusions that honesty or integrity tests provide valid information about an applicant's potential to engage in dysfunctional job behaviours (Sackett and Wanek, 1996).

Nonetheless, honesty tests do have disadvantages. Test scores from honesty tests, like those from any other personality measure, are open to misinterpretation and may constitute an invasion of the applicant's privacy. There is some evidence that job applicants do not hold favourable views of personality measures as selection instruments (Steiner and Gilliland, 1996). Applicants may form a negative impression of the organization that uses integrity tests, although there is no evidence that this happens or that it affects the applicant's reaction to the company (Dwight and Alliger, 1997). Existing data do suggest that honesty tests may have a high number of false positives; that is, they may tend to screen out a large number of applicants who are truly honest but do poorly on the test (Camara and Schneider, 1994). An applicant who is falsely rejected may feel stigmatized and take legal action (Arnold, 1991).

Finally, there is a practical problem. Most publishers of integrity tests require the proprietary testing forms to be returned to the publisher, who only releases an overall total score and subscale scores. The publishers of the Reid Report have become more responsible about the administration and reporting of scores (Neuman and Baudoun, 1998). The HR specialist is not able to review the correctness of the responses and must rely on the publisher's interpretation of the scores in the context of the publisher's proprietary normative data, which cannot be inspected (Camara and Schneider, 1994).

GRAPHOLOGY   There are several indirect methods for assessing personality. These methods require an individual to respond in some fashion to an ambiguous stimulus such as a drawing or picture. The ink blot, or Rorschach test, is an example of a projective technique that has been popularized through movies and television. The premise of such tests is that individuals project something about their personality into their responses. In the case of handwriting, the assumption is that the unique characteristics of the handwriting indirectly reflect something about personality traits, which a graphologist or graphoanalyst can interpret. While several projective techniques are useful diagnostic tools in clinical psychology, graphology does not fall into this category. There is little, if any, scientific evidence that supports the use of graphology in personnel selection. Whatever success graphologists appear to have had seems to be based on inferences drawn from information contained in the content of the writing and not in the handwriting itself (Ben-Shukhar, Bar-Hillel, Bilu, Ben-Abba, and Flug, 1986).

Nonetheless, the lack of scientific support has not deterred companies from using graphology to select employees, particularly at the executive level. Graphology is most popular in Western Europe, with reports estimating its use as a selection tool in over 50 percent of companies in France and Germany. Despite its apparent widespread use, potential French job applicants ranked it ninth out of ten selection procedures in terms of effectiveness and fairness; the only procedure to receive lower ratings was honesty testing (Steiner and Gilliland, 1996).

Although there are no firm figures, a few Canadian companies and consultants are beginning to use graphology either by itself or in conjunction with other selection devices, although they are often ashamed to admit it, partly because of human rights issues that might be involved ("A New Slant," 1994). The shame is understandable; any company making hiring or placement decisions with the aid of graphology should be aware that there is no scientific evidence to support its use. They should also consider the negative impact that such a procedure may have on potential applicants.

LEGAL CONSIDERATIONS Personality measures, particularly those based on the Big Five structure, effectively predict job performance; as well, integrity tests predict counterproductive work behaviours (Goodstein and Lanyon, 1999). Both types of tests are legally defensible and can be used as part of selection systems. Of course, such tests are subject to the same legal standards as other selection measures. These include establishing that the personality traits or dimensions are related to job or contextual performance through job analysis procedures and that the traits or dimensions are required for effective job performance. Without this type of supporting documentation, a company will almost certainly lose any litigation involving use of the personality or integrity measures (Hogan et al., 1996). Adherence to professional guidelines, such as those presented earlier in this chapter, that are designed to protect the human rights of job applicants will also enhance the chance of winning any court challenges.

Fairness does not appear to be an issue with respect to personality or integrity testing. There is no evidence that psychometrically sound personality inventories and integrity tests have adverse impact on any protected group (Hogan et al., 1996). In fact, it appears that adding personality or integrity tests to a selection system that includes measures of cognitive ability may reduce the bias in selection (Ones et al., 1993). Personality measures may help persons with disabilities demonstrate their qualifications as they do not differ significantly on personality from the remainder of the population (Hogan et al., 1996). The concerns about privacy still remain and may prove troublesome to the point that they limit the use of personality tests. It is essential that to avoid costly litigation personality testing be carried out by trained professionals guided by relevant legal and ethical standards.

ABILITY AND APTITUDE TESTS

As we have seen in earlier chapters, job-related KSAOs, including competencies, play an important role in successful job performance. Applicants for a position of electronic repair technician might be expected to have a high degree of finger dexterity (to perform repairs on circuit boards), colour vision (to tell the difference between different wires), and a potential for acquiring knowledge related to electronics (to achieve an understanding of basic circuit theory).

Selection programs seek to predict the degree to which job applicants possess the KSAOs related to the job. Many different tests have been developed to measure specific human abilities and aptitudes. In the case of electronic repair technicians, we would seek to employ those applicants with the highest levels of finger dexterity and colour vision, and the most aptitude for learning electronics.

ABILITY TESTS Abilities are attributes that an applicant brings to the employment situation. **Abilities** are general traits or characteristics on which people differ. It is of no importance whether an ability has been acquired through experience or inheritance. Abilities are simply general traits that people bring with them to the new work situation. Finger dexterity is the ability to carry out quick, coordinated movements of fingers on one or both hands and to grasp, place, or move very small objects (Fleishman and Reilly, 1992).

An ability can underlie performance on a number of specific tasks; finger dexterity might be required to operate a computer keyboard and to assemble electronic components. One keyboard operator may have taken several months of practice to develop the finger dexterity needed to type 100 words per minute; another may have come by that ability naturally. Both have the same ability, regardless of how it was acquired.

Skill, on the other hand, refers to the degree of proficiency on a given task, based on both ability and practices that have developed while performing the task. Two keyboard operators may have the same level of finger dexterity; however, one may have learned to type with hands raised at an inappropriate angle in relation to the keyboard. As a result, the two have different skill levels, or proficiencies, in using a keyboard despite having the same ability. Similarly, a keyboard operator and an electronics assembler might have the same level of finger dexterity but the keyboard operator might be more skilled at word processing than the assembler is at wiring circuit boards. **Aptitude** is simply a prediction, based on a measure of ability or skill, that an individual will do well in future performance.

Based on a test of finger dexterity, a human resources manager might predict that a job applicant has an aptitude for operating a keyboard, or for assembling electronic components. Over the years, Fleishman and his associates (e.g., Fleishman and Quaintance, 1984) have identified 52 distinct human abilities, which can be grouped into four broad categories: cognitive, psychomotor, physical, and sensory/perceptual abilities. Over time, many psychometrically sound tests have been developed to assess these different abilities.

COGNITIVE ABILITY TESTS **Cognitive abilities** are related to intelligence or intellectual ability. These abilities include verbal and numerical ability, reasoning, memory, problem solving, and processing information, among others.

Ability—a general trait or characteristic on which people differ and which they bring to a work situation.

Skill—refers to the degree of proficiency on a given task that develops through performing the task.

Aptitude—a prediction that an individual will perform well on a task that requires an ability or skill.

Cognitive ability—refers to intelligence or intellectual ability.

The first wide-scale, systematic use of cognitive ability testing took place during World War I, when a group of industrial psychologists developed the U.S. Army Alpha test. This was a paper-and-pencil test that could be efficiently administered to groups of army recruits to determine how those recruits could best be employed. The Army Alpha test sought to measure intellectual or basic mental abilities that were thought to be essential to performing military duties. Today, an extensive array of paper-and-pencil tests are available to measure specific cognitive abilities. Most likely you have taken one or more of these during your student career. Box 9.8 presents examples of types of items that could be used to assess verbal and quantitative cognitive abilities.

More recently, there has been a move away from assessing many individual, specific abilities to a more general cognitive ability. General cognitive ability, or general mental ability (abbreviated g or GMA) is thought to be the primary ability among those that make up intellectual capacity. General cognitive ability is believed to promote effective learning, efficient and accurate problem solving, and clear communications. General cognitive ability can be thought of as a manager of other, specific cognitive abilities, similar to a computer's operating system managing other software programs. General cognitive ability has been related to successful job performance in many different types of occupations (Ree and Carretta, 1998). It is related to how easily people may be trained to perform job tasks, how well they can adjust and solve problems on the job, and how well satisfied they are likely to be with the demands of the job (Gottfredson, 1986).

BOX 9.8 Examples of Items Used to Measure Cognitive Abilities

VERBAL REASONING

Dog is to house as bird is to _____.
a) song   b) nest   c) bath   d) people

Which one of the following items does not belong in the group?
a) magazine   b) newspaper   c) book   d) radio

The word "comfort" means the same as which of the following?
a) relief   b) support   c) relaxation d) ease

Which word best completes the following sentence?
We will start the demonstration _____ the guests have arrived.
a) when   b) unless   c) but   d) until

QUANTITATIVE REASONING

Which number, when multiplied by 5, is equal to 2/5 of 100?
a) 2   b) 4   c) 6   d) 8

Which of the following is correct?
a) $6 + 4 = 15$ b) $5 + 21 = 25$ c) $3 - 9 = -6$
d) $8 - 4 = -4$

If fabric costs $3.00 per square metre, what will it cost to buy a piece that is 9 metres long and 12 metres wide?
a) $36.00   b) $256.00   c) $324.00
d) $515.00

What is the next number in the series 3, 6, 12, __ ?
a) 15   b) 18   c) 21   d) 24

A test of general cognitive ability can provide a quick and efficient basis for selecting applicants for more extensive, and costly, testing. The National Football League (NFL) has given the Wonderlic Personnel Test, a test of general cognitive ability, to potential recruits since 1968. According to Charles Wonderlic, president of the testing company, "The test measures a person's ability to learn, solve problems and adapt to new situations" (Bell, 1996). Wonderlic test scores, along with information on the candidate's physical prowess and ability, are available to each NFL team for use in drafting players (i.e., making selection decisions). The Wonderlic has a maximum possible score of 50. The average score for factory workers is 17, for lawyers, 30, and for NFL prospects, 21, which is the overall average for the test. A low score on the test does not eliminate an NFL prospect but red flags him as someone who may not

BOX 9.9 What? I'm Too Smart for This Job?

When job applicants are asked to take a cognitive ability test, there is an underlying assumption that those with the best scores will qualify for a job offer. Job applicants do their best to achieve a high score on the test. What if the company or organization is actually looking for applicants whose cognitive ability falls *below* a specific level? The company may feel that people with high cognitive ability will become bored in the job, dissatisfied with the work, and soon leave. What are the likely consequences of adopting such a procedure?

Recently, the *Boston Globe* (Barry, 1999) reported a case in which the Southeastern Connecticut Law Enforcement Consortium rejected a police force applicant, Robert Jordan, who scored 33 out of 50 points on the Wonderlic Personnel Test. Mr. Jordan was disqualified from the competition along with 62 other high-scoring applicants. The Wonderlic Test Manual recommends that applicants for police officer positions have a score in the range of 20–27. The New London, Connecticut, police chief is quoted as saying, "Police work, believe it or not, is a boring job. What happens if you get certain people who can't accept being involved in that sort of occupation is it becomes very frustrating. Either the day they come in they want to be chief of police, or they become very frustrated and leave."

Mr. Jordan went to Federal Court but lost his case. After reviewing evidence about the validity of the Wonderlic and job analysis requirements for "police officer," the judge ruled that it was reasonable to reject people who scored higher than the requirements set out for the position. Mr. Jordan may have had the last laugh as the report quotes him as saying, "I made them the laughingstock of the country. Jay Leno made up this great song. The theme music was 'Dumb cops, dumb cops, watcha gonna do, with a low IQ.' People can't get over it that they want to cultivate this kind of department."

Laughter and questions of legality aside, there is an important consideration here for practitioners. Is it ethical to seek applicants with average or less-than-average intelligence when applicants expect that doing well on a test will lead to a job offer? It may be, provided there is strong job analysis data to support that position. But then another problem arises: Applicants taking employment tests are to be fully informed of the purpose of the test and how it is going to be used. The applicants would have to be told that, contrary to expectations, those with high scores would be disqualified (Lowman, 1998). In that circumstance, how many applicants are likely to do well on the test? Furthermore, while high IQ might predict high turnover in certain jobs, it also strongly predicts job performance: Higher cognitive ability, higher performance. Turnover may not be the most appropriate criterion in cases like this. So, maybe Jay Leno was right.

be able to meet the demands of a game that is becoming ever more cognitively complex. The Wonderlic is used as part of a battery of tests to develop a psychological profile on each candidate.

Measures of general cognitive ability, which have an average validity coefficient of .50, are among the most powerful predictors of success in training and job performance for a variety of occupational groups ranging from retail clerks to skilled workers to managers and executives (see Gottfredson, 1997; Ree and Carretta, 1998). The growing demands on workers to learn new tasks quickly as they move among assignments and encounter ever-changing technology will not diminish. Accordingly, the power of general cognitive ability measures to predict job success is likely to strengthen. Cognitive ability testing is extremely cost-effective and has withstood court challenges both in Canada (Cronshaw, 1986) and the United States (Gottfredson, 1986). With very few exceptions then, a measure of general cognitive ability can be used for selection in almost all occupations.

MULTIPLE APTITUDE TEST BATTERIES   Over the years a number a specific cognitive abilities have been identified; for example, verbal and numerical ability and inductive and deductive reasoning (see Fleishmann and Reilly [1992] for a comprehensive list). Psychometrically sound tests exist for these specific cognitive abilities. The question is whether assessing specific abilities provides improvement on predictions made from measures of general mental ability. One line of research suggests that specific abilities add only marginally to predictions based on g (Ree and Carretta, 1998). On the other hand, specific ability tests do provide significant, although small, increases in predictive validity from those made solely on the basis of general mental ability (McHenry, Hough, Toquam, Hanson, and Ashworth, 1990). As well, tests of specific abilities such as verbal and numerical ability and reasoning provide validity coefficients in the same range as g (Levine, Spector, Menon, Narayanan, and Cannon-Bowers, 1996). Proponents of g suggest that the validities of specific ability tests occur because they and g are measuring the same construct (Ree and Carretta, 1998).

The Canadian Forces use cognitive testing as part of its selection process. Potential recruits into the Forces complete the Canadian Forces Aptitude Test (CFAT), which validly predicts performance in a wide range of military occupations. The CFAT is an example of a Multiple Aptitude Test Battery. Tests like the CFAT include subtests related to specific cognitive abilities; as well, they may include tests of noncognitive abilities. The CFAT includes subtests related to problem solving, spatial ability, and verbal skills. Similarly, the U.S. military administers a test battery primarily based on cognitive abilities, the Armed Services Vocational Aptitude Battery (ASVAB), to over one million high-school students each year as well as to all applicants. The ASVAB is the best overall predictor of U.S. Army applicant performance, particularly for performance on technical jobs (Campbell, 1990b). The ASVAB is similar to the General Aptitude Test Battery (GATB), which is used as part of the selection process for jobs throughout the U.S. federal government. A version of the GATB has been developed for use at Human Resources Canada Centres.

Tests such as the ASVAB take up to three hours to complete. The question that a practitioner must answer is whether the small increase in validity that testing specific abilities provides over g is worth the time and money spent in testing the specific abilities, particularly since the measures of the specific abilities tend to be highly correlated with measures of g (Ree and Carretta, 1998).

PRACTICAL INTELLIGENCE/JOB KNOWLEDGE Sternberg and his associates (Sternberg, Wagner, Williams, and Horvath, 1995) distinguish practical intelligence from intellectual or academic ability and argue that while tests of cognitive ability predict intellectual performance, those tests are not as successful as they should be in predicting job success. To obtain that success, measures of cognitive ability need to be supplemented by measures of practical intelligence. The distinction between academic intelligence and **practical intelligence** is similar to the difference between declarative knowledge and procedural knowledge described in Chapter 5. Procedural knowledge, or tacit knowledge, is related to knowing how to get things done without the help of others. Consider two department managers competing to increase their respective budgets. Both have the intellectual ability to put together a rational proposal based on facts and figures to support their positions. The successful manager knows that the proposal alone will not succeed; the successful manager will know how to craft the report to demonstrate that the budget increase will also accomplish the goals of the decision makers and will know whom to lobby in the organization for support of the proposal. The successful manager knows how to get things done.

> **Practical intelligence—** knowing how to get things done without the help of others.

Unfortunately, recent empirical evidence does not provide support for practical intelligence as a predictor of job success. Taub (1999) compared general mental ability and practical intelligence as predictors of real-world success among a sample of university students. Taub found that intellectual and practical intelligence were, indeed, independent constructs, but he could not find any evidence to support the proposition that practical intelligence was a better predictor of real-world success than general mental ability.

Lobsenz (1999) found similar results when he used a measure of practical intelligence to predict job performance of entry-level telecommunications managers. Practical intelligence did not improve on the predictions that could be made from general mental ability. While the concept of practical intelligence remains an intriguing concept, it is premature to use measures of practical intelligence to make workplace decisions about job applicants or employees.

A concept related to practical intelligence or tacit knowledge is job knowledge. In fact, Schmidt and Hunter (1993) argue that practical intelligence is a narrow, specialized case of job knowledge. **Job knowledge** tests examine the degree to which job applicants or employees are knowledgeable about issues or procedures that are deemed essential to successful job performance—in other words, knowing how to do the job. Members of many professions

> **Job knowledge—the** degree to which a job applicant or employee is knowledgeable about issues or procedures that are essential for successful job performance.

must submit to an examination of their knowledge related to important professional practices and procedures before they are allowed entry into the profession. To practise law, a law school graduate must first have served a form of apprenticeship (articling) to gain knowledge and experience about legal procedures and then to pass a written "bar exam," which is a test of legal knowledge and procedures. Job knowledge tests have validities that average .45 with job performance. These types of tests tend to have higher validity when used to select people for high-complexity jobs. Job knowledge tests are more effective when they are job-specific, that is, when a unique knowledge test is developed for each occupation or profession (Dye, Reck, and McDaniel, 1993).

EMOTIONAL INTELLIGENCE   Recently, the media, business press, and Oprah Winfrey have discovered **emotional intelligence**. Daniel Goleman popularized this term in two recent books—*Emotional Intelligence* (1995) and *Working with Emotional Intelligence* (1998). He defines emotional intelligence (EQ) as

Emotional intelligence— the ability to perceive accurately, appraise, and express emotion.

> *a set of abilities which include self-control, zeal and persistence, and the ability to motivate oneself. He expresses this as the ability to persist in the face of frustration; to control impulse and delay gratification, to regulate one's moods and keep distress from swamping the ability to think, to empathize and to hope.*
> (Goleman, 1995)

Olive (1998) quotes Goleman as saying that, "In top management posts, emotional intelligence abilities like initiative and self-confidence or collaboration matter twice as much as IQ. And the higher you go in the organization, the more EQ matters. For the top leaders, it's about 85% of what characterizes the star performer." This is an alluring, though controversial, concept that has led consulting companies (e.g., Hay Group—http://ei.haygroup.com/) to offer services for identifying and selecting individuals with high levels of EQ. Is there empirical support for Goleman's position? Are there measures of emotional intelligence that can validly predict job success?

The short answer to these questions is that there is scant evidence to justify the use of EQ as part of a selection program. There are two primary reasons for this conclusion. First, there is lack of clarity about what constitutes EQ. Goleman based his ideas on the work of Salovey and Mayer (1990), who proposed that emotional intelligence represents a group of abilities that are distinct from the traditional verbal-propositional/spatial-performance dimensions of intelligence. Mayer and Salovey later defined EQ as:

> *the ability to perceive accurately, appraise and express emotion; the ability to access and/or generate feelings when they facilitate thought; the ability to understand emotions and emotional knowl-*

edge; and the ability to regulate emotions to promote emotional and intellectual growth. (Mayer and Salovey, 1997, 6)

Goleman's (1995) and Mayer and Salovey's (1997) definitions are not the same. As well, people working in this area have a tendency to change the definition of EQ to suit their purposes. There is also disagreement about whether emotional intelligence is more an inherent potential, or whether it is a set of learned "abilities," "competencies," or "skills." Others have argued that components of EQ, as defined by Goleman, are simply aspects of the Big Five personality dimensions (Polednik and Greig, 2000). This lack of agreement makes it difficult to know what is really meant by the construct and to identify it as a job requirement.

The second major impediment to using EQ in selection systems is the lack of measures that can provide us with valid inferences about the construct. At present there are four measures of EQ (See Box 9.2). Bar-On's (1997) EQi is the oldest of these measures; it has been in development the longest and is arguably the most commonly used measure of EQ. Many of the factors it measures are not included in either Goleman's or Mayer and Salovey's conceptions of EQ; nor are they very different from traditional personality factors. Newsome, Day, and Catano (in press), in fact, showed that there were moderate to high correlations between the EQi subscales and the Big Five personality measures. The EQi did not predict academic success, whereas a Big Five factor, conscientiousness, did. The EQi did not improve on any predictions about success that could be made from measures of cognitive ability and personality, lending support to Polednik and Greig's (2000) position that a personality measure may be a more effective predictor of organizational performance. Whether the newer measures of EQ, which are based more closely on either Mayer and Salovey's or Goleman's conceptions of EQ, have more success remains to be determined.

At the present, there are inadequate data to justify incorporating EQ into a selection system, despite the claims of the popular press and test publishers. Additional research needs to be done on the EQ construct; foremost is the need to come to an agreement on a definition of EQ. Nonetheless, EQ remains an appealing concept as emotions and moods may be better predictors of specific, short-term workplace behaviours than more stable personality traits (Arvey, Renz, and Watson, 1998).

PSYCHOMOTOR ABILITY TESTS **Psychomotor abilities** involve controlled muscle movements that are necessary to complete a task. Examples of psychomotor abilities include finger dexterity, multi-limb coordination, reaction time, arm–hand steadiness, and manual dexterity. Many tasks, from simple to complex, require coordinated movements for their success. Psychomotor abilities are often overlooked in selecting people for jobs. Consider a drummer

Psychomotor abilities— traits or characteristics that involve the control of muscle movements.

who must independently move all four limbs and exercise hand–wrist coordination, all in a controlled and coordinated fashion; imagine an orchestra whose drummer had an extensive knowledge of music theory but very little psychomotor ability. While a test of cognitive ability might predict ability to learn to read and understand music, it would not predict the level of motor coordination.

Tests of psychomotor ability tend to be very different from cognitive ability tests. They generally require the applicant to perform some standardized task on a testing apparatus that involves the psychomotor ability in question. Cognitive ability tests, on the other hand, are generally paper-and-pencil tests. For example, the Purdue Pegboard Test, which is a measure of finger dexterity, requires applicants to insert as many pegs as possible into a pegboard in a given time. This test has good predictive validity for many industrial jobs including watchmaking and electronics assembly. Canadian dental schools also use tests of finger and manual dexterity as part of their selection process; all applicants are required to carve a tooth from a block of soap, which is subsequently judged by a panel of dentists. Although psychomotor tests can be quite successful in predicting performance (Levine et al., 1996), they are not as popular as cognitive tests. Psychomotor tests involve individual testing on a specialized piece of equipment, and require more time and expense to administer than paper-and-pencil cognitive tests.

PHYSICAL AND SENSORY/PERCEPTUAL ABILITY TESTS   **Physical abilities** are those characteristics involved in the physical performance of a job or task. These abilities generally involve the use or application of muscle force over varying periods of time either alone or in conjunction with an ability to maintain balance or gross body coordination. Physical abilities include both static and dynamic strength, body flexibility, balance, and stamina. Physical requirements for occupational tasks generally fall into three broad physical ability categories: strength, endurance, and quality of movement (Hogan, 1991).

Sensory/perceptual abilities involve different aspects of vision and audition. These abilities include near and far vision, colour discrimination, sound localization, and speech recognition, among others (Fleishman and Reilly, 1992). Although they focus on different sets of abilities, physical abilities and sensory/perceptual abilities are very similar in their relation to job performance and in how they are assessed.

The performance of many jobs or tasks may require the worker to possess one or more physical or sensory/perceptual ability. A firefighter may need the strength to carry a body out of a burning building; a pilot may need adequate near and far vision to fly a plane; a soldier may need the strength and stamina to carry 100 kg of equipment for a long period of time and still be ready for combat; a construction worker may need strength to lift material and balance to keep from falling off a roof. These ability tests predict performance in jobs that are physically demanding or require sensory or perceptual skills. People who possess greater amounts of these abilities perform better in jobs where

Physical abilities—traits or characteristics that involve the use or application of muscle force over varying periods of time either alone or in conjunction with an ability to maintain balance or gross body coordination.

Sensory/perceptual abilities—traits or characteristics that involve different aspects of vision, audition, as well as the other senses.

such abilities play an important role (Campion, 1983). Physical tests of strength and endurance tests are routinely used in selecting police officer applicants and other protective services personnel such as firefighters (Arvey, Landon, Nutting, and Maxwell, 1992). As part of its comprehensive selection procedures, the Royal Canadian Mounted Police tests all applicants for physical ability.

Statistics from the National Institute of Occupational Safety and Health in the United States indicate that workers are three times more likely to be injured while performing jobs for which they have not demonstrated the required strength capabilities. Although medical and physical fitness exams (which are discussed later in this chapter) provide a measure of wellness, they do not give sufficient indication of whether the candidate can perform the task requirements safely. Thus, physical ability testing can aid employers in selecting workers who are capable of performing strenuous tasks, with such selections leading to a reduction in accidents, injuries, and associated costs, as well as potential increases in productivity (Dunn and Dawson, 1994).

Tests of sensory/perceptual abilities generally require the use of specialized tests or equipment that have been designed to assess each sensory or perceptual ability. Almost everyone has had their vision examined through the use of a Snellen Chart, which contains letters of various sizes. This test assesses an individual's far vision ability. Similarly, many people have experienced a test of their hearing sensitivity when they are asked to recognize a series of tones, which are presented at different levels of intensity and pitches to either or both ears through a headset.

Tests of physical ability are quite varied but involve physical activity on the part of the applicant. Only a few physical ability tests require equipment. For example, a hand dynamometer is used to measure static strength. The hand dynamometer resembles the hand grips used in most gyms. The applicant squeezes the grips with full strength and the resultant force is measured by an attached scale. Pull-ups or push-ups are used to measure dynamic strength, sit-ups are used to assess body trunk strength, while 1500-metre runs, step tests, and treadmill tests are used to measure stamina and endurance.

The performance of the applicants on these measures must be related to normative data, which compare the physical performance on the test with that obtained from actual job occupants. It is reasonable to expect applicants to run 1500 metres in under six minutes if 90 percent of all army recruits meet that performance standard; it would be unreasonable to select only those applicants for the army who could run the 1500 metres in under four minutes. The selection would be based on performance standards higher than those in force.

Establishing cutoff scores on physical tests often leads to litigation, with unsuccessful applicants challenging the appropriateness of the scores that were chosen. This was precisely the situation that led to the Supreme Court decision we discussed in Chapter 2 in which an employed forest firefighter lost her job because she failed to complete a 2.5 km run in the required time, even though she had passed the other physical ability tests. The Court upheld a labour arbitrator's decision to reinstate the dismissed firefighter. It held that the established cutoff had not taken into account differences in aerobic capacity between men and women and that most women could not raise their aerobic capacity to the required level even with training. The Court found that the employer had not shown that the cutoff adopted by the employer was reasonably necessary to identify individuals who could perform in a satisfactory manner as firefighters. Neither did the employer demonstrate that accommodating women would cause undue hardship (*British Columbia (Public Service Employee Relations Commission) v. BCGSEU*, 1999).

In some cases, *physical standards*, rather than physical ability or sensory/perceptual ability tests, are used for selection purposes. A police department may require all applicants to meet certain height and weight requirements and to have uncorrected 20/20 vision. The physical standards are being used as a substitute for actual physical testing. It is assumed that people who fall within the specified range should have the physical abilities required for successful job performance. It is often very difficult to justify that the physical standards in use meet legitimate job requirements. Indeed, many physical standards were set in the past to exclude members of certain groups, particularly women. When physical standards are set in such an arbitrary fashion, they are open to challenge before human rights tribunals with the employer subject to severe penalties. It is reasonable to set physical requirements for jobs as long as those standards are job-related and nondiscriminatory. The Supreme Court, in its decision involving the aerobic standard for firefighters, upheld this position and laid out a series of important questions that must be answered in establishing physical or sensory/perceptual standards (see Chapter 2, pages 47–48).

Physical Fitness and Medical Examinations

Many employers routinely administer physical fitness tests as part of the hiring process. The intent of these physical fitness tests is not to identify job-related physical abilities, but rather to screen out unhealthy or unfit employees who may pose a liability to the employer. The employer is concerned that placing physically unfit employees in jobs that require some degree of physical effort may lead to injury or illness, or that the work will be carried out in an unsafe manner. From the employer's view, hiring physically unfit workers means lost productivity, replacement costs, and legal damages from fellow workers and customers who have been injured through their actions.

The intent of physical fitness tests is to ensure that an applicant meets minimum standards of health to cope with the physical demands of the job. Canadian federal regulations also require physical or medical testing of applicants for certain dangerous occupations (e.g., deep-sea diver), or for jobs that may bring them in contact with dangerous chemical substances such as lead or asbestos. In addition to identifying any health problems, the examinations provide baseline data for comparison of any job-related changes in the applicant's health that may be covered through workers' compensation or other insurance programs.

WHEN SHOULD PHYSICAL/MEDICAL EXAMS BE GIVEN? Fitness testing or physical or medical examinations should be administered only after the applicant has been given an offer of employment, which is made conditional on the applicant's passing the test or exam. The physical or medical exam is generally the last step in the selection process. The employer must demonstrate that the health or fitness requirement is related to carrying out the job in question "safely, reliably and efficiently." Physical fitness testing is no different from any other assessment procedure and must meet the same technical standards. In Canada, various human rights acts require that medical or physical examinations of job candidates be job-related.

PEOPLE WITH DISABILITIES Requiring physical examinations before any offer of employment is made raises issues of privacy and also leaves the prospective employer open to charges of discrimination. This last concern is a major issue in hiring people who may have a disability. In the United States, the Americans with Disabilities Act of 1990 prevents employers from excluding applicants who have disabilities that are not job-related solely on the grounds of that disability. The act further requires employers to make accommodations in the workplace for people with disabilities. An employer could not refuse to hire an applicant who was the best computer programmer simply because the programmer used a wheelchair and the employer had no provision for such disabilities in the workplace. The employer would be required to make suitable accommodations. While there is no equivalent act in Canada at present, the many decisions rendered by human rights tribunals and the judiciary have produced the same effects as the Americans with Disabilities Act.

HIV AND AIDS TESTING Employers are becoming increasingly sensitive to hiring individuals who have acquired immune deficiency syndrome (AIDS) or the human immunodeficiency virus (HIV). However, Canadian organizations are prohibited from testing job applicants for the presence of either (Belcourt, Sherman, Bohlander, and Snell, 1996). The Canadian Human Rights Commission has accepted only three narrow grounds to justify treating employees or job applicants with AIDS differently from other employees:

1. The individual carries out invasive procedures such as surgery.
2. The individual is required to travel to countries where AIDS carriers are denied entry.
3. A sudden deterioration of the brain or central nervous system would compromise public safety.

Following these guidelines, the commission ruled that the Canadian Forces was wrong in dismissing a seaman after he tested HIV-positive, and

BOX 9.10 Canadian Human Rights Commission Policy on HIV/AIDS

Everyone has the right to equality and to be treated with dignity and without discrimination, regardless of HIV/AIDS status.

To ensure the fulfillment of this principle the Commission has adopted the following policies:

I. COMPLAINTS

The Canadian Human Rights Act prohibits discrimination on the basis of disability. Individuals with HIV/AIDS may therefore seek protection under the Canadian Human Rights Act. People who are not HIV positive may also be subject to discrimination by virtue of their real or perceived membership in a risk group or their association with a person or people with HIV/AIDS. These individuals may also seek protection under the Canadian Human Rights Act on the basis of perceived disability.

The Commission will expedite the investigation of complaints alleging HIV/AIDS–related discrimination.

2. BFOR/BFJ

The Commission will not accept being free from HIV/AIDS as a bona fide occupational requirement (BFOR) or a bona fide justification (BFJ) unless it can be proven that such a requirement is essential to the safe, efficient, and reliable performance of the essential functions of a job or is a justified requirement for receiving programs or services.

As a result of new drugs and forms of intervention, people with HIV infection are now able to continue productive lives for many years. If individuals with the requisite workplace accommodation are able to continue to work

they should be allowed to do so. Any decision made by an organization relying on health and safety considerations to exclude a person must be based on an individual assessment supported by authoritative and up-to-date medical and scientific information.

3. PRE- AND POST-EMPLOYMENT TESTING

HIV-positive persons pose virtually no risk to those with whom they interact in the workplace. The Commission, therefore, does not support pre- or post-employment testing for HIV. Such testing could result in unjustified discrimination against people who are HIV positive.

4. PUBLIC EDUCATION

The Commission will assist in fostering improved public understanding of HIV/AIDS. The level of misunderstanding about HIV/AIDS remains high and contributes to the discriminatory treatment of people who are HIV positive or who are perceived to be so.

5. WORKPLACE POLICIES

The Commission will encourage employers to develop an HIV/AIDS workplace policy to ensure employees are accurately informed about HIV/AIDS as it affects them in the workplace. This will avoid unnecessary fears about the disease and its transmission which could lead to discriminatory acts. June 1996

Source: Canadian Human Rights Commission, June 1996. Reproduced with the permission of the Minister of Public Works and Government Services Canada.

---

ordered the payment of compensation. Employers are required to accommodate the needs of people with AIDS, which is a disability, by redefining work duties and implementing temporary reassignments (Belcourt et al., 1996).

GENETIC SCREENING   The Health Law Institute at the University of Alberta reported that 24 percent of genetic specialists believed employers should have access to an employee's confidential medical records to determine whether the employee is likely to develop a genetic disease that might be costly to the employer ("Specialists," 1995). Undoubtedly, many employers agree. **Genetic screening** is a controversial issue that proposes that job applicants be screened for genetic propensity or susceptibility to illness resulting from various workplace chemicals or substances. For example, applicants who have an inherited sensitivity to lead would not be hired for work in a lead battery plant. Genetic screening raises many ethical and legal considerations (Yanchinski, 1990).

The Human Genome Project, a $4 billion international effort to map all genetic material, has the potential to have a profound effect on how workers and their employers look at health hazards, privacy, and medical information. In the United States, where most health-care programs are privately funded by employers, there have been reports that applicants are being denied employment on the grounds that they are genetically more likely to develop cancer or environmentally related illnesses. In response to these concerns, the U.S. government amended the Americans with Disabilities Act to define genetic predisposition as a disability and to prohibit discrimination on the basis of genetic information. Over half of U.S. states have followed suit in banning the use of genetic information in making workplace decisions. There is less incentive for employers to do genetic screening in Canada to exclude potential employees with certain genetic predispositions because of publicly funded health care in Canada (Sabourin, 1999).

At present, there is no ban on using genetic information to make employment decisions in Canada and it is probable that some use has occurred. It is very likely, however, that any workplace discrimination on the basis of genetic information would be excluded under existing provisions of the Charter of Rights and the various provincial human rights acts. A genetic predisposition would likely be considered a disability that would have to be reasonably accommodated by an employer.

THE NEED FOR ACCOMMODATION   Canadian employers cannot discriminate on the basis of a medical, genetic, or physical condition unless that condition poses a serious and demonstrable impediment to the conduct of the work or poses serious threats to the health and safety of people. Employers have an obligation to accommodate workers with medical or physical conditions on an *individual* basis. As stated by the Supreme Court of Canada in its BC firefighter decision, "the legislatures have determined that the standards governing the performance of work should be designed to reflect all members of society, in so far as this is reasonably possible." The Court reinforced the need for accommodation by noting:

> *Courts and tribunals should be sensitive to the various ways in which individual capabilities may be accommodated. Apart from individual testing to determine whether the person has the aptitude or qualification that is necessary to perform the work, the possibility that there may be different ways to perform the job while still accomplishing the employer's legitimate work-related*

Genetic screening—the testing of genetic material to determine a genetic propensity or susceptibility to illness resulting from various workplace chemicals or substances.

purpose should be considered in appropriate cases. The skills, capabilities and potential contributions of the individual claimant and others like him or her must be respected as much as possible. Employers, courts and tribunals should be innovative yet practical when considering how this may best be done in particular circumstances.

Drug and Alcohol Testing

Inevitably, societal changes find their way into the workplace. One of the most profound changes in North American society has been the increased use of drugs as a recreational activity that may carry over into the workplace. Employers often believe that workplace drug and alcohol use is an added expense through costs associated with employee accidents, absenteeism, turnover, and tardiness. Additionally, there may be costs associated with reduced product quality and productivity on the part of employees who use drugs and alcohol in the workplace. In some cases, drug or alcohol use by employees while working may result in threats to the safety of the public and co-workers. In the United States, where many workers receive health insurance through their employer, employers may face the escalating costs of health-care insurance due to the presence of a significant number of drug users. For these reasons, many employers, with support from both their employees and the public, believe that they are justified in screening job applicants for drug and alcohol use. The screening programs generally apply to all employees and job applicants and not just those in safety-sensitive positions.

Are these concerns justified? The empirical evidence in support of alcohol and drug testing is far from clear. The relationship between drug use and turnover is relatively small, ranging from .04 to .08. While there are some links between drug and alcohol use and accidents, the magnitude of the relationship is probably smaller than people have assumed. Self-reported drug use on the job does appear to be related to how workers behave in the workplace and interact with their co-workers, including antagonistic behaviours such as arguing with co-workers. In almost every workplace there is some expression of deviant behaviour that is not related to substance abuse. When that general deviant behaviour is taken into account, the relationship between substance abuse and job performance becomes insignificant (Harris and Trusty, 1997). Notwithstanding the empirical evidence, workplace drug and alcohol testing programs have become quite common in the United States.

Drug Testing Methods   Methods for drug testing include analysis of samples of urine, blood, or hair obtained from the applicant. In the case of alcohol, breath samples may also be taken. Urinalysis is the most common means of testing; it is also prone to being unreliable. Reliability is estimated through splitting the urine sample and testing both halves. However, if the initial sample is contaminated or the laboratory procedures are inadequate, both halves may produce results that, while consistent, are erroneous. As part of the reliability and validity checks, laboratory personnel, testing protocols, and procedures are subject to standards and outside scrutiny as a means of ensuring quality control. The reliability of urinalysis has improved since the technique was first introduced. Paper-and-pencil tests designed to identify drug users have performed poorly and are rarely used (Harris and Trusty, 1997). Drug tests must meet the same standards of reliability and validity that we expect of psychological tests.

POSITIVE DRUG TEST RESULTS   Positive results pose a dilemma for an employer. The positive results on a drug test only indicate that a person may have used the drug in the past; they do not indicate that the person is currently using the drug, or how far in the past the drug use took place. Neither can the testing identify the extent of past use. Additionally, certain foods or legitimate nonprescription drugs may produce positive results; for example, eating poppy seeds, which are used in many baked goods, will produce test results similar to those from banned substances. Therefore, a positive result may mean that the applicant is a casual user, an addict, or not a user at all.

DRUG TESTING IN CANADIAN ORGANIZATIONS   Random or mandatory drug testing by Canadian companies is not as common as it is in the United States. Only 2 percent of Canadian companies had a drug testing program in place, compared with 75 percent of U.S. companies that participated in an American Management Association survey ("Storm over Drug Testing," 1992). Based on recent Canadian court decisions, that percentage is not likely to increase. In 1990, the Toronto-Dominion Bank became one of the first Canadian organizations to require employees to undergo drug testing. It required all new or returning employees to take a drug test within 48 hours of receiving a job offer. If they tested positive for heroin, cocaine, or marijuana on two different tests, the employees were required to undergo counselling. Refusal to take the test or failure of the test for a third time after counselling led to dismissal. The drug testing policy was challenged by the Canadian Civil Liberties Association and submitted to a tribunal under the Human Rights Act. In 1994, the tribunal ruled that Toronto-Dominion's policy was not discriminatory because it applied to all employees. Subsequently, the tribunal's ruling was challenged before the Federal Court of Canada; the ruling was set aside and the matter referred back to the tribunal with instructions that if it could not link the drug testing to job performance it must find that the policy contravenes the Canadian Human Rights Act (Gibb-Clark, 1996).

Toronto Dominion appealed this decision to the Federal Appeals Court. In 1998, the court ruled that T-D's mandatory pre-employment drug testing policy was a prohibited discriminatory practice as the Canadian Human Rights Act protects individuals with disabilities, including any previous or existing dependence on a drug. The court concluded that the policy was indefensible as either a bona fide occupational requirement or as reasonable accommodation. The court stated that the Toronto-Dominion Bank had not shown that drug use by employees had an effect on job performance or that it led to workplace crime. The T-D Bank suspended the policy following the Appeal Court's ruling (Ayed, 1998).

In *Entrop v. Imperial Oil*, the Ontario Division Court ruled that a drug and alcohol testing policy in place at Imperial Oil violated the Ontario Human

---

BOX 9.11 Canadian Human Rights Commission Policy on Drug Testing

The Canadian Human Rights Act prohibits discrimination on the basis of disability, and defines disability to include those with a previous or existing dependence on a drug. Subject to a limited exception for safety-sensitive positions, as outlined below, the requirement to take a drug test as a condition of employment will usually constitute a prima facie case of discrimination. Persons with a previous or existing dependence who lose or are denied employment as a result of testing positively for past drug use may file a complaint under the Canadian Human Rights Act. In addition, individuals may also claim discrimination by virtue of a perceived dependence on drugs.

While the Commission will judge each case on its merits, the following principles, based on current case law and understanding of the nature and significance of drug testing, will inform Commission decisions:

1. In the normal course of events, drug testing cannot be justified for positions where safety is not an issue. This is because drug tests do not measure the level of impairment arising from drug use and therefore cannot be used to judge the ability of an individual to perform the job.

2. Drug testing, including pre-employment or random testing, may be permissible for jobs where safety is of fundamental importance, provided the employer can demonstrate that there is no other feasible method to assure employees are not incapacitated on the job. Pre-employment testing, however, must be undertaken only after a job offer has been made and only in relation to safety-sensitive jobs.

3. In any situation where testing is justified in relation to a safety-sensitive job, employees who test positive must be accommodated. Where Employee Assistance or equivalent programs are available, this could mean that the employee is referred to a substance abuse professional to determine if in fact he or she is drug-dependent. If the employee is determined not to be substance dependent, the employee should be returned to his or her position. If the employee is found to be dependent, he or she should be referred to rehabilitation.

4. If the employee is unsuccessful in rehabilitation, including testing positive for drug use during the course of treatment or refusing to follow the specified treatment, further accommodation may not be required.

5. If rehabilitation is successful, the employee should be returned to his or her position. Follow-up testing may be a condition of continued employment where safety continues to be of fundamental importance. If follow-up testing reveals continuing drug use, further employer action, up to dismissal, may be justified.

Note: For the purpose of this policy, "drug testing" refers to testing for the past use of various drugs, but does not refer to alcohol testing.

APPLICATION

In the event that a drug testing policy practice is challenged, the onus will be on the employer to establish it has a bona

---

BOX 9.11 Continued

fide occupational requirement for the policy. To do this, the employer must establish that the policy or practice:

- is reasonably necessary to assure the safe, efficient, and economic performance of the work; and,

- is rationally connected to the job, and is proportional, i.e., that there is no less discriminatory alternative.

The following issues are pertinent to the investigation:

Is drug testing applied only to those in, or applying for, safety-sensitive jobs? If not, the policy may be discriminatory.

Is the job for which the testing is being applied truly safety-sensitive? A safety-sensitive job is one in which incapacity due to drug impairment could result in direct and significant risk of injury to the employee or others.

If the job for which the testing is being applied is truly safety-sensitive, are there other possible ways of determining whether an individual is drug impaired? Testing may not be acceptable if the individual occupying the job has regular contact with co-workers or a supervisor during the course of performing his or her job duties, even if the contact is not continuous.

Where safety-sensitivity is an issue, is "pre-employment" testing carried out only after a job offer? If not, the policy may be discriminatory.

Is appropriate accommodation provided in the event of a positive test result? Where these are generally available, referral to an Employee Assistance Program or its equivalent would be considered appropriate accommodation. Other measures would also be acceptable, as required, if they were rehabilitative in nature or otherwise protected the employment rights of the individual.

Presented to the Canadian Human Rights Commission on October 18, 1999.

Source: Canadan Human Rights Commission, October 18, 1999. Reproduced with the permission of the Minister of Public Works and Government Services Canada.

Rights Act because it failed to link drug or alcohol use to impairment and discriminated with respect to a perceived disability. The decision prohibited the use of pre-employment drug or alcohol testing and the use of random testing among Imperial's employees. The court did recognize a limited right of the employer to test for drugs or alcohol following drug-related incidents or to certify an employee for a safety-sensitive job ("Courts Overrule," 1998). Imperial Oil appealed the lower court's ruling to the Ontario Court of Appeal, but, to date, no decision has been released.

The Ontario Labour Relations Board, influenced by the Division Court's ruling in *Entrop v. Imperial Oil*, went one step further in concluding that mandatory drug and alcohol testing in safety-sensitive positions is unlawful (Currie, 1999). Imperial Oil had required all of its contractors, as a term of doing business, to institute drug and alcohol testing programs. Unionized workers at Sarnia Crane Ltd. challenged the policy as a violation of their collective agreement with Sarnia Crane. The board ruled that the imposition of the policy violated nondiscrimination clauses in the collective agreement. The board went on to provide guidelines for companies that are concerned about drug- and alcohol-related problems:

1. Introduce an employee assistance program (EAP).

2. Train staff to identify a person's state of impairment from visual cues.

3. Introduce health promotion programs designed to stop smoking, to manage weight and stress, and to improve nutrition as a support to the EAP.

4. Train supervisors to confront employees about substandard performance that may be drug or alcohol related and offer to help the employee through the EAP. If the employee fails to respond, the employee may be subject to future discipline.

5. Introduce peer intervention on the assumption that workers are jointly responsible for others and that some behaviours in the workplace, such as drug or alcohol abuse, are unacceptable.

The Toronto-Dominion and Imperial Oil cases illustrate the pitfalls associated with implementing a drug or alcohol testing policy in Canada. Court and tribunal decisions prohibit pre-employment screening and limit the use of such procedures to the narrowest circumstances, where a direct link can be established with respect to job performance or to the safety and health of people. Even then, the substance abuse must be considered a disability that must be accommodated. The effect of these court decisions is to make drug and alcohol testing impractical in most work situations unless the organization is willing to spend millions of dollars and several years in court pursuing the drug and alcohol testing policy. The guidelines suggested by the Ontario Labour Relations Board appear to be a much more practical and realistic alternative.

WORK SAMPLES AND SIMULATION TESTS

In Chapter 6 we discussed two types of testing that were used to develop criterion measures of work performance: work samples and simulations. Both of these procedures are more commonly used as part of the selection process. They tend to be used to assess skills and competencies that are less amenable to traditional cognitive ability and personality testing. For example, written communication skills are best assessed by obtaining a sample of the candidate's writing; oral communication skills are best assessed by watching the candidate give an oral presentation; leadership and influence within teams are best assessed by observing the candidate participate in a simulated unstructured group situation.

Work samples and simulations require the job candidate to produce behaviours related to job performance under controlled conditions that approximate those found in the real job. The candidate is not asked to perform the real job for several reasons. Actual job performance may be affected by many factors other than the applicant's proficiency or aptitude for the job; these factors could affect candidates differentially so that two applicants with

Work samples and simulations—testing procedures that require job candidates to produce behaviours related to job performance under controlled conditions that approximate those found in the job. Work samples provide a closer approximation to the actual job and work environment.

the same proficiency might perform differently. Placing the applicant in the job may also be extremely disruptive, costly, and time-consuming, if not outright dangerous in some situations. The major difference between work samples and simulations is the degree of their approximation of the real work situation. The major difference between both of these tests and a job knowledge test is that work samples and simulations rely on the reproduction of job-related behaviours whereas written responses to a job knowledge test are used to make inferences about the applicant's potential to perform required job behaviours.

Work samples tests include major tasks taken from the job under consideration; these tasks are organized into an assignment, which the applicant is asked to complete. The work sample and the scoring of an applicant's performance are standardized, allowing for comparisons of skill or aptitude across candidates. Work samples include both motor and verbal behaviours (Asher and Sciarrino, 1974). Motor work samples require the applicant to physically manipulate some machinery or tools; verbal work samples require the applicant to solve problems that involve communication or interpersonal skills.

For example, a secretary's job might include using a computer and related software to type letters and reports, to manage the office budget, to track purchases, to send data files electronically to other people, together with operating the phone and voice-mail systems, scheduling appointments, and receiving people into the office. A work sample test given to applicants for this position might include both a motor work sample, using a computer to type and to electronically transmit a standardized letter, and a verbal work sample, dealing with a message from the boss that asks the secretary to reschedule several important appointments to allow the boss to keep a dental appointment.

The work sample test would not seek to include every aspect of the job but only those deemed to be the most important. The work sample test could be given to the candidate in the actual place of employment or in an off-work setting. Regardless of where the testing takes place, it would be carried out using standardized instructions, conditions, and equipment. The results of the work sample test tell how well the applicant performed on the work sample tasks. Work sample performance is only an estimate, or prediction, of actual job performance.

Recall our discussion of typical versus maximum performance in Chapter 6; work sample performance is clearly a case of maximum performance where the applicant's motivation may be quite different from that exhibited through typical, day-to-day job performance. Like any test, the validity of a work sample test must be established as part of the selection procedure; however, work sample tests, if developed properly, will predict job performance in a reliable and valid manner (Asher and Sciarrino, 1974). Because they incorporate aspects of the job into selection, work samples have the potential to attain relatively high levels of validity. At the same time, however, work samples may require expenditures on expensive equipment and personnel to administer the test to each applicant individually. As is the case with simulations, these costs may be more than offset by the increased benefits of improved selection.

Simulations, like work sample tests, attempt to duplicate salient features of the job under consideration. Candidates perform the set of designated tasks and are given an objective score based on their performance. The score is used to predict aptitude or proficiency for job performance. Unlike work samples, the tasks and the setting in which they are carried out represent less of an approximation of the actual job. That is, the simulation asks the candidate to carry out critical job tasks in a more artificial environment than work sample testing.

The most distinguishing feature of a simulation is its fidelity, the degree to which it represents the real environment. Simulations can range from those with low fidelity (e.g., using a computer game as an indicator of managerial decision making) to those with high fidelity (e.g., using performance in a flight simulator that highly resembles a cockpit to predict pilot behaviour). High-fidelity simulations can be quite expensive, but in some cases there may be no alternative. The simulation allows a type of hands-on performance in an environment that provides substantial safety and cost benefits compared with allowing the applicant to perform in the actual job. While a computer-controlled flight simulator may cost several million dollars to develop and construct, it is far preferable to having prospective pilots demonstrate their flying proficiency in an actual aircraft where a mistake can be deadly, as well as much more costly.

High-fidelity computer-assisted flight simulators are normally used as part of training programs and are used by Air Canada and other Canadian airlines in that capacity. The Canadian Forces, however, is one of the few organizations to use a simulator in selecting candidates for flight school; performance on the high-fidelity simulator is a much better predictor of flying success on the part of future pilots than a battery of cognitive and psychomotor tests (Spinner, 1990). Generally, the savings from reductions in training failures and training time more than offset the initial cost of the simulator.

Situational exercises are a form of work sample testing used in selecting managers or professionals. Situational exercises attempt to assess aptitude or proficiency in performing important job tasks, but do so by using tasks that are more abstract and less realistic than those performed on the job. To a large extent, situational exercises are really a form of low-fidelity simulation. The situational exercise involves the types of skills that a manager or professional may be called on to use in the actual job.

Situational exercises have been designed to assess problem-solving ability, leadership potential, and communication skills. The Kitchener, Ontario, Prison for Women, for example, hired a professional actor to play the part of an inmate to assess a candidate's handling of difficult interpersonal situations (Thompson, 1995).

The two most prominent situational exercises are the leaderless group discussion and the in-basket test. In a **leaderless group discussion**, a group of candidates for a managerial position might be asked to talk about or develop a position or statement on a job-related topic. In the leaderless group discussion

Situational exercises— assess aptitude or proficiency in performing important job tasks by using tasks that are abstract and less realistic than those performed on the actual job.

Leaderless group discussion— a simulation exercise designed to assess leadership, organizational, and communication skills.

used by IBM, candidates must advocate the promotion of a staff member. In a leaderless group discussion, the group is not provided with any rules to conduct the discussion; nor is any structure imposed on the group. The primary purpose of the exercise is to see which of the candidates emerges as a leader by influencing other members of the group. Each candidate is assessed on a number of factors by a panel of judges; these factors might include communication and organizational skills, interpersonal skills, and leadership behaviour.

The **in-basket test** seeks to assess the applicant's organizational and problem-solving skills. The Public Service Commission of Canada uses an in-basket test in selecting applicants for certain managerial and professional positions in the federal civil service. As part of an in-basket test, each candidate is given a standardized set of short reports, notes, telephone messages, and memos of the type that most managers would have to deal with on a daily basis. The applicants must set priorities for the various tasks, determine which can be deferred or delegated, and which must be dealt with immediately. They must also indicate how they would approach the different problems the material suggests they will encounter as a manager. Each candidate's performance on the in-basket test is scored by a panel of judges.

> **In-basket test**—a simulation exercise designed to assess organizational and problem-solving skills.

The in-basket has a great intuitive appeal as a selection test for managers because it resembles what managers actually do; unfortunately, empirical evidence suggests that it does not have high validity as a selection instrument (Schippman, Prien, and Katz, 1990). In part, this may be due to the lack of agreed-on scoring procedures for the in-basket test; successful managers who complete the in-basket do not always arrive at the same conclusions. Additionally, those judging the in-basket performance often fail to distinguish among various target abilities that are supposed to be measured by the in-basket exercise, calling into question the accuracy of inferences made about potential managerial performance that are based on in-basket scores (Rolland, 1999).

Most types of work samples and situational tests discussed here are labour-intensive and costly to develop and administer. However, the importance of making the right selection decision increases where organizations expect more from fewer employees. Particularly for small businesses, selecting the right individual is critical to their success. Additionally, because the relationship of work samples and situational tests to the job is so transparent, candidates from different gender and ethnic groups tend to perceive them as fair. This is most desirable given the growing minority segment of the workforce. For these reasons, the use of work samples and simulation tests is likely to increase in coming years. It will become even more important to ensure that scoring of candidates is done systematically and objectively.

ASSESSMENT CENTRES

Although situational exercises can be used as stand-alone selection tests, they generally play a prominent role in testing carried out as part of an **assessment centre**. The term "assessment centre" is somewhat misleading. It does not refer

> **Assessment centre**—a standardized procedure that involves the use of multiple measurement techniques to evaluate candidates for selection, classification, and promotion.

to a physical place but rather to a standardized assessment procedure that involves the use of multiple measurement techniques to evaluate candidates for selection, classification, and promotion purposes. Assessment centres had their origin in World War II, when they were used by both Germany and Britain to assess the military leadership potential of recruits. Following the war, the procedure was adapted by AT&T in the United States to assess managerial potential. Today, the procedure is mostly used to assess applicants for managerial or administrative positions.

While the assessment centre is used as a procedure to select external applicants, it is typically used by most organizations for internal selection, that is, promotion. While some assessment procedures (e.g., an interview) may involve only one candidate, the vast majority of assessment centre procedures involve group activity. The candidates are evaluated in groups by a panel of trained assessors. The assessment centre is also unique in including managers along with psychologists and other human resources professionals on the assessment team. The managers are trained in the use of the assessment techniques and scoring procedures. The managers selected to be assessors are those who are familiar with the job for which the candidates are being selected (Finkle, 1976). The key features of an assessment centre are outlined in Box 9.12.

BOX 9.12 Essential Elements of an Assessment Centre

1. Job analysis is used to identify job dimensions, tasks, and attributes that are important to job success.

2. Behaviour of candidates is observed by trained assessors and related to KSAOs.

3. Assessment techniques must provide information related to the dimensions and attributes identified in the job analysis.

4. Multiple assessment procedures are used to elicit a variety of behaviours and information relevant to the selected dimensions and attributes.

5. A sufficient number of job-related simulations must be included in the procedure to allow opportunities to observe behaviour on the selected dimensions.

6. Multiple assessors, diverse in ethnicity, age, gender, and functional work areas are used to observe and assess each candidate.

7. Assessors must receive thorough training and meet performance standards before being allowed to evaluate candidates.

8. Systematic procedures must be used by assessors to record specific behavioural observations accurately at the time of their occurrence.

9. Assessors must prepare a report or record of observations made during each exercise in preparation for consolidating information across assessors.

10. Data from all assessor reports must be pooled or integrated either at a special meeting of assessors or through statistical methods.

Source: Task Force on Assessment Center Guidelines (1989).

ASSESSMENT CENTRE TESTING While the specific testing procedures may vary from one assessment centre to another, depending on the purpose of the assessment, assessment centres generally include tests or procedures from each of the following categories:

- ability and aptitude tests
- personality tests, both objective and projective
- situational exercises
- interviews

Following completion of all the assessment centre components, the team of assessors reviews each individual's performance on a number of variables. The variables represent different dimensions, including administrative skills, cognitive skills, human relations skills, decision-making ability, problem-solving skills, leadership potential, motivation, resistance to stress, and degree of flexibility, among several others (Bray, Campbell, and Grant, 1974). Based on the ratings and observations made over the period of the assessment, the team prepares a report summarizing the information obtained through the various techniques. Candidates are provided with feedback on their performance at the assessment centre.

SCORING PERFORMANCE AT THE ASSESSMENT CENTRE When the assessment is conducted for selection purposes, the various ratings are combined into an overall assessment centre score, which can be used to rank the applicants. Generally, some score is established as the minimum needed for consideration, with employment offers made to the highest-ranking applicant and proceeding downward until all the positions have been filled. When the assessments are made for other purposes, the assessment centre score and report may be used to predict the candidate's long-range managerial potential and likelihood of promotion. Some organizations, like AT&T, require all managers at a particular level to attend an assessment centre as a means of identifying those with potential for advancement in the company. Also, the assessment centre information can be used to develop training programs for individuals within the organization, to increase their chances of future advancement.

USE OF ASSESSMENT CENTRES IN CANADA In Canada, assessment centre procedures are used by the Public Service Commission of Canada to select candidates for senior managerial positions in the federal civil service and as part of its executive development and education program. They are also used extensively by Ford Motor Company, General Motors, Ontario Hydro, Northern Telecom, and Weyerhaeuser Canada, among many others. Assessment centres are also used by the Canadian Forces to select applicants for training as naval officers.

LOCATION AND COST OF THE ASSESSMENT CENTRE The assessment procedure can be quite extensive and usually takes place over two or three days. The assessment centre may be located in the company but is generally held at an off-site location. Given the length of time and the number of personnel involved in the procedure, it should not be surprising that assessment centres are an expensive proposition. They require a substantial investment on the part of an organization both to develop and to operate. This cost factor generally limits their use to larger organizations that have ongoing selection and promotion programs.

EFFECTIVENESS OF ASSESSMENT CENTRES Do assessment centres improve on other selection techniques? Are they worth the cost? Both organizations and candidates who have gone through an assessment centre attest to their satisfaction with the procedure. The objective data supporting their effectiveness, however, are equivocal. For example, personality predicted job performance and promotability of forestry products managers as well as an assessment centre procedure; however, the predictive validity improved when both measures were used (Goffin, Rothstein, and Johnston, 1996). While many research studies have confirmed the validity of the procedure, a troubling number have not shown any improvement in validity that can be attributed to the assessment centre. A meta-analytic evaluation of 50 assessment centres reported a validity coefficient of .37 (Gaugler, Rosenthal, Thornton, and Bentson, 1987), while a study of one assessment centre evaluated across 16 sites found a much lower validity of .08 to .16, depending on the criterion measure (Schmitt, Schneider, and Cohen, 1990).

In part, these mixed results may be due to the lack of standardization and wide variability in the exercises carried out at different assessment centres. Another factor that may affect validity is the role played by the assessor. Considerable research has investigated how assessors rate candidates. There is some indication that assessors may base their ratings on a candidate's past job experience or performance rather than on how the candidate performs at the assessment centre (Klimoski and Brickner, 1987).

First-hand experience with candidates through the extensive interaction at the assessment centre may allow assessors to identify and to weight important information from the candidate's previous experience. The assessor's expertise, cognitive ability, and personality are all factors that may affect assessment centre validity. For example, assessors who are tender-minded and warmhearted tend to rate candidates more leniently (Bartels and Doverspike, 1997).

Assessment centres are likely to increase in popularity as a procedure for assessing potential for managerial or professional careers. The procedure produces a wealth of information, which is useful throughout the candidate's career within the organization. It provides a comprehensive assessment of an individual and identifies strengths and weaknesses that form the basis of future development programs. Organizations have started to use assessment centres as a means of providing realistic job previews to job applicants and as a source of organizational and employee development (Howard, 1997).

Cautions are in order: assessment procedures may not be the best selection procedure in all cases. The worth of an assessment centre, like any selection device, rests on an evaluation of its psychometric properties and its utility.

EVALUATING TESTING EFFECTIVENESS

Throughout this chapter we have emphasized that tests used as part of selection procedures must exhibit sound psychometric properties, particularly reliability and validity. The tests must be constructed and used in accordance with accepted professional standards and must meet any legal requirements that govern their use. These selection procedures involve the expenditure of time and money; in the case of assessment centres, these can be considerable. Therefore, it is not sufficient to simply demonstrate that a selection test or procedure has acceptable psychometric properties. A more important question is whether the new selection tests improve on the outcomes that are expected from the existing selection system. Also at issue is whether the new selection system will produce benefits or advantages that exceed the cost of operating the selection system. Utility analysis is a method that can be used to evaluate the performance of different selection systems by comparing the net gains that accrue to the organization through their use. We present an introduction to utility analysis in Chapter 11 and illustrate that discussion with several examples. You may wish to read ahead and review that section now.

COMPARING SELECTION PREDICTORS

With the exception of the employment interview, which will be discussed in the next chapter, we have reviewed the most commonly used predictors that are used in personnel selection. Which, if any of these, are the better predictors? Which should be considered for adoption as part of a selection system? In large part the answers to these questions depend on the specific information that is being sought, as determined through a job analysis. Each of these predictors has different strengths and weaknesses and may be more suited to specific uses. Most of all, the selection measure must provide information that is related to the specific job, or class of jobs, that are being staffed. Consideration must also be given to the type of criterion measure that will be used. The validity of predictors may vary among criteria such as training performance, job tenure, performance ratings, and promotion.

Selection measures must meet prevailing psychometric and professional standards. They must also be reviewed in the context of fairness and legal and organizational policies. Table 9.1 has been compiled from meta-analytic studies that have reviewed the validity of different selection measures. The validities reported here are averaged across job performance criteria and are presented in descending order based on their mean, corrected validity coefficient. While these validities may be influential, the difference in utility provided by different predictors may also influence choice of a measure. The potential net gains from using different predictors in the hiring situation should be compared before making any final decision on which predictor to use.

Table 9.1 also presents data on the percentage of Canadian companies that report using some of these predictors. Data are not available for all of the selection instruments that we have discussed; nonetheless, it appears that

TABLE 9.1 MEAN VALIDITIES FOR PREDICTORS USED IN SELECTION

PREDICTOR	MEAN VALIDITY	USED BY CANADIAN COMPANIES[#]	
		SMALL/MEDIUM	LARGE
Work samples *	.54	—	—
Cognitive ability *	.51	39%	57%
Interview—structured *	.51	—	—
Job knowledge tests	.48	—	—
Integrity tests*	.41	—	—
Interview—unstructured*	.38	—	—
Assessment centre *	.37	—	—
Biographical data *	.35	24%	26%
Psychomotor ability **	.35	—	—
Perceptual ability **	.34	—	—
Physical ability ***	.32	—	—
Conscientiousness*	.31	18%	28%
Reference checks *	.26	72%	63%
Résumé components		94%	100%
Grade point average****	.32		
Job experience*	.18		
Years of education*	.10		
Graphology*	.02		

Sources:

* Schmidt and Hunter (1998)

** Hunter and Hunter (1984)

*** Schmitt, Gooding, Noe, and Kirsch (1984)

**** Roth, BeVier, Switzer, and Schippmann (1996)

Thacker and Cattaneo (1987)

Canadian firms, particularly small and medium-sized ones, are more likely to use traditional selection instruments, which have lower validity. Larger companies are more open to using employment testing and are benefiting from the higher returns from improved selection procedures. Given the advances in selection technology, there is no economic reason why small and medium firms cannot make use of newer selection procedures. Their economic survival may depend on their ability to do so.

Recall from Chapter 3 that test fairness includes the reaction of applicants to selection procedures. Adverse reactions to selection tests and procedures may impair the ability of an organization to recruit and hire the best applicants. It may also lead to costly litigation. Table 9.2 presents reactions of potential job applicants to different personnel selection techniques derived from two studies. In the first study, potential job applicants in the United States and France rated both the effectiveness and fairness of personnel selection methods (Steiner and Gilliland, 1996). Despite differences in language and culture, both groups gave favourable ratings to interviews, résumés, work samples, biographical data, ability tests, and references. The French group also rated personality tests favourably, while the U.S. group rated them slightly lower. Both groups gave the lowest ratings to personal contacts (selection based on the influence of a connection in the company), honesty testing, and graphology.

TABLE 9.2 EFFECTIVENESS AND FAIRNESS OF SELECTION TECHNIQUES AS PERCEIVED BY APPLICANTS

DEGREE OF FAVOURABILITY*	UNITED STATES	FRANCE
Above average	Interviews Résumés Work samples	Work samples Interviews
Average	Biographical data Ability tests References	Résumés Ability tests Personality tests References Biographical data
Below average	Personality tests Honesty tests Personal contacts	Graphology Personal contacts Honesty tests
Well below average	Graphology	

* Selection techniques are arranged in order of favourability within each degree of favourability.

Sources: Steiner and Gilliland (1996); Stinglhamber et al., (1999).

Similarly in the second study, French-speaking job applicants in Belgium reacted very positively to selection interviews and less so, but positively, to personality, ability, and work samples tests. Graphology provoked strongly negative reactions. The applicants' reactions to the selection procedures influenced their intentions to recommend the organization to others as a place to work and their intentions to buy its products (Stinglhamber, Vandenberghe, and Brancart, 1999). While data for Canadian applicants are not available, there is no reason to believe that they would be substantially different from those summarized in Table 9.2. Canadian organizations that are considering using honesty tests, graphology, and the use of personal contacts in their hiring process should consider the possible negative consequences on their ability to recruit and hire the best available people.

SUMMARY

Psychological testing can be carried out for many purposes, including selection of personnel. Employment testing must meet acceptable professional and legal standards and should be carried out by professionals who are knowledgeable about tests and testing procedures. Only those tests that are psychometrically sound should be used for employment purposes. The rights of job applicants asked to take employment tests must be respected at all times. A fundamental issue is whether the test provides information that is related to those dimensions identified through job analysis.

A variety of tests can be used for selection purposes. Personality tests have not had a good reputation as selection predictors, although more recent studies suggest a Big Five construction of personality may improve prediction of certain job performance dimensions. Personality tests are also increasingly being used to assess honesty or integrity with a considerable degree of predictive accuracy. Ability tests, both general cognitive ability and more specialized tests, consistently provide highly valid information about future job performance for a broad class of occupations. Employers are increasingly seeking information on applicant physical fitness and drug use. Collection of this type of information poses a threat to the applicant's privacy and must conform to human rights guidelines.

Work samples and simulations attempt to base selection on the ability of job applicants to perform actual job components either directly or in some abstract form. Assessment centres appear to be well suited for the selection of managers and professionals and provide a wealth of information. All of these approaches are alternatives to more traditional selection procedures. Some of these new selection tools are expensive, and their costs of selection may offset the benefits they provide. Before adopting specific selection techniques, consideration must be given to their perceived fairness and utility.

KEY TERMS

EXERCISES

1. Consult the government agency responsible for monitoring the use of selection tests, including physical fitness and drug testing, in your locality. This may be a human rights agency or other government body. Determine whether that agency has a policy on the use of selection tests. Compare that policy with the principles and standards identified in this chapter.

2. Survey 10 companies or organizations in your community to determine whether they use selection tests as part of their hiring procedure. List the tests that are used. Did any organization report using honesty, fitness, or drug tests? If the company did not use any type of testing, report the procedures they used and its reasons, if any, for not using selection tests.

3. Use the information you developed as part of completing Chapter 6's exercises to develop a work sample test, including scoring procedure, that could be used to select teachers or some other profession (although your instructor may be more knowledgeable about the former occupation).

4. Design an assessment centre that could be used to select teachers. Describe the rationale for selecting the various procedures that would be included in the centre.

5. Your workplace, by the nature of the work, has a high level of airborne dust particles. You are concerned about hiring people with environmental sensitivities. Assume that there is an accurate genetic

screening device to identify people who might be susceptible to the dust particles. Under what circumstances should you institute the test as part of your hiring procedures? Should it be voluntary or mandatory? How would you implement the test? Who would have access to the results? What would you tell applicants who tested positive?

CASE

Applicants to the Royal Canadian Mounted Police must pass a written examination, an interview, and a physical ability test before being accepted for basic training at the RCMP's training centre in Regina. As a federally regulated agency, the RCMP falls under the jurisdiction of the Employment Equity Act, designed to further the employment of women, visible minorities, and other designated groups. The RCMP has had difficulty meeting recruiting targets of 20 percent women, 4.5 percent Aboriginals, and 8.3 percent visible minorities that were set in compliance with the objectives of the act. A review of testing data showed that Aboriginals and visible minorities scored slightly lower than other groups on the written tests and that 40–50 percent of women applicants fail the physical ability test, a rate considerably higher than that for men.

In response to concerns over failing to meet its recruiting objectives, the RCMP is undertaking a revision of the current examination, which presently includes measures of written composition, logic, and mathematical computation; that is, the current test assesses cognitive ability. The new test will retain "academic" items related to composition and computation, but it will also have new items in the form of scenarios that are directed at problem solving. The new questions will be more job-directed and operational in nature. Test items will be rewritten to minimize the impact of different regional language styles to ensure that the questions are fair and equitable for all applicants.

With respect to the physical ability test, women had particular difficulty with the upper-body strength requirements. To deal with this problem the RCMP instituted a six-week pre-training fitness program to help women prepare for the fitness test. It also eased the physical standards for women.

These changes did not meet with unanimous approval, even from groups the changes were designed to help. A lawyer for the Federation of Saskatchewan Indian Nations is quoted as saying, "Instead of watering down their exams, the RCMP should try and change their relationship with Native people. The RCMP is trying to send the message that they want more Natives in the force, but the message to non-Natives is that the Indians are getting an easier ride. Indian people aren't stupid." A Reform MP in Saskatchewan added that "the RCMP should set high physical standards and even higher intellectual standards for their recruits. Public safety should not be compromised for political correctness." The changes, however, were applauded by members of

Nova Scotia's black community, which sees more minority officers as necessary to preventing racial strife. A black leader said that while math may have clear-cut answers, "everyone's general knowledge is not exactly the same ... [General knowledge] is based on experience and exposure to certain things. I think our experiences are different in many respects." He noted that the black community was very different from the Aboriginal community.

Sources: *Alberta Report* (January 19, 1998); *Canadian Press* Newswire (August 11, 1996; January 4, 1998); *The Globe and Mail* (October 14, 1997).

DISCUSSION QUESTIONS

1. Is the RCMP doing the right thing in revising its written examination and fitness test? Has the RCMP reduced its entrance requirements? Base your response on what you have learned in this chapter.

2. It appears that the RCMP is trying to incorporate a "practical intelligence" component into its examinations. Is this appropriate? What type of "job knowledge" should applicants be asked?

3. If physical ability is a job requirement for police officers, is it appropriate to have different standards for male and female applicants for the RCMP?

4. Is the existing test fair and equitable for all candidates? Will the new procedures discriminate against white males?

5. Can you design a recruiting campaign to attract more women and visible-minority applicants to the RCMP? What would it look like?

6 Chapter 11 looks at another method that can be used to improve the number of minority applicants: banding. This procedure is also controversial. You may want to read that section now and discuss this as an option. How would the public likely react to using banding?

REFERENCES

Alliger, G.M., and S.A. Dwight. 2000. "A Meta-Analytic Investigation of the Susceptibility of Integrity Tests to Faking and Coaching." *Educational and Psychological Measurement* 60: 59-73.

Alliger, G.M., S.O. Lilienfeld, and K.E. Mitchell. 1996. "The Susceptibility of Overt and Covert Integrity Tests to Coaching and Faking." *Psychological Science* 7: 32–39.

Americans with Disabilities Act of 1990, 1993. West, 42 USCA § 12101 et seq.

Arnold, D.W. 1991. "To Test or Not To Test: Legal Issues in Integrity Testing." *Forensic Psychology* 4: 62–67.

Arvey, R.D., T.E. Landon, S.M. Nutting, and S.E. Maxwell. 1992. "Development of Physical Ability Tests for Police Officers: A Construct Validation Approach." *Journal of Applied Psychology* 77: 996–1009.

Arvey, R.D., G.L. Renz, and T.W. Watson. 1998. "Emotionality and Job Performance: Implications for Personnel Selection." In G.R. Ferris, ed., *Research in Personnel and Human Resource Management*, vol. 16. Stamford, CT: JAI Press, 103–47.

Asher, J.J, and J.A. Sciarrino. 1974. "Realistic Work Sample Tests." *Personnel Psychology* 27: 519–33.

Ashton, M.C. 1998. "Personality and Job Performance: The Importance of Narrow Traits." *Journal of Organizational Behavior* 19: 289–303

Ayed, N, 1998. "TD Drug Testing Policy Discriminatory." *Canadian Press Newswire* (July 24, 1998).

Bar-On, R. 1997. *Emotional Quotient Inventory: Technical Manual*. Toronto: Multi-Health Systems.

Barrick, M.R., and M.K. Mount. 1991. "The Big Five Personality Dimensions and Job Performance: A Meta-Analysis." *Personnel Psychology* 44: 1–26.

———. 1993. "Autonomy as a Moderator of the Relationships between the Big Five Personality Dimensions and Job Performance." *Journal of Applied Psychology* 78: 111–18.

Barry, E. 1999. "Smarter than the Average Cop." *The Boston Globe* (September 10): B1.

Bartels, L.K., and D. Doverspike, 1997. "Assessing the Assessor: The Relationship of Assessor Personality to Leniency in Assessment Center Ratings." *Journal of Social Behavior and Personality* 12: 179–90.

Belcourt, M., A.W. Sherman, Jr., G.W. Bohlander, and S.A. Snell. 1996. *Managing Human Resources*. Toronto: Nelson Canada.

Bell, J. 1996. "Brain Power Counts, Too, When Evaluating Prospects." *USA Today* (April 10): 3C.

Ben-Shukhar, G., M. Bar-Hillel, Y. Bilu, E. Ben-Abba, and A. Flug. 1986. "Can Graphology Predict Occupational Success? Two Empirical Studies and Some Methodological Ruminations." *Journal of Applied Psychology* 71: 645–53.

Borman, W.C., and S.J. Motowidlo. 1993. "Expanding the Performance Domain to Include Elements of Contextual Performance." In N. Schmitt, W.C. Borman, and Associates, *Personnel Selection in Organizations*. San Francisco, CA: Jossey-Bass, 71–98.

———. 1997. "Task Performance and Contextual Performance: The Meaning for Personnel Selection Research." *Human Performance* 10: 99–109.

Bray, D.W., R.J. Campbell, and D.L. Grant. 1974. *Formative Years in Business: A Long-Term AT and T Study of Managerial Lives*. New York: Wiley.

British Columbia (Public Service Employee Relations Commission) v. BCGSEU. Supreme Court of Canada decision rendered September 9, 1999.

Camara, W.J., and D.L. Schneider. 1994. "Integrity Tests: Facts and Unresolved Issues. *American Psychologist* 49: 112–19.

Campbell, J.P. 1990a. "Modeling the Performance Prediction Problem in Industrial and Organizational Psychology." In M.D. Dunnette and L.M. Hough, eds., *The Handbook of Industrial and Organizational Psychology*, vol. 1. 2nd ed. San Diego: Consulting Psychologists Press, 687–32.

———. 1990b. "An Overview: The Army Selection and Classification Project (Project A)." *Personnel Psychology* 43: 231–41.

Campion, M.A. 1983. "Personnel Selection for Physically Demanding Jobs: Review and Recommendation." *Personnel Psychology* 36: 527–50.

Canadian Human Rights Commission. 1985. *Bona Fide Occupational Requirement and Bona Fide Justification: Interim Policies and Explanatory Notes.* Ottawa.

Canadian Psychological Association. 1986. *Canadian Code of Ethics for Psychologists.* Ottawa.

Canadian Psychological Association. 1987. *Guidelines for Educational and Psychological Testing.* Ottawa.

Collins, J.D., and F.L. Schmidt. 1993. "Personality, Integrity, and White Collar Crime: A Construct Validity Study." *Personnel Psychology* 46: 295–311.

"Courts Overrule Drug and Alcohol Testing Policies." 1998. *Worklife Report* 11: 6, 9.

Cronbach, L.J. 1990. *Essentials of Psychological Testing,* 5th ed. New York: Harper and Row.

Cronshaw, S.F. 1986. "The Status of Employment Testing in Canada: A Review and Evaluation of Theory and Professional Practice." *Canadian Psychology* 27: 183–95.

Currie, M.B. 1999. "Taking Another Hit: A Labour Relations Board Has Again Come up with Reasons to Rule against Drug and Alcohol Testing for Safety-Sensitive Jobs." *Occupational Health and Safety* 15: 48–48.

Digman, J.M. 1990. "Personality Structure: Emergence of the Five Factor Model." In M. Rosenzweig and L.W. Porter, eds., *Annual Review of Psychology.* Palo Alto, CA: Annual Reviews.

Dwight, S.A., and G.M. Alliger. 1997. "Reactions to Overt Integrity Testing Items." *Educational and Psychological Measurement* 50: 587–99.

Dunn, K., and E. Dawson. 1994. "The Right Person for the Right Job." *Occupational Health and Safety Canada* 10: 28–31.

Dye, D.A., M. Reck, and MA. McDaniel 1993. "The Validity of Job Knowledge Measures." *International Journal of Selection and Assessment* 1: 153–57.

Ellington, J.E., P.R. Sackett, and L.M. Hough. 1999. "Social Desirability Corrections in Personality Measurement: Issues of Applicant Comparison and Construct Validity." *Journal of Applied Psychology* 84: 155–66.

Finkle, R.B. 1976. "Managerial Assessment Centers." In M.D. Dunnette, ed., *Handbook of Industrial and Organizational Psychology.* Chicago: Rand McNally.

Fleishman, E.A., and M.K. Quaintance. 1984. *Taxonomies of Human Performance: The Description of Human Tasks.* Orlando, FL: Academic Press.

Fleishman, E.A., and M.E. Reilly. 1992. *Handbook of Human Abilities.* Palo Alto, CA: Consulting Psychologists Press.

Gaugler, B.B., D.B. Rosenthal, G.C. Thornton, and C. Bentson. 1987. "Meta-Analysis of Assessment Center Validity." *Journal of Applied Psychology* 72: 493–511.

Getkake, M., P. Hausdorf, and S.F. Cronshaw. 1992. "Transnational Validity Generalization of Employment Tests from the United States to Canada." *Canadian Journal of Administrative Sciences* 9: 324–35.

Gibb-Clark, M. 1996. "Drug-Testing Ruling Set Aside." *The Globe and Mail* (April 24): B1, B4.

Goffin, R.D., M.G. Rothstein, and N.G. Johnston. 1996. "Personality Testing and the Assessment Center: Incremental Validity for Managerial Selection." *Journal of Applied Psychology* 81: 746–56.

Goleman, D. 1995. *Emotional Intelligence*. New York: Bantam Books.

Goleman, D. 1998. *Working with Emotional Intelligence*. New York: Bantam Books.

Gottfredson, L. 1986. "Societal Consequences of the G Factor in Employment." *Journal of Vocational Behavior* 29: 379–411.

Gottfredson, L. 1997 "Why *g* Matters: The Complexity of Everyday Life." *Intelligence* 24: 79–132.

Goodstein, L.D., and R.I. Lanyon. 1999. "Applications of Personality Assessment to the Workplace: A Review." *Journal of Business and Psychology* 13: 291–322.

Guion, R.M. 1965. *Personnel Testing*. New York: McGraw Hill.

Guion, R.M., and R.F. Gottier. 1965. "Validity of Personality Measures in Personnel Selection." *Personnel Psychology* 18: 135–64.

Hall, C.S., and G. Lindzey. 1970. *Theories of Personality*. New York: Wiley.

Harris, M.M., and M.L. Trusty. 1997. "Drug and Alcohol Programs in the Workplace: A Review of Recent Literature." In C.L. Cooper and I.T. Robertson, eds., *International Review of Industrial and Organizational Psychology*, vol. 12. London: John Wiley and Sons, 289–315.

Hogan, J. 1991. "Structure of Physical Performance in Occupational Tasks." *Journal of Applied Psychology* 76: 495–507.

Hogan, J., and R. Hogan. 1989. "How to Measure Employee Reliability." *Journal of Applied Psychology* 74: 273–79.

Hogan, R., J. Hogan, and B.W. Roberts. 1996. "Personality Measurement and Employment Decisions: Questions and Answers." *American Psychologist* 51: 469–77.

Hough, L.M.. 1998. "Effects of Intentional Distortion in Personality Measurement and Evaluation of Suggested Palliatives." *Human Performance* 11: 209–44.

Hough, L.M., N.K. Eaton, M.D. Dunnette, J.D. Kamp, and R.A. McCloy. 1990. "Criterion-Related Validities of Personality Constructs and the Effect of Response Distortion on Those Validities." [Monograph]. *Journal of Applied Psychology* 75: 581–95.

Howard, A. 1997. "A Reassessment of Assessment Centers: Challenges for the 21st Century." *Journal of Social Behavior and Personality* 12: 13–52.

Hunter, J.E., and R.F. Hunter. 1984. "Validity and Utility of Alternative Predictors of Job Performance." *Psychological Bulletin* 96: 72–98.

Jenkins, C.D., S.J. Zyzanski, and R.H. Rosenman. 1979. *Jenkins Activity Survey Manual*. New York: Psychological Corporation.

Jones, J., ed. 1991. *Pre-Employment Honesty Testing: Current Research and Future Directions*. New York: Quorum Books.

Kichuk, S.L., and W.H. Wiesner. 1996. *The Effect of the 'Big Five' Personality Factors on Team Performance: Implications for Selecting Optimal Performance*. Paper presented at the Fourth Annual Advanced Concepts Conference on Work Teams, Dallas, TX.

Kichuk, S.L., and W.H. Wiesner. 1998. "Work Teams: Selecting Members for Optimal Performance." *Canadian Psychology* 39: 23–32.

Klimoski, R.J., and M. Brickner. 1987. "Why Do Assessment Centers Work? The Puzzle of Assessment Center Validity." *Personnel Psychology* 40: 243–60.

Levine, E.L., P.E. Spector, S. Menon, S. Narayanan, and J. Cannon-Bowers. 1996. "Validity Generalization for Cognitive, Psychomotor, and Perceptual Tests for Craft Jobs in the Utility Industry." *Human Performance* 9: 1–22.

Lindsay, D. 1998, "True Lies—An Applicant Writes an 'Integrity' Test." *This Magazine* 31: 4.

Lobsenz, R.E. 1999. "Do Measures of Tacit Knowledge Assess Psychological Phenomena Distinct from General Ability, Personality, and Social Knowledge?" *Dissertation Abstracts International: Section B—The Sciences and Engineering* 59: 05147.

Lowman, R.L., ed. 1998. *The Ethical Practice of Psychology in Organizations.* Bowling Green, OH: The Society for Industrial and Organizational Psychology.

Mayer, J.D., and P. Salovey. 1997. "What Is Emotional Intelligence?" In P. Salovey and D. Sluyter, eds., *Emotional Development and Emotional Intelligence: Implications for Educators.* New York: Basic Books.

McHenry, J.J., L.M. Hough, J.L. Toquam, M.A. Hanson, and S. Ashworth. 1990. "Project A Validity Results: The Relationship between Predictor and Criterion Domains." *Personnel Psychology* 43: 335–54.

McManus, M.A., and M.L. Kelly. 1999. "Personality Measures and Biodata: Evidence Regarding Their Incremental Predictive Value in the Life Insurance Industry." *Personnel Psychology* 52: 137–48.

Mitrovica, A. 2000. "CSIS Urged to End Polygraph Testing." *The Globe and Mail* (June 12): A5.

Mount, M.K., M.R. Barrick, and G.L. Stewart. 1998. "Five-Factor Model of Personality and Performance in Jobs Involving Interpersonal Interactions." *Human Performance* 11: 145–65.

Neuman, G.A., and R. Baudoun. 1998. "An Empirical Examination of Overt and Covert Integrity Tests." *Journal of Business and Psychology* 13: 65–79.

"A New Slant on Job Applicants: How Grapho-Analysis, the Study of Handwriting, Can Play a Role in the Management Hiring Process." 1994. *This Week in Business* (August 1): F3–F4.

Newsome, S., A.L. Day, and V.M. Catano. In Press. "Assessing the Predictive Validity of Emotional Intelligence." *Personality and Individual Differences.*

Olive, D. 1998. "EQ, not IQ, is Ticket to Top for Psych Guru." *Financial Post/National Post* (November 23): C12.

Ones, D., and C. Viswesvaran. 1996. "Bandwidth-Fidelity Dilemma in Personality Measurement for Personnel Selection." *Journal of Organizational Behavior* 17: 609–26

Ones, D., and C. Viswesvaran. 1998. "The Effects of Social Desirability and Faking on Personality and Integrity Testing for Personnel Selection." *Human Performance* 11: 245–69.

Ones, D., C. Viswesvaran, and F.L. Schmidt. 1993. "Comprehensive Meta-Analysis of Integrity Test Validities: Findings and Implications for Personnel Selection and Theories of Job Performance." *Journal of Applied Psychology* 78: 679–703.

Ontario Commissioner's Report. 1994. "Workplace Privacy." *Worklife Report* 9: 8–9.

Paunonen, S.V., M.G. Rothstein, and D.N. Jackson. 1999. "Narrow Reasoning about the Use of Broad Personality Measures for Personnel Selection." *Journal of Organizational Behavior* 20: 389–405.

"Personality Tests Flourishing as Employers Try to Weed out Problem Hires." 1999. *Financial Post/National Post* (August 5): C7.

Polednik, L., and E. Greig. 2000. "Personality and Emotional Intelligence." *The British Journal of Administrative Management* 19: 9.

Prociuk, T.J. 1988. "Applied Psychology in the Canadian Forces: An Overview of Current Research." *Canadian Psychology* 29: 94–102.

Ree, M.J., and T.R. Carretta. 1998. "General Cognitive Ability and Occupational Performance." In C.L. Cooper and I.T. Robertson, eds., *International Review of Industrial and Organizational Psychology*, vol. 13. London: John Wiley and Sons, 159–84.

Rolland, J.P. 1999. "Construct Validity of In-Basket Dimensions." *European Revue of Applied Psychology* 49: 251–59.

Rosse, J.G., M.D. Steecher, J.L. Miller, and R.A Levin. 1998. "The Impact of Response Distortion on Preemployment Personality Testing and Hiring Decisions." *Journal of Applied Psychology* 83: 634–44.

Roth, P.L., C.A. BeVier, F.S. Switzer, III, and J.S. Schippmann. 1996. "Meta-Analyzing the Relationship between Grades and Job Performance." *Journal of Applied Psychology* 81: 548–56.

Sabourin, M. 1999. "Bad Blood: Issues surrounding Workplace Genetic Testing." *Occupational Health and Safety* 15: 34–41.

Sackett, P.R., L.R. Burris, and C. Callahan. 1989. "Integrity Testing for Personnel Selection: An Update." *Personnel Psychology* 42: 491–529.

Sackett, P.R., and J.E. Wanek. 1996. "New Developments in the Use of Measures of Honesty, Integrity, Conscientiousness, Dependability, Trustworthiness, and Reliability for Personnel Selection." *Personnel Psychology* 49: 787–827.

Salgado, J.F. 1997. "The Five Factor Model of Personality and Job Performance in the European Community." *Journal of Applied Psychology* 82: 30–43.

———. 1998. "Big Five Personality Dimensions and Job Performance in Army and Civil Occupations: A European Perspective. *Human Performance* 11: 271–88.

Salovey, P., and J.D. Mayer. 1990. "Emotional Intelligence." *Imagination, Cognition, and Personality* 9: 185–211.

Schippman, J.S., E.P. Prien, and J.A. Katz. 1990. "Reliability and Validity of In-Basket Performance." *Personnel Psychology* 43: 837–59.

Schmidt, F.L., and J.E. Hunter. 1993. "Tacit Knowledge, Practical Intelligence, General Mental Ability, and Job Knowledge." *Current Directions of Psychological Science* 2: 8–9.

———. 1998. "The Validity and Utility of Selection Methods in Personnel Psychology: Practical and Theoretical Implications of 85 Years of Research Findings." *Psychological Bulletin* 124: 262–74.

Schmitt, N.A., R.Z. Gooding, R.D. Noe, and M. Kirsch. 1984. "Meta-Analyses of Validity Studies Published between 1964 and 1982 and Investigation of Study Characteristics." *Personnel Psychology* 37: 407–22.

Schmitt, N.A., J.R. Schneider, and S.A. Cohen. 1990. "Factors Affecting Validity of a Regionally Administered Assessment Center." *Personnel Psychology* 43: 2–11.

Simner, M.L. 1994. *Recommendations by the Canadian Psychological Association for Improving the Safeguards that Help Protect the Public against Test Misuse.* Ottawa: Canadian Psychological Association.

Society for Industrial and Organizational Psychology, Inc. 1987. *Principles for the Validation and Use of Personnel Selection Procedures*, 3rd ed. College Park, MD.

"Specialists Back Genetic Testing—Study." 1995. *Halifax Daily News* (December 23): 10.

Spinner, B. 1990. *Predicting Success in Basic Flying Training from the Canadian Automated Pilot Selection System* (Working Paper 90-6). Willowdale, ON: Canadian Forces Personnel Applied Research Unit.

Steiner, D.D., and S.W. Gilliland. 1996. "Fairness Reactions to Personnel Selection Techniques in France and the United States." *Journal of Applied Psychology* 81: 131–41.

Sternberg, R.J., R.K. Wagner, W.M. Williams, and J.A. Horvath. 1995. "Testing Common Sense." *American Psychologist* 50: 912–27.

Stinglhamber, F., C. Vandenberghe, and S. Brancart. 1999. "Les réactions des candidats envers les techniques de sélection de personnel: Une étude dans un contexte francophone." *Travail Humain* 62: 347–61.

"Storm Over Drug Testing: U.S.-Style Mandatory Programs Face Heavy Weather in Canada." 1992. *Financial Post* (April 21): 19.

Strauss, M. 2000. "Retailers Plagued by Thieving Employees." *The Globe and Mail* (March 28): A1.

Task Force on Assessment Center Guidelines. 1989. "Guidelines and Ethical for Assessment Center Operations." *Public Personnel Management* 18: 457–70.

Taub, G.E. 1999. "Predicting Success: A Critical Analysis of R.J. Sternberg and R.K. Wagner's Theory of Practical Intelligence: Is This an Ability beyond *g*?" *Dissertation Abstracts International: Section B—The Sciences and Engineering* 60: 0863.

Taylor, H.C., and J.F. Russell. 1939. "The Relationship of Validity Coefficients to the Practical Effectiveness of Tests in Selection: Discussion and Tables." *Journal of Applied Psychology* 23: 565–78.

Temple, W. 1992. "Counterproductive Behaviour Costs Millions." *British Journal of Administrative Management* (April/May): 20–21.

Tett, R.P., D.N. Jackson, and M. Rothstein. 1991. "Personality Measures as Predictors of Job Performance: A Meta-Analytic Review." *Personnel Psychology* 44: 703–42.

Thacker, J.W., and R.J. Cattaneo. 1987. "The Canadian Personnel Function: Status and Practices." *Proceedings of the Administrative Sciences Association of Canada Annual Meeting*, 56–66.

Thompson, C.T. 1995. "Actress to Help Test Applicants for Jobs at Prison." *Kitchener Record* (July 13): B1.

"Uniform Guidelines on Employee Selection Procedures." 1978. *Federal Register* 43: 38290–315.

Yanchinski, S. 1990. "Employees under a Microscope." *The Globe and Mail* (January 3): D3.

Zickar, M., and F. Drasgow. 1996. "Detecting Faking on a Personality Instrument Using Appropriateness Measurement." *Applied Psychological Measurement* 20: 71–87.

10

SELECTION III:
INTERVIEWING

CHAPTER GOALS

This chapter presents new and more effective alternatives to the traditional approaches to employment interviewing.

After reading this chapter you should

- understand the purposes and uses of employment interviews;
- appreciate the selection errors associated with traditional approaches to employment interviewing;
- understand the elements of employment interview structuring;
- understand different structured interviewing techniques and their relative advantages and disadvantages;
- appreciate the legal and predictive advantages of structured employment interviewing methods;
- begin developing competence in the design of effective interview questions and scoring guides;
- appreciate innovations and future directions in interview research and practice; and

- appreciate the role of employment interviews in the changing organizational environment.

The employment interview is one of the oldest and most widely used of all selection procedures (Rowe, Williams, and Day, 1994). In fact, surveys reveal that up to 99 percent of Canadian organizations use the interview as part of the selection process (Kane, 1988; Thacker and Cattaneo, 1993). Moreover, when making selection decisions, recruiters tend to have more confidence in the interview than in information provided from application forms, references, test results, or any other source of information about the applicant (Kane, 1988; Kinicki, Lockwood, Hom, and Griffeth, 1990). Given its importance to the employee selection process, it is worth devoting close attention to this selection technique.

PURPOSES AND USES OF THE INTERVIEW

Although interviews are often used as preliminary screening devices (e.g., in armed forces recruitment centres), they are most frequently one of the last stages of the selection process. Leaving the interview until the end allows the other selection instruments (e.g., tests) to screen out unqualified applicants and thus reduces the number of people who must be interviewed. It is usually desirable to reduce the number of interviewees because interviews are relatively expensive, compared with other selection instruments such as tests or the screening of résumés.

The interview is often used to collect information that has not been provided in the résumé or application form. Interviewers are typically supervisors or line managers who have little interview training (Guion, 1998). They tend to have little time available for preparing interview questions and often use standard questions, which they hear others using or which they remember having been asked when they were interviewees. In the majority of organizations, applicants are interviewed by several interviewers, either simultaneously (panel or board interviews) or in sequence (sequential or serial interviews) (Cox, Schlueter, Moore, and Sullivan, 1989; Kane, 1988).

Although interviews can be and have been used to assess job knowledge and cognitive ability, they are probably best suited to the assessment of noncognitive attributes such as interpersonal relations or social skills, initiative, conscientiousness, dependability, perseverance, teamwork, leadership skills, adaptability or flexibility, and organizational citizenship behaviour (e.g., Campion, Campion, and Hudson, 1994; Latham and Skarlicki, 1995; Motowidlo et al., 1992; Pulakos and Schmitt, 1995).

Interviews are also used to sell the job to the applicant. They provide the applicant with an opportunity to ask questions about the job or the organization and to make a decision as to whether the job and the organization are appropriate for him or her. However, research evidence suggests that interviewers' effects on applicant job choice are minimal (Rynes, 1991; Stevens, 1998). Factors such as pay, the job itself, promotion opportunities, or geographical location tend to be much more important.

Sometimes, especially in recent years, interviews are used in the termination of employees. As organizations downsize or "rightsize," jobs are eliminated and employees must compete for a smaller number of redesigned jobs. The interview serves to assist in identifiying employees who have the necessary knowledge, skills, abilities, and other attributes (KSAOs) to perform well in the redesigned jobs and thus to remain employed by the organization. Although there is considerable debate about the merits of downsizing as a cure for ailing organizations (e.g., Cascio, 1993), such interviews have become commonplace (Anonymous, 1989; Cameron, Freeman, and Mishra, 1991).

TRADITIONAL APPROACHES TO INTERVIEWING

The traditional, and still most common, approach to employment interviewing is one that has become known as an **unstructured interview**. In such interviews, the interviewer typically engages in a freewheeling conversation with the interviewee. There are no constraints on the kinds of questions that may be asked, and, furthermore, many of the questions used in the interview may not occur to the interviewer until part-way through the interview. However, most interviewers appear to rely on a common set of questions that they have heard others use. Box 10.1 presents a list of questions often used by interviewers. An examination of the list reveals that the questions invite applicants to evaluate themselves or to describe the evaluations of others. Naturally, applicants who want to create a positive impression are likely to evaluate themselves in much more favourable terms than perhaps they should when such questions are asked. Moreover, many interviewees have learned to respond to such questions with standard answers. For example, common responses to the question, "What are your weaknesses?" include "I get too involved in my work" and "I'm too much of a perfectionist." Answers to such questions reveal very little useful information about the applicant. The interviewer is forced to take on the role of an amateur psychologist trying to read meaning into vague self-evaluations, verbal expressiveness, or body language.

Some interviewees are particularly skilled at **impression management**, that is, creating a favourable impression of themselves by picking up cues from the interviewer concerning what answers the interviewer wishes to hear. They are able to monitor and change their own responses and behaviours in order to align them with those they perceive to be desired by the interviewer. By artfully guiding the conversation and making effective use of nonverbal behaviours, the polished interviewee is able to impress the interviewer and obfuscate the true purpose of the interview (Stevens and Kristof, 1995). Thus, instead of hiring the best *candidate*, the interviewer is likely to hire the most skillful *interviewee*. In fact, skillful interviewees can divert the conversation from relevant

Unstructured interview— a traditional method of interviewing that involves no constraints on the questions asked, no requirements for standardization, and a subjective assessment of the candidate.

Impression management—attempts by applicants to create a favourable impression of themselves by monitoring interviewer reactions and responding accordingly.

BOX 10.1 Commonly Used Interview Questions

1. Why did you leave your last job? (or Why do you want to leave your current job?)

2. What do you consider to be your strengths? What are your weaknesses?

3. What were your strongest subjects at school? What were your weakest subjects?

4. How would other people describe you as an individual?

5. What is your greatest accomplishment?

6. What were the most enjoyable aspects of your last job? What were the least enjoyable aspects?

7. Why do you want this job? What are you looking for from this job (or from us)?

8. Why should we hire you? What can you do for us?

9. What are your long-range plans or goals? (or Where do you plan to be five years from now?)

10. Tell me about yourself.

and important interview topics to topics that result in pleasant but uninformative conversations that cast themselves in a more favourable light. For example, upon noticing the golf trophy in an interviewer's office, such an interviewee may engage the interviewer in an amiable conversation about the game of golf that lasts most of the interview. The interviewer, left with a good feeling about the applicant, is likely to hire him or her without actually having obtained any job-relevant information from the applicant during the interview.

Another characteristic typical of unstructured interviews is that no systematic rating procedure is used. Interviewers are free to interpret interviewee responses in any manner they choose as there are no guidelines for evaluating the responses. In fact, rather than evaluating responses or answers to interview questions, the interviewer uses the interview to get a "feeling" or a "hunch" about the applicant. The interviewer emerges from the interview with a global, subjective evaluation of the applicant, which is biased by personal views and preferences and, therefore, is likely to be inaccurate. In fact, many interviewers report that they rely on such "gut feelings" in making their hiring decisions. Worse yet, some writers are still recommending such practices (e.g., Buhler, 1998).

Webster (1964, 1982) and his colleagues at McGill University, as well as Dipboye (1992) and others, have documented the numerous biases and perceptual and information-processing errors that plague the unstructured employment interview (see Box 10.4). For example, interviewers rate applicants more favourably if the applicants are perceived as being similar to themselves (e.g., Graves and Powell, 1996). Moreover, interview ratings are susceptible to first impressions (e.g., Dougherty, Turban, and Callender, 1994; Macan and Dipboye, 1990). That is, an interviewer's initial impression of an applicant, such as might be formed upon reading the résumé, affects the way he or she conducts the interview, the questions asked, and his or her

BOX 10.2 Some of the Worst Questions Asked in Actual Interviews

Although not as common as the interview questions listed in Box 10.1, the questions listed below must certainly rank among the worst used in employment interviews:

- Discuss morals.
- What's your worldview?
- Are you sure this job is right for you?
- Tell me 10 things about my desk.
- What does your dad do for a living?
- How was your childhood?
- What's your favourite fairytale and why?
- Why is an attractive woman like you not yet married?
- Why is your name hyphenated? Is it because you keep getting married and adding on names?
- We don't need another happy-go-lucky man looking for a wife working here! (to a recent social work graduate after he answered "no" to the question, "Are you married?")

- You must be inept not to have found a job by now!
- It must have been nice to not have to work all these years (to a recent college graduate).
- If you were part of a chicken, what part would you want to be?
- We like to see our team as a fruit basket, with each member complementing one another. Which piece of fruit will you be in this basket?
- We need people desperately. Would you mind taking a 10% pay cut and join us?
- We don't pay anyone what they are worth. How will you motivate yourself to excel and increase company profits without personal financial incentive?
- I know who I want to fill this position. What can you say to change my mind?

Adapted from: Gary Will. 1997. *Interview Horrors!* http://members.xoom.com/_XMCM/gwwork.

BOX 10.3 Job Interviews That Didn't Go Well

Interviewers are not the only ones mishandling interviews. Applicants do their share of bungling as well. A survey of company managers indicates that the behaviour of some graduates can be counterproductive to their primary objective: landing a job. The survey, conducted by OfficeTeam, a temporary staffing service, asked managers about funny things that happened in job interviews. Below are some of the responses.

- An extremely nervous recent graduate arrived at an interview wearing a beautiful new suit with all the tags still on the sleeve.
- An applicant brought in a pet lizard to display his "creativity."
- An applicant asked his mother to call the company while he was interviewing to see if he could be given an entry-level vice-president of operations position.

- An applicant brought his family and baby-sitter to watch the children in the company's lobby. After the interview, the family came in and asked questions such as when he would be able to start and when their health-care benefits would begin.
- A recent graduate was doing well until she said she'd be ideal for the job since she would need a year of this kind of training before starting her own company.
- A candidate's cellular phone rang. She said, "excuse me," and promptly answered the call—during the interview.

Source: Adapted from Anonymous, "Job Interviews That Didn't Go Well," *Canadian Banker* 104 (1997): 8. Reprinted with permission *Canadian Banker*, Vol. 104, No. 1, p. 8.

BOX 10.4 Research Findings on the Unstructured Interview

INTERVIEW DECISIONS

- Interviewers tend to make a hire/not hire decision before completing the interview (i.e., before all the information has been collected).

- Once a "not hire" decision is made, it is unlikely to be changed (however, tentative "hire" decisions can be reversed if negative information comes to light).

INTERVIEWER SET

- Unfavourable information provided by the applicant has greater impact on interview ratings than favourable information.

- Once interviewers have formed an impression of an applicant, they tend to look for information that will confirm their impression.

TEMPORAL PLACEMENT OF INFORMATION

- Interviewers remember information provided at the beginning of the interview better than information provided in the middle (primacy effect).

- Information provided at the end of the interview is also remembered better than information provided in the middle (recency effect).

ORDER OF INTERVIEWEES

- Interviewers seeing a series of applicants tend to remember best the first and the last applicants (they tend to confuse applicants in the middle with each other).

- An applicant's interview rating is affected by the preceding applicant (contrast effects)—they benefit if the preceding applicant was relatively poor but suffer if the preceding applicant was relatively good.

EFFECTS OF INFORMATION

- Impressions formed by the interviewer as a result of information obtained about the applicant prior to the interview (e.g., by reading the résumé) affect how the applicant is treated and rated in the interview.

- Interviewers who have more information about the job tend to have a more accurate perception (template) of what the "ideal" applicant should look like.

STEREOTYPES

- Interviewers tend to see female applicants as more suitable for certain jobs, whereas male applicants are seen as more appropriate for other jobs.

- Interviewers tend to give higher ratings to applicants who are most like them (similar-to-me effect).

VERBAL/NONVERBAL BEHAVIOUR

- An applicant's verbal skills and expressiveness affect interview ratings.

- An applicant's appearance (e.g., physical attractiveness, posture, age, clothing) and mannerisms (e.g., eye contact, handshake) affect interview ratings.

RELIABILITY AND VALIDITY

- Agreement on ratings among interviewers interviewing the same applicants tends to be quite low (low reliability).

- Correlations between interview scores and job performance ratings (for those hired) tend to be fairly low (low criterion validity).

evaluation of the candidate's answers. In addition, interview ratings are influenced by visual cues such as physical attractiveness of the applicant, eye contact, body orientation, smiling, and hand gestures as well as vocal cues such as rate of speaking, number and duration of pauses, variablility in loudness, and pitch (e.g., lower voices tend to be rated more positively than higher voices for management positions) (DeGroot and Motowidlo, 1999). Box 10.4 summarizes some of the research findings pertaining to the unstructured employment interview. These biases and errors have contributed to the poor reliability and validity of unstructured interviews.

ATTEMPTS TO IMPROVE INTERVIEW EFFECTIVENESS

Given the research on the biases and errors inherent in the unstructured interview, past reviews of employment interview research have, understandably, been rather pessimistic concerning the reliability and validity of the interview as a selection instrument (e.g., Schmitt, 1976). In contrast, the interview has remained popular among employers who seem to have considerable confidence in its usefulness for employee selection. However, over the last two decades exciting developments in interview research have changed the picture. In the early 1980s a number of researchers began working on new approaches to employment interviewing, which have become known as **structured interviews** (e.g., Janz, 1982; Latham and Saari, 1984; Latham, Saari, Pursell, and Campion, 1980). Reviews of the employment interview literature at the time indicated that structuring an interview appears to contribute to increased interview reliability and validity (Arvey and Campion, 1982; Harris, 1989; Webster, 1982). In fact, meta-analytic investigations of interview validity reveal that structured selection interviews have significantly greater reliability and predictive validity than traditional, unstructured interviews (e.g., Conway, Jako, and Goodman, 1995; Huffcutt and Arthur, 1994; McDaniel, Whetzel, Schmidt, and Maurer, 1994; Wiesner and Cronshaw, 1988). Moreover, among the variables investigated, interview structure was found to be, by far, the strongest moderator of interview validity. The effects of structure are displayed in Table 10.1, which summarizes the results of Wiesner and Cronshaw's (1988) and Huffcutt and Arthur's (1994) meta-analyses. Note the similarity of the findings in these two meta-analyses.

> **Structured interview**—an interview consisting of a standardized set of job-relevant questions and a scoring guide.

References to interview structure in selection interview literature tend to give the impression that structure is a dichotomous variable (i.e., that interviews are either structured or unstructured). However, interview structure is a function of several factors and it can vary along a continuum, ranging from very unstructured to highly structured. In fact, Huffcutt and Arthur (1994) found that interview validity increases as the degree of interview structure increases. It is therefore useful to gain an understanding of what is meant by interview "structure."

STRUCTURING EMPLOYMENT INTERVIEWS

Although there has been an apparently sudden discovery of structured employment interview techniques in recent years, their development is actually due to the contributions of numerous researchers over more than half a

TABLE 10.1 CRITERION-RELATED VALIDITY OF SELECTION INTERVIEWS

INTERVIEW SOURCE	SAMPLE SIZE[1]	NUMBER OF COEFFICIENTS	UNCORRECTED VALIDITY	CORRECTED VALIDITY[2]
Wiesner and Cronshaw (1988)				
All Studies	51 459	150	.26	.47
All Unstructured Interviews	5 518	39	.17	.31
Unstructured Individual	2 303	19	.11	.20
Unstructured Board	3 134	19	.21	.37
All Structured Interviews	10 080	48	.34	.62
Structured Individual	7 873	32	.35	.63
Structured Board	2 104	15	.33	.60
Huffcutt and Arthur (1994)				
All Studies	18 652	114	.22	.37
Structure Level 1[3]	7 308	15	.11	.20
Structure Level 2	4 621	39	.20	.35
Structure Level 3	4 358	27	.34	.56
Structure Level 4	2 365	33	.34	.57

Source: The above table is adapted from Wiesner and Cronshaw (1988) and Huffcutt and Arthur (1994).

[1]Not all studies used in the Wiesner and Cronshaw meta-analysis provided sufficient information to classify interviews as structured or unstructured.

[2]Validity coefficients are corrected for restriction of range and unreliability of the criterion measure.

[3]Structure Level 1 represents very unstructured interviews and is directly comparable to Wiesner and Cronshaw's unstructured classification. Levels 2, 3, and 4 represent increasing structure, with Level 4 representing the most highly structured interviews. Levels 3 and 4 are comparable to Wiesner and Cronshaw's structured classification.

century. These researchers sought to address what were perceived as the short-comings of the traditional, unstructured interview by applying psychometric principles to employment interview design. Over time, researchers uncovered a number of structuring elements that seemed to contribute to interview reliability and validity. Although not all interviews referred to as "structured" make use of all elements, the more of these elements that are part of the interview the more structured it is. In other words, employment interviews can be structured in a number of ways and to varying degrees. Below is a summary of components that can contribute to employment interview structure, extracted from the detailed review provided by Campion, Palmer, and Campion (1997).

1. Interview questions are derived from a job analysis (they are job-related).

2. Interview questions are standardized (all applicants are asked the same questions).

3. Prompting, follow-up questioning, probing, or elaboration on questions are limited.

4. Interview questions focus on behaviours or work samples rather than opinions or self-evaluations.

5. Interviewer access to ancillary information (e.g., résumés, letters of reference, test scores, transcripts) is controlled.

6. Questions from the candidate are not allowed until after the interview.

7. Each answer is rated during the interview using a rating scale tailored to the question (this is preferable to rating dimensions at the end of the interview and certainly preferable to making an overall rating or ranking at the end).

8. Rating scales are "anchored" with behavioural examples to illustrate scale points (e.g., examples of a "1,", "3," or "5" answer).

9. Total interview score is obtained by summing across scores for each of the questions.

10. Detailed notes are taken during the interview (such notes should be a record of applicant behaviours as related in the interview rather than evaluations of applicants; see Burnett, Fan, Motowidlo, and DeGroot, 1998).

Campion et al. (1997) also recommend using board or **panel interviews** (i.e., interviews conducted by two or more interviewers together or at the same time) or sequential or **serial interviews** (i.e., interviews conducted by two or more interviewers separately or in sequence). Such interviews should reduce the impact of biases held by an individual interviewer because each interviewer is accountable to the other interviewers. Each interviewer contributes a different perspective that should increase accuracy, and the aggregation of multiple judgments should cancel out random errors. The recall of information should also be better with multiple interviewers.

In addition, Campion et al. (1997) recommend using the same interviewer(s) across all candidates for greater standardization, not permitting interviewers to discuss candidates or answers between interviews, and providing interviewers with extensive training.

It is worth noting that Huffcutt and Arthur (1994) found no significant difference between validity coefficients for structure level 3 and structure level 4 (see Table 10.1). Their level 3 structure is characterized by partial standardization of questions. That is, interviewers may use probes or follow-up questions and, in some instances, select from a set of questions (e.g., Janz, 1982). Level 4 involves complete standardization of questions, and applicant responses to individual questions are rated during the interview using a behaviourally anchored scale (e.g., Green, Alter, and Carr, 1993; Latham et al., 1980). Huffcutt and Arthur's (1994) results suggest that even moderate levels of structure (i.e., level 3) can contribute to high interview validity.

Panel interview—an interview conducted by two or more interviewers together at one time.

Serial interviews—a series of interviews where the applicant is interviewed separately by each of two or more interviewers.

BOX 10.5 Structured Interviewing Process

Preparing for the Interview

1. Determine the amount of time available for the interview and how many questions you will be able to ask, without rushing, in that length of time.

2. Construct the interview questions, based on a job analysis such as the critical incidents technique to ensure their job relevance. Situational, patterned behaviour description, behavioural sample questions may be asked.

3. Develop a scoring guide with benchmark or sample answers. A five-point scale can be used to rate responses.

4. Make a standardized list of interview questions so that all applicants are asked the same questions, in the same order. Allow space or provide a notepad for taking notes.

5. If possible, "pilot test" the questions on some job applicants or recently hired employees in order to ensure that the questions are clear and that the scoring guide reflects the range of answers actually given by the "applicants" in your pilot study. Revise the questions or scoring guides as needed.

6. Use an office or arrange for an interview room where you can have privacy, freedom from distractions, and quiet. Ensure good lighting and ventilation, a comfortable temperature, and comfortable seating for yourself and the applicant. If applicants are to be interviewed by a panel, make sure the room is large enough to accommodate all the interviewers and the applicant comfortably and arrange for sufficient seating for all. Also, determine who will ask which questions (if asking of questions is to be shared among panel members).

7. Schedule the interviews with sufficient time for a brief break between interviews and to allow for some interviews to run a bit overtime.

8. Arrange to hold all calls and prevent interruptions during the interview. If you are interrupted to attend to a critical matter, apologize to the applicant and resolve the matter as quickly as possible, delegating it if you can.

9. Although familiarizing yourself with the applicant's résumé and references before the interview can facilitate rapport building and communicate your interest, it can bias your evaluation of the applicant during the interview. Either restrict your review of the résumé to relatively objective information, such as education or previous employment, or explain to the applicant that you have purposefully avoided reading the résumé and references to allow the interview to give you a fresh, unbiased perspective.

Conducting the Interview

1. Spend a few minutes at the beginning of the interview putting the applicant at ease. Greet the applicant by name. Introduce yourself and other interview panel members (if there are others). Indicate where the applicant is to sit. Provide the applicant with an overview of the interview process, indicating the general time frame and what topics you will be exploring in the interview. Tell the applicant that you will be taking notes during the interview and that you will be happy to answer questions at the end.

2. Ask each question in turn without omitting or skipping any. Let the candidate know he or she has lots of time to answer and you don't mind him or her taking time to think. Allow silence.

3. If the applicant seems confused or stuck, rephrase the question but don't do so too quickly. If the applicant still has difficulty, indicate you will come back to the question later.

4. Take detailed notes of the applicant's responses, focusing on behaviours described by the applicant. Your notes should not be evaluative.

BOX 10.5 Continued

5. Use the scoring guides to score the answers to interview questions as soon as possible—either during the interview or immediately after.

6. Sum the scores across interview questions to arrive at a total score for the interview.

7. Allow the applicant to ask questions at the end of the interview and answer them to the best of your ability without committing to a decision or any kind of preference.

8. Follow the same procedures for each applicant and retain interview documentation for future reference.

CLOSING THE INTERVIEW

1. Tell the candidate when he or she should expect to hear from you, or someone else in your organization, and how you will communicate your decision (e.g., telephone, e-mail, letter).

2. If you are likely to contact referees or call the applicant back for a second interview, inform the applicant.

3. Thank the applicant for coming in for the interview. Escort him or her to the door and take your leave.

4. Review your notes and make your ratings (if you have not already done so). If the interview was conducted by a panel, briefly meet with the panel and compare your ratings. Discuss and resolve large discrepancies. Either average the ratings (if discrepancies are not large) or arrive at a consensus rating.

5. Combine the interview scores with scores from other selection instruments, such as tests, references, or application forms, to arrive at a total rating for each candidate (see Chapter 11).

6. Make sure you inform all candidates of your decision when you have made it. It's a common practice to hold back on informing second- or third-choice candidates in case the first- and/or second-choice candidates turn down the offer. If you do so, inform the remaining candidates as soon as the offer has been accepted. Thank the candidates who were not accepted for their interest in the job and the organization.

STRUCTURED EMPLOYMENT INTERVIEW TECHNIQUES

THE SITUATIONAL INTERVIEW

One of the recent approaches to structured interviewing is the **situational interview** (SI) used by Latham and others (see Latham, 1989). The interviewer describes to the applicant hypothetical situations that are likely to be encountered on the job and asks the applicant what he or she would do in the situations. The interviewer then uses a **scoring guide** consisting of sample answers to each question to evaluate and score the applicant's answers. The scoring guide is designed using the critical incidents technique (Flanagan, 1954), in

Situational interview—a highly structured interview in which hypothetical situations are described and applicants are asked what they would do.

Scoring guide—a behavioural rating scale consisting of sample answers to each question used by the interviewer to evaluate and score the applicant's answers.

which examples of actual job-related behaviours that varied in effectiveness in particular situations are collected and refined to serve as sample answers. Thus, numerical values on the scale are illustrated with examples of answers that would be worth a 1 or a 3 or a 5. An example of an SI question is provided in Table 10.2. Please note that the scoring guide is only visible to the interviewer(s), not to the interviewee. Cover up the scoring guide in Table 10.2 with your hand and try answering the question. Once you have answered the question, compare your answer with the scoring guide.

The scoring guide for an SI question should be based on behaviours that have been shown to be either effective or ineffective in that situation in the past. However, because organizations differ, what is an effective response in one organization may not be effective in another. Thus, the scoring guide might differ from one company to another. In the example in Table 10.2, applicants who indicate that they would ignore the supervisor's remarks and insist on following through on the initial decision would be ignoring potentially important information. The result might be a serious mistake, which could cost the company considerable money. Such a response would not score well. Doing what the supervisor suggests or openly discussing the merits of the supervisor's suggestion might result in a good decision being made. However, this course of action would likely undermine the new manager's authority.

The ideal answer does not have to be given exactly as written in the scoring guide. However, the interviewer would be looking for evidence that the applicant recognizes the dynamics at play in the situation and understands basic principles of human behaviour. First, it is important to recognize that

TABLE 10.2 EXAMPLE OF A SITUATIONAL INTERVIEW QUESTION

You have just been hired as the manager of our purchasing department and it's your first day on the job. After carefully reviewing product and price information, you make a decision to purchase parts from a particular supplier. Your immediate subordinate, an experienced supervisor who is considerably older than you, questions your judgment in front of other employees and seems quite convinced that you are making a mistake. The employees look to you for a response, some of them smirking. What would you do?

Scoring Guide

1—I would tell the supervisor that I'm in charge and I am going with my initial decision.

3—I would do what the supervisor suggests as he knows the suppliers and materials better than I do *or* I would openly discuss the merits of his suggestion versus my own judgment.

5—Take the supervisor to a private place, thank him for the information, but instruct him never to question you in front of the employees again. Then, after asking him for information on the best supplier and dismissing him, I would think about the options again and after a brief period announce *my* decision to go with the supplier suggested in our private conversation.

there is the potential for a serious mistake if the manager persists in the original course of action. Second, the applicant should recognize that the manager's authority is being undermined, whether intentionally or not. The fact that the supervisor raises the issue in front of the employees and some of them are smirking suggests that there might be a test of leadership going on. Thus, the manager needs to determine the truthfulness of the supervisor's remarks and to assert authority. Recognizing that these objectives would best be accomplished in a private conversation reveals an understanding of human nature. Confronting the supervisor in public might make the supervisor defensive and evoke a need for him to "save face" in front of the employees. As much as possible, the manager needs to claim the final decision as his or her own.

The interviewer's task is to compare the applicant's answers with the examples on the scoring guides and to score the answers accordingly. There may be instances where an answer falls somewhere between two scoring guide examples (e.g., better than a 3 answer but not as good as a 5 answer). Under such circumstances, the interviewer has the discretion of assigning an intermediate score (e.g., a 4 or even a 4.5).

The assumption underlying the SI approach is that intentions are related to subsequent behaviours (Fishbein and Ajzen, 1975). Critics of this approach have argued that what applicants say they would do in a given situation and what they actually do may be quite different. However, a convincing counter-argument is that just *knowing* what the appropriate response should be can differentiate effective from ineffective performers. In a recent meta-analysis of the situational interview across 18 studies, Latham and Sue-Chan (1999) obtained a criterion validity coefficient of .35 (.47 with corrections for criterion unreliability and range restriction). Although not reported in the meta-analysis, a cursory review of the published studies suggests that the mean inter-rater reliability is in excess of .80.

THE COMPREHENSIVE STRUCTURED INTERVIEW

Campion, Pursell, and Brown (1988), in what has become known as the **comprehensive structured interview** (CSI) (Harris, 1989), combine situational interview questions with questions assessing job knowledge, job simulation questions, and worker characteristic or willingness questions. The job knowledge questions assess the degree to which the applicant possesses relevant job knowledge (e.g., "When putting a piece of machinery back together after repairing it, why would you clean all the parts first?"). The job simulation questions assess job-relevant verbal skills (e.g., "Many jobs require the operation of a forklift. Please read this [ninety-word] forklift procedure aloud."). Finally, the worker willingness questions assess the applicant's willingness to engage in particular activities (e.g., "Some jobs require climbing ladders to a height of a five-storey building and going out on a catwalk to work. Give us your feeling about performing a task such as this."). Campion et al. (1988) were

Comprehensive structured interview—a highly structured interview consisting of a combination of situational interview, job knowledge, job simulation, and worker characteristic or willingness questions.

able to predict job performance as well using this approach ($r = .34$ [.56 with corrections for criterion unreliability and range restriction]; reliability is estimated at .88).

THE BEHAVIOUR DESCRIPTION INTERVIEW

Behaviour description interview—a structured interview in which the applicant is asked to describe what he or she did in given situations in the past.

Finally, Janz (1982; 1989), following up on a suggestion made by Latham et al. (1980) and based on Ghiselli's (1966) findings, used another approach, which he refers to as the patterned behaviour description interview (PBDI). Recent variations of this approach are called behavioural interviews (BI) or **behaviour description interviews** (BDI). The interviewer is asked to predict the interviewee's behaviours in a given job situation based on the interviewee's descriptions of his or her behaviours in similar situations in the past. Table 10.3 provides an example of a BDI question based on the same critical incidents, and thus the same dynamics, as were used in the development of the SI question in Table 10.2. However, because BDI questions are concerned with past behaviours in a potentially wide variety of settings, their inquiry must be more general. Therefore, the goal in designing BDI questions is to make the questions apply to as wide a variety of previous experiences or situations as possible. A comparison of the questions in Tables 10.2 and 10.3 reveals that the BDI question is likely to generate responses with considerably broader scope than the SI question. Whereas the SI question relates to a very specific situation, the BDI could elicit descriptions of a wide variety of situations, depending on the applicants' experiences. One applicant might relate an experience as the chair on the board of directors of an organization, whereas another applicant might discuss his or her experience as a member of a group working on an assignment at school.

Probes—follow-up questions or prompts used by the interviewer to guide the applicant's descriptions of situations or events or to provide elaboration of answers.

The broad nature of BDI questions and probable responses makes it likely that the interviewer will need to clarify the applicant's answers in order to allow them to be scored accurately. Follow-up questions or **probes** are used to guide the applicant's descriptions of situations or events until sufficient information is obtained to permit scoring. Some probes are written in advance, as in the example in Table 10.3, in anticipation of probable responses and with consideration of the information that will be required for scoring. However, the interviewer is permitted to supplement the list of probes with additional probes during the interview if the information obtained is insufficient to make a rating. Probing to obtain required information without giving away the content of the ideal answer requires considerable skill on the part of the interviewer.

The example in Table 10.3 contains a scoring guide similar to the one used for the SI question. Initial approaches to BDI did not include the use of scoring guides but, rather, had interviewers rate applicants on various dimensions or traits (e.g., motivation) based on their responses to interview questions (see Janz, Hellervik, and Gilmore, 1986). The process of translating answers to dimension ratings was a rather subjective one, for scores would be derived on

TABLE 10.3 EXAMPLE OF A PATTERNED BEHAVIOUR DESCRIPTION INTERVIEW QUESTION

We all encounter situations in which our judgment is challenged. Tell me about a time when you were not certain you had made the right decision and then someone openly challenged your decision. What did you do?

Probes: What aspect of your decision were you uncertain about?
Did the person who challenged you have essential information that you did not possess?
Could anyone overhear the person's challenge?
What issues and possible consequences did you consider in responding to this person's challenge?
What was your final decision and what was the outcome?

Scoring Guide

1—I told the person that I was in charge and I was sticking with my decision.

3—I changed my mind and did what the person suggested *or* I openly discussed the merits of his/her suggestion (in front of others).

5—I took the person to a private place and thanked him or her for the advice but asked not to be questioned in front of other people. Then, after asking the person for suggestions, I took some time to reconsider the options and consequences. I made the decision that had the greatest probability of success, regardless of where the ideas came from, but made it clear it was *my* decision.

---

the basis of impressions gained by interviewers listening to answers to various questions. There was no direct correspondence between any one question and any one dimension. Such an approach would be expected to compromise interview reliability and validity (see the next section below). Recent approaches to the BDI or BI have incorporated scoring guides (e.g., Green et al., 1993; Motowidlo et al., 1992).

Note that the BDI question in Table 10.3 requests information that the applicant might construe as negative and might thus be reluctant to provide. When asking questions that might be viewed as requesting negative information, it is helpful to begin the question with what is called a *disarming statement*. In the example, the disarming statement communicates to the applicant that it is normal and perfectly acceptable to have had one's judgment challenged. The disarming statement is intended to reduce the likelihood that the applicant will deny having experienced this situation and to set the applicant at ease about discussing it freely.

Like the SI and CSI, the BDI is an attempt to apply Wernimont and Campbell's (1968) suggestion that the predictor should sample behaviours that are representative of criterion behaviours (i.e., a work sample). However, in contrast to the SI, the BDI approach is based on the premise that the best predictor of future behaviour is past behaviour. Critics of this approach have argued that people learn from past mistakes and that situational factors (e.g., relations with supervisors, tasks, organizational norms) constrain behaviour. Therefore, past behaviours will not necessarily be repeated in the future, particularly if the situation is somewhat different or if learning has taken place. However, after describing negative experiences, applicants can be asked to indicate if they would repeat the behaviour next time or to relate an experience where they were successful in a similar situation. A number of researchers (Campion et al., 1994; Green et al., 1993; Janz, 1982; Latham and Saari, 1984; Motowidlo et al., 1992; Orpen, 1985; Pulakos and Schmitt, 1995) obtained significant criterion-related validity coefficients using the BDI (mean weighted r across studies = .32 [uncorrected], inter-rater reliability is .73).

COMPARISON OF THE STRUCTURED INTERVIEW APPROACHES

According to the research evidence available to date (see above), validity coefficients for the SI, CSI, and BDI seem to be quite similar (.35, .34, and .32, respectively [uncorrected]). However, these comparisons are indirect because, in most studies, researchers examined either the SI or the BDI (there very few studies of the CSI). A few competitive tests of the BDI and SI approaches have been conducted (Campion et al., 1994; Latham and Saari, 1984; Latham and Skarlicki, 1995; Mosher, 1991; Pulakos and Schmitt, 1995). Unfortunately, the results of these studies are conflicting and inconclusive and, taken together, do not suggest that either approach has an advantage in terms of predictive validity.

Predictive validity issues notwithstanding, the BDI appears to be more appropriate in some selection situations whereas the SI and CSI appear to be more appropriate in others. In particular, the BDI seems best suited to the selection of candidates who have had prior work experience (especially in related areas of work) or have been engaged in relevant volunteer activities or hobbies. The job knowledge questions, and possibly the job simulation and worker characteristics questions, of the CSI also appear better suited to applicants with related experience. However, the situational questions of the CSI and the SI are useful with both experienced and inexperienced applicants. Experienced applicants may still have some advantage over inexperienced applicants competing for the same job when situational questions are asked, but the difference would likely be reduced.

As noted above, interviewers appear to require a fair degree of skill in order to conduct the BDI effectively. The SI or CSI might therefore be more foolproof in the hands of supervisors and line managers when they do the interviewing. The SI and CSI seem to require less skill or training because the interviewer simply reads the questions and compares the answers given with the scoring guide examples. Probing is not permitted. If the BDI is to be used, a thorough training program is highly recommended.

It is important to recognize that the above discussion of the relative merits of the two approaches is somewhat speculative. More research is needed to investigate the relative merits of the BDI and the SI in various situations and with varying degrees of interviewer training and experience. In addition to addressing the theoretical questions surrounding the relationships of past behaviour and behavioural intentions with subsequent behaviour, such research would provide highly useful information for improving the design of structured interviews. It may well be that both SI and BDI approaches could be used effectively in tandem within one interview session. Applicants who have difficulty answering a BDI question because of a lack of relevant work experience could be asked a corresponding SI question. Alternatively, SI questions could be followed by corresponding BDI questions in order to determine whether the behavioural intentions are consistent with past behaviours.

INTERVIEW PRACTICE AND THE LAW

As noted above, one of the hallmarks of structured interviews is the standardization of interview questions. When interviews are standardized, applicants can be compared on the basis of the same criteria and the interviewer obtains a better picture of the merits of each applicant relative to other applicants. In fact, a number of researchers have suggested that standardization may contribute to increased interview reliability and validity (see Campion et al., 1997).

Equally, if not more important, the standardized treatment of applicants is perceived as being fairer than nonstandardized treatment in today's society. The likelihood of organizations that use standardized interview questions becoming embroiled in selection-related litigation is therefore reduced. Moreover, when such organizations do go to court, the courts tend to rule in their favour (Gardiner and Hackett, 1996; Gatewood and Feild, 1998; Hackett, Rose, and Pyper, 1999; Williamson et al., 1997). Standardization therefore gives the interviewer and organization some measure of protection from discrimination suits.

Another aspect of structured interviews that appears to have a strong impact on the organization's ability to defend itself against litigation is the exclusive use of job-related questions (i.e., questions based on a formal job analysis). Questions that probe areas not directly relevant to the job run the risk of being interpreted as having discriminatory intent by the applicant and by the courts (Gardiner and Hackett, 1996; Gatewood and Feild, 1998; Hackett et al., 1999; Williamson et al., 1997). A question such as "Do you plan to have children?" which is frequently posed to female but not to male applicants, is not only unrelated to job requirements but treats male and female applicants differently (i.e., is unstandardized). Such questions are particularly troublesome from a human rights perspective.

The job relevance of interview questions has a significant impact on interview validity as well (Campion et al., 1997). Structured interviews may have greater predictive validity, in part, because structuring an interview increases its reliability and accuracy in differentiating between applicant competencies on job-relevant dimensions. Moreover, the greater job relevance of structured interview questions may direct the interviewer's attention away from irrelevant information and focus it on job-relevant information. This focusing of interviewer attention may reduce the potential effects of the biases and processing errors inherent in the unstructured interview. Therefore, the degree to which structured interview questions are job-relevant and interview ratings are reliable appears to determine the validity of the interview. However, the job relevance of interview questions does not, by itself, guarantee the reliability of interview ratings. Interviewers often disagree in their ratings of the same dimensions or characteristics for a given applicant and even give different ratings for the same answer to an interview question. Therefore, some kind of job-relevant rating or scoring guide is essential if high reliability among raters is to be achieved and if the interview ratings are to be based on job-relevant criteria. In fact such scoring guides appear to increase interview reliability, and therefore validity, particularly when they are used to assess the answers given by interviewees rather than trait dimensions (Campion et al., 1997).

The use of a standardized, job-relevant scoring system for assessing and comparing candidates may also contribute to an effective defence against litigation (Cronshaw, 1989; Gardiner and Hackett, 1996; Hackett et al., 1999). The courts have been particularly concerned when there is evidence that applicants giving the same responses are treated differently on the basis of gender or race or any other grounds on which discrimination is forbidden. To build on a previous example, it is insufficient for an employer to standardize the interview by asking both male and female applicants whether they intend to have children if a male's response to the question is irrelevant to the selection decision whereas a female's response might determine whether or not she is offered the job (i.e., the *scoring* of responses is not standardized).

Latham et al.'s (1980) approach requires interviewers to sum the scores given for each individual question to give an overall interview score, rather than permitting interviewers to make global judgments. The final score can then be used to make the selection decision by ranking candidates or by determining cutoff scores, which must be exceeded by candidates if they are to qualify for the job. In essence, this approach relieves the interviewer of much of the decision-making function and isolates the selection decision from the interviewer's biases and stereotypes (Webster, 1982). The selection decision, then, is a statistical or actuarial process that has greater criterion-related validity than the error-prone judgmental processes typically engaged in by interviewers when they make overall ratings or recommendations (see Campion et al., 1997). This advantage for the statistical combination of scores does not appear to hold, however, when low-job-relevance interview questions are used. Rather than evaluating behaviours, interviewers using such questions make subjective judgments with respect to each answer given (Wiesner, 1989). The total interview score for such questions therefore represents the sum of several subjective judgments, which do not differ significantly from a single overall subjective rating.

It should be emphasized, with respect to the discussion above, that interview validity and reliability issues are very much related in that reliability can place an upper limit on validity (e.g., Nunnally, 1978). In fact, Wiesner and Cronshaw (1988) found that interview validity and reliability were correlated at .48 in the studies they examined. Conditions that serve to make interviews more reliable should therefore be the same as those that make them more valid.

Although unstructured interviews are vulnerable targets of potential litigation, several researchers have examined and found comparatively little evidence of bias in structured interviews. Arvey et al. (1987) found no evidence of age or gender bias in their semi-structured interviews. Similarly, in their investigation of over 27 000 structured interviews for 18 different jobs, Blankenship and Cesare (1993) found no evidence of bias on the basis of age. Although Lin, Dobbins, and Farh (1992) also found no evidence of age bias in their structured interview, they found a very small effect for race. That is, interview panels or boards consisting of all black interviewers gave slightly higher scores to black applicants than did panels or boards made up of all white interviewers (ratings did not differ for white or Hispanic applicants). However, Lin et al. (1992) found less evidence of race bias when structured interviews were used than when unstructured interviews were used. Moreover, they note that the true performance levels of the applicants are unknown. Nevertheless, they recommended the use of mixed-race interview boards to reduce the potential for bias.

Paullin (1993) reviews seven studies, including four conducted by Motowidlo et al. (1992), and finds no consistent trends for bias with respect to gender or race or ethnic group. Any differences that do exist tend to be less than half a standard deviation and do not consistently favour any group. Finally, Huffcutt and Roth (1998) conducted a meta-analysis of 31 studies to assess racial group differences in employment interview scores. Like Lin et al. (1992), they found differences in ratings were quite small for structured interviews and much less than for unstructured interviews. The studies represent a variety of jobs including marketing, entry-level management, nonmanagerial telecommunications jobs, and firefighting. Not only are structured interviews less vulnerable to bias than unstructured interviews, but applicants perceive them as more job-related and, thus, fairer (Harris, 1993; Williamson et al., 1997). Consequently, applicants are less likely to contest decisions made on the basis of structured interviews.

DESIGNING INTERVIEW QUESTIONS

Although a variety of job analysis methods can be used to develop structured interview questions, the most common is the critical incidents technique (Campion et al., 1997). The critical incidents technique has been the basis of both the SI and the BDI. Examples of effective and ineffective as well as typical behaviours that contributed to the success or failure of employees in particular situations or tasks on the job should be collected. Each important task or situation should thus be linked with several examples of typical, effective, and ineffective behaviours. This information can be obtained from incumbents and their supervisors through interviews, focus group sessions, and questionnaires.

Once the critical incidents have been collected, the situations on which they are based can be turned into CSI, BDI, or SI questions. For SI questions, the situation should be described in sufficient detail to allow an applicant to visualize it accurately and should be followed by a "what would you do?" question. For each situation, the best critical incidents (i.e., most representative and most likely to be used as answers by interviewees) demonstrating effective, typical, and ineffective behaviours serve as behavioural anchors for the scoring guide (i.e., poor, average, and good answer, respectively). Scores are assigned so that 1 represents the poor answer, 3 an average answer, and 5 a good answer.

Care should be taken to select situations and phrase questions in a way that does not make the best answer readily apparent to the applicant. Situations where there is tension between competing demands or options are ideal if the options appear equally aversive or attractive to inexperienced individuals (i.e., there is a dilemma). Questions and scoring guides should be pretested on a group of applicants or recently hired employees to ensure that the questions are clear and elicit a range of responses. For example, if the poor answer is never given, the answers that are given should be examined to determine whether some of them reflect an alternative critical incident representing ineffective performance. Alternatively, the question should be reworked to create more tension.

BDI questions are designed by examining each task or situation in order to identify the behavioural dimension underlying the situation (e.g., meeting deadlines). The dimensions are turned into BDI questions, which retain the essence rather than the details of the original situation. In other words, the BDI question applies to a variety of situations that share the underlying behavioural dimension (e.g., meeting deadlines in a job, at school, when sending birthday cards, etc.). As with the SI, critical incidents are used to develop a scoring guide. However, the scoring guide anchors also need to be rephrased to make them more generally applicable to a variety of situations. The underlying behavioural dimensions rather than the actual incidents serve as anchors (e.g., "planning ahead, setting up contingency plans, monitoring progress" instead of "working long hours at the last minute, asking for extensions, missing the deadline").

Probes are developed by anticipating the kinds of responses that applicants from different backgrounds or with different levels of experience are likely to give to a BDI question. For example, applicants with limited work experience might never have been in a situation where they disagreed with a superior. A probe might then focus on responses to a disagreement with parents or friends in a situation similar to the one of relevance to the job. The probes should provide a clear understanding of the situation, the behaviour, and the outcome so that the applicant's response can be accurately scored. General probes like "What led up to the situation?" "What did you do?" "What happened?" "What was your reason for ...?" or "Can you tell me more about ...?" seem to apply in most circumstances.

Job knowledge or job simulation questions can also be derived from critical incidents. The situations that lead to ineffective or effective behaviours can be simulated during the interview. For example, if problems have occurred on the job because solvents have been mixed or used inappropriately and if a contributing factor is functional illiteracy, applicants could be asked to read the directions on a solvent container aloud and then to explain in their own words what the directions mean. Similarly, an applicant could be asked to "sell" a product to interviewers playing the roles of the kinds of customers who have been challenging for salespeople in the past.

INTERVIEWER TRAINING

Interviewer training has tended to focus on reducing common sources of bias and inaccuracy such as halo error, similar-to-me effects, contrast effects, and leniency and severity errors. Interviewers are also taught to put the applicant at ease, ask open-ended questions, develop good listening skills, maintain control of the interview, take appropriate notes, and ignore or interpret correctly the nonverbal behaviours occurring in the interview. Unfortunately, such training efforts have achieved mixed results at best (Dipboye, 1992). Most studies report that interviewer training designed to eliminate halo and other rating biases has minimal effect on interviewer behaviour and interview outcomes, particularly when shorter training programs are examined.

Training interviewers to administer a structured interview is a considerably different endeavour than training them to avoid errors and biases or develop good listening skills. Although rapport building is an important skill, interviewers using structured interviews need to learn how to evaluate answers and use scoring guides as well as how to take notes (Campion et al., 1997). For example, interviewers require training on how to score an answer when it does not match the examples in the scoring guide. The training should provide interviewers with decision rules to use in such circumstances. Interviewers using techniques that allow more discretion, such as the BDI, might require more extensive training than those using more standardized approaches such as the SI. When there is discretion, interviewers need to learn how to select questions or probes and when to probe. They need to learn how to use probes effectively without giving away the ideal answer. Demonstrations, behavioural role modelling, and opportunities for active practice are likely to be essential training techniques in any such training program (Campion et al., 1997; Dipboye, 1992). Training that focuses on the evaluation and scoring of applicant answers has been found to contribute to higher interview reliability and validity (Conway et al., 1995; Huffcutt and Woehr, 1999).

FUTURE DIRECTIONS FOR INTERVIEW RESEARCH AND PRACTICE

THE BEHAVIOURAL SAMPLE INTERVIEW

Behavioural sample interview—one of several structured interview techniques, including job knowledge interviews, work sample interviews, and walk-through interviews, that require the demonstration of behaviours in the present.

A relatively new concept in selection interviewing is what might be referred to as the work sample interview or **behavioural sample interview** (BSI). Whereas the SI focuses on future behaviours (behavioural intentions) and the BDI focuses on past behaviours, the BSI is concerned with behaviour in the present. It could be argued that a sampling of an applicant's current behaviour should be a better predictor of job performance than either behavioural intentions or past behaviours. What applicants say or even believe they will do and what they actually do in a given situation can be quite different. Similarly, because applicants can learn from mistakes and change over time, a past behaviour may not be repeated in the future.

Several approaches have been taken to behavioural sample interviewing, but they are all concerned with current behaviour. Campion et al. (1988) used job knowledge questions as well as work sample questions in their comprehensive structured interview, and Wright et al. (1989) describe the use of similar questions by themselves and by Kennedy (1985). Examples of these job knowledge and work sample questions are provided in the section on comprehensive structured interviews. Essentially, work sample questions require the applicant to demonstrate a skill or competence (i.e., provide work sample) during the interview (e.g., "If this item costs $5.67 and I give you $10, how much change should I get?" or "Sell me this paperweight.").

A related approach to work sample interviewing involves role-playing. One of the interviewers or an assistant plays a foil to the role played by the applicant while the interviewer or others observe and evaluate. The Edmonton Police Service uses such a role-play to assess assertiveness in candidates. The applicant is to assume he or she has just set up a chair to watch a parade. The chair happens to be similar to ones set up by the city for public use. The applicant is told to assume that he or she has left the chair unattended in order to get a drink and returns to find the chair occupied (by the foil). The applicant's task is to convince the foil to vacate the chair without resorting to aggressive behaviour (physical or verbal).

Another approach to the BSI is the walk-through interview used by Hedge and Teachout (1992) and Ree, Earles, and Teachout (1994) to select U.S. Air Force enlistees. The walk-through interview involves asking the interviewees to describe in detail, step-by-step, how they perform a job-related task while visualizing themselves performing the task.

Like the SI and BDI, the behavioural sample interview can be derived from the critical incidents through focused group sessions. Scoring guides should also be developed using the procedures described for the SI and BDI. However, in some respects, the BSI may be a little more difficult to construct than either the SI or BDI. Care must be taken when simulating situations in the interview setting to ensure fidelity to the actual situation. Due to the length of time required to administer some of the BSI questions, fewer of them are likely usable in one session. They should therefore be selected judiciously to assess the most important performance domains. Nevertheless, the behavioural sample interview offers yet-unexplored potential for predicting job performance.

LONG-DISTANCE INTERVIEWS

Many organizations recruit candidates across the country or internationally. However, the costs of flying candidates in for interviews and paying for their accommodations or, conversely, flying recruiters across the country or overseas can be prohibitive. As a result, some organizations have turned to telephone interviews, videoconference interviews, or computerized interviews as alternatives to face-to-face interviews. Although preliminary evidence suggests that long-distance, structured interviews can be valid predictors of job performance (e.g., Schmidt and Rader, 1999), there is also evidence that the use of technology can, in some circumstances, make the interview an unsatisfying, or even unpleasant, experience for both the applicant and the interviewer (e.g., Martin and Nagao, 1989). Moreover, there are a number of obstacles, such as limited access to videoconferencing facilities, high costs, and technical limitations (e.g., picture and sound quality) that need to be overcome if such technology is to be used effectively (e.g., Meckenbach, 1997). More research is needed on applicant and interviewer reactions as well as on the validity of such technology-dependent interviews compared with face-to-face interviews.

OTHER RESEARCH ISSUES

Although there is indisputable evidence that structured interviews are good predictors of job performance, we do not have a clear understanding of why they predict (Campion et al., 1997). More research based on good theoretical models of the structured interview is needed to provide a better understanding of the mechanisms responsible for interview effectiveness. Such research would contribute greatly to improvements in interview design and performance. Despite the predictive validity of structured interviews, many employers and applicants have responded negatively to them. Some employers resist using structured interviews or modify them, possibly because they want more control of the interview process. Likewise, some applicants do not like structured interviews, possibly because they have less influence on the interview process. Research is needed to find ways of improving user reactions to structured interviews and making them easier to use.

THE CHANGING WORKPLACE

Organizations are undergoing change at an accelerating rate (Daft, 1997). They must adapt to unanticipated innovations in technology, global competition, changing labour force demographics, and increasing government regulation and societal pressures for conformity to ethical, environmental, and human rights standards if they are to survive (Porter, 1991). The need for organizations to be responsive to such pressures for change is having a profound impact on the way jobs are defined. Until recently, job descriptions remained relatively static or evolved gradually over time as the need arose. In many occupations (e.g., secretary-typist) the kind of work employees did at the beginning of their career was not substantially different from the work done prior to retirement. Job requirements have become much more dynamic, however, because of the increased need for organizations to change in order to remain competitive. In secretarial occupations, for example, typewriters have been replaced by word processors and word processors, in turn, are undergoing rapid evolution. It is not at all inconceivable that in the very near future the requirements for a given job may be very different from one year to the next.

The increasingly dynamic nature of most job requirements has a number of important implications for developments in the field of employee selection in general and for the employment interview in particular. Until recently, the accepted approach to employee selection involved conducting a job analysis, determining employee specifications (KSAOs required to do the job as defined by the job analysis) using a panel of job experts, and developing or specifying selection instruments that are most appropriate for assessing the KSAOs (Gatewood and Feild, 1998). The job analysis typically involves using one or more methods to gather detailed information about worker activities or behaviours, what is produced or accomplished, the equipment used, the context and other factors of the work environment, and the personal characteristics that incumbents need to do the job. The most basic level of analysis is the individual tasks that are performed.

This approach provides a fairly accurate view of the job at the time the job analysis is conducted. However, given the increasing pressure for organizational change and innovation outlined above, the job might be substantially changed several months (or even weeks) later. Under such conditions the job analysis provides accurate and useful information for only a limited time. In fact, by the time the job analysis information has been used to develop selection instruments and these instruments are being used to select applicants, the job information, and therefore the selection instrument, may no longer be valid. Even if an applicant is appropriately selected, a year or two later the job may have changed sufficiently to require a different set of abilities or skills that the employee may not possess.

In addition, many organizations are beginning to rotate employees through a number of positions in order to maintain flexibility. The tasks such employees are asked to perform are determined by need and such needs are often difficult to predict. These employees must therefore be flexible as well as multiskilled. The prospect of rapidly evolving jobs and the creation of new jobs obviously calls for a more effective approach to employee selection.

In recent years, researchers have turned their attentions to aspects of job performance such as organizational citizenship, prosocial behaviour, and contextual performance, which are distinct from task performance (e.g., Motowidlo and Van Scotter, 1994; Organ and Konovsky, 1989). Organizational citizenship, prosocial behaviour, and contextual performance involve discretionary and predispositional variables such as demonstrating initiative, volunteering, making an extra effort, persisting, helping, cooperating, following rules, and supporting the organization in various ways. It is quite likely that such aspects of job performance will become more important in the changing workplace because they tend to apply across a wide variety of tasks or jobs (e.g., Borman and Motowidlo, 1993; Organ, 1988).

Of course, basic knowledge or skills pertinent to the occupation will continue to be important. A secretary, for example, will generally need to know how to type (although there are indications that in the near future keyboards, as we know them, will disappear). However, specific knowledge or skills, such as knowledge of a particular word-processing software package, will diminish in importance. Specific or specialized skills and knowledge are the most susceptible to change. For example, word-processing software is constantly being revised and may well be replaced by different software from another company if that software better meets the needs of the organization. Rather than trying to keep pace with the specific skill requirements for a job, employers would be well advised to focus more on the enduring competencies related to organizational citizenship or contextual performance. Given the continual changes to be faced by employees in innovative organizations, some additional applicant characteristics that are likely to become vital include adaptability or flexibility, ability to handle ambiguity and stress, ability to learn (and relearn), creativity and problem-solving abilities, and various prosocial skills. Structured employment interviews are well suited to assessing most of the abilities or competencies listed above and have been successfully used for this purpose (e.g., Campion et al., 1994; Frese, Fay, Hilburger, Leng, and Tag, 1997; Latham and Skarlicki, 1995).

Summary

Employment interviews are still a popular selection procedure among employers. However, most employers continue to use traditional, unstructured approaches to interviewing. These unstructured interviews have poor validity and place the employer in a legally vulnerable position. Structured approaches to employment interviewing, such as situational interviews, comprehensive structured interviews, patterned behaviour description interviews, and recent innovations such as behavioural sample interviews, provide improved predictive validity and are more legally defensible. Such interviews need to be based on a job analysis so that they assess only job-relevant attributes. Interview questions should be nontransparent and tend to be most effective when they centre on situations involving tension between competing demands. Appropriate scoring guides and rater training are essential to maintaining high rating accuracy. As job requirements change in response to the ever-changing workplace, organizations are beginning to shift the focus of selection from specific job skills to organizational fit, transferable skills, and personality attributes. Structured employment interviews are well suited to assessing such attributes and will continue to play an important role in selection for the workplace of tomorrow.

KEY TERMS

Behavioural sample interview, p. 422

Behaviour description interview, p. 414

Comprehensive structured interview, p. 413

Impression management, p. 403

Panel interview, p. 409

Probes, p. 414

Scoring guide, p. 411

Serial interviews, p. 409

Situational interview, p. 411

Structured interview, p. 407

Unstructured interview, p. 403

EXERCISES

Interview Question Writing

1. Are the following good interview questions? If not, how would you change them?

"How did you get along with your supervisor?"

"Do you follow policies, rules, and procedures carefully?"

2. "Are you an organized worker?" is obviously not a good interview question because it is transparent and requests a self-evaluation. Is the following wording satisfactory? If not, why not, and how would you change it?

"Can you give me an example of how organized you are?"

3. Rewrite the following questions to make them more effective.

   a. Are you able to handle stress?

   b. How are you at meeting deadlines?

   c. Do you have problems working closely with others?

   d. When you make a mistake, what do you do to fix it?

   e. How are you at solving problems?

   f. Do have any problems communicating with people?

   g. How do you feel about staying late to finish a project?

   h. Are you a good leader? Can you motivate others?

   i. What do you do when you encounter obstacles to meeting your goals?

   j. Are you a good planner?

Discussion Question

Organizations exist in an increasingly dynamic environment. As a result, jobs change and employees are required to move around the organization, to do a variety of tasks, to develop multiple skills, and to "retool" or upgrade themselves on an ongoing basis. Employees are being hired less for specific job skills and more for their abilities to fit themselves to the needs of the organization. Organizations are looking for employees who are innovative, flexible, willing to learn, conscientious, and who fit into the organizational culture (i.e., are good organizational citizens).

1. Can the employment interview be used to assess such personality characteristics effectively? How?

2. Are there better selection tools than the interview for assessing these characteristics? If so, what are they and why are they superior? If not, why not?

3. Does the assessment of organizational fit and relevant personality attributes pose a danger to human rights? If so, how? If not, why not? How might you reduce the dangers of human rights violations while still pursuing employees who fit into the organizational culture?

Interview Construction

1. Select a job you have done or know well. Identify the *five* most important tasks for this job.

2. For each of the five tasks, think of examples of both effective and ineffective performance that you have observed or have been a part of (i.e., critical incidents).

3. For each task, write an SI or a BDI question. Use the critical incidents to develop a three-point scoring guide (example of a poor answer, a typical answer, and a good answer).

This exercise can be completed individually or in small groups of three to five. The product of the exercise is used in the role-play that follows. An alternative to selecting a job with which participants are familiar is to have participants develop an interview for the job of "Course Instructor."

Interview Role-Play

1. Form small groups of between three and five. Assign the role of applicant to one group member and the role of interviewer to another. The remaining members of the group serve as observers. The applicant is to be interviewed for one of the jobs selected for the interview construction exercise.

2. As a group, select *five* self-evaluation questions from the list in Box 10.1, page 404. The interviewer is to use these questions to begin interviewing the applicant for the job.

3. Next the interviewer is to continue, using the five job-relevant questions developed in the interview construction exercise.

4. While the interviewer is conducting the interview, the observers should record their answers to the following questions:
   a. How do the answers to the first five questions differ from the answers to the second five questions?
   b. Does one set of questions provide better information on which to base a selection decision? Which?
   c. Is there a difference between the two question sets in terms of how much time the applicant spends talking? If so, which takes more time and why?
   d. Of the second set of questions, are there any questions that don't seem to work as well as they should? If so, why? How would you improve these questions?
   e. How useful is the scoring guide? Would you recommend any modifications to the scoring guide? If so, how would you change it?

5. After the interview, the observers are to debrief the interviewer and applicant. How did they perceive the relative effectiveness of the two sets of questions? Where did they experience difficulties? The observers should also provide feedback to both the interviewer and applicant as to how they might improve their interview performance.

This role-play can be conducted as a class demonstration with one interviewer and one applicant as role-players and the remainder of the class as observers. A discussion of the relative effectiveness of the two question sets and the effectiveness of the interviewer and applicant can be held with the entire class.

CASE

Cuts in health-care funding have led to restructuring of the health-care delivery system across Canada. In Kitchener, Ontario, the operations and administration of Kitchener-Waterloo General Hospital and Freeport Hospital were merged under the new name of Grand River Hospital Corporation. The duplication of services was eliminated by moving some services completely to one facility and all other services to the other facility. Similarly, duplication of administration was eliminated by merging jobs across the two hospitals so that where there were once two positions, there was now only one. For example, prior to restructuring, each hospital had its own director of human resources. However, there was only room for one director of human resources in the restructured Grand River Hospital. Thus, as jobs were merged, positions were eliminated. In some cases, due to funding cuts, as many as three or four jobs were merged into one. As a consequence, incumbents in most administrative jobs lost their original jobs and had to compete for the new, restructured positions.

A couple of the authors of this text were asked by Grand River Hospital to assist in designing structured employment interviews for the new positions. They met with teams of subject-matter experts (SMEs—employees who knew the job well) for each of the new positions in order to conduct job analyses and develop interview questions and scoring guides. The two merging hospitals were represented by roughly equal numbers of SMEs on each of the teams. Importantly, the authors acted only as consultants and facilitators—it was the teams of SMEs who developed the questions and scoring guides.

Clearly, the SMEs had the best understanding of the relevant jobs and the peculiarities of each hospital, but having them develop the questions and scoring guides also ensured their acceptance of the interview process and the outcome. In addition to developing the interview questions and scoring guides, the teams or panels of SMEs were responsible for interviewing the candidates for the new positions. The authors participated in the interviews as observers and in the post-interview discussions as facilitators and consultants.

As the interviews progressed, an interesting phenomenon emerged. Not surprisingly, interview panel members from Freeport Hospital tended to favour candidates from Freeport Hospital, whereas interview panel members from Kitchener-Waterloo General Hospital tended to favour candidates from their home hospital. What was unexpected was the degree to which many argued for changes to the scoring guide or wanted to disregard the scoring system when the results were not favourable for their preferred candidate. Remember that all interview panel members had agreed on the questions and the scoring guides when they developed the interviews. Now some claimed that their preferred candidate knew more than was reflected in his or her answer. Some argued that their preferred candidate was too nervous to think clearly. Others claimed that the interview questions or scoring guides reflected the working conditions at the other hospital more than those at their own hospital. Some argued that the range of opportunities to gain work experience was greater at the other hospital and that their preferred candidate was disadvantaged as a result. Still others felt the questions were not clear enough or that the scoring guide was too rigid. Yet the panel members who expressed such concerns when their preferred candidates did not do well tended to argue strongly in support of the interview process and scoring system when their preferred candidates did well. Needless to say, the authors were called on to mediate some lively discussions.

Discussion Questions

1. How is this situation different from that of the typical selection interview?

2. What factors need to be taken into consideration in this situation that don't normally apply in a selection interview?

3. Why do you think some of the interview panel members sought to sidestep the interview scoring process that they had helped develop in the first place?

4. If you had been one of the consultants on this project, how would you have responded to the concerns expressed by some of the interview panel members? Given the strong disagreements among interview panel members, what would you have done to facilitate agreement on an interview score for each candidate?

5. Is there anything the consultants on this project could have done to strengthen the acceptance of and adherence to the scoring process and minimize the potential for conflict? If so, what should they have done? If nothing, why?

REFERENCES

Anonymous. 1989. "Corporate Hiring and Executive Search Will Dramatically Change in the 1990s." *Canadian Manager* (Fall): 21–22.

Arvey, R.D., and J.E. Campion. 1982. "The Employment Interview: A Summary and Review of Recent Research." *Personnel Psychology* 35: 281–322.

Arvey, R.D., H.E. Miller, R. Gould, and P. Burch. 1987. "Interview Validity for Selecting Sales Clerks." *Personnel Psychology* 40: 1–12.

Blankenship, M.H., and S.J. Cesare. 1993. "Age Fairness in the Employment Interview: A Field Study." In R.D. Arvey, chair, *Perceptions, Theories, and Issues of Fairness in the Employment Interview*. Symposium presented at the 101st Annual Convention of the Psychological Association, Toronto, Ontario.

Borman, W.C., and S.J. Motowidlo. 1993. "Expanding the Criterion Domain to Include Elements of Contextual Performance." In N. Schmitt and W.C. Borman, eds., *Personnel Selection in Organizations*. San Francisco: Jossey-Bass.

Buhler, P. 1998. "Selecting the Right Person for the Job: No Small Challenge." *Supervision* (January): 7–9.

Burnett, J.R., C. Fan, S.J. Motowidlo, and T. DeGroot. 1998. "Interview Notes and Validity." *Personnel Psychology* 51: 375–96.

Cameron, K., S.J. Freeman, and A.K. Mishra. 1991. "Best Practices in White-Collar Downsizing: Managing Contradictions." *Academy of Management Executive* 5: 57–73.

Campion, M.A., J.E. Campion, and P.J. Hudson. 1994. "Structured Interviewing: A Note on Incremental Validity and Alternative Question Types." *Journal of Applied Psychology* 79: 998–1002.

Campion, M.A., D.K. Palmer, and J.E. Campion. 1997. "A Review of Structure in the Selection Interview." *Personnel Psychology* 50: 655–702.

Campion, M.A., E.D. Pursell, and B.K. Brown. 1988. "Structured Interviewing: Raising the Psychometric Properties of the Employment Interview." *Personnel Psychology* 41: 25–42.

Cascio, W.F. 1993. "Downsizing: What Do We Know? What Have We Learned?" *Academy of Management Executive* 7: 95–104.

Conway, J.M., R.A. Jako, and D.F. Goodman. 1995. "A Meta-Analysis of Interrater and Internal Consistency Reliability of Selection Interviews." *Journal of Applied Psychology* 80: 565–79.

Cox, J.A., D.W. Schlueter, K.K. Moore, and D. Sullivan. 1989. "A Look behind Corporate Doors." *Personnel Administrator* (March): 56–59.

Cronshaw, S.F. 1989. "Legal Implications for the Employment Interview in Canada." In S.F. Cronshaw, chair, *Improving Interview Validity and Legal Defensibility through Structuring.* Symposium conducted at the 50th Annual Convention of the Canadian Psychological Association (June).

Daft, R.L. 1997. *Organization Theory and Design.* St. Paul, MN: West Publishing Company.

DeGroot, T., and S.J. Motowidlo. 1999. "Why Visual and Vocal Interview Cues Can Affect Interviewers' Judgments and Predict Job Performance." *Journal of Applied Psychology* 84: 986–93.

Dipboye, R.L. 1992. *Selection Interviews: Process Perspectives.* Cincinnati, OH: South-Western Publishing.

Dougherty, T.W., D.B. Turban, and J.C. Callender. 1994. "Confirming First Impressions in the Employment Interview: A Field Study of Interviewer Behavior." *Journal of Applied Psychology* 79: 659–65.

Fishbein, M., and I. Ajzen. 1975. *Belief, Attitude, Intention, and Behavior: An Introduction to Theory and Research.* Reading, MA: Addison-Wesley.

Flanagan, J.C. 1954. "The Critical Incident Technique." *Psychological Bulletin* 51: 327–58.

Frese, M., D. Fay, T. Hilburger, K. Leng, and A. Tag. 1997. "The Concept of Personal Initiative: Operationalization, Reliability and Validity in Two German Samples." *Journal of Occupational and Organizational Psychology* 70: 139–61.

Gardiner, H.P., and R.D. Hackett. 1996. *The Employment Interview in Canadian Law: An Analysis of Human Rights Cases.* Unpublished manuscript. McMaster University.

Gatewood, R.D., and H.S. Feild. 1998. *Human Resource Selection,* 4th ed. Fort Worth, TX: The Dryden Press.

Ghiselli, E.E. 1966. "The Validity of the Personnel Interview." *Personnel Psychology* 19: 389–94.

Graves, L.M., and G.N. Powell. 1996. "Sex Similarity, Quality of the Employment Interview and Recruiters' Evaluation of Actual Applicants." *Journal of Occupational and Organizational Psychology* 69: 243–61.

Green, P.C., P. Alter, and A.F. Carr. 1993. "Development of Standard Anchors for Scoring Generic Past-Behaviour Questions in Structured Interviews." *International Journal of Selection and Assessment* 1: 203–12.

Guion, R.M. 1998. *Assessment, Measurement, and Prediction for Personnel Decisions*. Mahwah, NJ: Lawrence Erlbaum Associates.

Hackett, R.D., J.B. Rose, and J. Pyper. 1999. *Canadian Labour Arbitration Decisions Involving the Employment Interview*. Unpublished manuscript. McMaster University

Harris, M.M. 1989. "Reconsidering the Employment Interview: A Review of Recent Literature and Suggestions for Future Research." *Personnel Psychology* 42: 691–726.

———. 1993. "Fair or Foul: How Interview Questions Are Perceived." In R.D. Arvey, chair, *Perceptions, Theories, and Issues of Fairness in the Employment Interview*. Symposium presented at the 101st Annual Convention of the American Psychological Association, Toronto, Ontario.

Hedge, J.W., and M.S. Teachout. 1992. "An Interview Approach to Work Sample Criterion Measurement." *Journal of Applied Psychology* 77: 453–61.

Huffcutt, A.I., and W. Arthur, Jr. 1994. "Hunter and Hunter (1984) Revisited: Interview Validity for Entry-Level Jobs." *Journal of Applied Psychology* 79: 184–90.

Huffcutt, A.I., and P.L. Roth. 1998. "Racial Group Differences in Employment Interview Evaluations." *Journal of Applied Psychology* 83: 179–89.

Huffcutt, A.I., and D.J. Woehr. 1999. "Further Analysis of Employment Interview Validity: A Quantitative Evaluation of Interviewer-Related Structuring Methods." *Journal of Organizational Behavior* 20: 549–60.

Janz, T. 1982. "Initial Comparisons of Patterned Behavior Description Interviews versus Unstructured Interviews." *Journal of Applied Psychology* 67: 577–80.

———. 1989. "The Patterned Behavior Description Interview: The Best Prophet of the Future Is the Past." In R.W. Eder and G.R. Ferris, eds., *The Employment Interview: Theory, Research, and Practice*. Newbury Park, CA: Sage Publications, Inc.

Janz, T., L. Hellervik, and D.C. Gilmore. 1986. *Behavior Description Interviewing: New, Accurate, Cost Effective*. Boston, MA: Allyn and Bacon.

Kane, J.R. 1988. *Selection Procedures: Research vs. Reality*. Paper presented at the 49th Annual Convention of the Canadian Psychological Association, Montreal (June).

Kennedy, R. 1985. "Validation of Five Structured Interviews." Unpublished Master's thesis. East Carolina University.

Kinicki, A.J., C.A. Lockwood, P.W. Hom, and R.W. Griffeth. 1990. "Interviewer Predictions of Applicant Qualifications and Interviewer Validity: Aggregate and Individual Analysis." *Journal of Applied Psychology* 75: 477–86.

Latham, G.P. 1989. "The Reliability, Validity, and Practicality of the Situational Interview." In R.W. Eder and G.R. Ferris, eds., *The Employment Interview: Theory, Research, and Practice*. Newbury Park, CA: Sage Publications.

Latham, G.P., and L.M. Saari. 1984. "Do People Do What They Say? Further Studies on the Situational Interview." *Journal of Applied Psychology* 69: 569–73.

Latham, G.P., L.M. Saari, E.D. Pursell, and M.A. Campion. 1980. "The Situational Interview." *Journal of Applied Psychology* 65: 422–27.

Latham, G.P., and D.P. Skarlicki. 1995. "Criterion-Related Validity of the Situational and Patterned Behavior Description Interviews with Organizational Citizenship Behavior." *Human Performance* 8: 67–80.

Latham, G.P., and C. Sue-Chan. 1999. "A Meta-Analysis of the Situational Interview: An Enumerative Review of Reasons for Its Validity." *Canadian Psychology* 40: 56–67.

Lin, T.R., G.H. Dobbins, and J.L. Farh. 1992. "A Field Study of Age and Race Similarity Effects on Interview Ratings in Conventional and Situational Interviews." *Journal of Applied Psychology* 77: 363–71.

Macan, T.H., and R.L. Dipboye. 1990. "The Relationship of Pre-Interview Impressions to Selection and Recruitment Outcomes." *Personnel Psychology* 43: 745–68.

Martin, C.L., and D.H. Nagao. 1989. "Some Effects of Computerized Interviews on Job Applicant Responses." *Journal of Applied Psychology* 74: 72–80.

McDaniel, M.A., D.L. Whetzel, F.L. Schmidt, and S.D. Maurer. 1994. "The Validity of Employment Interviews: A Comprehensive Review and Meta-Analysis." *Journal of Applied Psychology* 79: 599–616.

Meckenbach, G. 1997. "Your Next Job Interview Might Be at Home." *Computing Canada* 16: 1–4.

Mosher, M.R. 1991. *Development of a Behaviorally Consistent Structured Interview*. Paper presented at the 27th International Applied Military Psychology Symposium, Stockholm, Sweden (June).

Motowidlo, S.J., G.W. Carter, M.D. Dunnette, N. Tippins, S. Werner, J.R. Burnett, and M.J. Vaughan. 1992. "Studies of the Structured Behavioral Interview." *Journal of Applied Psychology* 77: 571–87.

Motowidlo, S.J., and J.R. Van Scotter. 1994. "Evidence that Task Performance Should Be Distinguished from Contextual Performance." *Journal of Applied Psychology* 79: 475–80.

Nunnally, J.C. 1978. *Psychometric Theory*, 2nd ed. New York: McGraw-Hill.

Organ, D.W. 1988. *Organizational Citizenship Behavior: The Good Soldier Syndrome*. Lexington, MA: Lexington Books.

Organ, D.W., and M.A. Konovsky. 1989. "Cognitive versus Affective Determinants of Organizational Citizenship Behavior." *Journal of Applied Psychology* 74: 157–64.

Orpen, C. 1985. "Patterned Behavior Description Interviews versus Unstructured Interviews: A Comparative Validity Study." *Journal of Applied Psychology* 70: 774–76.

Paullin, C. 1993. "Features of Structured Interviews Which Enhance Perceptions of Fairness." In R.D. Arvey, chair, *Perceptions, Theories, and Issues of Fairness in the Employment Interview*. Symposium presented at the 101st Annual Convention of the American Psychological Association, Toronto.

Porter, M.E. 1991. *Canada at the Crossroads: The Reality of a New Competitive Environment*. Ottawa, ON: The Business Council on National Issues.

Pulakos, E.D, and N. Schmitt. 1995. "Experience-Based and Situational Interview Questions: Studies of Validity." *Personnel Psychology* 48: 289–308.

Ree, M.J., J.A. Earles, and M.S. Teachout. 1994. "Predicting Job Performance: Not Much More than *g*." *Journal of Applied Psychology* 79: 518–24.

Rowe, P.M., M.C. Williams, and A.L. Day. 1994. "Selection Procedures in North America." *International Journal of Selection and Assessment* 2: 74–79.

Rynes, S. 1991. "Recruitment, Job-Choice, and Post-Hire Consequences: A Call for New Research Directions." In M.D. Dunnette and L.M. Hough, eds., *Handbook of Industrial and Organizational Psychology*, vol. 2. Palo Alto, CA: Consulting Psychologists Press.

Schmidt, F.L., and M. Rader. 1999. "Exploring the Boundary Conditions for Interview Validity: Meta-Analytic Validity Findings for a New Interview Type." *Personnel Psychology* 52: 445–64.

Schmitt, N. 1976. "Social and Situational Determinants of Interview Decisions: Implications for the Employment Interview." *Personnel Psychology* 29: 79–101.

Stevens, C.K. 1998. "Antecedents of Interview Interactions, Interviewers' Ratings, and Applicants' Reactions." *Personnel Psychology* 51: 55–85.

Stevens, C.K., and A.L. Kristof. 1995. "Making the Right Impression: A Field Study of Applicant Impression Management during Job Interviews." *Journal of Applied Psychology* 80: 587–606.

Thacker, J.W., and R.J. Cattaneo. 1993. *Survey of Personnel Practices in Canadian Organizations: A Summary Report to Respondents* (Working Paper Series no. W92-04). Windsor, ON: University of Windsor.

Webster, E.C. 1964. *Decision Making in the Employment Interview*. Montreal: Industrial Relations Centre, McGill University.

———. 1982. *The Employment Interview: A Social Judgement Process*. Schomberg, ON: S.I.P. Publications.

Wernimont, P.F., and J.P. Campbell. 1968. "Signs, Samples, and Criteria." *Journal of Applied Psychology* 52: 372–76.

Wiesner, W.H. 1989. "The Contributions of Job Relevance, Timing, and Rating Scale to the Validity of the Employment Interview." In S.F. Cronshaw, chair, *Improving Interview Validity and Legal Defensibility through Structuring*. Symposium conducted at the 50th Annual Convention of the Canadian Psychological Association.

Wiesner, W.H., and S.F. Cronshaw. 1988. "A Meta-Analytic Investigation of the Impact of Interview Format and Degree of Structure on the Validity of the Employment Interview." *Journal of Occupational Psychology* 61: 275–90.

Williamson, L.G., J.E. Campion, S.B. Malos, M.V. Roehling, and M.A. Campion. 1997. "Employment Interview on Trial: Linking Interview Structure with Litigation Outcomes." *Journal of Applied Psychology* 82: 900–12.

Wright, P.M., P.A. Lichtenfels, and E.D. Pursell. 1989. "The Structured Interview: Additional Studies and a Meta-Analysis." *Journal of Occupational Psychology* 62: 191–99.

11

....

DECISION MAKING

CHAPTER GOALS

This chapter considers ways of reducing subjectivity and error in making selection decisions by using scientific methods that maximize selection effectiveness and efficiency. It also discusses utility analysis, decision-making procedures that may be used to evaluate the overall performance of selection systems.

   After reading this chapter you should

- appreciate the complexity of decision making in the employee selection context;

- be familiar with the sources of common decision-making errors in employee selection;

- understand the distinction between judgmental and statistical *collection* of applicant information;

- understand the distinction between judgmental and statistical *combination* of applicant information;

- understand the advantages and disadvantages of various decision-making models;

- appreciate issues involved with group decision making;
- understand basic principles in the application of cutoff scores;
- understand basic principles involved in top-down selection processes;
- understand principles and issues involved in banding; and
- be familiar with utility analysis as one way to evaluate personnel selection systems.

"The purpose of selection is to discriminate." This statement may sound strange in the context of our discussion of employment equity in Chapter 2. Unfortunately, the term *discrimination* has acquired a negative connotation because of its frequent association with the word "unfair." In fact, we do not want to discriminate unfairly, but we do want to discriminate on the basis of applicants' abilities to do the work. Just as we discriminate in the grocery store between the desirable fruit or vegetables and those we do not want, our task in selection is to discriminate between those applicants we believe will become effective employees and those who will not. Thus, selection involves making decisions about which applicants to hire and which not to hire, based on the information available.

Unfortunately, humans are imperfect decision makers (Simon, 1957). The use of phrases such as "I'm only human," as justification for having made mistakes, reflects our common understanding of this principle. Factors other than logic typically enter into our decisions. Decisions are influenced by emotional reactions to applicants, by political motives, as well as by a variety of constraints (Bazerman, 1986; Janis and Mann, 1977). Decision makers often make decisions based on inadequate or erroneous information. As a result, employers frequently make poor hiring decisions. The purpose of this chapter is to provide information and tools that can assist employers in making better selection decisions.

THE CONTEXT OF SELECTION DECISIONS

Employers typically have to contend with a number of constraints and competing demands when making selection decisions. Often, time pressures prevent them from making logical or objective choices. If they need to fill vacant positions quickly they will tend to *satisfice* (Simon, 1957). That is, rather than searching for the best candidates, they will select the first applicants they encounter who meet minimum levels of acceptability. Similarly, if an insufficient number of suitable applicants is available or if the level of applicant qualifications is quite low, employers' standards of acceptability tend to drop (Ross and Ellard, 1986). They will often accept less-qualified applicants rather than continue their recruitment efforts in order to generate applications from better-qualified candidates.

Sometimes, rather than selecting for a specific job, employers select applicants for the organization. Their selection decisions are based on perceptions of applicants' overall suitability for the organization, or *organizational fit*. They do not concern themselves with which job a candidate should be placed in until after the hiring decision has been made. Such organizations tend to have *promote-from-within* policies, flexible job descriptions, dynamic jobs, or to practise job rotation or rapid promotion.

Another form of selection involves promotion or transfer. Although promotions or transfers are often made on the basis of seniority or merit, they are most effective if treated as selection decisions. The candidates selected should be those most qualified for the vacant positions. When candidates are selected on the basis of merit or good job performance, the selection decision is based on the assumption that good performance in one job is indicative of good performance in another. However, the best salesperson or machinist will not necessarily make the best sales manager or shop supervisor. In fact, he or she might be quite incompetent in the new job (Peter and Hull, 1969). On the other hand, promotions based on seniority are based on the assumption that the most experienced employee would be most effective. But the most experienced salesperson might not even be the best salesperson, let alone the best sales manager. Therefore, just as in other selection decisions, candidates for promotion or transfer should be assessed in terms of the knowledge, skills, abilities, and other attributes (KSAOs) they possess relevant to the positions for which they are being considered.

SELECTION ERRORS

Many employers believe they have a knack for making good selection decisions. Some look for a firm handshake, unswerving eye contact, or upright posture in the applicant. Others look for confidence, enthusiasm, or personality. Most employers hold *implicit theories* about how certain behaviours, mannerisms, or personality characteristics go together. *Implicit theories* are personal beliefs that are held about how people or things function, without objective evidence and often without conscious awareness. For example, an employer might believe that unswerving eye contact reveals honesty, directness, and confidence. However, such an assumption is not necessarily warranted. Maintaining eye contact could be an interview tactic learned by the applicant or it could even reflect hostility. Moreover, in some cultures maintaining direct eye contact is considered rude and inappropriate behaviour. Applicants from these cultures would be disadvantaged if eye contact becomes a factor in the selection decision.

Many other employers make subjective decisions based on gut feelings about the applicant. They hire applicants simply because they like them or seem to get along well with them, at least based on the few minutes they spend

BOX 11.1 What Do Employers Look for in an Applicant?

Employers have long hired applicants for a variety of reasons that do not appear to be job-related. You be the judge as to the merits of the selection techniques described below:

One employer asked applicants to lunch in order to observe them eating. The employer believed that those who eat quickly are energetic workers, that they eat quickly in order to be able to get on with their work. Conversely, those who eat slowly are expected to take longer at lunch and coffee breaks, as well as to work more slowly. It appears the employer believed in a variation of the well-known maxim, "You are *how* you eat."

Another employer looked for the same characteristic by observing how applicants walked into the office for their interviews. Those who had a spry, determined step were more likely to be hired than those who ambled into the office or those who seemed hesitant as they entered.

The employer believed that an energetic, determined walk is indicative of an energetic, determined worker.

Yet another employer didn't like to hire applicants who have a lot of hobbies or who are involved in a lot of extracurricular activities. The employer reasoned that people who are active outside of work or who have a lot of nonwork interests will be too distracted by their hobbies to sufficiently devote themselves to their work and that they might use some of their work time to pursue their own interests.

Finally, one employer had a tendency to hire applicants who seemed to desperately need the job. It appears the applicants' needs triggered the employer's sense of social responsibility and compassion. The employer felt good about being able to help these needy individuals and reasoned that the more-capable applicants can easily find employment elsewhere.

What advice would you have for each of these employers?

---

together in the interview. Invariably, such gut feelings, as well as the implicit theories, lead to poor selection decisions, as we discussed in Chapter 3.

Although employers assess a considerable amount of (often complex) information about each candidate, they must simplify this information to produce a dichotomous decision. Candidates are classified as either acceptable or unacceptable and hired or not hired on the basis of this assessment. Sometimes these decisions turn out to be correct. The applicant who is hired becomes a productive and valued employee. Other times (more often than many employers care to admit) employers make mistakes by hiring individuals who turn out to be unsuitable. The four possible outcomes of a selection decision are presented in Table 11.1.

Two of the outcomes in Table 11.1, the true positive and the true negative, are correct decisions, or "hits." In the *true positive* outcome, the employer has hired an applicant who turns out to be a successful employee. In the *true negative* outcome, the employer did not hire an applicant who would have been considered a failure as an employee if hired. Obviously, an employer would wish to maximize both these "hits" or correct predictions but, as we will demonstrate later in this chapter, that can be quite difficult to accomplish. The two other outcomes represent selection errors or "misses."

A **false positive error** occurs when an applicant is assessed favourably and is hired but proves to be unsuccessful on the job. This is a costly error and

False positive error— occurs when an applicant who is assessed favourably turns out to be a poor choice.

TABLE 11.1 OUTCOMES OF THE SELECTION PROCESS

Criterion Measures of Job Performance		Not Hired	Hired
	Success	False Negative (Miss)	True Positive (Hit)
	Failure	True Negative (Hit)	False Positive (Miss)
		Selection Decision	

may even be disastrous in some jobs. Productivity, profits, and the company's reputation may suffer when such errors are made. It may be difficult to terminate the employees once hired, termination can be costly, and grievance proceedings could result from the termination. Moreover, replacements for the unsuccessful employee must be recruited, selected, and trained, all at additional cost. Some organizations use probationary periods (e.g., between one and six months) for new employees in order to reduce the costs of false positive errors. In fact, tenure for professors is really a probation system—in this case the probationary period is five or six years.

A **false negative error** is one in which the applicant is assessed unfavourably and is not hired but would have been successful if hired. Such errors tend to go unnoticed because there are usually no obvious negative consequences for the employer as there are with false positive errors. The employer rarely finds out about the quality of the applicant who was not hired. Only in high-profile occupations such as professional sports does a false negative error become readily apparent. When an athlete who is turned down by one team becomes a star pitcher, goalie, or fullback with a competing team, the first team is constantly faced with its mistake.

However, even though false negative errors are rarely that obvious in most organizations, they can be costly. Applicants for key jobs (e.g., a software designer) might develop highly successful products for the competing organization that did hire them. Furthermore, when an organization turns down a number of good candidates who are then hired by a competitor, even for nonkey jobs, the competitor could gain a significant advantage in productivity. In addition, false negative errors might adversely affect minority applicants and could result in human rights litigation.

False negative error—occurs when an applicant who is rejected would have been a good choice.

Although it is not possible to entirely avoid or even recognize all errors when making selection decisions, they can be minimized. Valid selection methods and systematic procedures will serve to improve the probability of making correct selection decisions. One particular challenge faced by employers is how to make sense of the various, and sometimes conflicting, sources of information about applicants in order to make an informed decision. The next section considers different ways of combining complex information and suggests some systematic procedures for making selection decisions.

COLLECTION AND COMBINATION OF INFORMATION

Before a selection decision can be made, information about the applicants must be collected from various sources and combined in some way. Typically, employers collect this information on application forms or from résumés, in employment interviews, and through reference checks. Many employers also administer ability, personality, and/or other tests, collect and score biographical information, or make use of assessment centres. These methods of collecting applicant information are discussed in detail in Chapters 8, 9, and 10.

Sometimes all information is in agreement and the decision can be straightforward. Other times the information is contradictory and the decision is more difficult. For example, if one applicant looks very good "on paper" (i.e., in the résumé), has a high score on a mental ability test, and receives glowing recommendations from the references, but does poorly in the interview, while another applicant does well on everything except the mental ability test, what is the appropriate decision? The employer must find some way of making sense of this information so that the best possible selection decision can be made.

Information collected from some sources, such as test scores, tends to be more objective. A good test provides a reliable and valid measure of some attribute, which can be readily used to compare applicants on a numerical or statistical basis. That is, no (or very little) human judgment is involved in collecting this score. We shall refer to these methods of collecting applicant information or data as *statistical*. Information collected from more subjective sources, such as unstructured interviews, rely much more, or even exclusively, on human judgment. We shall refer to these methods of collecting applicant information or data as *judgmental* (some authors refer to these as "clinical" methods).

Just as applicant data can be collected statistically or judgmentally, the data can be *combined* using statistical and judgmental methods. Data combined mathematically, using a formula, has been synthesized in a more objective fashion, which we shall call *statistical* combination. Combining data through human judgment or an overall impression is a more subjective process, which we shall refer to as *judgmental* combination. Thus, a number of permutations are possible. Judgmentally collected data can be combined in either a judgmental or statistical manner, and statistically collected data can be combined in either a judgmental or a statistical manner. Moreover, it is possible that some of the data are collected judgmentally (e.g., unstructured interview) whereas other data are collected statistically (e.g., test scores). This composite of judgmental and statistical data can also be combined in either a judgmental or statistical manner. The possible permutations of methods of data collection and combination are presented in Table 11.2.

In the **pure judgment approach**, judgmental data are collected and combined in a judgmental manner. The decision maker forms an overall impression of the applicant based on gut feeling or implicit theories rather than explicit, objective criteria. In this approach, the decision maker both collects information and makes a decision about the applicant. An employer making a selection decision based on an unstructured interview is representative of this approach. The employer who hires applicants because he feels sorry for them is using intuition or pure judgment to make his decisions.

Pure judgment approach—an approach in which judgmental data are combined in a judgmental manner.

The **trait rating approach** is one in which judgmental data are combined statistically. A number of judgmental ratings are made (e.g., based on interviews, application forms or résumés, or reference checks). The ratings are combined using an arithmetic formula, which produces an overall score for each applicant. Although the decision makers collect the information and make ratings on each of the components, the decision is based on the overall score generated by the mathematical formula.

Trait rating approach—an approach in which judgmental data are combined statistically.

The **profile interpretation** strategy involves combining statistical data in a judgmental manner. Data are collected from objective sources such as tests or biographical inventories. The decision maker examines these data to form an overall, subjective impression of the applicant's suitability for the job. The selection decision is based on this overall impression or gut feeling.

Profile interpretation—an approach in which statistical data are combined in a judgmental manner.

In the **pure statistical approach**, statistically collected data are combined statistically. Test scores or scores from other objective sources such as biographical inventories or weighted application blanks are fed into a formula or

Pure statistical approach—an approach in which data are combined statistically.

TABLE 11.2 METHODS OF COLLECTING AND COMBINING APPLICANT INFORMATION

Method of Collecting Data	Method of Combining Data	
	Judgmental	Statistical
Judgmental	Pure Judgment	Trait Ratings
Statistical	Profile Interpretation	Pure Statistical
Both	Judgmental Composite	Statistical Composite

Sources: Adapted from Sawyer (1966).

regression equation, which produces an overall combined score. Applicants are then selected in order of their scores (i.e., the top scorer, then the second highest, and so on until the desired number of applicants has been selected).

Judgmental composite—an approach in which judgmental and statistical data are combined in a judgmental manner.

The **judgmental composite** involves collecting both judgmental and statistical data and then combining them judgmentally. A decision maker might conduct interviews and reference checks (judgmental data) and have access to test scores (statistical data). The decision maker then examines the test scores and considers the impressions of the applicants gained from the interviews and reference checks in order to form an overall impression and make a decision concerning who should be hired. This is probably the most common method used by employers to make selection decisions.

Statistical composite—an approach in which judgmental and statistical data are combined statistically.

The **statistical composite** also involves collecting both judgmental and statistical data, but the data are combined statistically. Ratings or scores are given or obtained from each component, such as an interview, a reference check, a personality test, and a mental ability test. The ratings or scores are combined in a formula or regression equation to produce an overall score for each applicant. Selection decisions are thus based on the applicants' scores.

Although all six of the basic decision-making approaches described above have been used in employee selection, they are not equally effective. A considerable body of research indicates that the pure statistical and the statistical composite approaches are generally superior to the other methods in predicting performance (Meehl, 1954; Sawyer, 1966). Both of these approaches involve combining information in a statistical manner.

There are several possible explanations for the superiority of statistical methods over judgmental methods of combining information (Kleinmuntz, 1990). First, as noted previously, implicit theories are more likely to bias evaluations and contribute to error when judgmental methods are used. Irrelevant factors such as the applicant's appearance or mannerisms are likely to unduly influence the decision. Second, it is difficult for decision makers to take into account the complexity of all the information available to them when they use judgmental processes to make decisions. Because the ability to remember and process information is easily overloaded, decision makers tend to oversimplify or inappropriately simplify information to create applicant summaries that are inaccurate. Third, it is virtually impossible to assign appropriate weights to all the selection instruments when judgmental procedures are used. How important should reference checks be in comparison to ability tests or interviews? It is difficult to give even equal weighting to all selection information in a subjective manner. Sometimes particular applicant data, such as test scores, are largely ignored in favour of impressions based on other sources, such as the interview. Statistical approaches are likely to provide better decisions, even when scores from all the selection instruments are weighted equally, because all applicant information is taken into consideration in a systematic manner.

It is worth noting that statistical approaches are compromised when poor quality information goes into the selection equation. The maxim "garbage in, garbage out" applies just as well to employee selection methods as it does to computer programming. Erroneous or irrelevant information, such as might be obtained from unstructured interviews, non-valid tests, or inaccurate references, will contribute error variance to the equation and reduce the likelihood of making good selection decisions. It is therefore important to ensure that only data coming from reliable and valid selection measures are combined to yield an overall score for each applicant.

WHY DO EMPLOYERS RESIST USING STATISTICAL APPROACHES?

Although statistical approaches to decision making are clearly superior to judgmental approaches, employers tend to resist them (Gatewood and Feild, 1998). They prefer relying on gut feelings or instinct. There are probably several reasons why employers cling to judgmental approaches. Employers might find it difficult to give up the personal control that judgmental approaches give them. They can choose to ignore or discount information that is at odds with gut feelings and they can emphasize or rely solely on information that is in accord with their feelings. When they use statistical approaches, their role becomes simply that of information collectors rather than judgmental decision makers.

Employers also tend to be overconfident in their decision-making abilities (Bazerman, 1986; Kleinmuntz, 1990). They generally believe that they are quite successful in selecting good job candidates. Unfortunately, few employers bother to keep track of their success or "hit" rates by reviewing the job performance of those they hired. If they did, they would become much more concerned about their abilities to judge applicant competence. Granted, there might be a very small minority of employers who might be able to assess job applicants with reasonable accuracy (e.g., Zedeck, Tziner, and Middlestadt, 1983), but even they are outperformed by statistical models based on their own decision rules (known as *bootstrapping*; see Kleinmuntz, 1990). Unfortunately, most employers are not very good judges of job applicant potential. Finally, some employers use judgmental approaches because they feel they can't afford the time or money required to develop a statistical selection model. However, statistical models can be quite simple and need not be expensive. Moreover, as discussed in the utility analysis section of this chapter, any costs incurred can be more than recouped in savings generated by an effective selection system.

One method we have used quite effectively in workshops to demonstrate to managers the inaccuracy of their judgments is to show them videotapes of actual employment interviews. In fact, the applicants appearing on the videotapes had been hired and we had obtained job performance ratings from their supervisors after they had been working at least half a year. We asked the managers to rate the applicants and predict their job performance. We were then able to compare the managers' ratings and predictions with the applicants' actual job performance ratings. It was quite a surprise for most of the managers to discover how badly they had misjudged the applicants.

GROUP DECISION MAKING

Although most employee selection research has explored individual models of decision making, several surveys indicate that in most organizations selection decisions are made by groups (Cox, Schlueter, Moore, and Sullivan, 1989; Kane, 1988; Robertson and Makin, 1986). Some researchers suggest that groups can be poor decision makers (Brandstatter, Davis, and Stocker-Kreichgauer, 1983; Janis and Mann, 1977; Steiner, 1972). Power motives, politics, conformity to the group, and other factors serve to reduce the objectivity of group decisions. However, in spite of all the potential problems encountered in group decision making, many researchers conclude that groups are generally better at problem solving and decision making than the average individual (Hill, 1982; Michaelson, Watson, and Black, 1989; Shaw, 1981). As indicated in Chapter 10, Wiesner and Cronshaw (1988) found that selection interview boards or panels are better at predicting job performance than individual interviewers when the interview is unstructured and as good as individual interviewers when the interview is structured (see Table 10.1).

In most organizations there appears to be an intuitive understanding that groups might make better selection decisions than individuals; thus, selection teams or panels are commonplace. Having two or more individuals make the selection decision can reduce the effects of the biases that any one individual might have. Selection team or panel members are more likely to be careful in their assessments when they have to justify their ratings to other team members. The fact that differences of opinion concerning an applicant must be resolved to everyone's satisfaction will tend to reduce the impact of biases. Also, with more individuals examining applicant information it is less likely that particular information will be overlooked or distorted.

A less commendable reason for organizations using selection teams or panels is that such teams make it easier to share the blame for poor decisions. Individual members could be somewhat less conscientious than they should be because they can evade personal responsibility and consequences for their decisions. Nevertheless, based on the research evidence, it is advisable that any judgmental information be collected by a selection team or panel. In fact, numerous Canadian human rights tribunals have cited the use of selection panels as an important factor in defending against discrimination suits (Gardiner and Hackett, 1996; Hackett, Rose, and Pyper, 1999).

One recent development in the Canadian workplace is the increasing use of teams to do work. Selecting appropriate team members has thus become an important challenge and the focus of some recent research (e.g., Kichuk and Wiesner, 1996; Stevens and Campion, 1994). Not only job-related abilities but also personality and interpersonal factors must be taken into consideration when selecting for a team.

When teams make selection decisions, there are often disagreements among team members as to appropriate ratings or who should be hired. It is

SC Johnson Ltd. produces a wide variety of products, including Pledge furniture polishes, Glade air fresheners, Windex glass and surface cleaners, Raid insecticides, Off insect repellants, Edge shaving gels, Ziploc bags, Saran Wrap, Shout stain remover, and Scrubbing Bubbles bathroom cleaners. The Canadian plant, located in Brantford, Ontario, was at one time one of the poorest-producing plants in the Johnson family. However, management and employees at the plant were able to turn the plant into one of Johnson's star performers. They attribute much of their success to the implementation of a team-based manufacturing process.

Teams at the Brantford plant construct and take apart assembly lines as needed to manufacture seasonal products such as insect repellants and citronella candles. The team members may choose who does what tasks on the assembly line, may rotate tasks, may elect their team leader, and may also interview and select new members.

Having work teams select new members for the team makes a lot of sense and seems to work well for SC Johnson. The existing team members intimately know the work that has to be done and have a good sense of the personal qualities that will contribute to effective team membership. They are likely to make better decisions than a manager who has relatively limited knowledge of the work and the team. In addition, existing team members probably have a good sense as to which individuals they are most likely to get along with.

More research is needed to determine whether work teams do make better selection decisions than their supervisors or managers. In any case, it is just as important for such work teams to use objective, validated selection methods as it is for managers to use such methods.

important that such differences be resolved as objectively as possible. The easiest way to resolve differences is to average the team members' individual scores to arrive at a combined score for each applicant (this is analogous to statistical combination). However, as noted in the section on the collection and combination of information, such combinations can be misleading if some of the team members submit erroneous or biased ratings. As a general rule, when there is close agreement among team members' ratings, the individual ratings can be safely averaged. But when there is disagreement (e.g., a range of two or more points), team members should discuss the reasons for their ratings until they arrive at a consensus. By discussing their rationales for the ratings, team members are likely to uncover some of the misperceptions, biases, and errors in recollection that can contribute to differences in scores.

SETTING CUTOFF SCORES

In the next section we will consider different models of decision making. Several of these models make use of a *cutoff score*, so it will be necessary to gain an understanding of cutoff scores before we discuss the models. **Cutoff scores** serve as criteria or thresholds in selection decisions. Applicants who score below the cutoff on a given predictor (e.g., test, interview) are rejected. Thus,

Cutoff score—a threshold; those scoring at or above the score pass, those scoring below fail.

cutoff scores ensure that applicants meet some minimum level of ability or qualification to be considered for a job. In college or university, a grade of 50 percent often serves as a cutoff. A student whose grade is lower than 50 percent fails the course. This cutoff has been established by convention. In most organizations, cutoffs are established based on the predictor scores of individuals who are successful on the job being selected for, or based on expert judgments concerning the difficulty of the predictor items (Schmitt and Klimoski, 1991).

One method of establishing cutoff scores involves identifying the proportion of applicants who are to be hired and determining how stringent the cutoff score should be to select only the desired number of applicants. First, the expected **selection ratio** is calculated (number of individuals to be hired divided by the expected number of applicants). Next, the distribution of the applicants' scores on the predictor is estimated by examining the predictor score distributions of past groups of applicants or of current employees (i.e., predictive or concurrent validation data). Finally, the cutoff score is established by applying the selection ratio to the predictor score distribution in order to determine the score that only the top applicants (the proportion to be hired) would attain.

For example, if a fire department seeks to hire five firefighters and 150 people are expected to apply, the selection ratio will be .03 (5/150). About 3 percent of expected applicants will be accepted, or, conversely, about 97 percent of expected applicants will have to be rejected. The cutoff score should therefore be set at the 97th percentile of the distribution of predictor scores (plus or minus one standard error of measurement). That is, the cutoff score is set so that only 3 percent of applicants would be expected to meet or exceed the score (or 97 percent would fall below it). This approach is limited to setting cutoffs for a single predictor. When more than one predictor is to be used, it is common to use expert judges.

There are several ways in which expert judges can be used to establish cutoffs, but they differ only slightly in their methods. We will consider the general approach and readers are encouraged to consult Cascio (1991) or Gatewood and Feild (1998) for more detailed treatments of the various methods. Experienced employees, supervisors, or managers who know the job well or industrial psychologists typically serve as expert judges. Essentially, the expert judges are asked to rate the difficulty of test items (or interview questions) and to indicate what score on each item should be attained by a minimally competent applicant. These ratings are summed for all items to yield a pass threshold or cutoff score. Cutoff scores can be established in this manner for each of the predictors used in the selection process.

Selection ratio—the proportion of applicants who are hired.

DECISION-MAKING MODELS

There are several different decision-making models that involve combining applicant information statistically (regardless of how that information was collected). These models are *multiple regression*, *multiple cutoffs*, *multiple hurdle*, *combination*, and *profile matching* (Gatewood and Feild, 1998). We will now consider the models in terms of their usefulness for different purposes and under different conditions.

MULTIPLE REGRESSION MODEL

In the multiple regression model, the applicant's scores on each predictor (e.g., tests, interviews, reference checks) are weighted and summed to yield a total score (e.g., predicted job performance). The appropriate regression weights or *b* values are determined through prior research, where the unique contributions of each predictor (X) to predicting job performance (Y) are investigated.

Table 11.3 provides some hypothetical data for purposes of illustration. The scores of four applicants on each of four predictors—the maximum scores, regression weights, cutoff scores, and mean or average scores for each predictor—are presented in the table. Applicants for a retail sales position wrote a cognitive ability test, completed an extroversion scale, were interviewed, and provided references, which were scored. The maximum score on the cognitive ability test (X_1) is 50 and the regression weight (b_1) is 1. The maximum score on the extroversion scale (X_2) is 40 and the regression weight (b_2) is 0.5 (i.e., the extroversion score contributes only half as much as the cognitive ability score to the prediction of job performance). The maximum interview score (X_3) is 30 and the weighting for the interview score (b_3) is 0.7, while the maximum reference check score (X_4) is 15 and the score for the reference check is given a weight (b_4) of 0.6. The regression equation for predicting job performance in this case is

$$Y = b_1X_1 + b_2X_2 + b_3X_3 + b_4X_4$$

TABLE 11.3 EXAMPLES OF SALES APPLICANT DATA

Applicant	Predictor Scores			
	Cognitive Ability Test	Extraversion Scale	Structured Interview	Reference Check
Mr. A	36	30	27	11
Ms. B	32	37	16	10
Mr. C	44	22	24	13
Ms. D	37	27	28	14
Maximum Possible Scores	50	40	30	15
Regression Weights	1.0	.5	.7	.6
Cutoff Scores	30	24	18	10
Mean Scores	35	27	23	11

Predicted job performance = Cognitive Ability Score + 0.5 Extroversion Score + 0.7 Interview Score + 0.6 Reference Check Score. A predicted job performance score can thus be calculated for each applicant.

Applying the regression equation to the data in Table 11.3 yields a total predicted score of 76.5 for Mr. A, 67.7 for Ms. B, 79.6 for Mr. C, and 78.5 for Ms. D. The applicants can now be ranked based on their total predicted scores: (1) Mr. C, (2) Ms. D, (3) Mr. A, and (4) Ms. B. They can be selected on a top-down basis until the desired number of candidates has been obtained. If two candidates are needed, Mr. C and Ms. D would be selected.

The multiple regression model assumes that the predictors are linearly related to the criterion and that a low score on one predictor can be compensated for by a high score on another predictor. An applicant could do very poorly in the interview (e.g., receive a score of zero) and still do well if he or she receives high scores on the tests and the reference check. However, the assumptions made by the multiple regression model are not necessarily warranted. First, very high scores on some predictors might be as undesirable as very low scores. For example, while an extreme introvert might have difficulty relating to customers in a retail sales position, an extreme extrovert might annoy them and drive them away. Second, there might be a minimum level of competence required on each of the predictors for the individual to perform acceptably in the job. For example, a very low interview score might indicate that the applicant has such poor interpersonal and communication skills that he or she cannot function acceptably in retail sales, regardless of high cognitive ability and extroversion scores. The multiple regression approach also has the disadvantage of being expensive, particularly for large applicant pools, because all applicants must be assessed on all predictors.

Nevertheless, the multiple regression approach does have several advantages. It is an efficient method of combining multiple predictors in an optimal manner and it minimizes errors in prediction. Moreover, different regression equations can be produced for different jobs even if the same predictors are used for all jobs. Thus, if applicants are being selected for more than one job, they can be placed in the job for which their total score is the highest or they can be placed in the job where their total score is the furthest above the minimum score necessary for acceptable job performance. The multiple regression approach is probably the most efficient decision-making approach if the assumptions underlying the model are not violated (Cascio, 1991).

MULTIPLE CUTOFF MODEL

In the multiple cutoff model, scores on all predictors are obtained for all applicants, just as in the multiple regression model. Using the data in Table 11.3 to illustrate, all applicants would write the cognitive ability and extroversion tests, all would be interviewed, and reference check information would be scored for all. However, in this model, applicants are rejected if their scores on any of the predictors fall below the cutoff scores. In our example, both Mr. A and Ms. D score above the cutoffs on all four predictors. Ms. B's score falls below the cutoff on the structured interview and Mr. C's score falls below the cutoff on the extroversion scale. Ms. B and Mr. C would thus be rejected. Note that this is quite a different result from the multiple regression approach, where Mr. C obtained the highest score and would have been selected.

The multiple cutoff model assumes that a minimum level is required on each of the attributes measured by the predictors for successful job performance (i.e., there is a nonlinear relationship among the predictors and job performance). The model also assumes that the predictors are not compensatory (i.e., it is not possible to compensate for a low score on one predictor with a high score on another predictor).

A disadvantage of the multiple cutoff model is that, just like the multiple regression approach, it requires that all applicants be assessed on all procedures. This requirement makes it expensive to administer. Another disadvantage is that the model only identifies those applicants who have minimum qualifications for the job. There is no way of distinguishing among those who have passed the minimum cutoffs. If 10 applicants have passed the cutoffs but the employer only wants to select five candidates, how is the employer to decide which ones to select?

In spite of its disadvantages, the multiple cutoff model does serve to narrow the pool of applicants to a smaller set of minimally qualified candidates and it is an easy model for managers to understand. It is probably most useful when minimum levels of certain physical abilities are required for job performance (Gatewood and Feild, 1998). For example, some occupations such as law enforcement, firefighting, or heavy manufacturing have minimum specifications for eyesight, colour vision, or strength.

MULTIPLE HURDLE MODEL

In the multiple hurdle model, applicants must pass the minimum cutoff for each predictor, in turn, before being assessed on the next predictor. As soon as an applicant has failed to meet the cutoff on a given predictor, he or she ceases to be a candidate for the job and is not assessed on any of the remaining predictors. In our example in Table 11.3, all four applicants pass the cognitive ability test and go on to write the extroversion scale. Mr. C fails to meet the cutoff on the extroversion scale and is dropped from further consideration. Only Mr. A, Ms. B, and Ms. D go on to the structured interview, where Ms. B fails to meet the cutoff and is rejected. Reference checks are performed only for Mr. A and Ms. D, who both pass and become candidates for the job.

The result is identical to the one for the multiple cutoff model but the approach is less expensive because fewer applicants need to be assessed at each stage of the selection process. Both models make the same assumptions but differ in the procedure used for collecting predictor information. The multiple cutoff approach uses a nonsequential procedure whereas the multiple hurdle procedure is sequential (i.e., applicants must pass each predictor cutoff, in sequence, before going on to the next predictor). Like the multiple cutoff approach, the multiple hurdle model narrows the pool of applicants to a smaller set of candidates meeting minimum qualifications and is also an easy model to understand.

The multiple hurdle approach has the disadvantage of being more time-consuming than the multiple regression or multiple cutoff approaches. Applicants need to be assessed and scored on each predictor before a decision can be made on whether to assess them on the next predictor. It also makes it difficult to estimate the validity of each procedure, particularly in later stages of the selection process. Relatively fewer applicants are being assessed on predictors toward the end of the sequence (e.g., interview and reference check, in our example), so restriction of range becomes a problem for estimating the validity of these predictors. One other disadvantage is that, like the multiple cutoff model, this model only identifies those applicants who have minimum qualifications for the job and does not distinguish among those who have passed all the cutoffs.

Like the multiple cutoff approach, the multiple hurdle approach is most appropriate when minimum levels of particular KSAOs are necessary for job performance and cannot be compensated for by higher levels on other KSAOs. Moreover, the multiple hurdle approach is most useful when the applicant pool is large and some of the selection procedures are expensive (Gatewood and Feild, 1998). In such circumstances, the less expensive procedures (e.g., tests) can be used as hurdles at the beginning in order to screen out inappropriate applicants and reduce the applicant pool. Thus, the more expensive procedures (e.g., interviews) are used on a smaller pool of select applicants.

COMBINATION MODEL

In the combination model, all applicants are measured on all predictors and those falling below the cutoff on any of the predictors are rejected, just as in the multiple cutoff model. Then, multiple regression is used to calculate the total scores of those applicants who pass the cutoffs. The applicants are ranked by total score and selected on a top-down basis, as in the multiple regression method. The combination model is therefore a mixture of the multiple cutoff and multiple regression approaches. If we apply this model to the data in Table 11.3, Ms. B and Mr. C would be rejected because they do not pass all the cutoffs. So far, this result is identical to the result for the multiple cutoff model. Now the regression equation is applied to the remaining applicants, Mr. A and Ms. D. Recall from the section on the multiple regression model that Mr. A's total score is 76.5 and Ms. D's total score is 78.5. Ms. D is therefore ranked first and Mr. A second. If we were hiring only one candidate, Ms. D would be selected.

Like the multiple cutoff model, the combination model assumes that a minimum level of each of the KSAOs is required for effective job performance. A further assumption is that, once minimum levels have been reached, high scores on one predictor can compensate for low scores on another predictor. As might be expected, the combination model has the same advantages as the multiple cutoff model but has the additional advantage of providing a means of selecting from among those candidates who pass all the cutoffs. However, the combination approach is just as expensive as the multiple cutoff approach because all applicants are assessed on all predictors.

Obviously, the combination model is useful as long as the assumptions underlying the approach hold. It is an appropriate model when selection instruments do not vary greatly in cost and is particularly useful when a considerable number of applicants tend to pass all the cutoffs. When more applicants than can be hired pass the cutoffs, the combination model facilitates selection among those applicants.

PROFILE MATCHING

In the profile matching model, current employees who are considered successful on the job are assessed on several predictors. Their average scores on each predictor are used to form an *ideal* profile of scores required for successful job performance. One should also try to obtain average predictor scores for current employees who are considered poor or marginal performers. Obtaining scores for poor or marginal employees is not always easy because such employees are often dismissed or leave of their own accord soon after being hired or, if a valid selection system is used, tend not to be hired in the first place. If it is possible to obtain scores for poor performers, their average predictor scores should be compared with the average predictor scores of good performers to ensure that the predictors differentiate between good and poor performers. Those predictors that do not differentiate should not be included in the ideal profile of scores.

Once an ideal profile of scores has been established, applicants' predictor scores can be compared with the ideal profile. Those applicants whose profiles are most similar to the ideal profile can then be selected. One of two methods can be used to determine the degree of similarity between applicant profiles and the ideal profile: the correlation method or the D^2 method. The correlation method involves correlating an applicant's scores on the predictors with the predictor scores of the ideal profile. The higher the correlation, the greater the similarity between the applicant's profile and the ideal profile. The D^2 method involves calculating differences between an applicant's scores and ideal profile scores on each predictor, squaring the differences, and summing the squared differences to yield D^2. The larger D^2 is, the poorer is the match between the applicant's profile and the ideal profile. The D^2 method is preferred because it considers the magnitude of applicants' mean scores across the predictors, the degree to which applicant scores differ from the ideal scores, and the pattern or shape of applicant scores relative to the ideal profile. The correlation method only considers the pattern or shape of the scores (Nunnally, 1978).

In our example in Table 11.3, the mean scores across the predictors (i.e., the ideal profile) can be correlated with the applicants' scores across the predictors to produce a correlation coefficient for each of the applicants. The resulting correlation coefficients are as follows: Mr. A ($r = .987$), Ms. B ($r = .825$), Mr. C ($r = .910$), and Ms. D ($r = .979$). Using the D^2 method requires the subtraction of the mean score for each predictor from each applicant's score on that predictor to obtain a difference. The resulting differences are squared and the squares summed across predictors for each applicant to obtain a D^2 score. Our applicants in Table 11.3 obtained the following D^2 scores: Mr. A ($D^2 = 26$), Ms. B ($D^2 = 159$), Mr. C ($D^2 = 111$), and Ms. D ($D^2 = 38$). Recall that the smaller the D^2 score is, the better the match. Thus, in this example, the rank order for both the correlation and D^2 method are the same: (1) Mr. A, (2) Ms. D, (3) Mr. C, and (4) Ms. B.

Although the two methods produced identical rank orders in this example, the resulting rank orders are not always the same. Moreover, the correlation method often yields very high correlation coefficients, which barely differentiate applicants from each other. The D^2 method can also produce misleading results. An applicant whose scores substantially *exceed* the mean scores will have a high D^2 score and rank below an applicant whose scores fall close to the mean scores (whether slightly above or even below the means). Thus, this model is based on the assumption that scores that are higher than the ideal are as undesirable as scores that are lower than the ideal. In fact, the model assumes that there is one best profile, whereas there could be several profiles that predict success just as well.

As noted previously, the profile matching model cannot be implemented if the predictors do not differentiate between employees who are poor performers and those who are good performers. Moreover, restriction of range can be a problem because truly poor performers are often difficult to find (i.e., they are asked to leave or are not hired in the first place). Also, because the profiles of successful employees could change over time, ideal profiles need to be checked periodically.

Profile matching does have the advantage of permitting the ranking of applicants based on their similarities to the ideal profile. It is an appropriate method to use when there is clearly a best type of employee for the job and when it can be demonstrated that poor employees tend to score higher as well as lower on the predictors than good employees (i.e., there is a curvilinear relationship between predictor scores and job performance). As these conditions rarely apply, multiple regression remains a more appropriate approach in virtually all circumstances (Gatewood and Feild, 1998).

MAKING SELECTION DECISIONS

Regardless of which decision-making model is used, the eventual aim of the selection process is to decide which applicants to hire. The models described in the previous sections lend themselves to one of two basic approaches: *top-down selection* and *banding*. Each method is based on particular assumptions and has certain advantages and disadvantages.

TOP-DOWN SELECTION

Top-down selection involves ranking applicants on the basis of their total scores and selecting from the top down until the desired number of candidates has been selected. This approach is based on the assumption that individuals scoring higher on the predictors will be better performers on the job than individuals scoring lower on the predictors (i.e., there is a linear relationship between predictor scores and job performance). As long as this assumption is not violated, top-down selection is considered the best approach for maximizing organizational performance (Gatewood and Feild, 1998). Only the top performers are hired.

One difficulty with using top-down selection is that it can have adverse impact against certain minority groups. For example, blacks tend to have slightly lower average scores than whites on certain tests. Selecting from the top down could therefore result in disproportionately more whites than blacks being hired. *Race norming* or *within-group scoring* has been suggested as a method of preventing such adverse impact. Applicants can be ranked on their predictor scores within their relevant minority groups. For example, whites could be ranked on their predictor scores relative to other whites, and blacks could be rank-ordered on their predictor scores relative to other blacks. Then the top-ranking black candidate and the top-ranking white candidate could be selected, followed by the black and white candidates ranking second, and so on until the desired number of candidates is selected. Although top-down selection across all groups would result in the best-quality candidates being hired, on average, ranking within groups permits employers to achieve employment equity goals while still hiring high-quality applicants (Gatewood and Feild, 1998).

Although the American Civil Rights Act of 1991 prohibits race norming, the adjustment of scores, or the use of different cutoff scores for different minority groups in the United States, there is no such legislation in Canada. Nevertheless, employment equity initiatives can be difficult to implement, as one Canadian fire department discovered. The Kitchener Fire Department attempted to increase minority representation in the department by reducing the cutoff score for women. Whereas male applicants needed a score of 85 to pass, the cutoff score for females was set at 70. The public outcry was so great that the department had to abandon this approach. Many individuals perceived this method as an example of reverse discrimination (i.e., discrimination against the white male applicants).

BANDING

An alternative approach to accomplishing employment equity is banding. **Banding** involves grouping applicants based on ranges of scores. The grouping process takes into account the concept of *standard error of measurement* (from classical test theory). Essentially, the standard error of measurement

Banding—grouping applicants based on ranges of scores.

(SEM) reflects the fact that almost any measurement contains an error as well as a true score component. For example, if you obtain a score of 83 percent on an exam, part of that score reflects your true knowledge of the material tested but part of it reflects other factors such as your level of alertness during testing, level of stress, distractions, and luck. Not sleeping well the night before the test, experiencing personal problems, or spending considerable time studying material that turns out to be a very small component of the exam can reduce your test score so that it underrepresents your true knowledge. On the other hand, if you study only some of the course material but, as luck would have it, that very material constitutes most of the test, or if you obtain some advance knowledge of test content, or if you simply make some lucky guesses, your test score overrepresents your true knowledge. Such errors of measurement are taken into account by the SEM, a statistic that reflects the reliability of an individual's score.

Bands around a given score are calculated as plus or minus two times the SEM (i.e., the score ± 2SEM). Assuming that the error is randomly distributed, we would be correct 95 percent of the time in asserting that an individual's true score lies within the band defined by plus or minus 2SEM. If the SEM in our example above is 2.53, we can establish a band of 5.06 points (2.53 × 2) around your score of 83. That is, there is a 95 percent probability that your true score is somewhere between 77.94 and 88.06 (83 ± 5.06).

Now, let's assume you have a friend who wrote the same exam and scored 80 percent. Before you belittle your friend's lower grade, consider the effects of measurement error. If we construct a band around your friend's score of 80, we discover that his or her true score is somewhere between 74.94 and 85.06 (with a 95 percent probability). It is therefore possible that your friend's true score is higher than yours! Because there is an overlap in the bands around your scores, we can assert that your scores are not statistically different from each other. From a measurement perspective, both of you can be viewed as being at the same level of proficiency with respect to the course material. In fact, in this example, both of you would receive a grade of A–. Of course, SEM is not used to differentiate grades of A– from B+ or B+ from B, but such grades are a form of banding.

Banding is applied to selection decisions by calculating a band from the top score downwards. If the top score on a test is 96 and the SEM is 2.5, then the band extends from 96 down to 91 (96 – 5). There is no need to extend the band above 96 as 96 is the top score. Any scores falling within the band from 91 to 96 are considered equal because the differences among them are not statistically significant. We are therefore free to select any applicants we wish within the band. In fact, as long as their scores fall within the same band, we could select minority applicants ahead of nonminority applicants in order to accomplish employment equity objectives.

Bands can be constructed in one of two ways: fixed or sliding. *Fixed bands* are calculated starting at the top score, as described above. All the applicants within the band must be selected before a new band can be calculated. A new band is calculated starting from the highest score among those applicants who were not included in the first band. This process continues until the desired number of applicants has been hired. Table 11.4 illustrates both fixed and sliding bands with hypothetical data. The scores of 19 applicants have been ranked and some of them have been identified as minority applicants. If we assume that the SEM is 2.5, then the first band ranges from 91 to 96 (as described above). Using the fixed bands approach, we would select the applicants scoring 93 and 96 and then construct a second fixed band from 89 (the new highest score) down to 84. Within the second fixed band, we would select the minority applicants first and then the remainder of the applicants until all the required applicants scoring within the band have been selected. If we required additional candidates, we would construct a third fixed band from 82 down to 77.

With *sliding bands,* not every applicant in the band needs to be selected before the next band is constructed. Once the top scorer in the band has been selected, a new band is constructed from the next highest score. In this manner, the band slides down each time the top scorer within the band is selected. Applying the sliding band approach to the data in Table 11.4, we would first

TABLE 11.4	FIXED VERSUS SLIDING BANDS FOR THE SELECTION OF MINORITY APPLICANTS							
Fixed Bands	**Applicant Scores and Minority Status**		**Sliding Bands**					
Band 1	96		1					
	93	Minority						
Band 2	89			2				
	89	Minority						
	87				3			
	86							
	85					4		
	85	Minority						
	85	Minority					5	
	84							
Band 3	82	Minority						6
	82							
	81							7
	80							
	80							
	79	Minority						
	78	Minority						
	78							
	77							

select the minority applicant scoring 93 and then the applicant scoring 96. Once we've selected the top scorer (96), we would construct the second sliding band from 84 to 89. Within this band we would select the three minority applicants and then the highest remaining scorer (89). Once the highest scorer has been selected, we would construct the third sliding band from 82 to 87 and so on.

The sliding band approach provides a larger number of applicants to select from than does the fixed band approach and therefore provides greater likelihood of selecting minority applicants. To illustrate, assume we wish to select seven candidates from among the applicants represented in Table 11.4. Using the traditional top-down approach, we would select as few as two and at the most three minority applicants. The fixed band approach would result in the selection of four minority candidates, whereas the sliding band approach would result in the selection of five minority applicants. Of course, the number of minority applicants selected in any particular situation depends on a number of factors such as the proportion of applicants who are minority group members, the distribution of minority scores, and selection ratios (Murphy, Osten, and Myors, 1995). Nevertheless, on average, banding should contribute to the hiring of a greater proportion of minority applicants provided minority status is used as the criterion of selection within bands.

Although there has been some debate concerning the logic and psychometric soundness of banding (e.g., Cascio, Outtz, Zedeck, and Goldstein, 1995; Schmidt, 1995; Murphy and Myors, 1995), the principle of banding has survived legal scrutiny in the United States. Nevertheless, U.S. courts have ruled that it is not permissible to use minority status as a primary criterion for selection within bands because they consider that a form of race norming (Gutman and Christiansen, 1997). Employers may select within bands on the basis of secondary criteria such as education, experience, or professional conduct. However, minority status may only be used as a tie-breaker among individuals with the same scores. Under such circumstances, banding is not likely to significantly reduce adverse impact (Murphy, Osten, and Myors, 1995). In Canada there is no legislation prohibiting preferential selection of minority applicants. As a result, banding might be a workable means of achieving affirmative action objectives in a manner that is likely to be more acceptable to nonminority applicants and employees than race norming, particularly if the principles behind banding are explained to them (Truxillo and Bauer, 1999).

PRACTICAL CONSIDERATIONS

A variety of decision-making models and methods are available for making selection decisions. Which model or method is best in a given situation depends on a number of factors. The number of applicants expected, the amount of time available before selection decisions have to be made, and the costs associated with the selection instruments all have to be considered in making a choice. However, whenever they are feasible, linear models appear to outperform other approaches to decision making.

BOX 11.3 Banding in Toronto

Some writers suggest that U.S. companies might withstand litigation if applicants were *randomly* selected within bands rather than on the basis of minority status (Gatewood and Feild, 1998). However, given that minority applicants are not strongly represented in a given band, they are no more likely to be selected randomly within bands than through a top-down process. The City of Toronto made this discovery when it used such a procedure in the hiring of 24 firefighters in 1996. Applicants were split into three bands based on test and interview scores. The 13 candidates in the top band (all white males) were hired and then the city implemented what was believed to be a fair system by holding a random draw of the 83 applicants in the second

band. Not surprisingly, given the small number of minority applicants, no minority applicants were drawn.

A complaint was lodged against the city by the Ontario Human Rights Commission because all 24 of the applicants hired were white males. Had the city used a preferential selection procedure (i.e., based on minority status), some minority applicants would likely have been selected and the city might have averted the complaint. Of course, the City of Toronto might still have experienced some problems because of its banding procedure. The rather large second band suggests that the bands were set somewhat arbitrarily rather than being based on the SEM.

Many of the models discussed in this chapter assume large applicant pools or frequent and regular selection activity. Yet small businesses, which constitute a growing proportion of the Canadian economy, often hire small numbers of applicants on an infrequent basis. How can selection decisions in such small businesses be made more effectively?

Most of the rating procedures described in this chapter can be simplified to serve the needs of a small-business owner or manager (Schneider and Schmitt, 1986). He or she can conduct an "armchair" job analysis by considering what tasks the employee would be expected to perform and how job performance would be assessed. Next the owner or manager should determine what behaviours related to these tasks could best be assessed in an interview and/or in simulations. Subjective weights could be attached, in advance, to each of the behaviours assessed and the owner or manager should ensure that all applicants are evaluated systematically and fairly on the same criteria. Thus, although applicant information may be collected in a judgmental fashion or in a judgmental and statistical fashion, the information is combined statistically (i.e., trait rating or statistical composite) to yield a total score for each applicant. This total score can then be used to make the selection decisions.

CONCLUSIONS

Although valid selection instruments are necessary for making good selection decisions, they are not sufficient. Good selection procedures must be used as well. Selection systems can be made more effective if some of the following recommendations are followed (Gatewood and Feild, 1998):

1. Use valid selection instruments.

2. Dissuade managers from making selection decisions based on gut feelings or intuition.

3. Encourage managers to keep track of their own selection "hits" and "misses."

4. Train managers to make systematic selection decisions using one of the approaches described in this chapter.

5. Periodically evaluate or audit selection decisions in order to identify areas needing improvement.

UTILITY ANALYSIS

At this point, you may be asking yourself whether the cost of developing a valid selection system is worth all of the aggravation and actually produces any benefits. Utility analysis is a procedure that may allow you to come up with answers to this question. If you review the selection model presented in Figure 8.3 (page 292), you will see that one of the last steps in developing and implementing a selection system is to conduct a utility analysis.

A selection system takes time and money to develop and implement with no guarantee that it will be free of bias or that it will be perceived as fair. Furthermore, validity coefficients that have not been adjusted to account for range restriction, attenuation, and sampling error mostly fall in the range from 0.30 to 0.40, accounting for 16 percent or less of the variability in outcome measures. Decisions based on the selection system have important implications for both applicants and the company. HR managers must be able to demonstrate that a selection system produces benefits or advantages to the organization that exceed the cost of operating the selection system. HR managers must know if the cost of implementing a new selection system will produce benefits that exceed those produced by the old system. **Utility analysis** is a decision-making procedure that is used to evaluate selection systems by determining the net gains that accrue to the organization from their use.

Utility analysis—a decision-making procedure used to evaluate selection systems.

TAYLOR-RUSSELL UTILITY MODEL

Taylor and Russell (1939) developed a procedure to demonstrate the practical effectiveness of selection systems. The procedure relied not only on the validity coefficient but also on two other conditions that influenced the worth of the system: the selection ratio and base rate. The selection ratio is the proportion of job applicants selected for positions in the company. **Base rate** is the proportion of applicants who would be successful had all the applicants been hired. The base rate can be estimated from available employment data. For the performance data presented in Table 3.1 (page 90), a company considers any

Base rate—the proportion of applicants who would be successful had all the applicants for a position been hired.

employee who obtains a score of 6 or above to be a success. Figure 11.1 shows that five of the employees are at or above this level of performance; therefore, the base rate is 0.50. Half the workers hired through the current selection system are satisfactory. What if only four positions were open when these people originally applied for work, and selection had been based on cognitive ability? The selection ratio would be 0.40 (i.e., 4 out of 10 applicants are hired). Using the regression line previously established for this group in Chapter 3, cognitive ability scores equal to or greater than 7 predict performance scores that are equal to or greater than 6. Selecting the four applicants with the highest cognitive ability scores would lead to the employment of Mr. E, Ms. M, Mr. H, and Mr. K.

The intersection of the lines representing the base rate and selection ratio divide the scatterplot into four quadrants, representing four different outcomes of the selection process described in Table 11.1. Mr. E, Ms. M, and Mr. H represent applicants who are true positives (those predicted to be successful and who turn out to be successful). Mr. K. is an example of a false positive (predicted to be unsuccessful and would fail if hired). Mr. L and Mr. N are false negatives (predicted to be unsatisfactory but would be successful if hired). Ms. F, Mr. G, Mr. I, and Ms. J. are true negatives (those predicted to be unsatisfactory and would be so if hired). Taylor and Russell defined the **success rate** as the proportion of applicants hired through the selection system who are judged satisfactory. Three of the four people hired fall into this category, producing a success rate = 0.75. If the success rate is greater than the base rate, as it is here (0.75 vs. 0.50), the selection system is considered to be useful since it

Success rate—the proportion of applicants hired through the selection system who are judged satisfactory.

FIGURE 11.1 COGNITIVE ABILITY AND JOB PEFORMANCE

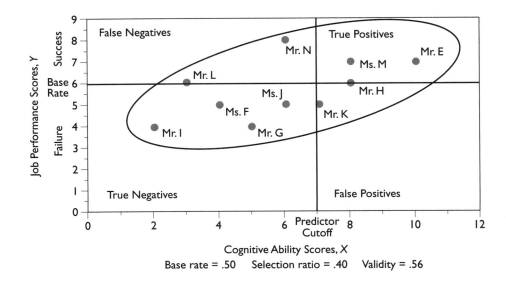

Base rate = .50   Selection ratio = .40   Validity = .56

leads to a greater proportion of successful hires than would otherwise be the case.

The success rate is determined by the specific base rate, selection ratio, and validity that apply in any given situation. Changing the selection ratio, effectively moving the cutoff line to the left or right in Figure 11.1, or the base rate, moving the base rate line up or down, would alter the number of people falling in each quadrant and would have an impact on the success rate. A different validity, changing the orientation or shape of the oval, would also affect the success rate. Taylor and Russell produced a series of tables that estimate the success rate for any given combination of validity, base rate, and selection ratio.

Brogden/Cronbach/Gleser Utility Model

The Taylor-Russell model evaluates the worth of a selection system in terms of an increase in the percentage of successful workers who are hired through the system. It assumes that workers fall into only two categories: successful or unsuccessful. However, most workers vary in the degree of success they exhibit in doing their jobs. Those who are more successful are more valuable employees because they increase the overall productivity of an organization. Can this overall increase in productivity, or utility, be established for selection systems? If so, then comparison of the utility figures reflects the relative worth of different selection systems. Higher utility values indicate that the selection process has added well-qualified, more-productive workers to the organization.

Over the years several researchers have developed a formula for calculating the utility of a selection test or system (Brogden, 1949; Cronbach and Gleser, 1965):

$$u = nr_{xy}sd_y\bar{z}_x - c$$

where u = the increase in utility or productivity in one year from hiring n employees through the selection system;

n = the number of employees hired with the selection system;

r_{xy} = the criterion-related validity coefficient;

sd_y = the standard deviation of job performance;

$\bar{z}_x$ = the average, standardized predictor score of the employees hired through the selection system; and

c = the total costs involved in obtaining the new employees, including pro-rated costs associated with development of the system.

This formula shows that the benefit that accrues from each person hired through the selection system is related not only to the size of the validity coefficient but also to the standard deviation of job performance of the employees and the average predictor score of the hired employees. A large standard deviation suggests that there is great variability in job performance among the workers. A selection system, for any validity coefficient, will be more valuable in this situation, since the outcome of the selection process may result in hiring someone who is either exceptionally good or exceptionally bad. If all the workers, once hired, perform at relatively the same level, the selection system will have less impact on productivity.

The average standardized score on the predictor, which is related to the selection ratio, indicates the extent to which top candidates were hired. Average Z scores closer to zero suggest that people of average ability were hired, while average Z scores greater than 1.0 suggest that on average the best candidates were selected. The best candidates should add more value to the organization. The net benefit is obtained by subtracting the cost of developing and operating the selection system. Costs can be quite variable, ranging from a few dollars to administer a paper-and-pencil test to several million to develop a system to select jet pilots.

Different estimation procedures can be used to express sd_y as a dollar value, which then allows a dollar figure to be placed on the actual productivity gain (Boudreau, 1991), although not everyone agrees on the appropriateness or need to do this (Latham and Whyte, 1994). The dollar-valued gain in productivity can be considerable when a large number of employees are being hired, giving rise to questions about the credibility of such values to managers, and may lead to less support for valid selection procedures (Whyte and Latham, 1997). For example, Cronshaw (1986) showed that the use of a selection test battery by the Canadian Forces resulted in a gain of close to $3 million per year for the 417 people selected for a clerical/administrative trade group. If this figure is multiplied by the number of years an average person remains in this job category, the utility increases to over $51 million.

It is not clear whether the large values or how the utility analysis is "sold" to management leads to the loss of credibility (Cronshaw, 1997). Managers with less understanding of utility information do seem to react more favourably when utility information is presented as an opportunity cost rather than as a monetary gain (Hazer and Highhouse, 1997). Nevertheless, the utility formula, either in dollar or nondollar form, allows a comparison of different selection systems in terms of the productivity they bring to an organization. If nothing else, the Brogden-Cronbach-Gleser model demonstrates the significant gains that may accrue through a scientifically based selection system.

An Illustration of Utility Analysis

In Canada, the federal government offers second-language training to selected employees. Suppose that 50 percent of all applicants for second-language training are accepted and that of those accepted only 20 percent become fully bilingual. That is, the program has a selection ratio of .50 and a base rate of .20. In an attempt to improve the outcome, a second-language aptitude test (SLAT) is developed to select applicants for training. The validity of the SLAT turns out to be .35. From the tables developed by Taylor and Russell (1939), for these values of validity, selection ratio, and base rate, the success rate will be .36, or an increase of 16 percent in utility. That is, for every 100 applicants, 18 out of the 50 candidates ($.36 \times 50$) selected for language training with the SLAT should succeed at becoming bilingual. This change represents an increase of 8 over the 10 ($.20 \times 50$) who would be successful under the old system. If some effort were put into improving the SLAT so that its validity reached .50, the success rate would increase to .44, representing a gain of 8 percent over the older version of the SLAT and a 24 percent increase over the base rate. Both versions of the SLAT could be considered successful in that they increased the number of successful candidates selected in every group of 50 applicants.

While the improved SLAT produced an 8 percent gain over the older version, it is difficult to say whether that increase offsets the costs of the improvement. The Taylor-Russell utility model does not provide an easy means of integrating costs and benefits. The Brogden-Cronbach-Gleser model allows such cost-benefit comparisons. We would need to assemble some additional information before we could use this model. First we would need to calculate the cost of improving the SLAT validity; let's set this cost at $100 000. Next, we need to determine the average score, in standardized form, of all those selected with the improved SLAT; let $\overline{z}_x = 1.25$. The value of both these variables would be obtained from data associated with the test development and with the testing. Finally, we need to estimate sd_y the standard deviation of performance in dollars. There are several estimation techniques that do this and that according to managers produce estimates that are accurate enough for decision-making purposes (Morrow, 1997).

One procedure, which seems to produce conservative estimates, is simply to let this value equal 40 percent of the salary and benefits of the position. For our example, let salary and benefits total $40 000; we would then use $16 000 as an estimate of sd_y. The utility of selecting 50 employees with the improved SLAT would be:

$$U_{\text{New}} = (50) \ [(.50)(1.25) \ (\$16\ 000)] - \$100\ 000 = \$500\ 000 - \$100\ 000 = \$400\ 000.$$

However, this figure assumes that the utility of the old selection system is zero. We know that this is not the case as the validity of the old SLAT was .35. If we assume that the old SLAT had long since paid for itself and that the only costs were the cost of purchasing and administering the test, let's say $10 per selected applicant, then its utility was:

$$U_{\text{Old}} = (50)[(.35)(1.25)(\$16\ 000)] - \$500 = \$350\ 000 - \$500 = \$349\ 500$$

The net gain would be the difference between the two utility values:

$$U_{\text{Net}} = U_{\text{New}} - U_{\text{Old}} = \$400\ 000 - \$349\ 500 = \$50\ 500$$

Of course, if we had decided to amortize the cost of development over the life span of the test, the utility would appear to be much greater. For example, having "paid" the development costs up front, the next 50 candidates selected, and every other group of 50 selected applicants, would return a net benefit of

$150 000, compared with using the old SLAT, assuming the same administration costs of $10 per selected applicant. Over time the return on the investment to improve the test could be quite substantial. The net utility represents the benefits associated with the improved productivity that is obtained from hiring better-qualified applicants through use of the selection system, minus the costs of that system.

Evaluating testing programs through utility analysis is more complicated than the simple illustrations presented here. Often, many assumptions have to be made about the appropriate way to calculate costs and to estimate the other parameters needed by the models. Also, does utility provide the kind of information that managers want when making human resource decisions? Nonetheless, utility analysis does provide a means of comparing different selection systems and can provide quite useful information for the human resources specialist. Utility models can demonstrate, in quite convincing fashion, whether the implementation of personnel testing programs will produce productivity gains for the organization.

SUMMARY

Employers face a difficult task in trying to combine and make sense of complex applicant information in order to make selection decisions. They are vulnerable to numerous biases and errors and they often oversimplify information because their information processing abilities are overloaded. Although several approaches to making selection decisions can be used, methods that involve combining applicant information in a statistical manner are generally superior to other methods in reducing errors and predicting job performance. Methods such as multiple regression, multiple cutoff, multiple hurdle, combination, and profile matching can be used to make effective selection decisions when used under appropriate conditions. Selection teams or panels can also assist in improving selection decisions. Banding is suggested as an alternative to conventional top-down selection because banding satisfies affirmative action objectives, while still enabling the hiring of top-quality applicants. Finally, utility analysis is presented as a means to evaluate the effectiveness of selection systems.

KEY TERMS

Banding, p. 453

Base rate, p. 458

Cutoff score, p. 445

False negative error, p. 439

False positive error, p. 438

Judgmental composite, p. 442

Profile interpretation, p. 441

Pure judgment approach, p. 441

Pure statistical approach, p. 441

Selection ratio, p. 446

Statistical composite, p. 442

Success rate, p. 459

Trait rating approach, p. 441

Utility analysis, p. 458

EXERCISES

Selection Decision

Assume you occasionally hire cashiers for a small store. You generally do not hire more than two or three at a time. Using the information presented in the table below, determine which of the applicants would be selected and/or, where appropriate, what their rank would be under the following decision-making models:

a. multiple regression
b. multiple cutoff
c. combination
d. profile matching (D^2 only)

Predictor Scores

Applicant	Cognitive Test	Conscientious-ness Scale	Biodata Form	Structured Interview	Reference Check
Ms. Z	47	26	18	47	6
Mr. Y	36	36	15	45	8
Ms. W	46	36	16	32	9
Ms. V	44	30	10	36	7
Mr. U	39	38	14	41	10
Maximum Possible Scores	50	40	20	50	10
Regression weights	1.4	.4	.5	.9	.4
Cutoff scores	36	27	12	35	7
Mean scores	40	35	16	39	8

Which of the selection models discussed do you believe is best suited to this situation? Why?

Discussion Question

You are human resources specialists trying to improve selection procedures in your organization. Under the current system, application forms are screened by relevant department managers to determine who should be interviewed. References are also collected. The managers do their own interviewing using individual, unstructured interviews and base their selection decisions almost exclusively on these interviews. They tend to have a lot of confidence in their gut feelings about candidates and believe they've been doing a pretty good job of selecting the right applicants. How would you go about trying to convince them that they should adopt a more structured, objective (i.e., statistical) decision-making system? What objections to your suggestion do you anticipate would be raised by the managers? How would you address these objections?

Applied Project

Conduct an interview with a knowledgeable individual in a local company concerning the selection system used in the organization. During the interview ask the following questions:

1. How many positions are filled annually? How many applications are received for each vacant position?

2. What selection devices or methods (e.g., tests, interviews, references) are used?

3. Have these selection devices been validated? If so, how?

4. What role does each of these selection devices play in selection decisions?

5. What kind of selection system is used by the organization (i.e., do they use statistical or judgmental combination)?

6. Are selection decisions made on the basis of a total score? If not, how are they made?

7. Are weightings applied to applicant data? If so, how are the weightings determined?

8. Does the organization attempt to evaluate the effectiveness of its selection system? If so, how? If not, why not? Did the company use utility analysis as part of the evaluation? If so, which model did it use?

9. Assume that Figure 11.1 represents the relationship between the company's selection system or predictor and performance. Discuss why the company would not want to set the predictor cutoff extremely high. What would an extremely high predictor cutoff mean in terms of recruitment?

Assess the information you obtain from the organization in light of the material presented in this chapter. Write a report detailing the strengths of the organization's selection system and making recommendations for improvements, where needed.

CASE

Dofasco is one of Canada's largest and most successful steel producers. Headquartered in Hamilton, Ontario, the company has a subsidiary in Southfield, Michigan, and has also been engaged in strategic joint ventures with various steel mills and mines in Ontario, Quebec, and the United States. Almost 10 000 employees are engaged in these operations.

Steel making has become an increasingly sophisticated activity and, as a result, the levels of skills required have been rising. Not surprisingly, training and development have become vital elements of Dofasco's success. Dofasco has always prided itself on its relations with employees. In fact, the company slogan, "our product is steel, our strength is people," reflects Dofasco's commitment to developing and motivating its workforce. One of the ways Dofasco motivates employees is through its promote-from-within policy. As a result, when Dofasco hires employees, the company not only is concerned with their ability to do entry-level jobs but is also looking for evidence of promotion potential (e.g., leadership potential) and organizational fit.

Given Dofasco's commitment to employee relations and development, the company has one of the lowest turnover rates in the manufacturing sector. In fact, the extremely low turnover rate has created a bit of a problem for Dofasco. Over the next 10 years about one-half of Dofasco's workforce (including management) will be retiring. The challenge for Dofasco will be to fill the many vacated entry-level positions with employees who have the potential to quickly acquire the skills necessary to promote them into various technical and leadership positions that will also need to be filled.

DISCUSSION QUESTIONS

Pretend you have been put in charge of staffing at Dofasco. Your job is to plan and execute a selection strategy for Dofasco over the next 10 years. Assume that the rate of retirements will be fairly evenly distributed over the next 10 years.

1. What steps can you take now, in preparation for the large-scale selection task that lies ahead? What information will you need to collect? How can this information be used? What strategy will you put in place to deal with the large number of employees who will need to be hired each year? Will you maintain a promote-from-within policy? If so, how? If not, what consequences do you anticipate and how will you deal with them?

2. What selection tools might be appropriate to assess the potential of applicants to acquire knowledge and skills quickly? How might you assess leadership potential? How about organizational fit? Justify your choices.

3. Design a selection system for entry-level employees, specifying the various selection tools you will use (e.g., structured interviews, personality tests,

reference checks, etc.), the order in which you will apply them, and the weight you will assign to each of the selection tools. What decision-making model will you use? How will you determine whether your selection system is working (i.e., selecting the best possible employees)? Should you find your system is not working as well as it should, how might you go about improving it? How will you determine whether your selection system has adverse impact on minority applicants? Should you discover your system does adversely affect minorities, what steps will you take to address the problem? Provide a detailed rationale for your design.

REFERENCES

Bazerman, M.H. 1986. *Judgment in Managerial Decision Making*. New York: Wiley.

Boudreau, J.W. 1991. "Utility Analysis for Decisions in Human Resource Management." In M.D. Dunnette and L.M. Hough, eds., *The Handbook of Industrial and Organizational Psychology*, vol. 2. 2nd ed. Palo Alto: Consulting Psychologists Press, 621–745

Brandstatter, M., J.H. Davis, and G. Stocker-Kreichgauer, eds. 1983. *Group Decision Processes*. London: Academic Press.

Brogden, H.E. 1949. "When Testing Pays Off." *Personnel Psychology* 2: 171–83.

Cascio, W.F. 1991. *Applied Psychology in Personnel Management*. 4th ed. Engelwood Cliffs, NJ: Prentice-Hall.

Cascio, W.F., J. Outtz, S. Zedeck, and I.L. Goldstein. 1995. "Statistical Implications of Six Methods of Test Score Use in Personnel Selection. *Human Performance* 8: 133–64.

Cox, J.A., D.W. Schlueter, K.K. Moore, and D. Sullivan. 1989. "A Look behind Corporate Doors." *Personnel Administrator* (March): 56–59.

Cronbach, L., and G. Gleser. 1965. *Psychological Tests and Personnel Decisions*. Urbana, IL: University of Illinois Press.

Cronshaw, S.F. 1986 . "The Utility of Employment Testing for Clerical/Administrative Trades in the Canadian Military. *Canadian Journal of Administrative Sciences* 3: 376–85.

Cronshaw, S.F. 1997. "Lo! The Stimulus Speaks: The Insider's View on Whyte and Latham's 'The Futility of Utility Analysis.' " *Personnel Psychology* 50: 611–15.

Gardiner, H.P., and R.D. Hackett. 1996. *The Employment Interview in Canadian Law: An Analysis of Human Rights Cases*. Unpublished manuscript. McMaster University, Hamilton, ON.

Gatewood, R.D., and H.S. Feild. 1998. *Human Resource Selection*. Toronto: The Dryden Press.

Gutman, A., and N. Christiansen. 1997. "Further Clarification of the Judicial Status of Banding." *The Industrial-Organizational Psychologist* 35: 75–81.

Hackett, R.D., J.B. Rose, and J. Pyper. 1999. *Canadian Labour Arbitration Decisions Involving the Employment*

Interview. Unpublished manuscript. McMaster University, Hamilton, ON.

Hazer, J.T., and S. Highhouse 1997. "Factors Influencing Managers' Reactions to Utility Analysis: Effects of SD_y Method, Information Frame, and Focal Intervention. *Journal of Applied Psychology* 82: 104–12.

Hill, G.W. 1982. "Group versus Individual Performance: Are N + 1 Heads Better than One?" *Psychological Bulletin* 91: 517–39.

Janis, I.L., and L. Mann. 1977. *Decision Making: A Psychological Analysis of Conflict, Choice, and Commitment*. New York: The Free Press.

Kane, J.R. 1988. *Selection Procedures: Research vs. Reality*. Paper presented at the 49th Annual Convention of the Canadian Psychological Association, Montreal, Quebec (June).

Kichuk, S.L., and W.H. Wiesner. 1996. *The Effects of the Big 5 Personality Factors on Team Performance: Implications for Selecting Optimal Teams*. Advanced Concepts Conference of the Interdisciplinary Centre for the Study of Work Teams. Dallas, TX (May).

Kleinmuntz, B. 1990. "Why We Still Use Our Heads Instead of Formulas: Toward an Integrative Approach." *Psychological Bulletin* 107: 296–310.

Latham, G.P., and G. Whyte. 1994. "The Futility of Utility Analysis." *Personnel Psychology* 47: 31–46.

Meehl, P.E. 1954. *Clinical Versus Statistical Prediction: A Theoretical Analysis and a Review of the Evidence*. Minneapolis, MN: University of Minnesota Press.

Michaelson, L.K., W.E. Watson, and R.H. Black. 1989. "A Realistic Test of Individual versus Group Consensus Decision Making." *Journal of Applied Psychology* 74: 834–39.

Morrow, C.C. 1997. "Human Resource Utility Models: An Investigation of Current Models' Assumptions and Perceived Accuracy." *Dissertation Abstracts International: Section B—The Sciences and Engineering* 57: 4763.

Murphy, K.R., and B. Myors. 1995. "Evaluating the Logical Critique of Banding." *Human Performance* 8: 191–201.

Murphy, K.R., K. Osten, and B. Myors. 1995. "Modeling the Effects of Banding in Personnel Selection." *Personnel Psychology* 48: 61–84.

Nunnally, J.C. 1978. *Psychometric Theory*. 2nd ed. New York: McGraw-Hill.

Peter, L.J., and R. Hull. 1969. *The Peter Principle*. New York: William Morrow.

Robertson, I.T., and P.J. Makin. 1986. "Management Selection in Britain: A Survey and Critique." *Journal of Occupational Psychology* 59: 45–57.

Ross, M., and J.H. Ellard. 1986. "On Winnowing: The Impact of Scarcity on Allocators' Evaluations of Candidates for a Resource." *Journal of Experimental Social Psychology* 22: 374–88.

Sawyer, J. 1966. "Measurement and Prediction, Clinical and Statistical." *Psychological Bulletin* 66: 178–200.

Schmidt, F.L. 1995. "Why All Banding Procedures in Personnel Selection Are Logically Flawed." *Human Performance* 8: 165–77.

Schmitt, N.W., and R.J. Klimoski. 1991. *Research Methods in Human Resources Management*. Cincinnati, OH: South-Western.

Schneider, B., and N.W. Schmitt. 1986. *Staffing Organizations*. Glenview, IL: Scott Foresmann.

Shaw, M.E. 1981. *Group Dynamics: The Psychology of Small Group Behavior*, 3rd ed. New York: McGraw-Hill.

Simon, H.A. 1957. *Administrative Behavior,* 2nd ed. New York: Free Press.

Steiner, I.D. 1972. *Group Process and Productivity.* New York: Academic Press.

Stevens, M.J., and M.A. Campion. 1994. "The Knowledge, Skill, and Ability Requirements for Teamwork: Implications for Human Resource Management." *Journal of Management* 20: 503–30.

Taylor, H.C., and J.F. Russell. 1939. "The Relationship of Validity Coefficients to the Practical Effectiveness of Tests in Selection: Discussion and tables." *Journal of Applied Psychology* 23: 565–78.

Truxillo, D.M., and T.N. Bauer. 1999. "Applicant Reactions to Test Score Banding in Entry-Level and Promotional Contexts." *Journal of Applied Psychology* 84: 322–39.

Whyte, G., and G.P. Latham 1997. "The Futility of Utility Analysis Revisited: When Even an Expert Fails." *Personnel Psychology* 50: 601–10.

Wiesner, W.H., and S.F. Cronshaw. 1988. "A Meta-Analytic Investigation of the Impact of Interview Format and Degree of Structure on the Validity of the Employment Interview." *Journal of Occupational Psychology* 61: 275–90.

Zedeck, S., A. Tziner, and S.E. Middlestadt. 1983. "Interviewer Validity and Reliability: An Individual Analysis Approach." *Personnel Psychology* 36: 355–70.

Index

To the owner of this book

We hope that you have enjoyed *Recruitment and Selection in Canada*, Second Edition (ISBN 0-17-616843-5), and we would like to know as much about your experiences with this text as you would care to offer. Only through your comments and those of others can we learn how to make this a better text for future readers.

School _____   Your instructor's name _____

Course _____   Was the text required? _____   Recommended? _____

1. What did you like the most about *Recruitment and Selection in Canada*?

    _____
    _____
    _____

2. How useful was this text for your course?

    _____
    _____
    _____

3. Do you have any recommendations for ways to improve the next edition of this text?

    _____
    _____
    _____

4. In the space below or in a separate letter, please write any other comments you have about the book. (For example, please feel free to comment on reading level, writing style, terminology, design features, and learning aids.)

    _____
    _____
    _____
    _____

Optional

Your name _____   Date _____

May Nelson Thomson Learning quote you, either in promotion for *Recruitment and Selection in Canada* or in future publishing ventures?

Yes _____   No _____

Thanks!

You can also send your comments to us via e-mail at
college@nelson.com

PLEASE TAPE SHUT. DO NOT STAPLE.

TAPE SHUT

TAPE SHUT

- - - - - - - - - - - FOLD HERE - - - - - - - - - - -

MAIL POSTE
Canada Post Corporation
Société canadienne des postes
Postage paid   Port payé
if mailed in Canada si posté au Canada
Business Reply   Réponse d'affaires

0066102399   01

NELSON
★
THOMSON LEARNING™

0066102399-M1K5G4-BR01

NELSON THOMSON LEARNING
HIGHER EDUCATION
PO BOX 60225 STN BRM B
TORONTO ON M7Y 2H1

TAPE SHUT

TAPE SHUT